Teacher Edition

SCIENCE FUSiON

fusion [FYOO • zhuhn] a combination of two or more things that releases energy

HOLT McDOUGAL

HOUGHTON MIFFLIN HARCOURT

Professional Development

Houghton Mifflin Harcourt and NSTA, the National Science Teacher's Association, have partnered to provide customized professional and development resources for teachers using *ScienceFusion*.

The Professional Development Resources in the NSTA Learning Center include:

—do-it-yourself resources, where you can study at your own pace.

—live and archived online seminars.

—journal articles, many of which include lesson plans.

—fee-based eBooks, eBook chapters, online short courses, symposia, and conferences.

Access to the NSTA Learning Center is provided in the *ScienceFusion* Online Resources.

Acknowledgments for Covers

Skier (bg) ©David Stoecklein/Corbis; *pacific wheel* (l) ©Geoffrey George/Getty Images; *snowboarder* (cl) ©Jonathan Nourok/Photographer's Choice/Getty Images; *water droplet* (cr) ©L. Clarke/Corbis; *molecular structure* (r) ©Stockbyte/ Getty Images.

Interior, digital screens: *giraffes* ©Corbis.

Contents in Brief

About the Program

Teaching Tools

Units at a Glance

Resources

Consulting Authors

Michael A. DiSpezio

Global Educator
North Falmouth, Massachusetts

Michael DiSpezio is a renaissance educator who moved from the research laboratory of a Nobel Prize winner to the K–12 science classroom. He has authored or coauthored numerous textbooks and written more than 25 trade books. For nearly a decade, he worked with the JASON Project under the auspices of the National Geographic Society, where he designed curriculum, wrote lessons, and hosted dozens of studio and location broadcasts.

Over the past two decades, he has developed supplementary material for organizations and shows that include PBS's *Scientific American Frontiers*, *Discover* magazine, and the Discovery Channel. He has extended his reach outside the United States and into topics of crucial importance today. To all his projects, he brings his extensive background in science and his expertise in classroom teaching at the elementary, middle, and high school levels.

Marjorie Frank

Science Writer and
Content-Area Reading Specialist
Brooklyn, New York

An educator and linguist by training, a writer and poet by nature, Marjorie Frank has authored and designed a generation of instructional materials in all subject areas, including past HMH Science programs. Her other credits include authoring science issues of an award-winning children's magazine; writing game-based digital assessments in math, reading, and language arts; and serving as instructional designer and coauthor of pioneering school-to-work software

for Classroom Inc., a nonprofit organization dedicated to improving reading and math skills for middle and high school learners. She wrote lyrics and music for *SCIENCE SONGS*, which was an American Library Association nominee for notable recording. In addition, she has served on the adjunct faculty of Hunter, Manhattan, and Brooklyn Colleges, teaching courses in science methods, literacy, and writing.

Michael R. Heithaus

Director, School of Environment and Society
Associate Professor, Department of Biological Sciences
Florida International University
North Miami, Florida

Mike Heithaus joined the Florida International University Biology Department in 2003. He has served as Director of the Marine Sciences Program and is now Director of the School of Environment and Society, which brings together the natural and social sciences and humanities to develop solutions to today's environmental challenges. While earning his doctorate, he began the research that grew into the Shark Bay Ecosystem Project in Western Australia, with which he still works. Back in the United States, he served as a Research Fellow with National Geographic, using remote imaging in his research and hosting a 13-part *Crittercam* television series on the National Geographic Channel. His current research centers on predator-prey interactions among vertebrates, such as tiger sharks, dolphins, dugongs, sea turtles, and cormorants.

Donna M. Ogle

Professor of Reading and Language
National-Louis University
Chicago, Illinois

Creator of the well-known KWL strategy, Donna Ogle has directed many staff development projects translating theory and research into school practice in middle and secondary schools throughout the United States. She is a past president of the International Reading Association and has served as a consultant on literacy projects worldwide. Her extensive international experience includes coordinating the Reading and Writing for Critical Thinking Project in Eastern Europe, developing an integrated curriculum for a USAID Afghan Education Project, and speaking and consulting on projects in several Latin American countries and in Asia. Her books include *Coming Together as Readers; Reading Comprehension: Strategies for Independent Learners; All Children Read;* and *Literacy for a Democratic Society.*

Program Reviewers

Content Reviewers

Paul D. Asimow, PhD
*Professor of Geology
and Geochemistry*
Division of Geological and Planetary Sciences
California Institute of Technology
Pasadena, CA

Laura K. Baumgartner, PhD
Postdoctoral Researcher
Molecular, Cellular, and Developmental Biology
University of Colorado
Boulder, CO

Eileen Cashman, PhD
Professor
Department of Environmental Resources Engineering
Humboldt State University
Arcata, CA

Hilary Clement Olson, PhD
Research Scientist Associate V
Institute for Geophysics, Jackson School of
Geosciences
The University of Texas at Austin
Austin, TX

Joe W. Crim, PhD
Professor Emeritus
Department of Cellular Biology
The University of Georgia
Athens, GA

Elizabeth A. De Stasio, PhD
*Raymond H. Herzog Professor
of Science*
Professor of Biology
Department of Biology
Lawrence University
Appleton, WI

Dan Franck, PhD
Botany Education Consultant
Chatham, NY

Julia R. Greer, PhD
*Assistant Professor of Materials Science and
Mechanics*
Division of Engineering and Applied Science
California Institute of Technology
Pasadena, CA

John E. Hoover, PhD
Professor
Department of Biology
Millersville University
Millersville, PA

William H. Ingham, PhD
Professor (Emeritus)
Department of Physics and Astronomy
James Madison University
Harrisonburg, VA

Charles W. Johnson, PhD
*Chairman, Division of Natural Sciences,
Mathematics, and Physical Education*
Associate Professor of Physics
South Georgia College
Douglas, GA

Tatiana A. Krivosheev, PhD
Associate Professor of Physics
Department of Natural Sciences
Clayton State University
Morrow, GA

Joseph A. McClure, PhD
Associate Professor Emeritus
Department of Physics
Georgetown University
Washington, DC

Mark Moldwin, PhD
Professor of Space Sciences
Atmospheric, Oceanic, and Space Sciences
University of Michigan
Ann Arbor, MI

Russell Patrick, PhD
Professor of Physics
Department of Biology, Chemistry, and Physics
Southern Polytechnic State University
Marietta, GA

Patricia M. Pauley, PhD
Meteorologist, Data Assimilation Group
Naval Research Laboratory
Monterey, CA

Stephen F. Pavkovic, PhD
Professor Emeritus
Department of Chemistry
Loyola University of Chicago
Chicago, IL

L. Jeanne Perry, PhD
Director (Retired)
Protein Expression Technology Center
Institute for Genomics and Proteomics
University of California, Los Angeles
Los Angeles, CA

Kenneth H. Rubin, PhD
Professor
Department of Geology and Geophysics
University of Hawaii
Honolulu, HI

Brandon E. Schwab, PhD
Associate Professor
Department of Geology
Humboldt State University
Arcata, CA

Marllin L. Simon, Ph.D.
Associate Professor
Department of Physics
Auburn University
Auburn, AL

Larry Stookey, PE
Upper Iowa University
Wausau, WI

Kim Withers, PhD
Associate Research Scientist
Center for Coastal Studies
Texas A&M University-Corpus Christi
Corpus Christi, TX

Matthew A. Wood, PhD
Professor
Department of Physics & Space Sciences
Florida Institute of Technology
Melbourne, FL

Adam D. Woods, PhD
Associate Professor
Department of Geological Sciences
California State University, Fullerton
Fullerton, CA

Natalie Zayas, MS, EdD
Lecturer
Division of Science and Environmental Policy
California State University, Monterey Bay
Seaside, CA

Teacher Reviewers

Ann Barrette, MST
Whitman Middle School
Wauwatosa, WI

Barbara Brege
Crestwood Middle School
Kentwood, MI

Katherine Eaton Campbell, M Ed
Chicago Public Schools-Area 2 Office
Chicago, IL

Karen Cavalluzzi, M Ed, NBCT
Sunny Vale Middle School
Blue Springs, MO

Katie Demorest, MA Ed Tech
Marshall Middle School
Marshall, MI

Jennifer Eddy, M Ed
Lindale Middle School
Linthicum, MD

Tully Fenner
George Fox Middle School
Pasadena, MD

Dave Grabski, MS Ed
PJ Jacobs Junior High School
Stevens Point, WI

Amelia C. Holm, M Ed
McKinley Middle School
Kenosha, WI

Ben Hondorp
Creekside Middle School
Zeeland, MI

George E. Hunkele, M Ed
Harborside Middle School
Milford, CT

Jude Kesl
Science Teaching Specialist 6–8
Milwaukee Public Schools
Milwaukee, WI

Joe Kubasta, M Ed
Rockwood Valley Middle School
St. Louis, MO

Mary Larsen
Science Instructional Coach
Helena Public Schools
Helena, MT

Angie Larson
Bernard Campbell Middle School
Lee's Summit, MO

Christy Leier
Horizon Middle School
Moorhead, MN

Helen Mihm, NBCT
Crofton Middle School
Crofton, MDL

Jeff Moravec, Sr., MS Ed
Teaching Specialist
Milwaukee Public Schools
Milwaukee, WI

Nancy Kawecki Nega, MST, NBCT, PAESMT
Churchville Middle School
Elmhurst, IL

Mark E. Poggensee, MS Ed
Elkhorn Middle School
Elkhorn, WI

Sherry Rich
Bernard Campbell Middle School
Lee's Summit, MO

Mike Szydlowski, M Ed
Science Coordinator
Columbia Public Schools
Columbia, MO

Nichole Trzasko, M Ed
Clarkston Junior High School
Clarkston, MI

Heather Wares, M Ed
Traverse City West Middle School
Traverse City, MI

Power up with

SCIENCE Fusion

Print

The **Write-in Student Edition** teaches science content through constant **interaction** with the text.

Labs and Activities

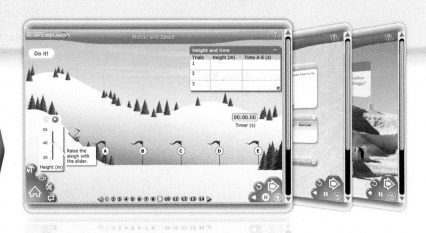

Lab Manual

Motion, Forces, and Energy

Digital

The parallel **Digital Curriculum** provides **e-learning digital lessons and virtual labs** for every print lesson of the program.

Energize your students through a multimodal blend of Print, Inquiry, and Digital experiences.

Unit Assessment

Formative Assessment
Strategies RTI
Throughout TE

Lesson Reviews SE

Unit PreTest

Summative Assessment
Alternative Assessment
(1 per lesson) RTI

Lesson Quizzes

Unit Tests A and B

Unit Review RTI
(with answer remediation)

Practice Tests
(end of module)

Project-Based Assessment

See the Assessment Guide for quizzes and tests.

Go Online to edit and create quizzes and tests.

See RTI teacher support materials.

The Hands-on Labs and Virtual Labs

provide meaningful and exciting inquiry experiences.

Print

The **Write-in Student Edition** teaches science content through constant **interaction** with the text.

Write-in Student Edition

360° of Inquiry

The *ScienceFusion* write-in student edition promotes a student-centered approach for

- learning and applying inquiry skills in the student edition
- building STEM and 21st Century skills
- keeping digital natives engaged and interactive

Research shows that an interactive text teaches students how to relate to content in a personal, meaningful way. They learn how to be attentive, energetic readers who reach a deep level of comprehension.

Big Ideas & Essential Questions

Each unit is designed to focus on a Big Idea and supporting lesson-level Essential Questions.

Connect Essential Questions

At the close of every unit, students build enduring understandings through synthesizing connections between different Essential Questions.

Active Reading

Annotation prompts and questions throughout the text teach students how to analyze and interact with content.

S.T.E.M.

STEM activities in every unit ask students to apply engineering and technology solutions in scenario-based learning situations.

Think Outside the Book

Students may wish to keep a Science Notebook to record illustrations and written work assignments. Blank pages at the end of each unit can also be used for this purpose.

Visualize It!

As concepts become more abstract, Visualize It! provides additional support for conceptual understanding.

Labs and Activities

The **Hands-on Labs** and **Virtual Labs** provide meaningful and exciting inquiry experiences.

S.T.E.M. Engineering & Technology

STEM activities in every unit focus on
- engineering and technology
- developing critical thinking and problem solving skills
- building inquiry, STEM, and 21st Century skills

Scenario-Based STEM Activity

You Try It!

Hands-On and Virtual

Three levels—directed, guided, and independent—of labs and activities plus lesson level Virtual Labs give students wall-to-wall options for exploring science concepts and building inquiry skills.

Hands-On Labs and Activities

Virtual Lab

Digital

The parallel-to-print **Digital Curriculum** provides **e-learning digital lessons and virtual labs** for every print lesson of the program.

360° of Inquiry

Digital Lessons and Virtual Labs

Digital Lessons and Virtual Labs provide an e-Learning environment of interactivity, videos, simulations, animations, and assessment designed for the way digital natives learn. An online Student Edition provides students anytime access to their student book.

Digital Lessons

Online Student Edition

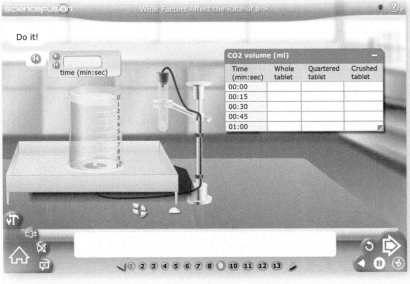

Virtual Labs

Video-Based Projects

Also available online:

- NSTA *SciLinks*
- Digital Lesson Progress Sheets
- Video-Based Projects
- Virtual Lab Datasheets
- People in Science Gallery
- Media Gallery
- Extra Support for Vocabulary and Concepts

Assessment

All paths lead to a full suite of print and online
Assessment Options right at your fingertips.

Classroom Management
Integrated Assessment Options

The *ScienceFusion* assessment options give you maximum flexibility in assessing what your students know and what they can do. Both the print and digital paths include formative and summative assessment. See the **Assessment Guide** for a comprehensive overview of your assessment options.

Teacher Online Management Center

Print Assessment

The print **Assessment Guide** includes

- **Lesson Quizzes**
- **Unit Tests**
- **Unit Performance Assessments**

Online Assessment

The **Digital Assessment** includes

- **assignable leveled assessments for individuals**
- **customizable lesson quizzes and unit tests**
- **individual and whole class reporting**

Customizing Assessment for Your Classroom

Editable quizzes and tests are available in ExamView and online at 🌐 **thinkcentral.com.** You can customize a quiz or test by adding or deleting items, revising difficulty levels, changing formats, revising sequence, and editing items. Students can also take quizzes and tests directly online.

Choose Your Options

with two powerful teaching tools— a comprehensive **Teacher Edition** and the **Teacher Online Management Center.**

Classroom Management   Teacher Edition

Lesson level teaching support, includes activities, probing questions, misconception alerts, differentiated instruction, and interpreting visuals.

- Lessons organized around a 5E lesson format

- Comprehensive support—print, digital, or hands-on—to match all teaching styles.

- Extension strategies for every lesson give teacher more tools to review and reinforce.

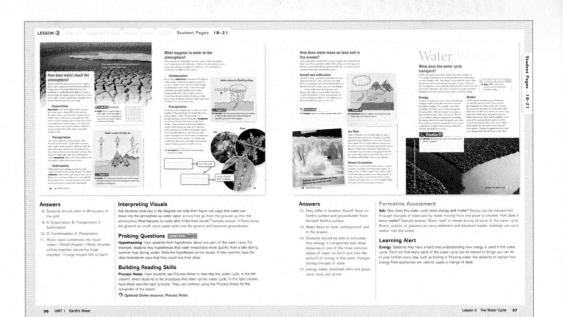

- Easy access to NSTA's e-professional development center, *The Learning Center*

- SciLinks provide students and teachers content-specific online support.

Additional support for STEM activities focuses on 21st century skills and helping students master the multi-dimensional abilities required of them in the 21st century.

Response to Intervention

Response to Intervention is a process for identifying and supporting students who are not making expected progress toward essential learning goals.

Probing Questions *Inquiry*

Lesson level questions and suggestions provide teachers with options for getting students to think more deeply and critically about a science concept.

Professional Development

Unit and lesson level professional development focuses on supporting teachers and building educator capacity in key areas of academic achievement.

Learning Alert *MISCONCEPTION*

The Learning Alert section previews Inquiry Activities and Lessons to gather and manage the materials needed for each lesson.

Classroom Management
Online teaching and planning

ScienceFusion is a comprehensive, multimodal science program that provides all the digital tools teachers need to engage students in inquiry-based learning. *The Teacher Online Management Center,* at ⊘ thinkcentral.com, is designed to make it easier for teachers to access program resources to plan, teach, assess, and track.

▶ Program resources can be easily previewed in PDF format and downloaded for editing.

▶ Assign and schedule resources online, and they will appear in your students' inboxes.

▶ All quizzes and tests can be taken and automatically scored online.

▶ Easily monitor and track student progress.

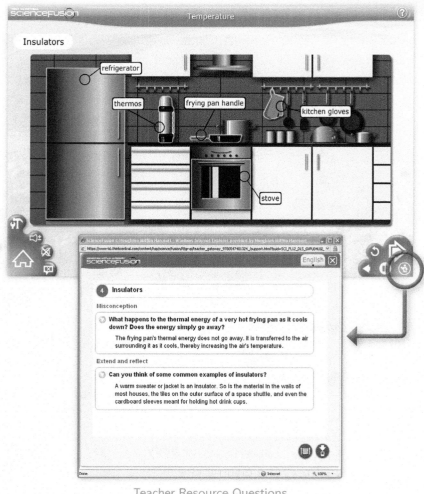

Teacher Resource Questions

Teaching with Technology Made Easy

ScienceFusion's 3,000+ animations, simulations, videos, & interactivities are organized to provide

▶ flexible options for delivering exciting and engaging digital lessons

▶ Teacher Resource Questions, for every lesson, to ensure that the important information is learned

▶ multimodal learning options that connect online learning to concepts learned from reading, writing, and hands-on inquiry

Student Edition Contents

When can lying down help you go faster? When you are on a bicycle! Lowering your body reduces the energy you need to travel faster.

Probably invented more than 40,000 years ago, the bow is a complex machine that is still used today.

Assignments:

_____

_____

_____

_____

_____

_____

_____

_____

_____

_____

Student Edition Contents

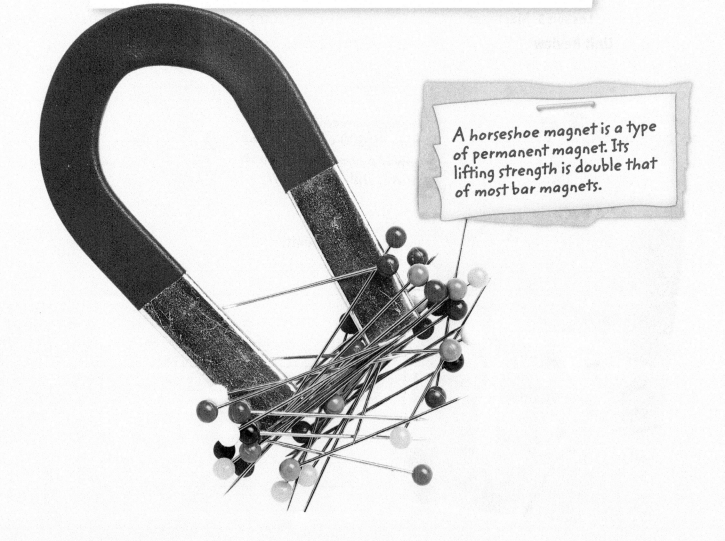

A horseshoe magnet is a type of permanent magnet. Its lifting strength is double that of most bar magnets.

Assignments:

_____
_____
_____
_____
_____
_____
_____
_____
_____
_____
_____
_____
_____
_____
_____
_____
_____
_____
_____
_____
_____

Program Scope and Sequence

ScienceFusion is organized by five major strands of science. Each strand includes Big Ideas that flow throughout all grade levels and build in rigor as students move to higher grades.

ScienceFusion Grade Levels and Units

	GRADE K	GRADE 1	GRADE 2	GRADE 3
Nature of Science	**Unit 1** Doing Science	**Unit 1** How Scientists Work	**Unit 1** Work Like a Scientist	**Unit 1** Investigating Questions
STEM	**Unit 2** Technology All Around Us	**Unit 2** Technology and Our World	**Unit 2** The Engineering Process	
Life Science	**Unit 2** Animals **Unit 3** Plants **Unit 4** Habitats	**Unit 3** Animals **Unit 4** Plants **Unit 5** Environments	**Unit 3** All About Animals **Unit 4** All About Plants **Unit 5** Environments for Living Things	**Unit 3** Plants and Animals **Unit 4** Ecosystems and Interactions

GRADE 4	GRADE 5	GRADES 6-8

Unit 1 Studying Science	**Unit 1** How Scientists Work	**Module K** Introduction to Science and Technology
		  Unit 1 The Nature of Science
		  Unit 2 Measurement and Data

Unit 2 The Engineering Process	**Unit 2** The Engineering Process	**Module K** Introduction to Science and Technology **Unit 3** Engineering, Technology, and Society

Unit 3 Plants and Animals
Unit 4 Energy and Ecosystems
	Unit 3 Cells to Body Systems
	Unit 4 Living Things Grow and Reproduce
	Unit 5 Ecosystems
	Unit 6 Energy and Ecosystems
		Module A Cells and Heredity
		  Unit 1 Cells
		  Unit 2 Reproduction and Heredity
		Module B The Diversity of Living Things
		  Unit 1 Life over Time
		  Unit 2 Earth's Organisms
		Module C The Human Body
		  Unit 1 Human Body Systems
		  Unit 2 Human Health
		Module D Ecology and the Environment
		  Unit 1 Interactions of Living Things
		  Unit 2 Earth's Biomes and Ecosystems
		  Unit 3 Earth's Resources
		  Unit 4 Human Impact on the Environment

ScienceFusion Grade Levels and Units

	GRADE K	GRADE 1	GRADE 2	GRADE 3
Earth Science	**Unit 5** Day and Night **Unit 6** Earth's Resources **Unit 7** Weather and the Seasons	**Unit 6** Earth's Resources **Unit 7** Weather and Seasons **Unit 8** Objects in the Sky	**Unit 6** Earth and Its Resources **Unit 7** All About Weather **Unit 8** The Solar System	**Unit 5** Changes to Earth's Surface **Unit 6** People and Resources **Unit 7** Water and Weather **Unit 8** Earth and Its Moon
Physical Science	**Unit 8** Matter **Unit 9** Energy **Unit 10** Motion	**Unit 9** All About Matter **Unit 10** Forces and Energy	**Unit 9** Changes in Matter **Unit 10** Energy and Magnets	**Unit 9** Matter **Unit 10** Simple and Compound Machines

GRADE 4	GRADE 5	GRADES 6-8

Unit 5 Weather
Unit 6 Earth and Space
	Unit 7 Natural Resources
	Unit 8 Changes to Earth's Surface
	Unit 9 The Rock Cycle
	Unit 10 Fossils
	Unit 11 Earth's Oceans
	Unit 12 The Solar System and the Universe
		Module E The Dynamic Earth
		  Unit 1 Earth's Surface
		  Unit 2 Earth's History
		  Unit 3 Minerals and Rocks
		  Unit 4 The Restless Earth
		Module F Earth's Water and Atmosphere
		  Unit 1 Earth's Water
		  Unit 2 Oceanography
		  Unit 3 Earth's Atmosphere
		  Unit 4 Weather and Climate
		Module G Space Science
		  Unit 1 The Universe
		  Unit 2 The Solar System
		  Unit 3 The Earth-Moon-Sun System
		  Unit 4 Exploring Space

Unit 7 Properties of Matter
Unit 8 Changes in Matter
Unit 9 Energy
Unit 10 Electricity
Unit 11 Motion
	Unit 13 Matter
	Unit 14 Light and Sound
	Unit 15 Forces and Motion
		Module H Matter and Energy
		  Unit 1 Matter
		  Unit 2 Energy
		  Unit 3 Atoms and the Periodic Table
		  Unit 4 Interactions of Matter
		  Unit 5 Solutions, Acids, and Bases
		Module I Motion, Forces, and Energy
		  Unit 1 Motion and Forces
		  Unit 2 Work, Energy, and Machines
		  Unit 3 Electricity and Magnetism
		Module J Sound and Light
		  Unit 1 Introduction to Waves
		  Unit 2 Sound
		  Unit 3 Light

ScienceFusion

Video-Based Projects

Available in Online Resources

This video series, hosted by program authors Michael Heithaus and Michael DiSpezio, develops science learning through real-world science and engineering challenges.

Ecology

Leave your lab coat at home! Not all science research takes place in a lab. Host Michael Heithaus takes you around the globe to see ecology field research, including tagging sharks and tracking sea turtles. Students research, graph, and analyze results to complete the project worksheets.

Module	Video Title
A	Photosynthesis
B	Expedition Evolution Animal Behavior
D	A Trip Down Shark River The Producers of Florida Bay
E	Transforming Earth
I	Animals in Motion
J	Animals and Sound
K	Invaders in the Everglades Data from Space

S.T.E.M. Science, Technology, Engineering, and Math

Host Michael DiSpezio poses a series of design problems that challenge students' ingenuity. Each video follows the engineering process. Worksheets guide students through the process and help them document their results.

Module	Video Title
A	An Inside View**
C	Prosthetics Robotic Assist**
D	Got Water?
E	Seismic Monitoring
F	When the Wind Blows Tornado Warning
G	Soft Landing
H	Just Add Heat
I	Take the Long Way

** In partnership with Children's Hospital Of Boston

Enduring Understandings

Big Ideas, Essential Questions

It goes without saying that a primary goal for your students is to develop understandings of science concepts that endure well past the next test. The question is, what is the best way to achieve that goal?

by Marjorie Frank

Research and learning experts suggest that students learn most effectively through a constructivist approach in which they build concepts through active involvement in their own learning. While constructivism may lead to superior learning on a lesson-by-lesson basis, the approach does not address how to organize lessons into a program of instruction. Schema theory, from cognitive science, suggests that knowledge is organized into units and that information is stored in these units, much as files are stored in a digital or paper folder. Informed by our understanding of schema theory, we set about organizing *ScienceFusion*. We began by identifying the Big Ideas of science.

> **Big Ideas** are generalizations—broad, powerful concepts that connect facts and events that may otherwise seem unrelated. Big Ideas are implicit understandings that help the world make sense. Big Ideas define the "folders," or units, of *ScienceFusion*. Each is a statement that articulates the overarching teaching and learning goals of a unit.

Essential Questions define the "files," or information, in a unit. Each Essential Question identifies the conceptual focus of a lesson that contributes to your students' growing understanding of the associated Big Idea. As such, Essential Questions give your students a sense of direction and purpose.

With *ScienceFusion*, our goal is to provide you with a tool that helps you help your students develop Enduring Understandings in science. Our strategy for achieving that goal has been to provide lesson plans with 5E-based learning experiences organized in a framework informed by schema theory.

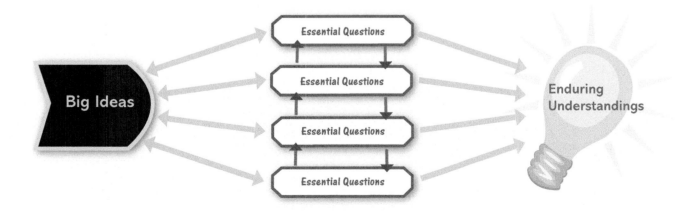

21st Century Skills/STEM

Skills Redefined

Our world has changed. Globalization and the digital revolution have redefined the skill set that is essential for student success in the classroom and beyond. Known collectively as 21st Century Skills, these areas of competence and aptitude go beyond the three Rs of reading, writing, and arithmetic. 21st Century Skills incorporate a battery of high-level thinking skills and technological capabilities.

by Michael A. DiSpezio

21st Century SKILLS A Sample List

Learning and Innovation Skills

- Creativity and Innovation
- Critical Thinking and Problem Solving
- Communication and Collaboration

Information, Media, and Technology Skills

- Information Literacy
- Media Literacy
- ICT (Information, Communications, and Technology) Literacy

Life and Career Skills

- Flexibility and Adaptability
- Initiative and Self-Direction
- Productivity and Accountability
- Leadership and Responsibility

S.T.E.M.

Curriculum that integrates Science, Technology, Engineering, and Mathematics

21st Century Skills are best taught in the context of the core subject areas. Science makes an ideal subject for integrating these important skills because it involves many skills, including inquiry, collaboration, and problem solving. An even deeper level of incorporating these skills can be found with Science, Technology, Engineering, and Mathematics (STEM) lessons and activities. Hands-on STEM lessons that provide students with engineering design challenges are ideal for developing Learning and Innovation Skills. Students develop creativity and innovation as they engineer novel solutions to posed problems. They communicate and collaborate as they engage higher-level thinking skills to help shape their inquiry experience. Students assume ownership of the learning. From this emerges increased self-motivation and personal accountability.

With STEM lessons and activities, related disciplines are seamlessly integrated into a rich experience that becomes far more than the sum of its parts. Students explore real-world scenarios using their understanding of core science concepts, ability for higher level analysis, technological know-how, and communication skills essential for collaboration. From this experience, the learner constructs not only a response to the STEM challenge, but the elements of 21st Century Skills.

ScienceFusion provides deep science content and STEM lessons, activities, and Video-Based Projects that incorporate and develop 21st Century Skills. This provides an effective learning landscape that will prepare students for success in the workplace—and in life.

Differentiated Instruction

Reaching All Learners

Your students learn in different ways, at different speeds, and through different means. Channeling the energy and richness of that diversity is part of the beauty of teaching. A classroom atmosphere that encourages academic risk-taking encourages learning. This is especially true in science, where learning involves making predictions (which could turn out to be inaccurate), offering explanations (which could turn out to be incomplete), and doing things (which could result in observable mistakes).

by Marjorie Frank

Like most people, students are more likely to take risks in a low-stress environment. Science, with its emphasis on exploring through hands-on activities and interactive reading, provides a natural vehicle for low-stress learning. Low stress, however, may mean different things to different people. For students with learning challenges, low stress may mean being encouraged to respond at the level they are able. Another factor in meeting the needs of diverse students is the instructional tools. Are they flexible? Inviting? *ScienceFusion* addresses the needs of diverse students at every step in the instructional process.

As You Plan

Select from these resources to meet individual needs.

- For each unit, the Differentiated Instruction page in the Teacher Edition identifies program resources specifically geared to diverse learners.

- Leveled activities in the Lesson Planning pages of the Teacher Edition provide additional learning opportunities for students with beginning, intermediate, or advanced proficiency.

- A bibliography contains notable trade books with in-depth information on content. Many of the books are recommendations of the National Science Teachers Association and the Children's Book Council.

- Online Resources: Alternative Assessment worksheets for each lesson provide varied strategies for learning content.

- Online Resources: Digital lessons, virtual labs, and video-based projects appeal to all students, especially struggling readers and visual learners.

- Student Edition with Audio is online as PDF files with audio readings for use with students who have vision impairments or learning difficulties.

- Student Edition reading strategies focus on vocabulary, concept development, and inquiry skills.

As You Teach

Take advantage of these point-of-use features.

- A mix of Directed Inquiry and Independent Inquiry prompts suitable for different kinds of learners

- Short-cut codes to specific interactive digital lessons

Take It Home

As you reach out to families, look for these school-home connections.

- Take It Home activities found at the beginning of many units in the Student Edition

- Additional Take It Home worksheets are available in the Online Resources

- School-Home Connection Letters for every unit, available online as files you can download and print as-is or customize

The 5E Model and Levels of Inquiry

How do students best learn science? Extensive research and data show that the most effective learning emerges from situations in which one builds understanding based upon personal experiences. Learning is not transmitted from instructor to passive receiver; instead, understanding is constructed through the experience.

by Michael A. DiSpezio

The 5E Model for Effective Science Lessons

In the 1960s, Robert Karplus and his colleagues developed a three-step instructional model that became known as the Learning Cycle. This model was expanded into what is today referred to as the 5E Model. To emulate the elements of how an actual scientist works, this model is broken down into five components for an effective lesson: Engage, Explore, Explain, Extend (or Elaborate), and Evaluate.

Engage—The engagement sets the scene for learning. It is a warm-up during which students are introduced to the learning experience. Prior knowledge is assessed and its analysis used to develop an effective plan to meet stated objectives. Typically, an essential question is then posed; the question leads the now motivated and engaged students into the exploration.

Explore—This is the stage where the students become actively involved in hands-on process. They communicate and collaborate to develop a strategy that addresses the posed problem. Emphasis is placed on inquiry and hands-on investigation. The hands-on experience may be highly prescribed or open-ended in nature.

Explain—Students answer the initial question by using their findings and information they may be reading about, discussing with classmates, or experiencing through digital media. Their experience and understanding of concepts, processes, and hands-on skills is strengthened at this point. New vocabulary may be introduced.

Extend (or Elaborate)—The explanation is now extended to other situations, questions, or problems. During this stage the learner more closely examines findings in terms of context and transferable application. In short, extension reveals the application and implication of the internalized explanation. Extension may involve connections to other curriculum areas.

Evaluate—Although evaluation is an ongoing process, this is the stage in which a final assessment is most often performed. The instructor evaluates lesson effectiveness by using a variety of formal and informal assessment tools to measure student performance.

The 5E lesson format is used in all the *ScienceFusion* Teacher Edition lessons.

Levels of Inquiry

It wasn't that long ago that science was taught mostly through demonstration and lecture. Today, however, most instructional strategies integrate an inquiry-based approach to learning science. This methodology is founded in higher-level thinking and facilitates the students' construction of understanding from experience. When offered opportunities to ask questions, design investigations, collect and analyze data, and communicate their findings, each student assumes the role of an active participant in shaping his or her own learning process.

The degree to which any activity engages the inquiry process is variable, from highly prescribed steps to a completely learner-generated design. Researchers have established three distinct levels of inquiry: directed (or structured) inquiry, guided inquiry, and independent (or open) inquiry. These levels are distinguished by the amount of guidance offered by the instructor.

DIRECTED inquiry

In this level of inquiry, the instructor poses a question or suggests an investigation, and students follow a prescribed set of instructions. The outcome may be unknown to the students, but it is known to the instructor. Students follow the structured outline to uncover an outcome that supports the construction of lesson concepts.

GUIDED inquiry

As in Directed Inquiry, the instructor poses to the students a question to investigate. While students are conducting the investigation, the instruction focuses on developing one or more inquiry skills. Focus may also be provided for students to learn to use methods or tools of science. In *ScienceFusion*, the Teacher Edition provides scaffolding for developing inquiry skills, science methods, or tools. Student pages accompany these lessons and provide prompts for writing hypotheses, recording data, and drawing conclusions.

INDEPENDENT inquiry

This is the most complex level of inquiry experience. A prompt is provided, but students must design their own investigation in response to the prompt. In some cases, students will write their own questions and then plan and perform scientific investigations that will answer those questions. This level of inquiry is often used for science fair projects. Independent Inquiry does not necessarily mean individual inquiry. Investigations can be conducted by individual students or by pairs or teams of students.

Response to Intervention

In a traditional model, assessment marks the end of an instructional cycle. Students work through a unit, take a test, and move on, regardless of their performance. However, current research suggests that assessment should be part of the instructional cycle, that it should be ongoing, and that it should be used to identify students needing intervention. This may sound like a tall order—who wants to give tests all the time?—but it may not be as difficult as it seems. In some ways, you are probably doing it already.

by Marjorie Frank

Assessment

Every student interaction has the potential to be an assessment. It all depends on how you perceive and use the interaction.

- Suppose you ask a question. You can just listen to your student's response, or you can assess it. Does the response indicate comprehension of the concept? If not, intervention may be needed.

- Suppose a student offers an explanation of a phenomenon depicted in a photo. You can assess the explanation. Does it show accurate factual knowledge? Does it reveal a misconception? If so, intervention may be needed.

- Suppose a student draws a diagram to illustrate a concept. You can assess the diagram. Is it accurate? If not, intervention may be needed.

As the examples indicate, assessing students' understandings can—and should—be an integral part of the instructional cycle and be used to make decisions about the next steps of instruction. For students making good progress, next steps might be exploring a related concept, a new lesson, or an additional challenge. For students who are not making adequate progress, intervention may be needed.

Assessment and intervention are tightly linked. Assessment leads to intervention—fresh approaches, different groupings, new materials—which, in turn, leads to assessment. Response to Intervention (RTI) gives shape and substance to this linkage.

RTI ▶ Response to Intervention

Response to Intervention is a process for identifying and supporting students who are not making expected progress toward essential learning goals.

RTI is a three-tiered approach based on an ongoing cycle of superior instruction, frequent monitoring of students' learning (assessments), and appropriate interventions. Students who are found not to be making expected progress in one Tier move to the next higher Tier, where they receive more intense instruction.

- **Tier I:** Students receive whole-class, core instruction.
- **Tier II:** Students work in small groups that supplement and reinforce core instruction.
- **Tier III:** Students receive individualized instruction.

How RTI and *ScienceFusion* Work

ScienceFusion provides many opportunities to assess students' understanding and many components appropriate for students in all Tiers.

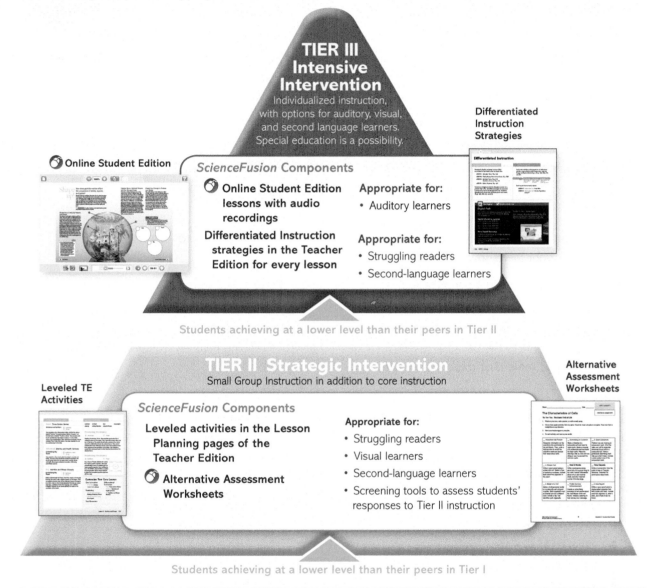

TIER III Intensive Intervention

Individualized instruction, with options for auditory, visual, and second language learners. Special education is a possibility.

Online Student Edition

Differentiated Instruction Strategies

ScienceFusion Components

Online Student Edition lessons with audio recordings

Differentiated Instruction strategies in the Teacher Edition for every lesson

Appropriate for:
- Auditory learners

Appropriate for:
- Struggling readers
- Second-language learners

Students achieving at a lower level than their peers in Tier II

TIER II Strategic Intervention

Small Group Instruction in addition to core instruction

Leveled TE Activities

Alternative Assessment Worksheets

ScienceFusion Components

Leveled activities in the Lesson Planning pages of the Teacher Edition

Alternative Assessment Worksheets

Appropriate for:
- Struggling readers
- Visual learners
- Second-language learners
- Screening tools to assess students' responses to Tier II instruction

Students achieving at a lower level than their peers in Tier I

TIER I Core Classroom Instruction

With the help of extensive point-of-use strategies that support superior teaching, students receive whole-class instruction and engage productively in small-group work as appropriate.

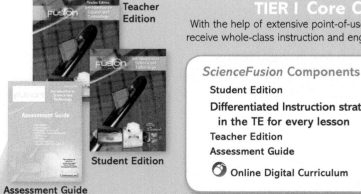

Teacher Edition

Student Edition

Assessment Guide

Digital Curriculum

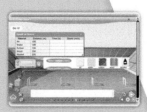

ScienceFusion Components

Student Edition

Differentiated Instruction strategies in the TE for every lesson

Teacher Edition

Assessment Guide

Online Digital Curriculum

Appropriate for:
- Screening tools to assess students' responses to Tier I instruction
- Tier I intervention for students unable to complete the activity independently

Active Reading

Reading is a complex process in which readers use their knowledge and experience to make meaning from text. Though rarely accompanied by obvious large-muscle movement, reading is very much an active endeavor.

by Marjorie Frank

Think back to your days as a college student when you pored over your textbooks to prepare for class or for an exam—or, more recently, concentrated on an article or book with information you wanted to remember.

▶ You probably paid close attention to the text.

▶ Perhaps you paused to ask yourself questions.

▶ You might have broken off temporarily to look up an important, but unfamiliar, word.

▶ You may have stopped to reread a challenging passage or to "catch up" if your mind wandered for a moment.

If you owned the reading material, you also may have used a pencil or marker to interact with the text right there on the page (or in a digital file).

In short, you were having a conversation with yourself about the text. You were engaged. You were thinking critically.

These are the characteristics of active readers. This is precisely the kind of reader you want your students to be, because research suggests that active reading enables readers to understand and remember more information.

Active Reading involves interacting with text cognitively, metacognitively, and quite literally. You can actually see active readers at work. They are not sitting quietly as they read; they're underlining, marking, boxing, bracketing, drawing arrows, numbering, and writing comments. Here is what they may be noting:

▶ key terms and main ideas

▶ connections between ideas

▶ questions they have, opinions, agreements, and disagreements

▶ important facts and details

▶ sequences of events

▶ words, such as *because, before,* and *but,* that signal connections between ideas

▶ problems/solutions

▶ definitions and examples

▶ characteristics

The very process of interacting actively with text helps keep readers focused, thinking, comprehending, and remembering. But interacting in this way means readers are marking up the text. This is exactly why *ScienceFusion* Student Editions are consumable. They are meant to be marked up.

Active Reading and *ScienceFusion*

ScienceFusion includes Active Reading prompts throughout the Student Editions. The prompts appear as part of the lesson opener and on most two-page spreads.

Students are often given an Active Reading prompt before reading a section or paragraph. These prompts ask students to underline certain words or number the steps in a process. Marking the text in this way is called *annotating*, and the students' marks are called *annotations*. Annotating the text can help students identify important concepts while reading. Other ways of annotating the text include placing an asterisk by vocabulary terms, marking unfamiliar or confusing terms and information with a question mark, and underlining main ideas. Students can even invent their own systems for annotating the text. An example of an annotation prompt is shown at right.

> **Active Reading** 5 **Identify** As you read, underline sources of energy for living things.

In addition, there are Active Reading questions throughout each lesson. These questions have write-on lines accompanying them, so students can answer right on the page. Students will be asked to **describe** what they've just read about, **apply** concepts, **compare** concepts, **summarize** processes, and **identify cause-and-effect** relationships. By answering these Active Reading questions while reading the text, students will be strengthening those and other critical thinking skills that are used so often in science.

> **Active Reading** 16 **Compare** What is the difference between the pulmonary and systemic circulations?
>
> _____
> _____
> _____

Students' Responses to Active Reading Prompts

Active Reading has benefits for you as well as for your students. You can use students' responses to Active Reading prompts and the other interactive prompts in *ScienceFusion* as ongoing assessments. A quick review of students' responses provides a great deal of information about their learning.

▶ Are students comprehending the text?

▶ How deeply do they understand the concepts developed?

▶ Did they get the main idea? the cause? the order in which things happen?

▶ Which part of a lesson needs more attention? for whom?

Answers to these questions are available in students' responses to Active Learning prompts throughout a lesson—long before you might see poor results on an end-of-lesson or end-of-unit assessment. If you are following Response to Intervention (RTI) protocols, these frequent and regular assessments, no matter how informal, are integral parts of an effective intervention program.

The Active Reading prompts in *ScienceFusion* help make everyone a winner.

Project-Based Learning

For a list of the *ScienceFusion* Video-Based Projects, see page xxiv.

by
Michael R. Heithaus

When asked why I decided to become a biologist, the answer is pretty simple. I was inspired by spending almost every day outdoors, exploring under every rock, getting muddy in creeks and streams, and fishing in farm ponds, rivers, and—when I was really lucky—the oceans. Combine that with the spectacular stories of amazing animals and adventure that I saw on TV and I was hooked. As I've progressed in my career as a biologist, that same excitement and curiosity that I had as a ten-year-old looking for a salamander is still driving me.

But today's kids live in a very different world. Cable and satellite TV, Twitter, MP3 players, cell phones, and video games all compete with the outdoors for kids' time and attention. Education budget cuts, legal issues, and the pressures of standardized testing have also limited the opportunities for students to explore outdoors with their teachers.

How do we overcome these challenges so as to inspire kids' curiosity, help them connect with the natural world, and get them to engage in science and math? This is a critical issue. Not only do we need to ensure our national competitiveness and the conservation of our natural resources by training the next generation of scientists, we also need to ensure that every kid grows up to understand how scientists work and why their work is important.

To overcome these challenges, there is no question that we need to grab students' attention and get them to actively engage in the learning process. Research shows that students who are active and engaged participants in their learning have greater gains in concept and skills development than students who are passive in the classroom.

Project-based learning is one way to engage students. And when the stimulus for the project is exciting video content, engaged and active learning is almost guaranteed. Nothing captures a student's attention faster than exciting video. I have noticed that when my university students have video to accompany a lesson, they learn and retain the material better. It's no different for younger students! Videos need to do more than just "talk at" students to have a real impact. Videos need to engage students and require participation.

Teachers and students who use *ScienceFusion* video-based projects have noticed the following:

- The videos use captivating imagery, dynamic scientists, and cool stories to inspire kids to be curious about the world around them.
- Students connect to the projects by having the videos present interesting problems for them to solve.
- The videos engage students with projects woven into the story of the video so students are doing the work of real scientists!

The start-to-finish nature of the video projects, where students do background research and develop their own hypotheses, should lead to students' personal investment in solving the challenges that are presented. By seeing real scientists who are excellent role models gather data that they have to graph and interpret, students will not only learn the science standards being addressed, they will see that they can apply the scientific method to their lives. One day, they too could be a scientist!

Based on my experiences teaching in the university classroom, leading field trips for middle school students, and taking the first project-based videos into the classroom, project-based learning has considerable benefits. The video-based projects generate enthusiasm and curiosity. They also help students develop a deeper understanding of science content as well as how to go about a scientific investigation. If we inspire students to ask questions and seek answers for themselves, we will go a long way toward closing achievement gaps in science and math and facilitate the development of the next generation of scientists and scientifically literate citizens.

Developing Visual Literacy

Science teachers can build the bridges between students' general literacy and their scientific literacy by focusing attention on the particular kinds of reading strategies students need to be successful. One such strategy is that of knowing how to read and interpret the various visual displays used in science.

by Donna M. Ogle

Many young readers receive little instruction in reading charts, tables, diagrams, photographs, or illustrations in their language arts/reading classes. Science is where these skills can and must be developed. Science provides a meaningful context where students can learn to read visually presented forms of information and to create their own visual representations. Research studies have shown that students take longer to read science materials containing combinations of visual displays and narrative texts than they do to read narrative text alone. The process of reading the combination materials is slower and more difficult because the reader must relate the visual displays to the narrative text and build a meaning that is based on information from both.

We also know that students benefit when teachers take time to explain how each visual form is constructed and to guide students in the thinking needed to make sense of these forms. Even the seemingly simple act of interpreting a photograph needs to be taught to most students. Here are some ways to help students develop the ability to think more critically about what they view:

▶ Model for students how to look carefully at a photograph and list what they notice.

▶ Divide the photograph into quadrants and have students think more deeply about what the photographer has used as the focus of the image and what context is provided.

▶ Have students use language such as *zoom, close-up, foreground, background*, or *panorama views* to describe photographs.

The ability to interpret a photograph is clearly a part of the scientific skill of engaging in careful observation. This skill helps students when they are using print materials, observing nature, and making their own photographs of aspects of their experiments.

Attention to the other forms of visual displays frequently used in science is also important to students' learning of scientific concepts and processes. For example, students in grades 4 through 8 need to learn to interpret and then construct each of the types of graphs, from circle graphs and bar graphs to more complex line graphs.

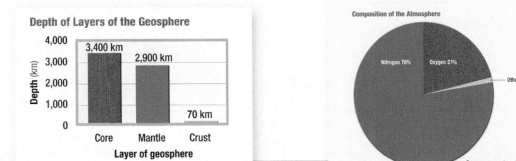

Students also need to be able to read diagrams and flow charts. Yet, in a recent study asking students to think aloud and point to how they visually scan tables and diagrams, we learned how inadequate many students were as readers of these visual forms. Because so much of the scientific information students will encounter is summarized in these visual formats, it is essential that students learn to interpret and construct visual displays.

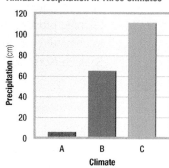

Annual Precipitation in Three Climates

A second aspect of interpreting visual displays is connecting the information in the visual formats with the narrative text information. Some students misinterpret what they see in visuals when even a few words differ between the text and the illustration. For example, in the excerpt below from a middle school Student Edition, the text says, "the arm of a human, the front leg of a cat, and the wing of a bat do not look alike . . . but they are similar in structure. "

The diagram labels (lower right) showing the bat wing and the cat's leg use *front limb*, not *wing* or *leg*. For students who struggle with English, the differing terms may cause confusion unless teachers show students how to use clues from later in the paragraph, where limb and wing/arm are connected, and how to connect this information to the two drawings. In some cases teachers have students draw lines showing where visual displays connect with the more extensive narrative text content. Developing students' awareness of how visual and narrative information support each other and yet provide different forms in which information can be shared is an important step in building scientific literacy.

Jenny's Bike Ride

Reading science requires students to use specific reading strategies. The more carefully science teachers across grade levels assess what students already know about reading scientific materials, the more easily they can focus instruction to build the scaffolds students need to gain independence and confidence in their reading and learning of science. Time spent explaining, modeling, and guiding students will yield the rewards of heightened student enjoyment, confidence, and engagement in the exciting world of scientific inquiry.

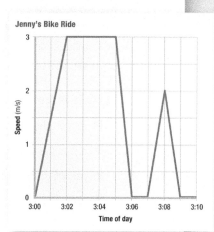

Common Structures

Scientists have found that related organisms share structural traits. Structures reduced in size or function may have been complete and functional in the organism's ancestor. For example, snakes have traces of leglike structures that are not used for movement. These unused structures are evidence that snakes share a common ancestor with animals like lizards and dogs.

Scientists also consider similar structures with different functions. The arm of a human, the front leg of a cat, and the wing of a bat do not look alike and are not used in the same way. But as you can see, they are similar in structure. The bones of a human arm are similar in structure to the bones in the front limbs of a cat and a bat. These similarities suggest that cats, bats, and humans had a common ancestor. Over millions of years, changes occurred. Now, these bones perform different functions in each type of animal.

front limb of a bat

front limb of a cat

Visualize It!

10 Relate Do you see any similarities between the bones of the bat and cat limbs and the bones of the human arm? If so, use the colors of the bat and cat bones to color similar bones in the human arm. If you don't have colored pencils, label the bones with the correct color names.

Science Notebooking

Science Notebooks are powerful classroom tools. They lead your students deep into the learning process, and they provide you with a window into that process as well as a means to communicate about it. Most middle-school students will have had some experience using a Science Notebook during their elementary years.

Why Use a Science Notebook?

A Science Notebook contains the writer's ideas, observations, and perceptions of events and endeavors. A Science Notebook also contains ideas and observations of scientific processes, data, conclusions, conjectures, and generalizations.

Inquiry Skills A Science Notebook is especially important when students do inquiry-based activities. It offers students a single place to record their observations, consider possibilities, and organize their thoughts. As such, it is a learner's version of the logs that professional scientists keep.

In their Science Notebooks, students can

▶ sketch their ideas and observations from experiments and field trips

▶ make predictions about what will happen in an experiment

▶ reflect on their work and the meaning they derived from experiments

▶ make inferences based on the data they have gathered

▶ propose additional experiments to test new hypotheses

▶ pose new questions based on the results of an activity or experiment

Process Skills A Science Notebook is an excellent extension of the textbook, allowing students to further practice and hone process skills. Students will not only apply these skills in relation to the specific science content they are learning, they will be gaining a deeper insight into scientific habits of mind.

In their Science Notebooks, students can

▶ record and analyze data

▶ create graphs and charts

▶ infer outcomes

▶ draw conclusions

▶ collect data from multiple experimental trials

▶ develop 21st Century organizational skills

A student's Science Notebook entry for a *ScienceFusion* Quick Lab
▼

Quick Lab: Balancing Act

Partner: Evan

Answers

2. Me: 12 adjustments
   Evan: 10 adjustments

3. No, I was not aware of my muscles making adjustments the first time. I think I didn't notice because I was concentrating more on just staying on one leg.

4. Yes, I was aware of my muscles making adjustments the second time. I think my muscles worked harder the second time because my leg was getting tired.

5. 12 times

6. Your body is always having to make adjustments to maintain a balanced internal environment. Most of these adjustments aren't even noticed by a person, just like I didn't notice my leg muscles adjusting during the first balancing test.

Science Notebooks and *ScienceFusion*

In many ways, the *ScienceFusion* worktexts are Science Notebooks in themselves. Students are encouraged to write answers directly in the text and to annotate the text for better understanding. However, a separate Science Notebook can still be an invaluable part of your student's learning experience with *ScienceFusion*. Student uses for a Science Notebook along with the worktext include:

▶ writing answers for the Unit Review

▶ writing responses to the Think Outside the Book features in each lesson

▶ planning for and writing answers to the Citizen Science feature in each unit

▶ working through answers before writing them in the worktext

▶ writing all answers if you choose not to have students work directly in the worktext

▶ taking notes on additional materials you present outside of the worktext

▶ making observations and recording data from Daily Demos and additional activities provided in the Teacher Edition

▶ collecting data and writing notes for labs performed from the Lab Manual

▶ making notes and writing answers for Digital Lessons and Virtual Labs

▶ collecting data and writing answers for the Project-Based Videos

The Benefits (for You and Your Students) of Science Notebooking

No doubt, it takes time and effort to help students set up and maintain Science Notebooks, not to mention the time it takes you to review them and provide meaningful feedback. The payoff is well worth it. Here's why:

Keeping a Science Notebook:

▶ leads each learner to engage with ideas

▶ engages students in writing—an active, thinking, analytical process

▶ causes students to organize their thinking

▶ provides students with multiple opportunities and modes to process new information

▶ makes learning experiences more personal

▶ provides students with a record of their own progress and accomplishments

▶ doubles as a study guide for formal assessments

▶ creates an additional vehicle for students to improve their reading and writing skills

As you and your students embrace Science Notebooking, you will surely find it to be an engaging, enriching, and very valuable endeavor.

Using the *ScienceFusion* Worktext

Research shows that an interactive text teaches students how to relate to content in a personal, meaningful way. They learn how to be attentive, energetic readers who reach a deep level of comprehension. Still, the worktext format may be new to you and your students. Below are some answers to questions—both pedagogical and practical—you may have about *ScienceFusion's* worktext format.

How does the worktext format help my students learn?

▶ In this format, your students will interact with the text and visuals on every page. This will teach them to read expertly, to think critically, and to communicate effectively—all skills that are crucial for success in the 21st century.

▶ The use of images and text on every page of the *ScienceFusion* worktext accommodates both visual and verbal learners. Students are engaged by the less formal, magazine-like presentation of the content.

▶ By the end of the school year, the worktexts become a record of the knowledge and skills your students learned in class. Students can use their books as a study guide to prepare for tests.

What are some features that make the *ScienceFusion* worktext different from a regular textbook?

Some of the special features of the *ScienceFusion* worktext include these prompts for writing directly in the worktext:

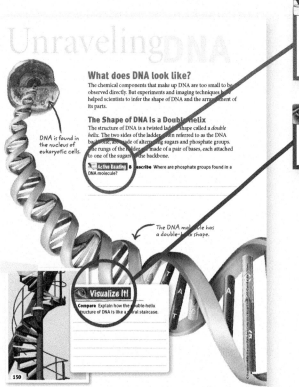

Active Reading

Annotation prompts and questions throughout the worktext teach students how to analyze and interact with content as they read.

Visualize It!

Questions and completion prompts that accompany images help develop visual literacy.

Engage Your Brain

Math problems, with on-page guidance, allow students to understand the relationships between math and science and to practice their math skills.

Do the Math

Interesting questions and activities on the lesson opener pages help prepare students for the lesson content.

Are my students really supposed to write directly in the book?

Yes! Write-on lines are provided for students to answer questions on-page, while the student is reading. Additional prompts are given for students to annotate the pages. You can even encourage your students to experiment with their own systems of annotation. More information can be found in "A How-To Manual for Active Reading" in the Look It Up! Section at the end of the Student Edition and Teacher Edition.

You might wish to encourage your students to write in the worktexts using pencils so that they can more easily revise their answers and notes as needed.

We will have to use the same set of worktexts for several years. How can students use the worktexts if they can't write in them?

Though *ScienceFusion* is set up in a worktext format, the books can still be used in a more traditional fashion. Simply tell your students that they cannot write in the textbooks but should instead use their Science Notebooks for taking notes and answering questions. (See the article titled "Science Notebooking" for more information about using Notebooks with *ScienceFusion*.)

How do I grade my students' answers in the worktext?

The pages in the worktext are conveniently perforated so that your students can turn in their work. Or you may wish for your students to leave the pages in the book, but turn in the books to you on a daily or weekly basis for you to grade them.

The Lesson Reviews and Unit Reviews are designed so students can turn in the pages but still keep their annotated pages for reference when moving on to the next lesson or unit or for review before a lesson or unit test.

- Tour the classroom while students are writing in their worktexts. Address any issues you see immediately or make note of items that need to be addressed with students later.

- Have students do 'self checks' and 'partner checks.' Choose a question in the worktext, and have all students check their responses. Or, have students trade their worktext with a partner to check each other's responses.

- Once a week, have students copy five questions and their responses from the worktext onto a sheet of notebook paper. You can review student answers to ensure they're using the worktext correctly without having students turn in worktext pages or the books themselves.

- Use a document camera to show students correct worktext answers.

- Every two weeks, review and grade one class's worth of student worktext answers per day. Or, grade a class's worktexts while the students are taking a test.

Pacing Guide

You have options for covering the lesson materials: you may choose to follow the digital path, the print path, or a combination of the two. Customize your Pacing Guide to plan print, inquiry, digital, and assessment mini-blocks based on your teaching style and classroom needs.

Pressed for Time? Follow the faster-paced compressed schedule.

	Traditional 1 = 45 min	Block 1 = 90 min	Compressed (T/B)	Print Path	Inquiry Labs & Activities	Digital Path	Review & Assess
UNIT 1 Motion and Forces							
Unit Project	3	1.5	3 (1.5)				
Lesson 1 Motion and Speed	6	3	5 (2.5)				
Lesson 2 Acceleration	3	1	2 (1)				
Lesson 3 Forces	6	3	5 (2.5)				
Lesson 4 Gravity and Motion	4	2	3 (1.5)				
Lesson 5 Fluids and Pressure	6	3	5 (2.5)				
Unit Review	2	1	1 (0.5)				
Total Days for Unit 1	30	14.5	24 (12)				
UNIT 2 Work, Energy, and Machines							
Unit Project	3	1.5	3 (1.5)				
Lesson 1 Work, Energy, and Power	4	2	3 (1.5)				
Lesson 2 Kinetic and Potential Energy	4	2	3 (1.5)				
Lesson 3 Machines	6	3	5 (2.5)				
Unit Review	2	1	1 (0.5)				
Total Days for Unit 2	19	9.5	15 (7.5)				

Total Days (spanning Traditional, Block, Compressed). Customize Your Pacing Guide (spanning Print Path, Inquiry Labs & Activities, Digital Path, Review & Assess).

	Total Days			Customize Your Pacing Guide				
	Traditional 1 = 45 min	Block 1 = 90 min	Compressed (T/B)	Print Path	Inquiry Labs & Activities	Digital Path	Review & Assess
UNIT 3 Electricity and Magnetism							
Unit Project	3	1.5	3 (1.5)				
Lesson 1 Electric Charge and Static Electricity	4	2	3 (1.5)				
Lesson 2 Electric Current	3	1	2 (1)				
Lesson 3 Electric Circuits	5	2.5	4 (2)				
Lesson 4 Magnets and Magnetism	4	2	3 (1.5)				
Lesson 5 Electromagnetism	6	3	5 (2.5)				
Lesson 6 Electronic Technology	4	2	3 (1.5)				
Unit Review	2	1	1 (0.5)				
Total Days for Unit 3	31	15	24 (12)				

The Big Idea and Essential Questions

This Unit was designed to focus on this Big Idea and Essential Questions.

Big Idea Unbalanced forces cause changes in the motion of objects, and these changes can be predicted and described.

Lesson	ESSENTIAL QUESTION	Student Mastery	PD Professional Development	Lesson Overview
LESSON 1 Motion and Speed	*How are distance, time, and speed related?*	To analyze how distance, time, and speed are related	Content Refresher, TE p. 6	TE p. 14
LESSON 2 Acceleration	*How does motion change?*	To analyze how acceleration is related to time and velocity	Content Refresher, TE p. 7	TE p. 32
LESSON 3 Forces	*How do forces affect motion?*	To describe different types of forces and explain the effect force has on motion	Content Refresher, TE p. 8	TE p. 44
LESSON 4 Gravity and Motion	*How do objects move under the influence of gravity?*	To describe the effect that gravity, including Earth's gravity, has on matter	Content Refresher, TE p. 9	TE p. 60
LESSON 5 Fluids and Pressure	*What happens when fluids exert pressure?*	To explain why fluids exert pressure and how the resulting pressure causes motion and the buoyant force	Content Refresher, TE p. 10	TE p. 76

©Gary I. Rothstein/epa/Corbis

Professional Development   Science Background

Use the keywords at right to access

- Professional Development from **The NSTA Learning Center**
- **SciLinks** for additional online content appropriate for students and teachers

Keywords

fluids   gravity

forces   motion

Options for Instruction

Two parallel paths provide coverage of the Essential Questions, with a strong **Inquiry** strand woven into each. Follow the Print Path, the **Digital Path,** or your customized combination of print, digital, and inquiry.

	LESSON 1 Motion and Speed	LESSON 2 Acceleration	LESSON 3 Forces
Essential Questions	*How are distance, time, and speed related?*	*How does motion change?*	*How do forces affect motion?*
Key Topics	• Motion • Speed • Distance-Time Graphs • Velocity	• Acceleration • Acceleration as a Vector	• Introduction to Forces • Net Forces • Newton's Laws
Print Path	Teacher Edition pp. 14–28 Student Edition pp. 4–17	Teacher Edition pp. 32–43 Student Edition pp. 20–27	Teacher Edition pp. 44–58 Student Edition pp. 28–41
Inquiry Labs	Lab Manual **Quick Lab** Investigate Changing Positions **Quick Lab** Create a…Graph **S.T.E.M. Lab** Investigate Average Speed	Lab Manual **Quick Lab** Acceleration… Slope **Quick Lab** Mass and Acceleration **S.T.E.M. Lab** Investigate Acceleration	Lab Manual **Quick Lab** Net Force **S.T.E.M. Lab** Newton's Laws of Motion Virtual Lab Sliding Downhill
Digital Path	Digital Path TS665131	Digital Path TS665132	Digital Path TS665181

LESSON 4	LESSON 5	UNIT 1
Gravity and Motion	Fluids and Pressure	Unit Projects

LESSON 4
Gravity and Motion

How do objects move under the influence of gravity?

- Gravity
- Law of Universal Gravitation
- Orbits

Teacher Edition
pp. 60–72

Student Edition
pp. 42–51

Lab Manual
Quick Lab Gravity and Distance

Quick Lab Free-Fall Distances

 **Virtual Lab**
What Factors Affect
Gravitational Attraction?

Digital Path
TS665212

LESSON 5
Fluids and Pressure

What happens when fluids exert pressure?

- Introduction to Pressure and Fluids
- Atmospheric Pressure and Water Pressure
- Pressure and Fluid Flow
- Buoyant Force

Teacher Edition
pp. 76–90

Student Edition
pp. 54–67

Lab Manual
Quick Lab Finding the Buoyant Force

Quick Lab Pressure Differences

Field Lab Pressure in Fluids

Digital Path
TS675255

UNIT 1
Unit Projects

Citizen Science Project
What's in a Vane?

Teacher Edition p. 13

Student Edition
pp. 2–3

Video-Based Projects
Animals in Motion

Unit Assessment
Formative Assessment
Strategies RTI
Throughout TE
Lesson Reviews SE
Unit PreTest

Summative Assessment
Alternative Assessment
(1 per lesson) RTI
Lesson Quizzes

Unit Tests A and B
Unit Review RTI
(with answer remediation)
Practice Tests
(end of module)

Project-Based Assessment
See the Assessment Guide for quizzes and tests.

Go Online to edit and create quizzes and tests.

Response to Intervention

See RTI teacher support materials on p. PD6.

Differentiated Instruction

English Language Proficiency

Strategies for **English Language Learners (ELL)** are provided for each lesson, under the Explain tabs.

LESSON 1 *Definition Differences,* TE p. 19

LESSON 2 *Acceleration Terms,* TE p. 37

LESSON 3 *Newton's Laws of Motion,* TE p. 49

LESSON 4 *Cause and Effect,* TE p. 65

LESSON 5 *Double-Door Fold,* TE p. 81

Vocabulary strategies provided for all students can also be a particular help for ELL. Use different strategies for each lesson or choose one or two to use throughout the unit. Vocabulary strategies can be found under the Explain tab for each lesson (TE pp. 19, 37, 49, 65, and 81).

Leveled Inquiry

Inquiry labs, activities, probing questions, and daily demos provide a range of inquiry levels. Preview them under the Engage and Explore tabs starting on TE pp. 16, 34, 46, 62, and 78.

 Levels of **Inquiry**

DIRECTED inquiry	GUIDED inquiry	INDEPENDENT inquiry
introduces inquiry skills within a structured framework.	develops inquiry skills within a supportive environment.	deepens inquiry skills with student-driven questions or procedures.

Each long lab has two inquiry options:

LESSON 1 S.T.E.M. Lab *Investigate Average Speed*

LESSON 2 S.T.E.M. Lab *Investigate Acceleration*

LESSON 3 S.T.E.M. Lab *Newton's Laws of Motion*

LESSON 5 Field Lab *Pressure in Fluids*

Go Digital! 🔊 thinkcentral.com

Digital Path

The Unit 1 Resource Gateway is your guide to all of the digital resources for this unit. To access the Gateway, visit thinkcentral.com.

Digital Interactive Lessons

Lesson 1 Motion and Speed TS665131

Lesson 2 Acceleration TS665132

Lesson 3 Forces TS665181

Lesson 4 Gravity and Motion TS665212

Lesson 5 Fluids and Pressure TS675255

More Digital Resources

In addition to digital lessons, you will find the following digital resources for Unit 1:

People in Science: Steve Okamoto

Video-Based Project: Animals in Motion
(previewed on TE p. 12)

Virtual Labs: Sliding Downhill
(previewed on TE p. 47)
What Factors Affect Gravitational Attraction?
(previewed on TE p. 63)

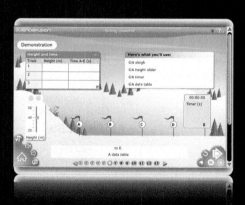

RTI Response to Intervention

Response to Intervention (RTI) is a process for identifying and supporting students who are not making expected progress toward essential learning goals. The following *ScienceFusion* components can be used to provide strategic and intensive intervention.

Component	Location	Strategies and Benefits
STUDENT EDITION Active Reading prompts, Visualize It!, Think Outside the Book	**Throughout each lesson**	Student responses can be used as screening tools to assess whether intervention is needed.
TEACHER EDITION Formative Assessment, Probing Questions, Learning Alerts	**Throughout each lesson**	Opportunities are provided to assess and remediate student understanding of lesson concepts.
TEACHER EDITION Extend Science Concepts	**Reinforce and Review, TE pp. 20, 38, 50, 66, 82** **Going Further, TE pp. 20, 38, 50, 66, 82**	Additional activities allow students to reinforce and extend their understanding of lesson concepts.
TEACHER EDITION Evaluate Student Mastery	**Formative Assessment, TE pp. 21, 39, 51, 67, 83** **Alternative Assessment, TE pp. 21, 39, 51, 67, 83**	These assessments allow for greater flexibility in assessing students with differing physical, mental, and language abilities as well as varying learning and communication modes.
TEACHER EDITION Unit Review Remediation	**Unit Review, TE pp. 92–94**	Includes reference back to Lesson Planning pages for remediation activities and assignments.
INTERACTIVE DIGITAL LESSONS and VIRTUAL LABS	**thinkcentral.com** **Unit 1 Gateway** **Lesson 1 TS665131** **Lesson 2 TS665132** **Lesson 3 TS665181** **Lesson 4 TS665212** **Lesson 5 TS675255**	Lessons and labs make content accessible through simulations, animations, videos, audio, and integrated assessment. Useful for review and reteaching of lesson concepts.

Content Refresher

Professional Development

Motion and Speed

ESSENTIAL QUESTION
How are distance, time, and speed related?

1. Motion

Motion occurs when an object travels from one point to another.

Position describes the location of an object. A reference point is a location to which you compare other locations. Motion is a change in position over time. Distance depends on the path you take; the distance between two points can be different depending on how it is measured. The standard unit of length with which to measure distance is the meter (m). Longer distances are measured in kilometers (km), and shorter distances are measured in centimeters (cm). Very short distances can be measured in millimeters (mm).

In eighteenth-century France, some 2,000 different units of measurement were used because different locales had their own systems. The French Revolution (1789–1799) set the stage for a new, universal system of measurement. A commission decided on a basic unit of measurement, the meter. They designed a decimal system that uses base names (such as *meter* and *gram*) and prefixes to indicate fractional and multiple units (such as *milligram* and *kilogram*). In 1795, the French government adopted the metric system.

2. Speed

Distance and time are used to calculate speed.

Speed is a measure of how fast something moves, or how far it moves in a given amount of time. It is the distance that an object travels divided by the time the object takes to travel that distance. Average speed is a way to calculate the speed of an object that may not always be moving at a constant speed. To calculate average speed (s), divide the total distance (d) by the total time (t): $s = d/t$.

3. Distance-Time Graphs

You can analyze speed with a distance-time graph.

A distance-time graph plots the distance traveled by an object on the y-axis and the time on the x-axis. To calculate the speed of an object using a distance-time graph, calculate the steepness, or slope, of the line (change in y over change in x, or "rise over run"). As an object moves, the distance it travels increases with time. On a distance-time graph, this is shown as a rising line. A flat line on a distance-time graph indicates that the object is not moving—that is, the speed is zero. Steeper lines on a distance-time graph show intervals where the speed is greater than intervals with less steep lines.

The fastest-running mammal is the cheetah, a large cat native to Africa. The cheetah can reach a speed of 110 kilometers per hour (about 70 miles per hour) when chasing prey. By contrast, the fastest Olympic runner can reach a speed of about 37 kilometers per hour (about 23 miles per hour). Neither the cheetah nor the runner, however, can maintain their speed for very long.

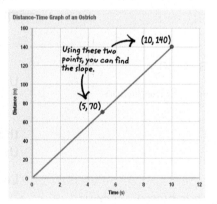

Distance-Time Graph of an Ostrich

(10, 140)

Using these two points, you can find the slope.

(5, 70)

4. Velocity

Velocity consists of speed and direction.

A vector is a quantity that has both size and direction.

Velocity is a vector. It specifies both speed and direction. Because velocity has a direction, it is possible for two objects to have the same speed but different velocities. Such objects move at the same speed but in different directions.

Teacher (to) Teacher

Jennifer Eddy
Lindale Middle School
Linthicum, MD

Lesson 1 Motion and Speed   In my classes, I use sports examples (including video footage) to show students how distance, time, and speed are related. Then, I have groups of students write and perform a "sports broadcast" to explain how the distance traveled in a certain amount of time affects the speed of an object or person. I encourage students to use examples from all different types of sports.

Lesson 2

Acceleration
ESSENTIAL QUESTION
How does motion change?

1. Acceleration

Acceleration occurs when velocity changes.

Acceleration is the rate of change in velocity. It is the difference between the velocity an object starts with and the velocity an object ends with, divided by time. Average acceleration is a way to calculate the acceleration of an object that may not always be moving at a constant acceleration.

$$a = \frac{v_2 - v_1}{t_2 - t_1}$$

Acceleration is measured in meters per second per second, or meters per second squared (m/s^2).

Producing acceleration requires force.

In order to produce an acceleration, a force must be applied to an object. The nature of the acceleration produced depends on the magnitude and direction of the force, and the direction of motion of the object being acted upon. For example, a force acting in the same direction as the velocity will only change the speed of the object, not its direction.

Everyday versus physical science usage.

In everyday life, the word acceleration is used to mean an increase in speed and the word deceleration is used to mean a decrease in speed. In physics, acceleration refers to any change in speed—either increase or decrease.

2. Acceleration as a Vector

Acceleration occurs when there is a change in speed or direction.

Acceleration is a vector, so acceleration can be the result of a change in speed, a change in direction, or both. An object that is changing direction experiences acceleration even when it does not speed up or slow down.

Acceleration can be positive or negative.

If the velocity of an object is increasing, the object is experiencing positive acceleration. If the velocity of an object is decreasing, the object is experiencing negative acceleration.

Objects experiencing centripetal acceleration are always changing direction.

Acceleration that results in circular motion, where an object is always changing direction but not necessarily speed, is called centripetal acceleration. The object always experiences acceleration because it is always changing direction. Examples of objects experiencing centripetal acceleration are a satellite orbiting Earth, which has a fairly uniform speed but is constantly changing direction, or an object tied to the end of a string being swung around in a circle. That object would likely have changes in speed as well as direction.

Sir Isaac Newton coined the word centripetal when he discovered centripetal force. He derived it from the Latin *centrum*, which means "center," and *petere*, which means "to rush."

 COMMON MISCONCEPTIONS RTI

ACCELERATION MEANS SPEEDING UP Students often think of acceleration as an object speeding up. They may not realize that if an object slows down it is accelerating, too—that is, it has negative acceleration.

This misconception is addressed in the Daily Demo on p. 35 and the Learning Alert on p. 41.

Content Refresher (continued)

Professional Development

Forces

ESSENTIAL QUESTION
How do forces affect motion?

1. Introduction to Force

Students will learn what a force is and how to discriminate between contact forces and forces that act at a distance.

A force is a push or a pull exerted on an object that can change the motion of the object. Force is measured in SI units called newtons (N). *SI* is an abbreviation for the French *le Système International d'Unités*, or International System of Units. SI is the most widely used system of measurement. Force can also be measured in English units called pounds. Force is a vector, meaning that every force has both magnitude and direction. Forces can transfer energy through direct contact, such as friction or normal force. Forces can also transfer energy at a distance, as with gravity, magnetism, and electrical charges.

2. Net Force

Students will learn the concept of net force and how to use it to determine the direction of motion.

The net force acting on any object is the combination of all the forces acting on that object. When these forces acting on an object at rest produce a net force of zero, the forces are balanced. Balanced forces result in no change in the motion of the object. This means if the object is at rest, it will remain at rest. If an object is moving with constant velocity (speed and direction), it will remain moving with the same velocity. When the forces acting on an object at rest are not balanced, the object will accelerate in the same direction as the direction of the net force.

These dogs are pulling with equal force on the toy. The net force is 0 N, and the toy will not move.

3. Newton's Laws

Students will learn Newton's three laws of motion.

Isaac Newton developed three laws that, taken together, explain how and why objects move as they do. Newton's first law of motion states that an object at rest will remain at rest, and an object in motion will remain moving at a constant velocity unless and until it experiences an unbalanced force. This is universally known as the law of inertia. Inertia is the tendency of an object to resist a change in its motion. Two common outside forces that influence moving objects on Earth are friction and gravity.

Newton's second law states that the acceleration of an object produced by the net force of all outside forces will be directly proportional to the magnitude of the force and inversely proportional to the mass of the object. In other words, for a given force, the greater the mass of the object, the smaller will be the acceleration produced by that force. This relationship can be expressed by the mathematical formula $F = ma$.

Newton's third law is known as the law of action and reaction. It states that whenever one object exerts a force on a second object, the second object exerts a force on the first object that is equal in magnitude and opposite in direction. In other words, forces always act in pairs. Action and reaction forces occur at the same time. But the action and reaction forces never act on the same object—the action force will act on one of a pair of interacting objects, while the reaction force will act on the other. For example, when a person walks across a floor, the person's feet push against the floor and the floor pushes against the feet, and the whole body moves. The forces in a force pair do not always have equal effects; if one object in a force pair has a larger mass, it will undergo a smaller acceleration from the force acting upon it.

One of these dogs is pulling with more force on the toy. The toy will move in the direction of the larger dog.

Gravity and Motion

ESSENTIAL QUESTION

How do objects move under the influence of gravity?

1. Gravity

Masses attract each other.

Gravity is the force objects exert on each other because of their mass. We feel the effects of Earth's gravity constantly; Earth's gravity pulls people and all other objects on and around Earth toward its center. Gravity plays a large role in the organization of celestial bodies. The moon's orbit around Earth and Earth's own orbit around the sun are due to gravity.

The force of gravity between Earth and an object, which is equivalent to weight, is equal to the mass of the object m multiplied by the acceleration due to gravity g. The formula F = mg represents this relationship. Gravitational acceleration equals 9.8 m/s^2 at Earth's surface.

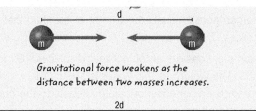

Gravitational force weakens as the distance between two masses increases.

2. Law of Universal Gravitation

Gravity depends on mass and distance.

The two factors that affect gravity are mass and distance. There is always gravitational force, or attraction, between two objects. However, when the mass of one or both of those objects increases, the gravitational force between them increases. Gravitational force also increases when distance decreases, or the objects get closer together. Gravitational force changes as the square of the distance.

3. Orbits

Gravity keeps objects in orbit.

An orbit is an elliptical path that one object takes around another object. An orbital path is the result of the speed of the orbiting body and the gravitational pull between the two objects.

The speed an object must have to escape the gravitational pull of another body, such as a spacecraft leaving a planet, is called escape velocity. If the object is not projected straight up, speeds lower than the escape velocity will result in orbital motion.

A spacecraft and its contents in orbit are in free fall. The environment is such that an astronaut can't feel gravity.

▨▨ COMMON MISCONCEPTIONS ▨▨ RTI

WEIGHT AND MASS Students frequently think that weight and mass are terms that can be used interchangeably. This sometimes happens because on Earth, the two are virtually interchangeable in a practical—not scientific—sense. In fact, mass is the amount of matter an object contains, and it remains the same no matter where the object is. Weight depends on the force of gravity exerted upon an object.

This misconception is addressed in the Discussion on p. 62 and in the Learning Alert on p. 70.

Content Refresher (continued)

Professional Development

Fluids and Pressure

ESSENTIAL QUESTION
What happens when fluids exert pressure?

1. Introduction to Pressure and Fluids

Students will learn that pressure is a force and that fluids can be liquids or gases.

The term *pressure* is the amount of force exerted on a given area. Quantitatively, pressure is defined by the following equation:

pressure = force/area

The SI unit for measuring pressure is the pascal (Pa). One pascal is equivalent to one newton per meter squared (N/m^2). SI units refer to *Système Internationale d'Unités*, which are international standards for measuring quantities.

Fluids are substances that can flow and take on the shape of a container, and includes gases and liquids. The kinetic theory of matter explains the pressure that fluids exert. Because particles are in constant motion, they collide with their container, and these collisions exert a force. The pressure increases when the force of the collisions increases or when the area of the container decreases.

2. Atmospheric Pressure and Water Pressure

Students will learn that the atmosphere and water both exert pressure.

Atmospheric pressure is the pressure caused by the weight of Earth's atmosphere. We typically do not notice atmospheric pressure because the pressure inside our bodies is roughly equal to atmospheric pressure.

Water pressure is the pressure caused by the weight of water.

Both atmospheric pressure and water pressure increase with the weight of air or water above them. Pressure increases as you move from the upper atmosphere to sea level to the ocean floor.

3. Pressure and Fluid Flow

Students will learn that pressure affects the movement of fluids.

Fluids at about the same altitude flow from regions of higher pressure to regions of lower pressure. This explains why air moves in and out during respiration. During an inhalation, an expanding chest cavity causes pressure in the lungs to decrease and air to move into the lungs from the outside. During an exhalation, the reverse processes occur.

Wind is a result of differences in atmospheric pressure near Earth's surface. Winds blow from regions of high pressure to regions of low pressure.

4. Buoyant Force

Students will learn that buoyant force and Archimedes' principle explain why objects sink, float, or buoy up.

Fluids exert forces in all directions. The upward force that a fluid exerts on an object is called the buoyant force. Archimedes, a mathematician, first proposed that the buoyant force on an object equals the weight of the fluid that it displaces. This is now called Archimedes' principle.

For example, consider an object that displaces 10 cm^3 of water. The weight of this water is about 0.1 N, which according to Archimedes' principle is equal to the buoyant force on the object.

Archimedes' principle also helps explain why objects sink, float, or buoy up. The buoyant force does not depend upon the weight or the shape of the submerged object; it depends upon the weight of the displaced fluid.

The density of an object equals its mass divided by its volume. A steel ship can float because it contains air, which makes the ship less dense than water.

©Corbis

Teacher Notes

Advance Planning

These activities may take extended time or special conditions.

Unit 1

Video-Based Project Animals in Motion, p. 12
  multiple activities spanning several lessons

Project What's in a Vane?, p. 13
  design and test windmill vanes

Graphic Organizers and Vocabulary pp. 19, 20, 37, 38, 49, 50, 65, 66, 81, 82
  ongoing with vocabulary

Lesson 1

Quick Lab Create a Distance-Time Graph, p. 17
  copy scenarios onto index cards

Lesson 2

Quick Lab Mass and Acceleration, p. 35
  pulleys

Lesson 3

Quick Lab First Law of Skateboarding, p. 47
  skateboards and dolls

S.T.E.M. Lab Newton's Laws of Motion, p. 47
  requires two 45-min periods

Lesson 5

Daily Demo Water Flow, p. 78
  prepare demonstration materials

Field Lab Pressure in Fluids, p. 79
  conduct lab outdoors

What Do You Think?

Have students think about how applying force can change the motion of an object.

Ask: Imagine you want to move a shopping cart. How do you make it move forward? You push it. How do you make it move backward? You pull it. How do you make it turn? Sample answer: You push with one hand and pull with the other.

Ask: A solid object can apply a force to an object to change its motion. Can a liquid or a gas also apply a force to an object? Give an example. Sample answer: Yes. An ocean wave can knock over a sandcastle. Wind can spin the blades of a pinwheel.

Ask: What do you think applies a force to a parachute to make an object such as this shuttle slow down? the air

UNIT 1
Motion and Forces

Big Idea
Unbalanced forces cause changes in the motion of objects, and these changes can be predicted and described.

The parachute helps slow the shuttle down.

What do you think?
How do you change the direction in which an object is moving? By applying force, of course. Can you tell what force helps the shuttle slow down? What allows the rocket in the photo to lift off?

1

Video-Based Project
Animals in Motion

⊛ Go Online to preview the videos, access teacher support pages, and print student activity worksheets.

Dr. Mike Heithaus and graduate students Katy Cameron and Erica Olson study animals in motion by tagging tiger sharks and loggerhead turtles in Australia's Shark Bay.

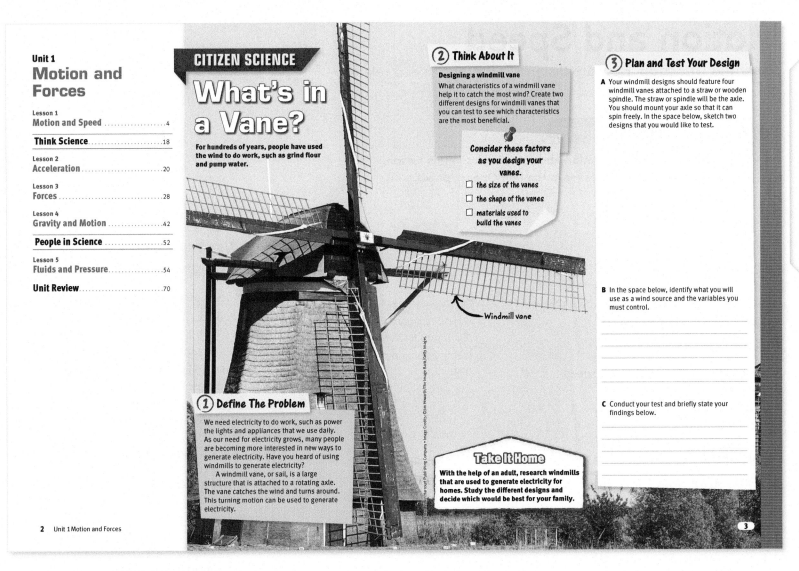

CITIZEN SCIENCE
What's in a Vane?

For hundreds of years, people have used the wind to do work, such as grind flour and pump water.

① Define The Problem
We need electricity to do work, such as power the lights and appliances that we use daily. As our need for electricity grows, many people are becoming more interested in new ways to generate electricity. Have you heard of using windmills to generate electricity?

A windmill vane, or sail, is a large structure that is attached to a rotating axle. The vane catches the wind and turns around. This turning motion can be used to generate electricity.

② Think About It
Designing a windmill vane
What characteristics of a windmill vane help it to catch the most wind? Create two different designs for windmill vanes that you can test to see which characteristics are the most beneficial.

Consider these factors as you design your vanes.
- ☐ the size of the vanes
- ☐ the shape of the vanes
- ☐ materials used to build the vanes

③ Plan and Test Your Design
A Your windmill designs should feature four windmill vanes attached to a straw or wooden spindle. The straw or spindle will be the axle. You should mount your axle so that it can spin freely. In the space below, sketch two designs that you would like to test.

B In the space below, identify what you will use as a wind source and the variables you must control.

C Conduct your test and briefly state your findings below.

Take It Home
With the help of an adult, research windmills that are used to generate electricity for homes. Study the different designs and decide which would be best for your family.

2 Unit 1 Motion and Forces

CITIZEN SCIENCE

Unit Project What's in a Vane?

3. Plan and Test Your Design

A. Students only need to show the designs for the vanes. The two designs should be different from each other.

B. Students may choose to use a desk fan to create "wind." Students may identify many different variables they need to control, such as the speed of the wind, the angle at which the wind hits the vanes, the distance from the fan, the height of the fan, and so on.

C. Students should make sure that all of the variables except the vane design remain as constant as possible throughout the tests. Students should be able to articulate their findings in terms of which vane design was more efficient, how they determined efficiency, and possibly why.

Optional Online rubric: Design Your Own Investigations: Experiments

Take It Home

Ask students to provide you with a brief oral description of the different kinds of windmills they were able to research, which design they chose, and why.

Optional Online rubric: Oral Presentations

Motion and Speed

Essential Question How are distance, time, and speed related?

🍎 **Professional Development**

For more detailed information about the topics in this lesson, refer to the Content Refresher in the Unit Opener pages.

Opening Your Lesson

Begin the lesson by assessing students' prerequisite and prior knowledge.

Prerequisite Knowledge

- General knowledge of distance, speed, and time
- General knowledge of graphs and graphing

Accessing Prior Knowledge

Ask: How do you measure speed? Sample answer: by measuring the total distance something travels in a certain amount of time

Ask: If a car traveled 50 mi/h and a person walked 5 km/h, which traveled the greatest distance? Sample answer: There isn't enough information to tell because you have to know how much time each traveled to know the total distance.

Customize Your Opening

☐ **Accessing Prior Knowledge,** above
☐ Print Path Engage Your Brain, SE p. 5
☐ Print Path Active Reading, SE p. 5
☐ **Digital Path** Lesson Opener

Key Topics/Learning Goals	Supporting Concepts
Motion 1 Define *position, reference point,* and *motion.* 2 Identify common distance units.	• Position describes the location of an object. • A reference point is a location to which you compare other locations. • Motion is a change in position over time. • Distance depends on the path you take. The distance between two points can differ. • The standard units of length for measuring distance are the meter and the kilometer.
Speed 1 Define *speed.* 2 Differentiate between speed and average speed. 3 Calculate average speed.	• Speed is a measure of how fast something moves in a given amount of time. It is the distance that an object travels divided by the time the object takes to travel that distance. • Average speed is a way to calculate the speed of an object that may not always be moving at a constant speed. • To calculate average speed, divide the total distance by the total time: $s = d/t$
Distance–Time Graphs 1 Graph distance versus time. 2 Determine speed from a distance–time graph. 3 Analyze the relationship between speed and line steepness on a graph.	• A distance–time graph plots distance on the *y*-axis and time on the *x*-axis. • To calculate speed using a graph, calculate the steepness/slope of the line. • The distance an object travels increases with time. This is shown as a rising line. • A flat line shows an object is not moving. • Steeper lines show greater speed.
Velocity 1 Define *vector* and *velocity.* 2 Differentiate between speed and velocity.	• A vector is a quantity with size and direction. • Velocity is a vector. It is speed in a direction. • It is possible for two objects to have the same speed but different velocities.

Options for Instruction

Two parallel paths provide coverage of the Essential Questions, with a strong Inquiry strand woven into each. Follow the Print Path, the Digital Path, or your customized combination of print, digital, and inquiry.

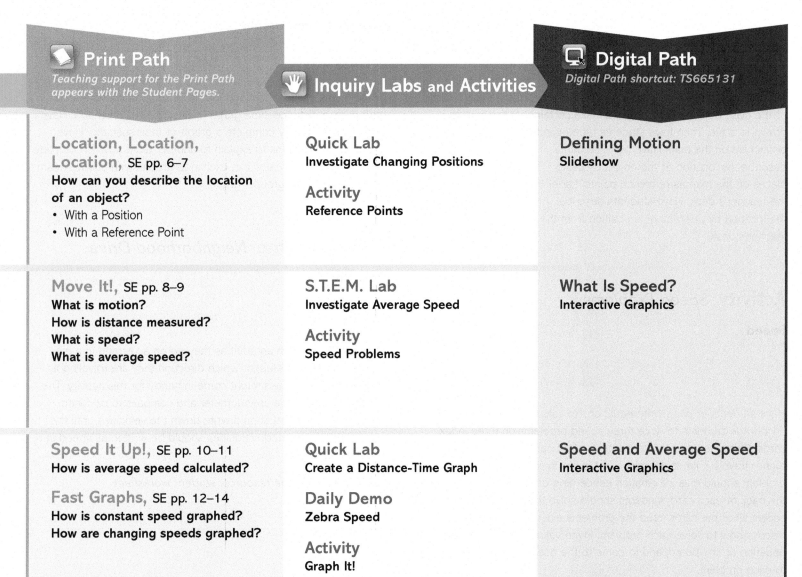

Print Path
Teaching support for the Print Path appears with the Student Pages.

Inquiry Labs and Activities

Digital Path
Digital Path shortcut: TS665131

Location, Location, Location, SE pp. 6–7
How can you describe the location of an object?
• With a Position
• With a Reference Point

Quick Lab
Investigate Changing Positions

Activity
Reference Points

Defining Motion
Slideshow

Move It!, SE pp. 8–9
What is motion?
How is distance measured?
What is speed?
What is average speed?

S.T.E.M. Lab
Investigate Average Speed

Activity
Speed Problems

What Is Speed?
Interactive Graphics

Speed It Up!, SE pp. 10–11
How is average speed calculated?

Fast Graphs, SE pp. 12–14
How is constant speed graphed?
How are changing speeds graphed?

Quick Lab
Create a Distance-Time Graph

Daily Demo
Zebra Speed

Activity
Graph It!

Speed and Average Speed
Interactive Graphics

Follow Directions, SE p. 15
What is velocity?

Activity
Speed and Motion Game

Speed and Velocity
Interactive Graphics

Options for Assessment

See the Evaluate page for options, including Formative Assessment, Summative Assessment, and Unit Review.

Engage and Explore

Activities and Discussion

Activity *Reference Points*

Engage

Motion

👥 small groups or whole class
🕐 15 min
Ⓘ **GUIDED** inquiry

Have groups or the whole class work together to draw a large map of the classroom. Students should make certain that the map is drawn to scale. Then have students tape objects or stickers on the map. Have other students describe the location of the object by using places on the map as reference points. Label the teacher's desk. Have students describe the location by describing its position from the teacher's desk.

Activity *Speed Problems*

Speed

👥 individuals or pairs, then whole class
🕐 15 min
Ⓘ **INDEPENDENT** inquiry

Have students or pairs write equations to calculate average speed. Encourage students to write three speed problems on three index cards. Write the following sentence on the board as an example: A runner travels 3 km in 15 min. What is her average speed? Each problem should give information concerning distance and time. On the back of each card, students should solve the problems. Then collect all of the cards, read the problems aloud, and let students discuss how to solve each problem. Invite volunteers to write each equation on the board, and to come to the board to show the solution to each problem.

Ⓘ **INDEPENDENT** inquiry variation Interested students can extend this activity by writing and solving equations for variables other than speed; for example, students can write problems that include data on average speed and distance, or average speed and time. Students can then figure out how to write and solve for the unknown variable.

Activity *Graph It!*

Distance–Time Graphs

👥 small groups
🕐 15 min
Ⓘ **GUIDED** inquiry

Have teams invent a scenario that involves motion and speed, and draw a distance–time graph to describe that scenario. Have teams only partially complete a graph of their scenario. Have them write directions to explain to another team how to complete their graph. Then teams can exchange graphs with another team to solve the other group's graph.

Take It Home *Neighborhood Drive*

Velocity

👥 adult–student pairs
🕐 15 min
Ⓘ **GUIDED** inquiry

Students travel with an adult as they go on an errand in a car. The adult tells the student which direction they are traveling as they drive. A compass might come in handy for this activity. The student watches the speedometer and compass to calculate velocity. The student should write down the velocities until the destination is reached. Velocities should be written as speed in a certain direction.

🌀 *Optional Online resource: student worksheet*

Customize Your Labs

🔲 *See the Lab Manual for lab datasheets.*

🌀 *Go Online for editable lab datasheets.*

Levels of **Inquiry**

| **DIRECTED** inquiry | **GUIDED** inquiry | **INDEPENDENT** inquiry |
| introduces inquiry skills within a structured framework. | develops inquiry skills within a supportive environment. | deepens inquiry skills with student-driven questions or procedures. |

Labs and Demos

Daily Demo *Zebra Speed*

Engage

Distance–Time Graphs

👥 whole class
🕐 10 min
📋 **DIRECTED** inquiry

PURPOSE **To help students understand relationships in a distance–time graph**

MATERIALS

* zebra cutout

1 Draw the axes of a distance–time graph on the board. Label the vertical axis *y* and the horizontal axis *x*. Use a cutout to represent a zebra.

2 Remind students that the *y*-axis shows distance, and the *x*-axis shows time. Ask a student to point out the *y*-axis and the *x*-axis.

3 Invite an interested student to move the zebra cutout up the *y*-axis. Tell the student that when you say, "Go," he or she should move the zebra slowly for a few seconds, stop for a few seconds, and then move the zebra more quickly up the *y*-axis.

4 Say, "Go." As the student moves the zebra cutout up the *y*-axis, draw a line moving to the right that starts at (0, 0). Draw at a constant rate but match the height of the zebra cutout.

5 Compare what you have graphed to the actual motion of the paper zebra. Point out that the line is flat when the zebra is not moving, and that the line rises more steeply when the zebra is moving more quickly.

Distance-Time Graph of a Zebra

🌐 💻 S.T.E.M. Lab *Investigate Average Speed*

Speed

👥 individuals
🕐 45 min
📋 **GUIDED** or **INDEPENDENT** inquiry

PURPOSE **To build and test a simple model car and then calculate its average speed**

MATERIALS

* balance
* board, wood
* books (4 or 5)
* clay, modeling
* film canister lids (4)
* ruler
* scissors
* stopwatch
* straw
* string
* toothpicks (2–4)

🌐 💻 Quick Lab *Investigate Changing Positions*

PURPOSE **To investigate how a change in reference point affects how an object appears to move**

See the Lab Manual or go Online for planning information.

🌐 💻 Quick Lab *Create a Distance-Time Graph*

PURPOSE **To create a distance-time graph to show the speed of an object, or its distance traveled over time**

See the Lab Manual or go Online for planning information.

Activities and Discussion

☐ **Activity** Reference Points
☐ **Activity** Speed Problems
☐ **Activity** Graph It!
☐ **Take It Home** Neighborhood Drive

Labs and Demos

☐ **Daily Demo** Zebra Speed
☐ **S.T.E.M. Lab** Investigate Average Speed
☐ **Quick Lab** Changing Positions
☐ **Quick Lab** Distance-Time Graph

Your Resources

Explain Science Concepts

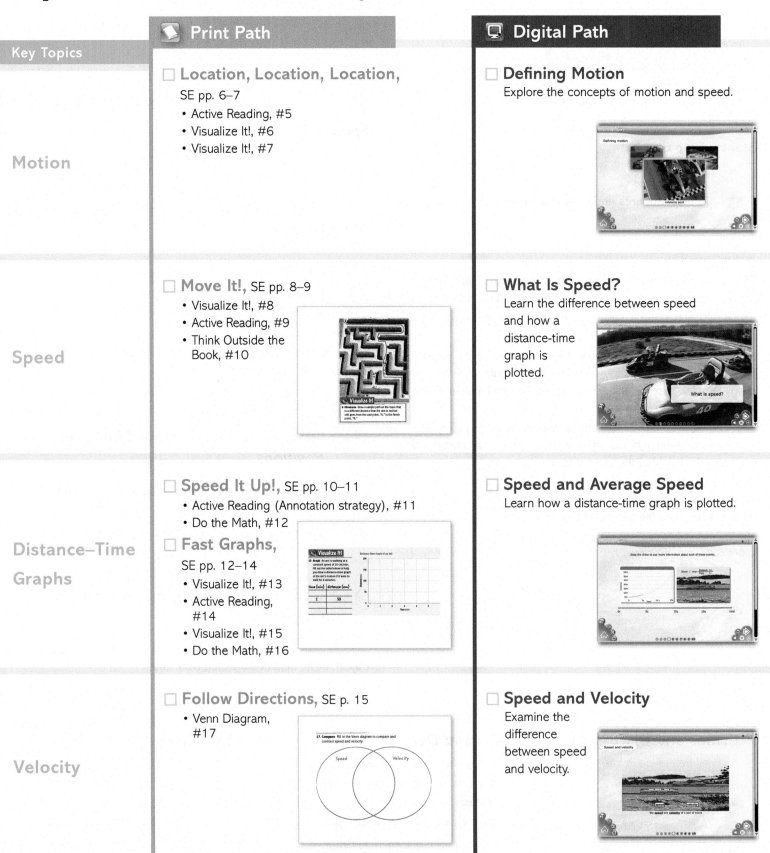

Key Topics	📖 Print Path	💻 Digital Path
Motion	☐ **Location, Location, Location,** SE pp. 6–7 • Active Reading, #5 • Visualize It!, #6 • Visualize It!, #7	☐ **Defining Motion** Explore the concepts of motion and speed.
Speed	☐ **Move It!,** SE pp. 8–9 • Visualize It!, #8 • Active Reading, #9 • Think Outside the Book, #10	☐ **What Is Speed?** Learn the difference between speed and how a distance-time graph is plotted.
Distance–Time Graphs	☐ **Speed It Up!,** SE pp. 10–11 • Active Reading (Annotation strategy), #11 • Do the Math, #12 ☐ **Fast Graphs,** SE pp. 12–14 • Visualize It!, #13 • Active Reading, #14 • Visualize It!, #15 • Do the Math, #16	☐ **Speed and Average Speed** Learn how a distance-time graph is plotted.
Velocity	☐ **Follow Directions,** SE p. 15 • Venn Diagram, #17	☐ **Speed and Velocity** Examine the difference between speed and velocity.

Differentiated Instruction

Basic *Calculating Speed and Velocity*

Synthesizing Key Topics

👥 individuals or small groups
🕐 10 min

On a broad, flat surface, mark with tape a start line and a finish line. Have a student roll a toy car the length of the course. Ask students to measure how much time the car takes to roll from start to finish. Next, direct them to measure the length of the course. Then, have students calculate the speed of the car. Finally, ask two students to roll two cars in opposite directions on the course. Encourage students to figure out the velocity of each car.

Advanced *Graphing Distance and Time*

Distance–Time Graphs

👥 individuals
🕐 15 min

Encourage interested students to make a distance–time graph that shows how a school bus might travel in one day. Invite students to make the graph as complicated as they can. Ask students to write a detailed explanation of exactly what the graph shows the bus is doing. Display students' graphs and their associated explanations around the classroom.

ELL *Definition Differences*

Synthesizing Key Topics

👥 pairs
🕐 15 min

Four Square EL or struggling students may not be clear about the differences between motion, speed, and velocity. Have students draw a 2 × 2 matrix with a circle at the center for each of these words. Direct them to write the word in the circle, and then fill in the surrounding cells with the definition, characteristics, examples, and nonexamples for each one.

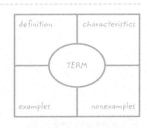

🌐 *Optional Online resource: Four Square support*

Lesson Vocabulary

motion	position	reference point
speed	vector	velocity

Previewing Vocabulary

👥 whole class
🕐 10 min

Other Meanings Explain that some words have different meanings in everyday life and in science. Also, some words can have more than one scientific meaning.
- **Velocity** in science is speed in a certain direction. **Ask:** How might you use *velocity* in everyday speech? Sample answer: People often use *velocity* simply to mean speed.
- A **vector** in science is a quantity that has both size and direction. Tell students that *vector* has other meanings in science, too. For example, in medicine, a *vector* is an organism, such as a mosquito, that transmits disease.

Reinforcing Vocabulary

👥 individuals
🕐 ongoing

Key-Term FoldNote Have students make Key-Term FoldNotes. On the outside of each tab, students write a vocabulary term; underneath, they write the term's definition.

🌐 *Online resource: Key-Term FoldNote support*

Customize Your Core Lesson

Core Instruction
☐ **Print Path** choices
☐ **Digital Path** choices

Vocabulary
☐ **Previewing Vocabulary**
  Other Meanings
☐ **Reinforcing Vocabulary**
  Key-Term FoldNote

Differentiated Instruction
☐ **Basic** Calculating Speed and Velocity
☐ **Advanced** Graphing Distance and Time
☐ **ELL** Definition Differences

Your Resources

Extend Science Concepts

Reinforce and Review

Activity *Speed and Motion Game*

Synthesizing Key Topics
👥 whole class
🕐 10 min

Four Corners Pick four corners of the classroom to represent *speed, velocity, motion,* and *position*. Label each corner. Read the following relationships to students. After each one, ask students to stand in the corner they think best fits the description. Tell students they should only pick *motion* if they cannot tell whether speed or velocity applies. Give each student in the correct corner a point. You can continue the game with additional examples provided by student volunteers.

1. A car travels 40 km/h. speed
2. A plane travels 800 km/h heading northwest. velocity
3. A blue jay flies from a tree branch to the ground. motion
4. His desk is in the front of the classroom. position
5. I walked four blocks in 5 min. speed
6. The ball is under the car near the right rear tire. position
7. In 1 min, I jogged south six blocks. In another minute, I walked west for two blocks. velocity
8. She walked from the front of the classroom to the back. motion
9. Ed biked 12 km west in 1 h. velocity
10. Ava biked 1 km in 5 min. speed
11. My home is five blocks south and two blocks east of the school. position

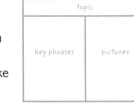

Graphic Organizer

Synthesizing Key Topics
👥 individuals
🕐 10 min

Combination Notes Have students summarize this lesson using Combination Notes. For each idea or concept, have them write a summary or explanation in the left column. In the right column, have them make and label a sketch to illustrate the concept.

🖰 *Optional Online resource: Combination Notes support*

Going Further

Math Connection

Synthesizing Key Topics
👥 individuals
🕐 20 min

Have interested students write the equation for speed ($s = d/t$). Then have them figure out the equations for distance ($d = s \times t$), and time ($t = d/s$). Encourage students to write math problems using each of the equations. Remind them to use the appropriate units of measurement when writing their problems. Invite students to share their problems with a partner or the class.

Physical Education Connection

Synthesizing Key Topics
👥 individual
🕐 20 min

Invite interested students to measure speeds of runners during a track meet or PE lesson. Remind students that they will need data on distances run. Students can use the data they collect to make distance–time graphs that compare different information. For example, students could graph data from several different runners to compare their speeds; alternatively, they could graph and compare several runs made by the same runner. Tell students to use a different color for each line on their graphs to make it easier to read.

Customize Your Closing

🖰 *See the Assessment Guide for quizzes and tests.*

🖰 *Go Online to edit and create quizzes and tests.*

Reinforce and Review

☐ **Activity** Speed and Motion Game
☐ **Graphic Organizer** Combination Notes
☐ **Print Path** Visual Summary, SE p. 16
☐ **Digital Path** Lesson Closer

Evaluate Student Mastery

Formative Assessment

See the teacher support below the Student Pages for additional Formative Assessment questions.

Ask: On a distance-time graph, what do you show on the *x*-axis? Answer: time **Ask:** What is an example of speed? Sample answer: a cyclist riding 2 km in 10 min **Ask:** What is an example of velocity? Answer: a cyclist riding north at 10 kilometers per hour **Ask:** How would you describe my position? Sample answer: in front of the board, next to the desk

Reteach

Formative assessment may show that students need reinforcement for certain topics. The resources below are recommended for reteaching. If students were introduced to a topic through the Print Path, you can also use the Digital Path to reteach, or vice versa.

🎧 *Can be assigned to individual students*

Motion
Activity Reference Points

Quick Lab Investigate Changing Positions

Speed
Activity Speed Problems 🎧

Distance–Time Graphs
Activity Graph It!

Quick Lab Create a Distance-Time Graph 🎧

Velocity
Take It Home Neighborhood Drive 🎧

Summative Assessment

Alternative Assessment
A Need for Speed

🕐 *Online resource: student worksheet, optional rubrics*

Motion and Speed

Tic-Tac-Toe: *A Need for Speed*

1. Work on your own, with a partner, or with a small group.

2. Choose three quick activities from the game. Check the boxes you plan to complete. They must form a straight line in any direction.

3. Have your teacher approve your plan.

4. Do each activity, and turn in your results.

__ Location	__ Average Speed	__ Velocity
Describe your location in the classroom from the reference point of the doorway. You don't need actual measurements for this, as you can use classroom objects to describe the location. Then describe your location in the classroom from a reference point on the moon.	Calculate the average speed of a plane that travels 1,000 miles in 2.5 hours.	1. Draw a diagram that shows two objects going in the same direction but with different velocities. 2. Draw two objects traveling at the same speed but with different velocities. 3. Draw two objects with identical velocities. Describe speed and velocity in each diagram.
__ Modeling Speed	__ Map It	__ Graph It
Use two toy cars. Make two ramps of different lengths using classroom objects. Put one car at the top of each ramp. Release the cars together. Which car is faster? Explain why.	Draw a map of your classroom that shows the locations of the desks and other major features in the room. Describe how to get from your desk to the door and your desk to a window.	Make a graph that shows a car traveling at different rates for 10 hours. What is the average speed? What is the distance that the car traveled in 10 hours?
__ A-Mazing	__ Changing Speeds	__ Speed But No Velocity?
Use graph paper to draw a maze. Pick two points (the start and the finish) and find the distance between the two points if you travel though the maze. Measure the distance in a straight line (as the crow flies) from the start to the finish.	Draw a graph that shows the changing speed of a fictional runner during a 26-mile marathon. At times, the runner speeds up; at other times, he or she slows down. Occasionally the runner stops to rest or to get a drink. Show these changes on your graph.	Draw a diagram or sketch that shows an object that has traveled a certain distance at a specific speed but has zero average velocity.

Going Further
- ☐ Math Connection
- ☐ Physical Education Connection

Formative Assessment
- ☐ **Strategies** Throughout TE
- ☐ **Lesson Review** SE

Summative Assessment
- ☐ **Alternative Assessment** A Need for Speed
- ☐ **Lesson Quiz**
- ☐ **Unit Tests A and B**
- ☐ **Unit Review** SE End-of-Unit

Your Resources

_____   _____

_____   _____

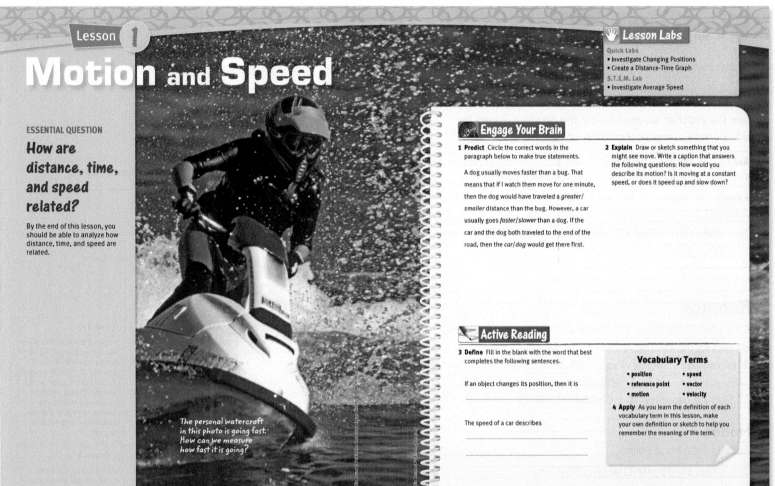

Answers

Answers for 1–3 should represent students' current thoughts, even if incorrect.

1. greater; faster; car

2. Pictures should show an object that can be in motion. Captions should describe how the object is moving and whether it is going at a constant speed.

3. in motion; how fast it goes

4. Students should define or sketch each vocabulary term in the lesson.

Opening Your Lesson

Discuss students' answers to item 3 to assess their understanding of speed and motion. Most students should understand motion and speed, and will likely share their everyday experiences of them.

Prerequisites Students should already have some general knowledge of making and reading line graphs. They should also have a basic understanding of distance, speed, and time.

Learning Alert

Everyday Definitions Ask students how they have heard the word *velocity* used. Explain that *velocity* is often used to mean *speed*, but in science *velocity* is more than speed. It includes both speed and direction. Explain that if a plane travels 800 km/h north, this is the plane's velocity. If a plane travels 800 km/h, this is the plane's speed. Invite students to suggest other examples of speed versus velocity.

Location, location, location

How can you describe the location of an object?

Have you ever gotten lost while looking for a specific place? If so, you probably know that the description of the location can be very important. Imagine that you are trying to describe your location to a friend. How would you explain where you are? You need two pieces of information: a position and a reference point.

With a Position

Position describes the location of an object. Often, you describe where something is by comparing its position with where you currently are. For example, you might say that a classmate sitting next to you is two desks to your right, or that a mailbox is two blocks south of where you live. Each time you identify the position of an object, you are comparing the location of the object with the location of another object or place.

With a Reference Point

When you describe a position by comparing it to the location of another object or place, you are using a reference point. A **reference point** is a location to which you compare other locations. In the example above of a mailbox that is two blocks south of where you live, the reference point is "where you live."

Imagine that you are at a zoo with some friends. If you are using the map to the right, you could describe your destination using different reference points. Using yourself as the reference point, you might say that the red panda house is one block east and three blocks north of your current location. Or you might say the red panda house is one block north and one block east of the fountain. In this example, the fountain is your reference point.

Active Reading 5 **Apply** How would you describe where this question is located on the page? Give two different answers using two different reference points.

_____
_____
_____
_____

6 Unit 1 Motion and Forces

ZOO MAP

Guest Services
- Restrooms
- Food
- First Aid
- Information

Visualize It!

6 **Apply** One of your friends is at the southeast corner of Monkey Island. He would like to meet you. How would you describe your location to him?

_____
_____
_____

7 **Apply** You need to go visit the first aid station. How would you describe how to get there?

_____
_____
_____

7

Answers

5. Sample answer: three paragraphs from the start of the page; about four inches from the bottom of the page

6. Go three blocks south and one block east.

7. Go one block west, one block north, and then two blocks west.

Probing Questions

Analyzing **Ask:** If someone gives you a location in relation to a reference point, will you be able to find that location? Sample answer: It depends on how well you know the reference point. **Ask:** Has someone ever given you directions that you thought were clear, but then you got lost? Why do you think this happens? Sample answer: It is easy to leave out a turn, or forget to describe a reference point. Someone following the directions might miss a reference point, especially if it is dark.

Interpreting Visuals

Invite students to look carefully at the map of a zoo. **Ask:** From the Information Booth, how would you get to the closest place to eat? Go east two blocks, south one block, and east two more blocks. **Ask:** Without going back the way you just came, how do you get to the nearest restroom? Go three blocks north and two blocks east. **Ask:** How do you get to the carousel from the entrance to the Red Panda house? Go two blocks west, one block south, and then one block west.

MOVE It!

What is motion?

An object moves, or is in motion, when it changes its position relative to a reference point. **Motion** is a change in position over time. If you were to watch the biker pictured to the right, you would see him move. If you were not able to watch him, you might still know something about his motion. If you saw that he was in one place at one time and a different place later, you would know that he had moved. A change in position is evidence that motion has happened.

If the biker returned to his starting point, you might not know that he had moved. The starting and ending positions cannot tell you everything about motion.

↖ This biker is in motion.

How is distance measured?

Suppose you walk from one building to another building that is several blocks away. If you could walk in a straight line, you might end up 500 meters from where you started. The actual distance you travel, however, would depend on the exact path you take. If you take a route that has many turns, the distance you travel might be 900 meters or more.

The way you measure distance depends on the information you want. Sometimes you want to know the straight-line distance between two positions, or the displacement. Sometimes, however, you might need to know the total length of a certain path between those positions.

When measuring any distances, scientists use a standard unit of measurement. The standard unit of length is the meter (m), which is about 3.3 feet. Longer distances can be measured in kilometers (km), and shorter distances in centimeters (cm). In the United States, distance is often measured in miles (mi), feet (ft), or inches (in).

↗ The distance from point A to point B depends on the path you take.

Visualize It!

8 Illustrate Draw a sample path on the maze that is a different distance than the one in red but still goes from the start point, "A," to the finish point, "B."

8 | Unit 1 Motion and Forces

What is speed?

A change in an object's position tells you that motion took place, but it does not tell you how quickly the object changed position. The **speed** of an object is a measure of how far something moves in a given amount of time. In other words, speed measures how quickly or slowly the object changes position. In the same amount of time, a faster object would move farther than a slower moving object would.

What is average speed?

The speed of an object is rarely constant. For example, the biker in the photo above may travel quickly when he begins a race but may slow down as he gets tired at the end of the race. *Average speed* is a way to calculate the speed of an object that may not always be moving at a constant speed. Instead of describing the speed of an object at an exact moment in time, average speed describes the speed over a stretch of time.

Active Reading **9 Compare** What is the difference between speed and average speed?

Think Outside the Book Inquiry

10 Analyze Research the top speeds of a cheetah, a race car, and a speed boat. How do they rank in order of speed? Make a poster showing which is fastest and which is slowest. How do the speeds of the fastest human runners compare to the speeds you found?

Lesson 1 Motion and Speed | 9

Answers

8. Students' paths should correctly complete the maze using a different path than the one given.

9. Speed measures how fast an object is moving at a specific moment in time. Average speed measures how far an object moves in a given period of time.

10. Posters should display animal speed. Their speeds should be given in correct units, and the units should all be the same so that different animals can be compared.

Probing Question

Recognizing Relationships Tell students that an object that is not moving in relation to one reference point might be moving in relation to a different reference point because a reference point can also move. Encourage students to imagine that they are seated on an airplane with their seat belts on during a flight. Ask them to pick different reference points, and discuss whether they are moving in relation to that reference point. Sample answers: Reference point: the cockpit of the plane; no, I am not moving in relation to the cockpit of the plane. Reference point: the school; yes, I am moving in relation to the school. Encourage students to think about reference points for Earth. **Ask:** Is Earth moving? Sample answer: Reference point: the sun; yes, Earth is moving. Explain that there is no perfect reference point—many different reference points are valid.

Learning Alert

Different Types of Rates Speed is a rate, that is, a measure of how one quantity (distance) changes compared with another (time). Explain that there are many other types of rates that we use in our everyday lives. Encourage students to think of other types of rates. Sample answers: Heart rate or pulse is a measure of the number of heartbeats per minute; fuel efficiency of cars is measured in miles per gallon.

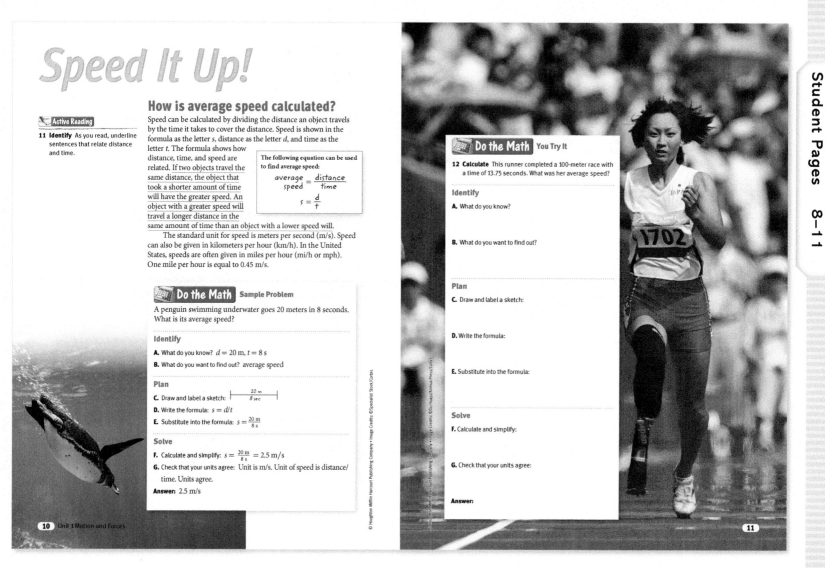

Speed It Up!

How is average speed calculated?

Active Reading

11 Identify As you read, underline sentences that relate distance and time.

Speed can be calculated by dividing the distance an object travels by the time it takes to cover the distance. Speed is shown in the formula as the letter s, distance as the letter d, and time as the letter t. The formula shows how distance, time, and speed are related. If two objects travel the same distance, the object that took a shorter amount of time will have the greater speed. An object with a greater speed will travel a longer distance in the same amount of time than an object with a lower speed will.

The following equation can be used to find average speed:

$$\text{average speed} = \frac{distance}{time}$$

$$s = \frac{d}{t}$$

The standard unit for speed is meters per second (m/s). Speed can also be given in kilometers per hour (km/h). In the United States, speeds are often given in miles per hour (mi/h or mph). One mile per hour is equal to 0.45 m/s.

Do the Math Sample Problem

A penguin swimming underwater goes 20 meters in 8 seconds. What is its average speed?

Identify

A. What do you know? $d = 20\,\text{m}, t = 8\,\text{s}$

B. What do you want to find out? average speed

Plan

C. Draw and label a sketch: |———20 m———| 8 sec

D. Write the formula: $s = d/t$

E. Substitute into the formula: $s = \frac{20\,\text{m}}{8\,\text{s}}$

Solve

F. Calculate and simplify: $s = \frac{20\,\text{m}}{8\,\text{s}} = 2.5\,\text{m/s}$

G. Check that your units agree: Unit is m/s. Unit of speed is distance/time. Units agree.

Answer: 2.5 m/s

Do the Math You Try It

12 Calculate This runner completed a 100-meter race with a time of 13.75 seconds. What was her average speed?

Identify

A. What do you know?

B. What do you want to find out?

Plan

C. Draw and label a sketch:

D. Write the formula:

E. Substitute into the formula:

Solve

F. Calculate and simplify:

G. Check that your units agree:

Answer:

10   Unit 1 Motion and Forces

11

Answers

11. *See students' pages for annotations.*

12. A: distance = 100 m, time = 13.75 s;
    B: average speed;
    C: Sketches should include both the distance and time given in the problem;
    D: $s = d/t$;
    E: $s = 100\,\text{m}/13.75\,\text{s}$;
    F: $s = 100\,\text{m}/13.75\,\text{s} = 7.27\,\text{m/s}$;
    G: Units is m/s. Unit of speed is distance/time. Units agree;
    Answer: 7.27 m/s

Do the Math

If students need extra help to solve the problem about the average speed of the runner, ask them the following questions. What is the first thing you need to figure out? distance and time Where do you find that information? at the top of the page What is the equation to figure out the speed? $s = d/t$ Ask students how they can be sure they have stated their answers using the correct units. Sample answer: You check to see if the units in the answer match the units given at the beginning of the problem, in this case, meters and seconds. Invite students to name some other units of distance and time. Sample answers: miles, feet, kilometers, inches; hours, weeks, months, minutes

Formative Assessment

Suppose a race is 50 m, and it takes an athlete 15 s to run it. **Ask:** Is that enough information to calculate speed? Yes; the formula is $s = d/t$, and both time and distance are given. **Ask:** If you know that a dog ran across a park that is 200 m long, do you know how fast the dog ran? no, because you don't know if the dog ran in a straight line so you don't know distance, and you don't know how much time it took **Ask:** If you look at the speedometer of a car and it says 55 mi/h and it took an hour to reach your destination, do you know the distance traveled? Answer: no, because the driver may not have traveled at a constant speed of 55 mph for the entire trip.

Fast Graphs

How is constant speed graphed?

A convenient way to show the motion of an object is by using a graph that plots the distance the object has traveled against time. This type of graph is called a distance-time graph. You can use it to see how both distance and speed change with time.

How far away the object is from a reference point is plotted on the *y*-axis. So the *y*-axis expresses distance in units such as meters, centimeters, or kilometers. Time is plotted on the *x*-axis, and can display units such as seconds, minutes, or hours. If an object moves at a constant speed, the graph is a straight line.

You can use a distance-time graph to determine the average speed of an object. The slope, or steepness, of the line is equal to the average speed of the object. You calculate the average speed for a time interval by dividing the change in distance by the change in time for that time interval.

Suppose that an ostrich is running at a constant speed. The distance-time graph of its motion is shown below. To calculate the speed of the ostrich, choose two data points from the graph below and calculate the slope of the line. The calculation of the slope is shown below. Since we know that the slope of a line on a distance-time graph is its average speed, then we know that the ostrich's speed is 14 m/s.

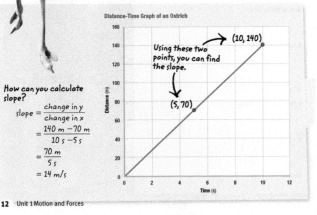

How can you calculate slope?

$$\text{slope} = \frac{\text{change in } y}{\text{change in } x}$$
$$= \frac{140 \text{ m} - 70 \text{ m}}{10 \text{ s} - 5 \text{ s}}$$
$$= \frac{70 \text{ m}}{5 \text{ s}}$$
$$= 14 \text{ m/s}$$

Distance-Time Graph of an Ostrich

Using these two points, you can find the slope.

(10, 140)

(5, 70)

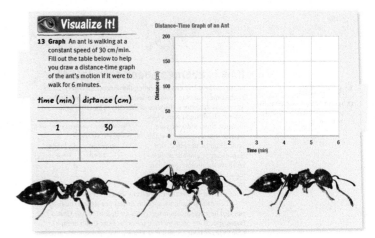

Visualize It!

13 Graph An ant is walking at a constant speed of 30 cm/min. Fill out the table below to help you draw a distance-time graph of the ant's motion if it were to walk for 6 minutes.

time (min)	distance (cm)
1	30

Distance-Time Graph of an Ant

How are changing speeds graphed?

Some distance-time graphs show the motion of an object with a changing speed. In these distance-time graphs, the change in the slope of a line indicates that the object has either sped up, slowed down, or stopped.

As an object moves, the distance it travels increases with time. The motion can be seen as a climbing line on the graph. The slope of the line indicates speed. Steeper lines show intervals where the speed is greater than intervals with less steep lines. If the line gets steeper, the object is speeding up. If the line gets less steep, the object is slowing. If the line becomes flat, or horizontal, the object is not moving. In this interval, the speed is zero meters per second.

For objects that change speed, you can calculate speed for a specific interval of time. You would choose two points close together on the graph. Or, you can calculate the average speed over a long interval of time. You would choose two points far apart on the graph to calculate an average over a long interval of time.

Active Reading **14 Analyze** If a line on a distance-time graph becomes steeper, what has happened to the speed of the object? What if it becomes a flat horizontal line?

_____

_____

_____

Answers

13. Sample answer: data points for the table include: 0 min and 0 cm, 2 min and 60 cm, 3 min and 90 cm, and 6 min and 120 cm. Graphs should correctly plot this data. Lines will be straight and constantly increasing.

14. a steeper line indicates increasing speeds; a flat line indicates zero speed, or no motion

Building Graphing Skills

Explain that in a distance–time graph, speed is measured by the steepness, or slope, of a line. In mathematics, *slope* is defined as the change in *y*-values divided by the change in *x*-values. Here, slope is calculated by dividing the change in distance by the change in time for a given interval. Walk students through calculating the ostrich's speed using one data point that is different from the ones used in the book. Direct them to re-use the final data point (10 s, 140 m). Ask students which data point would be the simplest to use. (0 s, 0 m) **Ask:** What is the change in *y* (distance)? 140 m − 0 m = 140 m **Ask:** What is the change in *x* (time)? 10 s − 0 s = 10 s **Ask:** What is the change in *y* divided by the change in *x*? 140 m/10 s = 14 m/s **Ask:** What are the units? m/s **Ask:** What is the ostrich's average speed? 14 m/s **Ask:** Does this answer agree with the answer in the book, which was calculated using two different points on the line? yes

Probing Question

Ask: What would a line on a graph look like if a runner ran at a constant speed, stopped for a drink, and then ran faster than before? Answer: The line would slope upward at a constant rate, become flat while the runner stops for a drink, and then become steeper than before.

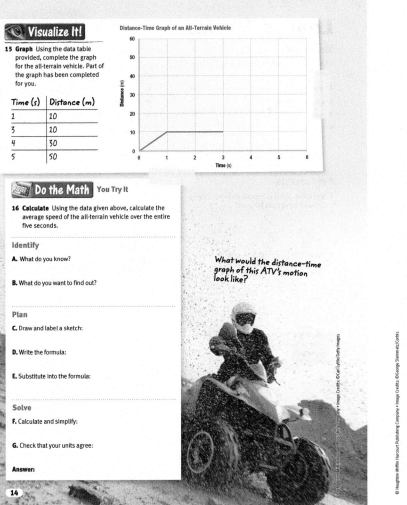

Visualize It!

15 Graph Using the data table provided, complete the graph for the all-terrain vehicle. Part of the graph has been completed for you.

Time (s)	Distance (m)
1	10
3	10
4	30
5	50

Distance-Time Graph of an All-Terrain Vehicle

Do the Math — You Try It

16 Calculate Using the data given above, calculate the average speed of the all-terrain vehicle over the entire five seconds.

Identify

A. What do you know?

B. What do you want to find out?

Plan

C. Draw and label a sketch:

D. Write the formula:

E. Substitute into the formula:

Solve

F. Calculate and simplify:

G. Check that your units agree:

Answer:

What would the distance-time graph of this ATV's motion look like?

14

Follow Directions

What is velocity?

Suppose that two birds start from the same place and fly at 10 km/h for 5 minutes. Why might they not end up at the same place? Because the birds were flying in different directions! There are times when the direction of motion must be included in a measurement. A **vector** is a quantity that has both size and direction.

In the example above, the birds' speeds were the same, but their velocities were different. **Velocity** [vuh•LAHS•ih•tee] is speed in a specific direction. If a police officer gives a speeding ticket for a car traveling 100 km/h, the ticket does not list a velocity. But it would list a velocity if it described the car traveling south at 100 km/h.

Because velocity includes direction, it is possible for two objects to have the same speed but different velocities. In the picture to the right, the chair lifts are going the same speed but in opposite directions: some people are going up the mountain while others are going down the mountain.

Average velocity is calculated in a different way than average speed. Average speed depends on the total distance traveled along a path. Average velocity depends on the straight-line distance from the starting point to the final point, or the displacement. A chair lift might carry you up the mountain at an average speed of 5 km/h, giving you an average velocity of 5 km/h north. After a round-trip ride, your average traveling speed would still be 5 km/h. Your average velocity, however, would be 0 km/h because you ended up exactly where you started.

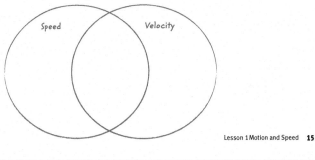

These chair lifts have opposite velocities because they are going at the same speed but in opposite directions.

17 Compare Fill in the Venn diagram to compare and contrast speed and velocity.

Speed | Velocity

Lesson 1 Motion and Speed 15

Answers

15. Graphs after 3 seconds should have a constant increasing upward slope.

16. A: $d = 50$ m, $t = 5$ s;
    B: average speed;
    C: sketches should show distance and time;
    D: $s = d/t$; E: $s = 50$ m/5 s;
    F: $s = 50$ m/5 s = 10 m/s;
    G: Units is m/s. Unit of speed is distance/time, so units agree;
    Answer: 5 m/s

17. left: distance in a time; middle: describe how fast something moves; right: distance in a time and a direction

Probing Questions

Applying Imagine that your battery-operated car has gotten away from you in the park. You know that the car travels at a constant speed of 1 km/h. **Ask:** Is this enough information to determine the location of the car if it has been gone for 20 min? no A neighbor tells you that she saw your toy car heading north. **Ask:** Now do you have enough information to determine the location of the car? yes, if it hasn't changed direction.

Formative Assessment

Ask: If two scooters are moving at the same speed but in opposite directions, is their velocity the same? No, they are going in different directions. **Ask:** If two dogs are moving in the same direction but at different speeds, what can you say about their velocity? Sample answer: The velocities are different.

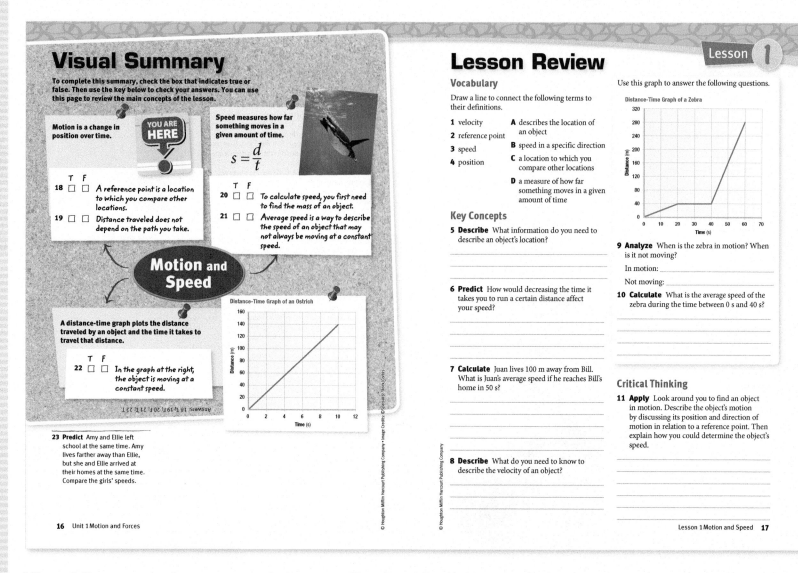

Visual Summary

To complete this summary, check the box that indicates true or false. Then use the key below to check your answers. You can use this page to review the main concepts of the lesson.

Motion is a change in position over time.

YOU ARE HERE

Speed measures how far something moves in a given amount of time.

$$s = \frac{d}{t}$$

T F
18 ☐ ☐ A reference point is a location to which you compare other locations.

19 ☐ ☐ Distance traveled does not depend on the path you take.

T F
20 ☐ ☐ To calculate speed, you first need to find the mass of an object.

21 ☐ ☐ Average speed is a way to describe the speed of an object that may not always be moving at a constant speed.

Motion and Speed

A distance-time graph plots the distance traveled by an object and the time it takes to travel that distance.

T F
22 ☐ ☐ In the graph at the right, the object is moving at a constant speed.

Distance-Time Graph of an Ostrich

Answers: 18 T, 19 F, 20 F, 21 T, 22 T

Image Credits: ©SpecialP Stock/Corbis

23 Predict Amy and Ellie left school at the same time. Amy lives farther away than Ellie, but she and Ellie arrived at their homes at the same time. Compare the girls' speeds.

16 Unit 1 Motion and Forces

© Houghton Mifflin Harcourt Publishing Company

Lesson Review

Lesson 1

Vocabulary

Draw a line to connect the following terms to their definitions.

1 velocity
2 reference point
3 speed
4 position

A describes the location of an object
B speed in a specific direction
C a location to which you compare other locations
D a measure of how far something moves in a given amount of time

Key Concepts

5 Describe What information do you need to describe an object's location?

6 Predict How would decreasing the time it takes you to run a certain distance affect your speed?

7 Calculate Juan lives 100 m away from Bill. What is Juan's average speed if he reaches Bill's home in 50 s?

8 Describe What do you need to know to describe the velocity of an object?

Use this graph to answer the following questions.

Distance-Time Graph of a Zebra

9 Analyze When is the zebra in motion? When is it not moving?

In motion: _____

Not moving: _____

10 Calculate What is the average speed of the zebra during the time between 0 s and 40 s?

Critical Thinking

11 Apply Look around you to find an object in motion. Describe the object's motion by discussing its position and direction of motion in relation to a reference point. Then explain how you could determine the object's speed.

© Houghton Mifflin Harcourt Publishing Company

Lesson 1 Motion and Speed 17

Visual Summary Answers

18. T
19. F
20. F
21. T
22. T
23. Amy's average speed was faster than Ellie's because Amy went a farther distance in the same amount of time.

Lesson Review Answers

1. B
2. C
3. D
4. A
5. An object's location is described using a position and a reference point.
6. It would increase your speed.
7. 2 m/s
8. distance, time, and direction
9. In motion: between 0 and 20 s and between 40 and 60 s. Not moving: between 20 and 40 s.
10. $s = d/t = (40\ m - 0\ m)/(40\ s - 0\ s)$
    $= 40\ m/40\ s = 1\ m/s$

11. Answers should use a position and reference point. They should explain that the speed can be calculated if they measure how fast the object goes in a certain amount of time.

Interpreting Graphs

Purpose To learn how to interpret graphs and other visual displays of information

Learning Goals
- Collect and organize data in graphs and other visual displays.
- Interpret data in graphs and other visual displays.

Informal Vocabulary
visual display, data points, axes

Prerequisite Knowledge
- Motion and speed
- Velocity and acceleration

Discussion *Seeing Is Believing*

👥 whole class   🕐 10 min
                   (inquiry) **GUIDED** inquiry

Ask the class to think about what they already know about graphs. **Ask:** What kinds of graphs do you know about? Sample answers: bar graph, line graph, pie chart Have students describe each kind of graph, and sketch an example of each on the board. **Ask:** Why might you want to display data in a graph instead of in a table of values? Sample answers: A graph can make it easier to read the data. A graph can help you compare the data or find patterns.

For greater depth, provide students with a set of data and walk them through the process of making it into a graph.
🌐 *Optional Online resource: Class Discussion rubric*

Differentiated Instruction

Basic *What Does It Show?*

👥 pairs   🕐 15 min

Provide pairs of students with a few simple graphs. Have pairs discuss the graphs and analyze what they show, using the steps in the tutorial. Tell students to write a sentence or two on each graph that summarizes the information presented.

Variation Provide graphs that are well labeled but which have no titles. Ask students to write a title for each graph.

Advanced *Graph It*

👥 individuals   🕐 25 min

Posters Provide each student with a simple data set. For example, the data set could give the heights of every student in an imaginary classroom. Have students use the data to create a graph. Remind them to clearly label their graphs and to write a descriptive title.

For greater depth, provide students with different data sets. After they have completed their graphs, have students pair up and interpret each other's graphs.

ELL *Parts of a Graph*

👥 pairs   🕐 15 min

Provide each pair with a simple, clearly labeled graph. Have pairs work to identify the title, the *x*-axis, and the *y*-axis. Then have them use the steps in the tutorial to discuss what the graph shows. Remind them to pay close attention to the units of the *x*- and *y*-axes to help them understand what kind of data is being presented.

Customize Your Feature

☐ **Discussion** Seeing Is Believing

☐ Basic What Does It Show?
☐ Advanced Graph It
☐ ELL Parts of a Graph
☐ Building Graphing Skills
☐ Take It Home

Think Science

Interpreting Graphs

A visual display, such as a graph or table, is a useful way to show data that you have collected in an experiment. The ability to interpret graphs is a necessary skill in science, and it is also important in everyday life. You will come across various types of graphs in newspaper articles, medical reports, and, of course, textbooks. Understanding a report or article's message often depends heavily on your ability to read and interpret different types of graphs.

Tutorial

Ask yourself the following questions when studying a graph.

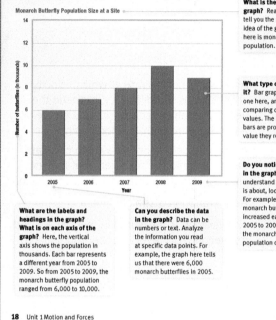

Monarch Butterfly Population Size at a Site

What is the title of the graph? Reading the title can tell you the subject or main idea of the graph. The subject here is monarch butterfly population.

What type of graph is it? Bar graphs, like the one here, are useful for comparing categories or total values. The lengths of the bars are proportional to the value they represent.

Do you notice any trends in the graph? After you understand what the graph is about, look for patterns. For example, here the monarch butterfly population increased each year from 2005 to 2008. But in 2009, the monarch butterfly population decreased.

What are the labels and headings in the graph? What is on each axis of the graph? Here, the vertical axis shows the population in thousands. Each bar represents a different year from 2005 to 2009. So from 2005 to 2009, the monarch butterfly population ranged from 6,000 to 10,000.

Can you describe the data in the graph? Data can be numbers or text. Analyze the information you read at specific data points. For example, the graph here tells us that there were 6,000 monarch butterflies in 2005.

You Try It!

A member of your research group has made the graph shown below about an object in motion. Study the graph, then answer the questions that follow.

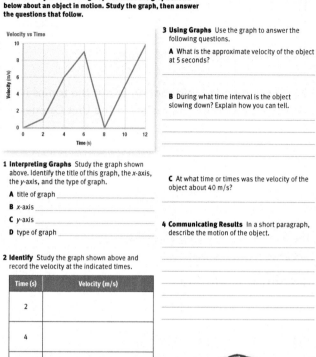

Velocity vs Time

1 Interpreting Graphs Study the graph shown above. Identify the title of this graph, the *x*-axis, the *y*-axis, and the type of graph.

A title of graph _____

B *x*-axis _____

C *y*-axis _____

D type of graph _____

2 Identify Study the graph shown above and record the velocity at the indicated times.

Time (s)	Velocity (m/s)
2	
4	
6	
8	
10	

3 Using Graphs Use the graph to answer the following questions.

A What is the approximate velocity of the object at 5 seconds?

_____

B During what time interval is the object slowing down? Explain how you can tell.

_____

_____

_____

C At what time or times was the velocity of the object about 40 m/s?

_____

4 Communicating Results In a short paragraph, describe the motion of the object.

_____

_____

_____

_____

_____

_____

Take It Home

Find a newspaper or magazine article that has a graph. What type of graph is it? Study the graph and determine its main message. Bring the graph to class and be prepared to discuss your interpretation of the graph.

Answers

1. A. Velocity vs Time

   B. Time (s)

   C. Velocity (m/s)

   D. line graph

2. 1; 6; 9; 0; 5

3. A. 8 m/s.

   B. from 6–8 seconds; the line showing the velocity drops

   C. 3 s, 7.5 s, 9.5 s

4. Sample answer: the moving object started slowly, gained speed, then slowed and stopped briefly. It then started moving again.

Building Graphing Skills

Assist students in reading the graphs as needed. In the second graph, velocity can be thought of as the same thing as speed. Students may at first think the second graph is a trace of the position. Helps students see that the speed, not the location, is shown on the vertical axis. **Ask:** If an object has a velocity of zero, what is it doing? standing still **Ask:** What is happening from 0 s to 2 s? the object starts at rest and speeds up to 1 m/s

Take It Home

Tell students that the business section of the newspaper is a good place to find graphs and other visuals, but other sections will sometimes have visuals as well. Encourage students to follow the steps in the tutorial to help them analyze the graphic they choose.

Acceleration

Essential Question How does motion change?

Professional Development

For more detailed information about the topics in this lesson, refer to the Content Refresher in the Unit Opener pages.

Opening Your Lesson

Begin the lesson by assessing students' prerequisite and prior knowledge.

Prerequisite Knowledge

- The relationships between distance, speed, and time
- How to construct distance–time graphs

Accessing Prior Knowledge

Ask: What is acceleration? Sample answer: The rate at which an object increases its speed

Ask: Does acceleration have a direction like velocity, or no direction, like speed? Answers will vary.

You will probably discover that students have incomplete ideas about acceleration. Explain that the lesson will help them better understand acceleration.

Customize Your Opening

☐ **Accessing Prior Knowledge,** above

☐ Print Path Engage Your Brain, SE p. 21

☐ Print Path Active Reading, SE p. 21

☐ **Digital Path** Lesson Opener

Key Topics/Learning Goals

Acceleration

1 Define *acceleration*.
2 Identify common acceleration units.
3 Calculate average acceleration.

Acceleration as a Vector

1 Recognize that acceleration is a change in speed, direction, or both.
2 Predict the outcome of velocity and acceleration being in the same direction, and in opposite directions.

Supporting Concepts

- Acceleration is the rate at which velocity changes. It is the difference between the velocity an object starts with and the velocity an object ends with, divided by time.
- Average acceleration is a way to calculate the acceleration of an object that may not always be moving at a constant acceleration.
- Acceleration in a straight line: $a = \dfrac{v_2 - v_1}{t_2 - t_1}$
- Acceleration is measured in feet per second per second, or meters per second squared (m/s^2).

- Acceleration is a vector, so acceleration can be a change in speed OR a change in direction (or both).
- The acceleration of an object moving in a circular direction (changing direction but not speed) is called centripetal acceleration.
- If velocity and acceleration are in the same direction, the speed is increasing; if they are in opposite directions, the speed is decreasing.

Options for Instruction

Two parallel paths provide coverage of the Essential Questions, with a strong Inquiry strand woven into each. Follow the Print Path, the Digital Path, or your customized combination of print, digital, and inquiry.

Print Path
Teaching support for the Print Path appears with the Student Pages.

Inquiry Labs and Activities

Digital Path
Digital Path shortcut: TS665132

Getting Up to Speed,
SE pp. 22–23
How do we measure changing velocity?
• Acceleration Measures a Change in Velocity
How is average acceleration calculated?

S.T.E.M. Lab
Investigate Acceleration

Quick Lab
Mass and Acceleration

Quick Lab
Acceleration and Slope

Daily Demo
Toy Car Acceleration

Activity
Accelerometers

Changes in Velocity
Video

Acceleration Equation
Interactive Graphics

Centripetal Acceleration
Slideshow

What a Drag! SE pp. 24–25
How can accelerating objects change velocity?
• Accelerating Objects Change Speed
• Accelerating Objects Change Direction

Activity
Roller Coaster Cartoons

Activity
Acceleration Game

Acceleration
Image

Types of Acceleration
Interactive Graphics

Options for Assessment

See the Evaluate page for options, including Formative Assessment, Summative Assessment, and Unit Review.

Engage and Explore

Activities and Discussion

Probing Questions *Acceleration or Not?*

Engage

Acceleration

👥 small groups or whole class
🕐 15 min
Inquiry **GUIDED** inquiry

Recognizing If a car demonstrates acceleration, what happens? Sample answer: The car speeds up. Is this the only way a car can demonstrate acceleration? no Remind students that any change in speed or direction means there is a change in acceleration. **Ask:** Is a car slowing down experiencing accelerating? yes **Ask:** If a car turns a corner, is it accelerating? yes **Ask:** If a car starts moving after stopping, is it accelerating? yes **Ask:** Is a satellite orbiting Earth at a constant speed accelerating? yes Why? It is changing direction.

Activity *Roller Coaster Cartoons*

Acceleration as a Vector

👥 individuals or pairs
🕐 15 min
Inquiry **GUIDED** inquiry

Ask students how acceleration would change during a roller coaster ride, and how negative acceleration, positive acceleration, and centripetal acceleration might occur. Have students draw cartoons of three places on a roller coaster ride and label them to describe the acceleration happening.

Take It Home *Acceleration Detector*

Acceleration

👥 adult-student pairs
🕐 15 min
Inquiry **GUIDED** inquiry

Students work with an adult to use their bodies as acceleration detectors. The pairs pay close attention to how their bodies feel as they accelerate in different ways. The pairs record their observations after each type of movement.

🌐 *Optional Online resource: student worksheet*

Activity *Accelerometers*

Acceleration

👥 small groups
🕐 15 min
Inquiry **GUIDED** inquiry

Ask students what a thermometer measures. temperature Ask students if they can figure out what an accelerometer measures. acceleration Tell students that they are going to make their own accelerometers. First, draw a guide on the board to show students what they will be drawing. Draw a half circle with the flat edge at the top. Draw lines separating six equal segments on the half circle, so it looks like half of a pie cut into six wedges. Then give each student an index card and direct them to copy your drawing onto their index cards, using the longer perimeter at the top of the card for the flat edge of the half circle. Make sure they draw their half circles as large as the index card allows and that their lines segmenting the half circle are evenly spaced. Next, hand out a piece of string about 5 in. long, a washer, and a ruler to each student. Tell students to tie the washer to the bottom of the string and then tape the other end of the string to the center point of the flat edge of the half circle. Finally, direct students to tape their half circles to the rulers, with the end of the ruler in the middle of the card, flush with the flat edge of the card. The accelerometers should resemble little signs that students can hold up. Tell students to hold their accelerometers as steady as they can, and to move in different ways—walking slowly then speeding up, walking quickly then stopping or slowing down, and changing direction. Give students some time to experiment with their accelerometers as they move in different ways. Tell them to observe how the washer moves as they make different movements. Ask students to write down three observations about how the washer moves and share them with the class. Sample answer: The washer moves when I speed up. It also moves when I slow down or change direction.

© Purestock Images

Customize Your Labs

📄 *See the Lab Manual for lab datasheets.*

🌐 *Go Online for editable lab datasheets.*

Levels of **Inquiry**   **DIRECTED** inquiry   **GUIDED** inquiry   **INDEPENDENT** inquiry

introduces inquiry skills   develops inquiry skills   deepens inquiry skills
within a structured   within a supportive   with student-driven
framework.   environment.   questions or procedures.

Labs and Demos

Daily Demo *Toy Car Acceleration*

Engage

Acceleration

👥 whole class
🕐 5 min
🔵 **DIRECTED** inquiry

PURPOSE **To help students understand acceleration**

MATERIALS

- **small toy car**

1 Push a wheeled car on a flat surface at a steady speed. Explain that this car has a velocity because it has speed and direction. **Ask:** Is this car accelerating? no Why or why not? because there is no change in velocity

2 Push the car so that it is slowly gaining speed as it rolls. Explain that the car still has velocity because it has speed and a direction. **Ask:** Is the car accelerating? yes Ask students to explain their answers. The car is accelerating because it is gaining speed. **Ask:** What type of acceleration is this? positive acceleration

3 Finally, push the car so that it starts out fast then slows down. Explain that the car has speed and direction. **Ask:** Is the car demonstrating acceleration? yes Encourage students to explain why the slowing car has acceleration. It is demonstrating acceleration because its velocity is changing. **Ask:** Can you name the type of acceleration the slowing car is demonstrating? negative acceleration Explain that because the velocity is decreasing, the car is demonstrating negative acceleration.

🌐 💻 S.T.E.M. Lab *Investigate Acceleration*

Acceleration

👥 small groups
🕐 45 min
🔵 **GUIDED** or **INDEPENDENT** inquiry

Students investigate acceleration by constructing a simple accelerometer and observing how it behaves as they move backward, forward, or vertically.

PURPOSE **To determine the types of circumstances that lead to positive acceleration and to negative acceleration**

MATERIALS

- **cardboard**
- **glue**
- **scissors**
- **string**
- **washer**
- **safety goggles**

🌐 💻 Quick Lab *Mass and Acceleration*

PURPOSE **To investigate the effects of mass on acceleration**

See the Lab Manual or go Online for planning information.

🌐 💻 Quick Lab *Acceleration and Slope*

PURPOSE **To investigate the effect of ramp slope on an object's acceleration**

See the Lab Manual or go Online for planning information.

Activities and Discussion

☐ **Probing Question** Acceleration or Not?

☐ **Activity** Roller Coaster Cartoons

☐ **Take It Home** Acceleration Detector

☐ **Activity** Accelerometers

Labs and Demos

☐ **Daily Demo** Toy Car Acceleration

☐ **S.T.E.M. Lab** Investigate Acceleration

☐ **Quick Lab** Mass and Acceleration

☐ **Quick Lab** Acceleration and Slope

Your Resources

Explain Science Concepts

Key Topics

Print Path

☐ **Getting Up to Speed,** SE pp. 22–23
- Active Reading (Annotation strategy), #5
- Active Reading (Annotation strategy) #6
- Visualize It!, #7
- Visualize It!, #8

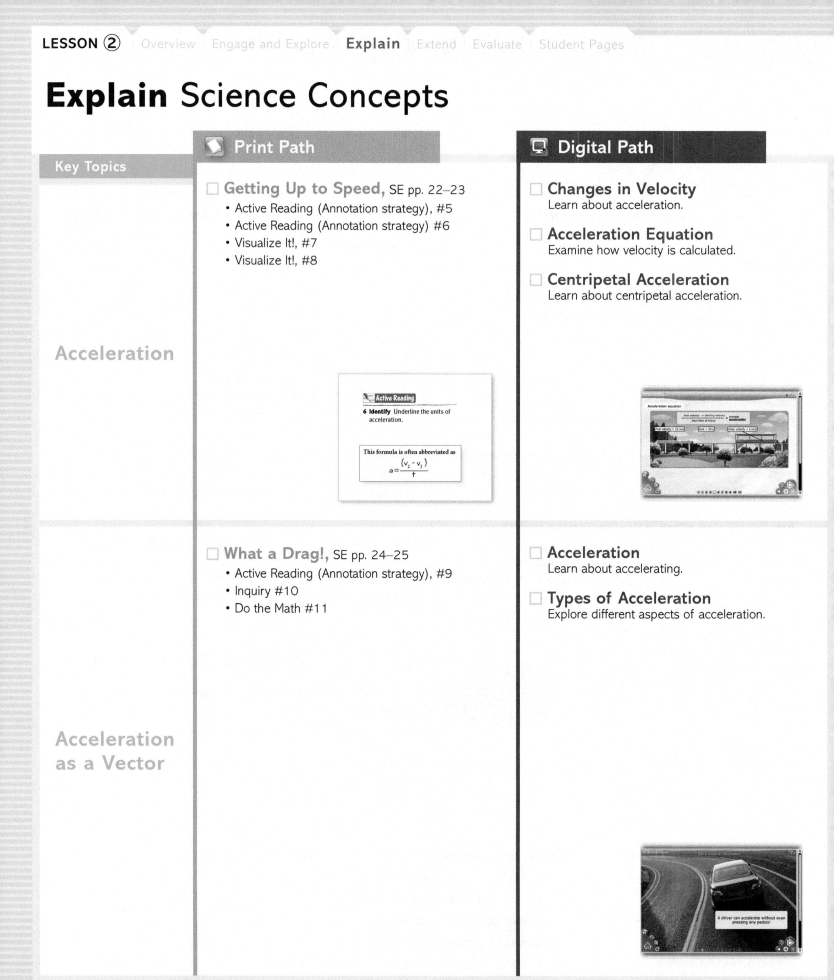

🖥 **Active Reading**

6 Identify Underline the units of acceleration.

This formula is often abbreviated as
$$a = \frac{(v_2 - v_1)}{t}$$

Digital Path

☐ **Changes in Velocity**
Learn about acceleration.

☐ **Acceleration Equation**
Examine how velocity is calculated.

☐ **Centripetal Acceleration**
Learn about centripetal acceleration.

Acceleration

☐ **What a Drag!,** SE pp. 24–25
- Active Reading (Annotation strategy), #9
- Inquiry #10
- Do the Math #11

☐ **Acceleration**
Learn about accelerating.

☐ **Types of Acceleration**
Explore different aspects of acceleration.

Acceleration as a Vector

A driver can accelerate without even pressing any pedals!

Basic *Everyday vs. Scientific Acceleration*

Acceleration

👥 individuals
🕐 10 min

Help students understand the difference between how the word *acceleration* is used in everyday speech and how it is used in physics. Encourage students to make a two-column chart. Have them write *Acceleration* across the top of the page, *Everyday Speech* at the top of one column, and *Physical Science* at the top of the other. In each column, have students write sentences using *acceleration*. For example, In the *Everyday* column, students could write, "Sarah is taking an accelerated math class."; in the *Science* column, they could write, "The runner exhibited acceleration as he slowed down." Ask students to put a star next to each use of *acceleration* in physical science that is not used in everyday speech, and a check next to each use of *acceleration* that could be both everyday and scientific. Encourage students to share their examples.

Advanced *Graphing Velocity and Time*

Velocity-Time Graphs

👥 individuals
🕐 15 min

Suppose you watched two runners in a race. One runner built speed rapidly and then slowed near the finish. The other built speed gradually throughout the race. Have students apply their knowledge of graphs and slope to draw one velocity-time graph that shows each runner's racing strategy. Remind students to graph velocity on the *y*-, or vertical, axis and time on the *x*-, or horizontal axis. The graph of the first runner would have a steep rise, a plateau, and a slow drop. The graph of the second would show a smoothly rising line.

ELL *Acceleration Terms*

Synthesizing Key Topics

👥 pairs
🕐 15 min

English language learners may not be familiar with the terms *speeding up, slowing down,* and *sharp turn*. These idioms may be confusing to ELLs who take them literally—in terms of direction (*up* and *down*) instead of acceleration. Explain that the terms refer to a change in velocity. Have students demonstrate with a toy car what speeding up, slowing down, and turning sharply mean.

acceleration   **centripetal acceleration**

Previewing Vocabulary

👥 whole class
🕐 10 min

Word Origins Share the following to help students remember terms:
- **Acceleration** comes from the Latin word *celerare*, which means "to quicken."
- **Centripetal** comes from the Latin word *centrum*, which means "center." **Ask:** How might the Latin meaning of these two words help you figure out the meaning of *centripetal acceleration*? Sample answer: You can figure out that centripetal acceleration likely has something to do with speeding around a center.

Reinforcing Vocabulary

👥 individuals
🕐 ongoing

Word Triangles Have students use the vocabulary words in Word Triangles. At the bottom of each triangle, they can write a term and its definition. In the center, they can write a sentence using the term. At the top, have them draw a diagram or illustration that helps explain the term.

Customize Your Core Lesson

Core Instruction
☐ **Print Path** choices
☐ **Digital Path** choices

Vocabulary
☐ **Previewing Vocabulary**
   Word Origins
☐ **Reinforcing Vocabulary**
   Word Triangles

Your Resources

Differentiated Instruction
☐ **Basic** Everyday vs. Scientific Acceleration
☐ **Advanced** Graphing Velocity and Time
☐ **ELL** Acceleration Terms

Extend Science Concepts

Reinforce and Review

Activity *Acceleration Game*

Synthesizing Key Topics 👥 whole class 🕐 10 min

Four Corners Pick four corners of the classroom to represent *positive acceleration, negative acceleration, centripetal acceleration,* and *unknown*. Label each corner. Read the following relationships to students. After each one, ask students to stand in the corner they think describes the relationship. Give each student in the correct corner a point. You can continue the game with additional examples provided by student volunteers.

1 A car goes from 40 km/h to 50 km/h in 2 min. positive acceleration

2 In 5 min, a plane goes from 800 km/h northwest to 700 km/h northwest. negative acceleration

3 A toy top spins in a circle. centripetal acceleration

4 A runner runs 1 km in 4 min, 30 s. unknown

5 Ana walked four blocks in 5 min. unknown

6 A ball that you roll slows down until it finally stops. negative acceleration

7 She walked from the front of the classroom to the back. unknown

8 A cowboy twirls a lasso over his head. centripetal acceleration

9 The jaguar put on a sudden burst of speed. positive acceleration

10 Max slowed down during the last leg of the race. negative acceleration

Graphic Organizer

Synthesizing Key Topics 👥 individuals 🕐 10 min

Venn Diagram Have students use a Venn diagram to compare and contrast velocity and acceleration. Where the two circles overlap, students can explain how the two concepts are similar. In the outer parts of each circle, students can explain how each concept is different.

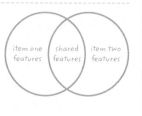
item one features · *shared features* · *item two features*

🕐 *Optional Online resource: Venn diagram support*

Going Further

Engineering Connection

Synthesizing Key Topics 👥 individuals or pairs 🕐 20 min

In-Depth Research You may have heard the saying "It doesn't take a rocket scientist to know that!" It does, however, take a rocket scientist to develop technology to accelerate rockets and to slow them down when it is time for them to re-enter our atmosphere. Spacecraft propulsion is the technology used to accelerate spacecraft, and there are many different types, such as chemical rockets and electric propulsion, or the more experimental ion thrusters. Invite students to research types of rocket propulsion. Encourage students to share their findings.

Health Connection

Synthesizing Key Topics 👥 individuals 🕐 20 min

Discussion In 2001, a race was planned at the Texas Motor Speedway. However, 2 h before the race, drivers refused to race. Why did they back out? While driving practice laps, drivers reached very high speeds, some over 239.9 mi/h. Many drivers were disoriented and dizzy. One driver even momentarily passed out! The symptoms were caused by the extreme acceleration, which reduced blood flow to the head. Some people believe that some extreme amusement park rides are dangerous in a similar way. Ask students if they have ever gone on rides with extreme positive or negative acceleration. Encourage students to share experiences and discuss whether they think these rides are safe.

Customize Your Closing

🗨 *See the Assessment Guide for quizzes and tests.*

🕐 *Go Online to edit and create quizzes and tests.*

Reinforce and Review

☐ **Activity** Acceleration Game

☐ **Graphic Organizer** Venn Diagram

☐ **Print Path** Visual Summary, SE p. 26

☐ **Digital Path** Lesson Closer

Evaluate Student Mastery

See the teacher support below the Student Pages for additional Formative Assessment questions.

Suppose you know the initial velocity of an airplane taking off and the final velocity when it is cruising high up in the air. **Ask:** Could you calculate the acceleration? Why or why not? Answer: No, you also need the time interval during which the airplane changed velocity. **Ask:** What is an example of positive acceleration? Sample answer: a car speeding up **Ask:** What is an example of negative acceleration? Sample answer: a runner slowing down **Ask:** What is an example of centripetal acceleration? Sample answer: a speed skater making a turn

Reteach

Formative assessment may show that students need reinforcement for certain topics. The resources below are recommended for reteaching. If students were introduced to a topic through the Print Path, you can also use the Digital Path to reteach, or vice versa.

🎧 *Can be assigned to individual students*

Acceleration

S.T.E.M. Lab Investigate Acceleration

Probing Question Acceleration or Not?

Daily Demo Toy Car Acceleration

Basic Everyday vs. Scientific Acceleration 🎧

ELL Acceleration Terms 🎧

Acceleration as a Vector

Activity Roller Coaster Cartoons 🎧

Summative Assessment

Alternative Assessment

Types of Acceleration

🔘 *Online resources: student worksheet, optional rubrics*

Acceleration

Climb the Ladder: *Types of Acceleration*

1. Work on your own, with a partner, or with a small group.

2. Choose one item from each rung of the ladder. Check your choices.

3. Have your teacher approve your plan.

4. Submit or present your results.

__ **Racing!**	__ **More Racing!**
Draw a graph of a runner who travels at several different speeds during a race. Circle the parts of the graph that show acceleration.	A runner in a 5K race is traveling 10 m/s when she crosses the finish line, 16 minutes after starting. What is her average acceleration?
__ **Speed**	__ **Show Speed**
A runner's velocity and acceleration are in the same direction. What can you say about the runner's speed? Explain in words or a diagram what happens to the runner's velocity and acceleration.	A runner's velocity and acceleration are in opposite directions. What can you say about the runner's speed? Draw a diagram or illustration that shows the runner's velocity and acceleration.
__ **Acceleration**	__ **Centripetal Acceleration**
A runner changes direction. What can you say about acceleration? Describe in writing what might happen to the runner's speed and direction.	Make a drawing that shows centripetal acceleration. Label acceleration, direction, and speed.

Going Further

☐ Engineering Connection

☐ Health Connection

Formative Assessment

☐ **Strategies** Throughout TE

☐ **Lesson Review** SE

Summative Assessment

☐ **Alternative Assessment** Types of Acceleration

☐ **Lesson Quiz**

☐ **Unit Tests A and B**

☐ **Unit Review** SE End-of-Unit

Your Resources

_____

_____

_____

_____

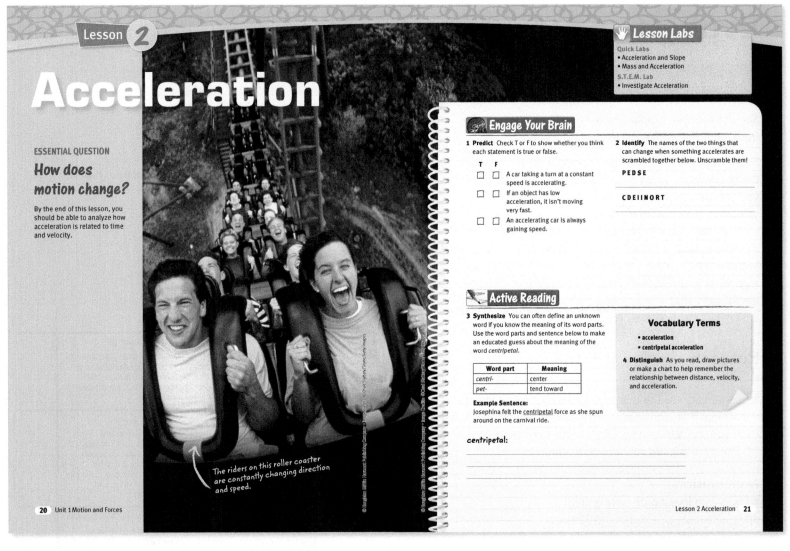

Lesson ②

Acceleration

ESSENTIAL QUESTION

How does motion change?

By the end of this lesson, you should be able to analyze how acceleration is related to time and velocity.

The riders on this roller coaster are constantly changing direction and speed.

20 Unit 1 Motion and Forces

Lesson Labs

Quick Labs
• Acceleration and Slope
• Mass and Acceleration
S.T.E.M. Lab
• Investigate Acceleration

Engage Your Brain

1 Predict Check T or F to show whether you think each statement is true or false.

T F
☐ ☐ A car taking a turn at a constant speed is accelerating.
☐ ☐ If an object has low acceleration, it isn't moving very fast.
☐ ☐ An accelerating car is always gaining speed.

2 Identify The names of the two things that can change when something accelerates are scrambled together below. Unscramble them!

P E D S E _____

C D E I I N O R T _____

Active Reading

3 Synthesize You can often define an unknown word if you know the meaning of its word parts. Use the word parts and sentence below to make an educated guess about the meaning of the word *centripetal*.

Word part	Meaning
centri-	center
pet-	tend toward

Example Sentence:
Josephina felt the centripetal force as she spun around on the carnival ride.

centripetal: _____
_____
_____

Vocabulary Terms
• acceleration
• centripetal acceleration

4 Distinguish As you read, draw pictures or make a chart to help remember the relationship between distance, velocity, and acceleration.

Lesson 2 Acceleration 21

Answers

Answers for 1–3 should represent students' current thoughts, even if incorrect.

1. T, F, F

2. speed; direction

3. See student work; Sample answer: moving around a center

4. Students' annotations will vary.

Opening Your Lesson

Discuss students' answers to item 1 to assess their understanding of acceleration. Many students will not have a clear understanding of acceleration at this point.

Prerequisites Students should already understand speed, motion, and velocity. They should also have a basic understanding of how distance and time relate to speed.

Interpreting Visuals

Ask students to examine the photograph on this page. Ask them the following questions. Based on what you already know about speed and velocity, what can you determine about the people on the roller coaster? Sample answers: Their direction changes as they go down and then up, so their velocity changes. Their speed probably also changes. They probably go faster when they are going down and slower when they are going up. What does *acceleration* mean to you? Sample answer: It means speeding up. Do the people on this roller coaster speed up? Sample answer: Yes, when they go downhill. Do the people on this roller coaster slow down? Sample answer: Yes, when they go uphill. Explain that slowing down is a type of acceleration too, and that students will learn more about this type of acceleration as they explore the lesson.

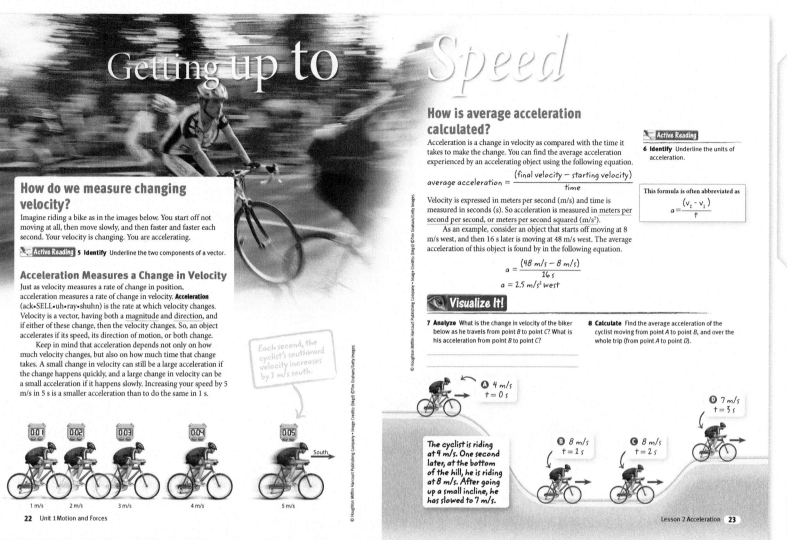

Getting up to *Speed*

How do we measure changing velocity?

Imagine riding a bike as in the images below. You start off not moving at all, then move slowly, and then faster and faster each second. Your velocity is changing. You are accelerating.

Active Reading **5 Identify** Underline the two components of a vector.

Acceleration Measures a Change in Velocity

Just as velocity measures a rate of change in position, acceleration measures a rate of change in velocity. **Acceleration** (ack•SELL•uh•ray•shuhn) is the rate at which velocity changes. Velocity is a vector, having both a magnitude and direction, and if either of these changes, then the velocity changes. So, an object accelerates if its speed, its direction of motion, or both change.

Keep in mind that acceleration depends not only on how much velocity changes, but also on how much time that change takes. A small change in velocity can still be a large acceleration if the change happens quickly, and a large change in velocity can be a small acceleration if it happens slowly. Increasing your speed by 5 m/s in 5 s is a smaller acceleration than to do the same in 1 s.

Each second, the cyclist's southward velocity increases by 1 m/s south.

1 m/s   2 m/s   3 m/s   4 m/s   5 m/s   South

22 Unit 1 Motion and Forces

How is average acceleration calculated?

Acceleration is a change in velocity as compared with the time it takes to make the change. You can find the average acceleration experienced by an accelerating object using the following equation.

$$\text{average acceleration} = \frac{(\text{final velocity} - \text{starting velocity})}{\text{time}}$$

Velocity is expressed in meters per second (m/s) and time is measured in seconds (s). So acceleration is measured in meters per second per second, or meters per second squared (m/s²).

As an example, consider an object that starts off moving at 8 m/s west, and then 16 s later is moving at 48 m/s west. The average acceleration of this object is found by in the following equation.

$$a = \frac{(48 \text{ m/s} - 8 \text{ m/s})}{16 \text{ s}}$$
$$a = 2.5 \text{ m/s}^2 \text{ west}$$

Active Reading
6 Identify Underline the units of acceleration.

This formula is often abbreviated as
$$a = \frac{(v_2 - v_1)}{t}$$

Visualize It!

7 Analyze What is the change in velocity of the biker below as he travels from point B to point C? What is his acceleration from point B to point C?

8 Calculate Find the average acceleration of the cyclist moving from point A to point B, and over the whole trip (from point A to point D).

A 4 m/s t = 0 s
B 8 m/s t = 1 s
C 8 m/s t = 2 s
D 7 m/s t = 3 s

The cyclist is riding at 4 m/s. One second later, at the bottom of the hill, he is riding at 8 m/s. After going up a small incline, he has slowed to 7 m/s.

Lesson 2 Acceleration **23**

Answers

5. *See students' pages for annotations.*

6. *See students' pages for annotations.*

7. The velocity is unchanged; 0 m/s²

8. from A to B: 4 m/s²; whole trip: 1 m/s²

Learning Alert ⚠ MISCONCEPTION ⚠

Students likely hold the misconception that *acceleration* is synonymous with *speeding up*. Mention that *speeding up* is only the casual meaning of *acceleration*; in physics, *acceleration* means any change in speed or direction. Review the last sentence of the first paragraph on this page. Emphasize that *any* change in velocity means an object is accelerating. Remind students that velocity includes the speed of an object *and* its direction. Invite students to suggest examples of acceleration in which an object does not speed up. An object slows down or changes direction.

Interpreting Visuals

Have students look at the illustration of the bicyclist on a hill. Ask students the following questions. Does the cyclist experience acceleration from point A to point B? Sample answer: Yes, because he starts traveling at point A at 4 m/s and ends up traveling at point B at 8 m/s. Also, even though the illustration does not show it, he must have changed direction as he bicycled down the slope. A change in direction is a change in acceleration. Does the cyclist's acceleration change from point C to point D? Sample answer: Yes, because he slows down from 8 m/s to 7 m/s. Also, he must have changed direction as he travelled up the incline.

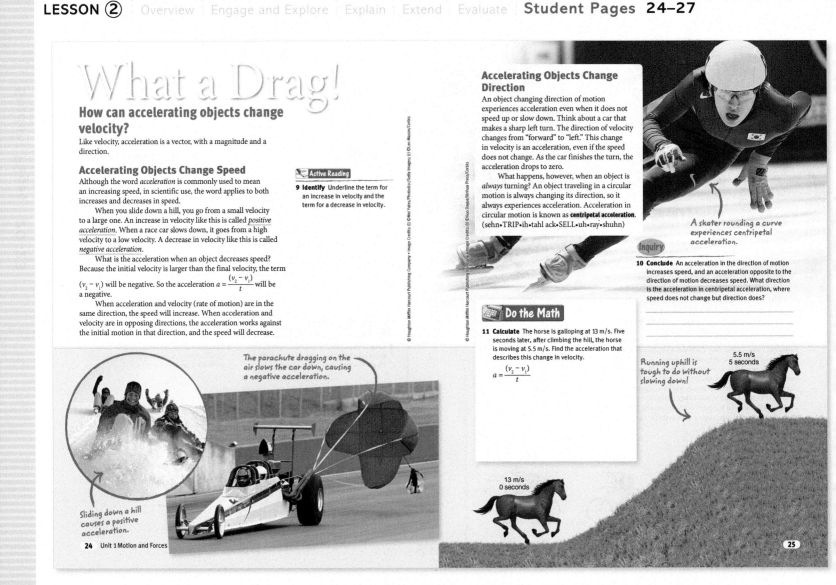

What a Drag!

How can accelerating objects change velocity?

Like velocity, acceleration is a vector, with a magnitude and a direction.

Accelerating Objects Change Speed

Although the word *acceleration* is commonly used to mean an increasing speed, in scientific use, the word applies to both increases and decreases in speed.

When you slide down a hill, you go from a small velocity to a large one. An increase in velocity like this is called *positive acceleration*. When a race car slows down, it goes from a high velocity to a low velocity. A decrease in velocity like this is called *negative acceleration*.

What is the acceleration when an object decreases speed? Because the initial velocity is larger than the final velocity, the term $(v_2 - v_1)$ will be negative. So the acceleration $a = \frac{(v_2 - v_1)}{t}$ will be a negative.

When acceleration and velocity (rate of motion) are in the same direction, the speed will increase. When acceleration and velocity are in opposing directions, the acceleration works against the initial motion in that direction, and the speed will decrease.

Active Reading

9 Identify Underline the term for an increase in velocity and the term for a decrease in velocity.

Accelerating Objects Change Direction

An object changing direction of motion experiences acceleration even when it does not speed up or slow down. Think about a car that makes a sharp left turn. The direction of velocity changes from "forward" to "left." This change in velocity is an acceleration, even if the speed does not change. As the car finishes the turn, the acceleration drops to zero.

What happens, however, when an object is *always* turning? An object traveling in a circular motion is always changing its direction, so it always experiences acceleration. Acceleration in circular motion is known as **centripetal acceleration**. (sehn•TRIP•ih•tahl ack•SELL•uh•ray•shuhn)

A skater rounding a curve experiences centripetal acceleration.

Inquiry

10 Conclude An acceleration in the direction of motion increases speed, and an acceleration opposite to the direction of motion decreases speed. What direction is the acceleration in centripetal acceleration, where speed does not change but direction does?

Do the Math

11 Calculate The horse is galloping at 13 m/s. Five seconds later, after climbing the hill, the horse is moving at 5.5 m/s. Find the acceleration that describes this change in velocity.

$$a = \frac{(v_2 - v_1)}{t}$$

The parachute dragging on the air slows the car down, causing a negative acceleration.

Sliding down a hill causes a positive acceleration.

Running uphill is tough to do without slowing down!

5.5 m/s
5 seconds

13 m/s
0 seconds

24 Unit 1 Motion and Forces

25

Answers

9. *See students' pages for annotations.*

10. perpendicular to the direction of motion

11. $(5.5 - 13)/5 = -1.5$ m/s^2

Probing Questions

Analyzing **Ask:** If a car gains speed as it backs up, is it demonstrating negative acceleration? No, it is demonstrating positive acceleration because it is speeding up. **Ask:** What is an example of negative acceleration? Sample answer: a car that slows down **Ask:** Is a bird that shifts direction demonstrating acceleration? Yes, because a change in direction is acceleration. **Ask:** What kind of acceleration does an arrow shooting out of a bow demonstrate? positive acceleration **Ask:** What kind of acceleration does a car that has run out of gas demonstrate as it rolls to a stop? negative acceleration

Formative Assessment

Ask: Suppose a car travels at a steady velocity. Will there be any acceleration? No, because acceleration occurs when there is a change in velocity. **Ask:** How do you calculate average acceleration (in a straight line)? average acceleration = (final velocity − starting velocity)/time A car traveling north at 50 mi/h speeds up to 55 mi/h. **Ask:** What type of acceleration is this? positive acceleration **Ask:** When might you travel at a low velocity, but with high acceleration? Sample answer: when you stop suddenly **Ask:** What type of acceleration does the second hand on a clock demonstrate? centripetal acceleration

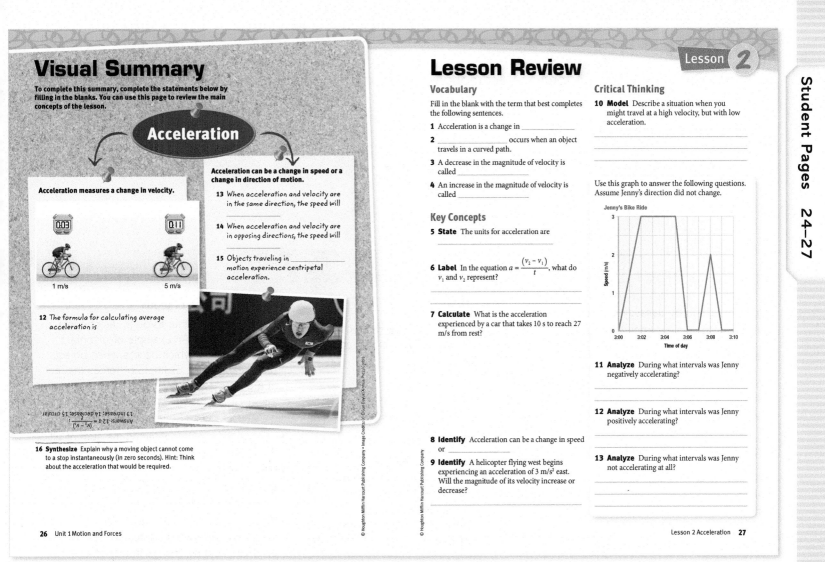

Visual Summary Answers

12. $a = \dfrac{(v_2 - v_1)}{t}$

13. increase

14. decrease

15. circular

16. The acceleration formula would have to divide by zero, which is impossible.

Lesson Review Answers

1. velocity

2. centripetal acceleration

3. negative acceleration

4. positive acceleration

5. meters per second squared, or m/s²

6. v_1 is the initial velocity, v_2 is the final velocity

7. 2.7 m/s²

8. direction

9. decrease

10. See student work; example: traveling in a car at 60 miles per hour without slowing down or speeding up

11. from 3:05 to 3:06 and from 3:08 to 3:09

12. from 3:00 to 3:02 and from 3:07 to 3:08

13. from 3:02 to 3:05, from 3:06 to 3:07, and from 3:09 to 3:10

Forces

Essential Question How do forces affect motion?

Professional Development

For more detailed information about the topics in this lesson, refer to the Content Refresher in the Unit Opener pages.

Opening Your Lesson

Begin the lesson by assessing students' prerequisite and prior knowledge.

Prerequisite Knowledge

- Basic definitions of *mass* and *vector*
- Basic definitions of *motion* and *acceleration*

Accessing Prior Knowledge

Ask: What is mass? the amount of matter in an object
Ask: What is a vector? an object with mass and direction
Ask: How do you describe motion? a change in position
Ask: What is acceleration? a change in motion over time; a change in speed or direction

Customize Your Opening

☐ **Accessing Prior Knowledge,** above

☐ Print Path Engage Your Brain, SE p. 29 1–2

☐ Print Path Active Reading, SE p. 29 3–4

☐ **Digital Path** Lesson Opener

Key Topics/Learning Goals	Supporting Concepts
Introduction to Force 1 Discriminate between contact forces and forces that act at a distance.	• A force is a push or a pull. • Forces can act either through direct contact or at a distance. An example of a contact force is friction, which occurs when objects touch each other. Example of forces that act at a distance are gravity and magnetism.
Net Force 1 Compare the effect of balanced and unbalanced forces on an object. 2 Apply the concept of net force to determine direction of motion.	• The net force on an object is the sum of all the forces acting on the object. • When two forces act in opposite directions, the smaller force can be subtracted from the larger force to determine the net force. • When all the forces applied to an object produce a net force of zero, the forces are balanced, and no change in motion occurs. • If forces acting on an object are not balanced, then the object accelerates in the direction of the net force.
Newton's Laws 1 Explain Newton's first law using the concept of inertia. 2 Describe the relationship among force, mass, and acceleration. (Newton's second law) 3 Calculate force, mass, or acceleration given two of the three variables. 4 Explain how forces act in pairs. (Newton's third law)	• Inertia is the tendency of an object to resist any change in motion. Newton's first law states that an object at rest remains at rest, and an object in uniform motion maintains its velocity unless a force acts on it. • Newton's second law states that the acceleration of an object depends on its mass and the magnitude of the force. Newton's second law can be expressed as $F = ma$, or force equals mass times acceleration. • Newton's third law of motion states that when one object exerts a force on a second object, the second object exerts an equal and opposite force on the first object.

Options for Instruction

Two parallel paths provide coverage of the Essential Questions, with a strong Inquiry strand woven into each.
Follow the Print Path, the Digital Path, or your customized combination of print, digital, and inquiry.

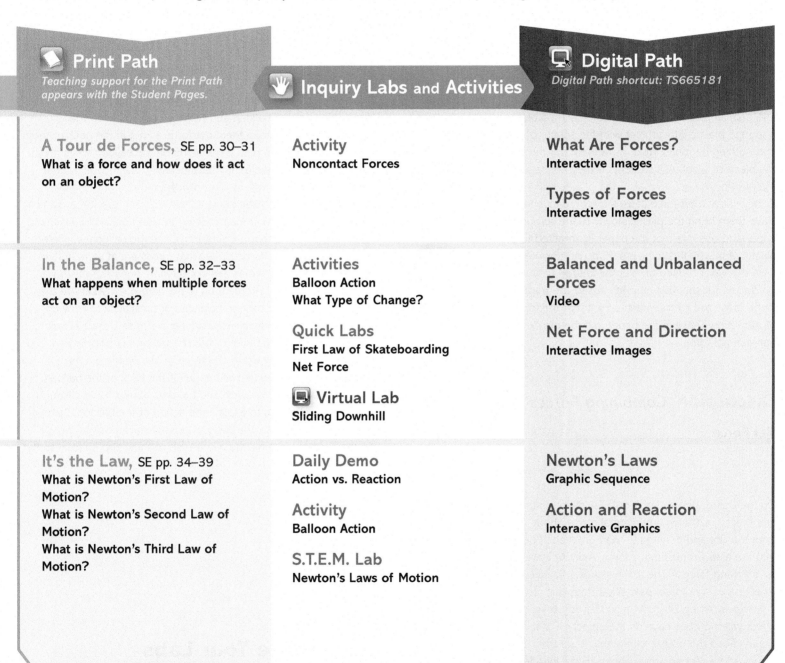

Print Path *Teaching support for the Print Path appears with the Student Pages.*	Inquiry Labs and Activities	Digital Path *Digital Path shortcut: TS665181*
A Tour de Forces, SE pp. 30–31 **What is a force and how does it act on an object?**	**Activity** Noncontact Forces	**What Are Forces?** Interactive Images **Types of Forces** Interactive Images
In the Balance, SE pp. 32–33 **What happens when multiple forces act on an object?**	**Activities** Balloon Action What Type of Change? **Quick Labs** First Law of Skateboarding Net Force **Virtual Lab** Sliding Downhill	**Balanced and Unbalanced Forces** Video **Net Force and Direction** Interactive Images
It's the Law, SE pp. 34–39 **What is Newton's First Law of Motion?** **What is Newton's Second Law of Motion?** **What is Newton's Third Law of Motion?**	**Daily Demo** Action vs. Reaction **Activity** Balloon Action **S.T.E.M. Lab** Newton's Laws of Motion	**Newton's Laws** Graphic Sequence **Action and Reaction** Interactive Graphics

Options for Assessment

See the Evaluate page for options, including Formative Assessment, Summative Assessment, and Unit Review.

Engage and Explore

Activities and Discussion

Activity *Noncontact Forces*

Engage

Introduction to Force

👥 small groups
🕐 10–15 min
🔵 **GUIDED** inquiry

Provide each group with a piece of hard plastic, such as a stirring rod, a small piece of wool, and some scraps of paper. Have students bring the plastic into contact with the scraps of paper and observe that nothing happens. Next, have them rub the plastic vigorously with the piece of wool. Ask students if they notice anything happening to the plastic. The action makes the plastic feel warmer. Ask students if they know what force causes the production of heat. friction Have them bring the plastic slowly to the scraps of paper and observe that the paper is attracted to the plastic. Ask why this happens. Rubbing the plastic with the wool caused an electric charge to build up on the plastic; this charge caused the paper to be attracted to the plastic. Elicit that the force of attraction between the paper and the plastic is a non-contact force.

Discussion *Combining Forces*

Net Force

👥 whole class
🕐 10–15 min
🔵 **DIRECTED** inquiry

On the board, draw a large dot. Tell students that the dot represents an object. Next draw a horizontal arrow about 50 cm long leading from the dot and pointing to the right. Label the arrow *x*. Tell students that the arrow represents a force. **Ask:** Why are arrows useful for showing forces? The arrows show the size (magnitude) and direction of the force. **Ask:** What does this arrow show? a force of *x* newtons acting or pulling on the object to the right **Ask:** What effect will the force have on the object? If the object is not moving, it will cause the object to move to the right, the direction of the force. Add a second arrow about 25 cm long leading from the dot and pointing to the left. **Ask:** Which force is stronger? How do you know? Force *x*; the arrow is longer. **Ask:** What is the net force acting on the object? *x* − *y* newtons If the object is not moving, in which direction will the object move? to the right

Activity *Balloon Action*

Net Force

👥 small groups
🕐 10–15 min
🔵 **GUIDED** inquiry

Provide each group with a balloon. Have one member of each group blow up the balloon and twist the neck to keep the balloon inflated. Instruct them not to tie a knot in the neck of the balloon. **Ask:** What forces were acting on the balloon while it was being inflated, and were they balanced or unbalanced? Sample answer: Air was being pushed into the balloon and the air was pushing against the sides of the balloon; the forces were unbalanced because the air moving into the balloon caused the sides of the balloon to stretch. Once the balloon is inflated, encourage students to describe what forces are at work in the inflated balloon. Air molecules are pushing against the sides of the balloon, and the balloon is pushing back. **Ask:** Are the forces acting on the balloon balanced or unbalanced? How do you know? Sample answer: Balanced, because the air is still pushing against the balloon, but the balloon is not moving; another force is balancing the force of the inside air. Ask students to predict what will happen if the neck of the balloon is released. Sample answer: The balloon will go flying through the air. Ask students to explain the action of the balloon. Sample answer: The sides of the balloon push inward against the air in the balloon causing the air to rush out and the balloon to fly through the air.

Customize Your Labs

🔲 *See the Lab Manual for lab datasheets.*

🔘 *Go Online for editable lab datasheets.*

Levels of **Inquiry**   **DIRECTED** inquiry   **GUIDED** inquiry   **INDEPENDENT** inquiry
introduces inquiry skills   develops inquiry skills   deepens inquiry skills
within a structured   within a supportive   with student-driven
framework.   environment.   questions or procedures.

Labs and Demos

Daily Demo *Action vs. Reaction*

Newton's Laws

👥 whole class
🕐 10–15 min
Inquiry GUIDED inquiry

Use this short demo after you have discussed Newton's third law.

PURPOSE **To demonstrate action-reaction forces**

MATERIALS

• spring scales (2)

Tell students that you are going to hook two spring scales together and pull on one scale while the other scale is kept motionless. Ask them to predict how the readings on the two scales will compare. Have them record their predictions. Hook two spring scales together. Have a student volunteer hold one of the scales while you pull gently on the other. Have students observe and record the readings on each scale. Next, both you and the student volunteer pull gently on the scales at the same time. Again, record the readings on each scale. In both cases, the readings on each scale will be the same, although the readings with both people pulling may be different. Invite students to discuss what this demonstration shows about force. Sample answer: equal and opposite action and reaction

🌐 💠 Quick Lab *Net Force*

PURPOSE **To compare the effect of balanced and unbalanced forces on an object**

See the Lab Manual or go Online for planning information.

🌐 💠 Quick Lab *First Law of Skateboarding*

PURPOSE **To investigate and describe how an unbalanced force acting on an object changes its speed, direction, and motion**

See the Lab Manual or go Online for planning information.

🌐 💠 S.T.E.M. Lab *Newton's Laws of Motion*

PURPOSE **To describe the relationship among force, mass, and acceleration and to explain how forces act in pairs**

See the Lab Manual or go Online for planning information.

🖥 Virtual Lab *Sliding Downhill*

Net Force

👥 flexible
🕐 45 min
Inquiry GUIDED inquiry

Students calculate the energy and speed of a moving object.

PURPOSE to determine the relationship between potential and kinetic energy and speed

---

Activities and Discussion

☐ **Activity** Noncontact Forces

☐ **Discussion** Combining Forces

☐ **Activity** Balloon Action

Labs and Demos

☐ **Daily Demo** Action vs. Reaction

☐ **Quick Lab** Net Force

☐ **Quick Lab** First Law of Skateboarding

☐ **S.T.E.M. Lab** Newton's Laws of Motion

☐ **Virtual Lab** Sliding Downhill

Your Resources

_____

_____

_____

_____

Explain Science Concepts

Key Topics	📖 Print Path	🖥 Digital Path
Introduction to Force	☐ **A Tour de Forces,** SE pp. 30–31 • Active Reading (Annotation strategy), #5 • Visualize It!, #6 • Visualize It!, #7	☐ **What Are Forces?** Learn about force and the relationship between force and energy. ☐ **Types of Forces** Explore different types of forces.
Net Force	☐ **In the Balance,** SE pp. 32–33 • Active Reading (Annotation strategy), #8 • Visualize It!, #9 • Visualize It!, #10	☐ **Balanced and Unbalanced Forces** Explore the effect balanced and unbalanced forces have on an object. ☐ **Net Force and Direction** Learn how net force determines the direction of motion.
Newton's Laws	☐ **It's the Law,** SE pp. 34–39 • Active Reading (Annotation strategy), #11 • Visualize It!, #12 • Think Outside the Book, #13 • Visualize It!, #14 • Active Reading (Annotation strategy), #15 • Do the Math, #16 • Visualize It!, #20 • Visualize It!, #21 • Describe, #22 	☐ **Newton's Laws** Learn about Newton's Laws of Motion. ☐ **Action and Reaction** Discover how forces work in pairs. 

Basic *Animated Acceleration*

Newton's Laws

👥 whole class
🕐 varied

Discussion Students likely have seen a character in an animated cartoon attempt to run on a carpet that slides backward into folds while the character remains in one place. Display or describe such a situation, and ask students to explain why the rug moves while the character remains in the same place. Sample answer: Friction between the carpet and the floor is less than that between the character's shoes and the carpet. The character's feet pushing against the carpet cause the carpet to slide along the floor while the character stays in the same place.

🌐 *Optional Online rubric: Class Discussion*

Advanced *Forces Acting at an Angle*

Net Force

👥 individuals or small groups
🕐 varied

Diagrams Have students predict the angle at which a soccer ball at rest will move when kicked with equal force from two directions. Ask students to predict what will happen if equal forces act on the ball at right angles to each other. Sample answer: The ball will move away at a 45° angle. Finally, challenge them to draw diagrams showing the different results.

ELL *Newton's Laws of Motion*

Newton's Laws

👥 small groups
🕐 15–20 min

Have students work in small groups. Instruct each group to choose one of Newton's three laws of motion to discuss. Be sure that each law is selected by at least one group. Have groups try to explain the laws in their own words. Then have each group create activities or draw illustrations to demonstrate how their law works. Have each group present its ideas to the class.

force   **net force**   **inertia**

Previewing Vocabulary

👥 whole class   🕐 5 min

Word Origins Share the following word origins to help students remember terms.
• **Force** comes from the Latin word *fortia*, meaning "strong."
• **Inertia** comes from the Latin word *iners*, meaning "not active."

Reinforcing Vocabulary

👥 individuals   🕐 15 min

Description Wheel Instruct students to create description wheels for each vocabulary term by writing each in the circle in the center. Then have them write details about each term on the spokes radiating out from the center circle.

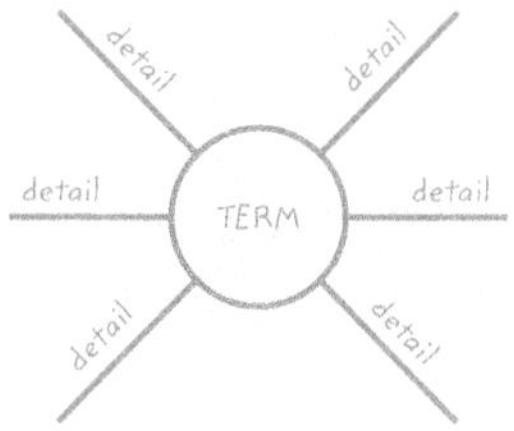

🌐 *Optional Online resource: Description Wheel support*

Customize Your Core Lesson

Core Instruction
☐ **Print Path** choices
☐ **Digital Path** choices

Vocabulary
☐ Previewing Vocabulary Word Origins
☐ Reinforcing Vocabulary Description Wheel

Your Resources

Differentiated Instruction
☐ **Basic** Animated Acceleration
☐ **Advanced** Forces Acting at an Angle
☐ **ELL** Newton's Laws of Motion

Extend Science Concepts

Reinforce and Review

Activity *What Type of Change?*

Synthesizing Key Topics   👥 small groups   🕐 30 min

Think Fast After completing the lesson, conduct a Think Fast exercise. Provide short statements or pose questions that require quick oral responses from students. Use the following ideas or come up with your own. You can also have student volunteers pose questions for classmates to answer.

- In what direction does an object at rest move when balanced forces act on it? The object does not move.
- What is the tendency to resist change in motion? inertia
- Name a force that acts at a distance. gravity or magnetic force
- What has a size and a direction? a vector
- What is required to change motion? force
- What does an unbalanced force cause? a change in motion
- What always occurs in pairs? forces
- What produces acceleration? an unbalanced force

Graphic Organizer

Synthesizing Key Topics   👥 individuals   🕐 30 min

Mind Map After students have studied the lesson, ask them to create and complete a Mind Map to help them classify and organize information about forces and Newton's laws.

🕐 *Optional Online resource: Mind Map support*

Going Further

Environmental Science Connection

Introduction to Force   👥 whole class   🕐 varied

Research Project On average, newer cars cause less air pollution than older cars do. One reason for this is that newer cars have more efficient engines than older cars do. Another reason is that new cars have less mass than older cars; in other words, they are less heavy. As a result, newer cars require less force to achieve the same acceleration as older, more massive cars. A less massive car with a smaller engine can still have good acceleration. Smaller engines burn less fuel, so they create less air pollution. Have students research three cars built in the same year and make a chart comparing the cars' masses and the average amount of fuel they use.

Real World Connection

Synthesizing Key Topics   👥 whole class   🕐 5 min

Ice Skating Have you ever watched ice skaters? You probably weren't thinking about the laws of motion while you watched, but they have a great deal to do with how ice skating works. Think of the blade of an ice skate as the first object, and the ice as the second. When a skater pushes the blade against the ice, he or she is applying a backwards force to the ice, which pushes the skater forward. The reduced friction from ice allows for longer glides than on other surfaces, such as grass or cement.

Customize Your Closing

📄 *See the Assessment Guide for quizzes and tests.*

🕐 *Go Online to edit and create quizzes and tests.*

Reinforce and Review

☐ **Activity** What Type of Change?

☐ **Graphic Organizer** Mind Map

☐ **Print Path** Visual Summary, SE p. 40

☐ **Print Path** Lesson Review, SE p. 41

☐ **Digital Path** Lesson Closer

Evaluate Student Mastery

See the teacher support below the Student pages for additional Formative Assessment questions.

Ask: What is a force? a push or a pull **Ask:** What can a force do? A force can change the speed or direction of an object. **Ask:** What are some forces that act at a distance? gravity, magnetic **Ask:** What is net force? the combination of all the forces acting on an object **Ask:** What happens when unbalanced forces act on an object? They produce a change in motion, such as speed or direction. **Ask:** What is inertia? the tendency of objects to resist a change in motion **Ask:** What are force pairs? When an object exerts a force on another, the second object exerts an equal and opposite force on the first.

Reteach

Formative assessment may show that students need reinforcement for certain topics. The resources below are recommended for reteaching. If students were introduced to a topic through the Print Path, you can also use the Digital Path to reteach, or vice versa.
Can be assigned to individual students

Introduction to Force
Activity Noncontact Forces

Net Force
Discussion Combining Forces

Quick Lab First Law of Skateboarding

Newton's Laws
Activity Balloon Action

Daily Demo Action vs. Reaction

Alternative Assessment
Forces, Motions, and Newton's Laws

Online resources: student worksheet, optional rubrics

Forces

Mix and Match: *Forces, Motion, and Newton's Laws*
Mix and match ideas to show what you've learned about forces.

1. Work on your own, with a partner, or with a small group.
2. Choose one static situation and one involving acceleration from Column A, six topics from Column B, and one option from Column C. Check your choices.
3. Have your teacher approve your plan.
4. Submit or present your results.

A. Choose Two Situations	B. Choose Six Things to Analyze	C. Choose One Way to Communicate Analysis
___ a tire hanging on a rope	___ friction	___ demonstration
___ a bicycle leaning against a building	___ gravity	___ model
___ a car rounding a corner	___ balanced forces	___ video
___ a sailboat moving in a breeze	___ unbalanced forces	___ labeled diagrams
___ a car in a driveway	___ contact force	___ skit
___ a weight lifter holding a heavy barbell overhead	___ Newton's first law	_____
___ a person skating on ice	___ Newton's second law	
___ a crash test dummy being restrained by a seat belt during a crash	___ Newton's third law	
_____		

Going Further
- [ ] Environmental Science Connection
- [ ] Real World Connection
- [ ] Print Path Why It Matters, SE p. 37

Your Resources

_____

_____

Formative Assessment
- [ ] Strategies Throughout TE
- [ ] Lesson Review SE

Summative Assessment
- [ ] Alternative Assessment Forces, Motions, and Newton's Laws
- [ ] Lesson Quiz
- [ ] Unit Tests A and B
- [ ] Unit Review SE End-of-Unit

_____

_____

Answers

Answers for 1–3 should represent students' current thoughts, even if incorrect.

1. Students should draw arrows indicating that gravity is pulling downward on the ball and that an upward force was exerted on the ball when it was tossed.

2. Caption should describe the effect of the foot in setting the ball in motion.

3. mesh-like material for catching fish; amount remaining after any subtractions or additions have been made to the starting amount

4. Students should define or sketch each vocabulary term in the lesson.

Opening Your Lesson

Discuss answers to item 1 to assess students' prerequisite knowledge and to estimate what they already know about the key topics.

Prerequisites Students should already be familiar with the concepts of energy, motion, speed, and acceleration.

Building Reading Skills

KWL Direct students to make a KWL chart by folding a sheet of paper lengthwise to form three columns. Have students title the columns: What I Know, What I Want to Find Out, and What I Learned. Allow students time to complete the first two columns of the chart to help them answer the Essential Question. Students can return to the chart to complete the last column at the end of the lesson.

🌐 *Optional Online resource: KWL support*

A Tour de Forces

What is a force, and how does it act on an object?

You have probably heard the word *force* used in conversation. People say, "Don't force the issue," or "Our team is a force to be reckoned with." Scientists also use the word *force*. What exactly is a force, as it is used in science?

A Force Is a Push or a Pull

Active Reading **5 Identify** As you read, underline the unit that is used to express force.

In science, a **force** is simply a push or a pull. All forces have both a size and a direction. A force can cause an object to change its speed or direction. When you see a change in an object's motion, one or more forces caused the change. The unit used to express force is the newton (N). You will learn how to calculate force a little later in this lesson.

Forces exist only when there is an object for them to act on. However, forces do not always cause an object to move. When you sit in a chair, the chair does not move. Your downward force on the chair is balanced by the upward force from the floor.

Visualize It!

6 Identify Draw arrows to represent the pushing forces in the image at left and the pulling forces in the image at right.

30 Unit 1 Motion and Forces

A Force Can Act Directly on an Object

It is not always easy to tell what is exerting a force or what is being acted on by a force. When one object touches or bumps into another object, we say that the objects are in contact with each other. A force exerted during contact between objects is a contact force. Friction is an example of a contact force between two surfaces. Suppose you slide a book across your desk. The amount of friction between the surface of the desk and the book cover determines how easily the book moves. Car tires rely on friction to keep a moving car from sliding off a road. Cars may slide on icy roads because ice lowers the force of friction on the tires.

A Force Can Act on an Object from a Distance

Forces can also act at a distance. One force that acts at a distance is called gravity. When you jump, gravity pulls you back to the ground even though you are not touching Earth. Magnetic force is another example of a force that can act at a distance. Magnetic force can be a push or a pull. A magnet can hold paper to a metal refrigerator door. The magnet touches the paper, not the metal, so the magnetic force is acting on the refrigerator door at a distance. Magnetic force also acts at a distance when the like poles of two magnets push each other apart. A magnetic levitation train floats because magnetic forces push the train away from its track.

Visualize It!

7 Identify The arrows in the picture below represent contact and distance forces. Label each arrow with a "C" if it is a contact force or "D" if it is a distance force.

31

Answers

5. *See students' pages for annotations.*

6. Students should draw an arrow to the right to show the force exerted by the martial artist; students should draw arrows pointing toward the dog and its owner to show the forces exerted on the toy.

7. C: ground to boy, boy to lawn mower; D: bird to ground, airplane to ground

Interpreting Visuals

Direct students to look at the photograph of the woman with the dog. Have students identify the direct forces that are acting on the toy. Sample answer: The dog is pulling on the toy in one direction; the woman is pulling in the opposite direction. Then, ask why the toy does not appear to be moving. The dog and the woman are pulling with the same amount of force.

Next, ask students to look at the photograph of the martial arts student. Tell students that the martial arts student is not the only person in the photograph exerting force. Ask students to identify the force being exerted by the person holding the block. This person is pushing back. Encourage students to identify how the forces being exerted by the two people interact. Sample answer: They are pushing in opposite directions, and the result is that the block breaks.

Formative Assessment

Ask: What is a force? a push or a pull **Ask:** What is the difference between contact forces and distance force? A contact force acts directly on an object and touches it; a distance force acts on an object from a distance.

In the Balance

What happens when multiple forces act on an object?

Usually, more than one force is acting on an object. The combination of all the forces acting on an object is called the **net force**. How do you determine net force? The answer depends on the directions of the forces involved.

When forces act in the same direction, you simply add them together to determine the net force. For example, when forces of 1 N and 2 N act in the same direction on an object, the net force is 1 N + 2 N = 3 N. When forces act in opposite directions, you subtract the smaller force from the larger force to determine the net force: 2 N – 1 N = 1 N.

Active Reading

8 Identify As you read, underline how one determines net force.

Visualize It!

9 Calculate Calculate the net force acting on the appliance box and use it to determine if the box will move.

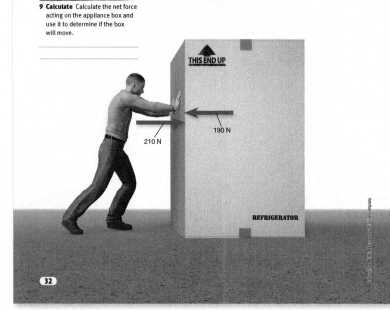

210 N   190 N

THIS END UP

REFRIGERATOR

32

The Forces Can Be Balanced

When the forces on an object produce a net force of 0 N, the forces are balanced. Balanced forces will not cause a change in the motion of a moving object or cause a nonmoving object to start moving. Many objects around you have only balanced forces acting on them. A light hanging from the ceiling does not move, because the force of gravity pulling downward on the light is balanced by the force of the chain pulling the light upward.

The Forces Can Be Unbalanced

When the net force on an object is not 0 N, the forces are unbalanced. Unbalanced forces produce a change in the object's motion. It could be a change in its speed or direction or both. This change in motion is called acceleration. The acceleration is always in the direction of the net force. For example, when a big dog and a small dog play with a tug toy, the bigger dog pulls with greater force, so the acceleration is in the direction of the bigger dog.

Visualize It!

10 Apply The arrows in the first image show that the forces on the rope are balanced. Draw arrows on the second image to show how the forces on the rope are unbalanced.

These two tug-of-war teams are pulling on the rope with equal force to produce a net force of 0 N. The rope does not move.

One of these teams is pulling on the rope with more force. The rope moves in the direction of the stronger team.

Lesson 3 Forces   33

Answers

8. *See students' pages for annotations*

9. *210 N – 190 N = 20 N; the box will move because the net force is greater than 0.*

10. In the upper photo, arrows should be equal in size but opposite in direction to show that forces are balanced. In the lower photo, the arrow pointing toward the stronger team should be longer than the arrow pointing toward the weaker team to indicate that the stronger team is exerting the greater force.

Probing Questions GUIDED Inquiry

Analyzing Have students look at the images of the tug-of-war players. **Ask:** If it was originally at rest, what direction would the rope move in if one side was pulling east with a 20 N force, and the other side was pulling west with 20 N force? The rope wouldn't move, because the forces would be balanced.

Identifying Note that arrows are used to represent forces in the illustrations. **Ask:** Why are arrows useful for representing forces? Forces are vectors—they have both size and direction. **Ask:** What does the length of an arrow show? the size of the force represented by the arrow

Formative Assessment

Ask: What is net force? Net force is the combination of all the forces acting on an object. **Ask:** What type of force is needed to change an object's motion? Sample answer: an unbalanced force **Ask:** What type of force is needed to make an object stop moving? Sample answer: an unbalanced force

It's the Law

What is Newton's First Law of Motion?

Force and motion are related. In the 1680s, British scientist Sir Isaac Newton explained this relationship between force and motion with three laws of motion.

Newton's first law describes the motion of an object that has a net force of 0 N acting on it. The law states: *An object at rest stays at rest, and an object in motion stays in motion at the same speed and direction, unless it experiences an unbalanced force.* Let's look at the two parts of this law more closely.

An Object at Rest Stays at Rest

Active Reading **11 Identify** As you read, underline examples of objects affected by inertia.

Newton's first law is also called the law of inertia. **Inertia** (ih•NER•shuh) is the tendency of all objects to resist a change in motion. An object will not move until a force makes it move. So a chair will not slide across the floor unless a force pushes the chair, and a golf ball will not leave the tee until a force pushes it off.

Visualize It!

12 Explain In your own words, explain why the dishes remain in place when the magician pulls the cloth out from under them.

_____

_____

An Object in Motion Stays in Motion

Now let's look at the second part of Newton's first law of motion. It states that an object in motion stays in motion at the same speed and direction, or velocity, unless it experiences an unbalanced force. Think about coming to a sudden stop while riding in a car. The car stops because the brakes apply friction to the wheel, making the forces acting on the car unbalanced. You keep moving forward until your seat belt applies an unbalanced force on you. This force stops your forward motion.

Both parts of the law are really stating the same thing. After all, an object at rest has a velocity—its velocity is zero!

Think Outside the Book Inquiry

13 Apply Create a model that demonstrates the concept of inertia. Share your results with the class.

When this car was in motion, the test dummy was moving forward at the same velocity as the car. When the car hit the barrier and stopped, the dummy kept moving until it, too, was acted on by a net backward force.

FO4305OZ02

000 1768

Visualize It!

14 Infer What forces acted on the test dummy to stop its forward motion?

_____

_____

_____

_____

34 | 35

Answers

11. *See students' pages for annotations.*

12. Inertia caused the plates to remain in place because the tablecloth did not exert a force on the plates great enough to make the plates move.

13. Students' concepts will vary but should show an object moving without stopping or remaining still.

14. The forces exerted by the air bag and seat belt acted on the dummy to stop its forward motion.

Building Reading Skills

Cluster Diagram After reading about Newton's First Law, direct students to draw a cluster diagram to summarize the information in the passage using the headings. Students should write "Newton's First Law of Motion" in the first circle and "An Object at Rest Stays at Rest" and "An Object in Motion Stays in Motion" in two circles branching off the first circle. They can then continue to add details or examples branching off those circles.

🌐 *Optional Online resource: Cluster Diagram support*

Using Annotations

Word Square Direct students to create a Word Square using the term *inertia* and the definition they underlined. Students should put the term in one square, the definition in a second square, a picture in a third square, and a sentence using the word in the fourth square. Encourage the students to share their Word Squares with the class.

🌐 *Optional Online resource: Word Square support*

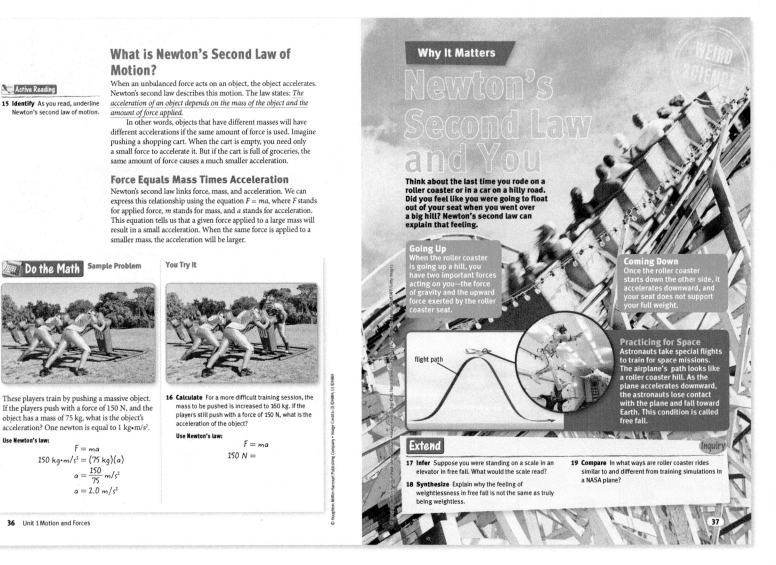

What is Newton's Second Law of Motion?

Active Reading

15 Identify As you read, underline Newton's second law of motion.

When an unbalanced force acts on an object, the object accelerates. Newton's second law describes this motion. The law states: *The acceleration of an object depends on the mass of the object and the amount of force applied.*

In other words, objects that have different masses will have different accelerations if the same amount of force is used. Imagine pushing a shopping cart. When the cart is empty, you need only a small force to accelerate it. But if the cart is full of groceries, the same amount of force causes a much smaller acceleration.

Force Equals Mass Times Acceleration

Newton's second law links force, mass, and acceleration. We can express this relationship using the equation $F = ma$, where F stands for applied force, m stands for mass, and a stands for acceleration. This equation tells us that a given force applied to a large mass will result in a small acceleration. When the same force is applied to a smaller mass, the acceleration will be larger.

Do the Math   Sample Problem   You Try It

These players train by pushing a massive object. If the players push with a force of 150 N, and the object has a mass of 75 kg, what is the object's acceleration? One newton is equal to 1 kg•m/s².

Use Newton's law:

$$F = ma$$
$$150 \text{ kg•m/s}^2 = (75 \text{ kg})(a)$$
$$a = \frac{150}{75} \text{ m/s}^2$$
$$a = 2.0 \text{ m/s}^2$$

16 Calculate For a more difficult training session, the mass to be pushed is increased to 160 kg. If the players still push with a force of 150 N, what is the acceleration of the object?

Use Newton's law:

$$F = ma$$
$$150 \text{ N} =$$

Why It Matters

Newton's Second Law and You

Think about the last time you rode on a roller coaster or in a car on a hilly road. Did you feel like you were going to float out of your seat when you went over a big hill? Newton's second law can explain that feeling.

Going Up When the roller coaster is going up a hill, you have two important forces acting on you—the force of gravity and the upward force exerted by the roller coaster seat.

Coming Down Once the roller coaster starts down the other side, it accelerates downward, and your seat does not support your full weight.

flight path

Practicing for Space Astronauts take special flights to train for space missions. The airplane's path looks like a roller coaster hill. As the plane accelerates downward, the astronauts lose contact with the plane and fall toward Earth. This condition is called free fall.

Extend   Inquiry

17 Infer Suppose you were standing on a scale in an elevator in free fall. What would the scale read?

18 Synthesize Explain why the feeling of weightlessness in free fall is not the same as truly being weightless.

19 Compare In what ways are roller coaster rides similar to and different from training simulations in a NASA plane?

37

Answers

15. *See students' pages for annotations.*

16.   150 N = (165 kg)(a)

   150 kg · m/s2 = (165 kg)(a)

   a = 150/165 · m/s²

17. The scale would read "0" because it and I are falling with the same acceleration.

18. Weight is the mass of an object times its acceleration due to gravity. During free fall, gravity is still exerting a force. The object still has a weight equivalent to its mass times the acceleration due to gravity. To be truly weightless, its acceleration must equal zero.

19. Answers may include that weightless feelings last longer on planes because the distance over which the person falls is greater during the airplane flight.

Do the Math

Ask students to look at the formula $F = ma$. Direct students to identify what each letter in the equation stands for. F = force, m = mass, and a = acceleration Next, help students solve the problem given. **Ask:** What is the force? 150 N **Ask:** What is the mass? 75 kg **Ask:** How would you write the equation? 150 N = (75 kg)a **Ask:** What step do you need to take next? You need to solve for a. **Ask:** How do you do this? Divide 150 N by 75 kg. **Ask:** How would you write this? $a = 150$ N/75 kg

Why It Matters

Newton's First Law Tell students that in addition to being an application of Newton's second law of motion, roller coasters also demonstrate Newton's first law of motion. **Ask:** What is Newton's first law of motion? An object at rest stays at rest, and an object in motion stays in motion unless it is acted upon by an unbalanced force. **Ask:** How does this apply to roller coasters or other amusement park rides? Sample answer: When a roller coaster suddenly turns a corner, your body feels a jerk because your body continues to travel in the same direction the roller coaster was originally traveling. Your body is experiencing inertia, the tendency to resist a change in motion.

What is Newton's Third Law of Motion?

Newton also devised a third law of motion. The law states: *Whenever one object exerts a force on a second object, the second object exerts an equal and opposite force on the first.*

So when you push against a wall, Newton's law tells you that the wall is actually pushing back against you.

Objects Exert Force on Each Other

Newton's third law also can be stated as: All forces act in pairs. Whenever one object exerts a force on a second object, the second object exerts an equal and opposite force on the first. There are action forces and reaction forces. Action and reaction forces are present even when there is no motion. For example, you exert a force on a chair when you sit on it. Your weight pushing down on the chair is the action force. The reaction force is the force exerted by the chair that pushes up on your body.

Forces in Pairs Have Equal Size but Opposite Directions

When an object pushes against another object, that object pushes back equally hard. But the second object pushes back in the opposite direction. In the pool below, the swimmer's feet push against the wall as he moves forward. This push is the action force. The wall also exerts a force on the swimmer. This is the reaction force, and it moves the swimmer forward. The forces do not act on the same object. Read on to find out why the swimmer moves but the wall does not!

Visualize It!

20 Apply The arrow below represents the action force exerted by the swimmer. Draw an arrow that represents the reaction force.

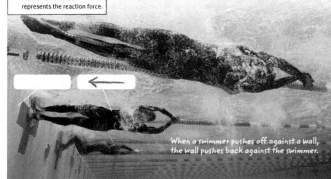

When a swimmer pushes off against a wall, the wall pushes back against the swimmer.

38 Unit 1 Motion and Forces

Forces Acting in Pairs Can Have Unequal Effects

Even though action and reaction forces are equal in size, their effects are often different. Gravitation is a force pair between two objects. If you drop a ball, gravity in an action force pulls the ball toward Earth. But the reaction force pulls Earth toward the ball! It's easy to see the effect of the action force. Why don't you see the effect of the reaction force—Earth being pulled upward? Newton's second law answers this question. The force on the ball is the same size as the force on Earth. However, Earth has much more mass than the ball. So Earth's acceleration is much smaller than that of the ball!

Visualize It!

21 Identify Label the action force and reaction force in the image below.

Forces Can Act in Multiple Pairs

An object can have multiple forces acting on it at once. When this happens, each force is part of a force pair. For example, when a baseball bat hits a baseball, the bat does not fly backward. A force is exerted on the ball by the bat. The bat does not fly backward, because the player's hands are exerting another force on the bat. What then keeps the player's hands from flying backward when the bat hits the ball? The bones and muscles in the player's arms exert a force on the hands. As you can see, a simple activity such as playing baseball involves the action of many forces at the same time.

22 Describe In your own words, explain Newton's third law of motion.

Lesson 3 Forces 39

Answers

20. Students should draw a right arrow of equal size to the action force to repre-sent the force exerted by the wall.

21. The action force label should be on the falling ball and the reaction force label on the arrow representing gravity.

22. Answers should include the idea that for every action there is an equal and opposite reaction.

Interpreting Visuals

Direct students to look at the photograph of the person swimming. The swimmer pushing off the wall is the action force. **Ask:** Why is that? because the swimmer makes the first action of the force pair, not the wall **Ask:** Why is the wall the reaction force? Because the wall pushes back on the swimmer; the text also states that action and reaction force pairs do not act on the same object. **Ask:** What object are the swimmer and the wall acting on? The force from the swimmer acts on the wall, and the force from the wall acts on the swimmer.

Formative Assessment

Ask: Imagine a person kayaking across a lake. Can you name a force pair at work? Sample answer: the force of the paddle on the water, the force of the water on the paddle **Ask:** Which is the action force? Sample answer: the force of the paddle on the water **Ask:** Which is the reaction force? Sample answer: the force of the water on the paddle Direct students to look at the photograph of the batter. **Ask:** What effect does the force of the ball have on the bat? It causes the bat to slow down. **Ask:** What type of force made the ball move toward the batter? Sample answer: an action force; the arm of the pitcher caused the ball to move

Visual Summary

To complete this summary, fill in the blanks with the correct word or phrase. Then use the key below to check your answers. You can use this page to review the main concepts of the lesson.

Forces

An object at rest will remain at rest and an object in constant motion will remain in motion unless acted upon by an unbalanced force.

When an unbalanced force acts on an object, the object moves with accelerated motion.

23 Newton's first law is also called the law of _____

24 In the formula F = ma, m stands for _____

Whenever one object exerts a force on a second object, the second object exerts an equal and opposite force on the first.

25 Forces in the same pair have equal size but opposite _____

Answers: 23: inertia; 24: mass; 25: direction

26 Synthesize A car designer is designing a new model of a popular car. He wants to use the same engine as in the old model, but improve the new car's acceleration. Use Newton's second law to explain how to improve the car's acceleration without redesigning the engine.

Lesson Review

Lesson 3

Vocabulary

Draw a line to connect the following terms to their definitions.

1 force   **A** resistance of an object to a change in motion

2 inertia

3 newton   **B** the unit that expresses force

   C a push or a pull

Key Concepts

4 Describe What is the action force and the reaction force when you sit down on a chair?

5 Summarize How do you determine net force?

6 Explain How do tests with crash dummies, seat belts, and air bags illustrate Newton's first law of motion?

Critical Thinking

Use this photo to answer the following questions.

7 Identify This rock, known as Balanced Rock, sits on a thin spike of rock in a canyon in Idaho. Explain the forces that keep the rock balanced on its tiny pedestal.

8 Calculate Balanced Rock has a mass of about 36,000 kg. If the acceleration due to gravity is 9.8 m/s², what is the force that the rock is exerting on its pedestal?

9 Infer What would happen to the moon if Earth stopped exerting the force of gravity on it?

Visual Summary Answers

23. inertia

24. mass

25. direction

26. Sample answer: Newton's second law states that *F = ma.* To improve the car's acceleration, the designer must decrease the force needed to move the car forward. If the designer wants to keep the same acceleration, he will have to decrease the car's mass to decrease the force needed to move it.

Lesson Review Answers

1. C

2. A

3. B.

4. The action force is your body press-ing down on the chair. The reaction force is the chair pressing up on your body.

5. Add forces that act in the same direction. Subtract the smaller force from the larger force when forces act in opposite directions.

6. Answers should include the idea that after the car stops, the dummy inside keeps going because of inertia until the seat belt and air bag exert contact forces on the dummy, causing its forward motion to stop.

7. Sample answer: Balanced Rock does not move because of inertia. The forces acting on the big rock are balanced. The force of the large rock pressing down on the spike of rock and the spike of rock pressing up on the large rock have a net force of 0 N.

8. Sample answer: $F = ma$
$F = 36,000 \text{ kg} \times 9.8 \text{ m/s2}$
$F = 352,800 \text{ kg} \cdot \text{m/s2}$, or 352,800 N

9. Sample answer: The moon stays in orbit around Earth because of Earth's gravity. If Earth no longer exerted force on the moon, the moon would travel in a straight line away from Earth in the direction it was traveling when the force of grav-ity stopped acting upon it.

Gravity and Motion

Essential Question How do objects move under the influence of gravity?

🍎 **Professional Development**

For more detailed information about the topics in this lesson, refer to the Content Refresher in the Unit Opener pages.

Opening Your Lesson

Begin the lesson by assessing students' prerequisite and prior knowledge.

Prerequisite Knowledge

- The effect of forces on objects
- Definitions of *mass*, *force*, and *matter*

Accessing Prior Knowledge

Ask: When you drop something, why does it fall down, not up? Sample answer: Gravity makes things fall down toward Earth.

Ask: What keeps us from floating off into space? Sample answer: Gravity pulls us down to Earth.

Customize Your Opening

- ☐ **Accessing Prior Knowledge,** above
- ☐ Print Path Engage Your Brain, SE p. 43 #1–2
- ☐ Print Path Active Reading, SE p. 43 #3–4
- ☐ **Digital Path** Lesson Opener

Key Topics/Learning Goals	Supporting Concepts
Gravity 1 Define and describe *gravity*. 2 Relate the force of gravity to the mass of an object.	• Gravity is an attractive force, acting at a distance, which exists between any pair of masses. • The force of Earth's gravity at its surface is given by the equation $F = mg$, where g is the acceleration due to gravity (about 9.8 m/s^2). This force is equivalent to weight. • Earth's gravity pulls everything toward the center of Earth. • Gravity is the major force in determining the motion and shape of celestial bodies. Gravity is difficult to notice on smaller scales.
Law of Universal Gravitation 1 Express the relation(s) among mass, distance, and gravitational force. 2 Describe the universality of gravity.	• The gravitational force between two bodies is proportional to each mass, and inversely proportional to the square of the distance between them (their centers of mass). • Gravitational attraction exists between any two bodies anywhere in the universe; nothing with mass is truly "weightless."
Orbits 1 Identify a situation in which one object is orbiting another. 2 Explain how gravity can keep objects in orbit.	• An object is orbiting when it travels around another object in space. • An object in orbit is in *free fall:* the motion of a body when the only force acting on the body is the force of gravity. • Gravity is the force that changes the direction of an orbiting object. • The force of gravity always points toward the center of the orbit, and provides the force that keeps objects in orbit.

Options for Instruction

Two parallel paths provide coverage of the Essential Questions, with a strong Inquiry strand woven into each. Follow the Print Path, the Digital Path, or your customized combination of print, digital, and inquiry.

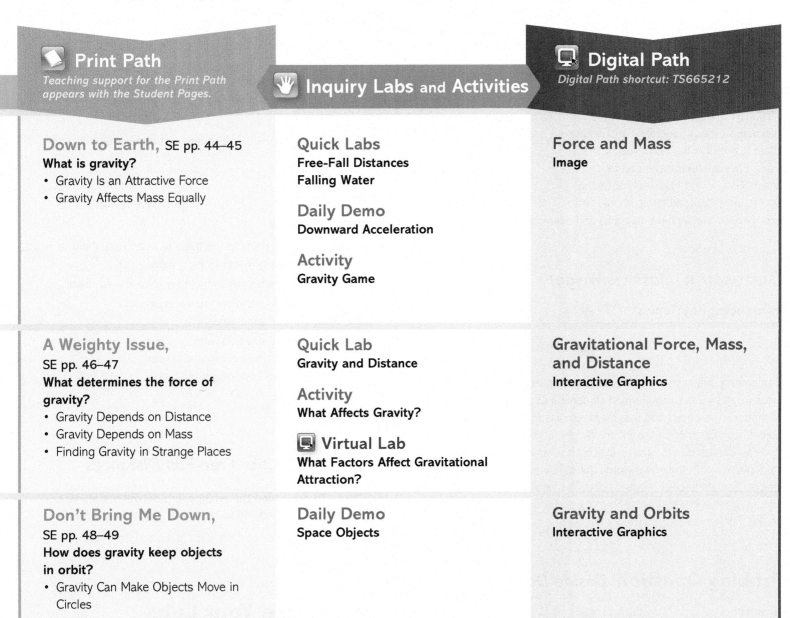

Print Path
Teaching support for the Print Path appears with the Student Pages.

Inquiry Labs and Activities

Digital Path
Digital Path shortcut: TS665212

Down to Earth, SE pp. 44–45
What is gravity?
- Gravity Is an Attractive Force
- Gravity Affects Mass Equally

Quick Labs
Free-Fall Distances
Falling Water

Daily Demo
Downward Acceleration

Activity
Gravity Game

Force and Mass
Image

A Weighty Issue,
SE pp. 46–47
What determines the force of gravity?
- Gravity Depends on Distance
- Gravity Depends on Mass
- Finding Gravity in Strange Places

Quick Lab
Gravity and Distance

Activity
What Affects Gravity?

Virtual Lab
What Factors Affect Gravitational Attraction?

Gravitational Force, Mass, and Distance
Interactive Graphics

Don't Bring Me Down,
SE pp. 48–49
How does gravity keep objects in orbit?
- Gravity Can Make Objects Move in Circles

Daily Demo
Space Objects

Gravity and Orbits
Interactive Graphics

Options for Assessment

See the Evaluate page for options, including Formative Assessment, Summative Assessment, and Unit Review.

Engage and Explore

Activities and Discussion

Activity *What Affects Gravity?*

Law of Universal Gravitation

👥 individuals
🕐 35 min
🔎 GUIDED inquiry

Have students create a Two-Panel Flip Chart to help them organize the information about how mass and distance affect gravity. On the outer flap of the sides, have students write *Distance Affects Gravity* and *Mass Affects Gravity*. On the inner flaps, students should write explanations that include diagrams and examples.

Discussion *Mass vs. Weight*

Introducing Key Topics

👥 whole class
🕐 10–15 min
🔎 GUIDED inquiry

Comparing Many students may believe that mass and weight measure the same thing. Remind students that mass is the amount of matter in an object and that mass remains the same whether the object is on Earth or on the moon. Weight, on the other hand, is the force on a mass due to gravity. Discuss the misconception and ask students to put in their own words the difference between mass and weight. Sample answer: Mass doesn't change when gravitational conditions change, so a person's mass on Earth is the same as it is on the moon even though weight changes.

Probing Question *Upside Down?*

Gravity

👥 whole class
🕐 15 min
🔎 GUIDED inquiry

Applying Why don't people in the Southern Hemisphere—the "bottom" of Earth—fall off? Prompt students to discuss how gravity attracts objects to Earth. Ask students to come up with other examples that illustrate how gravity works.

Labs and Demos

Daily Demo *Downward Acceleration*

Engage

Gravity

👥 whole class
🕐 10 min
🔎 GUIDED inquiry

Use this short demo after you have discussed how gravity affects mass equally.

PURPOSE **To introduce the relationship between gravity and mass**

MATERIALS

- golf ball
- smooth steel ball
- table tennis ball

1 Have a few volunteers hold the three balls and ask them to make observations about how heavy each feels.
2 Ask students to predict which ball they think will fall faster.
3 Take the balls back and drop them from the same height at the same time.
4 **Observing** Were the results what you had expected? Sample answer: I was surprised that the balls hit the floor at the same time. This supports the concepts that are introduced in the lesson.

⊘ 🗋 Quick Lab *Free-Fall Distances*

PURPOSE **To determine the relationship between a planet's gravitational force and the speed of an object in free fall**

See the Lab Manual or go Online for planning information.

Customize Your Labs

🗋 *See the Lab Manual for lab datasheets.*

⊘ *Go Online for editable lab datasheets.*

Daily Demo *Space Objects*

Orbits

👥 whole class
🕐 15 min
🔵 **DIRECTED** inquiry

PURPOSE **To illustrate how gravity keeps objects in orbit**

MATERIALS

- diagram of Earth with the moon and satellites orbiting around it, shown on a transparency
- diagram of the solar system on a transparency
- overhead projector

1 Show students the diagram of the solar system.

2 Point out that the planets move around the sun and that the sun's gravitational pull keeps the planets within the solar system, keeping them from floating off into space.

3 Show students the diagram of Earth with orbiting bodies shown.

4 Point out that the objects move in an orbit around Earth and that Earth's gravitational pull keeps these objects from floating away.

5 **Interpreting** How do these diagrams help you understand how gravity keeps objects in orbit? Sample answer: I can see that the planets keep moving around the sun and don't float away; I can see that Earth's gravitational pull keeps objects within its orbit.

🌑 🔲 Quick Lab *Gravity and Distance*

PURPOSE **To investigate the relationship between mass and gravitational force**

See the Lab Manual or go Online for planning information.

🌑 🔲 Quick Lab *Falling Water*

Gravity

👥 small groups
🕐 20 min
🔵 **DIRECTED** inquiry

Students drop a cup that has a hole in its side to compare the forces acting on the cup to the forces acting on the water inside it, normally and in free fall.

PURPOSE **To investigate how gravity affects objects close to Earth**

MATERIALS

- paper cup
- water
- paper towels
- safety goggles
- scissors
- lab apron
- plastic tub

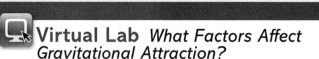

🖥️ Virtual Lab *What Factors Affect Gravitational Attraction?*

Law of Universal Gravitation

👥 flexible
🕐 45 min
🔵 **GUIDED** inquiry

Students investigate the gravitational force acting on a satellite in orbit.

PURPOSE **To examine the effect of mass and distance on gravitational force**

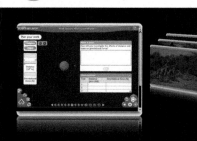

Activities and Discussion

☐ **Activity** What Affects Gravity?

☐ **Discussion** Mass vs. Weight

☐ **Probing Questions** Upside Down?

Labs and Demos

☐ **Daily Demo** Downward Acceleration

☐ **Quick Lab** Free-Fall Distances

☐ **Daily Demo** Space Objects

☐ **Quick Lab** Gravity and Distance

☐ **Quick Lab** Falling Water

☐ **Virtual Lab** What Factors Affect Gravitational Attraction?

Your Resources

_____

_____

_____

Explain Science Concepts

Key Topics	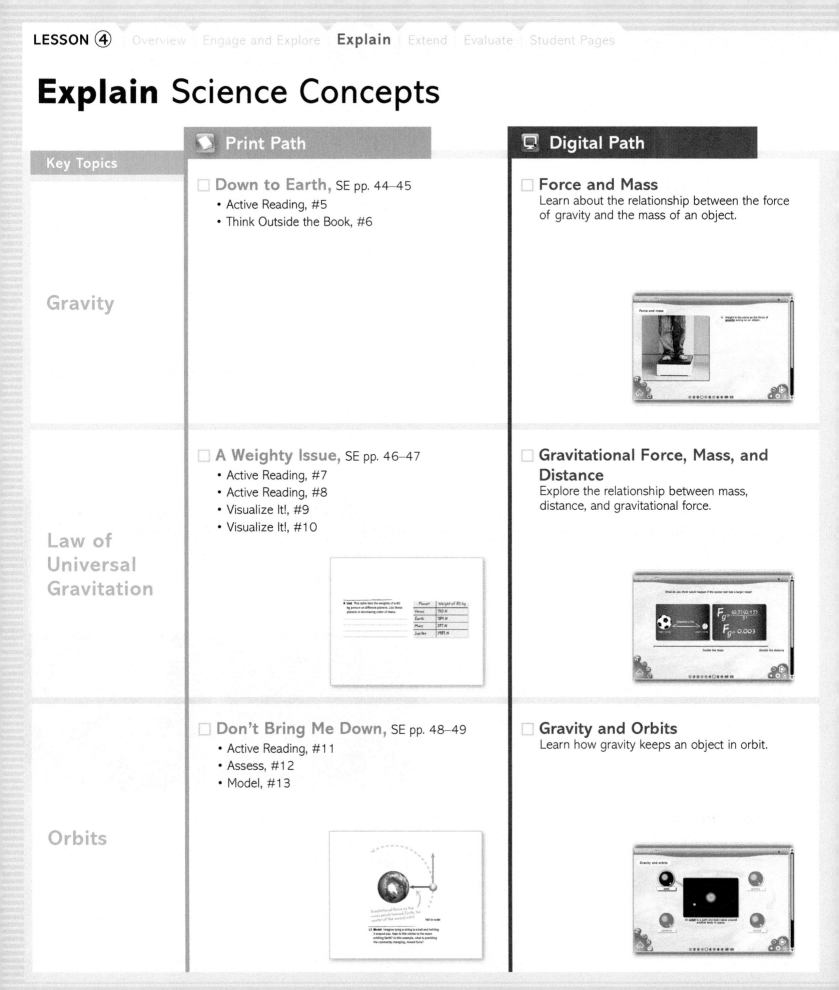 📖 **Print Path**	🖥 **Digital Path**
Gravity	☐ **Down to Earth,** SE pp. 44–45 • Active Reading, #5 • Think Outside the Book, #6	☐ **Force and Mass** Learn about the relationship between the force of gravity and the mass of an object.
Law of Universal Gravitation	☐ **A Weighty Issue,** SE pp. 46–47 • Active Reading, #7 • Active Reading, #8 • Visualize It!, #9 • Visualize It!, #10	☐ **Gravitational Force, Mass, and Distance** Explore the relationship between mass, distance, and gravitational force.
Orbits	☐ **Don't Bring Me Down,** SE pp. 48–49 • Active Reading, #11 • Assess, #12 • Model, #13	☐ **Gravity and Orbits** Learn how gravity keeps an object in orbit.

Differentiated Instruction

Basic *Gravity Web*

Synthesizing Key Topics

👥 individuals
🕐 ongoing

As students read the lesson, have them complete a Main Idea Web for gravity. Have students write *Gravity is a force that attracts objects to each other* in the center of the web. They can add details and examples that illustrate the main idea as they read.

Advanced *Planets*

Synthesizing Key Topics

👥 pairs
🕐 30 min

Have students pick one of the planets in our solar system to research. Encourage students to find out how long their planet takes to orbit the sun, the size of their planet relative to Earth, what the gravity is on their planet, how many moons orbit their planet, and whether anything else orbits their planet. For example, Jupiter takes about 12 years to orbit the sun and has at least 39 moons. Encourage students to present their research in a poster with illustrations, diagrams, and text. Display the posters around the classroom.

ELL *Cause and Effect*

Synthesizing Key Topics

👥 individuals
🕐 ongoing

This lesson contains many concepts that are explained by cause-and-effect relationships. To help students organize these ideas, introduce two types of cause-and-effect diagrams to them. Explain that one type models multiple causes that have a single effect and the other type models a single cause that has multiple effects. As they read, encourage students to look for sentences that contain clue words, such as *if, then, when,* and *as a result.*

🌐 *Optional Online resource: Cause and Effect Diagrams*

Lesson Vocabulary

gravity   free fall
orbit

Previewing Vocabulary

👥 whole class
🕐 15 min

Word History and Origins Share the following to help students remember terms.
• **Gravity** comes from the Latin word *gravis,* which means "heavy."
• **Orbit** comes from the Latin word *orbita,* which means "wheel track or course."

Reinforcing Vocabulary

👥 individuals
🕐 ongoing

Four Square Have students make a Four Square diagram for *gravity.* Have students draw a circle in the center of their papers and write *gravity* in it. After students draw four sections, have them write the definition of gravity, characteristics of gravity, examples of gravity, and nonexamples of gravity.

Customize Your Core Lesson

Core Instruction
☐ **Print Path** choices
☐ **Digital Path** choices

Vocabulary
☐ **Previewing Vocabulary** Word History and Origins
☐ **Reinforcing Vocabulary** Four Square

Your Resources

Differentiated Instruction
☐ **Basic** Gravity Web
☐ **Advanced** Planets
☐ **ELL** Cause and Effect

Extend Science Concepts

Reinforce and Review

Activity *Gravity Game*

Synthesizing Key Topics

small groups
30 min

Competitive Game

1 Divide students into groups of four or five.

2 Have students sit together and elect one student who will be the spokesperson for the group.

3 Working around the room, ask questions that you have developed or that are borrowed from exercises in the book.

4 After asking a group a question, give them a few minutes to discuss before having the spokesperson give the answer.

5 If the group is correct, the students earn a point. If they are incorrect, the next group has a chance to answer the question.

6 The group with the most points at the end of the game wins.

Sample Questions

- True or false: *Mass* is another word for *weight*. false
- Imagining that gravity is the only force acting on an object, what will happen if two objects of different masses were dropped from the same height? c
  a. The lighter object will hit the ground first.
  b. The heavier object will hit the ground first.
  c. The two objects will hit the ground at the same time.
- The law of gravitational force relates gravity, mass, and. distance
- True or false: All moons are spherical. false

Graphic Organizer

Synthesizing Key Topics

individuals
ongoing

Combination Notes Have students create a Combination Notes graphic organizer to organize important ideas about gravity. Have students write *gravity* across the top of the graphic organizer, and then record key phrases and draw pictures that illustrate important ideas about gravity such as *mass versus weight, the law of universal gravitation,* and *orbits.*

topic	
key phrases	pictures

🖉 *Optional Online resource: Combination Notes support*

Going Further

Engineering Connection

Gravity

whole class
15 min

Discussion Although engineers seek to ensure that all buildings are stable, some basic designs are more stable than others. One of the most stable structures is the geodesic dome, such as the one at Epcot Center in Florida. Its rounded shape excels at resisting damage from strong winds and heavy snows. One of its greatest advantages is that its shape spreads the force of gravity down the sides. The compression that gravity would otherwise cause is evenly distributed. Have students discuss how the geodesic dome is a good design for overcoming the effects of gravity. Then have them think of other examples that are good or bad designs for overcoming gravity, such as a pyramid or a skyscraper, and have them explain their thinking.

Physical Education Connection

Gravity

individuals or pairs
25 min

Research Project Remind students that astronauts experience free fall in space. Floating around in space means that astronauts don't use their bones and muscles as much as they do on Earth. This can cause their bodies to become very weak. Have students research and present a poster describing some of the ways that astronauts stay in shape while in space.

🖉 *Optional Online rubric: Written Pieces*

Customize Your Closing

📄 *See the Assessment Guide for quizzes and tests.*

🖉 *Go Online to edit and create quizzes and tests.*

Reinforce and Review

☐ **Activity** Gravity Game

☐ **Graphic Organizer** Combination Notes

☐ **Print Path** Visual Summary, SE p. 50

☐ **Digital Path** Lesson Closer

Evaluate Student Mastery

See the teacher support below the Student Pages for additional Formative Assessment questions.

Explain to students that gravity exists everywhere and even when astronauts travel to space, they are still being affected by gravity. Remind students that the size of the force of gravity depends on mass and distance. **Ask:** What are some examples that we've discussed about how gravity influences objects? Sample answers: The force of Earth's gravity makes objects fall to its surface and keeps us from floating away; Earth's gravity keeps objects, such as satellites and the moon, in orbit; the sun's gravity keeps Earth and other planets in orbit; the moon has less mass than Earth, so the gravity on the moon is not as strong.

Reteach

Formative assessment may show that students need reinforcement for certain topics. The resources below are recommended for reteaching. If students were introduced to a topic through the Print Path, you can also use the Digital Path to reteach, and vice versa.
🎧 *Can be assigned to individual students*

Gravity
Quick Lab Free-Fall Distances 🎧

Law of Universal Gravitation
Activity What Affects Gravity? 🎧

Quick Lab Gravity and Distance

Virtual Lab What Factors Affect Gravitational Attraction?

Orbits
Daily Demo Space Objects

Alternative Assessment
The Effects of Gravity

🌐 *Online resource: student worksheet, optional rubrics*

Gravity and Motion

Tic-Tac-Toe: *The Effects of Gravity*

1. Work on your own, with a partner, or with a small group.
2. Choose three quick activities from the game. Check the boxes you plan to complete. They must form a straight line in any direction.
3. Have your teacher approve your plan.
4. Do each activity, and turn in your results.

__ Poetry Slam	__ Orbiting Objects	__ Where in Space?
Write a poem using the word *gravity*. Highlight key ideas and phrases about gravity, including how mass and distance affect gravity and how objects stay in orbit. If you want, present your poem as a performance.	Draw a series of diagrams showing how one object orbits another somewhere in our solar system. Be sure to illustrate how the forward motion and gravity work together to keep an object in orbit.	Perform a skit that takes place on a planet with greater surface gravity than Earth. Imagine that you have encountered some kind of problem related to gravity. Use what you know about gravity to solve the problem.
__ Be the Teacher	__ Planetary Brochure	__ News Report
Write a quiz to test how well students have learned the material in this lesson. Check that your questions cover the main ideas and that the questions are fair. Include an answer key. Give the quiz to a partner to see if it works well.	Imagine that you live on a newly discovered planet. The air is breathable and the water is drinkable. However, the planet has a much lower surface gravity than Earth. Write a brochure encouraging people to visit. Describe all the benefits of living with lower surface gravity.	Write a Webcast. The topic should be related to gravity. For example, report on the launch of a space shuttle, a mysterious change in Earth's gravity, or a foreign object that has entered Earth's orbit. Make sure that your report includes an explanation of what scientists suspect is causing the event.
__ Comic Strip	__ Puzzle Time	__ www.gravity.net
Draw a comic strip with a character who is learning about gravity. Include at least three examples of everyday actions that help the character figure out how gravity works.	Make a crossword puzzle that uses key terms and ideas from the lesson. The puzzle should use at least ten terms including *mass, distance, orbit,* and *gravity*.	Design an imaginary Web page for the term *gravity*. Include on your web page definitions of key terms, images, and examples.

Going Further
- ☐ Engineering Connection
- ☐ Physical Education Connection

Formative Assessment
- ☐ Strategies Throughout TE
- ☐ Lesson Review SE

Summative Assessment
- ☐ Alternative Assessment The Effects of Gravity
- ☐ Lesson Quiz
- ☐ Unit Tests A and B
- ☐ Unit Review SE End-of-Unit

Your Resources

_____   _____

_____   _____

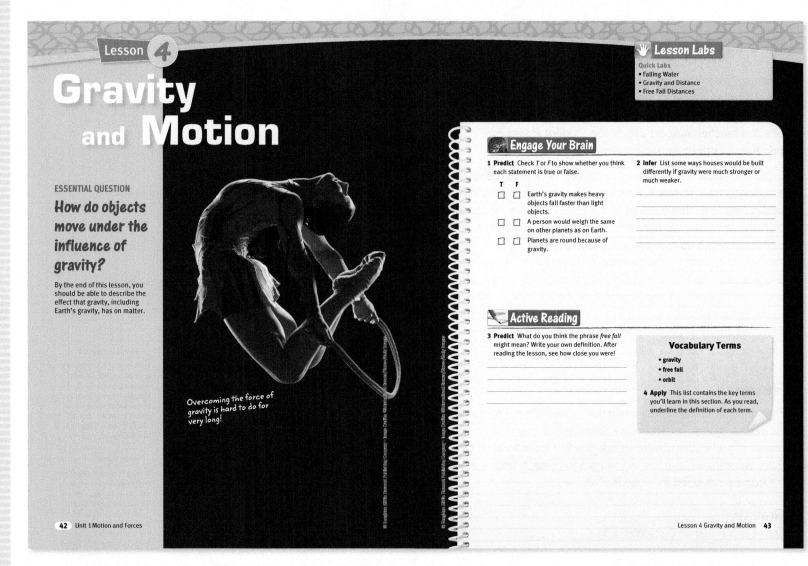

Answers

Answers for 1–3 should represent students' current thoughts, even if incorrect.

1. F, F, T

2. See students' annotations; responses could include number of stories, need for staircases, or placement of shelves.

3. See students' responses. Sample answer: falling without touching anything

4. Students' annotations will vary.

Opening Your Lesson

Discuss students' responses to item 2 to assess their prerequisite knowledge and to estimate what they already know about the key topics.

Prerequisites Students should already be familiar with the idea that forces cause changes in movement, shape, or other qualities. Students should also be familiar with the words *matter* and *mass*.

Before You Read

Photo Talk To help students start to think about the effects of gravity, encourage them to analyze the lesson opener photo. **Ask:** What makes this woman's accomplishment so impressive? Why isn't this something that just anyone can do? Sample answer: To do this kind of jump requires a great deal of practice and training. Most people would not succeed. **Ask:** Why would most people fail if they tried this jump? Sample answer: Gravity holds things to Earth, or brings them down to the ground. The woman seems to be doing something impossible. **Ask:** What do people mean by the phrase *defying gravity*? Sample answer: They mean that something seems as though it can fly and that it does not seem as if it is going to fall down.

Down to EARTH

Gravity pulls the skydiver, his clothes, and his parachute toward the Earth, all with the same acceleration.

This stop-action photo shows that when there is no air resistance, a feather and a billiard ball fall at the same rate.

Active Reading

5 Analyze What has to happen for a feather and a ball to fall at the same rate?

_____

_____

44 Unit 1 Motion and Forces

What is gravity?

If you watch video of astronauts on the moon, you see them wearing big, bulky spacesuits and yet jumping lightly. Why is leaping on the moon easier than on Earth? The answer is gravity. **Gravity** is a force of attraction between objects due to their mass. Gravity is a noncontact force that acts between two objects at any distance apart. Even when a skydiver is far above the ground, Earth's gravity acts to pull him downward.

Gravity Is An Attractive Force

Earth's gravity pulls everything toward Earth's center. It pulls, but it does not push, so it is called an attractive force.

You feel the force due to Earth's gravity as the heaviness of your body, or your weight. Weight is a force, and it depends on mass. Greater mass results in greater weight. This force of gravity between Earth and an object is equal to the mass of the object *m* multiplied by a factor due to gravity *g*.

$$F = mg$$

On Earth, *g* is about 9.8 m/s². The units are the same as the units for acceleration. Does this mean that Earth's gravity accelerates all objects in the same way? The surprising answer is yes.

Suppose you dropped a heavy object and a light object at the same time. Which would hit the ground first? Sometimes an object experiences a lot of air resistance and falls slowly or flutters to the ground. But if you could take away air resistance, all objects would fall with the same acceleration. When gravity is the only force affecting the fall, a light object and a heavy object hit the ground at the same time.

Acceleration depends on both force and mass. The heavier object experiences a greater force, or weight. But the heavier object is also harder to accelerate, because it has more mass. The two effects cancel, and the acceleration due to gravity is the same for all masses.

Gravity Affects Mass Equally

All matter has mass. Gravity is a result of mass, so all matter is affected by gravity. Every object exerts a gravitational pull on every other object. Your pencil and shoes are gravitationally attracted to each other, each to your textbook, all three to your chair, and so on. So why don't objects pull each other into a big pile? The gravitational forces between these objects are too small. Other forces, such as friction, are strong enough to balance the gravitational pulls and prevent changes in motion. Gravity is not a very powerful force—you overcome the attraction of Earth's entire mass on your body every time you stand up!

However, when enough mass gathers together, its effect can be large. Gravity caused Earth and other planets to become round. All parts of the planet pulled each other toward the center of mass, resulting in a sphere.

Some astronomical bodies do not have enough mass to pull themselves into spheres. Small moons and asteroids can maintain a lumpy shape, but larger moons such as Earth's have enough mass to form a sphere.

Gravity also acts over great distances. It determines the motion of celestial bodies. The paths of planets, the sun, and other stars are determined by gravity. Even the motion of our galaxy through the universe is due to gravity.

Galaxies, made up of billions of stars, have characteristic shapes and motions that are due to gravity.

Earth's moon has a diameter of more than 3,400 km. It has more than enough mass to pull itself into a sphere.

3,400 km

Deimos, one of the moons of Mars, is only about 15 km at its longest stretch. Deimos does not have enough mass to form a sphere.

15 km

Think Outside the Book

6 Incorporate Write a short story about a time when you had to overcome the force of gravity to get something done.

45

Answers

5. There must be no air resistance.

6. See student work. Students' responses will likely include lifting a heavy object.

Interpreting Visuals

Discuss why the photograph shows multiple feathers and balls. The photo is showing the position of the objects over time; the camera took several shots within a few moments.

Interpreting Visuals

Look at the photograph of the galaxy. **Ask:** What do you notice about its shape? Sample answer: It appears rounded. **Ask:** What do the feathery spirals coming off the center make you think of? Sample answer: They make it look as though it is moving, or rotating. **Ask:** What might the shape and motion have to do with gravity? Sample answer: Gravity pulls large masses into a rounded shape; perhaps it has pulled the galaxy into a rounded shape. Perhaps gravity keeps the stars in the galaxy revolving, like the planets revolve around the sun.

Building Math Skills

Estimation The captions above state that Deimos is about 15 km wide and Earth's moon is about 3,400 km wide. How can you use estimation to compare the two moons? Sample answer: You can round the moon's size down to 3,000 km, which is easier to compare to 15 km, because 15 divides into 3,000 evenly. Doing this helps me see that our moon is about 200 times the size of Deimos.

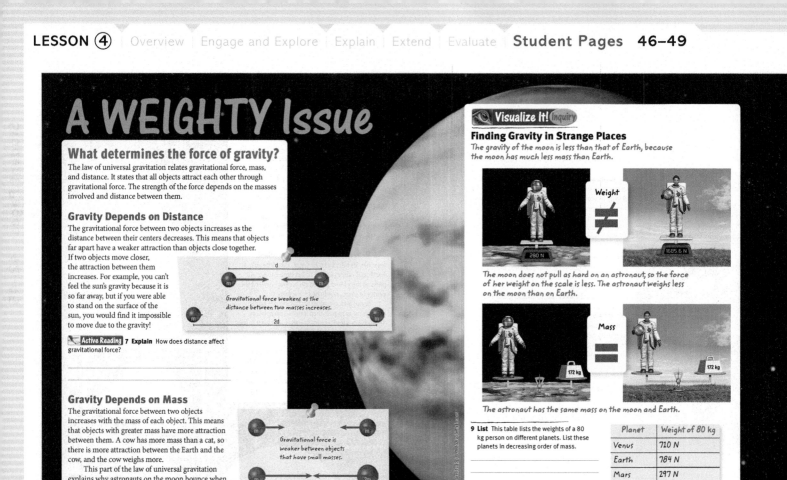

A WEIGHTY Issue

What determines the force of gravity?

The law of universal gravitation relates gravitational force, mass, and distance. It states that all objects attract each other through gravitational force. The strength of the force depends on the masses involved and distance between them.

Gravity Depends on Distance

The gravitational force between two objects increases as the distance between their centers decreases. This means that objects far apart have a weaker attraction than objects close together. If two objects move closer, the attraction between them increases. For example, you can't feel the sun's gravity because it is so far away, but if you were able to stand on the surface of the sun, you would find it impossible to move due to the gravity!

d

Gravitational force weakens as the distance between two masses increases.

2d

Active Reading 7 **Explain** How does distance affect gravitational force?

Gravity Depends on Mass

The gravitational force between two objects increases with the mass of each object. This means that objects with greater mass have more attraction between them. A cow has more mass than a cat, so there is more attraction between the Earth and the cow, and the cow weighs more.

This part of the law of universal gravitation explains why astronauts on the moon bounce when they walk. The moon has less mass than Earth, so the astronauts weigh less. The force of each step pushes an astronaut higher than it would on Earth.

Gravitational force is weaker between objects that have small masses.

2m

Gravitational force is stronger when one or more objects are more massive.

Notice that the force that each object experiences is of equal strength.

Active Reading 8 **Explain** How does mass affect gravitational force?

Visualize It! Inquiry

Finding Gravity in Strange Places

The gravity of the moon is less than that of Earth, because the moon has much less mass than Earth.

Weight ≠

280 N   1685.6 N

The moon does not pull as hard on an astronaut, so the force of her weight on the scale is less. The astronaut weighs less on the moon than on Earth.

Mass =

172 kg   172 kg

The astronaut has the same mass on the moon and Earth.

9 **List** This table lists the weights of a 80 kg person on different planets. List these planets in decreasing order of mass.

Planet	Weight of 80 kg
Venus	710 N
Earth	784 N
Mars	297 N
Jupiter	1983 N

10 **Justify** The weight of 80 kg of mass on Mercury is 296 N, almost identical to the weight of the same mass on Mars. But Mercury has much less mass than Mars! Explain how this can be. (What else could affect gravitational force?)

46   47

Answers

7. Gravitational force decreases as distance increases.

8. Gravitational force increases as mass increases.

9. Jupiter, Earth, Venus, Mars

10. Mercury also has a smaller radius than Mars has, so the distance used in the weight calculation is smaller, making the attractive force larger.

Building Reading Skills

Student Vocabulary The phrase *more massive* used in this section does not necessarily indicate that an object is very large. It simply means that it has more mass than another object. For example, an ant is more massive than an ant egg. Can you think of some small objects that are more massive than other objects? Sample answers: A pebble is more massive than a grain of sand. An eyelash is more massive than a gnat.

Learning Alert ⚠ MISCONCEPTION ⚠

Mass and Weight If a student reading a beam balance determines that a rock is 0.5 kg, what is the student measuring? Most students will answer "weight." Many students believe that mass and weight can be used interchangeably. Explain that an object's mass always stays the same, but weight is determined by gravity. Ask students what would happen to the weight of the rock if it were taken to the moon, which has one-sixth of Earth's gravity. It would weigh less. Ask them if the amount of matter—its mass—would change. no

Interpreting Visuals

What concept about mass and weight does the diagram of the astronaut illustrate? Sample answer: The diagram illustrates the concept that even though a person's weight changes when gravity changes, mass stays the same.

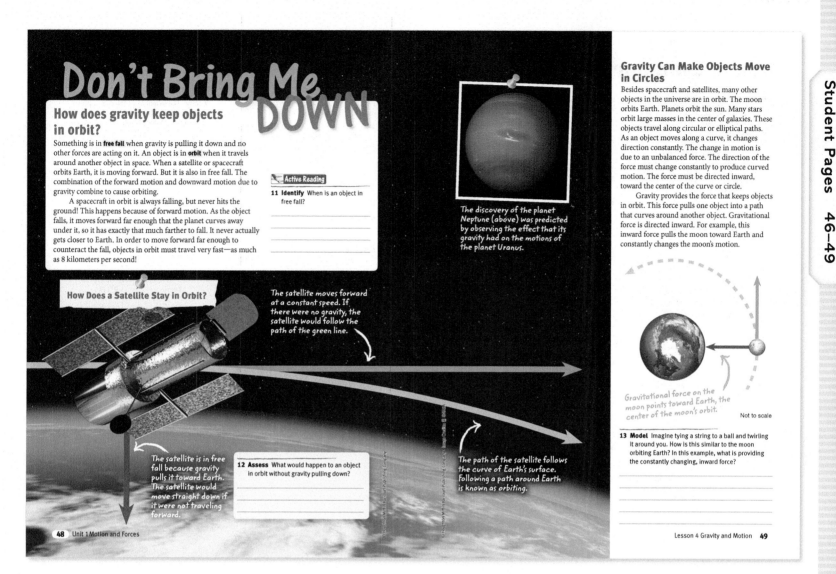

Don't Bring Me DOWN

How does gravity keep objects in orbit?

Something is in **free fall** when gravity is pulling it down and no other forces are acting on it. An object is in **orbit** when it travels around another object in space. When a satellite or spacecraft orbits Earth, it is moving forward. But it is also in free fall. The combination of the forward motion and downward motion due to gravity combine to cause orbiting.

A spacecraft in orbit is always falling, but never hits the ground! This happens because of forward motion. As the object falls, it moves forward far enough that the planet curves away under it, so it has exactly that much farther to fall. It never actually gets closer to Earth. In order to move forward far enough to counteract the fall, objects in orbit must travel very fast—as much as 8 kilometers per second!

Active Reading

11 Identify When is an object in free fall?

_____

_____

_____

How Does a Satellite Stay in Orbit?

The satellite moves forward at a constant speed. If there were no gravity, the satellite would follow the path of the green line.

The satellite is in free fall because gravity pulls it toward Earth. The satellite would move straight down if it were not traveling forward.

12 Assess What would happen to an object in orbit without gravity pulling down?

_____

_____

The path of the satellite follows the curve of Earth's surface. Following a path around Earth is known as orbiting.

The discovery of the planet Neptune (above) was predicted by observing the effect that its gravity had on the motions of the planet Uranus.

Gravity Can Make Objects Move in Circles

Besides spacecraft and satellites, many other objects in the universe are in orbit. The moon orbits Earth. Planets orbit the sun. Many stars orbit large masses in the center of galaxies. These objects travel along circular or elliptical paths. As an object moves along a curve, it changes direction constantly. The change in motion is due to an unbalanced force. The direction of the force must change constantly to produce curved motion. The force must be directed inward, toward the center of the curve or circle.

Gravity provides the force that keeps objects in orbit. This force pulls one object into a path that curves around another object. Gravitational force is directed inward. For example, this inward force pulls the moon toward Earth and constantly changes the moon's motion.

Gravitational force on the moon points toward Earth, the center of the moon's orbit.

Not to scale

13 Model Imagine tying a string to a ball and twirling it around you. How is this similar to the moon orbiting Earth? In this example, what is providing the constantly changing, inward force?

_____

_____

_____

_____

Answers

11. When gravity is the only force acting upon it, an object is in free fall.

12. The object would fly off into space along a straight line.

13. The ball travels in an orbit around you. The tension in the string provides the force.

Formative Assessment

Have students imagine that Earth suddenly disappeared along with its gravitational force. **Ask:** What would happen to the moon and the other objects that orbit Earth? Sample answer: Earth's gravitational force would not influence them anymore, so these objects would no longer orbit Earth's position. They might continue to orbit the sun.

Building Reading Skills

Text Structure: Cause and Effect Point out that the combination of forward motion and gravity has the effect of keeping objects in orbit. **Ask:** How does the section explain this cause-and-effect relationship? Sample answer: The text explains that objects in space are always moving forward, but that the force of gravity pulls them toward the center of their orbit; this combination keeps objects orbiting larger objects.

Probing Questions GUIDED Inquiry

Applying What are some ways that you are affected by gravity every day? Sample answers: The sun's gravitational pull keeps Earth in orbit around it, which means that we get sunlight on Earth. Gravity keeps me from floating away, but also makes me fall down and get hurt sometimes.

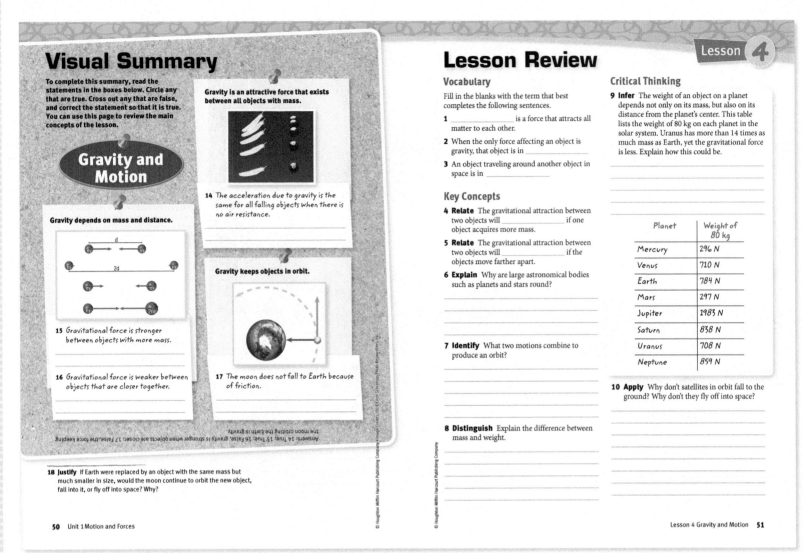

Visual Summary Answers

14. True

15. True

16. False, gravity increases as distance decreases.

17. False, the force keeping the moon orbiting the Earth is gravity.

18. The moon would continue to orbit the new object. Gravitational attraction between two objects depends only on their mass and the distance between their centers of mass. In this example, neither quantity changed, so the gravitational force will be the same and the moon would continue in its orbit.

Lesson Review Answers

1. gravity

2. free fall

3. orbit

4. increase

5. decrease

6. Because gravity pulls their mass into a ball

7. A forward and downward motion

8. Mass measures how much matter an object has. Weight is the force of gravity acting on that mass.

9. Uranus has a much bigger radius than Earth. The distance to the center of Uranus is greater, so the gravitational attraction is less.

10. They do not fall to the ground because they move forward so fast that the planet curves away beneath them, putting more distance between the satellite and the ground. This increases the distance they have to fall. They do not fly off into space because gravity keeps them falling towards the ground.

Steve Okamoto

Purpose To learn about the work and educational background of a roller coaster designer

Learning Goals
- Identify contributions made by a scientist.
- Recognize that scientists come from different backgrounds.
- Identify jobs in science fields.

Informal Vocabulary
mechanical engineering

Prerequisite Knowledge
- Mechanical energy
- Motion and speed

Activity *Math Careers*

individuals, then pairs, then whole class	20 min
	INDEPENDENT inquiry

Think, Pair, Share Understanding energy, forces, and motion requires a good understanding of math. Tell students to brainstorm careers in which they think they would have to know math. Then have students pair up and discuss their ideas with a partner. Encourage partners to talk about which careers they think would be most interesting. Finally, have pairs volunteer to share their ideas with the class.

To extend the activity, have pairs research one of the careers they brainstormed to learn more about what people in that career do, where they work, and what education they must acquire.

Optional Online resource: Think, Pair, Share support

Differentiated Instruction

Basic *Amusement Park*

small groups	20 min

Displays Have students work in groups to design an imaginary amusement park. Students should work together to think of a theme for their park and decide what types of rides to have. Then each student in the group should work individually to design one of the rides. Encourage them to keep in mind the information from the profile of Steve Okamoto in order to design rides that seem realistic. Students should then organize their designs into a display of the entire park.

Advanced *Product Designer*

individuals	20 min

Quick Research Have students find out more about how people become product designers. What schools can they attend? What kinds of classes do they take? What kinds of jobs can they do? Invite volunteers to share the product design jobs they found most interesting and the education required for such a job.

ELL *Compound Crazy*

pairs	10 min

These pages contain many compound words, including *blueprint, classroom, lifeguard, wheelchair,* and *armrest.* Help students identify and underline the compound words. Then have them draw a line between each word in the compound word. If pairs are unfamiliar with the meanings of any of the compounds, have them try to figure out the meanings based on the meanings of the words that make them up. They can use a dictionary to check if necessary.

Customize Your Feature

- ☐ **Activity** Math Careers
- ☐ **People in Science** Online
- ☐ **Basic** Amusement Park
- ☐ **Advanced** Product Designer
- ☐ **ELL** Compound Crazy
- ☐ **People in Science** News
- ☐ **Building Reading Skills**

People in Science

Steve Okamoto
ROLLER COASTER DESIGNER

A day in the life of a roller coaster designer is filled with twists and turns—just ask designer Steve Okamoto. As a kid, he became interested in roller coasters after a trip to Disneyland. To become a product designer, Steve studied subjects like math and science. He later earned a degree in product design that involved studying mechanical engineering and studio art.

Before he starts designing roller coasters, Steve has to think about all of the parts of a roller coaster and how it will fit in the amusement park. It's like putting together a huge puzzle. Different parts of the puzzle include the safety equipment needed, what the roller coaster will be made out of, and how the track will fit in next to other rides.

He also has to think about what visitors to the park will want to see and experience in a roller coaster ride.

As he is designing a roller coaster, Steve's math and science background comes in handy. For example, in order to make sure that a roller coaster's cars make it up each hill, he has to calculate the speed and acceleration of the cars on each part of the track. To create the curves, loops, and dips of the roller coaster track, he uses his knowledge of physics and geometry.

Acceleration from the downhill run provides the speed for the next climb.

52

JOB BOARD

Machinists

What You'll Do: Use machine tools, such as lathes, milling machines, and machining centers, to produce new metal parts.

Where You Might Work: Machine shops and manufacturing plants in industries including the automotive and aerospace industries.

Education: In high school, you should take math courses, especially trigonometry, and, if available, courses in blueprint reading, metalworking, and drafting. After high school, most people acquire their skills in an apprenticeship program. This gives a person a mix of classroom and on-the-job training.

Bicycle Mechanic

What You'll Do: Repair and maintain different kinds of bikes, from children's bikes to expensive road bikes.

Where You Might Work: Independent bicycle shops or large chain stores that carry bicycles; certain sporting events like Olympic and national trials.

Education: Some high schools and trade schools have shop classes that teach bicycle repair. Most bicycle mechanics get on-the-job training. To work as a mechanic at national and international cycling events, you will have to earn a bicycle mechanic's license.

PEOPLE IN SCIENCE NEWS

Mike Hensler

The Surf Chair
As a Daytona Beach lifeguard, Mike Hensler realized that the beach was almost impossible for someone in a wheelchair. Although he had never invented a machine before, Hensler decided to build a wheelchair that could be driven across sand without getting stuck. He began spending many evenings in his driveway with a pile of lawn-chair parts, designing the chair by trial and error.

The result looks very different from a conventional wheelchair. With huge rubber wheels and a thick frame of white PVC pipe, the Surf Chair not only moves easily over sandy terrain but also is weather resistant and easy to clean. The newest models of the Surf Chair come with optional attachments, such as a variety of umbrellas, detachable armrests and footrests, and even places to attach fishing rods.

Unit 1 People in Science 53

People in Science News

Encourage students to think of a product they would like to invent. Have them think about the audience for the product, how it would be of help to that audience, and how it would work. If possible, have students make a model of their imaginary product and share it with the class.

Building Reading Skills

Text Structure: Problem/Solution Help students identify the problem and solution in the surf chair article. Remind them that a problem is a question to be answered or a situation that presents a difficulty. A solution is the answer to a question or the method of overcoming a difficulty. Problem: It was almost impossible for someone in a wheelchair to go to the beach. Solution: Hensler built a wheelchair that could be driven across sand without getting stuck.

Fluids and Pressure

Essential Question What happens when fluids exert pressure?

Professional Development

For more detailed information about the topics in this lesson, refer to the Content Refresher in the Unit Opener pages.

Opening Your Lesson

Begin the lesson by assessing students' prerequisite and prior knowledge.

Prerequisite Knowledge

- A general understanding of the properties of liquids and gases
- A general understanding of the nature of forces

Accessing Prior Knowledge

Invite students to make a three-column KWL chart about what they know about fluids and pressure. Have students put what they know in the first column and what they want to know in the second column. After they have finished the lesson, they can complete the third column with what they have learned.

Customize Your Opening

- ☐ **Accessing Prior Knowledge,** above
- ☐ Print Path Engage Your Brain, SE p. 55
- ☐ Print Path Active Reading, SE p. 55
- ☐ **Digital Path** Lesson Opener

Key Topics/Learning Goals	Supporting Concepts
Introduction to Pressure and Fluids 1 Describe how pressure is related to force and area. 2 Calculate pressure in pascals. 3 Identify both liquids and gases as fluids and explain why they exert pressure.	• *Pressure* is the amount of force exerted on a given area. • Pressure is calculated using the equation $\text{pressure} = \frac{\text{force}}{\text{area}}$ • A fluid is any material that can flow and take the shape of its container. • Particles in fluids collide; each collision exerts a force. These forces cause pressure.
Atmospheric Pressure and Water Pressure 1 Explain what causes atmospheric pressure and water pressure. 2 Describe how pressure varies with depth.	• The pressure caused by gravity pulling on the atmosphere is atmospheric pressure. • Like atmospheric pressure, water pressure is caused by gravity pulling down on water. • Atmospheric pressure and water pressure increase with depth. Atmospheric pressure decreases as altitude increases. Water pressure increases with depth.
Pressure and Fluid Flow 1 Give examples of how differences in pressure result in fluid flow.	• Pressure differences can drive fluids from higher-pressure to lower-pressure areas. • Breathing and drinking through a straw are examples of fluid flowing due to pressure differences.
Buoyant Force 1 Define buoyant force and Archimedes' principle. 2 Predict whether an object will sink, float, or buoy up in a fluid.	• The upward force that fluids exert on matter is called buoyant force. Archimedes' principle states that the buoyant force on an object in a fluid is an upward force equal to the weight of the fluid that the object replaces. • An object will sink if its weight is greater than the buoyant force, float if its weight is equal, and buoy up if its weight is less.

Options for Instruction

Two parallel paths provide coverage of the Essential Questions, with a strong Inquiry strand woven into each. Follow the Print Path, the Digital Path, or your customized combination of print, digital, and inquiry.

Print Path
Teaching support for the Print Path appears with the Student Pages.

Inquiry Labs and Activities

Digital Path
Digital Path shortcut: TS675255

Feel the Pressure!
SE pp. 56–57
What are fluids?
Why do fluids exert pressure?
How is pressure calculated?

Daily Demo
The Magic Bottle

Activity
Pressure in Real Life!

What's a Fluid?
Interactive Images

What's Pressure?
Slideshow

Particle Model
Video

Under Pressure, SE pp. 58–59
What are two familiar fluids that exert pressure?
• The Atmosphere
• Water
How does depth affect fluid pressure?

Field Lab
Pressure in Fluids

Daily Demo
Water Flow

Depth and Pressure
Interactive Images

Thar She Blows! SE pp. 60–61
What are some examples of fluid motion due to pressure?
• Fluid Motion and Breathing
• Fluid Motion and Weather

Quick Lab
Pressure Differences

Activity
Quiz Show

How Do Fluids Flow?
Graphic Sequence

Fluids on the Move
Slideshow

Sink or Swim? SE pp. 62–65
What causes buoyant force?
How is buoyant force calculated?
What can happen as a result of weight and buoyant force?
What affects the density of an object?

Quick Lab
Finding the Buoyant Force

Buoyant Force
Interactive Images

Density
Interactive Images

Options for Assessment

See the Evaluate page for options, including Formative Assessment, Summative Assessment, and Unit Review.

Engage and Explore

Activities and Discussion

Activity *Pressure in Real Life!*

Introduction to Pressure and Fluids

👥 pairs or small groups
🕐 20 min
(Inquiry) **GUIDED** inquiry

Ask students to work together to make a list of everyday examples of relationships between fluids and pressure. Encourage them to think about the weather, biology, and technology for inspiration. Have them make a diagram that demonstrates one of those relationships. Discuss some of students' ideas about types of fluids and pressure.

Take It Home *Pressure During the Day*

Atmospheric Pressure and Water Pressure

👥 adult-students pairs
🕐 ongoing
(Inquiry) **GUIDED** inquiry

Student and adult pairs should work together to list different ways that air pressure and water pressure affect their lives throughout the day, both inside and outside the home.

🕐 *Optional Online resource: student worksheet*

Discussion *Icebergs*

Buoyant Force

👥 whole class
🕐 10 min

Tell students that icebergs are chunks of freshwater ice that have broken off from a glacier and are floating in salt water. Very large icebergs can be 75 meters high and 200 meters long. The average weight of icebergs is 100,000 to 200,000 tons. **Ask:** How is it possible that huge and heavy icebergs can float in the ocean? The density of freshwater ice is less than the density of salt water. **Ask:** Freshwater ice is about nine-tenths the density of salt water. What does this tell you about how much of an iceberg is above water versus below water? Encourage students to discuss and develop a hypothesis. Only about one-tenth of an iceberg is above water.

Labs and Demos

Daily Demo *Water Flow*

Engage ▸

Atmospheric Pressure and Water Pressure

👥 whole class
🕐 10 min
(Inquiry) **GUIDED** inquiry

NOTE: This demo can be done as a precursor to the Field Lab.

PURPOSE **To demonstrate how water pressure increases with the depth of water**

MATERIALS

• tin can
• a tool to puncture holes in the tin can
• water

1 Before class, punch holes in a vertical line from the bottom to the top of the tin can. Make sure the holes are approximately the same size and equidistant from each other.

2 **Observing** With students watching, cover the holes with tape or your fingers and fill the can with water.

3 **Predict** Encourage students to predict how quickly the water will come out of each hole.

4 Remove your fingers or the tape from the holes and allow the water to flow out of the holes.

5 **Observing** What do you notice? A greater volume of water is pouring out of the lowest hole. Why do you think this is? The water pressure is higher at the lower depth.

6 **Analyzing** How could this application be used in technology? How might this be applied in your house? Sample answers: Dams and power plants may use this principle. This principle also explains how water moves through pipes to homes.

To extend the activity, cover the holes and fill the can again, and place a lid on the top. Now turn the can on its side and uncover the holes. The water should have equal flow from each of its holes because the pressure differences throughout the can are less extreme.

©Mark Karrass/Corbis

Daily Demo *The Magic Bottle*

Engage

Introduction to Pressure and Fluids

👥 whole class
🕐 10 min
GUIDED inquiry

PURPOSE **To demonstrate the effects of pressure**

MATERIALS

• plastic bottle with lid, 2 L
• water, hot

1 Have students watch as you pour hot water into the bottle.

2 Wait a couple of minutes. Then empty the bottle and quickly screw on the lid.

3 **Observing** What is happening? Sample answer: The bottle is collapsing.

4 **Analyzing** Why is this happening? Sample answer: Because the air inside the bottle is warmer than the air outside, molecules inside the bottle are farther apart than those outside, so outside air pressure is greater.

🌐 💾 Quick Lab *Finding the Buoyant Force*

PURPOSE **To investigate and describe buoyant force**
See the Lab Manual or go Online for planning information.

🌐 💾 Quick Lab *Pressure Differences*

Pressure and Fluid Flow

👥 pairs
🕐 20 min
DIRECTED inquiry

Students investigate how the speed of air affects air pressure.

PURPOSE **To observe the effects of pressure differences**

MATERIALS

• cup, clear plastic
• food coloring
• marker, permanent
• straws, clear, 3
• ruler, metric
• water

🌐 💾 Field Lab *Pressure in Fluids*

Atmospheric Pressure and Water Pressure

👥 small groups
🕐 45 min
DIRECTED/GUIDED inquiry

Students form hypotheses about water squirting from a bottle, then test their hypotheses.

PURPOSE **To demonstrate the relationship between depth of water and water pressure**

MATERIALS

• bottles, 1 L
• bottles, 2 L
• cans, coffee
• containers, plastic
• funnels
• marker, permanent
• metersticks
• nails
• pencils, colored
• ruler, metric
• water

Customize Your Labs

💾 *See the Lab Manual for lab datasheets.*

🌐 *Go Online for editable lab datasheets.*

Activities and Discussion

☐ **Activity** Pressure in Real Life!

☐ **Take It Home** Pressure During the Day

☐ **Discussion** Icebergs

Labs and Demos

☐ **Daily Demo** Water Flow

☐ **Daily Demo** The Magic Bottle

☐ **Quick Lab** Finding the Buoyant Force

☐ **Quick Lab** Pressure Differences

☐ **Field Lab** Pressure in Fluids

Your Resources

Explain Science Concepts

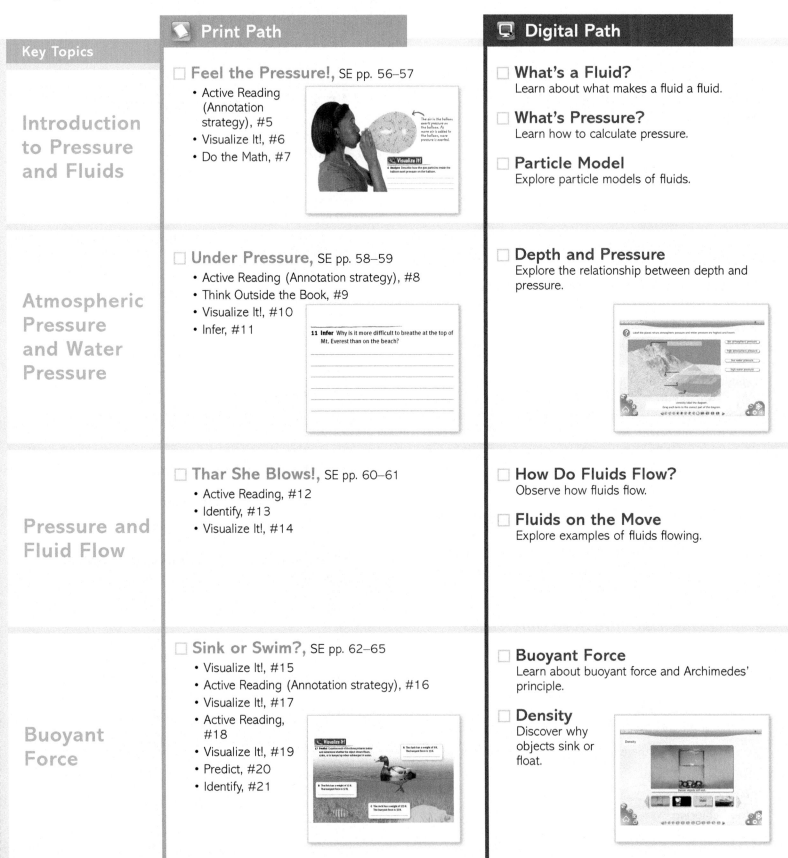

Key Topics	📖 Print Path	💻 Digital Path
Introduction to Pressure and Fluids	☐ **Feel the Pressure!,** SE pp. 56–57 • Active Reading (Annotation strategy), #5 • Visualize It!, #6 • Do the Math, #7	☐ **What's a Fluid?** Learn about what makes a fluid a fluid. ☐ **What's Pressure?** Learn how to calculate pressure. ☐ **Particle Model** Explore particle models of fluids.
Atmospheric Pressure and Water Pressure	☐ **Under Pressure,** SE pp. 58–59 • Active Reading (Annotation strategy), #8 • Think Outside the Book, #9 • Visualize It!, #10 • Infer, #11	☐ **Depth and Pressure** Explore the relationship between depth and pressure.
Pressure and Fluid Flow	☐ **Thar She Blows!,** SE pp. 60–61 • Active Reading, #12 • Identify, #13 • Visualize It!, #14	☐ **How Do Fluids Flow?** Observe how fluids flow. ☐ **Fluids on the Move** Explore examples of fluids flowing.
Buoyant Force	☐ **Sink or Swim?,** SE pp. 62–65 • Visualize It!, #15 • Active Reading (Annotation strategy), #16 • Visualize It!, #17 • Active Reading, #18 • Visualize It!, #19 • Predict, #20 • Identify, #21	☐ **Buoyant Force** Learn about buoyant force and Archimedes' principle. ☐ **Density** Discover why objects sink or float.

Differentiated Instruction

Basic *Floating Shapes*

Buoyant Force
    small groups
    20 min

Give each group of students an equal amount of modeling clay. Tell students that the modeling clay is denser than water and should sink. But if it is the right shape, it will float. Invite students to have a competition to see which group can create a "boat" out of modeling clay that floats without capsizing. When students are finished, encourage them to discuss what the shape of their clay has to do with whether their "boats" float or not.

Advanced *Air Pressure in Weather*

Synthesizing Key Topics
    individuals
    15 min

Encourage interested students to research three different weather phenomena, what causes each, and what air pressure and fluids have to do with each. Then have students create a display explaining their weather phenomena. Students can include diagrams, pictures, charts, and anything else that helps to explain their weather phenomena in terms of air pressure and fluids.

ELL *Double-Door Fold*

Introduction to Pressure and Fluids
    individuals or pairs
    10 min

Some students may have difficulty understanding that *fluid* and *liquid* do not mean the same thing in a scientific sense. Encourage students to make a double-door fold for these words to distinguish the concepts.

 Online resource: Double-Door Fold

Lesson Vocabulary

fluid	pressure	pascal
buoyant force	atmospheric pressure	Archimedes' principle

Previewing Vocabulary

    whole class
    10 min

Word Roots Tell students that the word *fluid* comes from the Latin *fluere*, meaning "to flow." Point out that many things flow, such as air, water, and natural gas.

Tell students that *buoyant* is related to the Spanish word *boyar*, which means "to float." Ask students to discuss what they think the term *buoyant force* refers to. Sample answer: the force that causes some things to float

Reinforcing Vocabulary

    individuals
    ongoing

Word Squares To help students remember the vocabulary terms, have them make word squares. In the top left square, they should write the term; below that, they should write both their definition and the dictionary definition. In the other two squares they should draw a picture of the term and use it in a sentence.

TERM / translation	symbol or picture
my meaning / dictionary definition	sentence

 Optional Online resource: Word Square support

Customize Your Core Lesson

Core Instruction

☐ **Print Path** choices

☐ **Digital Path** choices

Vocabulary

☐ **Previewing Vocabulary** Word Roots

☐ **Reinforcing Vocabulary** Word Squares

Your Resources

Differentiated Instruction

☐ **Basic** Floating Shapes

☐ **Advanced** Air Pressure in Weather

☐ **ELL** Double-Door Fold

Extend Science Concepts

Reinforce and Review

Activity *Quiz Show*

Synthesizing Key Topics　　👥 whole class
　　　　　　　　　　　　　　　　🕐 20 min

Quiz Show Divide the class into two groups. Ask one group to come up with at least ten questions and answers having to do with atmospheric pressure; ask the other group to come up with at least ten questions and answers having to do with water pressure, including buoyancy.

1 Each group selects two spokespeople for their team.

2 The spokespeople from each team alternate between asking the other team questions and, with the help of their entire team, answering the other team's questions.

3 The first team asks a question. The second team answers it.

4 If the team answering the question is correct, they get one point. If they are incorrect, the team asking the question supplies the answer. If this answer is incorrect, that team loses a point.

5 Play continues until one team has reached ten points.

FoldNote

Synthesizing Key Topics　　👥 individuals
　　　　　　　　　　　　　　　　🕐 10 min

Key-Term FoldNote Have students create a Key-Term FoldNote for topics they have studied. On the outside of each tab, have students write a word or topic, such as *pascal, fluid motion,* or *density*. Underneath each tab, have students describe how this word or topic is related to fluids and pressure.

🌐 *Online Resource: Key-Term Fold support*

Going Further

Health Connection

Atmospheric Pressure　　👥 individuals
and Water Pressure　　　🕐 varied

Research and Discuss Have students find and read an account of climbing Mt. Everest. They can find articles online or, if interested, read one of the many books written on the subject. When they have finished, discuss with students how pressure poses a hazard to climbers. Encourage students to discuss various ways that climbers can minimize this hazard.

Language Arts Connection

Atmospheric Pressure　　👥 individuals
and Water Pressure　　　🕐 20 min

Write a Science Fiction Story Invite students to write a story about a different world in which water or atmospheric pressure is different than on the Earth. How does that affect the life on that planet? How do beings on that planet live differently? What conflicts does this produce? Encourage students to illustrate and share their stories.

Customize Your Closing

📷 *See the Assessment Guide for quizzes and tests.*

🌐 *Go Online to edit and create quizzes and tests.*

Reinforce and Review

☐ **Activity** Quiz Show

☐ **FoldNote** Key-Term Fold

☐ **Print Path** Visual Summary, SE p. 66

☐ **Print Path** Lesson Review, SE p. 67

☐ **Digital Path** Lesson Closer

Evaluate Student Mastery

Formative Assessment

See the teacher support below the Student Pages for additional Formative Assessment questions.

Ask the following questions to assess student mastery of the material. **Ask:** What is pressure? Pressure is the force exerted on a given area. **Ask:** What unit is used to measure the size or magnitude of pressure? the pascal Describe this unit. One pascal is the force of one newton over one square meter. **Ask:** What are two properties of fluids? Fluids can flow and take on the shape of a container.

Reteach

Formative assessment may show that students need reinforcement for certain topics. The resources below are recommended for reteaching. If students were introduced to a topic through the Print Path, you can also use the Digital Path to reteach, or vice versa.
🎧 *Can be assigned to individual students*

Introduction to Pressure and Fluids
Activity Pressure in Real Life! 🎧

Atmospheric Pressure and Water Pressure
Daily Demo Water Flow

Pressure and Fluid Flow
Quick Lab Pressure Differences
Advanced Air Pressure in Weather 🎧

Buoyant Force
Discussion Icebergs

Summative Assessment

Alternative Assessment
Pressure Is Out of This World!

🌐 *Online resources: student worksheet, optional rubrics*

Fluids and Pressure

Tic-Tac-Toe: *Pressure Is Out of This World!*
You are a scientist from another world who is investigating the way that pressure affects Earth. You are conducting experiments and making observations.

1. Work on your own, with a partner, or with a small group.
2. Choose three quick activities from the game. Check the boxes you plan to complete. They must form a straight line in any direction.
3. Have your teacher approve your plan.
4. Do each activity, and turn in your results.

__ Can You Do It?	__ How Do They Breathe?	__ The Incredible Egg
You need to lift a pile of books using just a balloon. Explain how you will do it.	Create a diagram that shows how pressure differences allow animals to breathe.	You have an uncooked egg, salt, and a large glass filled with cold water. Explain how you can make the egg float.
__ Pressure News	__ Outer Space Town	__ Water System
Write a newscast that describes how air pressure affects the inhabitants of this planet.	You want to bring Earth creatures back to your home planet but the atmospheric pressure is much less there. Design a habitat on your planet that would protect Earth creatures from the lower atmospheric pressure.	Research the water that comes out of water fountains. Draw a diagram indicating the points at which pressure plays a part.
__ Ocean	__ Advertising Straws	__ What's Next?
You are exploring under the sea. Take notes about what you see that explains why fish and other objects float or sink.	Explain to your fellow citizens why straws are so amazing. Write an advertisement to help you sell the product to your planet that explains how pressure works in a straw.	Write a report to your planet explaining how pressure and fluids affect the daily lives of the people who live on Earth.

Going Further
☐ Health Connection
☐ Language Arts Connection

Formative Assessment
☐ Strategies Throughout TE
☐ Lesson Review SE

Summative Assessment
☐ Alternative Assessment Pressure Is Out of This World!
☐ Lesson Quiz
☐ Unit Tests A and B
☐ Unit Test SE End-of-Unit

Your Resources

Lesson 5

Fluids and Pressure

ESSENTIAL QUESTION

What happens when fluids exert pressure?

By the end of this lesson, you should be able to explain why fluids exert pressure and how the resulting pressure causes motion and the buoyant force.

The water in the river is a fluid. The air used to inflate the raft is also a fluid.

54 Unit 1 Motion and Forces

Lesson Labs
Quick Labs
• Finding the Buoyant Force
• Pressure Differences
Field Lab
• Pressure in Fluids

Engage Your Brain

1 Describe Fill in the blank with the word that you think correctly completes the following sentences.

A cork will _____ on top of water.

A rock will _____ in water.

An object that sinks in water is more _____ than water.

2 Describe Write your own caption to this photo. Include a description of the liquid's properties.

_____
_____
_____
_____

Active Reading

3 Apply Many scientific words, such as *pressure*, also have everyday meanings. Use context clues to write your own definition for each meaning of the word *pressure*.

Example sentence
Damien felt a lot of *pressure* because he knew the team was relying on him to hit a home run.

pressure:
_____
_____

Example sentence
When Jodie applied *pressure* to the clay, it started to flatten.

pressure:
_____

Vocabulary Terms
• fluid
• pressure
• pascal
• atmospheric pressure
• buoyant force
• Archimedes' principle

4 Identify As you read, create a reference card for each vocabulary term. On one side of the card, write the term and its meaning. On the other side, draw an image that illustrates or makes a connection to the term. These cards can be used as bookmarks in the text so that you can refer to them while studying.

Lesson 5 Fluids and Pressure 55

Answers

Answers for 1–3 should represent students' current thoughts, even if incorrect.

1. float; sink; dense

2. Students should describe the liquid and the general properties of liquids, such as the liquid flowing and taking the shape of the glass.

3. a stress or strain; a force that acts on something

4. Students should define or sketch each vocabulary term in the lesson.

Opening Your Lesson

Discuss students' answers to item #1 to assess their understanding of fluids and pressure.

Prerequisites Students should already have some understanding of forces. They should also have a basic understanding that the shape of a fluid depends on what container it is in.

Learning Alert

Difficult Concepts Students may confuse the terms *liquid* and *fluid*. Make sure that they understand that fluid refers to anything that takes the shape of a container and flows. Ask them to come up with several examples of fluids that are not liquids. Examples include helium in a balloon, air in a bike tire, and gas in a gas line. Have them repeat the properties of fluids so that they are confident in the definition.

Feel the Pressure!

What are fluids?

Active Reading **5 Identify** As you read, underline the characteristics of a fluid.

Can you think of a similarity between a container of water and a container of air? Water and air both take the shape of the container they are put into. Liquids and gases, like air, are fluids. A **fluid** is any material that can flow and that takes the shape of its container. A fluid can flow because its particles easily move past each other.

The water flows and takes the shape of the river channel.

Why do fluids exert pressure?

All fluids exert pressure. So, what is pressure? **Pressure** is the measure of how much force is acting on a given area. Any force exerted over an area, such as your body weight pushing down on the ground, creates pressure. When you pump up a bicycle tire, you push air into the tire. And like all matter, air is made of tiny particles that are constantly moving. Inside the tire, the air particles bump against one another and against the walls of the tire. The bumping of particles creates a force on the tire. The particles move in all directions and act on every part of the tire.

The air in the balloon exerts pressure on the balloon. As more air is added to the balloon, more pressure is exerted.

Visualize It!

6 Analyze Describe how the gas particles inside the balloon exert pressure on the balloon.

_____

_____

56

How is pressure calculated?

Pressure can be calculated by using the following equation:

$$pressure = \frac{force}{area}$$

The SI unit for pressure is the **pascal**. One pascal (1 Pa) is the force of one newton exerted over an area of one square meter (1 N/m²). This equation can be used to find the pressure exerted by fluids as well as other materials.

As you can see from the equation, a greater force results in greater pressure. Pressure also depends on the area over which the force is exerted. A greater area results in less pressure.

Water inside is exerting pressure on the tank in all directions.

Do the Math

Sample Problem
Calculate the pressure that water exerts on the bottom of a fish tank. The water presses down on the bottom with a force of 2,000 N, and the area of the bottom of the tank is 0.4 m².

Identify

A What do you know? area = 0.4 m², force = 2,000 N

B What do you want to find? pressure

Plan

C Write the formula: $pressure = \frac{force}{area}$

D Substitute the given values into the formula: $pressure = \frac{2,000 \ N}{0.4 \ m^2}$

Solve

E Divide: $\frac{2,000 \ N}{0.4 \ m^2} = 5,000 \ N/m^2$

F Check that your units agree: *A pascal is a N/m², so the units are correct.*

Answer: 5,000 Pa

You Try It

7 Calculate Calculate the pressure that the air outside exerts on a window pane that is 1.5 m². The force with which the air pushes on the window is 150,000 N.

Identify

A What do you know?

B What do you want to find?

Plan

C Write the formula:

D Substitute the given values into the formula:

Solve

E Divide:

F Check that your units agree:

Answer:

Lesson 5 Fluids and Pressure 57

Answers

5. *See students' pages for annotations.*

6. The air particles are always moving. They bump against each other and against the walls of the balloon. This movement creates pressure.

7. A: area = 1.5 m²; force = 150,000 N; B: pressure; C: pressure = force/area; D: pressure = 150,000 N / 1.5 m²; E: 150,000 N / 1.5 m² = 100,000 Pa; F: A pascal is a N/m², so the units agree; Answer: 100,000 Pa

Do the Math

Area Students may benefit from a tangible example of area. Use a meterstick to draw a 1 meter by 1 meter square on the board. Point out that the square measures 1 meter by 1 meter. Explain that multiplying the length by the width gives the area of the square, which is 1 square meter. Draw an additional 1 by 1 square right next to the first square. Point out that the shape now measures 2 meters by 1 meter and that multiplying the length and width of the shape gives an area of 2 square meters. Finally, draw 2 more squares on top of the first 2 so you have a 4 by 4 square. Point out how the area of the new shape is 4 square meters.

Newtons Explain to students that 1 newton is equal to about 0.225 pounds of force. In other words, there are about 4.5 newtons in a pound.

Probing Questions GUIDED (Inquiry)

Applying Do you think fluids exert force evenly or unevenly? Explain you answer. Sample answer: Evenly, because fluids flow into all the spaces available, and therefore I think the pressure would tend to be even.

What happens to the pressure inside and outside of a balloon when it pops? Sample answer: The pressure equalizes.

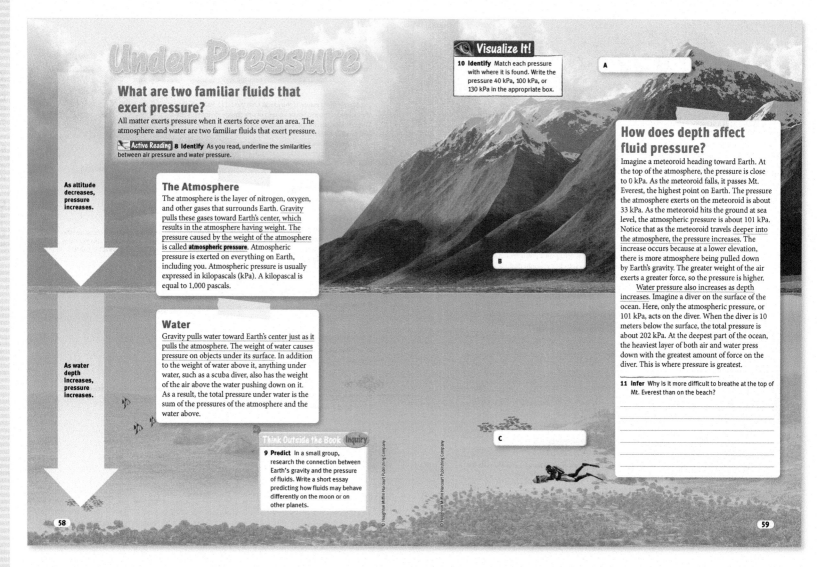

Under Pressure

What are two familiar fluids that exert pressure?

All matter exerts pressure when it exerts force over an area. The atmosphere and water are two familiar fluids that exert pressure.

Active Reading 8 Identify As you read, underline the similarities between air pressure and water pressure.

As altitude decreases, pressure increases.

The Atmosphere

The atmosphere is the layer of nitrogen, oxygen, and other gases that surrounds Earth. Gravity pulls these gases toward Earth's center, which results in the atmosphere having weight. The pressure caused by the weight of the atmosphere is called **atmospheric pressure**. Atmospheric pressure is exerted on everything on Earth, including you. Atmospheric pressure is usually expressed in kilopascals (kPa). A kilopascal is equal to 1,000 pascals.

Water

Gravity pulls water toward Earth's center just as it pulls the atmosphere. The weight of water causes pressure on objects under its surface. In addition to the weight of water above it, anything under water, such as a scuba diver, also has the weight of the air above the water pushing down on it. As a result, the total pressure under water is the sum of the pressures of the atmosphere and the water above.

As water depth increases, pressure increases.

Think Outside the Book Inquiry

9 Predict In a small group, research the connection between Earth's gravity and the pressure of fluids. Write a short essay predicting how fluids may behave differently on the moon or on other planets.

© Houghton Mifflin Harcourt Publishing Company

Visualize It!

10 Identify Match each pressure with where it is found. Write the pressure 40 kPa, 100 kPa, or 130 kPa in the appropriate box.

A

B

C

How does depth affect fluid pressure?

Imagine a meteoroid heading toward Earth. At the top of the atmosphere, the pressure is close to 0 kPa. As the meteoroid falls, it passes Mt. Everest, the highest point on Earth. The pressure the atmosphere exerts on the meteoroid is about 33 kPa. As the meteoroid hits the ground at sea level, the atmospheric pressure is about 101 kPa. Notice that as the meteoroid travels deeper into the atmosphere, the pressure increases. The increase occurs because at a lower elevation, there is more atmosphere being pulled down by Earth's gravity. The greater weight of the air exerts a greater force, so the pressure is higher.

Water pressure also increases as depth increases. Imagine a diver on the surface of the ocean. Here, only the atmospheric pressure, or 101 kPa, acts on the diver. When the diver is 10 meters below the surface, the total pressure is about 202 kPa. At the deepest part of the ocean, the heaviest layer of both air and water press down with the greatest amount of force on the diver. This is where pressure is greatest.

11 Infer Why is it more difficult to breathe at the top of Mt. Everest than on the beach?

_____
_____
_____
_____
_____

58

59

Answers

8. *See students' pages for annotations.*

9. Students should write about how the very weak gravity on the moon would make it almost impossible to notice the pressure exerted by fluids. Fluid pressure on other planets would depend on the force of gravity on a particular planet. Students may also note that air and water are absent on the moon, so no atmospheric or water pressure is observed there.

10. A: 40 kPa; B: 100 kPa; C: 130 kPa

11. The atmospheric pressure at the top of Mt. Everest is low compared to the atmospheric pressure at sea level. The low air pressure makes it difficult to take in air, and so it is harder to breathe.

Learning Alert

Diving Dangers Scuba divers take precautions to avoid decompression sickness using dive tables or dive computers to calculate how long they can stay down and how quickly they should surface. Decompression sickness results from the surrounding pressure decreasing too fast. Bubbles of inert gas can form in the body, which can be fatal. Sometimes decompression sickness is called the bends because air bubbles can collect in the joints, or bends, of the body.

Formative Assessment

Ask: What is a pascal? A pascal is the unit for pressure. **Ask:** How do you calculate pascals? pressure = force/area **Ask:** What is a fluid? A fluid is a substance that can flow and take on a container's shape. **Ask:** Describe pressure as you move from the outer atmosphere down to the ocean's bottom. As you move from the outer atmosphere towards the ground, pressure increases; it continues to increase from the ocean's surface to its bottom.

Thar She Blows!

This whale exhales air explosively through its blowhole before taking another breath. The exhaled air forms a stream of air and water vapor.

What are some examples of fluid motion due to pressure?

When you drink through a straw, you remove some of the air in the straw. Because there is less air inside the straw, the pressure in the straw is reduced. However, the atmospheric pressure on the surface of the liquid outside of the straw remains the same. So, there is a difference between the pressure inside the straw and the pressure outside the straw. The outside pressure forces the liquid up the straw and into your mouth. So, just by drinking through a straw, you can observe an important property of fluids: At any given altitude, fluids flow from areas of higher pressure to areas of lower pressure.

Fluid Motion and Breathing

When you take a deep breath, fluid flows from higher to lower pressure. As you inhale, your lungs expand. This expansion lowers the pressure in your lungs. The pressure in your lungs is now lower than the air pressure outside your lungs. Air flows into your lungs—from higher to lower pressure. When your lungs are filled, the pressure inside your lungs increases. When you exhale, the air in your lungs flows out from a region of higher pressure to a region of lower pressure.

Active Reading 12 Describe In your own words, describe the movement of air when you inhale.

_____
_____
_____

13 Identify Is greater pressure exerted inside the whale's body or outside the blowhole? Explain.

_____
_____
_____

Fluid Motion and Weather

At any given altitude in the atmosphere, there are areas of higher pressure and areas of lower pressure. Air moves from areas of higher pressure to areas of lower pressure. The movement of the air is known as wind.

Some of the damaging winds caused by tornadoes are the result of pressure differences. There is a great difference between the very low air pressure inside a tornado and the higher air pressure outside a tornado. This difference causes air to rush into the center of the tornado.

Visualize It!

14 Analyze Write *low pressure* or *high pressure* in each of the blank boxes.

A tornado acts like a giant vacuum cleaner. Objects are pushed toward the center of the tornado and sucked inside. The tornado can even carry them away.

A

B

Answers

12. As you take a breath, your lungs expand. This lowers the pressure in your lungs so that it is now lower than the air pressure outside your lungs. Air flows into your lungs from higher to lower pressure.

13. Air moves out of the whale's body. The pressure must be greater inside the whale's lungs. Air moves from areas of higher pressure to areas of lower pressure.

14. A: high pressure; B: low pressure

Building Reading Skills

Identifying Sequence To help students better understand what causes air to move from areas of higher pressure to areas of lower pressure, have them make a sequence diagram for breathing. They should begin with the diaphragm moving down. Challenge interested students to make sequence diagrams for wind.

🌐 *Optional Online resource: Sequence Diagram support*

Interpreting Visuals

Tornadoes Ask students to describe what they see in the image of a tornado. Sample answer: The tornado has sucked up a lot a material and is spinning it around. Encourage students to discuss how air pressure has caused this phenomenon. Sample answer: The inside of the tornado has much lower air pressure than the area outside the tornado, so air and objects move from the area of higher pressure into the area of lower pressure inside the tornado.

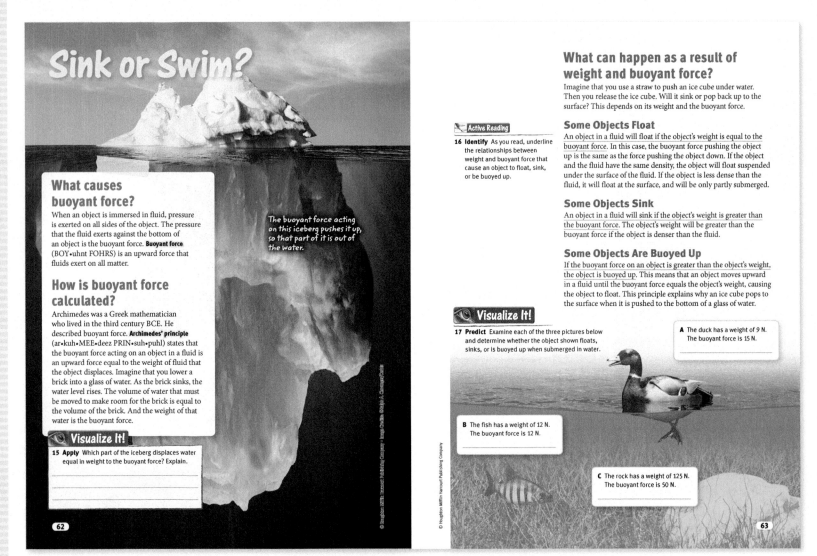

Sink or Swim?

What causes buoyant force?

When an object is immersed in fluid, pressure is exerted on all sides of the object. The pressure that the fluid exerts against the bottom of an object is the buoyant force. **Buoyant force** (BOY•uhnt FOHRS) is an upward force that fluids exert on all matter.

How is buoyant force calculated?

Archimedes was a Greek mathematician who lived in the third century BCE. He described buoyant force. **Archimedes' principle** (ar•kuh•MEE•deez PRIN•suh•puhl) states that the buoyant force acting on an object in a fluid is an upward force equal to the weight of fluid that the object displaces. Imagine that you lower a brick into a glass of water. As the brick sinks, the water level rises. The volume of water that must be moved to make room for the brick is equal to the volume of the brick. And the weight of that water is the buoyant force.

Visualize It!

15 Apply Which part of the iceberg displaces water equal in weight to the buoyant force? Explain.

_____

_____

The buoyant force acting on this iceberg pushes it up, so that part of it is out of the water.

62

What can happen as a result of weight and buoyant force?

Imagine that you use a straw to push an ice cube under water. Then you release the ice cube. Will it sink or pop back up to the surface? This depends on its weight and the buoyant force.

Active Reading

16 Identify As you read, underline the relationships between weight and buoyant force that cause an object to float, sink, or be buoyed up.

Some Objects Float

An object in a fluid will float if the object's weight is equal to the buoyant force. In this case, the buoyant force pushing the object up is the same as the force pushing the object down. If the object and the fluid have the same density, the object will float suspended under the surface of the fluid. If the object is less dense than the fluid, it will float at the surface, and will be only partly submerged.

Some Objects Sink

An object in a fluid will sink if the object's weight is greater than the buoyant force. The object's weight will be greater than the buoyant force if the object is denser than the fluid.

Some Objects Are Buoyed Up

If the buoyant force on an object is greater than the object's weight, the object is buoyed up. This means that an object moves upward in a fluid until the buoyant force equals the object's weight, causing the object to float. This principle explains why an ice cube pops to the surface when it is pushed to the bottom of a glass of water.

Visualize It!

17 Predict Examine each of the three pictures below and determine whether the object shown floats, sinks, or is buoyed up when submerged in water.

A The duck has a weight of 9 N. The buoyant force is 15 N.

_____

B The fish has a weight of 12 N. The buoyant force is 12 N.

_____

C The rock has a weight of 125 N. The buoyant force is 50 N.

63

Answers

15. The part that is below the water's surface; An object must be in a fluid to displace fluid. Only the bottom of the iceberg is submerged in the water.

16. *See students' pages for annotations.*

17. A: buoyed up; B: floats; C: sinks

Learning Alert

Buoyant Adaptations Tell students that fish and ducks have special adaptations to make them buoyant. Invite students to discuss what characteristics of a duck allow it to float. If there is time, allow students to research in the computer lab or at home. Sample answer: Duck feathers are covered with oil so they don't soak up water, and they have hollow bones; this keeps them lighter and more buoyant. Ducks also have internal air sacs that help them float.

Probing Questions DIRECTED Inquiry

Analyzing Sometimes, doctors recommend that people with pain in their joints exercise in water instead of on land. What does this have to do with Archimedes' principle? Sample answer: The upward buoyant force on a person in the water will be equal to the amount of water he or she displaces; therefore, that person will feel much lighter and exercise will be easier on their joints.

What affects the density of an object?

The density of an object is related to its ability to sink or float. Sometimes it is possible to change the density of an object to control whether it sinks or floats. Density is related to mass and volume. This relationship can be expressed in a mathematical formula.

$$density = \frac{mass}{volume}$$

Active Reading 18 Describe If an object's density is decreasing but its mass stays constant, what must be true of the object's volume?

_____

_____

A submarine rises to the surface when its density is less than that of water.

Its Mass

A submarine can travel both on the surface of the ocean and under water. Submarines have large ballast tanks that can be opened to allow seawater to flow in. As water is added, the submarine's mass increases, but its volume stays the same. The submarine's overall density increases so that it sinks below the surface. Adding more water allows the submarine to dive deeper. When the submarine needs to rise, air is added to its tanks and the water is blown out. The submarine's mass decreases as water is expelled, and so the density also decreases. The submarine rises to the surface.

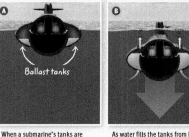

A Ballast tanks

B

C

When a submarine's tanks are mostly filled with air, the submarine floats on the surface.

As water fills the tanks from below and air escapes from the top, a submarine sinks.

As air is pumped into the tanks to force the water out, a submarine buoys up to the surface.

Visualize It!

19 Analyze Explain how the density of the submarine changes in each image.

_____

_____

_____

_____

_____

_____

64   Unit 1 Motion and Forces

Its Volume

Steel is almost eight times denser than water. Yet huge steel ships cruise the oceans with ease. How is this possible? It all depends on the shape of the ship. What if a ship were just a big block of steel? If you put that block into water, the block would sink because it is denser than water. So ships are built with a hollow shape. The amount of steel in the ship is the same as in the block. But the hollow shape increases the overall volume of the ship. An increase in the ship's volume leads to a decrease in its density. Ships float because their overall density is less than the density of water.

Like a submarine, some fish adjust their density to stay at a certain depth in the water. Most bony fish have an organ called a *swim bladder*. This organ is filled with gases. The inflated swim bladder increases the fish's volume, which decreases the fish's overall density. By adjusting the volume of gas in its swim bladder, the fish can move to different depths.

This fish uses its swim bladder to change its volume so that it can float at different depths in water.

20 Predict Each row of the table below shows the density of an object and the density of a fluid. Predict whether each object will sink or float on the surface of the fluid. Write your prediction, *sink* or *float*, in the table.

Object and its density	Fluid and its density	Prediction
cork, 0.24 g/cm³	water, 1.0 g/cm³	
penny, 8.96 g/cm³	mercury, 13.53 g/cm³	
boiled egg, 1.02 g/cm³	cooking oil, 0.93 g/cm³	
ice cube, 0.92 g/cm³	vinegar, 1.01 g/cm³	

21 Identify Placing the egg in which fluid would give a different result?

_____

_____

Lesson 5 Fluids and Pressure   65

Answers

18. Its volume is increasing.

19. A: Density remains constant since water is not added or released from ballast tanks; B: Mass increases with added water, and density increases; C: Mass is decreased by blowing water out of the ballast tanks, and density also decreases.

20. float; float; sink; float

21. Placing the egg in mercury will allow the egg to float instead of sink.

Interpreting Visuals

Direct students to look at the arrows in each of the diagrams. **Ask:** What do these arrows show? Sample answer: The arrows show the direction that air or water is flowing. **Ask:** What is the submarine in the middle illustration doing? How can you tell? Sample answer: It is diving or sinking. I can tell because the arrows show that air is flowing out and water is flowing in. This would make the submarine more dense, so it would sink.

Formative Assessment

Ask: Why does an object float? The upward, or buoyant, force acting on it is equal to the force acting downward. **Ask:** How can steel ships that are eight times denser than water float on the surface of the water? The hollow shape of the ship increases the ship's volume and leads to a decrease in density. This increases the ship's buoyancy and allows it to float at the water's surface. **Ask:** Why do some things float in salt water when they cannot in fresh water? Salt changes the density of water.

Visual Summary

To complete this summary, fill in the blanks with the correct word. Then use the key below to check your answers. You can use this page to review the main concepts of the lesson.

Pressure is the amount of force exerted on a given area.

Fluids and Pressure

22 Gases are one type of _____ because they flow and take the shape of their container.

Fluids flow from higher pressure areas to lower pressure areas.

23 The force of _____ causes atmospheric pressure by pulling down on the air.

Archimedes' principle explains buoyant force.

24 An object that has a weight greater than the buoyant force will _____

25 The mass of an object divided by its volume is its _____

Answers: 22. fluid; 23. gravity; 24. sink; 25. density

26 **Design** Imagine you want to design a toy boat from a block of clay. What would you need to consider to make sure that your boat can float?

Lesson Review

Lesson 5

Vocabulary

Draw a line to connect the following terms to their definitions.

1 pascal — **A** the amount of force exerted per unit area of a surface
2 fluid — **B** the SI unit of pressure
3 pressure — **C** a material that can flow and takes the shape of its container

Key Concepts

4 Compare A pebble sinks in water. A twig floats on top of the water. Compare the densities of the water, the pebble and the twig.

5 Describe Explain why atmospheric pressure changes as atmospheric depth changes.

6 Define What does Archimedes' principle state?

7 Calculate An object exerts 140 N of force on a surface that has an area of 2.0 m². How much pressure does the object exert?

8 Apply Describe the motion of air particles inside an inflated balloon.

Critical Thinking

Use this photo to answer the following questions.

9 Analyze What two properties show that the drink is a fluid?

10 Apply Explain how drinking through a straw illustrates fluid flowing from high-pressure to low-pressure areas.

11 Evaluate Your friend tells you that all heavy objects sink in water. Do you agree or disagree? Explain your answer in terms of buoyant force.

Visual Summary Answers

22. fluid
23. gravity
24. sink
25. density
26. Sample answer: Whether or not the boat would float depends on its density. I would have to make the volume of the boat large enough that the overall density of the boat is less than that of water.

Lesson Review Answers

1. B
2. C
3. A
4. The pebble has a higher density than water. The twig has a lower density than water.
5. As you go lower in the atmosphere, there is more air above. The weight of the air above is greater, so the pressure is greater.
6. The buoyant force on an object in a fluid is an upward force equal to the weight of the fluid that the object displaces.
7. 70 Pa
8. The particles collide with each other and with the balloon.
9. The drink flows and takes the shape of its container.
10. When a person sucks on a straw, some of the air is removed from the straw. The fluid flows from the high-pressure area to the low-pressure area inside the straw.
11. I disagree with the statement because whether an object sinks does not depend only on its weight. It also depends on buoyant force. If the buoyant force is greater than the object's weight, the object will float.

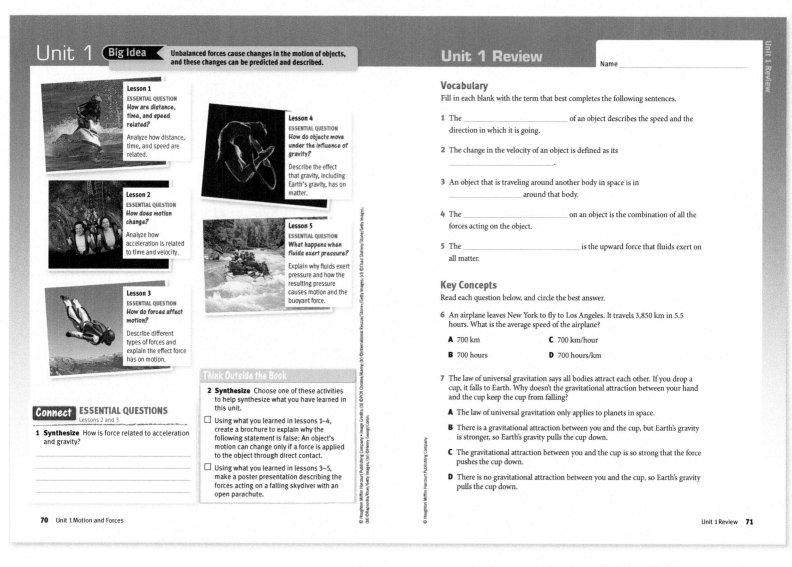

Unit Summary Answers

1. A change in force can change the direction or speed of acceleration. Gravity is a force that accelerates an object toward Earth's center.

2. Option 1: Students' brochures should state that some forces, such as gravity and magnetism, can act at a distance, causing an object's motion to change.

   Option 2: Students' presentations should illustrate different forces acting on the parachute and skydiver such as gravity and the force of collisions between the air particles and the inside of the parachute.

Unit Review Response to Intervention

A Quick Grading Chart follows the Answers. See the Assessment Guide for more detail about correct and incorrect answer choices. Refer back to the Lesson Planning pages for activities and assignments that can be used as remediation for students who answer questions incorrectly.

Answers

1. velocity Velocity is a vector, which is a quantity that has both size and direction. (Lesson 1)

2. acceleration Acceleration is a change in the speed and/or direction of a moving object. (Lesson 2)

3. orbit Gravity holds an object in orbit around another body. (Lesson 4)

4. net force Unbalanced forces on an object will cause the object to accelerate in the direction of the net force. (Lesson 3)

Unit 1 Review continued

Name _____

8 This distance-time graph shows the speeds of four toy cars.

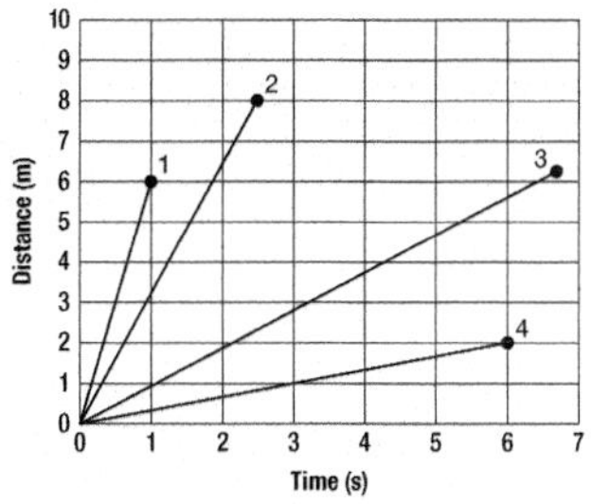

Which car is the fastest?

A Car 1   C Car 3

B Car 2   D Car 4

9 The diagram below shows the forces acting on a sneaker. As the force F is applied, the sneaker does not move.

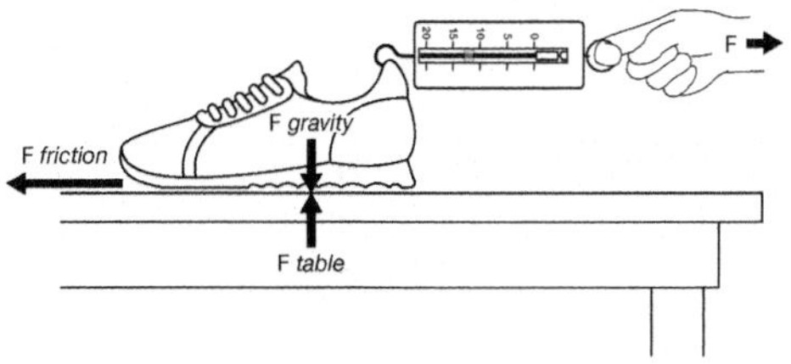

Which statement below correctly describes the forces?

A The net force is acting in an upward direction.

B The net force is acting to the left.

C The net force is moving to the right.

D The net force is zero and all the forces are balanced.

10 The diagram below shows a satellite in orbit around Earth. It is orbiting in the direction shown and is pulled toward Earth by gravity.

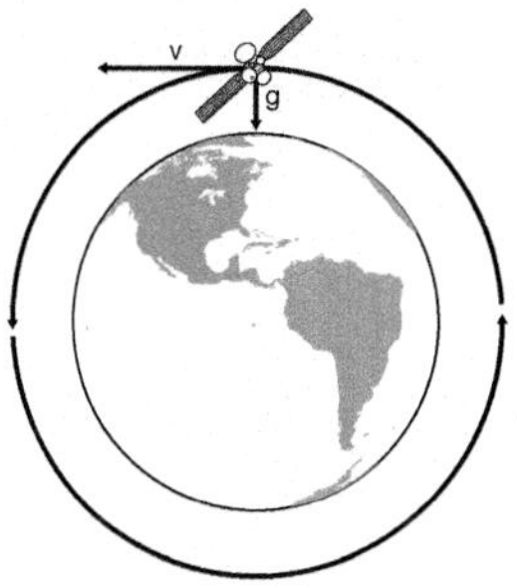

What would happen if Earth's gravity suddenly disappeared?

A The satellite would continue to orbit Earth.

B The satellite would fall to Earth.

C The satellite would move into space in a straight line.

D The satellite would stop moving.

11 Julia is in a car with her father. The car is undergoing centripetal acceleration. What is happening to the car?

A The car is changing direction at a constant speed.

B The car is changing direction and speeding up.

C The car is stopping suddenly.

D The car is slowing down.

12 Rajiv made a model of a boat. When he places it in water, it sinks. According to Archimedes' principle, why does the boat sink?

A The boat is too small.

B The buoyant force is less than the boat's weight.

C The buoyant force is equal to the boat's weight.

D The buoyant force is greater than the boat's weight.

Answers (continued)

5. buoyant force There is an upward force on an object placed in a fluid such as water. (Lesson 5)

6. Answer C is correct because 3,850 km divided by 5.5 hours equals 700 km/hour, which is a measurement of average speed. (Lesson 1)

7. Answer B is correct because the mass of your hand and the cup are very small compared to the mass of Earth. The gravitational attraction is there, but it is very small. (Lesson 4)

8. Answer A is correct because the distance-time line of car 1 is the steepest. Car 1 travels the greatest distance per second, so the speed is the fastest. (Lesson 1)

9. Answer D is correct because the sneaker is not moving at all—all four forces are equal. (Lesson 3)

10. Answer C is correct because without gravity, there is nothing to hold the satellite in orbit, so the satellite would continue in the direction of V. (Lesson 4)

11. Answer A is correct because centripetal acceleration means to change direction at a constant speed. (Lesson 2)

12. Answer B is correct because the downward force acting on the boat due to its weight is greater than the upward buoyant force. (Lesson 5)

13. Key Elements:
- Marek is pushing the box in the direction of the arrow.
- Friction is a force working in the opposite direction to the arrow.
- Gravity is a force pushing down on the box.
- The floor is pushing up with a force on the box. (Lesson 3)

14. Key Elements:
- $F = ma$ means the force on an object is equal to the mass of the object times its acceleration.
- The formula describes Newton's second law of motion. (Lesson 3)

Quick Grading Chart

Use the chart below for quick test grading. The lesson correlations can help you target reteaching for missed items.

Unit 1 Review continued

Critical Thinking

Answer the following questions in the space provided.

13 Marek is trying to push a box of sports equipment across the floor. The arrow on the box is a vector representing the force that Marek exerts.

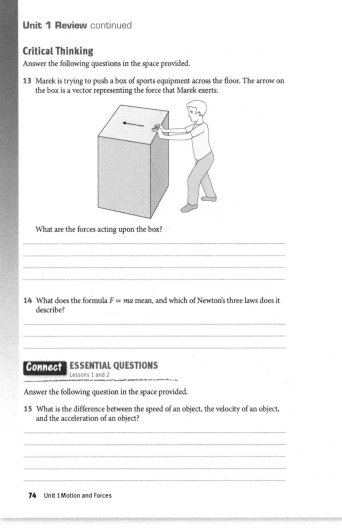

What are the forces acting upon the box?

_____

_____

_____

14 What does the formula $F = ma$ mean, and which of Newton's three laws does it describe?

_____

_____

Connect **ESSENTIAL QUESTIONS**
Lessons 1 and 2

Answer the following question in the space provided.

15 What is the difference between the speed of an object, the velocity of an object, and the acceleration of an object?

_____

_____

_____

_____

74   Unit 1 Motion and Forces

Item	Answer	Cognitive Complexity	Lesson
1.	—	Low	1
2.	—	Low	2
3.	—	Low	4
4.	—	Low	3
5.	—	Low	5
6.	C	Moderate	1
7.	B	Moderate	4
8.	A	Moderate	1
9.	D	Moderate	3
10.	C	Moderate	4
11.	A	Moderate	2
12.	B	Moderate	5
13.	—	Moderate	3
14.	—	Moderate	3
15.	—	Moderate	1, 2

Answers (continued)

15. Key Elements:

- The speed of an object is a measure of how fast the object is moving.

- The velocity of an object is a measure of how fast the object is moving and the direction in which the object is moving.

- The acceleration of an object is a measure of the object's change in velocity. (Lesson 1, 2)

Cognitive Complexity refers to the demand on thinking associated with an item, and may vary with the answer choices, the number of steps required to arrive at an answer, and other factors, but not the ability level of the student.

© Houghton Mifflin Harcourt Publishing Company

UNIT ② Work, Energy, and Machines

The Big Idea and Essential Questions

This Unit was designed to focus on this Big Idea and Essential Questions.

Big Idea Energy is transferred when a force moves an object.

Lesson	ESSENTIAL QUESTION	Student Mastery	(PD) Professional Development	Lesson Overview
LESSON 1 Work, Energy, and Power	How is work related to energy?	To relate work to energy and power	Content Refresher, TE p. 100	TE p. 106
LESSON 2 Kinetic and Potential Energy	What are kinetic and potential energy?	To calculate kinetic and potential energy and know how these two types of energy are related	Content Refresher, TE p. 101	TE p. 120
LESSON 3 Machines	How do simple machines work?	To describe different types of simple machines and to calculate the mechanical advantages and efficiencies of various simple machines	Content Refresher, TE p. 102	TE p. 138

©Chase Jarvis/Corbis

 **Professional Development** Science Background

Use the keywords at right to access

- Professional Development from **The NSTA Learning Center**
- **SciLinks** for additional online content appropriate for students and teachers

Keywords

energy	power
machines	work

NSTA National Science Teachers Association

SCiLINKS® THE WORLD'S A CLICK AWAY

Options for Instruction

Two parallel paths provide coverage of the Essential Questions, with a strong Inquiry strand woven into each. Follow the Print Path, the Digital Path, or your customized combination of print, digital, and inquiry.

	LESSON 1 Work, Energy, and Power	LESSON 2 Kinetic and Potential Energy	LESSON 3 Machines
Essential Questions	How is work related to energy?	What are kinetic and potential energy?	How do simple machines work?
Key Topics	• Work • Energy • Power	• Kinetic Energy • Potential Energy • Mechanical Energy	• Introduction to Machines • Mechanical Advantage and Mechanical Efficiency • Types of Machines

Print Path

	Teacher Edition pp. 106–118	Teacher Edition pp. 120–132	Teacher Edition pp. 138–152
	Student Edition pp. 78–87	Student Edition pp. 88–97	Student Edition pp. 102–115

Inquiry Labs

	Lab Manual **Quick Lab** Investigating Work **Quick Lab** Calculating Power **S.T.E.M. Lab** Using Water to Do Work	Lab Manual **Quick Lab** Investigate…Energy **Exploration Lab** Mechanical Energy 🖥 Virtual Lab Kinetic Energy	Lab Manual **Quick Lab** Mechanical Efficiency **Quick Lab** Investigate Pulleys **S.T.E.M. Lab** Compound Machines

Digital Path

	Digital Path TS696129	Digital Path TS665010	Digital Path TS675240

UNIT 2
Unit Projects

 Citizen Science Project
Day at the Races

Teacher's Edition **p. 105**

Student Edition
pp. 76–77

Take the Long Way

Unit Assessment
Formative Assessment
Strategies RTI
Throughout TE

Lesson Reviews SE

Unit PreTest

Summative Assessment
Alternative Assessment
(1 per lesson) RTI

Lesson Quizzes

Unit Tests A and B

Unit Review RTI
(with answer remediation)

Practice Tests
(end of module)

Project-Based Assessment
*See the Assessment Guide
for quizzes and tests.*

*Go Online to edit and create
quizzes and tests.*

Response to Intervention

See RTI teacher support
materials on p. PD7.

Differentiated Instruction

English Language Proficiency

Strategies for **English Language Learners (ELL)** are provided for each lesson, under the Explain tabs.

LESSON 1 *Combination Notes,* TE p. 111

LESSON 2 *Main Idea Web,* TE p. 125

LESSON 3 *Illustrated Machines,* TE p. 143

Vocabulary strategies provided for all students can also be a particular help for ELL. Use different strategies for each lesson or choose one or two to use throughout the unit. Vocabulary strategies can be found under the Explain tab for each lesson (TE pp. 111, 125, and 143).

Leveled Inquiry

Inquiry labs, activities, probing questions, and daily demos provide a range of inquiry levels. Preview them under the Engage and Explore tabs starting on TE pp. 108, 122, and 140.

Levels of **Inquiry**

DIRECTED inquiry	GUIDED inquiry	INDEPENDENT inquiry
introduces inquiry skills within a structured framework.	develops inquiry skills within a supportive environment.	deepens inquiry skills with student-driven questions or procedures.

Each long lab has two inquiry options:

LESSON 1 S.T.E.M. Lab *Using Water to Do Work*

LESSON 2 Exploration Lab *Mechanical Energy*

LESSON 3 S.T.E.M. Lab *Compound Machines*

🖥 **Go Digital!** ⦿ **thinkcentral.com**

Digital Path

The Unit 2 Resource Gateway is your guide to all of the digital resources for this unit. To access the Gateway, visit thinkcentral.com.

Digital Interactive Lessons

Lesson 1 Work, Energy, and Power TS696129

Lesson 2 Kinetic and Potential Energy TS665010

Lesson 3 Machines TS675240

More Digital Resources

In addition to digital lessons, you will find the following digital resources for Unit 2:

Video-Based Project: Take the Long Way
(previewed on TE p. 104)

Virtual Labs: Kinetic Energy
(previewed on TE p. 123)

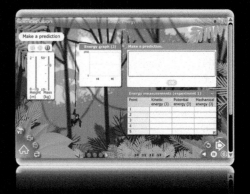

RTI Response to Intervention

Response to Intervention (RTI) is a process for identifying and supporting students who are not making expected progress toward essential learning goals. The following *ScienceFusion* components can be used to provide strategic and intensive intervention.

Component	Location	Strategies and Benefits
STUDENT EDITION Active Reading prompts, Visualize It!, Think Outside the Book	**Throughout each lesson**	Student responses can be used as screening tools to assess whether intervention is needed.
TEACHER EDITION Formative Assessment, Probing Questions, Learning Alerts	**Throughout each lesson**	Opportunities are provided to assess and remediate student understanding of lesson concepts.
TEACHER EDITION Extend Science Concepts	**Reinforce and Review, TE pp. 112, 126, 144** **Going Further, TE pp. 112, 126, 144**	Additional activities allow students to reinforce and extend their understanding of lesson concepts.
TEACHER EDITION Evaluate Student Mastery	**Formative Assessment, TE pp. 113, 127, 145** **Alternative Assessment, TE pp. 113, 127, 145**	These assessments allow for greater flexibility in assessing students with differing physical, mental, and language abilities as well as varying learning and communication modes.
TEACHER EDITION Unit Review Remediation	**Unit Review, TE pp. 154–156**	Includes reference back to Lesson Planning pages for remediation activities and assignments.
INTERACTIVE DIGITAL LESSONS and VIRTUAL LABS	**thinkcentral.com** **Unit 1 Gateway** **Lesson 1 TS696129** **Lesson 2 TS665010** **Lesson 3 TS675240**	Lessons and labs make content accessible through simulations, animations, videos, audio, and integrated assessment. Useful for review and reteaching of lesson concepts.

Content Refresher

Professional Development

Work, Energy, and Power

ESSENTIAL QUESTION
How is work related to energy?

1. Work

Students will learn that work is the use of force to move an object.

To do work on an object, a force must be applied to the object, and the object must move. Work is done only by the component of the force that acts in the same direction as the movement of the object. Work can be calculated by multiplying the force applied to an object by the distance the object moves while that force is being applied. The formula for calculating work is $W = F \cdot d$. The standard unit of measurement of work is the newton-meter, also called the joule. A *joule* equals one newton of force over one meter distance.

Students will learn that objects that are moving can do work.

- A moving object can apply a force to something, causing it to move.
- The gravitational force of Earth does work on water, which can then do work on other objects.
- People use moving objects to help them do work.

2. Energy

Students will learn that energy is transferred when work is done.

When work is done on an object, energy is transferred from whatever is exerting the force to the object.

The total amount of energy is constant.

The law of conservation of energy states that energy is neither created nor destroyed, although it can change into another form. Common forms of energy are mechanical, sound, thermal, chemical, nuclear, and electromagnetic energy. As a ball rolls down a ramp, the amounts of potential energy and kinetic energy change, but the total energy is the same.

3. Power

Students will learn how to calculate power.

Power is the rate at which work is done. When the power of an object increases, work is done faster. The equation for calculating power is

$$P = \frac{W}{t} \quad \textbf{or} \quad P = \frac{Fd}{t}.$$

The unit of measurement for power is the watt, equal to one joule of work done in one second.

Power can be calculated from energy and time.

Power can be thought of as the rate at which energy is transferred over a certain period of time. Power can be calculated from energy as well as from work. The formula for calculating power using energy and time is $P = \frac{E}{t}$.

©HMH

COMMON MISCONCEPTIONS RTI

WORK REQUIRES A FORCE Students might think that work continues even after a force ceases to be applied. In fact, an object can continue to move after the force is removed, but work is no longer being done.

This misconception is addressed in the Discussion on p. 108 and in the Learning Alert on p. 115

Teacher (to) Teacher

Lauren Baiocchi
Creekside Middle School
Castro Valley, CA

Lesson 2 Kinetic and Potential Energy   It can be easy and fun to model the differences between kinetic and potential energy. Stretch a rubber band, and explain that the band has potential energy. Release the rubber band (away from your students), and explain that it now has kinetic energy, energy of motion. A yo-yo is another easy, fun implement for demonstrating potential and kinetic energy.

Lesson 2

Kinetic and Potential Energy

ESSENTIAL QUESTION
What are kinetic and potential energy?

1. Kinetic Energy

Students will learn that kinetic energy is the energy an object has because of its motion, and how mass and speed of an object can be used to calculate this energy.

All moving objects possess kinetic energy. Every time people move, whether they are running in a marathon or turning the pages of a book, they have kinetic energy. Objects in motion also have kinetic energy, from a baseball zipping through the air to water tumbling down a stream.

The two factors that determine how much kinetic energy an object has are its mass and its speed. The greater an object's mass, the greater its kinetic energy. So, a school bus and a car traveling at the same speed would have differing amounts of kinetic energy due to their differing masses. Kinetic energy also varies with speed. Imagine two cars of equal mass. The car with the greater speed will have greater kinetic energy.

The speed and mass of an object form an equation that is used to represent the kinetic energy of an object: $KE = \frac{1}{2}mv^2$.

2. Potential Energy

Students will learn that potential energy is the stored energy an object has due to its position, condition, or chemical composition.

There are different forms of potential energy, such as chemical potential energy, elastic potential energy, and gravitational potential energy.

- Chemical potential energy is stored in substances and objects such as food, batteries, coal, and wood. The energy is released when we eat food, use batteries, or burn coal or wood.

- Elastic potential energy is stored in things that stretch, such as rubber bands. When the band is stretched, it has elastic potential energy because the band will try to return to its original shape. If the band is released, the elastic potential energy is transformed into kinetic energy.

- Gravitational potential energy is potential energy that is due to an object's position. The higher and heavier an object is, the greater gravitational potential energy it has. The mass, acceleration due to gravity, and height of an object form an equation that is used to represent the gravitational potential energy of an object: $GPE = mgh$.

Elastic potential energy and gravitational potential energy are two examples of mechanical potential energy.

3. Mechanical Energy

Students will learn that an object's mechanical energy is the sum of its potential energy and its kinetic energy.

Mechanical energy is the ability to do work. An object possesses mechanical energy due to its position or motion. For example, the barbells that weightlifters heft above their heads possess mechanical energy as a result of the barbells' position above the ground. The equation for calculating mechanical energy is $ME = PE + KE$. In this equation, only mechanical potential energy is considered.

Students may wonder why, if energy is conserved, an object such as a bouncing basketball does not continue to bounce forever. After all, its kinetic and potential energy are converted back and forth as the ball bounces up and down. Remind them that, with each bounce, some of the ball's mechanical energy is used to overcome friction. Therefore, the total mechanical energy of the basketball decreases with each bounce; so the sum of its potential and kinetic energy decreases with each bounce.

Content Refresher (continued)

Professional Development

Machines

ESSENTIAL QUESTION
How do simple machines work?

1. Introduction to Machines

Students will learn what a machine does and how machines can make work easier.

Machines are a common part of our lives. Most students are likely to think of machines in terms of technology. While computers, cars, and cell phones are machines in everyday terminology, they are not the kinds of machines relevant to this lesson. Guide students to think in more basic ways when teaching this lesson.

Students may need to review the scientific definitions of force and work to gain an understanding of how machines change the way work is done. Recall that there are two components of work—magnitude of the applied force and distance over which the force is applied. Machines cannot change the total amount of work required to do a task. So, any change in the magnitude of the applied force is accompanied by a corresponding change in the distance over which the force must be applied. For example, lifting a box vertically from the road to the back of a truck requires a large force exerted over a relatively short distance. The same amount of work is done pushing the box up a ramp from the road to the truck, but the magnitude of the required force is decreased, and the distance over which it is exerted is increased. Some machines change the direction of the applied force. These machines change the way work is done, but do not change the *amount* of work required to do a particular task.

2. Mechanical Advantage and Mechanical Efficiency

Students will learn definitions and applications of mechanical advantage and mechanical efficiency.

Some machines change the magnitude of the force required to do a task; the measurement of this change is mechanical advantage. Machines can have mechanical advantages of less than 1, exactly 1 (for those that change only the direction of the applied force), or greater than 1.

Mechanical efficiency is a percentage that compares the work output of a machine to the work input. Students might not initially grasp why these numbers are different. Explain that every machine uses some of the input work to overcome friction, and as a result no machine's mechanical efficiency can be greater than 100 percent.

3. Types of Machines

Students will learn about the six simple machines.

Levers are a familiar type of simple machine. Levers are categorized as first-class, second-class, or third-class by the relative position of the fulcrum, input force, and output force. The ideal mechanical advantage of a lever is calculated based upon the distance between the fulcrum and the input force and the distance between the fulcrum and the output force.

A steering wheel and a doorknob are both examples of wheel and axles. The mechanical advantage of a wheel and axle is calculated by dividing the radius of the input force by the radius of the output force.

Pulleys are classified as fixed, moveable, or block and tackle. Fixed pulleys change only the direction of a force, so their mechanical advantage is always 1. Moveable pulleys have a mechanical advantage of 2, and block and tackle pulley systems have a mechanical advantage of 2 or more.

An inclined plane is a simple machine that is a straight, slanted surface. The most common example of an inclined plane is a ramp. Inclined planes decrease the magnitude of the force needed to move an object and increase the distance over which the force must be applied. A wedge is a simple machine that is made up of two inclined planes that move. The mechanical advantage of a wedge depends upon its length and width. A screw is a simple machine that is an inclined plane wrapped around a cylinder. Its mechanical advantage depends on the length of the spiral on the screw and how close together the threads are.

Teacher Notes

Advance Planning

These activities may take extended time or special conditions.

Unit 2

Video-Based Project Take the Long Way, p. 104
 multiple activities spanning several lessons

Project A Day at the Races, p. 105
 design and plan

Graphic Organizers and Vocabulary pp. 111, 112, 125, 126, 143, 144
 ongoing with reading

Lesson 1

Quick Lab Calculating Power, p. 109
 roller skate

S.T.E.M. Lab Using Water to Do Work, p. 109
 2-liter bottle with hole drilled in bottom

Lesson 2

Daily Demo Roller Coaster Ride, p. 123
 foam pipe insulation, sliced in half lengthwise

Lesson 3

S.T.E.M. Lab Compound Machines, p. 141
 requires 90 min

Quick Lab Mechanical Efficiency, p. 141
 toy cart, approximately 400 g

What Do You Think?

Encourage students to think about what they know about work, energy, and machines.

Ask: List some devices or machines that people rely on and the energy sources that they use. Sample answers: cars: gasoline; air conditioning: electricity; sailboat: wind

Ask: What are some machines or tools you have used that are powered by your own energy or strength? Sample answers: a bicycle, a hammer, a wheelbarrow, scissors

Ask: Simple machines make work easier. What is an example of a simple machine that makes a task easier? Sample answer: A hammer makes it easier to pull a bent nail from a piece of wood.

UNIT 2

Work, Energy, and Machines

Big Idea

Energy is transferred when a force moves an object.

Machines are found everywhere—even in the skate park.

What do you think?

Machines make work and play easier. Skateboards are complex machines made of simple machines. Can you identify two basic parts of this skateboard?

Simple machines make up complex machines.

75

Video-Based Project

Take the Long Way

Go Online to preview the videos, access teacher support pages, and print student activity worksheets.

Students build a complex machine to accomplish a simple task.

©Jupiterimages/Getty Images

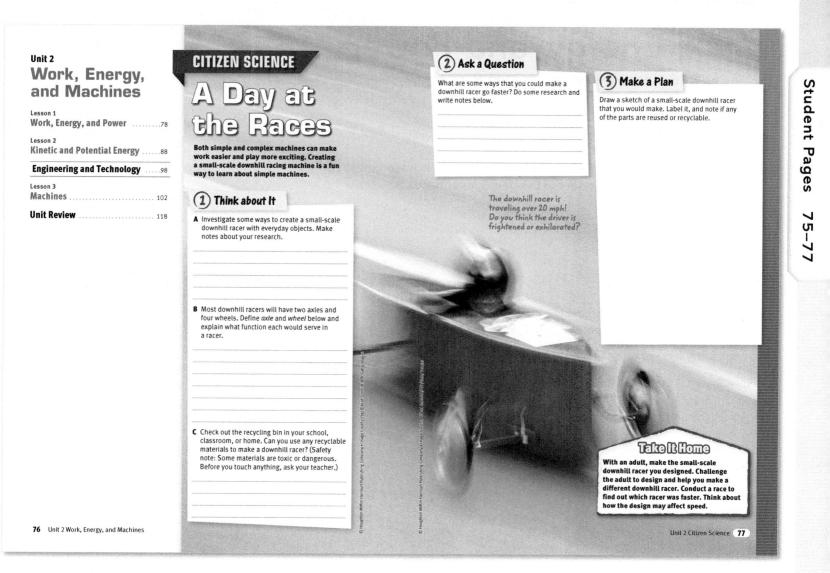

CITIZEN SCIENCE

A Day at the Races

Both simple and complex machines can make work easier and play more exciting. Creating a small-scale downhill racing machine is a fun way to learn about simple machines.

① Think about It

A Investigate some ways to create a small-scale downhill racer with everyday objects. Make notes about your research.

B Most downhill racers will have two axles and four wheels. Define *axle* and *wheel* below and explain what function each would serve in a racer.

C Check out the recycling bin in your school, classroom, or home. Can you use any recyclable materials to make a downhill racer? (Safety note: Some materials are toxic or dangerous. Before you touch anything, ask your teacher.)

② Ask a Question

What are some ways that you could make a downhill racer go faster? Do some research and write notes below.

③ Make a Plan

Draw a sketch of a small-scale downhill racer that you would make. Label it, and note if any of the parts are reused or recyclable.

The downhill racer is traveling over 20 mph! Do you think the driver is frightened or exhilarated?

Take It Home

With an adult, make the small-scale downhill racer you designed. Challenge the adult to design and help you make a different downhill racer. Conduct a race to find out which racer was faster. Think about how the design may affect speed.

76 Unit 2 Work, Energy, and Machines

Unit 2 Citizen Science 77

CITIZEN SCIENCE

Unit Project **A Day at the Races**

1. Think About It

Make sure students understand that a wheel is a circular device that can rotate on an axis. An axle is a shaft on which a pair of wheels revolves.

If students struggle with finding materials for a racer, share a basic plan for a racer with them. Encourage them to think about materials that could be used for each part of the racer.

2. Ask a Question

Discuss students' initial ideas as a class; this can provide support for students who are struggling.

3. Make a Plan

Students' sketches should present a racer that makes use of readily available everyday materials and objects and could reasonably be expected to operate. Plans should point out the materials that the student intends to use for each part of the racer.

Take It Home

Have students write two or three paragraphs evaluating the outcomes of the race and the designs of their racers. Encourage students to identify specific factors that affected speed, either positively or negatively. How would students redesign their racers if given the chance?

🖱 *Optional Online rubric: Written Pieces*

Work, Energy, and Power

Essential Question How is work related to energy?

Professional Development

For more detailed information about the topics in this lesson, refer to the Content Refresher in the Unit Opener pages.

Opening Your Lesson

Begin the lesson by assessing students' prerequisite and prior knowledge.

Prerequisite Knowledge

- Everyday definitions of work, energy, and power
- Understanding that moving an object requires effort

Accessing Prior Knowledge

Ask: What do the words *work, energy,* and *power* make you think of? Sample answers: work: homework, jobs, chores, sweating; energy: electricity, being tired, food; power: on and off switches, strength, authority

Ask: What is needed to move objects? Sample answers: You have to work to move objects; you must use energy; power is required. Force is also necessary.

Customize Your Opening

- [ ] **Accessing Prior Knowledge,** above
- [ ] **Print Path** Engage Your Brain, SE p. 79 #1–2
- [ ] **Print Path** Active Reading, SE p. 79 #3–4
- [ ] **Digital Path** Lesson Opener

Key Topics/Learning Goals	Supporting Concepts
Work 1 Define *work*. 2 Decide whether a force will do work or not, depending on the direction of motion of an object. 3 Calculate work given force and distance.	• Work is the use of force to move an object a distance. • Work is only done if the force or part of the force acts in the same direction as the motion of an object. • Work is force multiplied by distance. • Work is measured in either newton-meters (N•m) or joules (J).
Energy 1 Define *energy* in terms of work. 2 Explain that energy can be used to do work using many processes.	• Energy is the ability to do work. • Work transfers energy. • An example of energy transfer is wind turbines, which do work when they convert wind energy into electrical energy.
Power 1 Define *power*. 2 Calculate power given energy and time.	• Power is the rate at which work is done. It is also the rate at which energy is converted from one form to another. • Power equals energy divided by time. • Power is measured in watts (W). One watt is equal to one joule of work done in one second. It is also equal to one joule of energy transferred in one second.

Options for Instruction

Two parallel paths provide coverage of the Essential Questions, with a strong Inquiry strand woven into each. Follow the Print Path, the Digital Path, or your customized combination of print, digital, and inquiry.

Print Path
Teaching support for the Print Path appears with the Student Pages.

Inquiry Labs and Activities

Digital Path
Digital Path shortcut: TS696129

Print Path	Inquiry Labs and Activities	Digital Path
Work It Out, SE pp. 80–81 **What is work?** **How is work calculated?**	**S.T.E.M. Lab** Using Water to Do Work **Quick Lab** Investigating Work **Daily Demo** Working Model	**What is Work?** Interactive Images **Is Work Being Done?** Interactive Images
Energizing, SE pp. 82–83 **How are work and energy related?** • Energy Is the Ability to Do Work • Work Transfers Energy	**Activity** Input and Output **Activity** Work, Energy, Power Circle	**Calculate Work** Slideshow **What is Energy?** Slideshow
Superpower, SE pp. 84–85 **What is power?** **How is power calculated?**	**Quick Lab** Calculating Power **Activity** Calculation Practice **Activity** Organizer	**What is Power?** Video **Calculating Power** Interactive Images

Options for Assessment

See the Evaluate page for options, including Formative Assessment, Summative Assessment, and Unit Review.

Engage and Explore

Activities and Discussion

Activity *Input and Output*

Energy

👥 pairs
🕐 25 min
🔬 **GUIDED** inquiry

Have pairs of students analyze an everyday task, such as riding a bike, lifting a bag of groceries, or opening a door. Have the pair discuss how the activity transfers energy from one source to another. Then have students draw an Input/Output machine that illustrates how the activity transfers one type of energy into another type of energy. The input is the energy that is used for the activity, and the output is the energy that results from the activity.

Discussion *Misconceptions*

Introducing Key Topics

👥 whole class
🕐 20 min
🔬 **DIRECTED** inquiry

The concepts of work, energy, and power can be confusing to students. Discuss the following as you go through the lesson.

Work Ask students if they can determine how much work they have done if they throw a ball with a force of 50 newtons and it rolls 3 meters. If students answer yes, and that the work is 150 joules, they may believe that they are doing work on the ball even while it is rolling. Remind students that work is done only while a force is being applied to an object. For example, when you throw a ball, you are not doing work on the ball after it leaves your hand, because you are no longer applying a force.

Power The word *power* has multiple definitions. Ask students to write a few sentences using the word *power*. They will probably identify power with strength, rather than using the word as a rate. To help students think about the scientific definition of *power*, have them discuss the commercial versus the scientific use of the word. Ask what the company that supplies their electricity should be called—the energy company or the power company? Ask what the company delivers. energy or power; both are correct Tell students that electric meters in their homes measure how much energy, or power, is being delivered, measured in units called kilowatt hours (kWh).

Activity *Calculation Practice*

Synthesizing Key Topics

👥 pairs
🕐 20 min

Write out the formulas that can be used to calculate work, energy, and power on the board. Write the correct units for each calculation next to the corresponding formula. Then have students use the formulas to solve the following problems:

1 How much power is produced when a force of 4 newtons moves an object 20 meters in 50 seconds? 1.6 watts

2 How much force is required to move an object 10 meters if 20 joules of work is done? 2 newtons

3 How much work is done when a force of 20 newtons moves an object 100 meters? 2,000 joules

4 How much time does it take for 20 watts of power to produce 100 joules of work? 5 seconds

Activity *Organizer*

Synthesizing Key Topics

👥 individuals
🕐 ongoing
🔬 **GUIDED** inquiry

Have students create a grid, which they can use to organize information related to work, energy, and power. Students should use the grid to organize information about the three topics. Students might organize their grids in the following way:

Topic	Formula	Unit	Example
Work	W = Fd	joule (J)	It takes 1 joule of work to move 1 newton 1 meter.
Energy			
Power			

Customize Your Labs

📄 *See the Lab Manual for lab datasheets.*

🌐 *Go Online for editable lab datasheets.*

(b)©HMH; (t)©PhotoDisc/Getty Images

Levels of (Inquiry)

DIRECTED inquiry	GUIDED inquiry	INDEPENDENT inquiry
introduces inquiry skills within a structured framework.	develops inquiry skills within a supportive environment.	deepens inquiry skills with student-driven questions or procedures.

Labs and Demos

Daily Demo *Working Model*

Engage

Synthesizing Key Topics

👥 whole class
🕐 25 min
🔬 GUIDED inquiry

Use this short demo after you have discussed how to calculate work, energy, and power.

PURPOSE **To demonstrate work and power**

MATERIALS

- **medium-sized apple**
- **meterstick**

1 Point out to students that the concepts of this lesson can be confusing, but it helps if you can see a simple example.

2 Remind students that 1 joule of work is done when a force of 1 newton moves an object 1 meter. Hold up the apple, and tell students that an apple weighs about 1 newton. Hold a meterstick upright with one end on the floor. Set the apple down next to the meterstick. Lift the apple until it is at the top of the meterstick. Ask: How much work was done? 1 joule

3 Move the meterstick to the desk top and have a student lift the apple from the floor to the top of the stick. Ask: How much work was done? if the desk is 1 meter tall, 2 joules

4 Write the formula for calculating work, *W = Fd,* on the board. Below it, write a number sentence to model the demonstration: 1 joule equals 1 newton multiplied by 1 meter.

5 **Synthesizing** How many joules of work would be done if we lifted the apple 3 meters? 3 joules What if we wanted to lift 2 apples 1 meter? Two joules of work would be done.

🔬 **INDEPENDENT inquiry variation**

Have students use the same materials, but have them time how long it takes to lift the apple one meter. Have students use this information to calculate how much power (in watts) is produced by lifting the apple one meter in a given period of time.

🌐 📋 Quick Lab *Investigating Work*

PURPOSE **To investigate how much work students do**

See the Lab Manual or go Online for planning information.

🌐 📋 Quick Lab *Calculating Power*

PURPOSE **To investigate and calculate power needed**

See the Lab Manual or go Online for planning information.

🌐 📋 S.T.E.M. Lab *Using Water to Do Work*

Synthesizing Key Topics

👥 small groups
🕐 45 min
🔬 DIRECTED or GUIDED inquiry

Students construct and use a simple waterwheel.

PURPOSE **To investigate and calculate work and power**

MATERIALS

- **2-liter bottle with cap**
- **dowel, ¼ inch diameter**
- **funnel**
- **index cards, 8**
- **marker**
- **meterstick**
- **pitcher**
- **scissors**
- **stopwatch**
- **string, 1 meter**
- **tape**
- **water**
- **weight, 50g**
- **lab aprons**

Activities and Discussion

☐ **Activity** Input and Output

☐ **Discussion** Misconceptions

☐ **Activity** Calculation Practice

☐ **Activity** Organizer

Labs and Demos

☐ **Daily Demo** Working Model

☐ **Quick Lab** Investigating Work

☐ **Quick Lab** Calculating Power

☐ **S.T.E.M. Lab** Using Water to Do Work

Your Resources

Explain Science Concepts

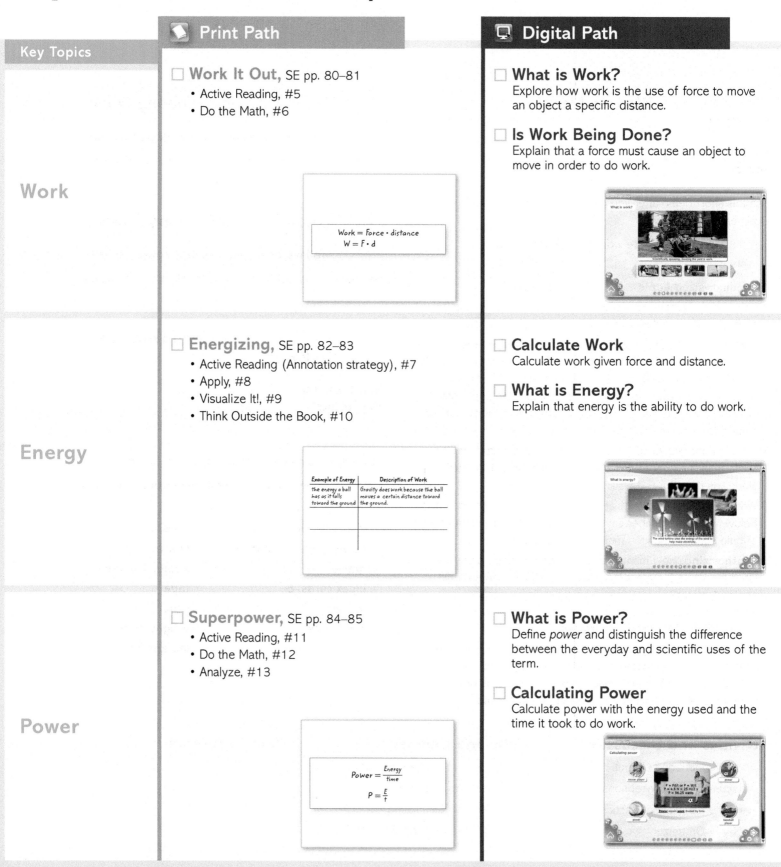

Key Topics	📖 Print Path	🖥 Digital Path
Work	☐ **Work It Out,** SE pp. 80–81 • Active Reading, #5 • Do the Math, #6 Work = force · distance W = F · d	☐ **What is Work?** Explore how work is the use of force to move an object a specific distance. ☐ **Is Work Being Done?** Explain that a force must cause an object to move in order to do work.
Energy	☐ **Energizing,** SE pp. 82–83 • Active Reading (Annotation strategy), #7 • Apply, #8 • Visualize It!, #9 • Think Outside the Book, #10	☐ **Calculate Work** Calculate work given force and distance. ☐ **What is Energy?** Explain that energy is the ability to do work.
Power	☐ **Superpower,** SE pp. 84–85 • Active Reading, #11 • Do the Math, #12 • Analyze, #13 Power = Energy / time P = E / t	☐ **What is Power?** Define *power* and distinguish the difference between the everyday and scientific uses of the term. ☐ **Calculating Power** Calculate power with the energy used and the time it took to do work.

Differentiated Instruction

Basic *Main Idea Web*

Synthesizing Key Topics

👥 individuals
🕐 ongoing

Remind students that the headings throughout a lesson often highlight the main ideas of the lesson. Encourage them to fill out a Main Idea Web with the lesson's headings and to add notes to the web to clarify their ideas. This method is similar to making an outline of the major concepts in the lesson. Summarizing important details in this way will help students learn by organizing new material.

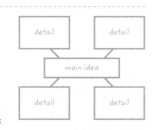

🌐 *Optional Online resource: Main Idea Web support*

Advanced *Moon Effect*

Work

👥 individuals
🕐 20 min

Challenge students to compare the amount of work done while lifting a notebook on Earth to the same task done on the moon. Students can conduct research about the moon to find that the force of gravity (and so the force needed to lift the book) is one-sixth of that on Earth. Since the weight of the notebook on the moon is one-sixth of its weight on Earth, one-sixth of the amount of work would be done when lifting the notebook on the moon.

ELL *Combination Notes*

Synthesizing Key Topics

👥 pairs
🕐 20 min

Have students make combination notes, one for each topic in the lesson—work, energy, and power. Students should write the term across the top. In the left column, students should write definitions and examples, and on the right side, they should make drawings or write equations to help them organize their thoughts.

Lesson Vocabulary

work   energy   power

Previewing Vocabulary

👥 whole class
🕐 15 min

Everyday Language vs. Scientific Meaning Terms in this lesson are often used in everyday language, but their scientific meanings are different. Share the following with students:

- The everyday meaning of *work* is "something you do or a place you go for your job." The scientific meaning of *work* is "the use of force to move an object some distance."
- The everyday meaning of *energy* is "the capacity for activity." The scientific meaning is "the ability to do work."
- The everyday meaning of *power* is "strength or authority." The scientific meaning is "the rate at which work is done."

Reinforcing Vocabulary

👥 individuals
🕐 ongoing

Word Triangle Have students complete Word Triangles for each new term. To make a Word Triangle, have students draw a triangle and split it into three sections. In the bottom third, students will write the term and its definition; in the middle third, students will write a sentence using the term; and in the top third, students will draw an illustration of the term.

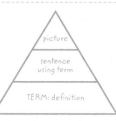

Customize Your Core Lesson

Core Instruction
☐ **Print Path** choices
☐ **Digital Path** choices

Vocabulary
☐ **Previewing Vocabulary**
Everyday Language vs. Scientific Meaning

Your Resources

☐ **Reinforcing Vocabulary**
Word Triangle

Differentiated Instruction
☐ **Basic** Main Idea Web
☐ **Advanced** Moon Effect
☐ **ELL** Combination Notes

Extend Science Concepts

Reinforce and Review

Activity *Work, Energy, Power Circle*

Synthesizing Key Topics

👥 whole class
🕐 30 min

Inside/Outside Circles

1 Pass out questions on index cards to students. Students write the answers on the back of their cards. Check students' answers, and have students adjust incorrect answers.

2 Have students pair up and form two circles. One partner is in an inside circle facing out, and the other is in an outside circle facing in.

3 Each student in the inside circle asks his or her partner a question. The partner answers. If the answer is incorrect, the student in the inside circle teaches the other student the correct answer. Repeat this step with the students in the outside circle asking the questions.

4 Have each student on the outside circle rotate one person to the right. He or she faces a new partner and gets a new question. Students rotate after each pair of questions.

Sample Questions

• What is the formula for calculating work? *W = Fd*
• What unit do we use for work? joules or newton-meters
• Fill in the blank: Work is the use of force to _____ an object. move
• What type of energy do wind turbines convert wind energy into? electrical
• Fill in the blank: Power is calculated by dividing energy by _____. time
• What unit do we use for power? watts or kilowatts

Layered Book FoldNote

Synthesizing Key Topics

👥 individuals
🕐 ongoing

Layered Book Have students create a Layered Book to cover the three key topic areas—Work, Energy, and Power. As students read each lesson, have them use the Layered Book to take notes.

🌐 *Online resource: Layered Book*

Going Further

Engineering Connection

Energy

👥 pairs or individuals
🕐 30 min

Design The first hill of a typical gravity-powered roller coaster is always the highest. A roller-coaster car has maximum potential energy and minimum kinetic energy at the top of the first hill. This potential energy changes to kinetic energy when the car begins to move downhill. Because some energy is lost to friction, the car could not climb the second hill if it were as high as the first hill. Each hill must be lower than the previous hill. Have students design a roller coaster illustrating this rule of engineering and label their designs with information about work, energy, and power.

Life Science Connection

Synthesizing Key Topics

👥 pairs or individuals
🕐 25 min

Illustrate Organisms are continually transforming energy from one type to another. A plant transforms electromagnetic energy (light) to chemical energy (sugar). Chemical energy fuels muscles, which can transform the chemical energy to mechanical energy. Shivering converts chemical energy to thermal energy. Have students research an example of energy being transferred between or within organisms. Encourage them to create a poster illustrating how energy is transferred in their example.

Customize Your Closing

📓 *See the Assessment Guide for quizzes and tests.*

🌐 *Go Online to edit and create quizzes and tests.*

Reinforce and Review

☐ **Activity** Work, Energy, Power Circle
☐ **FoldNote** Layered Book
☐ **Print Path** Visual Summary, SE p. 86
☐ **Print Path** Lesson Review, SE p. 87
☐ **Digital Path** Lesson Closer

Evaluate Student Mastery

See the teacher support below the Student Pages for additional Formative Assessment questions.

Have students create and then solve a math word problem that incorporates the lesson topics and uses formulas from the lesson. Sample question: Zach pulls a suitcase that weighs 100 newtons for 200 meters. It takes him 400 seconds to do this. How much work did Zach do, and how much power was required? Answer: 20,000 joules of work were done; 50 watts of power were required.

Reteach

Formative assessment may show that students need reinforcement for certain topics. The resources below are recommended for reteaching. If students were introduced to a topic through the Print Path, you can also use the Digital Path to reteach, or vice versa.
Can be assigned to individual students

Work
Daily Demo Working Model
S.T.E.M. Lab Using Water to Do Work

Energy
Activity Input and Output

Power
Activity Calculation Practice
Activity Organizer

Alternative Assessment
Using Energy

Online resources: student worksheet, optional rubrics

Work, Energy, and Power

Climb the Pyramid: *Using Energy*

1. Work on your own, with a partner, or with a small group.
2. Choose one item from each layer of the pyramid. Check your choices.
3. Have your teacher approve your plan.
4. Submit or present your results.

__ Concept Map
Create a concept map that shows how work, energy, and power are related. Make sure that your concept map includes data for force, distance, work, and power. Include information on how energy is transferred.

__ Figure It Out!	**__ Quiz**
Three students pull an object over a distance. Student 1 does 200 joules of work in 5 seconds; student 2 does 250 joules of work in 8 seconds; and student 3 does 300 joules of work in 10 seconds. Figure out the power exerted by each student.	Write a quiz for your class. Make sure your questions are not too complex. Be sure your quiz includes the following topics: work, energy, power, force, newtons, joules, watts, energy transfer, and formulas.

__ History in Science	**__ Concentration Cards**	**__ Chart**
Watt, Joule, and Newton were physical scientists. Research two of these scientists or two others who contributed to what we now know about work, energy, and power. Explain what you learned in a report or poster.	Design a concentration game to test knowledge of work, energy, and power. Then write two related pieces of information onto two cards— topic on one card; detail, information, or formula on another. Make at least 10 cards, and play concentration!	Imagine you are training for a marathon. Pretend you weigh 540 newtons; keep an imaginary training record. Record how far you ran (in meters) and your time (in seconds) for several sessions. Discuss your progress in term of joules and watts.

Going Further
☐ Engineering Connection
☐ Life Science Connection

Formative Assessment
☐ **Strategies** Throughout TE
☐ **Lesson Review** SE

Summative Assessment
☐ **Alternative Assessment** Using Energy
☐ **Lesson Quiz**
☐ **Unit Tests** A and B
☐ **Unit Review** SE End-of-Unit

Your Resources

_____   _____

_____   _____

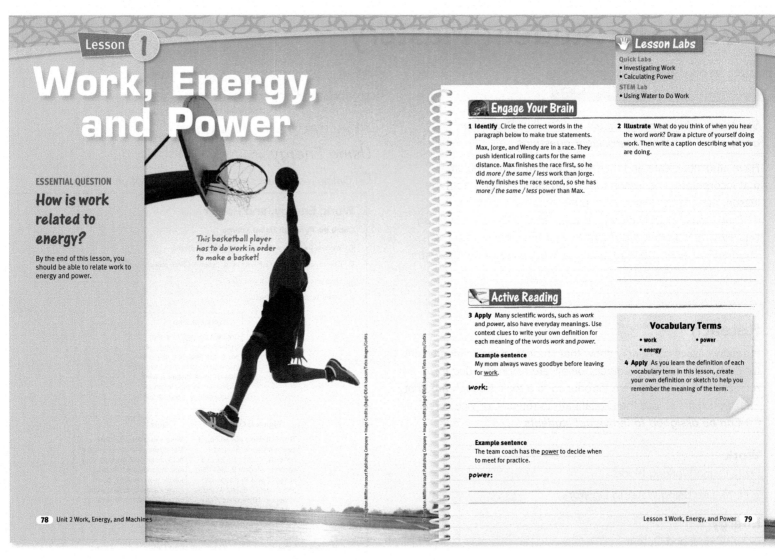

Lesson ①

Work, Energy, and Power

ESSENTIAL QUESTION

How is work related to energy?

By the end of this lesson, you should be able to relate work to energy and power.

This basketball player has to do work in order to make a basket!

78 Unit 2 Work, Energy, and Machines

✋ Lesson Labs

Quick Labs
• Investigating Work
• Calculating Power

STEM Lab
• Using Water to Do Work

🧠 Engage Your Brain

1 Identify Circle the correct words in the paragraph below to make true statements.

Max, Jorge, and Wendy are in a race. They push identical rolling carts for the same distance. Max finishes the race first, so he did *more / the same / less* work than Jorge. Wendy finishes the race second, so she has *more / the same / less* power than Max.

2 Illustrate What do you think of when you hear the word *work*? Draw a picture of yourself doing work. Then write a caption describing what you are doing.

📖 Active Reading

3 Apply Many scientific words, such as *work* and *power*, also have everyday meanings. Use context clues to write your own definition for each meaning of the words *work* and *power*.

Example sentence
My mom always waves goodbye before leaving for work.

work: _____

Example sentence
The team coach has the power to decide when to meet for practice.

power: _____

Vocabulary Terms

• work   • power
• energy

4 Apply As you learn the definition of each vocabulary term in this lesson, create your own definition or sketch to help you remember the meaning of the term.

Lesson 1 Work, Energy, and Power 79

Answers

Answers for 1–3 should represent students' current thoughts, even if incorrect.

1. more; less

2. Students should draw themselves doing work; captions should accurately describe the drawing.

3. Sample answers: a place where adults spend the day in order to make money; the ability to enforce decisions

4. Students should define or sketch each vocabulary term in the lesson.

Opening Your Lesson

Discuss student responses to the Engage Your Brain items to assess their prerequisite knowledge and to estimate what they already know about the key topics.

Prerequisites Students should already be familiar with the concept that forces act on objects and that an object's speed or direction changes as forces change.

Use the strategy below to assess students' prior knowledge about work, energy, and power.

Accessing Prior Knowledge To assess students' prior knowledge about work, energy, and power, you may wish to have them conduct a Textbook DRTA. Begin by explaining to students that *DRTA* stands for "directed reading/thinking activity." To complete a DRTA, tell students to 1) preview the selection, 2) write what they know, what they think they know, and what they think they'll learn about work, energy, and power, 3) read the selection, and 4) write what they learned. Discuss whether students' expectations were reasonable and whether they learned additional information that they did not anticipate.

🔘 *Optional Online resource: Textbook DRTA*

Work It Out

What is work?

What comes to mind when you think of work? Most people say they are working when they do anything that requires a physical or mental effort. But in physical science, **work** is the use of force to move an object some distance in the direction of the force. In scientific terms, you do work only when you exert a force on an object and move it. If you want to do work, you have to use force to move something.

Work is done only by the part of the force that is in the same direction as the motion. Imagine that you pull a sled through the snow. You pull the rope up at an angle while you pull the sled forward. Only the part of your force pulling the sled forward is doing work. The upward part of your force is not doing work, because the sled is not moving upward.

Active Reading 5 **Summarize** How does the scientific definition of work differ from the familiar definition?

_____

_____

How is work calculated?

Work is a measure of how much force is applied to move an object through a certain distance. You can calculate the work a force does if you know the size of the force applied to an object and the distance through which the force acts. The distance involved is the distance the object moved. You can calculate work using the following formula:

$$work = force \times distance$$
$$W = F \times d$$

Force can be expressed in newtons, and distance can be expressed in meters. When you multiply a force in newtons by a distance in meters, the product is a unit called the *newton-meter* (N·m), or the *joule*. The joule (J) is the standard unit used to express work. One joule of work is done when a force of one newton moves an object one meter. To get an idea of how much a joule of work is, lift an apple (which weighs about one newton) from your foot to your waist (about one meter).

80   Unit 2 Work, Energy, and Machines

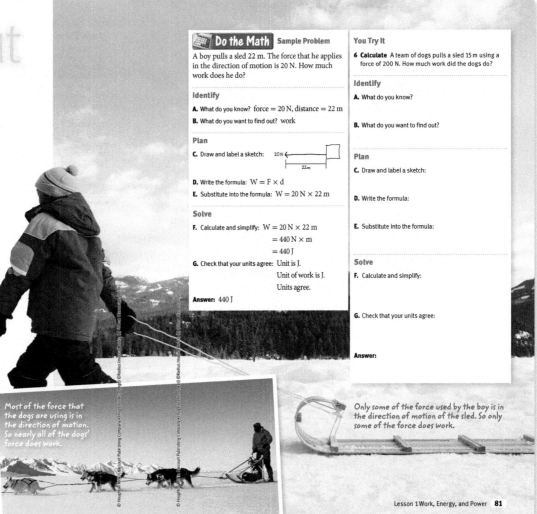

Do the Math   Sample Problem

A boy pulls a sled 22 m. The force that he applies in the direction of motion is 20 N. How much work does he do?

Identify

A. What do you know? force = 20 N, distance = 22 m

B. What do you want to find out? work

Plan

C. Draw and label a sketch: 20N

D. Write the formula: W = F × d

E. Substitute into the formula: W = 20 N × 22 m

Solve

F. Calculate and simplify: W = 20 N × 22 m
= 440 N × m
= 440 J

G. Check that your units agree: Unit is J.
Unit of work is J.
Units agree.

Answer: 440 J

You Try It

6 **Calculate** A team of dogs pulls a sled 15 m using a force of 200 N. How much work did the dogs do?

Identify

A. What do you know?

B. What do you want to find out?

Plan

C. Draw and label a sketch:

D. Write the formula:

E. Substitute into the formula:

Solve

F. Calculate and simplify:

G. Check that your units agree:

Answer:

Most of the force that the dogs are using is in the direction of motion. So nearly all of the dogs' force does work.

Only some of the force used by the boy is in the direction of motion of the sled. So only some of the force does work.

Lesson 1 Work, Energy, and Power   81

Answers

5. The scientific definition requires that force be used to move an object. The familiar definition doesn't require motion.

6. A. force = 200 N, distance = 15 m;
B. work;
C. sketches should show and label the correct force and distance;
D. W = F·d;
E. W = 200 N·15 m;
F. W = 200 N·15 m = 3,000 N·m = 3,000 J; G. Unit is J. Unit of work is J. Units agree.

Learning Alert 🚧 MISCONCEPTION 🚧

Work versus Movement Remind students that work is done only while a force is being applied to an object and the object is moving. For example, when you throw a flying disk, you are not doing work after the flying disk leaves your hand; force is no longer being applied. **Ask:** When does a person do work while skateboarding? A skateboarder does work while he or she is pushing on the ground with his or her foot.

Building Math Skills

Remind students that the formula for calculating work is $W = Fd$. Often word problems provide force and distance and ask the student to figure out how much work was done, but sometimes a problem gives the amount of work done plus another factor, and students must determine the value of the missing factor. **Ask:** How could you rewrite $W = Fd$ to help you figure out force and distance? for force: $F = W/d$; for distance: $d = W/F$

Formative Assessment

Ask: If you push very hard on an object but it does not move, have you done work? Explain. No; the object must move for work to be done. **Ask:** What two factors do you need to know to calculate how much work was done in any situation? force and distance

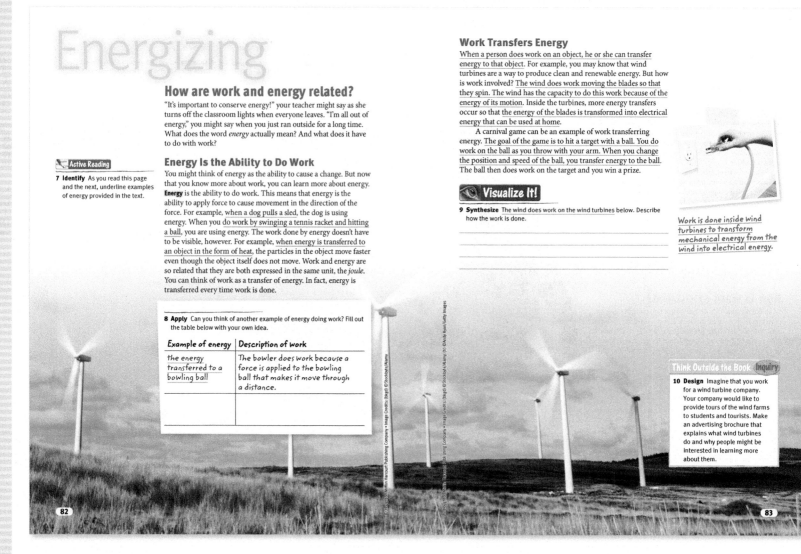

Energizing

How are work and energy related?

"It's important to conserve energy!" your teacher might say as she turns off the classroom lights when everyone leaves. "I'm all out of energy," you might say when you just ran outside for a long time. What does the word *energy* actually mean? And what does it have to do with work?

Active Reading

7 Identify As you read this page and the next, underline examples of energy provided in the text.

Energy Is the Ability to Do Work

You might think of energy as the ability to cause a change. But now that you know more about work, you can learn more about energy. **Energy** is the ability to do work. This means that energy is the ability to apply force to cause movement in the direction of the force. For example, when a dog pulls a sled, the dog is using energy. When you do work by swinging a tennis racket and hitting a ball, you are using energy. The work done by energy doesn't have to be visible, however. For example, when energy is transferred to an object in the form of heat, the particles in the object move faster even though the object itself does not move. Work and energy are so related that they are both expressed in the same unit, the *joule*. You can think of work as a transfer of energy. In fact, energy is transferred every time work is done.

8 Apply Can you think of another example of energy doing work? Fill out the table below with your own idea.

Example of energy	Description of work
the energy transferred to a bowling ball	The bowler does work because a force is applied to the bowling ball that makes it move through a distance.

Work Transfers Energy

When a person does work on an object, he or she can transfer energy to that object. For example, you may know that wind turbines are a way to produce clean and renewable energy. But how is work involved? The wind does work moving the blades so that they spin. The wind has the capacity to do this work because of the energy of its motion. Inside the turbines, more energy transfers occur so that the energy of the blades is transformed into electrical energy that can be used at home.

A carnival game can be an example of work transferring energy. The goal of the game is to hit a target with a ball. You do work on the ball as you throw with your arm. When you change the position and speed of the ball, you transfer energy to the ball. The ball then does work on the target and you win a prize.

Visualize It!

9 Synthesize The wind does work on the wind turbines below. Describe how the work is done.

_____

_____

_____

Work is done inside wind turbines to transform mechanical energy from the wind into electrical energy.

Think Outside the Book · Inquiry

10 Design Imagine that you work for a wind turbine company. Your company would like to provide tours of the wind farms to students and tourists. Make an advertising brochure that explains what wind turbines do and why people might be interested in learning more about them.

82 / 83

Answers

7. *See students' pages for annotations.*

8. Sample answer: Example of energy: the energy you use to lift a bag of groceries, Description of work: You do work because the bag moves in the direction of the force.

9. The work occurs when the blades of the wind turbine turn. The force comes from the wind and occurs when the blades accelerate. The distance is the amount that the blades move.

10. Students' brochures will vary, but should indicate an understanding that wind turbines use wind energy to generate electricity. Students should include that people may be interested in the benefits of wind energy but concerned about noise pollution and possible harm to flying animals.

Building Reading Skills

Main Idea and Detail Notes Tell students that periodically stopping as they read so they can take notes on the main ideas and details of a section is a good strategy for remembering important information. Have students reread the section on energy and take notes on the ideas they think are the most important. Ask students to share some notes they took on the section. Sample responses: Energy is related to work; energy is the ability to cause a change; energy can change from one form to another; energy changes when work is done.

Formative Assessment

Ask: What is the relationship between work and energy? When work is done, energy is transferred; an object must move for work to be done. **Ask:** When one form of energy changes into one or more other forms of energy, what happens to the total amount of energy? The total amount of energy stays the same.

Superpower

A crane's power depends on how quickly it lifts a crate.

What is power?

The word *power* has different common meanings. It is used to mean a source of energy, as in a power plant, or strength, as in a powerful engine. When you talk about a powerful swimmer, for example, you would probably say that the swimmer is very strong or very fast. However, if you use the scientific definition of power, you would instead say that a powerful swimmer is one who does the work of moving herself through the water in a short time.

Power is the rate at which work is done. For example, when two cranes lift the same crate the same height, they do the same amount of work. The one that lifts the crate the fastest is the more powerful crane. Because work is also a measure of energy transfer, you can also think of power as the rate at which energy is converted from one form to another.

How is power calculated?

Because power is a measure of how much energy is transferred in a given time, power can be calculated from energy and time. Sometimes you know that energy is being transferred, but you cannot directly measure the work being done. For example, you know that a TV uses energy. But there is no way to measure all of the work that every part of the TV does. To calculate the TV's power, divide the amount of energy used by the time it is used.

$$power = \frac{energy}{time}$$

$$P = \frac{E}{t}$$

Remember that energy is expressed in joules. So power is often expressed in joules per second. One joule of energy transferred in one second is equal to one *watt* (W). The watt is the unit of measurement for power. You have probably heard the term *watt* used in connection with light bulbs. A 60-watt light bulb requires 60 joules of energy every second to shine at its rated brightness.

 Active Reading

11 Apply What two things would you need to know to calculate the power of a microwave oven?

This is an incandescent light bulb.

Do the Math   Sample Problem

Here's an example of how to find the power used by an incandescent light bulb. A light bulb uses 600 J of energy in 6 s. What is the power of the light bulb?

To calculate power, divide energy by time.

$$P = \frac{E}{t}$$

$$P = \frac{600\ J}{6\ s}$$

$$P = \frac{100\ J}{s}$$

Unit is J/s. Unit for power is W, which is also J/s. Units agree.

$$P = 100\ W$$

You Try It

12 Calculate A compact fluorescent light bulb, called a CFL, is advertised as being just as bright as an incandescent 100 W light bulb but using less energy. The CFL uses only 156 J of energy in 6 s. What is the power of this CFL bulb?

13 Analyze Why might someone buy a more expensive CFL instead of an incandescent light bulb?

A compact fluorescent light bulb uses less energy each second than an equally bright incandescent light bulb.

Answers

11. the energy it uses and the time it uses that energy in

12. $P = \frac{E}{t}$

    $P = \frac{156\ J}{6\ s}$

    $P = 26\ W$

13. Sample answer: Since the CFL uses less power, you will pay less money in your electric bill, so the more expensive bulb will eventually save you money. Also, because the CFL lasts longer, you will buy replacement bulbs less often.

Building Math Skills

Point out to students that the kilowatt is a unit used to measure power. A kilowatt is equal to 1,000 watts. **Ask:** Which other units do you know that have a similar relationship? Sample answers: meter/kilometer; gram/kilogram; liter/kiloliter **Ask:** What makes the metric system easy to use? Sample answer: Converting between units is much simpler because you only have to multiply or divide by a multiple of ten.

Learning Alert

Power as a Rate Students can sometimes have difficulty with the concept that power is a rate. To emphasize this idea, discuss the following scenario: Encourage students to imagine that they are being paid to lift bricks onto a cart. How much they are paid depends on how many bricks they lift onto the cart in one hour. Ask students to discuss what power has to do with maximizing their earnings. Sample answer: If I lift 200 bricks onto the cart in one hour, I will be paid twice as much as if I lift 100 bricks. I will have to use more power to lift more bricks in the same amount of time. The more power I use, the more money I can earn.

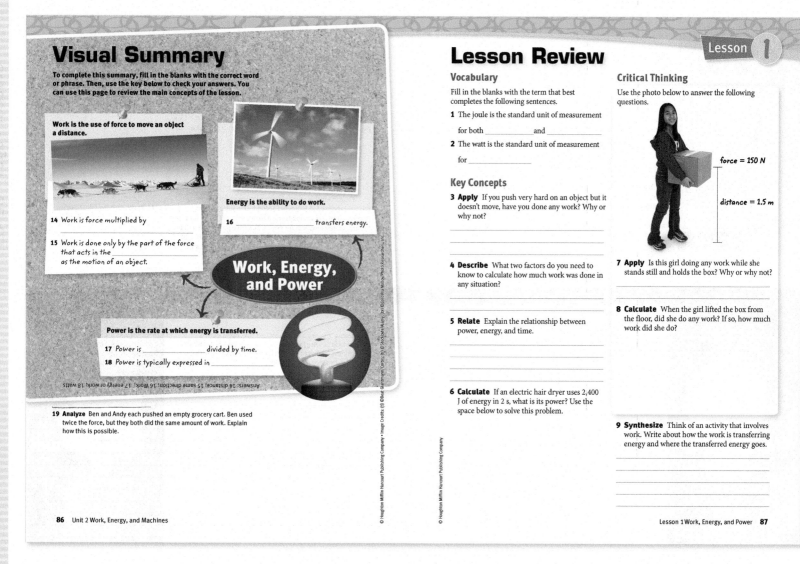

Visual Summary

To complete this summary, fill in the blanks with the correct word or phrase. Then, use the key below to check your answers. You can use this page to review the main concepts of the lesson.

Work is the use of force to move an object a distance.

14 Work is force multiplied by _____

15 Work is done only by the part of the force that acts in the _____ as the motion of an object.

Work, Energy, and Power

Energy is the ability to do work.

16 _____ transfers energy.

Power is the rate at which energy is transferred.

17 Power is _____ divided by time.

18 Power is typically expressed in _____

Answers: 14 distance; 15 same direction; 16 Work; 17 energy or work; 18 watts

19 Analyze Ben and Andy each pushed an empty grocery cart. Ben used twice the force, but they both did the same amount of work. Explain how this is possible.

86   Unit 2 Work, Energy, and Machines

Lesson Review   Lesson ①

Vocabulary

Fill in the blanks with the term that best completes the following sentences.

1 The joule is the standard unit of measurement for both _____ and _____

2 The watt is the standard unit of measurement for _____

Key Concepts

3 Apply If you push very hard on an object but it doesn't move, have you done any work? Why or why not?

4 Describe What two factors do you need to know to calculate how much work was done in any situation?

5 Relate Explain the relationship between power, energy, and time.

6 Calculate If an electric hair dryer uses 2,400 J of energy in 2 s, what is its power? Use the space below to solve this problem.

Critical Thinking

Use the photo below to answer the following questions.

force = 150 N

distance = 1.5 m

7 Apply Is this girl doing any work while she stands still and holds the box? Why or why not?

8 Calculate When the girl lifted the box from the floor, did she do any work? If so, how much work did she do?

9 Synthesize Think of an activity that involves work. Write about how the work is transferring energy and where the transferred energy goes.

Lesson 1 Work, Energy, and Power   87

Visual Summary Answers

14. distance
15. same direction
16. Work
17. energy
18. watts
19. If Ben used twice the force but did the same amount of work, then he must have gone half the distance that Andy went.

Lesson Review Answers

1. work; energy
2. power
3. No, you haven't done any work because the object has not moved a distance.
4. force and distance
5. Power can be calculated from energy and time.
6. $P = \frac{E}{t}$

   $P = \frac{2,400\ J}{2\ s}$

   $P = 1,200\ W$
7. No, she is not doing work on the box because the box has not moved a distance while she is just holding it.

8. Yes, the girl did work on the box when she lifted it because she moved the box a distance of 1.5 m. $W = F \cdot d = 150\ N \cdot 1.5\ m = 225\ J$

9. Sample answer: Moving a violin bow requires work. The work transfers my arm's energy into the bow, which then transfers energy to the violin strings.

Kinetic and Potential Energy

Essential Question What are kinetic and potential energy?

Professional Development

For more detailed information about the topics in this lesson, refer to the Content Refresher in the Unit Opener pages.

Opening Your Lesson

Begin the lesson by assessing students' prerequisite and prior knowledge.

Prerequisite Knowledge

- A general understanding of how energy can be transferred from one object or system to another

Accessing Prior Knowledge

Invite students to make a tri-fold FoldNote KWL chart about kinetic and potential energy. Students put what they know in the first column and what they want to know in the second column. After they finish the lesson, they complete the third column.

🌐 *Online resource, TriFold and KWL support*

Customize Your Opening

- ☐ **Accessing Prior Knowledge,** above
- ☐ **Print Path** Engage Your Brain, SE p. 89
- ☐ **Print Path** Active Reading, SE p. 89
- ☐ **Digital Path** Lesson Opener

Key Topics/Learning Goals

Kinetic Energy

1 Provide examples of kinetic energy.
2 Calculate an object's kinetic energy given its mass and speed.

Potential Energy

1 Provide examples of potential energy.
2 Calculate an object's gravitational potential energy given its mass and its height from the ground.

Mechanical Energy

1 Calculate an object's mechanical energy.

Supporting Concepts

- Kinetic energy is the energy of motion.
- Kinetic energy increases as mass increases. Kinetic energy increases as speed increases.
- The kinetic energy of a moving object can be calculated using the equation $KE = (\frac{1}{2})mv^2$

- Potential energy is stored energy due to an object's position, condition, or chemical composition.
- An example of chemical potential energy is the energy stored in the bonds of sugar molecules that make up carbohydrates.
- Examples of potential energy due to position, or mechanical potential energy, are the energy of a book up on a shelf and the energy of a stretched rubber band.
- Gravitational potential energy can be calculated using the equation $GPE = mgh$, where g is acceleration due to gravity, and h is the height of the object from the ground.

- Mechanical energy is kinetic energy plus potential energy due to position.
- Mechanical energy can be calculated by using the equation $ME = KE + PE$.
- If an object's only mechanical potential energy is due to gravitational potential energy, then the equation for its mechanical energy is $ME = (\frac{1}{2})mv^2 + mgh$.

Options for Instruction

Two parallel paths provide coverage of the Essential Questions, with a strong **Inquiry** strand woven into each.
Follow the **Print Path,** the **Digital Path,** or your customized combination of print, digital, and inquiry.

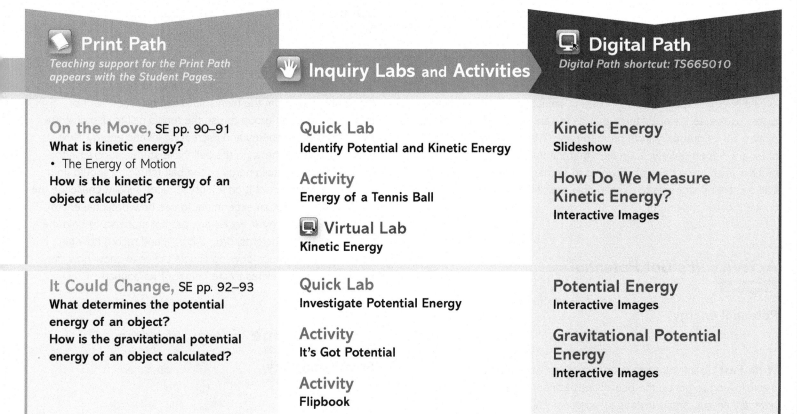

Print Path
Teaching support for the Print Path appears with the Student Pages.

Inquiry Labs and Activities

Digital Path
Digital Path shortcut: TS665010

On the Move, SE pp. 90–91
What is kinetic energy?
• The Energy of Motion
How is the kinetic energy of an object calculated?

Quick Lab
Identify Potential and Kinetic Energy

Activity
Energy of a Tennis Ball

Virtual Lab
Kinetic Energy

Kinetic Energy
Slideshow

How Do We Measure Kinetic Energy?
Interactive Images

It Could Change, SE pp. 92–93
What determines the potential energy of an object?
How is the gravitational potential energy of an object calculated?

Quick Lab
Investigate Potential Energy

Activity
It's Got Potential

Activity
Flipbook

Activity
Inside/Outside Circles

Potential Energy
Interactive Images

Gravitational Potential Energy
Interactive Images

It All Adds Up!, SE pp. 94–95
How is the mechanical energy of an object calculated?

Exploration Lab
Mechanical Energy

Daily Demo
Roller Coaster Ride

Mechanical Energy
Video

Energy of a Dive
Interactive Images

Options for Assessment

See the Evaluate page for options, including Formative Assessment, Summative Assessment, and Unit Review.

Engage and Explore

Activities and Discussion

Activity *Flipbook*

Engage ⟩

Kinetic Energy

👥 individuals
🕐 20 min
ⓘⁿᑫᵘⁱʳʸ **GUIDED** inquiry

Have students create a flipbook illustrating an object or organism with kinetic energy. Explain that a flipbook is similar to animation because it also uses a series of pictures that create an illusion of motion. Each picture varies gradually from page to page. When the pages of the book are flipped quickly, it appears that the images are in continuous motion. Encourage pairs of students to exchange their flipbooks. Call on several students to explain how their flipbooks illustrate the concept of kinetic energy.

Activity *It's Got Potential*

Engage ⟩

Potential Energy

👥 whole class
🕐 10 min
ⓘⁿᑫᵘⁱʳʸ **DIRECTED** inquiry

Write Fast To introduce the concept of potential energy, write the following terms on the board: *chemical potential energy*, *elastic potential energy*, and *gravitational potential energy*. Have students preview the text to learn about each of these types of potential energy, and then have students write the three terms across the top of a sheet of paper. Then, tell students that they have two minutes to make a list under each term of objects or substances with that type of potential energy. After the two minutes are up, call on volunteers to share some of the entries from their lists with the class. Discuss each example, and have students revise their lists if necessary.

Activity *Energy of a Tennis Ball*

Synthesizing Key Topics

👥 small groups
🕐 15 min
ⓘⁿᑫᵘⁱʳʸ **GUIDED** inquiry

Give each group of students a tennis ball. First, instruct students that in the classroom the tennis balls can be rolled but not thrown. Invite each group to use the tennis ball to demonstrate *increasing* kinetic energy and *decreasing* kinetic energy. Next, without rolling or throwing the ball, have students *increase* the gravitational potential energy of the ball (students should hold the ball up high, or set it on a high surface). Finally, challenge the groups to carry out an experiment to see how potential energy affects kinetic energy. If necessary, prompt students to hold the ball from different heights, drop the ball, and record how high it bounces. Have groups develop simple tables to show how the height of the ball relates to the height of its bounce.

Take It Home *Energy at Home*

Synthesizing Key Topics

👥 adult-student pairs
🕐 ongoing
ⓘⁿᑫᵘⁱʳʸ **GUIDED** inquiry

Direct students to work with adults to find examples of potential and kinetic energy in their homes and around their neighborhood. Students should record their observations in their charts. Students can compare their charts with others' in the class.

🌐 *Optional Online resource, student worksheet*

(r) ©Chase Jarvis/Corbis; (l) ©Artville/Getty Images

Customize Your Labs

📄 *See the Lab Manual for lab datasheets.*

🌐 *Go Online for editable lab datasheets.*

Levels of **Inquiry**

DIRECTED inquiry	**GUIDED** inquiry	**INDEPENDENT** inquiry
introduces inquiry skills within a structured framework.	develops inquiry skills within a supportive environment.	deepens inquiry skills with student-driven questions or procedures.

Labs and Demos

Daily Demo *Roller Coaster Ride*

Engage

Introducing Key Topics

👥 whole class
🕐 35 min
🔍 **GUIDED** inquiry

PURPOSE **To observe an object with potential and kinetic energy**

MATERIALS

* marbles
* foam pipe insulation, sliced in half lengthwise
* masking tape

1 With class input, use the foam pipe insulation and the tape to construct a model of a hilly section of a roller coaster.

2 **Predict** Set a marble at the top of the first hill. Have students predict what will happen when you start the marble rolling.

3 **Observe** Roll the marble through the model roller coaster.
Ask: What do you observe? Sample answer: The marble is not moving at first, but it starts moving faster as it goes downhill.

4 **Analyze** Have students discuss the energy of the marble.
Ask: How did the energy of the marble change when it started moving? Sample answer: The marble moved downhill, so its gravitational potential energy decreased. Its speed increased at first, so its kinetic energy increased.
Extend the activity by inviting students to use the materials to build their own roller coaster. Have students explain how their roller coaster demonstrates potential and kinetic energy.

🌐 🔲 Quick Lab *Investigate Potential Energy*

PURPOSE **To analyze the relationship between height and potential energy**

See the Lab Manual or go Online for planning information.

🌐 🔲 Quick Lab *Identify Potential and Kinetic Energy*

Synthesizing Key Topics

👥 small groups
🕐 20 min
🔍 **DIRECTED** inquiry

Students manipulate objects and make observations.

PURPOSE **To identify potential and kinetic energy**

MATERIALS

• ball	• spring toy	• tape, masking
• pencil	• string	• washer

🌐 🔲 Exploration Lab *Mechanical Energy*

PURPOSE **To determine how mechanical energy changes**

See the Lab Manual or go Online for planning information.

🖥 Virtual Lab *Kinetic Energy*

Kinetic Energy

👥 flexible
🕐 45 min
🔍 **DIRECTED** inquiry

Students observe the energy transformations that occur as a chimpanzee swings.

PURPOSE To study kinetic and potential energy

Activities and Discussion

☐ **Activity** Flipbook
☐ **Activity** It's Got Potential
☐ **Activity** Energy of a Tennis Ball
☐ **Take It Home** Energy at Home

Labs and Demos

☐ **Daily Demo** Roller Coaster Ride
☐ **Quick Lab** Potential Energy
☐ **Quick Lab** Identify Potential and Kinetic Energy
☐ **Exploration Lab** Mechanical Energy
☐ **Virtual Lab** Kinetic Energy

Your Resources

_____

_____

_____

Explain Science Concepts

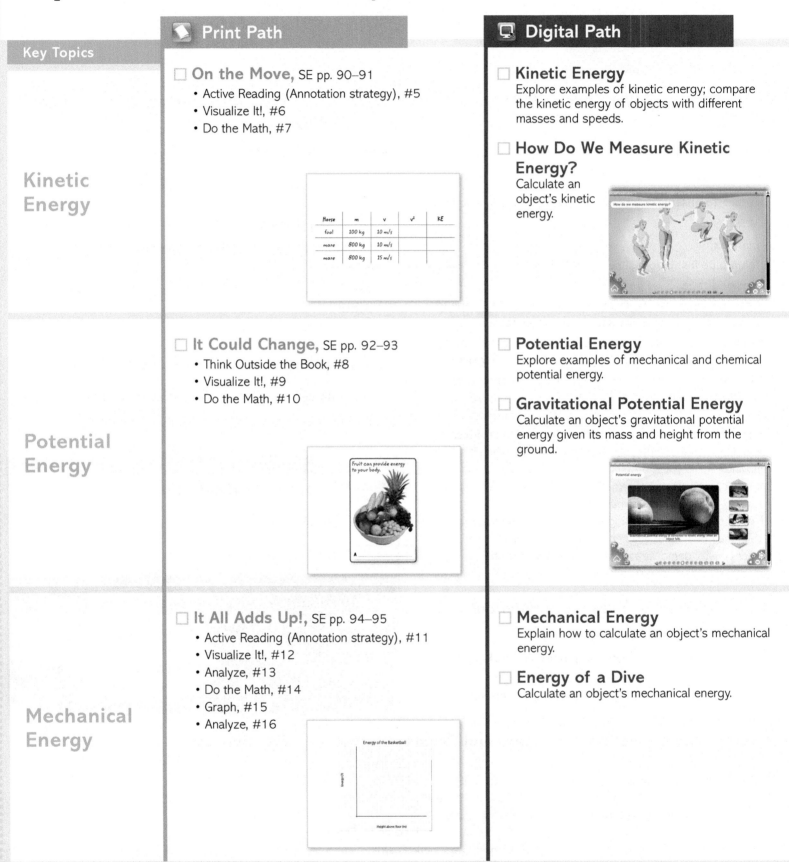

Key Topics	📖 Print Path	💻 Digital Path
Kinetic Energy	☐ **On the Move,** SE pp. 90–91 • Active Reading (Annotation strategy), #5 • Visualize It!, #6 • Do the Math, #7	☐ **Kinetic Energy** Explore examples of kinetic energy; compare the kinetic energy of objects with different masses and speeds. ☐ **How Do We Measure Kinetic Energy?** Calculate an object's kinetic energy.
Potential Energy	☐ **It Could Change,** SE pp. 92–93 • Think Outside the Book, #8 • Visualize It!, #9 • Do the Math, #10	☐ **Potential Energy** Explore examples of mechanical and chemical potential energy. ☐ **Gravitational Potential Energy** Calculate an object's gravitational potential energy given its mass and height from the ground.
Mechanical Energy	☐ **It All Adds Up!,** SE pp. 94–95 • Active Reading (Annotation strategy), #11 • Visualize It!, #12 • Analyze, #13 • Do the Math, #14 • Graph, #15 • Analyze, #16	☐ **Mechanical Energy** Explain how to calculate an object's mechanical energy. ☐ **Energy of a Dive** Calculate an object's mechanical energy.

Within the Print Path, a table is shown:

Horse	m	v	v²	KE
foal	100 kg	10 m/s		
mare	800 kg	10 m/s		
mare	800 kg	15 m/s		

Fruit can provide energy to your body.

Energy of the Basketball

Basic *Energy Calculations*

Synthesizing Key Ideas   individuals   10 min

Three-Column Chart Have students make a three-column chart with the following column headings: *Form of Energy, Description,* and *How It Is Calculated.* In the left column, have students list kinetic energy, gravitational potential energy, and mechanical energy. Then, have students write a short description of each form of energy in the middle column. In the right column, have students write the equation corresponding to that form of energy.

⊙ *Optional Online Support: Three-Column Chart*

Advanced *Mechanical Energy in Nature*

Mechanical Energy   pairs   30 min

Computer Presentation Invite pairs of students to use the Internet to find examples of mechanical energy that exist in nature. They can combine photographs, illustrations, and clip art into a computer presentation. Challenge pairs to start off with dramatic large-scale representations, such as Earth's rotation, and then gradually focus on smaller scale images, from waterfalls to a single drop of water. Students can add subtitles and audio components to their presentations. Have each pair of students present their work to the class.

ELL *Main Idea Web*

Potential Energy   individuals or pairs   10 min

Have students, individually or in pairs, create a main idea web to connect important concepts and details about potential energy. Tell students to write a main idea about potential energy in the center box. Then they can add boxes around it and fill them in with important details about chemical potential energy, elastic potential energy, and gravitational potential energy.

kinetic energy   potential energy   mechanical energy

Previewing Vocabulary

   whole class   10 min

Everyday Language *Kinetic* describes a type of energy; this adjective can also describe art. Kinetic art contains moving parts that can be powered by wind, electricity, water, or even a viewer pushing a button. Most kinetic art forms are sculptured works. Many of these sculptures are created with lightweight, modern materials including aluminum, plastic, and neon gas. Display photographs of the early kinetic sculptures of the 1920s, such as Alexander Calder's mobiles.

Reinforcing Vocabulary

   individuals   ongoing

Four Square To help students remember the terms introduced in the lesson, distribute a blank four-square graphic organizer. Have students place one of the vocabulary terms in the circle and then fill in the surrounding cells. Have students form small groups to share their completed graphic organizers.

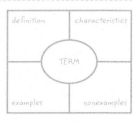

Customize Your Core Lesson

Core Instruction
☐ **Print Path** choices
☐ **Digital Path** choices

Vocabulary
☐ **Previewing Vocabulary**
   Everyday Language
☐ **Reinforcing Vocabulary**
   Four Square

Differentiated Instruction
☐ **Basic** Energy Calculations
☐ **Advanced** Mechanical Energy in Nature
☐ **ELL** Main Idea Web

Your Resources

Extend Science Concepts

Reinforce and Review

Activity *Reviewing Forms of Energy*

Synthesizing Key Topics   👥 whole class   🕐 20 min

Inside/Outside Circles Help students review the concepts they have learned by following these steps:

1 After students have read the lesson, give each an index card with a question based on the lesson material on one side and an answer on the other.

2 Students pair up and form two circles. One partner is in an inside circle; the other is in an outside circle. The students in the inside circle face out, and the students in the outside circle face in.

3 Each student in the inside circle asks his or her partner the question on the index card. The partner answers. If the answer is incorrect, the student in the inside circle teaches the other student the correct answer. Repeat this step with the outside-circle students asking the questions.

4 Have each student on the outside circle rotate one person to the right. He or she faces a new partner and gets a new question. Students rotate after each pair of questions and answers. (You can vary the rotation by moving more than one person, moving to the left, and so on, but try to make sure that partners are always new.)

Graphic Organizer

Synthesizing Key Topics   👤 individuals   🕐 10 min

Word Triangles Have students create word triangles for all of the different types of energy they are learning about. They should write a term and its definition in the bottom section of each word triangle. In the middle section, students should write a sentence in which the term is used correctly. Then they should draw an example of that particular form of energy in the small top section.

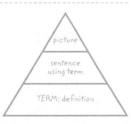

picture

sentence using term

TERM: definition

Going Further

Physical Education Connection

Synthesizing Key Topics   👥 pairs   🕐 20 min

Ready, Set, Go! Potential and kinetic energy can be observed in any sport or athletic activity. Have pairs of students take turns pantomiming favorite sports. While one student acts out different motions involved in the chosen sport, the other student should use a digital camera or a sketch pad to note poses that demonstrate potential energy and kinetic energy. Then, have the students in each pair switch roles and select another sport to pantomime.

Real World Connection

Kinetic Energy   👥 small groups   🕐 35 min

Kinetic Playground Recreational equipment such as an aerial merry-go-round can mimic kinetic art. Tell students to imagine that their class won a grant to design rides for a new community playground. Each group of students can brainstorm a piece of playground equipment that functions as a kinetic sculpture when it is not being used. Then groups can use found classroom materials to design a small-scale version of their swings, slides, seesaws, and other equipment. Have groups combine their equipment to form a model playground and demonstrate how each piece's moving parts combine to create a kinetic sculpture.

Customize Your Closing

🖥 *See the Assessment Guide for quizzes and tests.*

⟳ *Go Online to edit and create quizzes and tests.*

Reinforce and Review

☐ **Activity** Inside/Outside Circles
☐ **Graphic Organizer** Word Triangles
☐ **Print Path** Visual Summary, SE p. 96
☐ **Print Path** Lesson Review, SE p. 97
☐ **Digital Path** Lesson Closer

Evaluate Student Mastery

See the teacher support below the Student Pages for additional Formative Assessment questions.

Ask the following questions to assess student mastery of the material. **Ask:** Which has more kinetic energy: a boulder at the base of a mountain or a feather floating down from a bird's nest? Why? Sample answer: The feather has kinetic energy because it is in motion, while the boulder does not have kinetic energy because it is sitting still. **Ask:** What kind of energy exists in a stretched-out spring? elastic potential energy **Ask:** Give an example of a part of your body that requires energy to operate. Sample answer: My heart requires energy to pump blood throughout my body.

Reteach

Formative assessment may show that students need reinforcement for certain topics. The resources below are recommended for reteaching. If students were introduced to a topic through the Print Path, you can also use the Digital Path to reteach, and vice versa.
🎧 *Can be assigned to individual students*

Kinetic Energy
Quick Lab Identify Potential and Kinetic Energy

Daily Demo Roller Coaster Ride

Virtual Lab Kinetic Energy 🎧

Potential Energy
Quick Lab Investigate Potential Energy

Mechanical Energy
Quick Lab Mechanical Energy

Alternative Assessment
Kinetic and Potential Energy

🌐 *Online resources: student worksheet; optional rubrics*

Kinetic and Potential Energy

Points of View: *Forms of Energy*
Your class will work together to show what you've learned about kinetic and potential energy from several different viewpoints.

1. Work in groups as assigned by your teacher. Each group will be assigned to one or two viewpoints.

2. Complete your assignment, and present your perspective to the class.

Vocabulary Create a three-screen computer presentation about the lesson's vocabulary terms: *kinetic energy, potential energy,* and *mechanical energy.* Each slide should include a vocabulary term, a dictionary definition of the term, a definition of the term in your own words, and a sentence that correctly uses the term.

Examples Arrange a time to walk through the school building to find examples of objects or substances with potential energy, objects with kinetic energy, and objects with mechanical energy. Take videos or photographs of the examples you find. Share your videos or photographs with the class.

Illustrations Draw a poster of three cyclists conquering a mountain. One is biking up the mountain; another is resting at the mountaintop; and the third is coasting down the mountain. Then, use the poster to explain to a small group the concepts of potential energy, kinetic energy, and mechanical energy.

Details Write a short story from the point-of-view of a tennis ball, basketball, or baseball. Your short story can be creative and imaginative, but should correctly use the terms *potential energy, kinetic energy,* and *mechanical energy.*

Calculations Create a table that shows the kinetic energy of two runners in a race. In the first column, write the names of the runners. In the second column, write the mass of each runner in kilograms (kg). In the third column, write the speed of each runner in meters per second (m/s). Then square the speed in the fourth column. Finally, use the fifth column to calculate the kinetic energy of each runner.

Going Further
☐ Physical Education Connection
☐ Real World Connection

Formative Assessment
☐ **Strategies** Throughout TE
☐ **Lesson Review** SE

Summative Assessment
☐ **Alternative Assessment** Forms of Energy
☐ **Lesson Quiz**
☐ **Unit Tests A and B**
☐ **Unit Review** SE End-of-Unit

Your Resources
_____   _____

_____   _____

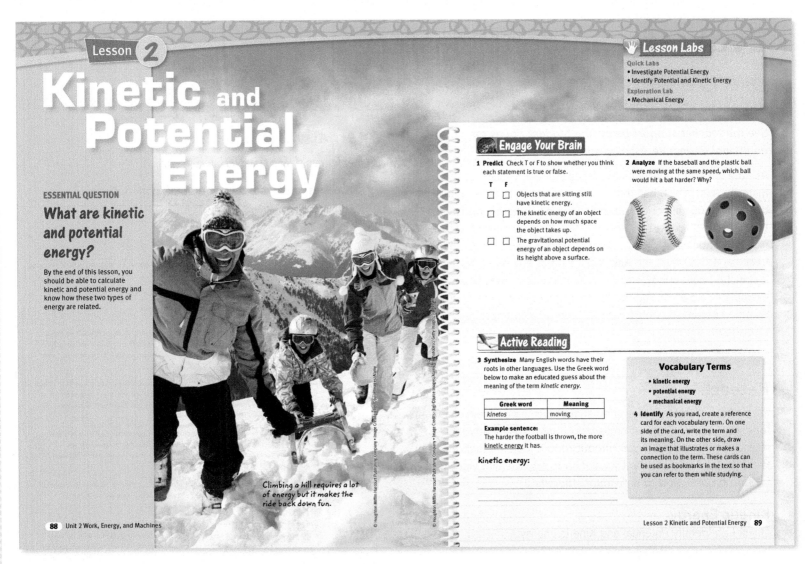

Answers

Answers to 1–3 should represent students' current thoughts, even if incorrect.

1. F; F; T

2. Sample answer: The baseball would hit harder because it has more mass than the plastic ball.

3. the energy of an object that is moving

4. Students should define or sketch each vocabulary term in the lesson.

Opening Your Lesson

Discuss students' answers to item 1 to assess their understanding of kinetic and potential energy.

Prerequisites Students should already have some understanding of how energy can be transferred between objects or systems. In this lesson, they will apply this understanding to discover how kinetic and potential energy are calculated.

Learning Alert

Difficult Concept Students may need to be reminded that energy can change from one form to another, and that energy is always conserved in these changes. In this lesson, students will need to understand that energy can change from potential energy to kinetic energy and back to potential energy. Remind them that energy is not created when these changes occur, and that energy is not destroyed, or "lost," during these changes.

On the Move

What is kinetic energy?

Energy is the ability to do work. There are different forms of energy. One form that you can find all around you is kinetic energy. **Kinetic energy** is the energy of motion. Every moving object has kinetic energy. For example, a hammer has kinetic energy as it moves toward a nail. When the hammer hits the nail, energy is transferred. Work is done when movement occurs in the direction of the force, and the nail is driven into a board.

The Energy of Motion

Active Reading **5 Identify** As you read, underline two factors that affect an object's kinetic energy.

What determines the amount of kinetic energy that an object has? The faster an object moves, the more kinetic energy it has. So kinetic energy depends, in part, on speed. Kinetic energy also depends on mass. If two objects move at the same speed, then the one that has more mass will have more kinetic energy. Imagine a bike and a car that are moving at the same speed. The car has more kinetic energy than the bike has because the car has more mass.

Visualize It!

6 Apply How does the rider's ability to stop the bike change as the bike moves down a steep hill?

_____

_____

The bike at the top of the hill is not moving. It does not have kinetic energy. The bike that is going down the hill has kinetic energy. As the bike moves faster, its kinetic energy increases.

90

How is the kinetic energy of an object calculated?

An object's kinetic energy is related to its mass and speed. The speed of an object is the distance that it travels in a unit of time. The following equation shows how kinetic energy is calculated.

$$\text{kinetic energy} = \frac{1}{2} mv^2$$

The letter m is the object's mass, and the letter v is the object's speed. When the mass is expressed in kilograms and the speed in meters per second, kinetic energy is expressed in _joules_ (J).

Do the Math

Sample Problem
The foal has a mass of 100 kg and is moving at 8 m/s along the beach. What is the kinetic energy (KE) of the foal?

Identify

A. What do you know? The mass, m, is 100 kg.
The speed, v, is 8 m/s.

B. What do you want to find? kinetic energy

Plan

C. Write the formula: $KE = \frac{1}{2}mv^2$

D. Substitute into the formula: $KE = \frac{1}{2}(100 \text{ kg})(8 \text{ m/s})^2$

Solve

E. Multiply: $KE = \frac{1}{2}(100 \text{ kg})(64 \text{ m}^2/\text{s}^2) = 3{,}200 \text{ kg} \cdot \text{m}^2/\text{s}^2 = 3{,}200 \text{ J}$

Answer: 3,200 J

You Try It

7 Calculate Complete the table at the right to calculate the kinetic energy of the horses.

Horse	m	v	v^2	KE
foal	100 kg	10 m/s		
mare	800 kg	10 m/s		
mare	800 kg	15 m/s		

Answers

5. _See students' pages for annotations._

6. Sample answer: As the bike moves down the hill, speed increases. It is much harder to stop the bike near the bottom than it is near the top of the hill.

7. For v^2, from top to bottom: 100 m²/s², 100 m²/s², 225 m²/s²; for KE, from top to bottom: 10,000 J, 80,000 J, 180,000 J

Do the Math

Remind students that in order to calculate the kinetic energy of a moving object, the object must be moving in a straight line at a constant speed. To complete the table in question 7, guide students to first calculate the square of the speed and then to use the equation $KE = \frac{1}{2}mv^2$ to calculate the kinetic energy of each object.

Annotation Strategy

Text Structure: Main Idea/Details Remind students that an important reading strategy for science is knowing how to identify the main idea and supporting details in text passages. Explain that a main idea is the central or most important point a writer tries to make in a paragraph or passage, while supporting details provide information about the main idea. Point out that when students complete this annotation strategy, they are underlining details that support the main idea "Kinetic energy is the energy of motion." Extend the activity by having each student locate one additional supporting detail that relates to this main idea. Call on several students to share their additional examples with the class.

🌐 _Optional Online resource: Text Structure: Main Idea/Details support_

It Could Change

What is potential energy?

Some energy is stored energy, or potential energy. **Potential energy** is the energy an object has because of its position, condition, or chemical composition. Like kinetic energy, potential energy is the ability to do work. For example, an object has *elastic potential energy* when it has been stretched or compressed. Elastic potential energy is stored in a stretched spring or rubber band. An object has *gravitational potential energy* due to its position above the ground. An object held above the ground has the potential to fall. The higher the object is above the ground, the greater its gravitational potential energy. Potential energy that depends on an object's position is referred to as *mechanical potential energy*. But there are other types of potential energy that do not depend on an object's position. For example, a substance stores *chemical potential energy* as a result of its chemical bonds. Some of that energy can be released during chemical reactions.

Think Outside the Book Inquiry

8 Classify With a partner, create a poster that shows examples of potential energy from everyday life. Label each example as gravitational, elastic, or chemical potential energy.

Visualize It!

9 Identify Fill in the type of potential energy that is illustrated in each image.

Fruit can provide energy to your body.

The boulder is high above the ground.

The archer pulls back on the string and stretches it.

A _____   B _____   C _____

How is the gravitational potential energy of an object calculated?

The following equation describes an object's gravitational potential energy.

$$\text{gravitational potential energy} = mgh$$

The letter m represents the object's mass expressed in kilograms. The letter g represents the acceleration due to Earth's gravity, which is $9.8\ \text{m/s}^2$. The letter h is the object's height from the ground in meters. The height is a measure of how far the object can fall. Like kinetic energy, potential energy is expressed in units of joules.

Do the Math

Sample Problem

The cat has a mass of 4 kg and is 1.5 m above the ground. What is the gravitational potential energy of the cat?

Identify

A. What do you know? mass = 4 kg, height = 1.5 m, acceleration due to gravity = 9.8 m/s²

B. What do you want to find? gravitational potential energy

Plan

C. Write the formula: $GPE = mgh$

D. Substitute the given values into the formula:
$GPE = (4\ kg)(9.8\ m/s^2)(1.5\ m)$

Solve

E. Multiply: $PE = (4\ kg)(9.8\ m/s^2)(1.5\ m) = 58.8\ kg \cdot m/s^2 = 58.8\ J$

Answer: 58.8 J

You Try It

10 Calculate Three books are on different shelves. Calculate the gravitational potential energy of each book based on its mass and its height above the floor.

Object	m	h	PE
picture book	0.2 kg	2 m	
picture book	0.2 kg	3 m	
textbook	1.5 kg	4 m	

Answers

9. A. chemical; B. gravitational; C. elastic
10. For PE, from top to bottom: 3.92 J, 5.88 J, 58.8 J

Formative Assessment

Ask: Describe one way that a rubber ball could gain potential energy. When the ball is thrown straight up in the air, it gains gravitational potential energy as it rises higher.
Ask: When would the ball have maximum potential gravitational energy? when the ball reaches its highest point before gravity pulls it back to the ground

Learning Alert

Elastic Potential Energy Objects such as springs and rubber bands have elastic potential energy, but living things can also store this energy. For example, the tendons in a kangaroo's legs can stretch like bungee cords. This helps some breeds of kangaroo leap 25 feet in a single bound and sprint at speeds of more than 35 miles per hour! The tendons pull tight when a kangaroo lands on the ground, giving its legs elastic potential energy. When the tendons stretch, the kangaroo uses kinetic energy to launch into its next hop.

Do the Math

Remind students that, in the equation used to calculate gravitational potential energy, g is a constant. Students should use the value $9.8\ \text{m/s}^2$ for g.

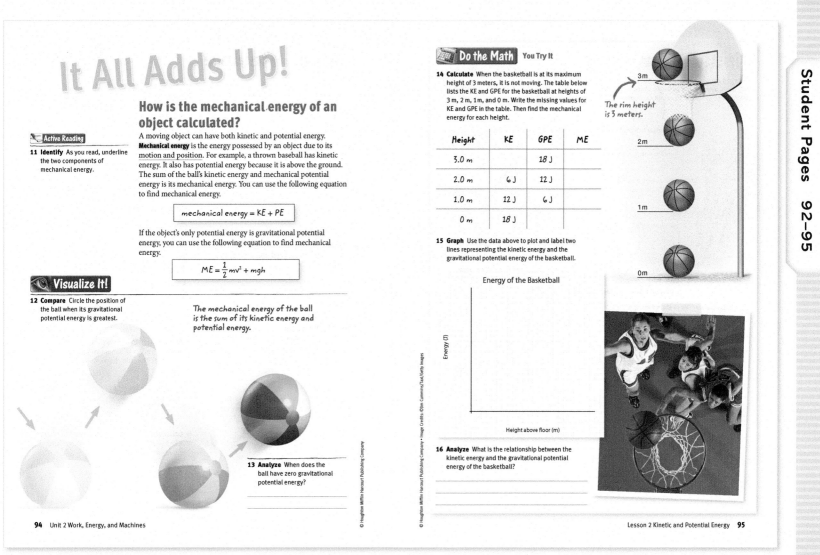

It All Adds Up!

How is the mechanical energy of an object calculated?

11 Identify As you read, underline the two components of mechanical energy.

A moving object can have both kinetic and potential energy. **Mechanical energy** is the energy possessed by an object due to its motion and position. For example, a thrown baseball has kinetic energy. It also has potential energy because it is above the ground. The sum of the ball's kinetic energy and mechanical potential energy is its mechanical energy. You can use the following equation to find mechanical energy.

$$mechanical\ energy = KE + PE$$

If the object's only potential energy is gravitational potential energy, you can use the following equation to find mechanical energy.

$$ME = \frac{1}{2}mv^2 + mgh$$

Visualize It!

12 Compare Circle the position of the ball when its gravitational potential energy is greatest.

The mechanical energy of the ball is the sum of its kinetic energy and potential energy.

13 Analyze When does the ball have zero gravitational potential energy?

94 Unit 2 Work, Energy, and Machines

© Houghton Mifflin Harcourt Publishing Company

Do the Math You Try It

14 Calculate When the basketball is at its maximum height of 3 meters, it is not moving. The table below lists the KE and GPE for the basketball at heights of 3 m, 2 m, 1 m, and 0 m. Write the missing values for KE and GPE in the table. Then find the mechanical energy for each height.

Height	KE	GPE	ME
3.0 m		18 J	
2.0 m	6 J	12 J	
1.0 m	12 J	6 J	
0 m	18 J		

15 Graph Use the data above to plot and label two lines representing the kinetic energy and the gravitational potential energy of the basketball.

Energy of the Basketball

Energy (J)

Height above floor (m)

16 Analyze What is the relationship between the kinetic energy and the gravitational potential energy of the basketball?

The rim height is 3 meters.

3m

2m

1m

0m

© Houghton Mifflin Harcourt Publishing Company • Image Credits: ©Tim Cummins/Taxi/Getty Images

Lesson 2 Kinetic and Potential Energy 95

Answers

11. *See students' pages for annotations.*

12. Students should circle the second ball from the left.

13. The ball has zero gravitational potential energy when it is touching the ground.

14. 0 J; 18 J; 18 J; 18 J; 0 J; 18 J

15. Students should draw the *y*-axis scale from 0 to 18 in units of 6. The *x*-axis scale is from 0 to 3 in units of 1. For kinetic energy, the points (0, 18), (1, 12), (2, 6), and (3, 0) are plotted and connected with a line. For GPE, the points (0, 0), (1, 6), (2, 12), and (3, 18) are plotted and connected with a line.

16. The sum of the two types of energy is always 18 J.

Annotation Strategy

Have students complete the annotation activity to reinforce that mechanical energy consists of both potential energy and kinetic energy. Extend the activity by having students circle the equation that summarizes this information. mechanical energy = *PE* + *KE*

Formative Assessment

Ask: Does a change in kinetic energy of a ball necessarily result in a change in the mechanical energy of the ball? Explain. No, if the change in kinetic energy is accompanied by a change in potential energy, the mechanical energy could stay consistent.

Do the Math

Remind students to use the equation *ME* = *PE* + *KE* to calculate the mechanical energy.

Building Graphing Skills

Ask: How does a line graph make it easier for you to see the gravitational potential energy of a basketball than when this data is presented in a table? Sample answer: The graph allows you to visualize data that change over time and is easier to interpret than a table.

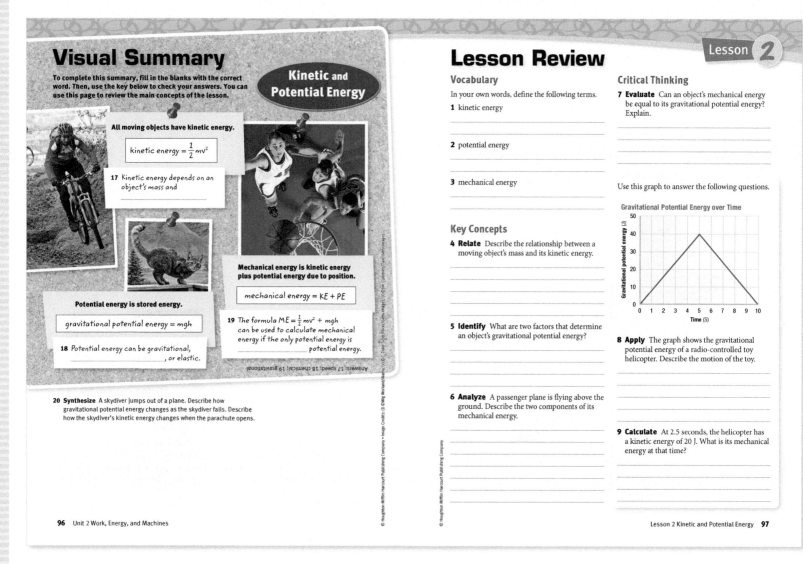

Visual Summary

To complete this summary, fill in the blanks with the correct word. Then, use the key below to check your answers. You can use this page to review the main concepts of the lesson.

Kinetic and Potential Energy

All moving objects have kinetic energy.

$$\text{kinetic energy} = \frac{1}{2}mv^2$$

17 Kinetic energy depends on an object's mass and _____

Potential energy is stored energy.

$$\text{gravitational potential energy} = mgh$$

18 Potential energy can be gravitational, _____, or elastic.

Mechanical energy is kinetic energy plus potential energy due to position.

$$\text{mechanical energy} = KE + PE$$

19 The formula $ME = \frac{1}{2}mv^2 + mgh$ can be used to calculate mechanical energy if the only potential energy is _____ potential energy.

Answers: 17 speed; 18 chemical; 19 gravitational

20 Synthesize A skydiver jumps out of a plane. Describe how gravitational potential energy changes as the skydiver falls. Describe how the skydiver's kinetic energy changes when the parachute opens.

96 Unit 2 Work, Energy, and Machines

Lesson Review

Lesson 2

Vocabulary

In your own words, define the following terms.

1 kinetic energy

2 potential energy

3 mechanical energy

Key Concepts

4 Relate Describe the relationship between a moving object's mass and its kinetic energy.

5 Identify What are two factors that determine an object's gravitational potential energy?

6 Analyze A passenger plane is flying above the ground. Describe the two components of its mechanical energy.

Critical Thinking

7 Evaluate Can an object's mechanical energy be equal to its gravitational potential energy? Explain.

Use this graph to answer the following questions.

Gravitational Potential Energy over Time

8 Apply The graph shows the gravitational potential energy of a radio-controlled toy helicopter. Describe the motion of the toy.

9 Calculate At 2.5 seconds, the helicopter has a kinetic energy of 20 J. What is its mechanical energy at that time?

Lesson 2 Kinetic and Potential Energy 97

Visual Summary Answers

17. speed

18. chemical

19. gravitational

20. Sample answer: The gravitational potential energy is greatest when the skydiver first jumps out of the plane. It decreases as the skydiver gets nearer to the ground. The skydiver's speed decreases when the parachute opens. This causes his kinetic energy to decrease.

Lesson Review Answers

1. Sample answer: the energy an object has due to motion

2. Sample answer: the energy an object has due to its position or chemical composition

3. Sample answer: the sum of an object's kinetic and potential energies

4. The greater the mass of an object moving at a given speed, the greater its kinetic energy.

5. the object's mass and the object's height

6. The two components of the mechanical energy of the plane are its kinetic energy due to mass and speed and its gravitational potential energy due to its mass and height above the ground.

7. Sample answer: Yes. If an object is not moving, it has zero kinetic energy. In this case, the sum of the kinetic energy and the potential energy would be the same as the gravitational potential energy.

8. Sample answer: The helicopter travels upwards at a steady rate for 5 seconds and then downwards at the same rate for 5 seconds.

9. 40 J

Testing a Simple Machine

Purpose
To build and test a simple machine

Learning Goals
- Measure the input and output force of a lifting device.
- Calculate the mechanical advantage of the lifting device.

Academic Vocabulary
simple machine, input force, output force, mechanical advantage

Prerequisite Knowledge
- Understanding of simple machines and the scientific concept of work
- Understanding of force and motion

Materials
blocks or stands

wooden board

wooden dowel

duct tape or masking tape

mass, 200-g to 1,000-g

meter stick or ruler

pulley

spring scale, calibrated in newtons

string

wheel and axle

Content Refresher

Professional Development

Simple Machines The six types of simple machines are levers, inclined planes, wheel and axles, screws, wedges, and pulleys.

Lever A lever is a rigid board or bar that rests on a pivot point, called a fulcrum. The lever moves an object, called the load. The closer a load is to the fulcrum, the easier it is to move. Bottle openers, crow bars, and seesaws are levers.

Inclined Plane An inclined plane is a flat surface higher at one end than the other. It takes less force to move a heavy object up vertically if you move it along an inclined plane. Loading ramps, slides, and ski slopes can all be inclined planes.

Wheel and Axle A wheel and axle is a large circle that rotates around a smaller circle. Often, turning the wheel turns the axle. Steering wheels, screwdrivers, and door knobs are examples.

Screw A screw is an inclined plane that winds around an axis. Some screws are used to lower and raise things, while others are used to hold things together. Jar lids, light bulbs, stools that spin, clamps, corkscrews, and drill bits all use screws.

Wedge A wedge is two inclined planes that meet to form an edge. A wedge can separate something, lift an object, or hold an object in place (for example, a door stop). Knives, axes, plow blades, scissors, chisels, and nails all have one or more wedges.

Pulley A pulley is a wheel on an axle. A rope usually runs around the wheel to change the direction of a force. Flag poles, cranes, clothes lines, sailboats, and blinds all have a pulley.

21st Century SKILLS
Theme: Financial, Economic, Business, and Entrepreneurial Literacy

Activities focusing on 21st Century Skills are included for this feature and can be found on the following pages.

These activities focus on the following skills:

- **Critical Thinking and Problem Solving**
- **ICT (Information, Communications, and Technology) Literacy**
- **Leadership and Responsibility**

You can learn more about the 21st Century Skills in the front matter of this Teacher's Edition.

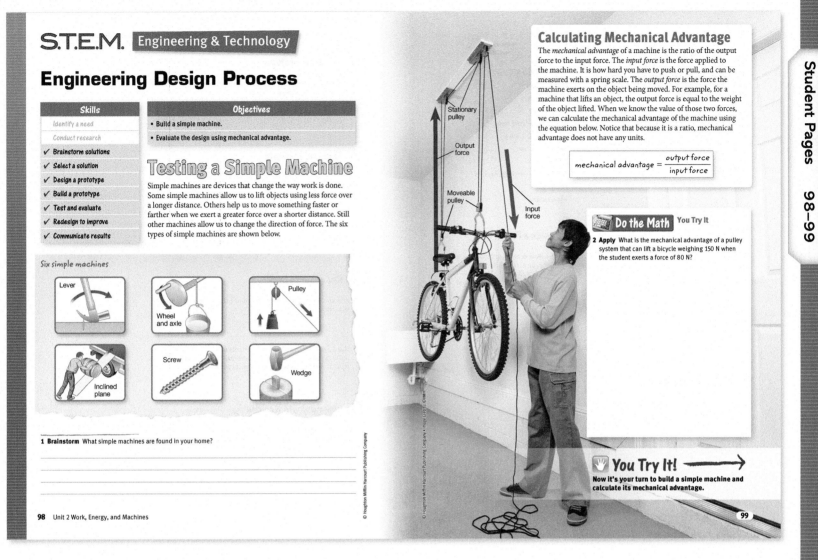

S.T.E.M. Engineering & Technology

Engineering Design Process

Skills
Identify a need
Conduct research
✓ Brainstorm solutions
✓ Select a solution
✓ Design a prototype
✓ Build a prototype
✓ Test and evaluate
✓ Redesign to improve
✓ Communicate results

Objectives
• Build a simple machine.
• Evaluate the design using mechanical advantage.

Testing a Simple Machine

Simple machines are devices that change the way work is done. Some simple machines allow us to lift objects using less force over a longer distance. Others help us to move something faster or farther when we exert a greater force over a shorter distance. Still other machines allow us to change the direction of force. The six types of simple machines are shown below.

Six simple machines

Lever

Wheel and axle

Pulley

Inclined plane

Screw

Wedge

1 Brainstorm What simple machines are found in your home?

Stationary pulley

Output force

Moveable pulley

Input force

Calculating Mechanical Advantage

The *mechanical advantage* of a machine is the ratio of the output force to the input force. The *input force* is the force applied to the machine. It is how hard you have to push or pull, and can be measured with a spring scale. The *output force* is the force the machine exerts on the object being moved. For example, for a machine that lifts an object, the output force is equal to the weight of the object lifted. When we know the value of those two forces, we can calculate the mechanical advantage of the machine using the equation below. Notice that because it is a ratio, mechanical advantage does not have any units.

$$\text{mechanical advantage} = \frac{\text{output force}}{\text{input force}}$$

Do the Math — You Try It

2 Apply What is the mechanical advantage of a pulley system that can lift a bicycle weighing 150 N when the student exerts a force of 80 N?

You Try It!

Now it's your turn to build a simple machine and calculate its mechanical advantage.

Answers

1. Sample answer: In the kitchen I have seen levers (tongs, scissors, fly swatter, salad tongs), a wheel and axle (rolling pin), a wedge (knife), and a pulley (windows blinds cord)

2. MA = output force / input force

   MA = 150 N / 80 N

   MA = 1.875

   This simple machine has a mechanical advantage of approximately 1.9.

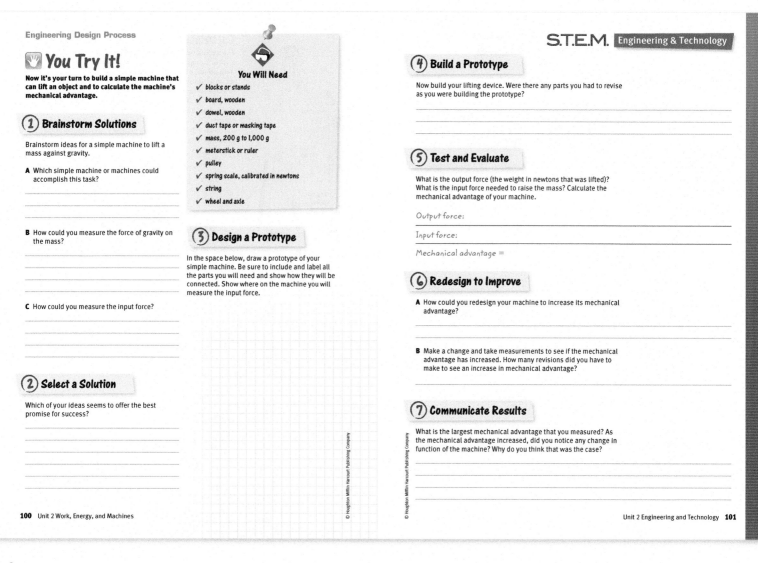

Answers

1. A. Sample answer: I could use a lever or a pulley.

   B. Sample answer: I will lift it with a spring scale that measures in newtons.

   C. Sample answer: I could use the spring scale to lift the weight with the lever or with the pulley.

2. Sample answer: I think the lever will work best.

3. Students' sketches should show a simple machine that can lift a mass. Labels should indicate where input force will be measured.

4. Sample answer: I had to tape the weight to the lever and tape the lever to the fulcrum.

5. Sample answer: input force = 4 N; output force = 10 N; mechanical advantage = 2.5

6. A. Sample answer: I could move the weight closer to the spring scale.

   B. Sample answer: I had to make two revisions.

7. Sample answer: The largest mechanical advantage I could measure was 3.3. I couldn't lift the weight as high because it was closer to the fulcrum and didn't move as much.

21st Century SKILLS

Learning and Innovation Skills

👥 pairs   🕐 30 min

Critical Thinking and Problem Solving Have pairs of students experiment with simple machines. How does changing the size, shape, angle, or other factors affect how a machine operates? (For example, how does a wedge behave differently if the angle between its two inclined planes is changed?) Challenge pairs to change one element of several simple machines. What effects does their change have? Encourage students to explain their results to the class.

Information, Media, and Technology Skills

👥 small groups   🕐 45 min

ICT (Information, Communications, and Technology) Literacy Have students use the Internet to research Rube Goldberg machines. These are deliberately over-engineered compound machines designed to do simple, often silly tasks. Invite small groups of students to design their own Rube Goldberg machine by putting together two or more simple machines to make a compound machine that accomplishes a silly task. Invite students to present their machines to the class.

Life and Career Skills

👥 small groups   🕐 ongoing

Leadership and Responsibility Challenge students to work together to solve problems using simple machines. Assign a different group leader for each simple machine the group investigates. Leaders should guide others in the group toward a specific goal. For example, one leader may want the group to design a way to use a wheel and axle to haul recycling bins outside. Another may want the group to use inclined planes to water a garden. Leaders should assign roles to other group members (for example, time keeper, materials person, builder/engineer) and should try to leverage the individual strengths of group members to accomplish the task. Have students share their solutions with the class.

Differentiated Instruction

Basic *Improving a Simple Machine*

👥 pairs   🕐 20 min

Invite pairs of students to demonstrate to each other their simple machines for lifting a mass against gravity. Ask student pairs to brainstorm ways in which each device could be improved. Then have pairs make changes to each machine to see if their ideas worked. Have pairs explain their ideas and reasoning to the class.

Advanced *Demonstrating a Pulley System*

👥 individuals or pairs   🕐 ongoing

Invite interested students to research fixed and moveable pulleys. Then have students put on a demonstration that shows how fixed and moveable pulleys can be used together to make a block-and-tackle pulley that makes it easier to lift heavy loads.

ELL *Machine Terms*

👥 individuals or pairs   🕐 10 min

Have students make word triangles for the six simple machines. At the top of each triangle, they can draw a picture of the machine. In the middle, they can write a sentence that uses the term. Finally, at the bottom of the triangle, they can define the term in their own words.

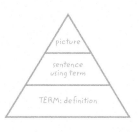

🔘 *Optional Online resource: Word Triangle support*

Customize Your Feature

☐ **21st Century Skills** Learning and Innovation Skills

☐ **21st Century Skills** Information, Media, and Technology Skills

☐ **21st Century Skills** Life and Career Skills

☐ **Basic** Improving a Simple Machine

☐ **Advanced** Demonstrating a Pulley System

☐ **ELL** Machine Terms

Machines

Essential Question How do simple machines work?

🍎 **Professional Development**

For more detailed information about the topics in this lesson, refer to the Content Refresher in the Unit Opener pages.

Opening Your Lesson

Begin the lesson by assessing students' prerequisite and prior knowledge.

Prerequisite Knowledge

- An understanding of work, energy, and power and the units used to measure each

Accessing Prior Knowledge

Have students share what they know about the purposes of machines. Identify several machines students have access to each day. Students may name objects that fit the common definition of machine rather than the scientific definition of simple machine. **Ask:** How do these machines make people's lives easier? Sample answers: Cars and buses help people move quickly from one place to another. A washing machine helps people wash clothing efficiently.

Customize Your Opening

☐ **Accessing Prior Knowledge,** above

☐ **Print Path** Engage Your Brain, SE p. 103

☐ **Print Path** Active Reading, SE p. 103

☐ **Digital Path** Lesson Opener

Key Topics/Learning Goals	Supporting Concepts
Introduction to Machines 1 Describe what a machine does. 2 Explain two ways that machines can affect force or work.	• A machine is a device that helps people do work by changing the way work is done • A machine does not decrease the amount of work. It only changes the way in which work is done. A machine can either change size or direction of the force needed to do work.
Mechanical Advantage and Mechanical Efficiency 1 Differentiate between the input and output force of a machine. 2 Calculate a machine's mechanical advantage given its input and output force. 3 Calculate a machine's mechanical efficiency given its input and output work.	• Input force is the force exerted on a machine; output force is the force that a machine exerts on an object. • Mechanical advantage is the number of times a machine multiplies its input force. Mechanical advantage = output force / input force. • Mechanical efficiency compares a machine's work output with its work input. It is usually expressed as a percentage. Mechanical efficiency = (work output/work input) × 100%.
Types of Machines 1 Identify the six types of simple machines. 2 Classify a lever as either first, second, or third class based on the position of its fulcrum. 3 Calculate the ideal mechanical advantage of a lever, a wheel and axle, and an inclined plane.	• A lever is a solid bar that pivots at a fixed point, called a fulcrum. • A wheel and axle is made of a wheel attached to a shaft, or axle. • A pulley is made of a wheel with a rope or cable that passes over it. • An inclined plane is a simple machine with a slanted surface. A wedge has one thick end and one thin end. A screw is an inclined plane wrapped around a cylinder or cone to form a spiral.

Options for Instruction

Two parallel paths provide coverage of the Essential Questions, with a strong **Inquiry** strand woven into each. Follow the **Print Path**, the **Digital Path**, or your customized combination of print, digital, and inquiry.

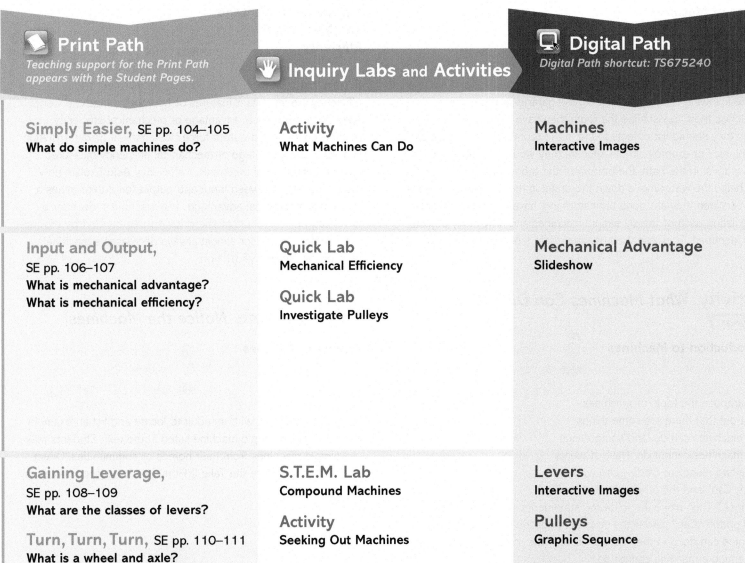

Print Path
Teaching support for the Print Path appears with the Student Pages.

Inquiry Labs and Activities

Digital Path
Digital Path shortcut: TS675240

Simply Easier, SE pp. 104–105
What do simple machines do?

Activity
What Machines Can Do

Machines
Interactive Images

Input and Output,
SE pp. 106–107
What is mechanical advantage?
What is mechanical efficiency?

Quick Lab
Mechanical Efficiency

Quick Lab
Investigate Pulleys

Mechanical Advantage
Slideshow

Gaining Leverage,
SE pp. 108–109
What are the classes of levers?

Turn, Turn, Turn, SE pp. 110–111
What is a wheel and axle?
What are the types of pulleys?

So Inclined, SE pp. 112–113
What are inclined planes?
What are wedges? What are screws?

S.T.E.M. Lab
Compound Machines

Activity
Seeking Out Machines

Levers
Interactive Images

Pulleys
Graphic Sequence

Wheel and Axle
Interactive Images

Inclined Planes
Interactive Images

Options for Assessment

See the Evaluate page for options, including Formative Assessment, Summative Assessment, and Unit Review.

Engage and Explore

Activities and Discussion

Activity *Seeking Out Machines*

Types of Machines

👥 pairs or small groups
🕐 15 min
🔵 **GUIDED** inquiry

Give pairs or groups a list of simple machines, and assign them one of the following rooms: the kitchen, the garage, or the bathroom. Challenge them to visualize the room they have been assigned. Then, they should list objects found in the room that include simple machines. For example, in the kitchen, they would list knives, which are wedges; in the bath, the bottom of the tub is an inclined plane that helps the water move down the drain; in the garage, a broom is a lever. When they are done brainstorming, have them make a data table listing each of the six simple machines and how many objects they identified. They can then use their data tables to make a graph.

Activity *What Machines Can Do*

Engage

Introduction to Machines

👥 whole class
🕐 10 min
🔵 **GUIDED** inquiry

To introduce the topic of machines, point out that there are some things that machines can do, and some things that machines cannot do. Have students make two response cards—one with the word "Can" and the other with the word "Cannot." Then make the following statements, and have students hold up the "Can" card if the statement describes something a machine can do, and the "Cannot" card if the statement describes something a machine cannot do.

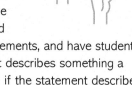

- change the way work is done (can)
- make work easier to do (can)
- decrease the size of the force needed to do a task (can)
- change the direction of a force (can)
- decrease the total amount of work needed to do a task (cannot)
- change the distance over which a force is applied to do a task (can)

Discussion *Compare and Contrast*

Mechanical Advantage and Mechanical Efficiency

👥 whole class
🕐 15 min
🔵 **GUIDED** inquiry

Explain that both mechanical advantage and mechanical efficiency are important features of how well a machine works. **Ask:** Does mechanical advantage or mechanical efficiency depend on input and output force? mechanical advantage **Ask:** Is mechanical advantage or mechanical efficiency measured using a percentage? mechanical efficiency **Ask:** Explain how the relationship between input and output force determines a machine's mechanical advantage. The machine's mechanical advantage is the result of the output force divided by the input force. **Ask:** What factor almost always decreases a machine's mechanical efficiency? friction

Take It Home *Notice the Machines!*

Types of Machines

👥 student-adult pairs
🕐 30 min
🔵 **INDEPENDENT** inquiry

Have students work with an adult to locate and list an example of each type of simple machine listed in the text. Students may use simple machines from their homes or communities. Direct students to complete the Take It Home worksheet to accompany this activity.

Customize Your Labs

◼ *See the Lab Manual for lab datasheets.*

🔴 *Go Online for editable lab datasheets.*

Levels of **Inquiry**

DIRECTED inquiry	GUIDED inquiry	INDEPENDENT inquiry
introduces inquiry skills within a structured framework.	develops inquiry skills within a supportive environment.	deepens inquiry skills with student-driven questions or procedures.

Labs and Demos

Daily Demo *Playground Machines*

Types of Machines

👥 whole class
🕐 15–20 min
Inquiry DIRECTED inquiry

PURPOSE **To demonstrate how a lever and fulcrum work**

MATERIALS

• **a stiff board made of plastic, wood, or cardboard**
• **a triangle-shaped block (triangle should be equilateral)**

1 Begin by reminding students that a lever is a simple machine that has a bar that pivots at a fulcrum.

2 Identify the piece of board as the bar and the triangle-shaped block as the fulcrum. Then tell students you will use these materials to demonstrate levers they might see on a playground.

3 Demonstrate a first-class lever for students by balancing the center of the board on the fulcrum. Have students identify the playground equipment this resembles. Then, ask students to classify this as a first-, second-, or third-class lever.

4 Then demonstrate a third-class lever for students by removing the triangle-block fulcrum and moving the board as if it were a baseball bat or tennis racket. The input force is now between the fulcrum (your hands) and the load. Have students identify the play equipment used in this way. Then, ask students to classify this as a first-, second-, or third-class lever.

🌐 🗎 Quick Lab *Mechanical Efficiency*

Mechanical Advantage and Mechanical Efficiency

👥 individuals
🕐 15 min
Inquiry DIRECTED inquiry

See the Lab Manual or go Online for planning information.

🌐 🗎 Quick Lab *Investigate Pulleys*

Mechanical Advantage and Mechanical Efficiency

👥 small groups
🕐 15 min
Inquiry DIRECTED inquiry

Students use a pulley system and calculate mechanical advantage. See the Lab Manual or go Online for planning information.

🌐 🗎 S.T.E.M. Lab *Compound Machines*

Types of Machines

👥 small groups
🕐 90 min
Inquiry DIRECTED or GUIDED inquiry

Students will design, build, and test a compound machine.

PURPOSE **To further explore simple machines and how they work**

MATERIALS

• cardboard box
• paper clip
• paper
• pencil
• rubber bands
• 2 rubber bands
• 3 metric rulers
• small masses, 10–100 g
• test mass, 100 g
• string, 20-cm length
• tape

Activities and Discussion

☐ **Activity** Seeking Out Machines
☐ **Activity** What Machines Can Do
☐ **Discussion** Compare and Contrast
☐ **Take It Home** Notice the Machines!

Labs and Demos

☐ **Daily Demo** Playground Machines
☐ **Quick Lab** Mechanical Efficiency
☐ **Quick Lab** Investigate Pulleys
☐ **S.T.E.M. Lab** Compound Machines

Your Resources

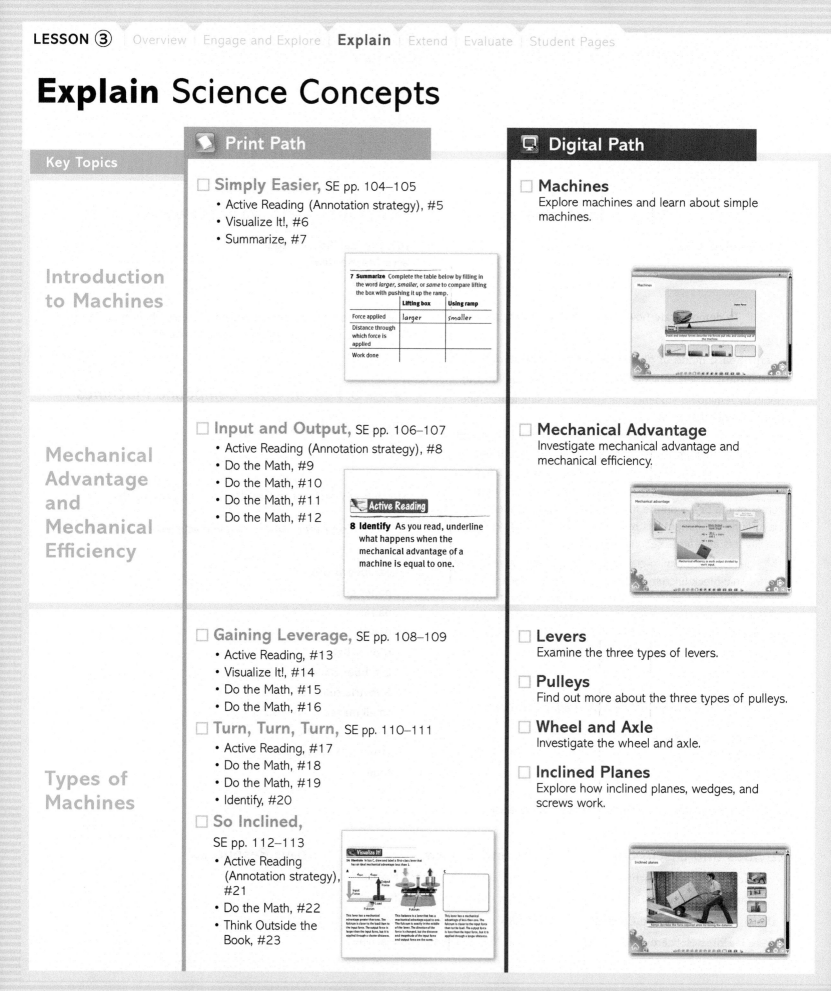

Explain Science Concepts

Key Topics	📖 Print Path	🖥 Digital Path
Introduction to Machines	☐ **Simply Easier,** SE pp. 104–105 • Active Reading (Annotation strategy), #5 • Visualize It!, #6 • Summarize, #7	☐ **Machines** Explore machines and learn about simple machines.
Mechanical Advantage and Mechanical Efficiency	☐ **Input and Output,** SE pp. 106–107 • Active Reading (Annotation strategy), #8 • Do the Math, #9 • Do the Math, #10 • Do the Math, #11 • Do the Math, #12	☐ **Mechanical Advantage** Investigate mechanical advantage and mechanical efficiency.
Types of Machines	☐ **Gaining Leverage,** SE pp. 108–109 • Active Reading, #13 • Visualize It!, #14 • Do the Math, #15 • Do the Math, #16 ☐ **Turn, Turn, Turn,** SE pp. 110–111 • Active Reading, #17 • Do the Math, #18 • Do the Math, #19 • Identify, #20 ☐ **So Inclined,** SE pp. 112–113 • Active Reading (Annotation strategy), #21 • Do the Math, #22 • Think Outside the Book, #23	☐ **Levers** Examine the three types of levers. ☐ **Pulleys** Find out more about the three types of pulleys. ☐ **Wheel and Axle** Investigate the wheel and axle. ☐ **Inclined Planes** Explore how inclined planes, wedges, and screws work.

Basic *Input/Output*

Types of Machines

individuals

20 min

Illustrations Have students find or draw an image of each of the six simple machines from the lesson. Then have them label where the input force and the output force. Students should compare their illustrations with a partner to check for errors in their work. Then students should collect their illustrations into a mini-book to save for future reference. Support students as needed.

Advanced *Friction*

Mechanical Advantage and Mechanical Efficiency

small groups

varies

Quick Research Direct small groups to investigate the role of friction in mechanical efficiency. Have students identify the factors that can increase the mechanical efficiency of a simple machine. Groups should prepare an oral presentation that they can present to the whole class; remind groups that each person should have a part in the presentation.

ELL *Illustrated Machines*

Types of Machines

individuals

20–30 min

Collage Have students choose one of the six simple machines described in the text. Then have them find images that show their chosen machine in use. Have students use those pictures to create a collage showing their chosen simple machine.

Lesson Vocabulary

machine	mechanical advantage	mechanical efficiency
lever	fulcrum	wheel and axle
pulley	inclined plane	

Previewing Vocabulary

whole class

10 min

Quick Pictures After an initial review of the lesson vocabulary, ask students to draw quick sketches of the following words: *machine, lever, fulcrum, wheel and axle, pulley,* and *inclined plane.* **Ask:** Using your sketches, name a job, or task, that each of the machines listed can do. Students should be able to identify a "job" for each machine listed based on their own personal experiences with simple machines.

Reinforcing Vocabulary

individuals

15 min

Description Wheel To help students remember the vocabulary terms in the lesson, have them develop a description wheel for each vocabulary word. Write the word in the center of the wheel. Then write the definition and details on the spokes. Students may add illustrations on any of the spokes.

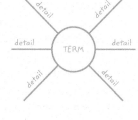

Customize Your Core Lesson

Core Instruction

☐ **Print Path** choices
☐ **Digital Path** choices

Vocabulary

☐ **Previewing Vocabulary** Quick Pictures
☐ **Reinforcing Vocabulary** Description Wheel

Your Resources

Differentiated Instruction

☐ **Basic** Input/Output
☐ **Advanced** Friction
☐ **ELL** Illustrated Machines

Extend Science Concepts

Reinforce and Review

Activity *Using Machines*

Synthesizing Key Topics
👥 whole class
🕐 15 min

Think, Pair, Share Present students with a problem. Tell them to imagine they have a very heavy box that must be moved from one location to another. They do not have a car at their disposal, but they do have access to all six simple machines. Give students five to ten minutes to devise a plan to move the heavy box from one location to another using one or all of the simple machines. Then have students join a partner to share their plans. Invite volunteers to share their various plans with the entire class.

FoldNotes

Types of Machines
👥 individuals
🕐 ongoing

Layered Book FoldNote After studying the lesson, have students develop a layered book to summarize the six simple machines described in the lesson: lever, pulley, wheel and axle, inclined plane, wedge, and screw.

When students have completed their layered books, have them compare their summaries with a partner to correct any errors or include any missing information. Support students as necessary throughout the writing process.

🌐 *Optional Online resource: Layered Book FoldNote*

Going Further

Life Science Connection

Synthesizing Key Topics
👥 individuals or small groups
🕐 varies

Have students research how animals, especially other primates, use tools in the wild. Have students create a visual and a short presentation to share their findings to the class. Students should include the types of materials animals use for tools, how those materials are used, and for what purposes they are used.

Social Studies Connection

Types of Machines
👥 small groups
🕐 varies

During World War II, a group of Allied prisoners engineered the escape of more than 70 men from a prison camp. Among the devices they used was a pulley system that let them pass notes quickly across long distances. Challenge students to invent such a note-delivery system. Provide them with materials they can use to build simple machines, such as spools, wire coat hangers, string, paper clips, straws, paper cups, and wooden clothespins. Encourage them to think creatively.

Customize Your Closing

🔲 *See the Assessment Guide for quizzes and tests.*

🌐 *Go Online to edit and create quizzes and tests.*

Reinforce and Review

☐ **Activity** Using Machines

☐ **FoldNote** Types of Machines

☐ **Print Path** Visual Summary, SE p. 114

☐ **Print Path** Lesson Review, SE p. 115

☐ **Digital Path** Lesson Closer

Evaluate Student Mastery

Formative Assessment

See the teacher support below the Student Pages for additional Formative Assessment questions.

Ask the following questions to assess student mastery of the material. **Ask:** What does a machine do? A machine changes the way work is done, making that work easier to do. **Ask:** Explain how to calculate mechanical advantage. MA = output force / input force **Ask:** How is mechanical efficiency expressed? as a percentage **Ask:** Name the six simple machines. lever, pulley, wheel and axle, inclined plane, wedge, screw

Reteach

Formative assessment may show that students need reinforcement for certain topics. The resources below are recommended for reteaching. If students were introduced to a topic through the Print Path, you can also use the Digital Path to reteach, and vice versa.
🎧 *Can be assigned to individual students*

Introduction to Machines
Activity Seeking Out Machines 🎧

Mechanical Advantage and Mechanical Efficiency
Basic Input/Output 🎧

Types of Machines
FoldNote Types of Machines 🎧
Daily Demo Playground Machines 🎧
ELL Illustrated Machines 🎧

Summative Assessment

Alternative Assessment
Machines

🌐 *Online resources: student worksheet; optional rubrics*

Machines

Take Your Pick: *Machines*
Choose from the assignments below to show what you have learned about machines.

1. Work on your own.
2. Choose items below for a total of 10 points. Check your choices.
3. Have your teacher approve your plan.
4. Submit or present your results.

2 Points

_____ **Acrostic** Using the word "Machines," create an acrostic to describe the importance of machines in human life. Use information from the lesson or extend the content by thinking beyond the lesson to everyday events.

_____ **Crossword** Create a crossword puzzle using all of the vocabulary words from the lesson. Include a key with your puzzle on a separate sheet of paper.

5 Points

_____ **Application Cards** Create at least five application cards to demonstrate real-world applications of the concepts and principles described in the lesson. Possible concepts to include are mechanical advantage, mechanical efficiency, force, or work. You may also include no more than two simple machines.

_____ **Quiz Cards** Develop a set of quiz cards based on the lesson. Make five cards for each key topic: Introduction to Machines, Mechanical Advantage and Mechanical Efficiency, and Types of Machines.

_____ **Design/Plan** Develop a simple demonstration to show how one of the six simple machines changes the way work is done. Write a plan and a short summary describing your demonstration.

_____ **Brochure** Develop a brochure advertising your choice of four simple machines. Include how the machines are used, how they change how work is done, and several uses for each type of machine.

8 Points

_____ **Worksheet** Develop a worksheet with questions that evaluate fellow students on the key topics from the lesson. Worksheets should be formatted so that students can write directly on the page.

_____ **Presentation** Create a short computer presentation that defines and explains mechanical advantage and mechanical efficiency. Present your slides to the teacher only, a small group, or the whole class.

Going Further
☐ Life Science Connection Using Tools
☐ Social Studies Connection Types of Machines

Formative Assessment
☐ Strategies Throughout TE
☐ Lesson Review SE

Summative Assessment
☐ Alternative Assessment Machines
☐ Lesson Quiz
☐ Unit Tests A and B
☐ Unit Review SE End-of-Unit

Your Resources
_____
_____

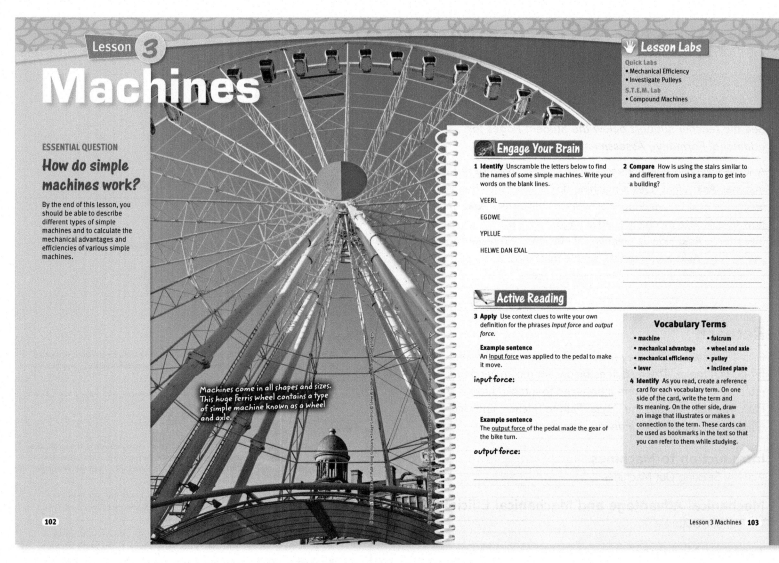

Lesson ③

Machines

ESSENTIAL QUESTION

How do simple machines work?

By the end of this lesson, you should be able to describe different types of simple machines and to calculate the mechanical advantages and efficiencies of various simple machines.

Machines come in all shapes and sizes. This huge Ferris wheel contains a type of simple machine known as a wheel and axle.

Lesson Labs

Quick Labs
• Mechanical Efficiency
• Investigate Pulleys

S.T.E.M. Lab
• Compound Machines

Engage Your Brain

1 Identify Unscramble the letters below to find the names of some simple machines. Write your words on the blank lines.

VEERL _____

EGDWE _____

YPLLUE _____

HELWE DAN EXAL _____

2 Compare How is using the stairs similar to and different from using a ramp to get into a building?

Active Reading

3 Apply Use context clues to write your own definition for the phrases *input force* and *output force*.

Example sentence
An input force was applied to the pedal to make it move.

input force:

_____

_____

Example sentence
The output force of the pedal made the gear of the bike turn.

output force:

_____

Vocabulary Terms

• machine
• mechanical advantage
• mechanical efficiency
• lever
• fulcrum
• wheel and axle
• pulley
• inclined plane

4 Identify As you read, create a reference card for each vocabulary term. On one side of the card, write the term and its meaning. On the other side, draw an image that illustrates or makes a connection to the term. These cards can be used as bookmarks in the text so that you can refer to them while studying.

102

Lesson 3 Machines 103

Answers

Answers 1–3 should represent students' current thoughts, even if incorrect.

1. lever; wedge; pulley; wheel and axle

2. Sample answer: Ramps make it easier for wheelchairs or anything with wheels to get into a building. Ramps are longer than stairs, but ramps and stairs are the same height. You end up in the same place using either a ramp or stairs.

3. a force that is put in or applied; a force that is produced

4. Students should define and sketch each vocabulary term in the lesson.

Opening Your Lesson

Begin by asking students to complete item 1 individually. Then have them compare their answers with a partner. Have students complete item 2 individually, and discuss their answers as a class.

Prerequisites Students should have a working understanding of the scientific concepts of work, energy, and power.

Learning Alert

Difficult Concept Some students may have difficulty imagining some of the simple machines listed in item 1. English language learners may or may not recognize the terms used. Display photos or pictures of each simple machine listed to improve students' understanding of the terms.

Simply Easier

5 Identify As you read, underline the types of simple machines.

What do simple machines do?

What do you think of as a machine—maybe a car or a computer? A **machine** is any device that helps people do work by changing the way work is done. The machines that make up other machines are called *simple machines*. The six types of simple machines are *levers*, *wheels and axles*, *pulleys*, *inclined planes*, *wedges*, and *screws*.

Change the Way Work Is Done

The wheelbarrow and rake shown below contain simple machines. They change the way you do work. Work is the use of force to move an object some distance. The force you apply to a machine through a distance is called the *input force*. The work that you do on a machine is called *work input*. You do work on a wheelbarrow when you lift the handles. You pull up on the handles to make them move. The wheelbarrow does work on the leaves. The work done by the machine on an object is called *work output*. The *output force* is the force a machine exerts on an object. The wheelbarrow exerts an output force on the leaves to lift them up.

Visualize It!

6 Identify The person raking leaves applies an input force to the handle of the rake. The output force is applied to the leaves. Label the input force and the output force on the rake.

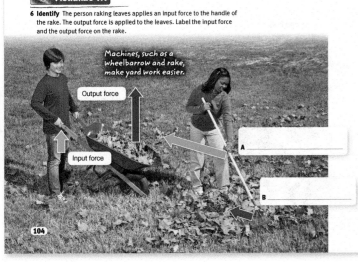

Machines, such as a wheelbarrow and rake, make yard work easier.

Output force

Input force

A _____

B _____

104

Change the Size of a Force and the Distance

Machines make tasks easier without decreasing the amount of work done. Work is equal to force times distance. If you apply less force with a machine, you apply that force through a longer distance. So the amount of work done remains the same. A ramp is an example of a machine that can change the magnitude, or size, of the force needed to move an object. You apply less force when you push a box up a ramp than when you lift the box. However, you apply the force through a longer distance. The amount of work you do is the same as when you lift the box to the same height, if friction is ignored. Other machines increase the amount of force needed, but you apply the force over a shorter distance.

Input force

The work done on the box is equal to the input force needed to lift the box times the height to which the box is lifted.

Input force

7 Summarize Complete the table below by filling in the word *larger*, *smaller*, or *same* to compare lifting the box with pushing it up the ramp.

	Lifting box	Using ramp
Force applied	larger	smaller
Distance through which force is applied		
Work done		

Less force is applied through a longer distance when the box is pushed up a ramp. But the work done on the box is the same.

Change the Direction of a Force

Some machines change the way you do work by changing the direction of a force. For example, you apply a downward force when you pull on the rope to raise a flag. The rope runs over a pulley at the top of the flagpole. The rope exerts an upward force on the flag, and the flag goes up. The direction of the force you applied has changed. But the magnitude of force and distance through which you apply the force are the same.

The pulley on the flagpole changed only the direction of the force. However, other machines can change the direction of a force, the magnitude of the force, and the distance through which the force is applied.

Pulling down on the rope pulls up the flag.

Input force

105

Answers

5. *See students' pages for annotations.*

6. A. input force; B. output force.

7. Students should fill in the table with the terms *smaller* (middle left), *larger* (middle right), *same* (bottom left), *same* (bottom right).

Using Annotations

Text Structure: Main Idea and Details Students are provided with the definition of a machine. Explain that the definition of a machine is one of the main ideas on these pages. Extend the activity by having students circle details that support this main idea.

Optional online resource: Main Idea/Details

Learning Alert

Difficult Concept Some students may feel overwhelmed by reading textual descriptions of math calculations. As students read the section on force, have them find the sentence that can be rewritten as a math statement. Then have them write a math statement that corresponds to that sentence and check their answers with the rest of the class. Sentence in text: "Work is equal to force times distance." Work = force × distance.

Formative Assessment

Ask: What elements of force might machines change? Machines are capable of changing the direction, size, and distance of force.

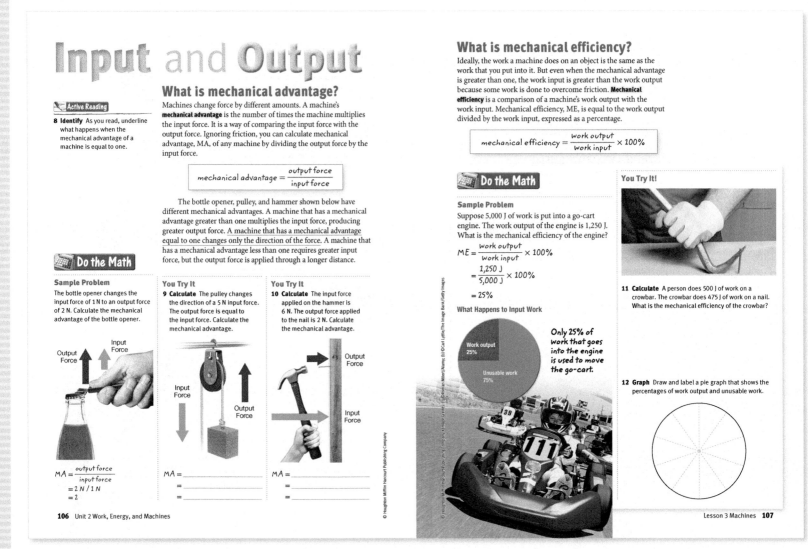

Input and Output

What is mechanical advantage?

8 Identify As you read, underline what happens when the mechanical advantage of a machine is equal to one.

Machines change force by different amounts. A machine's **mechanical advantage** is the number of times the machine multiplies the input force. It is a way of comparing the input force with the output force. Ignoring friction, you can calculate mechanical advantage, MA, of any machine by dividing the output force by the input force.

$$\text{mechanical advantage} = \frac{\text{output force}}{\text{input force}}$$

The bottle opener, pulley, and hammer shown below have different mechanical advantages. A machine that has a mechanical advantage greater than one multiplies the input force, producing greater output force. A machine that has a mechanical advantage equal to one changes only the direction of the force. A machine that has a mechanical advantage less than one requires greater input force, but the output force is applied through a longer distance.

Do the Math

Sample Problem

The bottle opener changes the input force of 1 N to an output force of 2 N. Calculate the mechanical advantage of the bottle opener.

Output Force / Input Force

$$MA = \frac{\text{output force}}{\text{input force}}$$
$$= 2\,N\,/\,1\,N$$
$$= 2$$

You Try It

9 Calculate The pulley changes the direction of a 5 N input force. The output force is equal to the input force. Calculate the mechanical advantage.

Input Force / Output Force

$$MA = \underline{\hspace{3cm}}$$
$$= \underline{\hspace{3cm}}$$
$$= \underline{\hspace{3cm}}$$

You Try It

10 Calculate The input force applied on the hammer is 6 N. The output force applied to the nail is 2 N. Calculate the mechanical advantage.

Output Force / Input Force

$$MA = \underline{\hspace{3cm}}$$
$$= \underline{\hspace{3cm}}$$
$$= \underline{\hspace{3cm}}$$

What is mechanical efficiency?

Ideally, the work a machine does on an object is the same as the work that you put into it. But even when the mechanical advantage is greater than one, the work input is greater than the work output because some work is done to overcome friction. **Mechanical efficiency** is a comparison of a machine's work output with the work input. Mechanical efficiency, ME, is equal to the work output divided by the work input, expressed as a percentage.

$$\text{mechanical efficiency} = \frac{\text{work output}}{\text{work input}} \times 100\%$$

Do the Math

Sample Problem

Suppose 5,000 J of work is put into a go-cart engine. The work output of the engine is 1,250 J. What is the mechanical efficiency of the engine?

$$ME = \frac{\text{work output}}{\text{work input}} \times 100\%$$
$$= \frac{1,250\ J}{5,000\ J} \times 100\%$$
$$= 25\%$$

What Happens to Input Work

Work output 25%

Unusable work 75%

Only 25% of work that goes into the engine is used to move the go-cart.

You Try It!

11 Calculate A person does 500 J of work on a crowbar. The crowbar does 475 J of work on a nail. What is the mechanical efficiency of the crowbar?

12 Graph Draw and label a pie graph that shows the percentages of work output and unusable work.

Answers

8. *See students' pages for annotations.*

9. MA = output force/input force = 5 N / 5 N = 1

10. MA = output force/input force = 2 N / 6 N = ⅓

11. mechanical efficiency = work output / work input × 100% = 475 J / 500 J × 100% = 95%

12. Students should make a pie graph that shows that 95% of the work input goes toward work output and that 5% of the work input goes toward unusable work.

Do the Math

Point out that the diagram on the far left provides an example of how to calculate mechanical advantage of a lever—in this case, a bottle opener. Remind students that the mechanical advantage of the pulley and the hammer are calculated in the same way, by dividing the output force by the input force.

Using Annotations

Have students complete the annotation strategy to note situations with mechanical advantages equal to 1. Extend the activity by having students work with a partner to restate in their own words each sentence they underline.

Do the Math

Remind students that, in machines, the work done to overcome friction plus the output work is always equal to the input work. Therefore, the total area of the circle graph is equal to the input work. This total amount is divided into two portions: the work that is converted to output work and the work that is used to overcome friction.

🌐 *Optional online resource: Circle Graph*

Gaining Leverage

What are the classes of levers?

What do hammers, seesaws, and baseball bats have in common? They are all levers. A **lever** is a simple machine that has a bar that pivots at a fixed point. This fixed point is called a **fulcrum**. Levers are used to apply a force to move an object. The force of the object is called the load.

Ideal mechanical advantage is the mechanical advantage of a simple machine that does not take friction into account. In other words, ideal mechanical advantage is the mechanical advantage of a machine that is 100% efficient. The ideal mechanical advantage of a lever is equal to the distance from input force to fulcrum (d_{input}) divided by the distance from output force to fulcrum (d_{output}).

$$\text{ideal mechanical advantage} = \frac{d_{input}}{d_{output}}$$

 **Visualize It!**

14 Illustrate In box C, draw and label a first-class lever that has an ideal mechanical advantage less than one.

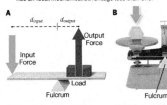 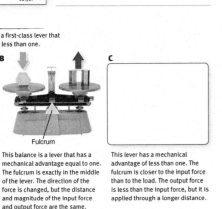

A

This lever has a mechanical advantage greater than one. The fulcrum is closer to the load than to the input force. The output force is larger than the input force, but it is applied through a shorter distance.

B

This balance is a lever that has a mechanical advantage equal to one. The fulcrum is exactly in the middle of the lever. The direction of the force is changed, but the distance and magnitude of the input force and output force are the same.

C

This lever has a mechanical advantage of less than one. The fulcrum is closer to the input force than to the load. The output force is less than the input force, but it is applied through a longer distance.

First-Class Levers

There are three classes of levers that differ based on the positions of the fulcrum, the load, and the input force. A seesaw is an example of a *first-class lever*. In a first-class lever, the fulcrum is between the input force and the load. First-class levers always change the direction of the input force. They may also increase the force or the distance through which the force is applied. The ideal mechanical advantage of first-class levers can be greater than one, equal to one, or less than one, depending on the location of the fulcrum.

Active Reading **13 Describe** Where is the fulcrum located in a first-class lever?

Second-Class Levers

In a *second-class lever*, the load is between the fulcrum and the input force. Second-class levers do not change the direction of the input force. They allow you to apply less force than the load. But you must exert the input force through a greater distance. The ideal mechanical advantage for a second-class lever is always greater than one. Wheelbarrows, bottle-cap openers, and staplers are second-class levers. A stapler pivots at one end when you push on the other end. The output force of the stapler drives the staple into the paper. The output force is applied between where you push and where the stapler pivots.

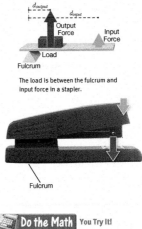

The load is between the fulcrum and input force in a stapler.

Do the Math You Try It!

15 Calculate The input force of a third-class lever is 5 cm away from the fulcrum. The output force is 20 cm away from the fulcrum. What is the ideal mechanical advantage of the lever?

Third-Class Levers

In a *third-class lever*, the input force is between the fulcrum and the load. Like second-class levers, third-class levers do not change the direction of the input force. The mechanical advantage for a third-class lever is always less than one. The output force is less than the input force. But the output force is applied through a longer distance. Hammers and baseball bats are examples of third-class levers. When you swing a baseball bat, the fulcrum is at the base of the handle. The output force is at the end of the bat where it hits the ball. A bat applies a force to the ball in the same direction as you swing the bat. Your hands move a much shorter distance than the end of the bat moves when you swing.

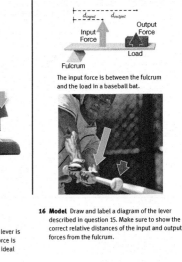

The input force is between the fulcrum and the load in a baseball bat.

16 Model Draw and label a diagram of the lever described in question 15. Make sure to show the correct relative distances of the input and output forces from the fulcrum.

Answers

13. A fulcrum is between the applied force and the load.

14. Students should draw a lever with the fulcrum closer to the input force than to the load. The fulcrum, input force, and load should be labeled.

15. ideal mechanical advantage = d_{input} / d_{output} = 5 cm / 20 cm = 0.25

16. Students should draw a third-class lever with an input force that is about 1/4 the distance of the output force from the fulcrum.

Formative Assessment

Ask: Define the terms *lever* and *fulcrum*. Sample answer: A lever is a simple machine that is made of a bar and a fulcrum. A fulcrum is the pivot point of a lever. **Ask:** What characteristic of a lever is used to classify it as a first-class, second-class, or third-class lever? the positions of the fulcrum, load, and input force **Ask:** Which type of levers change the direction of the input force? First-class levers change the direction of the input force.

Learning Alert

Difficult Concept Have students use visualization to understand the way a force changes direction when a lever is used. Ask students to imagine a seesaw. The fulcrum is at the center, and the direction of force changes when the riders move up and down. One rider is the load, and the other rider applies force to the lever by pushing up. This force is the input force, and it sends the first rider down while the second rider rises up. The roles are then reversed, and the first rider applies more input force to propel the second rider back to the ground. The lever pivots around the fulcrum at the center of the seesaw.

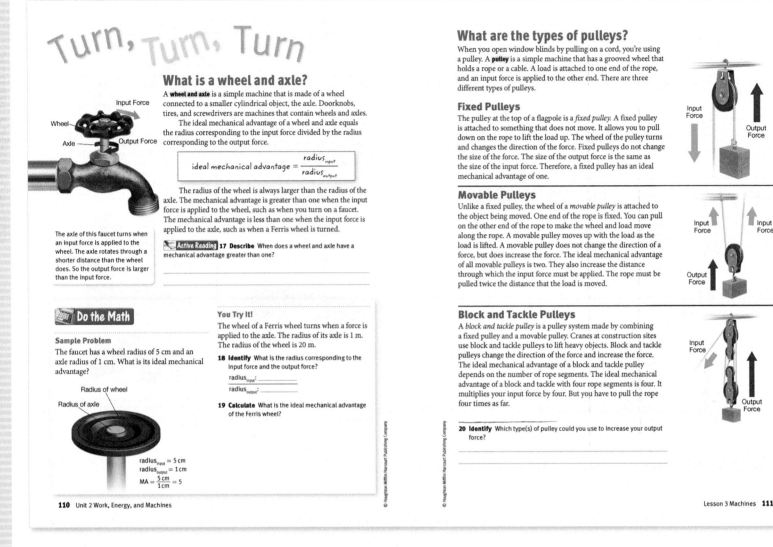

Turn, Turn, Turn

What is a wheel and axle?

A **wheel and axle** is a simple machine that is made of a wheel connected to a smaller cylindrical object, the axle. Doorknobs, tires, and screwdrivers are machines that contain wheels and axles.

The ideal mechanical advantage of a wheel and axle equals the radius corresponding to the input force divided by the radius corresponding to the output force.

$$\text{ideal mechanical advantage} = \frac{radius_{input}}{radius_{output}}$$

The radius of the wheel is always larger than the radius of the axle. The mechanical advantage is greater than one when the input force is applied to the wheel, such as when you turn on a faucet. The mechanical advantage is less than one when the input force is applied to the axle, such as when a Ferris wheel is turned.

Active Reading 17 Describe When does a wheel and axle have a mechanical advantage greater than one?

_____

_____

The axle of this faucet turns when an input force is applied to the wheel. The axle rotates through a shorter distance than the wheel does. So the output force is larger than the input force.

Do the Math

Sample Problem

The faucet has a wheel radius of 5 cm and an axle radius of 1 cm. What is its ideal mechanical advantage?

Radius of wheel
Radius of axle

$radius_{input} = 5\ cm$
$radius_{output} = 1\ cm$
$MA = \frac{5\ cm}{1\ cm} = 5$

You Try It!

The wheel of a Ferris wheel turns when a force is applied to the axle. The radius of its axle is 1 m. The radius of the wheel is 20 m.

18 Identify What is the radius corresponding to the input force and the output force?

$radius_{input}$: _____

$radius_{output}$: _____

19 Calculate What is the ideal mechanical advantage of the Ferris wheel?

110 Unit 2 Work, Energy, and Machines

What are the types of pulleys?

When you open window blinds by pulling on a cord, you're using a pulley. A **pulley** is a simple machine that has a grooved wheel that holds a rope or a cable. A load is attached to one end of the rope, and an input force is applied to the other end. There are three different types of pulleys.

Fixed Pulleys

The pulley at the top of a flagpole is a *fixed pulley*. A fixed pulley is attached to something that does not move. It allows you to pull down on the rope to lift the load up. The wheel of the pulley turns and changes the direction of the force. Fixed pulleys do not change the size of the force. The size of the output force is the same as the size of the input force. Therefore, a fixed pulley has an ideal mechanical advantage of one.

Movable Pulleys

Unlike a fixed pulley, the wheel of a *movable pulley* is attached to the object being moved. One end of the rope is fixed. You can pull on the other end of the rope to make the wheel and load move along the rope. A movable pulley moves up with the load as the load is lifted. A movable pulley does not change the direction of a force, but does increase the force. The ideal mechanical advantage of all movable pulleys is two. They also increase the distance through which the input force must be applied. The rope must be pulled twice the distance that the load is moved.

Block and Tackle Pulleys

A *block and tackle pulley* is a pulley system made by combining a fixed pulley and a movable pulley. Cranes at construction sites use block and tackle pulleys to lift heavy objects. Block and tackle pulleys change the direction of the force and increase the force. The ideal mechanical advantage of a block and tackle pulley depends on the number of rope segments. The ideal mechanical advantage of a block and tackle with four rope segments is four. It multiplies your input force by four. But you have to pull the rope four times as far.

20 Identify Which type(s) of pulley could you use to increase your output force?

_____

_____

Lesson 3 Machines 111

Answers

17. It is greater than 1 when the force is applied to the wheel.

18. 1 meter; 20 meters

19. ideal mechanical advantage = $radius_{input}$ / $radius_{output}$ = 1 / 20 = 0.05

20. movable or block and tackle pulley

Do the Math

Remind students that identical units of measurement cancel out in division problems. In the sample problem, point out that the radius of the wheel of the faucet and the axle is measured in centimeters (cm). When the mechanical advantage formula is used, the units of measurement must cancel out because they are the same.

Probing Questions GUIDED Inquiry

Analysis How is the fulcrum of a lever similar to an axle of a wheel and axle? Sample answer: It is the point around which another part of the simple machine rotates.

Interpreting Visuals

Have students use the diagrams to help interpret the information about the input and output force for each of the three types of pulleys.

So Inclined

What are inclined planes?

21 Identify As you read, underline how an inclined plane changes the force and the distance through which the force is applied.

Why is pushing furniture up a ramp easier than lifting the furniture? When you push something up a ramp, you are using a machine called an *inclined plane*. An **inclined plane** is a simple machine that is a straight, slanted surface. A smaller input force is needed to move an object using an inclined plane than is needed to lift the object. However, the force must be applied through a longer distance. So, the amount of work done on the object is the same. The ideal mechanical advantage of an inclined plane can be calculated by dividing the length of the incline by the height that the load is lifted.

$$\text{ideal mechanical advantage} = \frac{length}{height}$$

Do the Math

Sample Problem

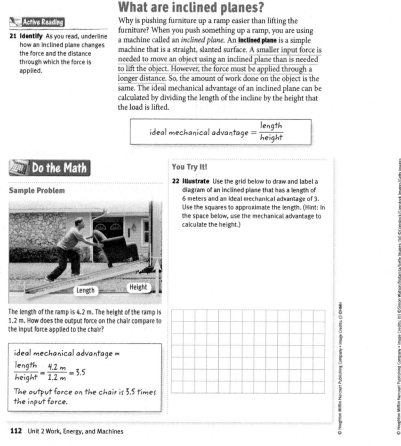

Length   Height

The length of the ramp is 4.2 m. The height of the ramp is 1.2 m. How does the output force on the chair compare to the input force applied to the chair?

ideal mechanical advantage =
$$\frac{length}{height} = \frac{4.2 \, m}{1.2 \, m} = 3.5$$

The output force on the chair is 3.5 times the input force.

You Try It!

22 Illustrate Use the grid below to draw and label a diagram of an inclined plane that has a length of 6 meters and an ideal mechanical advantage of 3. Use the squares to approximate the length. (Hint: In the space below, use the mechanical advantage to calculate the height.)

What are wedges?

Sculptors use chisels to break rock and wood. Chisels, ax heads, and knife blades are wedges. A *wedge* is a pair of inclined planes that move. They have one thick end and one thin end. Wedges are used to cut and split objects. For example, a sculptor applies an input force to the thick end of a chisel. The thin end of the chisel exerts an outward force that splits open the object. The output force of the wedge is greater than the input force, but the output force is applied through a shorter distance. The longer and thinner the wedge is, the greater its ideal mechanical advantage. So a longer chisel has a greater mechanical advantage than a shorter chisel that is the same width at the thick end.

Input Force — Width — Output Force — Length — Output Force

Wedges have two sloped sides and help split objects.

What are screws?

Screws are often used to hold wood together. A *screw* is an inclined plane that is wrapped in a spiral around a cylinder. Think of wrapping a long triangular piece of paper around a pencil, as shown below. The ridges formed by the paper are like the threads of a screw. When a screw is turned, a small force is applied through the distance along the inclined plane of the screw. The screw applies a large force through the short distance it is pushed.

Imagine unwinding the inclined plane of a screw. You would see that the plane is very long and has a gentle slope. The longer an inclined plane is compared with its height, the greater its ideal mechanical advantage. Similarly, the longer the spiral on a screw is and the closer together the threads are, the greater the screw's mechanical advantage.

The threads of a screw are made by wrapping an inclined plane around a cylinder.

Think Outside the Book   Inquiry

23 Apply Make a list of simple machines you use every day. In a small group, try to classify all the machines identified by the group members.

Answers

21. *See students' pages for annotations.*

22. Students should draw a triangle to represent an inclined plane that has a slope length of 6 units and a height of 2 units. The length of the inclined plane is three times the height.

23. Sample answers: clothesline (pulley); window blinds (pulley); seesaw (lever); fan (wheel and axle); bike wheels (wheel and axle); knife (wedge); wheelchair ramp (inclined plane); parking ramp (inclined plane)

Building Reading Skills

Context Clues: Restatement Direct students to read the sections on inclined planes, wedges, and screws. Then ask them to use context clues from the text to restate definitions or descriptions for each of these types of simple machine. Students can share their restatements with a partner or write them in their notebooks.

Optional online resource: Context Clues

Formative Assessment

Ask: Why does an inclined plane reduce the amount of force needed to move an object? A smaller amount of force can be applied to move the object over a longer distance.

Using Annotations

Have students complete the annotation strategy to emphasize the definition of an inclined plane. Then, to extend the activity, have students look for information about how wedges and screws are related to inclined planes.

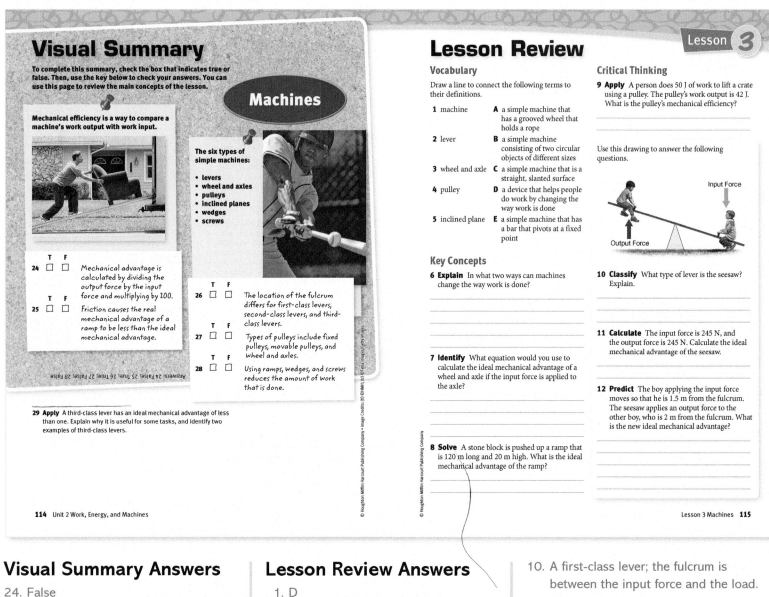

Visual Summary Answers

24. False

25. True

26. True

27. False

28. False

29. Sample answer: Third-class levers are useful when the output force is to be applied over a greater distance. Baseball bats and rakes are examples of third-class levers.

Lesson Review Answers

1. D

2. E

3. B

4. A

5. C

6. Machines can change the way work is done by changing the size and distance of the force used. They can also change the direction of a force.

7. ideal mechanical advantage = radius of input force / radius of output force = radius of axle / radius of wheel

8. ideal mechanical advantage = length / height = 120 m / 20 m = 6

9. mechanical efficiency = (work output / work input) × 100% = 42 / 50 × 100% = 84%

10. A first-class lever; the fulcrum is between the input force and the load.

11. MA = input force/output force = 245 N / 245 N = 1

12. MA = distance input force/distance output force = 1.5 m / 2 m = 0.75

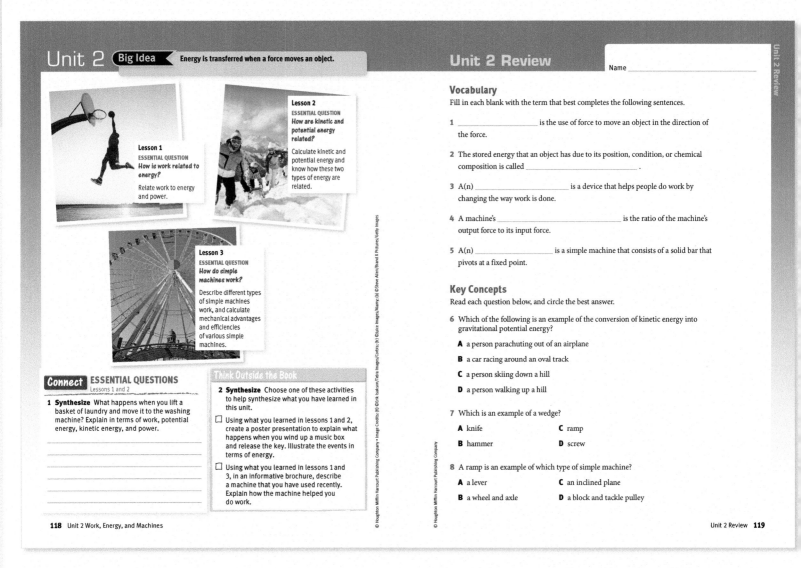

Unit 2 Big Idea Energy is transferred when a force moves an object.

Unit 2 Review   Name _____

Vocabulary

Fill in each blank with the term that best completes the following sentences.

1 _____ is the use of force to move an object in the direction of the force.

2 The stored energy that an object has due to its position, condition, or chemical composition is called _____ .

3 A(n) _____ is a device that helps people do work by changing the way work is done.

4 A machine's _____ is the ratio of the machine's output force to its input force.

5 A(n) _____ is a simple machine that consists of a solid bar that pivots at a fixed point.

Key Concepts

Read each question below, and circle the best answer.

6 Which of the following is an example of the conversion of kinetic energy into gravitational potential energy?

   A a person parachuting out of an airplane

   B a car racing around an oval track

   C a person skiing down a hill

   D a person walking up a hill

7 Which is an example of a wedge?

   A knife   **C** ramp

   B hammer   **D** screw

8 A ramp is an example of which type of simple machine?

   A a lever   **C** an inclined plane

   B a wheel and axle   **D** a block and tackle pulley

118 Unit 2 Work, Energy, and Machines

Unit 2 Review 119

Unit Summary Answers

1. Sample answer: When I lift a basket of laundry, I do work because I am using force to hold the basket. The basket has gravitational potential energy, and I have kinetic energy while I am walking. Power is the rate at which the work of lifting and carrying the basket is done.

2. Option 1: Students' presentations should illustrate that winding up a music box gives it potential energy. When released, this energy is converted to kinetic energy.

   Option 2: Answers will vary depending on the machines students choose.

Unit Review Response to Intervention

A Quick Grading Chart follows the Answers. See the Assessment Guide for more detail about correct and incorrect answer choices. Refer back to the Lesson Planning pages for activities and assignments that can be used as remediation for students who answer questions incorrectly.

Answers

1. Work Work is done only if the force acts in the same direction of the motion. (Lesson 1)

2. potential energy A book on a bookshelf has gravitational potential energy. A stretched rubber band has elastic potential energy. Chemical potential energy is the energy stored in chemical bonds. (Lesson 2)

3. machine Machines change the way work is done, not the amount of work that is done. (Lesson 3)

Unit 2 Review continued

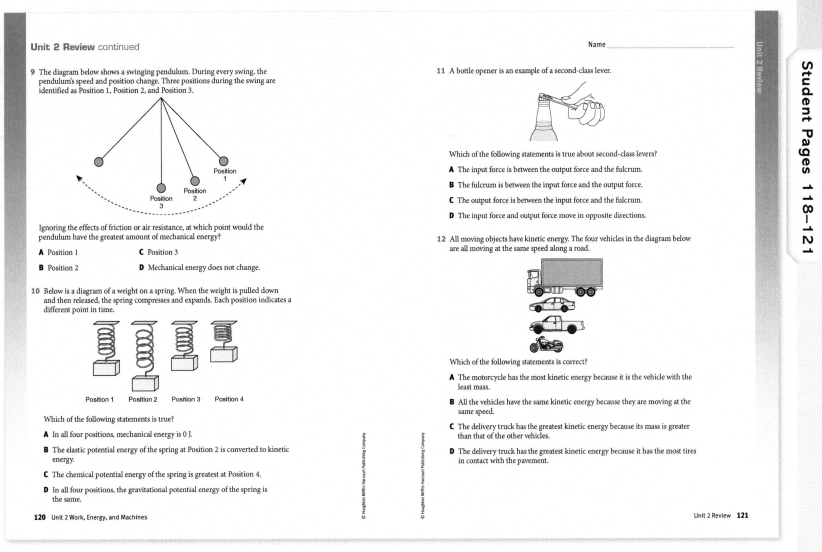

9 The diagram below shows a swinging pendulum. During every swing, the pendulum's speed and position change. Three positions during the swing are identified as Position 1, Position 2, and Position 3.

Ignoring the effects of friction or air resistance, at which point would the pendulum have the greatest amount of mechanical energy?

A Position 1

C Position 3

B Position 2

D Mechanical energy does not change.

10 Below is a diagram of a weight on a spring. When the weight is pulled down and then released, the spring compresses and expands. Each position indicates a different point in time.

Position 1   Position 2   Position 3   Position 4

Which of the following statements is true?

A In all four positions, mechanical energy is 0 J.

B The elastic potential energy of the spring at Position 2 is converted to kinetic energy.

C The chemical potential energy of the spring is greatest at Position 4.

D In all four positions, the gravitational potential energy of the spring is the same.

11 A bottle opener is an example of a second-class lever.

Which of the following statements is true about second-class levers?

A The input force is between the output force and the fulcrum.

B The fulcrum is between the input force and the output force.

C The output force is between the input force and the fulcrum.

D The input force and output force move in opposite directions.

12 All moving objects have kinetic energy. The four vehicles in the diagram below are all moving at the same speed along a road.

Which of the following statements is correct?

A The motorcycle has the most kinetic energy because it is the vehicle with the least mass.

B All the vehicles have the same kinetic energy because they are moving at the same speed.

C The delivery truck has the greatest kinetic energy because its mass is greater than that of the other vehicles.

D The delivery truck has the greatest kinetic energy because it has the most tires in contact with the pavement.

Answers *(continued)*

4. **mechanical advantage** Mechanical advantage is the output force divided by the input force. (Lesson 3)

5. **lever** The fixed point is called the fulcrum. There are three types of levers: first-class, second-class, and third-class levers. (Lesson 3)

6. Answer D is correct because the person is gaining gravitational potential energy as he or she climbs the hill. (Lesson 2)

7. Answer A is correct because when moving, such as when cutting something, a knife is a wedge; it is a combination of two inclined planes. (Lesson 3)

8. Answer C is correct because an inclined plane is a slanted surface that may be used to apply work over a long distance. A ramp is an example of an inclined plane. (Lesson 3)

9. Answer D is correct because mechanical energy remains the same when energy is transformed between potential energy and kinetic energy. (Lesson 2)

10. Answer B is correct because the spring is stretched and has stored elastic energy that can pull the weight back up. (Lesson 2)

11. Answer C is correct because this statement is true for second-class levers. (Lesson 3)

12. Answer C is correct because the object with the greatest mass has the greatest kinetic energy when the objects are moving at the same speed. (Lesson 2)

13. Answer D is correct because the formula for mechanical advantage = $radius_{input}/radius_{output}$ = 5/0.5 = 10. (Lesson 3)

14. Key Elements:

- Mechanical efficiency is a comparison of a machine's work output and a machine's work input.

- The formula for mechanical efficiency is (work output/work input) × 100%.

- Mechanical efficiency is expressed as a percentage. (Lesson 3)

Unit 2 Review continued

13 A faucet is an example of a simple machine, a wheel and axle. The faucet wheel has a radius of 5 cm. The axle has a radius of 0.5 cm. The input force is applied to the faucet wheel. What is the mechanical advantage of this simple machine?

A 0.1   C 5

B 1   D 10

Critical Thinking

Answer the following questions in the space provided.

14 What is mechanical efficiency, and how is it calculated?

_____

_____

_____

_____

15 Work is defined as the use of force to move an object in the direction of that force and is equal to the force times the distance the object moved. How do energy and power relate to work?

_____

_____

_____

_____

Connect ESSENTIAL QUESTIONS
Lessons 2 and 3

Answer the following question in the space provided.

16 Explain how an inclined plane makes loading a piano into a truck easier. Refer to the changing potential energy and kinetic energy of the piano as it (a) sits on the ground, (b) is being moved into the truck, and (c) sits in the truck.

_____

_____

_____

_____

_____

_____

© Houghton Mifflin Harcourt Publishing Company

122 Unit 2 Work, Energy, and Machines

Answers (continued)

15. Key Elements:
    - Energy is the ability to do work.
    - Work can transform one type of energy into another.
    - Power is the rate at which work is done. (Lesson 1)

16. Key Elements:
    - An inclined plane is a simple machine with a slanted surface.
    - The amount of work needed to raise a piano into the truck is not increased or decreased when a simple machine is used.
    - The inclined plane allows the work to be done over a longer distance.
    - (a) On the ground, the potential energy and kinetic energy equal zero. (b) As the piano moves up the inclined plane, the piano has kinetic energy and increasing gravitational potential energy. (c) When the piano is in the truck, the kinetic energy is zero and the potential energy is greater than when the piano was on the ground. (Lessons 2, 3)

Quick Grading Chart

Use the chart below for quick test grading. The lesson correlations can help you target reteaching for missed items.

Item	Answer	Cognitive Complexity	Lesson
1.	—	Low	1
2.	—	Low	2
3.	—	Low	3
4.	—	Low	3
5.	—	Low	3
6.	D	Moderate	2
7.	A	Moderate	3
8.	C	Moderate	3
9.	D	Moderate	2
10.	B	Moderate	2
11.	C	Moderate	3
12.	C	Moderate	2
13.	D	Moderate	3
14.	—	Moderate	3
15.	—	Moderate	1
16.	—	Moderate	2, 3

Cognitive Complexity refers to the demand on thinking associated with an item, and may vary with the answer choices, the number of steps required to arrive at an answer, and other factors, but not the ability level of the student.

The Big Idea and Essential Questions

This Unit was designed to focus on this Big Idea and Essential Questions.

Big Idea   An electric current can produce a magnetic field, and a magnetic field can produce an electric current.

Lesson	ESSENTIAL QUESTION	Student Mastery	Professional Development	Lesson Overview
LESSON 1 Electric Charge and Static Electricity	*What makes something electrically charged?*	To describe electric charges in objects and distinguish between electrical conductors and insulators	Content Refresher, TE p. 164	TE p. 172
LESSON 2 Electric Current	*What flows through an electric wire?*	To describe how electric charges flow as electric current	Content Refresher, TE p. 165	TE p. 186
LESSON 3 Electric Circuits	*How do electric circuits work?*	To describe basic electric circuits and how to use electricity safely	Content Refresher, TE p. 166	TE p. 198
LESSON 4 Magnets and Magnetism	*What is magnetism?*	To describe magnets and magnetic fields and explain their properties	Content Refresher, TE p. 167	TE p. 212
LESSON 5 Electromagnetism	*What is electromagnetism?*	To describe the relationship between electricity and magnetism and how this relationship affects our world	Content Refresher, TE p. 168	TE p. 230
LESSON 6 Electronic Technology	*What are electronics, and how have they changed?*	To describe what electronic devices do and how they change as technology changes	Content Refresher, TE p. 169	TE p. 246

©A. T. Willett/Alamy

Professional Development   Science Background

Use the keywords at right to access

- Professional Development from **The NSTA Learning Center**
- **SciLinks** for additional online content appropriate for students and teachers

Keywords
circuits
electric current
electricity
magnetism

NSTA National Science Teachers Association

SCiLINKS
THE WORLD'S A CLICK AWAY

Options for Instruction

Two parallel paths provide coverage of the Essential Questions, with a strong **Inquiry** strand woven into each. Follow the Print Path, the **Digital Path,** or your customized combination of print, digital, and inquiry.

	LESSON 1 Electric Charge and Static Electricity	LESSON 2 Electric Current	LESSON 3 Electric Circuits
Essential Questions	*What makes something electrically charged?*	*What flows through an electric wire?*	*How do electric circuits work?*
Key Topics	• Electric Charge • Electric Force • Conductors, Insulators, and Semiconductors	• Current • Voltage • Resistance	• Electric Circuits • Electric Safety
Print Path	Teacher Edition pp. 172–184 Student Edition pp. 126–135	Teacher Edition pp. 186–197 Student Edition pp. 136–143	Teacher Edition pp. 198–211 Student Edition pp. 144–155
Inquiry Labs	Lab Manual **Quick Lab** Investigate Conductors and Insulators Virtual Lab How Can Static Electric Charges Affect Each Other?	Lab Manual **Quick Lab** Investigate Electric Current **Quick Lab** Lemon Battery **S.T.E.M. Lab** Voltage, Current, and Resistance	Lab Manual **Exploration Lab** Model the Electric Circuits in a Room Virtual Lab How Can You Change Current in an Electric Circuit?
Digital Path	Digital Path TS675434	Digital Path TS675444	Digital Path TS675454

LESSON 4	LESSON 5	LESSONS 6 and
Magnets and Magnetism	Electromagnetism	UNIT 3 Unit Projects

What is magnetism?	**What is electromagnetism?**	*See the next page*

• Properties of Magnets • Properties of Magnetic Fields • Types of Magnets • Earth's Magnetic Field	• Electromagnetism • Electromagnets • Uses of Electromagnets • Induction	

Teacher Edition pp. 212–224	Teacher Edition pp. 230–244	**Unit Assessment**
Student Edition pp. 156–165	Student Edition pp. 170–183	*See the next page*

Lab Manual **Quick Lab** Making Magnets **Quick Lab** Studying Magnetism	Lab Manual **Quick Lab** Making an Electric Generator **Quick Lab** Building an Electromagnet **S.T.E.M. Lab** Building a Speaker

Digital Path TS675464	Digital Path TS675474

Options for Instruction

Two parallel paths provide coverage of the Essential Questions, with a strong **Inquiry** strand woven into each. Follow the **Print Path,** the **Digital Path,** or your customized combination of print, digital, and inquiry.

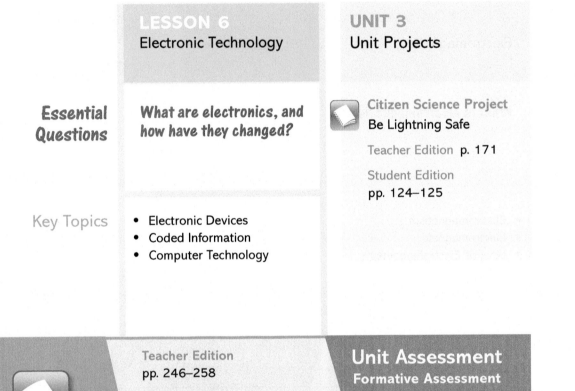

	LESSON 6 Electronic Technology	UNIT 3 Unit Projects
Essential Questions	**What are electronics, and how have they changed?**	Citizen Science Project **Be Lightning Safe** Teacher Edition p. 171 Student Edition pp. 124–125
Key Topics	• Electronic Devices • Coded Information • Computer Technology	

Print Path

Teacher Edition
pp. 246–258

Student Edition
pp. 184–193

Inquiry Labs

Lab Manual
Quick Lab The Speed of a Simple Computer

Quick Lab Investigate Satellite Imaging

Digital Path

Digital Path
TS675484

Unit Assessment

Formative Assessment

Strategies RTI
Throughout TE

Lesson Reviews SE

Unit PreTest

Summative Assessment

Alternative Assessment
(1 per lesson) RTI

Lesson Quizzes

Unit Tests A and B

Unit Review RTI
(with answer remediation)

Practice Tests
(end of module)

Project-Based Assessment

See the Assessment Guide for quizzes and tests.

Go Online to edit and create quizzes and tests.

Response to Intervention

See RTI teacher support materials on p. PD6.

Differentiated Instruction

English Language Proficiency

Strategies for **English Language Learners (ELL)** are provided for each lesson, under the Explain tabs.

LESSON 1 *Diagramming Charged Particles*, TE p. 177

LESSON 2 *Electricity Posters*, TE p. 191

LESSON 3 *Modified Cloze Sentences*, TE p. 203

LESSON 4 *Diagramming Magnets*, TE p. 217

Learning Poles, TE p. 217

LESSON 5 *Faraday Another Way*, TE p. 235

LESSON 6 *Computer Image*, TE p. 251

Vocabulary strategies provided for all students can also be of particular help for ELL. Use different strategies for each lesson, or choose one or two to use throughout the unit. Vocabulary strategies can be found under the Explain tabs for each lesson (TE pp. 177, 191, 203, 217, 235, and 251).

Leveled Inquiry

Inquiry labs, activities, probing questions, and daily demos provide a range of inquiry levels. Preview them under the Engage and Explore tabs starting on TE pp. 174, 188, 200, 214, 232, and 248.

 Levels of **Inquiry**

DIRECTED inquiry	**GUIDED** inquiry	**INDEPENDENT** inquiry
introduces inquiry skills within a structured framework.	develops inquiry skills within a supportive environment.	deepens inquiry skills with student-driven questions or procedures.

Each long lab has two inquiry options:

LESSON 2 S.T.E.M. Lab *Voltage, Current, and Resistance*

LESSON 3 Exploration Lab *Model the Electric Circuits in a Room*

LESSON 5 S.T.E.M. Lab *Building a Speaker*

🖥 Go Digital! ⏱ thinkcentral.com

Digital Path

The Unit 3 Resource Gateway is your guide to all of the digital resources for this unit. To access the Gateway, visit thinkcentral.com.

Digital Interactive Lessons

Lesson 1 Electric Charge and Static Electricity TS675434

Lesson 2 Electric Current TS675444

Lesson 3 Electric Circuits TS675454

Lesson 4 Magnets and Magnetism TS675464

Lesson 5 Electromagnetism TS675474

Lesson 6 Electronic Technology TS675484

More Digital Resources

In addition to digital lessons, you will find the following digital resources for Unit 3:

Virtual Labs: How Can Static Electric Charges Affect Each Other? (previewed on TE p. 175) How Can You Change Current in an Electric Circuit? (previewed on TE p. 201)

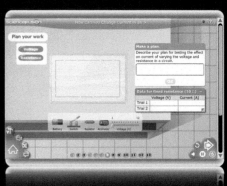

RTI ▶ Response to Intervention

Response to Intervention (RTI) is a process for identifying and supporting students who are not making expected progress toward essential learning goals. The following *ScienceFusion* components can be used to provide strategic and intensive intervention.

Component	Location	Strategies and Benefits
STUDENT EDITION Active Reading prompts, Visualize It!, Think Outside the Book	**Throughout each lesson**	Student responses can be used as screening tools to assess whether intervention is needed.
TEACHER EDITION Formative Assessment, Probing Questions, Learning Alerts	**Throughout each lesson**	Opportunities are provided to assess and remediate student understanding of lesson concepts.
TEACHER EDITION Extend Science Concepts	**Reinforce and Review, TE pp. 178, 192, 204, 218, 236, 252** **Going Further, TE pp. 178, 192, 204, 218, 236, 252**	Additional activities allow students to reinforce and extend their understanding of lesson concepts.
TEACHER EDITION Evaluate Student Mastery	**Formative Assessment, TE pp. 179, 193, 205, 219, 237, 253** **Alternative Assessment, TE pp. 179, 193, 205, 219, 237, 253**	These assessments allow for greater flexibility in assessing students with differing physical, mental, and language abilities as well as varying learning and communication modes.
TEACHER EDITION Unit Review Remediation	**Unit Review, TE pp. 260–263**	Includes reference back to Lesson Planning pages for remediation activities and assignments.
INTERACTIVE DIGITAL LESSONS and VIRTUAL LABS	**thinkcentral.com** **Unit 3 Gateway** **Lesson 1 TS675434** **Lesson 2 TS675444** **Lesson 3 TS675454** **Lesson 4 TS675464** **Lesson 5 TS675474** **Lesson 6 TS675484**	Lessons and labs make content accessible through simulations, animations, videos, audio, and integrated assessment. Useful for review and reteaching of lesson concepts.

Content Refresher

Professional Development

Lesson 1

Electric Charge and Static Electricity

ESSENTIAL QUESTION
What makes something electrically charged?

1. Electric Charge

Students will learn that electric charge is a fundamental physical property and that charges can be transferred.

Individual objects may carry a positive charge or a negative charge, or they may be electrically neutral. The charge an object has depends upon how the number of electrons compares to the number of protons present. The SI unit of electric charge is the coulomb (C) and is equal to 6.25×10^{18} electrons or protons.

Objects can become electrically charged in three ways—by friction, by contact, and by induction. Charging by friction occurs when electrons are "wiped" from the surface on one object and transferred onto the surface of another. Charging by contact, also called conduction, occurs when electrons move from one material that is in contact with another material. The materials do not need to be in motion. Charging by induction occurs when a charged object produces a temporary rearrangement of electrons in a second object. These materials do not need to be in contact with one another; they just need to be close enough for the charges to interact.

Static electricity results when electric charges build up on the surface of objects. When the object loses all or some of its electrical charge, a discharge occurs.

Electric charge is conserved. Thus, within the universe, the total amount of positive and negative charges is equal.

2. Electric Force

Students will learn that electric charges can be positive or negative and that electric force acts at a distance.

Objects that carry electric charges exert an electric force on each other. This force can act over a distance. Unlike the force of gravity, which acts only by pulling on objects, the electric force can both pull objects together and push them apart. The effect of the electric force on individual objects depends upon the kinds and numbers of charges the objects have as well as the distance between them. Electric force acts on objects having opposite charges by pulling them toward each other, while objects having the same charge (either + or −) are pushed apart. The amount of force is greater when the number of charges is greater or the distance is lessened.

3. Conductors, Insulators, and Semiconductors

Students will learn that materials are classified by how well they allow electric charges to move through them.

Materials that allow electric charges to move freely are classified as electrical conductors. A material that does not allow electric charges to move freely is an electrical insulator. Common insulators include plastic, glass, wood, and rubber.

Semiconductors do not conduct electric charge as well as electrical conductors but do not resist the flow of electric charge as well as insulators. Semiconductors are useful in many electronics applications because the flow of electric charge through the materials can be controlled.

©Corbis

COMMON MISCONCEPTIONS **RTI**

ELECTRON GAIN OR LOSS Students may think that to become positively charged, atoms gain protons.

This misconception is addressed in the Activity on p. 177 and the Learning Alert on p. 182.

Lesson 5 Electromagnetism Most students have seen the gigantic electro-magnets used at junkyards. However, students may not know that there are electromagnets in their own school! I take my students on a "mini" field trip to see the fire doors. Students see that there is a magnet holding the door open. I explain to them that when the fire alarm sounds, the electricity to these magnets is interrupted. The doors then close automatically.

Lesson 2

Electric Current

ESSENTIAL QUESTION
What flows through an electric wire?

1. Current

Students will learn about direct and alternating current and everyday devices that use each.

Electric current is the rate at which electric charges pass a given point. Electric current is measured in amperes. In direct current (DC), charge moves in a single direction between a positive and a negative terminal. Batteries produce direct current. Flashlights and media players are two everyday devices that run on batteries. In alternating current (AC), the direction of movement changes, or alternates, 60 times per second in the United States. The current delivered to a wall socket in the United States is 120 volt and 60 Hz. In Europe, it is generally 220 volt and 50 Hz, making it difficult or impossible to use American appliances in Europe.

2. Voltage

Students will learn that voltage is the amount of work it takes to move an electric charge.

Voltage, also called electric potential, is the amount of work it takes to move a unit electric charge between two points. It can be compared to the "pressure" pushing the electric charges. Voltage is measured in volts. The higher the voltage of an electric current, the greater the amount of energy the charges release as they move.

Electrical power is measured in watts. If you know how much electric current is in a wire and the voltage used in a particular area, you can find the amount of electrical power in watts using the equation power = current × voltage. Suppose you plug a blow dryer into a wall outlet. You measure the current to the blow dryer to be 10 A. This means that the blow dryer uses 1,200 watts: 120 V × 10 A = 1,200 watts.

It is relatively easy for a power company to change the voltage of alternating current using a transformer. This makes it inexpensive to transmit power over long distances. Power companies can transmit very high voltages, such as 1 million volts. Then they transform it to lower voltages for distribution. Eventually, for safety reasons, they drop the current down to 120 volts inside a home.

3. Resistance

Students will learn that resistance is the opposition to the movement of electric charges, and that several factors can affect resistance.

Some materials do not allow charges to move freely. This opposition to the movement of electric charge is called resistance. In comparing voltage to water pressure, current is similar to the rate of water flow. Resistance is similar to pipe diameter.

The higher the resistance of a material is, the lower the current in it will be at a particular voltage. Resistance is affected by the composition of a material. Good conductors of electric current, such as copper, have low resistance. Poor conductors of electric current, such as aluminum, have a higher resistance. Resistance of a wire depends on its thickness and length. A thick wire has less resistance than a thin wire (just as a wide pipe has less resistance than a narrow pipe). A short wire has less resistance than a long wire. Temperature can also affect the resistance of materials. In general, metals become more resistant to the movement of charges with rising temperature.

Current is equal to the voltage divided by the resistance. If you increase the voltage, the current will become greater.

(r) ©Getty Images

Content Refresher (continued)

Professional Development

Electric Circuits

ESSENTIAL QUESTION
How do electric circuits work?

1. Electric Circuits

Students will learn the components and structures of series and parallel circuits.

Electric circuits are part of our everyday world, but many times they are partly or completely hidden from view. Therefore, students will have a great amount of everyday experience with circuits but still might not understand that the light switch on the wall is a switch in a circuit.

Ohm's law, $V = IR$ (voltage is equal to current times resistance), is an equation that can be used to relate the voltage, current, and resistance in electric circuits. Ohm's law can help us understand how series circuits and parallel circuits differ.

In a series circuit, the resistance of the circuit is the sum of the resistances of each individual device in the circuit. Therefore, for a consistent voltage, each additional device added to the circuit increases resistance and decreases current. In a parallel circuit, each additional device added reduces the overall resistance (by giving the current another path to flow through). The voltage is the same in each branch of a parallel circuit, but the current is not.

Another difference between series and parallel circuits is how they are affected by a single broken device. In a series circuit, if one device is broken, there is no current in any part of the circuit, because current requires a closed loop in order to flow. In a parallel circuit, if one branch of the circuit is interrupted, current can still reach the other branches. In the past, strings of holiday lights were in series. Plugging the string of lights into a wall outlet completed the circuit, and each of the lights in the string lit up. However, if a single light in the entire string was broken, the entire string would not light. Parallel circuits avoid this problem, and most circuits in homes are parallel circuits for this reason.

2. Electrical Safety

Students will learn that precautions must be taken when using electrical appliances and during lightning storms.

Several characteristics of the human body make it vulnerable to harm by electric current. First, the body contains a great deal of water containing dissolved salts. This salty solution conducts electric current, so the water in the body allows current to move through the body. Secondly, electric current is involved in nerve impulses and in initiating and regulating the heartbeat. Therefore, electric current can disrupt movement and can cause irregular heartbeat, or it can cause the heart to stop beating. Electric current can also cause burns. For all these reasons, electrical safety is of utmost importance.

Homes are equipped with devices to enhance electrical safety. Fuses or circuit breakers are devices that are included in circuits in the home; these devices open the circuit if the current gets too high. Opening the circuit stops the flow of current. Circuit breakers are switches that can be reset; fuses need to be replaced after they are broken by excess current.

When voltage in a circuit increases significantly above what it is supposed to be, electronic devices can be harmed. These can be protected by surge protectors, which can divert excess electricity to an outlet's grounding wire.

Lightning storms also present danger due to electric current. Lighting can be conducted through the wiring or framework of buildings. Lightning rods are devices attached to homes and other buildings so that they are the highest point of the structure. If a lightning rod is struck by lightning, the electric current is carried safely to the ground to prevent damage to the building. People who are outside when a lightning storm strikes should move indoors if possible.

Magnets and Magnetism

ESSENTIAL QUESTION
What is magnetism?

1. Properties of Magnets

Students will understand that magnets exert force.

In ancient times, the Greeks and Chinese discovered the natural magnet lodestone, or magnetite. The Chinese observed three characteristics of magnetite: first, it attracted iron; second, when set afloat in water, magnetite aligns in a north-south direction; and third, magnetite could transfer its magnetic force to an iron needle. The ancient Chinese name for lodestone translates to "the stone that picks up iron."

Like gravity, a *magnetic force* can act on an object over a distance without having to contact the object directly.

2. Properties of Magnetic Fields

Students will be able to describe magnetic fields.

Each magnet generates a magnetic field that exits at the north pole of the magnet and enters at the south pole. The field consists of magnetic field lines (sometimes called lines of force). These lines are readily observed by pouring iron filings around a magnet. The rays of an aurora align in the same direction as the lines of Earth's magnetic field.

3. Types of Magnets

Students will understand various types of magnets.

Ferromagnetic materials can be turned into permanent magnets by placing them inside a strong magnetic field. Some substances, such as iron or alloys (such as a neodymium-iron-boron alloy), can produce extremely strong permanent magnets. An electromagnet is made from an iron core wrapped in coils of current-carrying wire. The power of an electromagnet can be increased or decreased by altering the amount of electric current that flows through the wire. A temporary magnet can be made by rubbing a needle or a pair of scissors with a magnet, briefly aligning its domains.

Heating, dropping, or striking a magnet disrupts the arrangement of the domains and thus damages the magnetic properties of the substance.

4. Earth's Magnetic Field

Students will understand Earth's magnetic field.

The movement of the atoms in Earth's core generates a magnetic field that surrounds the planet. In the magnetosphere, electrically charged particles form when solar radiation separates electrons from atoms. The magnetosphere is the site of auroras. Sometimes, Earth's magnetic field reverses—the north and south poles swap places. Fortunately, the magnetic field doesn't disappear during these reversals; in fact, the process takes thousands of years to complete. The study of Earth's magnetic history is called *paleomagnetism*.

 COMMON MISCONCEPTIONS RTI

COMPASSES Students often ask why the north pole of a compass points in a northern direction. Historically, the poles of a magnet were labeled "north" and "south." However, once an understanding was reached regarding the attraction of opposite forces, the poles of magnets became more properly labeled the "north-seeking" and "south-seeking" poles.

POLES Students may think Earth's geographic poles and its magnetic poles are the same, yet the two sets of poles are distinct. In 2009, researchers announced that the Northern Hemisphere's magnetic pole is moving towards Siberia at nearly 65 km/year.

These misconceptions are addressed on p. 223.

Content Refresher (continued)

Lesson 5

Electromagnetism
ESSENTIAL QUESTION
What is electromagnetism?

1. Electromagnetism

Students will learn that an electric current produces a magnetic field.

In 1820, Hans Oersted discovered that an electric current induced a changing magnetic field. In the early 1830s, physicists Michael Faraday and Joseph Henry discovered that an electric current could be induced by a magnetic field. Faraday's and Henry's work laid the foundation for the later development of the electric generator and the transformer.

Central to their work was the idea that both permanent and temporary magnets result from the magnetic field formed around a moving electric charge. Permanent magnets result from the spinning of unpaired electrons, which are electrically charged particles. Temporary magnets can also be formed in this manner, but the magnetic domains don't remain aligned.

2. Electromagnets

Students will learn how to build an electromagnet.

Temporary magnets known as electromagnets are produced by electric current, which consists of moving electric charges. In an electromagnet, coils of wire around an iron core create a magnet when electric charges flow. When the electric current stops, the magnetism stops.

3. Uses of Electromagnets

Students will become familiar with some devices that use electromagnets.

Electromagnets have many applications in modern industry. Students may be surprised to know that they are used in the following industries: robotics, security, environmental, manufacturing, transportation, research, and music.

4. Induction

Students will learn that magnets are used to generate an electric current.

The basis of electromagnetic induction is the generation of an electric current when magnetic fields change or are moved relative to a circuit. In electromagnetic induction, the magnet and the wire in which the current is present must be moving relative to each other.

A transformer uses induction to increase or decrease the voltage of an alternating current. An electric current in the primary coil sets up a magnetic field around the transformer iron. The magnetic field lines extend all around the transformer in continuous paths. As the current in the primary coil changes, the magnetic field around the transformer iron changes, which in turn induces a changing current in the secondary coil. A step-up transformer has more coils on the secondary side and therefore has a greater voltage output than input. The reverse is true for a step-down transformer.

A generator uses mechanical energy to rotate a coil in a magnetic field. As the coil rotates, the magnetic field it encounters changes. This changing magnetic field experienced by the coil induces an electric current.

 COMMON MISCONCEPTIONS  **RTI**

GENERATORS AND MOTORS Students might think that motors and generators do the same thing because they use the same parts. However, it is important for students to realize that it's more accurate to say that generators and motors perform "opposite" jobs.

This misconception is addressed in the Discussion on p. 232 and on p. 243.

Electronic Technology

ESSENTIAL QUESTION

What are electronics, and how have they changed?

1. Electronic Devices

Students will learn the difference between an electronic device and an electrical device.

Modern electronics began with the development of the vacuum tube. Thomas Edison found that an electric current could travel through an evacuated glass tube; but it was Sir John Ambrose Fleming, an English engineer, who invented the vacuum-tube diode in 1904. Vacuum tubes soon had a wide variety of applications. For example, although telegraph and telephone circuits could transmit and receive radio signals, the vacuum tube made it possible to manipulate radio signals.

In 1956, three American physicists—Walter Houser Brattain, John Bardeen, and William Bradford Shockley—won the Nobel Prize in physics for inventing the transistor. Transistors are electronic components used as amplifiers or switches in electric circuits. They are used extensively in control and communications. Transistors are the fundamental building blocks of computers. In 1961, a patent was awarded for the first integrated circuit, a piece of silicon that measured about 2 to 4 mm^2 that contained 15 to 20 transistors. Integrated circuits are constructed by using photolithography, the process of transferring a pattern onto a surface. Advances in photolithography have made it possible to make integrated circuits with millions of transistors.

2. Coded Information

Students will learn the difference between analog and digital signals.

All forms of communication involve codes. When we speak, the code is the pattern of sounds we make, which is then interpreted by the listener. Analog signals are signals that change or fluctuate. They have been traditionally used in broadcast and telephone technology. Their major disadvantage is that, because the signals fluctuate, distortion and interference can occur. Digital signals are not continuous, do not fluctuate, and are either "on" or "off." Digital signals are first converted to "bits" before they can be transmitted. Digital signals have less interference than analog signals and can be sent for longer distances. Until the 1980s, signals that transmitted sound messages were transmitted only in analog form. Older telephones, radios, and televisions are examples of analog devices. Many modern examples of these devices now send messages in digital form.

3. Computer Technology

Students will learn about the development of computers.

Most researchers point to the invention by French weaver Joseph Marie Jacquard, who created wooden punch cards to program the patterns on a loom, as the first important development in computer technology. The cards could be changed to create a new pattern, but the loom itself did not have to be adjusted. It was widely used in commercial weaving in the 1800s and is considered the first example of programming. Punch card technology was adopted in the earliest computing machines. Punch cards were used to indicate programming, with one program line per card.

The first general-purpose electronic computer was developed in 1946, financed by the U.S. Army. The Electronic Numerical Integrator and Computer (ENIAC) was fast and easily programmable. It was originally designed to create artillery firing tables for battle. Most of the work to develop the ENIAC was done in secret. The development of the microprocessor in 1971 led to the introduction of personal computers in the mid-1970s. Small tablet-size computers, smart phones, and e-book readers are just some of the ways that computers have become smaller and easier to use.

The advent of e-mail technology and the Internet now allow people to receive information and communicate quickly and easily. Both have affected more than computer development—they have transformed other information industries, including telephone, music, film, television, and print media.

Advance Planning

These activities may take extended time or special conditions.

Unit 3

Project Be Lightning Safe, p. 171
  research and plan

Graphic Organizers and Vocabulary pp. 177, 178, 191, 192, 203, 204, 217, 218, 235, 236, 251, 252
  ongoing with reading

Lesson 1

Activity Identifying Conductors and Insulators, p. 174
  spare extension cord, cut into pieces

Lesson 4

Differentiated Instruction (Basic) Magnetic Maze, p. 217
  arrange desks in classroom in advance

Lesson 5

S.T.E.M. Lab Building a Speaker, p. 233
  radio/mp3 player and cable

Lesson 6

Activity Circuit Boards, p. 248
  circuit boards for two different electronic devices

Daily Demo Analog Versus Digital, p. 249
  analog and digital recordings of the same song

What Do You Think?

Encourage students to think about what they know about electricity and magnetism.

Ask: What are some uses of electricity? Sample answers: lights, televisions, refrigerators, radios, toys, computers, cars

Ask: How does electricity get to our homes, schools, and other buildings? Sample answer: Wires carry it from power stations that generate electricity.

Ask: Describe some characteristics of magnets. Sample answers: Magnets are attracted to some kinds of metal. The ends of magnets sometimes attract each other and sometimes repel each other.

UNIT 3

Electricity and Magnetism

Lightning is the discharge of static electricity that builds up in clouds during a storm.

Big Idea
An electric current can produce a magnetic field, and a magnetic field can produce an electric current.

What do you think?
Static electricity can make your hair stand on end. What other effects of static electricity can you think of?

This Van de Graaff generator makes a safe but hair-raising demonstration.

123

Learning Alert

Van de Graaff Generators Some students may need help understanding the phenomenon shown in the picture of the girl touching the Van de Graaff generator. Tell students that a Van de Graaff generator is a device that can produce a large amount of static electricity. Explain that static electricity occurs when electric charges build up on an object. These charges can be positive or negative. Many Van de Graaff generators produce a build-up of negative charges. When a person touches a Van de Graaff generator, the negative charges move into the person's body and then spread throughout the body, even into the hair. In the picture, each hair on the girl's head has a build-up of static electricity. Because each hair has a similar charge, the hairs repel each other, causing them to stand up.

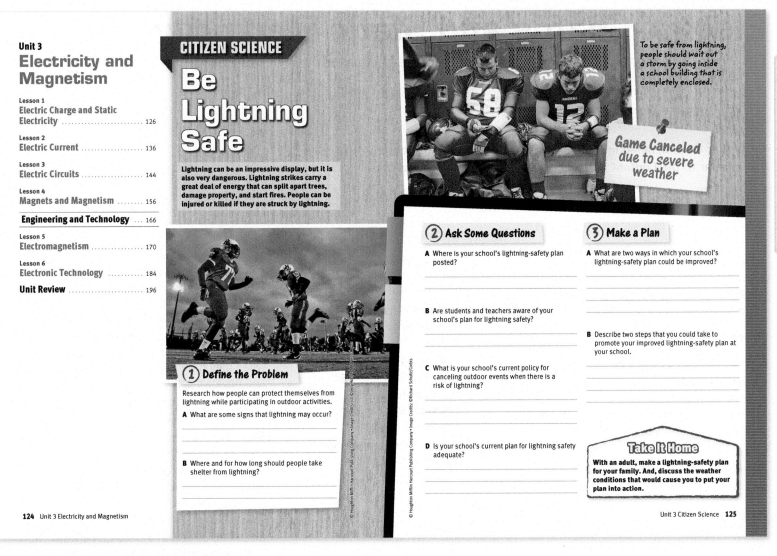

CITIZEN SCIENCE

Be Lightning Safe

Lightning can be an impressive display, but it is also very dangerous. Lightning strikes carry a great deal of energy that can split apart trees, damage property, and start fires. People can be injured or killed if they are struck by lightning.

To be safe from lightning, people should wait out a storm by going inside a school building that is completely enclosed.

Game Canceled due to severe weather

① Define the Problem

Research how people can protect themselves from lightning while participating in outdoor activities.

A What are some signs that lightning may occur?

B Where and for how long should people take shelter from lightning?

② Ask Some Questions

A Where is your school's lightning-safety plan posted?

B Are students and teachers aware of your school's plan for lightning safety?

C What is your school's current policy for canceling outdoor events when there is a risk of lightning?

D Is your school's current plan for lightning safety adequate?

③ Make a Plan

A What are two ways in which your school's lightning-safety plan could be improved?

B Describe two steps that you could take to promote your improved lightning-safety plan at your school.

Take It Home

With an adult, make a lightning-safety plan for your family. And, discuss the weather conditions that would cause you to put your plan into action.

124 Unit 3 Electricity and Magnetism

Unit 3 Citizen Science 125

CITIZEN SCIENCE

Unit Project Be Lightning Safe

1. Define the Problem

Have students research lightning safety on the Internet or in the library.

2. Ask Some Questions

Check on the status of the school's lightning safety plan before students begin the project. If the school does not have a formal plan, students can draft up recommendations for a lightning safety policy, which they can share with school leaders.

To gauge awareness of the current plan, encourage students to write a questionnaire to use with a few students and teachers.

3. Make a Plan

A. Have students brainstorm in small groups before writing down their ideas. Prompt students by asking what they think a good lightning safety plan should include.

B. As students brainstorm steps for promoting a lightning safety plan, encourage them to consider questions such as where the plan should be posted and how it should be communicated to students, teachers, and coaches.

Take It Home

Have students share the lightning safety plans they developed with an adult. Allow students to revise their plans after hearing some of the ideas of their peers.

🔵 *Optional Online rubric: Class Discussion*

Electric Charge and Static Electricity

Essential Question What makes something electrically charged?

Professional Development

For more detailed information about the topics in this lesson, refer to the Content Refresher in the Unit Opener pages.

Opening Your Lesson

Begin the lesson by assessing students' prerequisite and prior knowledge.

Prerequisite Knowledge

- Basic structure of an atom, including the charges of subatomic particles
- Knowledge of forces and an understanding that some forces act over a distance

Accessing Prior Knowledge

Ask: What particle of an atom has a negative charge? electron

Ask: What are forces? Sample answer: pushes and pulls **Ask:** Give an example of a force that acts over a distance. Sample answer: gravity

Customize Your Opening

- ☐ **Accessing Prior Knowledge,** above
- ☐ **Print Path** Engage Your Brain, SE, p. 127, #1–2
- ☐ **Active Reading,** SE p. 127, #3–4
- ☐ **Digital Path** Lesson Opener

Key Topics/Learning Goals	Supporting Concepts
Electric Charge **1** Describe electric charge as a fundamental property of matter. **2** Distinguish between the two types of electric charge. **3** Describe the ways in which objects can become electrically charged. **4** Describe the conservation of electric charge.	• Electric charge is a fundamental property that leads to the electromagnetic interactions among particles that make up matter. • Electric charge can be positive (+) or negative (−). Objects are electrically neutral when they have equal amounts of positive and negative charge. • An object can become electrically charged by friction, contact, or induction. • Static electricity is the buildup of electric charges on surfaces. • Electric charge is conserved. The total amount of charge (+) and (−) in the universe is equal.
Electric Force **1** Describe the nature of electric force between two charged objects.	• Electric force acts at a distance between two charged particles. The amount of charge and the distances between two electrically charged objects affect the magnitude of the electric force. • Like charges repel one another, and unlike charges attract one another.
Conductors, Insulators, and Semiconductors **1** Distinguish between an electrical conductor and an electrical insulator. **2** Describe what makes semiconductors so important to today's electronics.	• An electrical conductor allows electric charges to move freely; an electrical insulator does not allow electric charges to move freely. • Semiconductors do not conduct electrical charge as well as electrical conductors or as poorly as electrical insulators. Thus, they allow a greater control of the flow of electric charge.

Options for Instruction

Two parallel paths provide coverage of the Essential Questions, with a strong Inquiry strand woven into each. Follow the Print Path, the Digital Path, or your customized combination of print, digital, and inquiry.

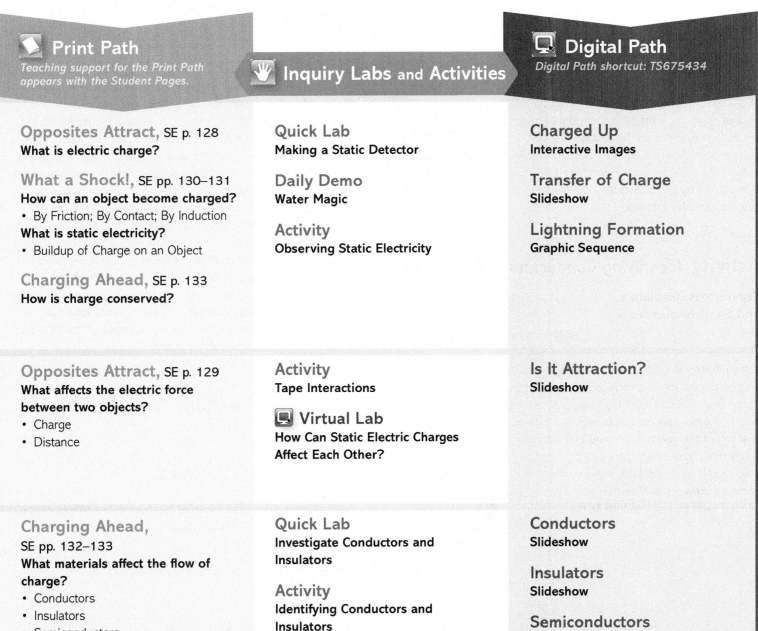

Print Path
Teaching support for the Print Path appears with the Student Pages.

Inquiry Labs and Activities

Digital Path
Digital Path shortcut: TS675434

Opposites Attract, SE p. 128
What is electric charge?

Quick Lab
Making a Static Detector

Daily Demo
Water Magic

Activity
Observing Static Electricity

Charged Up
Interactive Images

Transfer of Charge
Slideshow

Lightning Formation
Graphic Sequence

What a Shock!, SE pp. 130–131
How can an object become charged?
• By Friction; By Contact; By Induction
What is static electricity?
• Buildup of Charge on an Object

Charging Ahead, SE p. 133
How is charge conserved?

Opposites Attract, SE p. 129
What affects the electric force between two objects?
• Charge
• Distance

Activity
Tape Interactions

Virtual Lab
How Can Static Electric Charges Affect Each Other?

Is It Attraction?
Slideshow

Charging Ahead,
SE pp. 132–133
What materials affect the flow of charge?
• Conductors
• Insulators
• Semiconductors

Quick Lab
Investigate Conductors and Insulators

Activity
Identifying Conductors and Insulators

Conductors
Slideshow

Insulators
Slideshow

Semiconductors
Slideshow

Options for Assessment

See the Evaluate page for options, including Formative Assessment, Summative Assessment, and Unit Review.

Engage and Explore

Activities and Discussion

Activity *Observing Static Electricity*

Engage

Electric Charge

🖧 pairs
🕐 10 min
(Inquiry) **DIRECTED** inquiry

Distribute two inflated balloons and a piece of wool cloth to pairs of students. Tell students to rub the balloon against the cloth. Then have them slowly move the balloon toward their hair. **Ask:** What do you observe? Sample answer: The hair moves toward the balloon. Explain that this interaction is explained by static electricity, a phenomenon students are about to study.

Activity *Identifying Conductors and Insulators*

Conductors, Insulators, and Semiconductors

🖧 small groups
🕐 10 min
(Inquiry) **INDEPENDENT** inquiry

Cut an extension cord or another type of insulated wire into several smaller pieces. Provide each group of students with a piece of the cord. Have students work together to determine what purpose each part of the cord serves. Encourage students to make a cross-sectional drawing of the parts of the cord that includes labels that identify each part's function as a conductor or an insulator. Have students compare drawings and explain why they labeled each part of the cord as they did.

Activity *Tape Interactions*

Synthesizing Key Topics

🖧 individuals
🕐 10 min
(Inquiry) **DIRECTED** inquiry

Provide students with rolls of tape. Have them cut three pieces of tape of approximately the same size. Tell them to press two pieces of the tape onto their shirts. Then have them peel off the tape pieces and hold them near each other, without touching. **Ask:** What do you observe? Sample answer: The strips of tape repel each other. **Ask:** What can you conclude about the charges on the tape based on this reaction? Sample answer: Both pieces of tape have the same charge. Have students hold one of the strips of tape removed from their shirt near the third strip. **Ask:** What do you observe? Sample answer: The strips of tape attract one another. **Ask:** What can you conclude about the strip of tape removed from your shirt and the strip of tape that was not in contact with your shirt? Sample answer: The strips are oppositely charged because they attract one another. **Note:** Different types of tape may produce different results. Check the effectiveness of the tape prior to having students carry out the activity.

Take It Home *Static Cling*

Electric Charge

🖧 adult-student pairs
🕐 1 hour
(Inquiry) **GUIDED** inquiry

Adult-student pairs work together to observe the effects of static electricity in everyday life by examining static cling in freshly laundered clothing.

⏺ *Optional Online resource: student worksheet*

Customize Your Labs

◻ *See the Lab Manual for lab datasheets.*

⏺ *Go Online for editable lab datasheets.*

Levels of **Inquiry**

DIRECTED inquiry
introduces inquiry skills within a structured framework.

GUIDED inquiry
develops inquiry skills within a supportive environment.

INDEPENDENT inquiry
deepens inquiry skills with student-driven questions or procedures.

Labs and Demos

Daily Demo *Water Magic*

Engage

Electric Charge

👥 whole class
🕐 10 min
🔵 **GUIDED** inquiry

PURPOSE **To show how matter becomes charged by induction**

MATERIALS

• comb

• sink with working faucet

1 Turn on a faucet just enough to allow a thin stream of water to flow.

2 Have a student volunteer run a comb through his or her hair a few times.

3 **Observe** Tell the student to hold the comb near, but not touching, the stream of water. **Ask:** What do you observe? The comb attracts the stream of water. **Ask:** What does this indicate? The comb and the water have opposite electric charges.

4 **Predict** Ask students to predict what will happen to the charges of the comb and water if the comb is allowed to come in contact with the water. Sample answers: The charges of the water and comb will remain the same (opposite); the comb will give up its charges as the interaction results in a discharge.

5 **Observe** To test students' predictions, have the student volunteer pass the comb through the water. Then have them move the comb so that it is near but not touching the water. **Ask:** What do you observe? Sample answer: After touching the water, the comb no longer attracts the water.

🌐 🖥 Quick Lab *Making a Static Detector*

Electric Charge

👥 pairs
🕐 30 min
🔵 **DIRECTED** inquiry

Students use a charged balloon to move aluminum foil strips.

PURPOSE **To observe static electricity**

MATERIALS

• **aluminum foil**

• **inflated balloon**

• **modeling clay**

• **paper clip**

🌐 🖥 Quick Lab *Investigate Conductors and Insulators*

PURPOSE **To investigate which materials conduct electricity**

See the Lab Manual or go Online for planning information

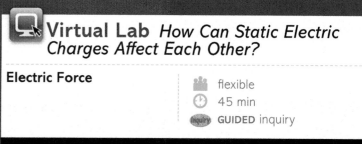

🖥 Virtual Lab *How Can Static Electric Charges Affect Each Other?*

Electric Force

👥 flexible
🕐 45 min
🔵 **GUIDED** inquiry

Students experiment with the amount and size of charges on objects.

PURPOSE **To explore how charge type and size affects interactions between objects**

Activities and Discussion

☐ **Activity** Observing Static Electricity

☐ **Activity** Identifying Conductors and Insulators

☐ **Activity** Tape Interactions

☐ **Take It Home** Static Cling

Labs and Demos

☐ **Daily Demo** Water Magic

☐ **Quick Lab** Making a Static Detector

☐ **Quick Lab** Conductors and Insulators

☐ **Virtual Lab** How Can Static Electric Charges Affect Each Other?

Your Resources

Explain Science Concepts

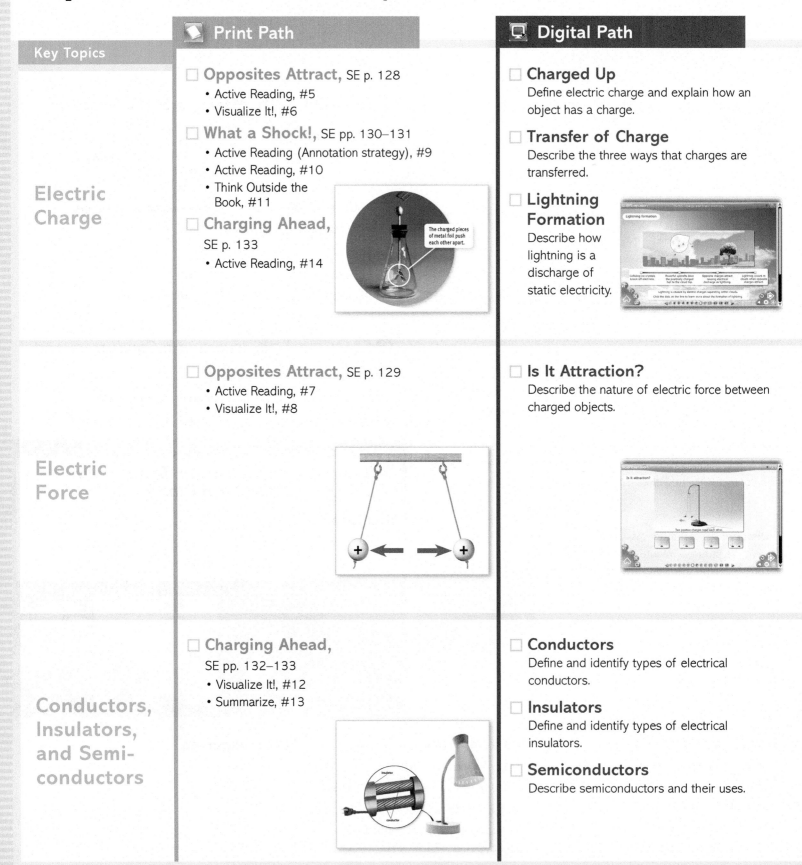

Key Topics	📖 Print Path	🖥 Digital Path
Electric Charge	☐ **Opposites Attract,** SE p. 128 • Active Reading, #5 • Visualize It!, #6 ☐ **What a Shock!,** SE pp. 130–131 • Active Reading (Annotation strategy), #9 • Active Reading, #10 • Think Outside the Book, #11 ☐ **Charging Ahead,** SE p. 133 • Active Reading, #14	☐ **Charged Up** Define electric charge and explain how an object has a charge. ☐ **Transfer of Charge** Describe the three ways that charges are transferred. ☐ **Lightning Formation** Describe how lightning is a discharge of static electricity.
Electric Force	☐ **Opposites Attract,** SE p. 129 • Active Reading, #7 • Visualize It!, #8	☐ **Is It Attraction?** Describe the nature of electric force between charged objects.
Conductors, Insulators, and Semi-conductors	☐ **Charging Ahead,** SE pp. 132–133 • Visualize It!, #12 • Summarize, #13	☐ **Conductors** Define and identify types of electrical conductors. ☐ **Insulators** Define and identify types of electrical insulators. ☐ **Semiconductors** Describe semiconductors and their uses.

The charged pieces of metal foil push each other apart.

Differentiated Instruction

Basic *Flow of Charge Display*

Conductors, Insulators, and Semiconductors

👥 individuals
🕐 varies

Have students develop an illustrated poster that identifies which materials are electrical conductors, electrical insulators, or semiconductors. Have students include labels to identify each object shown and write captions that explain what conductors, insulators, and semiconductors are.

🌐 *Optional Online rubrics: Posters and Displays*

Advanced *How Shocking!*

Electric Charge

👥 individuals
🕐 25 min

Have students use what they have learned about static electricity and how objects become charged to develop a sequence diagram that shows how charges can build up on an object and then cause a shock to a person who touches the object.

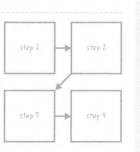

🌐 *Optional Online resource: Sequence Diagram support*

ELL *Diagramming Charged Particles*

Electric Charge

👥 pairs
🕐 30 min

Have English language learners pair up with non-English language learners. Hand out three note cards to each pair. Ask the students to work together to draw an atom that is electrically neutral on the first note card. Then have students draw the same atom to show how it would appear if it became a positively charged ion on the second note card. Have them repeat the process to show the atom becoming a negatively charged ion on the last note card. Have students label the subatomic parts in each drawing and write a caption explaining why the ion has the electrical charge that it does. Finally, encourage pairs to exchange their note cards with other pairs to see each others' work.

Lesson Vocabulary

electric charge   electrical conductor   semiconductor
static electricity   electrical insulator

Previewing Vocabulary

👥 small groups
🕐 20–25 min

Word Triangles Have students make Word Triangles for each vocabulary term. In their triangles, they should write the term and its definition, a sentence using the term, and an illustration. Have them share their Word Triangles with a partner.

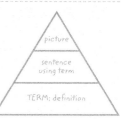

🌐 *Online Resource: Word Triangle support*

Reinforcing Vocabulary

👥 individuals
🕐 20–25 min

Paragraphs To help students remember the vocabulary terms introduced in this lesson, have them write a paragraph or two describing how objects gain electric charges, which materials can and cannot carry electric charges, and what causes static electricity. Encourage them to use all the vocabulary terms in their paragraphs. Explain that they should come up with descriptive paragraphs, not merely to list each term and its definition.

Customize Your Core Lesson

Core Instruction
☐ Print Path choices
☐ Digital Path choices

Vocabulary
☐ Previewing Vocabulary Word Triangles
☐ Reinforcing Vocabulary Paragraphs

Your Resources

Differentiated Instruction
☐ Basic Flow of Charge Display
☐ Advanced How Shocking!
☐ ELL Diagramming Charged Particles

Extend Science Concepts

Reinforce and Review

Activity *Electric Charge Carousel*

Synthesizing Key Topics

👥 small groups
🕐 25 min

Carousel Review Set up four sheets of chart paper. At the top of the first, write: *Describe factors that affect the electric force between two charged objects.* On the second, write: *What are three ways that objects become charged?* On the third, write: *What is the conservation of electric charge?* And on the last, write: *What are electrical conductors, electrical insulators, and semiconductors? Give an example of each.*

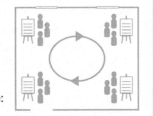

Divide students into small groups, and assign each group a chart. Give each group a different colored marker. Have groups review their questions, discuss their answers, and write a response. After five to ten minutes, have each group rotate to the next station. Groups should place a check next to each answer they agree with, comment on those they don't agree with, and add their own answers. Continue until all groups have reviewed all charts. Invite each group to share information with the class.

Graphic Organizer

Synthesizing Key Topics

👥 individual
🕐 25 min

Concept Map After students have studied the lesson, ask them to develop a Concept Map that describes electric charges and how they build up on objects or move through objects. Encourage students to use these terms in their concept maps: *electric charge, electric force, static electricity, electrical conductor, electrical insulator,* and *semiconductor*.

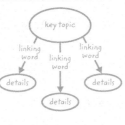

🕐 *Optional Online Resource: Concept Map support*

Going Further

Health Connection

Synthesizing Key Topics

👥 individuals
🕐 varied

Explain to students that television sets and computers can cause allergies to become worse. The static charge that builds up on the screens of televisions and computer monitors attracts dust from the air. Accompanying the dust are dust mites and their feces, which are common allergens that can bring on asthma attacks and other bronchial problems. Have students research allergies, asthma, or bronchitis to find out what the disorder is and what symptoms characterize it. Students should also determine what activities can help to prevent the onset of each disorder and what treatments are available during flare-ups. Then have them write a short report detailing what they found.

🕐 *Optional Online rubric: Written Pieces*

Physics Connection

Electric Charge

👥 individuals
🕐 varied

Sprites Sprites are high-altitude phenomena lasting only a few milliseconds that are associated with lightning storms. A sprite is an electrical discharge that occurs between thunderstorm clouds and the lower ionosphere. Unlike lightning, sprites are dimmer and seem to generate upward rather than downward toward Earth's surface. Have students research sprites to find out how scientists think they form. Students can prepare a short written or oral report of their findings.

Customize Your Closing

📖 *See the Assessment Guide for quizzes and tests.*

🕐 *Go Online to edit and create quizzes and tests.*

Reinforce and Review

☐ **Activity** Electric Charge Carousel

☐ **Graphic Organizer** Concept Map

☐ **Print Path** Visual Summary, SE p. 134

☐ **Print Path** Lesson Review, SE p. 135

☐ **Digital Path** Lesson Closer

Evaluate Student Mastery

Formative Assessment

See the teacher support below the Student Pages for additional Formative Assessment questions.

Describe for students or have them review the photograph showing a girl's hair standing on end when she touches a charged dome. **Ask:** What causes the student's hair to stand on end? Sample answer: Electric charges on the dome move through the student. **Ask:** What is static electricity? the buildup of charges on an object **Ask:** Why is a buildup of charges typically a buildup of electrons rather than protons? Sample answer: Electrons can move from atom to atom; protons cannot. **Ask:** Based on this example, are humans conductors, insulators, or semiconductors? conductors

Reteach

Formative assessment may show that students need reinforcement for certain topics. The resources below are recommended for reteaching. If students were introduced to a topic through the Print Path, you can also use the Digital Path to reteach, and vice versa.
🎧 *Can be assigned to individual students*

Electric Charge
Daily Demo Water Magic

Electric Force
Activity Tape Interactions 🎧
Virtual Lab How Can Static Electric Charges Affect Each Other?

Conductors, Insulators, and Semiconductors
Activity Identifying Conductors and Insulators 🎧
Quick Lab Investigate Conductors and Insulators 🎧

Summative Assessment

Alternative Assessment
Charge It!

🎧 *Online resources: student worksheet; optional rubrics*

Electric Charge and Static Electricity

Climb the Pyramid: *Charge It!*
Select options at each level to show what you know about electric charges and static electricity.

1. Work on your own, with a partner, or with a small group.
2. Choose one item from each layer of the pyramid. Check your choices.
3. Have your teacher approve your plan.
4. Submit or present your results.

__ Charge Demonstration
Use balloons and any other materials that are suitable to demonstrate how objects become charged by friction, contact, and induction. As you conduct your demonstration, explain how charges move from one object to another.

__ Static Charge and Discharge Poster	__ Graphic Arts
Find a dramatic photograph of lightning, and use it to make a poster that explains why lightning occurs. Include captions that identify the role of static electricity in lightning formation and labels that show where charges gather to form lightning.	Develop a graphic that can be used to explain how like and unlike electrical charges interact. Display and explain your graphic to the class.

__ Conservation Diagram	__ Material Display	__ Three-Column Chart
Develop a diagram that explains the conservation of charge.	Develop a display that defines and identifies examples of electrical conductors, electrical insulators, and semiconductors. Use your display as a basis for a class presentation that describes what each group of materials does and what types of materials make up each group.	Develop a three-column chart with the headings Electrical Conductors, Electrical Insulators, and Semiconductors. Provide a definition and examples for each term. Include at least 10 different examples of materials in your chart.

Going Further
☐ Health Connection
☐ Physics Connection

Formative Assessment
☐ Strategies Throughout TE
☐ Lesson Review SE

Summative Assessment
☐ Alternative Assessment Charge It!
☐ Lesson Quiz
☐ Unit Tests A and B
☐ Unit Review SE End-of-Unit

Your Resources

Answers

Answers for 1–3 should represent students' current thoughts, even if incorrect.

1. True; False; True; False

2. Sample answer: The student's hair is attracted to the balloon.

3. Sample answer: a fee or a cost for something; a property related to electricity

4. Students should define and sketch each vocabulary term in the lesson.

Opening Your Lesson

Have students share the ideas in their captions (item 2) to assess their prior knowledge about Key Topics.

Prerequisites Atoms are composed of a positively charged nucleus that contains protons and neutrons and negatively charged electrons that orbit the nucleus; forces are pushes and pulls; some forces, such as the force of gravity, can act on objects over a distance, while other forces act only when they are in contact with objects.

Accessing Prior Knowledge To assess students' prior knowledge about electric charges and static electricity, have them conduct a Textbook DRTA. Explain that DRTA stands for Directed Reading/Thinking Activity. To complete the activity, students need to (1) review the selection; (2) write what they know, what they think they know, and what they think they'll learn about electric charges and static electricity; (3) read the selection; and (4) write what they learned. At the conclusion of the lesson, discuss whether students' expectations were reasonable, and whether they learned additional information that they did not anticipate.

🌐 *Optional Online resource: Textbook DRTA support*

Opposites Attract

What is electric charge?

Have you ever touched a doorknob and felt a shock? Have you ever seen clothes cling to each other after they are taken from a dryer? Both of these events are due to a fundamental property of matter called *electric charge*. **Electric charge** is a property that leads to electromagnetic interactions between the particles that make up matter. An object can have a positive (+) charge, a negative (–) charge, or no charge. An object that has no charge is *neutral*.

The diagram below shows charges within an atom. All atoms have a dense center called a *nucleus*. The nucleus contains two types of particles: *protons* and *neutrons*. A proton has a charge of 1+. A neutron has no charge. *Electrons* are a third type of particle and are found outside the nucleus. An electron has a charge of 1–. When an atom has the same number of protons as electrons, the atom has no overall charge. This is because the charges of its protons and electrons add up to zero. However, atoms can lose or gain electrons. When this happens, the atom has an overall positive or negative charge and is called an *ion*. Positively charged ions have more protons than electrons. Negatively charged ions have fewer protons than electrons. The overall charge of an object is the sum of the charges of its atoms.

5 Apply An atom gains an additional electron. What is the overall charge of the ion that is formed? _____

Pieces of paper cling to a ruler due to the electric charge of the ruler.

Visualize It!

6 Label Complete the diagram by labeling the nucleus and an electron.

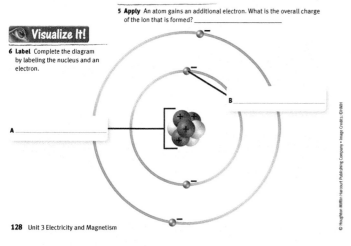

A _____

B _____

128 Unit 3 Electricity and Magnetism

What affects the electric force between two objects?

Any two charged objects exert a force on each other called an *electric force*. Like gravity, electric force acts between objects even when they do not touch. But gravity always pulls objects together. Unlike gravity, the electric force can either pull objects together or push them apart. How strongly the electric force pushes or pulls depends on the charge of each object and how close together the objects are.

Charge

If objects have like charges, they repel each other. The objects exert an electric force that pushes them apart. The balls in the diagram A at the right both have a positive charge. The arrows show the electric force acting on each ball.

Two objects with unlike charges attract each other. So an object with a positive charge and an object with a negative charge are attracted. Each object exerts a force on the other, pulling the objects together.

The amount of charge on each object also affects the strength of the electric force between them. The greater an object's charge is, the greater the electric force is. This is true whether the objects repel or attract each other.

Distance

The distance between two objects affects the size of the electric force, too. The closer together the charged objects are, the greater the electric force is. As charged objects move farther apart, they attract or repel each other less strongly.

Active Reading **7 Identify** What factors affect how strong the electric force is between two charged objects?

_____
_____
_____

Visualize It!

8 Analyze Label diagrams B and C with the missing charge signs. Then add a caption below each diagram to describe the forces between the objects.

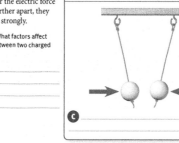

A The balls have like positive charges. They push each other apart.

B _____

C _____

Lesson 1 Electric Charge and Static Electricity **129**

Answers

5. 1–

6. A: nucleus; B: electron

7. the type and amount of charge on each object and the distance between the objects

8. B. Students should label the ball on the right with a minus sign; Sample caption: The balls have like negative charges. They push each other apart.

   C. Students should label one ball with a minus sign and the other ball with a plus sign; Sample caption: The balls have unlike charges. Each ball pulls the other ball toward it.

Probing Question

Evaluating Have students look closely at the atom shown in the illustration. After they label the diagram, ask them to use their responses and the information provided in the illustration to identify the overall charge of the atom. Challenge students to explain their response. Sample answer: The atom is neutral because it has equal numbers of protons and electrons.

Building Reading Skills

Text Structure: Comparison/Contrast The text compares electric force to the force of gravity. Students may find it helpful to list the similarities and differences between the two types of forces as they read.

🌀 *Online resource: Text Structure: Comparison/Contrast*

Interpreting Visuals

Remind students that like electric charges repel each other, while unlike charges attract. Point out to students that the arrows in each diagram indicate the direction in which the forces are acting (attracting or repelling). Have students use the direction in which the forces act as a clue to the identity of the missing charge in each diagram.

What a Shock!

How can an object become charged?

Objects become charged when their atoms gain or lose electrons. Three ways that objects can gain or lose electrons are by friction, contact, or induction.

Active Reading

9 Identify As you read, underline examples of objects becoming charged.

By Friction

Charging by friction occurs when two objects are rubbed together, causing a transfer of electrons between the objects. For example, rubbing a balloon on your hair moves electrons from your hair to the balloon. Your hair becomes positively charged, and the balloon becomes negatively charged. Similarly, when you rub your shoes on a carpet on a dry day, you may become charged. If you then touch a metal object such as a doorknob, you may feel a shock from the sudden release of electric charge.

By Contact

If a charged object and an uncharged object touch each other, the charged object can transfer some of its charge to the area it touches. The sphere at the right is part of a *Van de Graaff generator*. The generator places a charge on its dome. An uncharged object that touches the dome becomes charged by contact. This student's hair is standing on end because the charged hairs repel each other.

By Induction

Induction is a way of rearranging the charges within an object without touching it. For example, this ruler has a negative charge. When the ruler is brought near the metal knob, it repels electrons in the metal. Electrons move away from the ruler and down the metal rod. The knob now has a positive charge. The thin pieces of metal foil at the bottom of the metal rod now have a negative charge. Their like charges cause them to push each other apart.

The charged pieces of metal foil push each other apart.

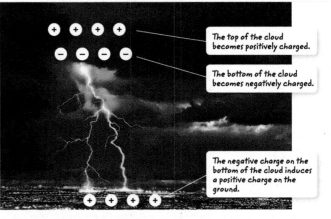

The top of the cloud becomes positively charged.

The bottom of the cloud becomes negatively charged.

The negative charge on the bottom of the cloud induces a positive charge on the ground.

What is static electricity?

After you take your clothes out of the dryer, they sometimes are stuck together. They stick together because of static electricity. **Static electricity** is the buildup of electric charge on an object. When something is static, it is not moving. Static electricity is the extra positive or negative charge that builds up on an object until it eventually moves elsewhere.

The Buildup of Charge on an Object

For an object to have static electricity, charge must build up on the object. For example, static electricity can build up inside storm clouds. The top of the cloud becomes positively charged. The bottom of the cloud becomes negatively charged. The negative charge in the bottom of the cloud can cause the ground to become positively charged by induction.

Charges that build up as static electricity eventually leave the object. This loss of charges is known as *electric discharge*. Electric discharge may happen slowly or quickly. Lightning is an example of rapid electric discharge. Lightning can occur between clouds. It can also occur between the negative part of the cloud and the positively charged ground. When lightning strikes, charged particles move toward places with opposite charge.

Active Reading **10 Analyze** During a lightning storm, what can cause the ground to become positively charged?

_____

_____

Think Outside the Book Inquiry

11 Apply Think of an everyday example of an object becoming charged. Draw and label a diagram that shows how charges moved. (Hint: You may need to use reference materials to learn more about the process you have chosen.)

Answers

9. *See students' pages for annotations.*

10. The negatively charged bottom of a storm cloud can induce a positive charge on the ground.

11. Students should draw diagrams showing the movement of negative charges in an everyday example such as brushing hair or the buildup of static charges on clothing. Students should be able to identify the method of charging.

Building Reading Skills

Combination Notes Have students use the Combination Notes strategy to outline the information about static electricity and how objects become charged. On the left side of a piece of paper, students can jot down notes. On the right side, students can make a sketch to illustrate the idea and label it.

🌐 *Online Resource: Combination Notes support.*

Learning Alert 🚧 MISCONCEPTION 🚧

Electron Gain or Loss Students may think that to become positively charged, atoms can gain protons. Remind students that atoms can only gain or lose electrons, which are negatively charged. An atom becomes a positively charged ion when it has a net loss of electrons and, thus, has more protons than electrons. By contrast, an atom becomes a negatively charged ion when it experiences a net gain of electrons.

Formative Assessment

Ask: What is the main way that charging by induction differs from charging by friction and by contact? Sample answer: Induction is a way for objects to become charged without touching. To be charged by friction or contact, objects must touch one another.

Charging Ahead

What materials affect the flow of charge?

Have you ever noticed that electrical cords are often made from both metal and plastic? Different materials are used because electric charges move through some materials more easily than they move through others.

Conductors

An **electrical conductor** is a material through which charges can move freely. Many electrical conductors are metals. Copper is a metal that is used to make wires because it is an excellent electrical conductor. When an electrically charged plastic ruler touches a metal conductor, the charge it transfers to the metal can move freely through the metal.

Insulators

An **electrical insulator** is a material through which charges cannot move easily. The electrons are tightly held in the atoms of the insulator. Plastic, rubber, glass, and dry air are all good electrical insulators. Plastic is often used to coat wires because electric charges cannot move through the plastic easily. This stops the charges from leaving the wire and prevents you from being shocked when you touch the lamp cord.

Visualize It!

12 Identify What is the purpose of the material surrounding the metal inside the lamp cord?

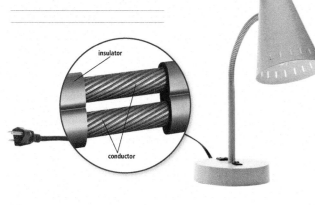

insulator

conductor

Semiconductors are used to make the computer chips found in electronic devices such as cell phones and calculators.

Semiconductors

Semiconductors are a special class of materials that conduct electric charge better than electrical insulators but not as well as electrical conductors. Their properties allow them to be used to control the flow of charge. Electrical devices use semiconductors to process electrical signals in many different ways. Silicon is the basis of many kinds of semiconductors. It is used to make computer chips found in electronic devices such as the ones shown above.

13 Summarize Fill in the table at the right to summarize what you have learned about conductors, insulators, and semiconductors.

	Example	Effect on the movement of charges
Conductor		
Insulator		
Semiconductor		

How is charge conserved?

All objects contain positive charges from the protons and negative charges from the electrons within their atoms. A neutral object becomes negatively charged when it gains one or more electrons and then has more negative charges than positive charges. Where do these electrons come from? They might come from a second object that loses the electrons and becomes positively charged. So electrons are not really lost. Charging objects involves moving electrons from one object to another. The total amount of charge always stays the same. This principle is called the conservation of charge.

Active Reading **14 Describe** What happens to the charge lost by an object?

© Houghton Mifflin Harcourt Publishing Company • Image Credits: ©HMH

© Houghton Mifflin Harcourt Publishing Company • Image Credits: (tl) ©Creatas/JupiterImages/Getty Images; (tr) ©HMH

Answers

12. Sample answer: The insulator surrounding the metal prevents charge from leaving the metal.

13. Students should fill in the table with the following terms: *copper* (top center), *allows charges to move freely* (top right), *plastic* (middle center), *does not allow charges to move freely* (middle right), *computer chip* (bottom center), *allows charges to move better than in insulators but not as well as in conductors* (bottom right).

14. Sample answer: It is gained by another object.

Learning Alert

Maintaining a Charge After students read about electrical conductors and insulators, lead a class discussion about the role of insulation in maintaining an object in a charged state. Point out that a conductor, such as a piece of wire, must be insulated from other conductors in order to remain charged. If the conductor is not insulated, electrons flow from one conductor to another. To assess students' understanding, **Ask:** Why is the metal rod in an electroscope able to maintain a charge? Sample answer: because it is insulated by the rubber stopper **Ask:** What would happen if someone touched the metal rod? Sample answer: It would become uncharged because electrons would flow between the rod and the person.

Formative Assessment

Ask: What are electrical conductors, electrical insulators, and semiconductors? Sample answer: An electrical conductor is a material that allows electric charges to flow through it easily. An electrical insulator is a material through which electric charges cannot move easily. A semiconductor is a material that conducts electric charges better than an electrical insulator and worse than an electrical conductor. **Ask:** If an object loses electrons to take on a positive charge, according to the conservation of electric charge, what happens to those electrons? Sample response: The electrons must move to another object because electric charge is conserved.

Visual Summary

To complete this summary, fill in the blanks with the correct word. Then use the key below to check your answers. You can use this page to review the main concepts of the lesson.

Electric Charge and Static Electricity

Like charges repel each other, while unlike charges attract each other.

15 An object that has a positive charge equal to its negative charge is _____

Electrical conductors allow electric charges to move freely, while electrical insulators do not.

insulator

conductor

17 A _____ is a material whose conductivity is between that of an electrical conductor and an electrical insulator.

Objects can become charged by friction, contact, or induction.

16 _____ is the buildup of electric charges on an object.

Electric charge is always conserved.

18 The electrons lost by one object are _____ by another.

Answers: 15 neutral; 16 Static electricity; 17 semiconductor; 18 gained

© Houghton Mifflin Harcourt Publishing Company • Image Credits: (t) ©MHS; (b) © Rob Matheson/Corbis

19 Predict Suppose an electrically charged ruler transfers some of its charge by contact to a tiny plastic sphere. Will the ruler and the sphere attract or repel afterwards? Why?

Lesson Review

Lesson ①

Vocabulary

Draw a line to connect the following terms to their definitions.

1 electric charge   **A** a material that allows electrons to flow easily

2 electrical conductor   **B** a material that does not allow electrons to flow easily

3 electrical insulator   **C** property that leads to electromagnetic interactions

Key Concepts

4 Explain Describe electric discharge.

_____

_____

_____

_____

5 Compare What properties of semiconductors make them useful in electronic devices?

_____

_____

_____

6 Predict Two objects have unlike charges. How would the electric force between the two objects change as they are moved apart?

_____

_____

_____

Critical Thinking

Use this diagram to answer the following questions.

Movement of electrons

Not to scale

7 Analyze Describe how charge is transferred from the ruler to the metal rod.

_____

_____

_____

8 Describe Explain how this transfer observes the conservation of charge.

_____

_____

_____

9 Evaluate A student places two charged objects near each other. The objects repel each other. The student concludes that the objects must both be negative. Do you agree? Explain.

_____

_____

_____

© Houghton Mifflin Harcourt Publishing Company

Visual Summary Answers

15. neutral

16. Static electricity

17. semiconductor

18. gained

19. They will repel because they have like charge.

Lesson Review Answers

1. C

2. A

3. B

4. Sample answer: Electric discharge occurs when an object loses some or all of its static charge. It is a movement of the electric charge somewhere else.

5. Sample answer: A semiconductor allows for the flow of charges to be controlled. This is useful in processing electrical signals.

6. Sample answer: The electric force would become weaker as the objects are moved apart. The objects would not attract each other as strongly.

7. Sample answer: The ruler is negatively charged. When it is in contact with the metal rod, electrons move from the ruler to the rod. The negative charges can move freely throughout the rod.

8. Sample answer: Charges are not created or destroyed. Charges lost by the ruler are gained by the rod.

9. Sample answer: Like charges repel. So the objects could both be negative, but they could also both be positive.

Electric Current

Essential Question What flows through an electric wire?

Professional Development

For more detailed information about the topics in this lesson, refer to the Content Refresher in the Unit Opener pages.

Opening Your Lesson

Begin the lesson by assessing students' prerequisite and prior knowledge.

Prerequisite Knowledge

- A general understanding of positive and negative charges.

Accessing Prior Knowledge

Direct students to draw a simple picture or schematic depicting their understanding of electric current. They should be as detailed as they are able, depending on their level of understanding of this topic. Use the pictures to assess what students may already know, and note any misconceptions that may be present.

Customize Your Opening

☐ **Accessing Prior Knowledge,** above
☐ Print Path Engage Your Brain, SE p. 137
☐ Print Path Active Reading, SE p. 137
☐ **Digital Path** Lesson Opener

Key Topics/Learning Goals	Supporting Concepts
Current 1 Describe electric current. 2 Compare direct to alternating current, and describe some everyday devices that use each.	• Electric current is the rate at which electric charges pass a given point. • Charges move in a single direction only in a direct current (DC). Batteries produce direct current. • Charges in an alternating current (AC) change, or alternate, direction. Most household appliances run on an alternating current.
Voltage 1 Describe voltage and its relationship to electric current.	• Voltage, measured in volts, is the amount of work to move a unit electric charge between two points. • When a higher voltage is applied to a given wire, the current in the wire increases.
Resistance 1 Describe resistance and its relationship to electric current. 2 Describe factors that can affect resistance.	• Opposition to the flow of electric charge is called *resistance*. • The resistance of a wire depends on its composition, thickness, length, and temperature. • Current flowing through materials with higher resistance will have a lower voltage.

Options for Instruction

Two parallel paths provide coverage of the Essential Questions, with a strong **Inquiry** strand woven into each.
Follow the **Print Path,** the **Digital Path,** or your customized combination of print, digital, and inquiry.

Print Path
Teaching support for the Print Path appears with the Student Pages.

Inquiry Labs and Activities

Digital Path
Digital Path shortcut: TS675444

Current Events, SE pp. 138–139
What is an electric current?
How is electric current measured?
What are two kinds of current?
- Direct Current (DC)
- Alternating Current (AC)

Quick Lab
Investigate Electric Current

Quick Lab
Lemon Battery

Activity
Current Diagram

Activity
Uses of Electricity

Electric Current and Direct Current
Interactive Images

Alternating Current
Slideshow

You've Got Potential,
SE p. 140
What affects electric current?
- Voltage

S.T.E.M. Lab
Voltage, Current, and Resistance

Activity
Modeling Current

Voltage and Resistance
Slideshow

You've Got Potential,
SE p. 140–141
What affects electric current?
- Resistance
What affects electrical resistance?

Daily Demo
Observing Resistance

Activity
Electric Topics

Factors Affecting Resistance
Slideshow

Options for Assessment

See the Evaluate page for options, including Formative Assessment,
Summative Assessment, and Unit Review.

Engage and Explore

Activities and Discussion

Discussion *Types of Electric Current*

Current

- 👥 whole class
- 🕐 10 min
- (Inquiry) **GUIDED** inquiry

Remind students that electric current is the rate at which electric charges pass a specific point. Then remind them of the two types of electric current: direct current and alternating current. **Ask:** What happens to the electric charges in a direct current? Sample answer: The charges in a direct current move in a single direction. **Ask:** What happens to charges in an alternating current? Sample answer: The charges in an alternating current change, or alternate, their direction as they move.

Activity *Current Diagram*

Current

- 👥 individuals then pairs
- 🕐 20 min
- (Inquiry) **INDEPENDENT** inquiry

Have students research circuit diagrams. Ask students to diagram a circuit with a single battery and a lamp. Students should be able to describe the movement of electric charges in their diagrams and then present and explain their drawings to their partners. Partners should give feedback to each other in order to correct any errors in the diagrams. Assist individual students and pairs as needed.

Activity *Modeling Current*

Voltage

- 👥 small groups
- 🕐 30 min
- (Inquiry) **INDEPENDENT** inquiry

Direct small groups to design a skit to demonstrate electric current. Groups can use the turnstile example from the student text as a guide for ideas for developing their own examples. Encourage students to use their demonstrations to show the difference between large and small currents and to show the relationship between voltage and electric current.

Activity *Uses of Electricity*

Current

- 👥 individuals
- 🕐 15 min
- (Inquiry) **GUIDED** inquiry

Think, Pair, Share Give students 3–5 minutes to list as many electrical devices as possible. After the time has elapsed, have them label each device as using AC or DC. If they need a hint, remind them that batteries use DC. Finally, have students share and check their results with a partner.

Customize Your Labs

📄 *See the Lab Manual for lab datasheets.*

🌐 *Go Online for editable lab datasheets.*

Levels of **Inquiry**

DIRECTED inquiry	**GUIDED** inquiry	**INDEPENDENT** inquiry
introduces inquiry skills within a structured framework.	develops inquiry skills within a supportive environment.	deepens inquiry skills with student-driven questions or procedures.

Labs and Demos

Daily Demo *Observing Resistance*

Resistance

👥 whole class
🕐 15–20 min
Inquiry GUIDED inquiry

PURPOSE **To show the differences in resistance levels for different materials**

MATERIALS

- batteries, 2
- battery holders (optional)
- bulbs, flashlight, 2
- copper wire, 3 very different lengths
- electrical tape

CAUTION **Do not allow students to touch the battery or other materials.**

1 Attach the medium length wire to the negative terminal of the battery, using electrical tape if necessary. Attach the other end of the wire to the bulb by wrapping it around the metal part of the bulb.

2 **Observe** Touch the bottom part of the bulb to the positive terminal. The bulb should light up.

3 Leave the circuit with the medium length wire lit. Connect the shortest wire to a battery and a bulb. Touch the bottom of the bulb to the positive terminal. Have students compare its brightness to the bulb attached to the medium length wire.

4 Finally, repeat this process using the longest length of wire.

5 **Observe Ask:** What did you notice about the demonstration? Sample answer: The longer the wire, the dimmer the light bulb.

6 **Analyze Ask:** How can wires made from the same material have different resistance levels? Sample answer: A shorter wire has less resistance than a longer wire.

🌐 🔲 Quick Lab *Investigate Electric Current*

Current

👥 small groups
🕐 30 min
Inquiry DIRECTED inquiry

Students construct a series circuit and check current with a multimeter.

PURPOSE **To observe current in a circuit**

MATERIALS

- batteries, AA 1.5 V in holder
- bulbs, flashlight, in base
- multimeter
- wire, insulated with alligator clips

🌐 🔲 Quick Lab *Lemon Battery*

PURPOSE **To explore how batteries work**

See the Lab Manual or go Online for planning information.

🌐 🔲 S.T.E.M. Lab *Voltage, Current, and Resistance*

Synthesizing Key Topics

👥 small groups
🕐 45 min
Inquiry DIRECTED/GUIDED inquiry

Students test pencil lead resistors in a DC circuit.

PURPOSE **To explore the electrical relationship** $V = IR$

MATERIALS

- battery, 9V
- calculator
- multimeter
- pencil pieces
- ruler, metrc
- wire, insulated with alligator clips, 2

Activities and Discussion

- ☐ **Discussion** Types of Electric Current
- ☐ **Activity** Current Diagram
- ☐ **Activity** Modeling Current
- ☐ **Activity** Uses of Electricity

Labs and Demos

- ☐ **Daily Demo** Observing Resistance
- ☐ **Quick Lab** Electric Current
- ☐ **Quick Lab** Lemon Battery
- ☐ **S.T.E.M. Lab** Voltage, Current, and Resistance

Your Resources

_____

_____

_____

Explain Science Concepts

	Print Path	Digital Path

Current

Print Path

☐ **Current Events,** SE pp. 138–139
- Active Reading (Annotation strategy), #5
- Visualize It!, #6
- Active Reading, #7

Digital Path

☐ **Electric Current and Direct Current**
Define electric current, and describe direct current.

☐ **Alternating Current**
Describe alternating current, and explain how it works.

Voltage

Print Path

☐ **You've Got Potential,** SE p. 140
- Visualize It!, #8

Digital Path

☐ **Voltage and Resistance**
Define voltage and resistance, and describe their relationship to electric current.

Resistance

Print Path

☐ **You've Got Potential,** SE pp. 140–141
- Think Outside the Book, #9
- Visualize It!, #10

Digital Path

☐ **Factors Affecting Resistance**
Explain what determines electrical resistance.

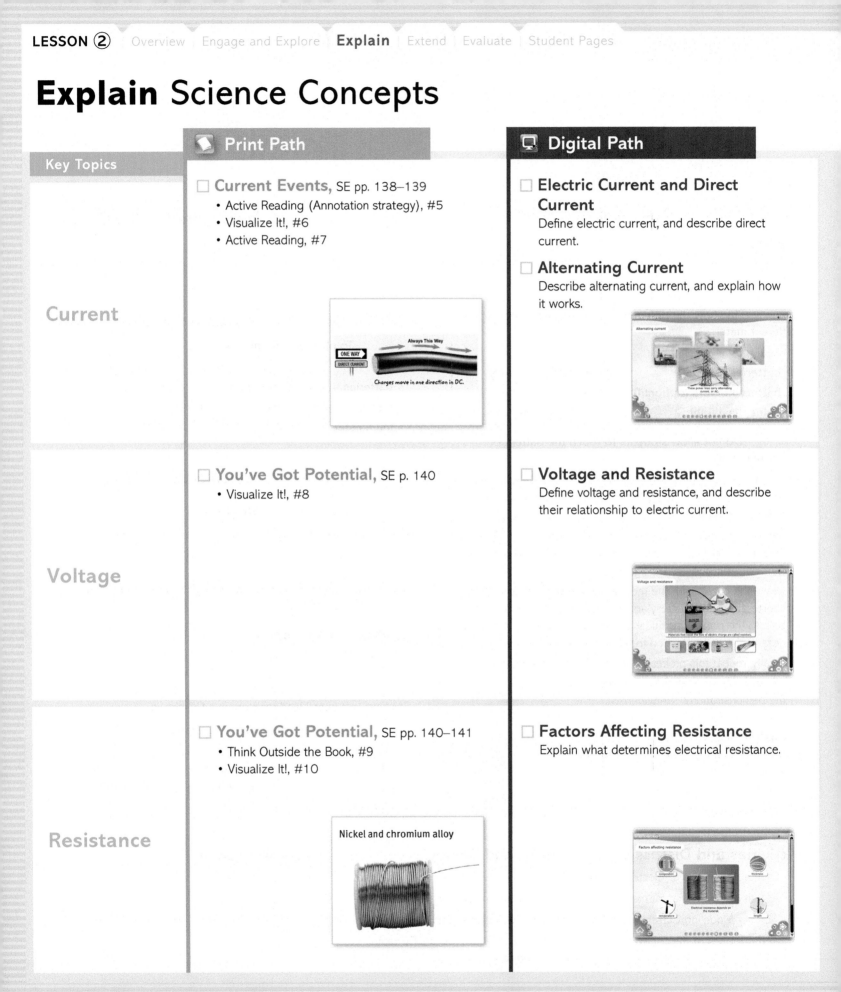

ONE WAY
DIRECT CURRENT
Always This Way
Charges move in one direction in DC.

Nickel and chromium alloy

Differentiated Instruction

Basic *Resistance Factors*

Resistance

👥 pairs
🕐 10 min

Have pairs of students write a short summary describing the factors that affect a conductor's electrical resistance. Each pair should share their summary with another pair. Pairs should check each other's work for errors and misconceptions.

Basic *AC and DC*

Current

👥 individuals
🕐 10 min

Double Door Fold After completing the lesson, have students create a double door fold to compare the characteristics of alternating current and direct current. On the outside of one fold, have students write "alternating current," and on the outside of the other fold, have students write "direct current." Underneath each flap, have students describe the characteristics of each type of current. Finally, have students include examples of each.

🌐 *Online resource: Double-Door Fold support*

Advanced *Developments in Electricity*

Synthesizing Key Concepts

👥 small groups
🕐 varies

Quick Research Have groups of students work together to research new developments in the light bulb. Have groups look into the differences and similarities between incandescent, fluorescent, and LED light bulbs. Groups should report their findings to the class in a short computer presentation.

ELL *Electricity Posters*

Synthesizing Key Concepts

👥 individuals or pairs
🕐 20 min

Posters Have individual students create drawings to show their understanding of AC, DC, voltage, and resistance. Then have students work with a partner to share and explain their drawings. Individual students should make any necessary revisions to their drawings before mounting them on a large sheet of paper or posterboard. If possible, display the posters in the classroom.

Lesson Vocabulary

electric current   **voltage**   **resistance**

Previewing Vocabulary

👥 whole class
🕐 10 min

Common Definitions Remind students that some words have both scientific and everyday meanings. Have students use dictionaries to find definitions for *current* and write one sentence for each definition, including the scientific definition used in this lesson.

Reinforcing Vocabulary

👥 individuals
🕐 15 min

Frame Game To help students remember what each vocabulary term in the lesson refers to, have them make a frame game for each one. Direct students to write the term in the center of the frame and then surround it with information about that term, such as a definition, a description, examples, and a drawing.

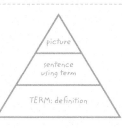

Customize Your Core Lesson

Core Instruction

☐ **Print Path** choices

☐ **Digital Path** choices

Vocabulary

☐ **Previewing Vocabulary**
   Common Definitions

☐ **Reinforcing Vocabulary**
   Frame Game

Your Resources

Differentiated Instruction

☐ Basic Resistance Factors

☐ Basic AC and DC

☐ Advanced Developments in Electricity

☐ ELL Electricity Posters

Extend Science Concepts

Reinforce and Review

Activity *Electric Topics*

Synthesizing Key Topics 👥 whole class 🕐 10 min

Write Fast Have students listen as you read the following questions. After each question is read, allow 1–2 minutes for students to write down their responses.

1 Describe an electric current. Sample answer: the rate at which electric charges pass a given point

2 Finish the statement: The higher the voltage applied to a given wire, the higher its _____. Sample answer: current

3 Resistance of a wire depends on what factors? Sample answer: composition, thickness, length, and temperature

Graphic Organizer

Synthesizing Key Concepts 👥 individuals 🕐 15–20 min

Cluster Diagram After studying the lesson, have students develop a cluster diagram to show the relationships between the lesson's key concepts. Make sure students include the terms *current, AC, DC, voltage,* and *resistance.*

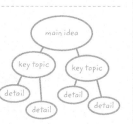

⏱ *Optional Online resource: Cluster Diagram support*

Going Further

Social Studies Connection

Synthesizing Key Topics 👥 individuals or small groups 🕐 varies

Timeline Have interested students research and create a timeline to describe the development of the electric light. Students can embellish their timelines with drawings and pictures from various time periods relevant to events on the timeline. Display completed timelines for the class.

Environmental Science Connection

Sources of Electrical Energy 👥 small groups 🕐 20 min

Poster Ask students to brainstorm a list of sources of electrical energy. Tell students that they should include both renewable and nonrenewable sources. Write student ideas on the board in two columns labeled Renewable and Nonrenewable. After you have listed energy sources, ask students to form small groups and choose several sources to research. Tell students that they should include both renewable and nonrenewable sources. Examples of renewable electrical energy sources students can research include wind power, solar power, and water power. Examples of nonrenewable sources include coal, oil, and natural gas. Invite students to create posters to communicate the information they have discovered about different sources of electrical energy. Display finished posters around the classroom.

Customize Your Closing

🗨 *See the Assessment Guide for quizzes and tests.*

⏱ *Go Online to edit and create quizzes and tests.*

Reinforce and Review

☐ **Activity** Electric Topics

☐ **Graphic Organizer** Cluster Diagram

☐ **Print Path** Visual Summary, SE p. 142

☐ **Print Path** Lesson Review, SE p. 143

☐ **Digital Path** Lesson Closer

Evaluate Student Mastery

See the teacher support below the Student Pages for additional Formative Assessment questions.

Ask the following questions to assess student mastery of the material. **Ask:** What are two types of electric current? alternating current (AC) and direct current (DC) **Ask:** What type of current powers a battery? direct current **Ask:** What is voltage? the amount of work to move an electric charge between two points **Ask:** What is resistance? the opposition to an electric charge **Ask:** What three factors affect the resistance of a copper wire? thickness, length, and temperature

Reteach

Formative assessment may show that students need reinforcement for certain topics. The resources below are recommended for reteaching. If students were introduced to a topic through the Print Path, you can also use the Digital Path to reteach, or vice versa.
🎧 *Can be assigned to individual students*

Current
Activity Current Diagram 🎧
Basic AC and DC 🎧
Quick Lab Investigate Electric Current

Voltage
Quick Lab Lemon Battery
S.T.E.M. Lab Voltage, Current, and Resistance

Resistance
Basic Resistance Factors
Daily Demo Observing Resistance

Alternative Assessment
Electric Currents

🔘 *Online resources: students worksheet; optional rubrics*

Electric Current

Choose Your Meal: *Electric Currents*
Create a balanced "meal" from the choices below to show what you have learned in this lesson.

1. Work on your own, with a partner, or with a small group.
2. Choose one item from each section of the menu, with an optional dessert. Check your choices.
3. Have your teacher approve your plan.
4. Submit or present your results.

Appetizers

_____ **Poem** Write a short poem that describes the factors that influence resistance.

_____ **Advertisement** Develop a print or web-based advertisement for a battery. Make sure to include information on the type of current the battery uses and how the battery works.

_____ **Experiment Design** Design an experiment to test the following question: Which material is the least resistant to an electric current: copper metal wire, a wooden dowel, or an aluminum can?

Main Dish

_____ **Essay** Write a two-paragraph essay explaining the key concepts of current and voltage from the lesson. Have a peer review your work and suggest possible edits. Edit and proofread your essay before publishing it.

Side Dishes

_____ **Quiz** Develop a 10-question quiz to test your classmates' knowledge on key topics from the lesson. Create a separate answer key for your quiz. If possible, give the quiz to a small group of students. Correct the quizzes and give each student in the group a grade.

_____ **Interview Questions** Develop 5-8 in-depth questions you would ask an expert in the field of electricity.

Desserts (optional)

_____ **Trading Cards** Create 4-6 trading cards that name a material used for conducting electricity. Various metals used for wiring are possible choices. Write the name of the material on the front of the card and include key information about the material on the back of the card, along with a rating that shows the material's effectiveness for conducting electricity.

_____ **Acrostic** Create an acrostic for one of the lesson's vocabulary terms: *electric current, voltage,* or *resistance,* with words and phrases that are relevant to the lesson.

Going Further
☐ Social Studies Connection
☐ Science Connection

Formative Assessment
☐ Strategies Throughout TE
☐ Lesson Review SE

Summative Assessment
☐ Alternative Assessment Electric Currents
☐ Lesson Quiz
☐ Unit Tests A and B
☐ Unit Review SE End-of-Unit

Your Resources

_____   _____

_____   _____

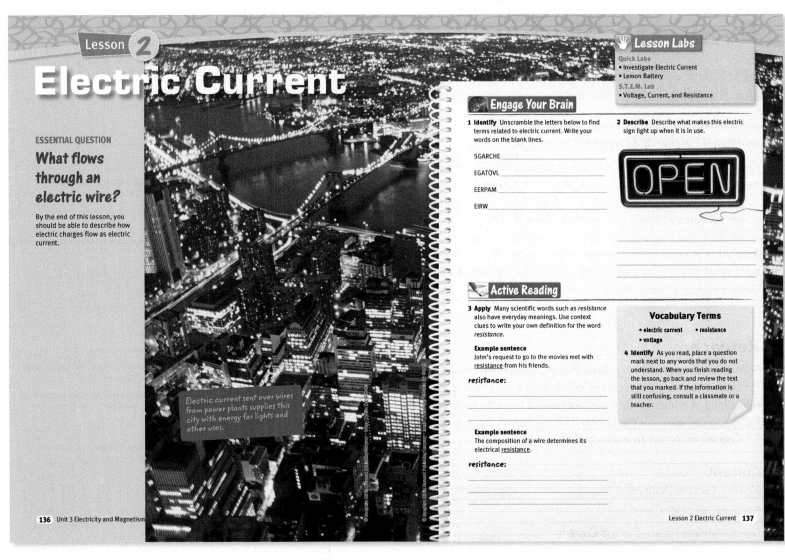

Answers

Answers for 1–3 should represent students' thoughts, even if incorrect.

1. charges; voltage; ampere; wire

2. Sample answer: Electric current in the wire powers the light. The current comes from a plug when it's placed in the wall.

3. Sample answer: hesitation, refusal to go along; opposition to the flow of charge in a wire

4. *See students' pages for annotations.*

Opening Your Lesson

Discuss students' descriptions of what makes the sign light up in item 2 to assess their understanding of electric current. Address any confusion students may have about the content at this point.

Prerequisites Students should have a basic understanding of how electrical energy powers their lights, computers, and other everyday appliances. They should also understand electric charges.

Learning Alert

Static Electricity versus Electric Current Static electricity and electric current both involve electric charge but are two different phenomena. Static electricity is the buildup of electric charge on the surface of an object. In contrast, electric current is the rate of flow of electric charges along a conductor. Electric current is normally controlled, while static electricity may rapidly discharge.

What is an electric current?

When you watch TV, use a computer, or even turn on a light bulb, you depend on moving charges to provide the electrical energy that powers them. *Electrical energy* is the energy of electric charges. In most devices that use electrical energy, the electric charges flow through wires. The rate of flow of electric charges is called **electric current**.

How is electric current measured?

Active Reading

5 Identify As you read, underline the units used to express electric current.

To understand an electric current, think of people entering the seating area for a sporting event through turnstiles. A counter in each turnstile records the number of people who enter. The number of people who pass through a turnstile each minute describes the rate of flow of people into the stadium. Similarly, an electric current describes the rate of flow of charges, such as the slow flow of many electrons through a wire. Electric current is the amount of charge that passes a location in the wire every second. Electric current is expressed in units called *amperes* (AM•pirz), which is often shortened to "amps." The symbol for ampere is A. A wire with a current of 2 A has twice as much charge passing by each second as a wire with a current of 1 A.

Visualize It!

6 Identify How can you express the rate of flow of people into a stadium? How can you express the rate of flow of charges through a wire?

What are two kinds of current?

Two kinds of electric current are *direct current* (DC) and *alternating current* (AC). Both kinds of current carry electrical energy. They differ in the way that the charges move.

Direct Current (DC)

In direct current, charges always flow in the same direction. The electric current generated by batteries is DC. Some everyday devices that use DC from batteries are flashlights, cars, and cameras.

ONE WAY **DIRECT CURRENT**

Always This Way

Charges move in one direction in DC.

Alternating Current (AC)

In alternating current, charges repeatedly shift from flowing in one direction to flowing in the reverse direction. The current *alternates* direction. The electric current from outlets in your home is AC. So, most household appliances run on alternating current. In the United States, the alternating current reverses direction and then returns back to the original direction 60 times each second.

TWO WAY **ALTERNATING CURRENT**

First This Way

Then This Way

Charges repeatedly change direction in AC.

Active Reading

7 Explain What alternates in alternating current?

Answers

5. *See students' pages for annotations.*

6. Sample answer: The rate of flow of people could be described in units of people per minute. The rate of flow of charges could be measured in amount of charge per second (amperes).

7. the direction of the flow of charges

Interpreting Visuals

Have students describe what they see in the photograph on the bottom of page 138. **Ask:** What aspect of electric current can the turnstile in the photograph be compared to? The turnstile can be compared to the specific, fixed point at which a current can be measured.

Learning Alert

AC Current Tell students that AC is the type of current usually delivered to homes and businesses around the world. **Ask:** What is the difference between AC and DC? Sample answer: Alternating current changes direction; direct current flows in one direction. **Ask:** Why do you think AC is used so much more? Answers may vary. Tell students that the voltage in alternating current can be controlled much more easily than that of direct current. Because the direction in AC changes, its voltage can be controlled by devices called *transformers*. High voltage current can be sent over long distances.

What affects electric current?

Two factors that can affect the current in a wire are *voltage* and *resistance*.

Voltage

Compare the two drink containers below. If you pour lemonade from a full container, your glass fills quickly. If the container is nearly empty, the flow of lemonade is weaker. The lemonade in the full container exerts more pressure due to its weight, causing a higher rate of flow. This pressure can be compared to voltage. **Voltage** is the amount of work required to move each unit of charge between two points. Just as higher pressure produces a higher rate of flow of lemonade, higher voltage produces a higher rate of flow of electric charges in a given wire. Voltage is expressed in units of volts (V). Voltage is sometimes called *electric potential* because it is a measure of the electric potential energy per unit charge.

👁 Visualize It!

8 Analyze How does the flow of the lemonade coming out of these containers relate to current and voltage?

_____

_____

_____

_____

Resistance

Think about the difference between walking around your room and walking around in waist-deep water. The water resists your movement more than the air, so you have to work harder to walk through water. If you walked in waist-deep mud, you would have to work even harder. Similarly, some materials do not allow electric charges to move freely. The opposition to the flow of electric charge is called **resistance**. Resistance is expressed in ohms (Ω, the Greek letter *omega*). Higher resistance at the same voltage results in lower current.

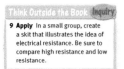

9 Apply In a small group, create a skit that illustrates the idea of electrical resistance. Be sure to compare high resistance and low resistance.

What affects electrical resistance?

A material's composition affects its resistance. Some metals, such as silver and copper, have low resistance and are very good electrical conductors. Other metals, such as iron and nickel, have a higher resistance. Electrical insulators such as plastic have such a high resistance that electric charges cannot flow in them at all. Other factors that affect the resistance of a wire are thickness, length, and temperature.

- A thin wire has higher resistance than a thicker wire.
- A long wire has higher resistance than a shorter wire.
- A hot wire has higher resistance than a cooler wire.

Conductors with low resistance, such as copper, are used to make wires. But conductors with high resistance are also useful. For example, an alloy of nickel and chromium is used in heating coils. Its high resistance causes the wire to heat up when it carries electric current.

Like lemonade in a drinking straw, electric charges move more easily through a short, wide pathway than through a long, narrow one.

👁 Visualize It!

10 Predict For each pair of images, place a check mark in the box that shows the material that has higher electrical resistance.

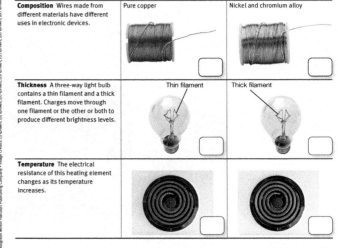

Composition Wires made from different materials have different uses in electronic devices.	Pure copper	Nickel and chromium alloy
Thickness A three-way light bulb contains a thin filament and a thick filament. Charges move through one filament or the other or both to produce different brightness levels.	Thin filament	Thick filament
Temperature The electrical resistance of this heating element changes as its temperature increases.		

Answers

8. Sample answer: The containers show how higher pressure results in a higher rate of flow of lemonade. This is similar to the idea that higher voltage results in a higher rate of flow of charges in a given wire.

9. Students should create a skit to illustrate resistance. They should indicate that higher-resistance materials hinder the flow of charge. You may wish to ask groups to perform their skits for the rest of the class.

10. Composition: second box; Thickness: first box; Temperature: second box

Learning Alert

Difficult Concepts Students may have difficulty understanding the usefulness of materials with higher electrical resistance. Expand on the example of the light bulb by pointing out that an incandescent light bulb gets quite hot while it is on. The material commonly used in light bulb filaments is tungsten, a metal with a very high melting point and high resistance. These qualities allow the tungsten filament to resist melting or burning out.

Formative Assessment

Ask: What is the difference between alternating current and direct current? The charges in an alternating current alternate, or change, direction, while the charges in a direct current move in only one direction. **Ask:** What factors affect a material's resistance? Sample answer: What the material is composed of, the shape of the material, and the temperature of the material. **Ask:** Which has a higher resistance, thin wires or thicker wires? Why? Sample answer: Thin wires; thicker wires allow a higher rate of flow of charges. **Ask:** How does temperature affect resistance in a wire? Sample answer: As temperature increases, the resistance of the metal wire also increases.

Visual Summary

To complete this summary, fill in the blanks with the correct word or phrase. Then use the key below to check your answers. You can use this page to review the main concepts of the lesson.

Electric current is the rate of flow of electric charges.

First This Way

Then This Way

11 In _____ current, the flow of charge changes direction and then reverses back to the original direction.

The opposition to the flow of electric charges is called resistance.

13 Four factors that determine the resistance of a wire are _____

Voltage is the amount of work to move an electric charge between two points.

12 If the voltage applied to a given wire increases, its current will _____

Electric Current

Answers: 11 alternating; 12 increase 13 composition, temperature, length, and thickness

14 Apply What might happen if a wire in an electronic device is replaced with a thinner, longer wire? Explain.

© Houghton Mifflin Harcourt Publishing Company • Image Credits: (b) ©Artville/Getty Images

---

Lesson Review

Vocabulary

Draw a line to connect the following terms to their definitions.

1 electric current

2 voltage

3 resistance

A the opposition to the flow of electric charges

B the rate of flow of electric charges

C the amount of work required to move each unit of electric charge between two points

Key Concepts

4 Compare How does direct current differ from alternating current?

5 Summarize Describe how resistance affects electric current.

6 Apply What happens to the electric current in a wire as voltage is increased?

7 Apply List two everyday devices that use DC and two everyday devices that use AC.

Critical Thinking

Use the diagram to answer the following questions.

Electrical Resistance of Various Materials

| Copper | Germanium | PVC Plastic |

Low resistance   High resistance

8 Analyze Which material is likely to slow the flow of electric charges the most? Explain.

9 Infer A certain voltage is applied to a copper wire and to a germanium wire of the same thickness and length. How will the current in the two wires compare?

10 Compare How do the currents produced by a 1.5 V flashlight battery and a 12 V car battery compare if the resistance is the same?

11 Infer What does it mean to say that the electric current from a wall socket is "120 V AC?"

© Houghton Mifflin Harcourt Publishing Company

Visual Summary Answers

11. alternating

12. increase

13. composition, temperature, length, and thickness

14. Sample answer: The current in the new wire will be lower because the resistance has increased. The device may not get enough electrical energy to operate properly.

Lesson Review Answers

1. B

2. C

3. A

4. In direct current, charges move in one direction. In alternating current, charges move in alternating directions.

5. At a constant voltage, higher resistance lowers electric current in a wire.

6. Electric current increases.

7. Sample answer: DC: cell phones and hearing aids that use batteries; AC: washing machines and lamps

8. PVC plastic; it has the highest resistance.

9. The copper wire will have a higher current than the germanium wire.

10. The 12 V car battery produces higher current than the 1.5 V flashlight battery.

11. Sample answer: It means that the wall socket provides alternating current at a voltage of 120 V.

Electric Circuits

Essential Question How do electric circuits work?

🍎 **Professional Development**

For more detailed information about the topics in this lesson, refer to the Content Refresher in the Unit Opener pages.

Opening Your Lesson

Begin the lesson by assessing students' prerequisite and prior knowledge.

Prerequisite Knowledge

- An understanding of electric charge and static electricity
- An understanding of electric current

Accessing Prior Knowledge

Tri-Fold Have students make a tri-fold KWL chart. Before students begin the lesson, have them complete the first two columns of the KWL chart. In the first column, students should record what they already know about electric currents. In the center column, students should record what they want to learn about this topic. The third column should be filled in after students have completed the lesson. In this column, students should record what they learned.

Customize Your Opening

- ☐ **Accessing Prior Knowledge,** above
- ☐ Print Path Engage Your Brain, SE p. 145
- ☐ Print Path Active Reading, SE p. 145
- ☐ **Digital Path** Lesson Opener

Key Topics/Learning Goals

Electric Circuits

1 Describe the parts of an electric circuit.
2 Distinguish between open and closed circuits.
3 Distinguish between a series circuit and a parallel circuit.

Electrical Safety

1 Describe why you must use precautions when using electrical appliances.
2 Describe some devices that make using electricity safer.
3 Describe safety measures that protect people and buildings during a lightning storm.

Supporting Concepts

- An electric circuit is a closed path through which electric charges can flow.
- Circuits usually contain an energy source such as a battery, connecting wires, and a load, such as a light bulb.
- Charges can flow in a closed circuit but cannot flow in an open circuit.
- Circuit diagrams use symbols to represent different components of the circuit.
- In a series circuit, all of the parts connect in a single loop.
- A parallel circuit is one in which the circuit splits up into different branches.

- The water in your body makes you a conductor of electric current.
- Frayed cords and exposed parts of circuits are an electrical hazard.
- Circuit breakers and fuses are devices designed to "break" an electric circuit when the current gets too high.
- Lightning is an electric discharge.
- When there is lightning, seek shelter.
- Lightning rods can be mounted at the highest point on a building. When lightning strikes a lightning rod, the electric charges are carried to Earth through the rod's wire.

Options for Instruction

Two parallel paths provide coverage of the Essential Questions, with a strong Inquiry strand woven into each. Follow the Print Path, the Digital Path, or your customized combination of print, digital, and inquiry.

 **Print Path**

Teaching support for the Print Path appears with the Student Pages.

Inquiry Labs and Activities

Digital Path

Digital Path shortcut: TS675454

A Complete Circuit,
SE pp. 146–147
The parts of an electric circuit:
• Energy Source; Electrical Conductor; Load

Around and Around,
SE pp. 148–149
How are circuits modeled?
• With Circuit Diagrams
How does current start and stop?

All Together?, SE pp. 150–151
How do series circuits and parallel circuits differ?
• Series: Charges Follow a Single Path
• Parallel: Charges Follow Multiple Paths

Exploration Lab
Model the Electric Circuits in a Room

Quick Lab
Compare Materials for Use in Fuses

Quick Lab
Compare Parallel and Series Circuits

Daily Demo
Will It Light?

Virtual Lab
How Can You Change Current in an Electric Circuit?

Simple Electric Circuit Diagram
Interactive Graphics

Open vs. Closed Circuits
Graphic Sequence

Series Circuits
Video

Parallel Circuits
Interactive Images

Safety First!, SE pp. 152–153
How can I use electricity safely?
• By Avoiding Exposure to Current
• By Using Electrical Safety Devices
• By Taking Precautions During a Lightning Storm

Activity
Safety Signs

Activity
Electric Circuits and Electrical Safety

Using Electricity Safely
Slideshow

Storm Safety
Slideshow

Options for Assessment

See the Evaluate page for options, including Formative Assessment, Summative Assessment, and Unit Review.

Engage and Explore

Activities and Discussion

Discussion *Staying Safe*

Engage

Introductory Activity

  👥 whole class
  🕐 10 min
  Inquiry **GUIDED** inquiry

Ask students if they have ever received a shock. Students will likely relate that they've been shocked by static electricity in situations such as walking on carpet and then touching a doorknob. Tell students that receiving a shock from electric current is far more painful than that. Ask students if they know how receiving a shock from electric current can harm a person. Sample answers: It can interfere with your heart beating; it can burn you. Tell students that electric shock can also cause muscles to tighten and lungs to constrict. Ask students to brainstorm electrical devices they use and ways to make sure they stay safe. Sample answers: You should never turn on a switch with wet fingers; never use a hair dryer near a shower or bath; never use cracked or frayed electrical cords, always keeps cords neatly coiled and stored; never fly a kite near a power line.

Activity *Safety Signs*

Engage

Electrical Safety

  👥 small groups
  🕐 10 min
  Inquiry **GUIDED** inquiry

Introduce students to the information in the lesson about electrical safety. Then, have students form small groups. Encourage the groups to brainstorm ideas for safety signs. Have them think about electrical safety signs they have noticed in the past, then come up with designs for signs that convey important information about staying safe around electric appliances and machines. Remind students to include effective graphics, not just words. Use the signs to launch a class discussion about electrical safety.

Labs and Demos

Daily Demo *Will It Light?*

Engage

Electric Circuits

  👥 whole class
  🕐 10 min
  Inquiry **DIRECTED** inquiry

PURPOSE **To introduce electric circuits**

MATERIALS

- battery, D-cell
- light bulb with holder
- wire, insulated, with alligator clips

1 Set the materials out on a table or desk. Ask students to predict whether or not the light bulb can be lit using only the materials on the table.

2 Then, assemble the components into a simple circuit, but do not attach the wires to the dry cell. After the circuit is constructed (while the wires are not connected), allow students to revise their predictions.

3 Then, complete the circuit by attaching the wires to the dry cell, allowing the bulb to light.

4 **Observing** What do you observe? The light bulb is lit.

5 **Analyzing** Could the light bulb be lit if any one of these components were removed? Explain. No, each one of these components is needed to construct this circuit so electric current flows.

6 **Evaluating Ask:** Were the predictions you made correct or incorrect? What information helped you reevaluate your prediction? At first my prediction was incorrect, because I didn't think we had everything we needed to make the light bulb light. After the components were assembled, I had more information and changed my prediction.

©Jupiterimages/Getty Images (r)

Customize Your Labs

📄 *See the Lab Manual for lab datasheets.*

🌐 *Go Online for editable lab datasheets.*

⊙ ◖ Quick Lab *Compare Parallel and Series Circuits*

Electric Circuits

👥 small groups
🕐 20 minutes
GUIDED inquiry

Students build a series circuit and a parallel circuit that include light bulbs.

PURPOSE **To determine the effects of parallel versus series circuits on the brightness of light bulbs**

MATERIALS

- battery, D-cell, in holder
- light bulb, with holder, 2
- wire, insulated with alligator clips, 4

⊙ ◖ Quick Lab *Compare Materials for Use in Fuses*

Electric Circuits

👥 small groups
🕐 30 min
DIRECTED inquiry

Students insert a strand of steel wool and a copper wire into an electric circuit and observe what happens.

PURPOSE **To explore the electrical resistance of two materials**

MATERIALS

- battery, 6V
- jar, clear glass
- steel wool, single strand
- stopwatch

- tape, duct
- wire, bare copper
- wire, insulated with alligator clips, 2

⊙ ◖ Exploration Lab *Model the Electric Circuits in a Room*

Electric Circuits

👥 small groups
🕐 two 45 min periods
GUIDED/INDEPENDENT inquiry

Students draw, build, and test an electric circuit.

PURPOSE **To investigate the parts of an electric circuit**

MATERIALS

- batteries, D-cell, with holders, 2
- light bulbs, small, with holders, 3
- markers, different colors
- paper
- shoe box

- switches
- tape, electrical
- tape, transparent
- wire cutter/stripper
- wire, insulated

▢ Virtual Lab *How Can You Change Current in an Electric Circuit?*

Electric Circuits

👥 flexible
🕐 45 min
DIRECTED inquiry

Students test conductors and record voltage, current, and resistance.

PURPOSE **To investigate factors that affect the flow of electric charges**

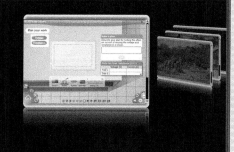

Activities and Discussion

☐ **Discussion** Staying Safe
☐ **Activity** Safety Signs

Labs and Demos

☐ **Daily Demo** Will It Light?
☐ **Quick Lab** Compare Parallel and Series Circuits

☐ **Quick Lab** Compare Materials for Use in Fuses
☐ **Exploration Lab** Model the Electric Circuits in a Room
☐ **Virtual Lab** How Can You Change Current in an Electric Circuit?

Your Resources

_____

_____

_____

_____

Explain Science Concepts

📖 **Print Path**

💻 **Digital Path**

☐ **A Complete Circuit,** SE pp. 146–147
- Active Reading (Annotation strategy), #5
- Think Outside the Book, #6
- Visualize It!, #7

☐ **Around and Around,** SE pp. 148–149
- Active Reading (Annotation strategy), #8
- Active Reading, #9
- Visualize It!, #10

☐ **All Together?,** SE pp. 150–151
- Active Reading (Annotation strategy), #11
- Visualize It!, #12
- Compare, #13

☐ **Simple Electric Circuit Diagram**
Name and describe parts of an electric circuit.

☐ **Open vs. Closed Circuits**
Distinguish between an open circuit and a closed circuit, and recognize these circuits from diagrams.

☐ **Series Circuits**
Explain the arrangement of parts in a series circuit, and describe the properties of a series circuit.

☐ **Parallel Circuits**
Explain the arrangement of parts in a parallel circuit, and describe the properties of a parallel circuit.

Electric Circuits

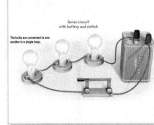

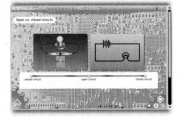

☐ **Safety First!,** SE pp. 152–153
- Active Reading (Annotation strategy), #14
- Active Reading, #15
- Infer, #16

☐ **Using Electricity Safely**
Recognize the reason it is important to take precautions when using electrical appliances, and list some devices that help protect against electric current.

☐ **Storm Safety**
Describe ways to stay safe during an electrical storm.

Electrical Safety

Basic *Circuit Diagrams*

Electrical Circuits

👥 individuals
🕐 15 min

Students will better understand how circuits function if they create a visual aid. Have students draw and label two diagrams of series circuits: one with two light bulbs and one with three. Help students remember the parts in a series circuit, such as a light bulb, wire, switch, and energy source. Remind students that all components in a circuit must connect. Help students label their diagrams and add notes and details next to each part.

Advanced *Teaching About Electrical Safety*

Electrical Safety

👥 pairs
🕐 30 min

Write a Book After students understand what a circuit is and what its parts are, have them write a children's book that conveys information about electrical safety. It may be helpful to supply several examples of books written for younger children that students can use as models. Encourage students to carefully select the information they will include in their books and to divide the tasks involved in making the book in a logical way. Have each pair of students present their completed book to the class.

ELL *Modified Cloze Sentences*

Electric Circuits

👥 individuals
🕐 10 min

Use the following modified cloze sentences to reinforce the main points of the lesson:

Every electric circuit has three parts, a _____ (conductor), an energy source, and a load.

A circuit must be a _____ (closed) loop for current to flow.

_____ (Series) circuits have a single path for current.

_____ (Parallel) circuits have more than one path for current.

electric circuit   **parallel circuit**   **series circuit**

Previewing Vocabulary

👥 whole class
🕐 15 min

Write these lesson vocabulary terms on the board:
parallel circuit   series circuit
Ask students what *parallel* means. Sample answer: side by side or at the same time Next, ask what *series* means. Sample answer: one after another Tell students that the following can help them remember the difference between the types of circuits: In a series circuit, electric charges flow through each component in a path, and each part must function for the circuit to be complete. In a parallel circuit, components are connected in parallel, and electric charges flow along separate, parallel paths.

Reinforcing Vocabulary

👥 pairs
🕐 15 min

Description Wheel Have one student in each pair complete the graphic organizer for the term *parallel circuit*; the other student should complete one for the term *series circuit*. After they are finished, have pairs trade completed graphic organizers with their partners to review their partner's work.

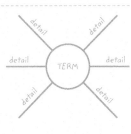

Customize Your Core Lesson

Core Instruction

☐ **Print Path** choices
☐ **Digital Path** choices

Vocabulary

☐ **Previewing Vocabulary**
☐ **Reinforcing Vocabulary**
    Description Wheel

Differentiated Instruction

☐ **Basic** Circuit Diagrams
☐ **Advanced** Teaching About Electrical Safety
☐ **ELL** Modified Cloze Sentences

Your Resources

_____

_____

Extend Science Concepts

Reinforce and Review

Activity *Electric Circuits and Electrical Safety*

Synthesizing Key Topics
👥 small groups
🕐 20 min

Carousel Review Help students review the material by following these steps:

1 After students have read the lesson, prepare three pieces of chart paper with the following questions: "What are the parts of an electrical circuit and what are some examples of each of these parts?" "How are series circuits and parallel circuits similar, and how are they different?" "What are some ways people can avoid exposure to electric current?"

2 Divide students into small groups and assign each group a chart. Give each group a different colored marker.

3 Have the groups review their question, discuss their answer, and write a response.

4 After five minutes, each group should rotate to the next chart. Groups should put a check by each answer they agree with, comment on answers they don't agree with, and add their own answers. Continue until all groups have reviewed all charts.

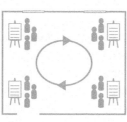

5 Invite each group to share information with the class.

Graphic Organizer

Synthesizing Key Topics
👥 individuals
🕐 10 min

Concept Map Distribute to students a blank Concept Map worksheet. Have the students add words and phrases to the ovals and use linking words to show how key topics from this lesson are related. Encourage students to include information about both electric circuits and electrical safety. Have several students share their completed concept maps with the class.

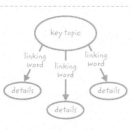

Going Further

History Connection

Synthesizing Key Topics
👥 small groups
🕐 20 min

Quick Research Ask students if they have ever experienced a power outage in their home due to weather. Ask students to describe what they had to "do without" as a result of the power outage—for example, television, lights, radio, and computer. Then ask students to think about life before homes were wired for electricity. Have students work with their groups to find out more about the history of electrical wiring and devices in homes. Encourage students to find out more about both the devices and circuits used, as well as advancements in home electrical safety that have been made over time. Have the students in each group give a short oral presentation to share what they have learned.

Health Connection

Electrical Safety
👥 Individuals or small groups
🕐 20 min

Quick Research Tell students that some scientists believe there may be a link between being exposed to higher-than-average electromagnetic fields, such as living near high-voltage power lines, and an increased incidence of certain kinds of cancer. Encourage interested students to research this possible link and write a short report on their findings. After they have completed their research, students may enjoy engaging in a debate on whether there is enough proof that electromagnetic field exposure causes cancer or not.

Customize Your Closing

🗅 *See the Assessment Guide for quizzes and tests.*

🕐 *Go Online to edit and create quizzes and tests.*

Reinforce and Review

☐ **Activity** Electric Circuits and Electrical Safety

☐ **Graphic Organizer** Concept Map

☐ **Print Path** Visual Summary, SE p. 154

☐ **Print Path** Lesson Review, SE p. 155

☐ **Digital Path** Lesson Closer

Evaluate Student Mastery

See the teacher support below the Student Pages for additional Formative Assessment questions.

Ask the following questions to assess student mastery of the material. **Ask:** What are some ways in which all circuits are similar? All circuits contain an energy source, at least one load, and a conductor. **Ask:** If one bulb in a circuit breaks, and current stops flowing in the entire circuit, what can you determine about this circuit? That it is a series circuit. **Ask:** What is the function of circuit breakers and fuses? To protect people and homes when too much current is flowing in a circuit.

Reteach

Formative assessment may show that students need reinforcement for certain topics. The resources below are recommended for reteaching. If students were introduced to a topic through the Print Path, you can also use the Digital Path to reteach, or vice versa.
🔵 *Can be assigned to individual students*

Electric Circuits
Basic Circuit Diagrams 🔵
Virtual Lab How Can You Change Current in an Electric Circuit? 🔵
Graphic Organizer Concept Map 🔵

Electrical Safety
Discussion Staying Safe
Activity Safety Signs

Summative Assessment

Alternative Assessment
Electric Circuits and Electrical Safety

⊘ *Online resources: student worksheet; optional rubrics*

Electric Circuits

Points of View: *Electric Circuits and Electrical Safety*
Your class will work together to show what you've learned about electrical circuits and electrical safety from several different viewpoints.

1. Work in groups as assigned by your teacher. Each group will be assigned to one or two viewpoints.

2. Complete your assignment, and present your perspective to the class.

 Vocabulary For the terms *series circuit* and *parallel circuit* make a poster that includes a dictionary definition of each term, a definition for each term in your own words, and diagrams representing each term.

Examples Research to learn more about electrical safety. Write a short report summarizing what you learn. Include at least one fact or piece of information that was not included in the lesson materials.

Illustrations Make a collage that shows images associated with either electrical circuits or electrical safety. For each image you include, describe how it is related to the main topic you have selected.

Analysis Electrical circuits vary in their structure, the type and number of devices they include, and the energy source used. Select one of these factors that can vary between circuits. Then, design an experiment to explore how changes in that factor affect the function of the circuit. For example, you might design an experiment to determine how the size of the battery used as an energy source affects the brightness of the light produced by a bulb. (Do not actually carry out your experiment.)

Observations Look for warning signs or symbols related to electrical safety in your school, your home, or your neighborhood. Include only those that can be observed safely. Sketch or photograph each of the signs or symbols, and share your observations with others. Discuss the meaning of each sign or symbol you observe.

 Details Imagine that you are a tour guide who has been asked to give a guided tour of an electrical circuit. You'll need to imagine that you and the tour participants are small enough to walk around inside an electrical circuit! Write a script of what you would say at each specific "point of interest" in your tour. Include interesting and factual information, as well as any relevant information you would share with the tour participants about electrical safety.

Going Further
☐ History Connection
☐ Health Connection

Formative Assessment
☐ Strategies Throughout TE
☐ Lesson Review SE

Summative Assessment
☐ Alternative Assessment Electric Circuits and Electrical Safety
☐ Lesson Quiz
☐ Unit Tests A and B
☐ Unit Review SE End-of-Unit

Your Resources

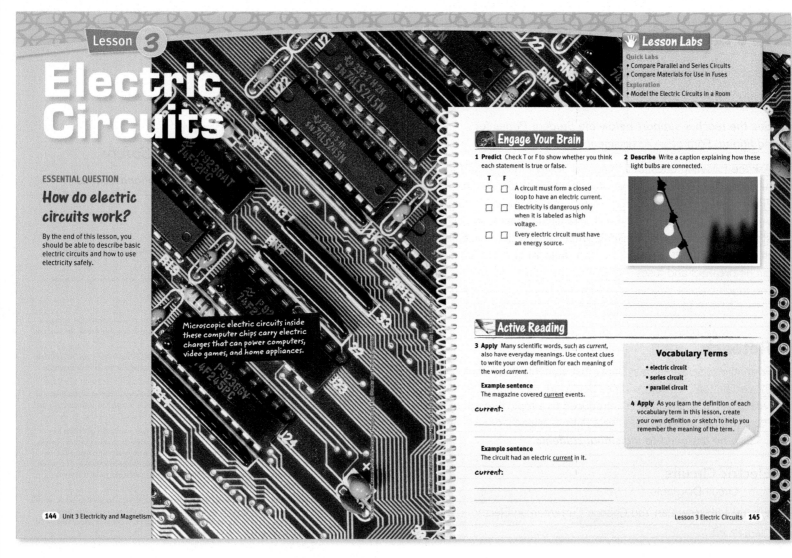

Answers

Answers should reflect student's current thoughts, even if incorrect.

1. T; F; T

2. Sample answer: The light bulbs are joined by metal wires that carry electric current.

3. Sample answer: of the present time; the rate of flow of electric charges

4. Students should define or sketch each vocabulary term in the lesson.

Opening Your Lesson

Discuss students' responses to the Engage Your Brain questions to assess their previous knowledge of electric circuits. If students' responses indicate that they have misconceptions about electric circuits, be certain to address those misconceptions as they complete the lesson materials.

Prerequisites Students should already know the definitions of the term *electric current* and should understand the distinction between static electricity and electric current.

Learning Alert

Similar-Sounding Terms Point out that terms *electric current* and *electric circuit* sound very similar. Remind students that electric current is the rate of flow of electric charges. Work with the class to develop a sentence that uses both terms and shows the relationship between them. For example, "Electric current can exist in an electric circuit."

A Complete Circuit

What are the parts of an electric circuit?

Think about a running track. It forms a loop. The spot where you start running around the track is the same as the spot where you end. This kind of closed loop is called a circuit. Like a track, an electric circuit also forms a loop. An **electric circuit** is a complete, closed path through which electric charges can flow. All electric circuits contain three basic parts: an energy source, an electrical conductor, and a load.

Active Reading

5 Identify As you read this page and the next, underline examples of energy sources, electrical conductors, and electrical loads used in an electric circuit.

Energy Source

The energy source converts some type of energy, such as chemical energy, into electrical energy. One common household energy source is a battery. A battery changes chemical energy stored inside the battery into electrical energy. A solar cell is an energy source that changes light energy into electrical energy.

Inside a power plant, a form of energy such as chemical or nuclear energy is changed into mechanical energy. Electric generators in the power plant change the mechanical energy into electrical energy. Power transmission lines deliver this energy to wall outlets in homes, schools, and other buildings.

Solar cell

Battery

Think Outside the Book Inquiry

6 Research Learn how your local power plant uses turbines and generators to produce electrical energy. Then write a short article about how the power plant generates the mechanical energy for the turbines.

Power plant

Electrical Conductor

Materials in which electric charges can move easily are called *electrical conductors*. Most metals are good conductors of electric current. Electric wires are often made of copper. Copper is a metal that is a good conductor and is inexpensive compared to many other metals. Conducting wires connect all the parts of an electric circuit.

To protect people from harmful electrical shocks, copper wire is often covered with an insulator. An *electrical insulator* is a material, such as glass, plastic, or rubber, through which electric charges cannot move easily.

Insulators

Copper wire is a conductor.

Load

A complete circuit also includes a *load*, a device that uses electrical energy to operate. The conductor connects the energy source to the load. Examples of loads include light bulbs, radios, computers, and electric motors. The load converts electrical energy into other forms of energy. A light bulb, for example, converts electrical energy into light and energy as heat. A doorbell produces sound waves, energy that is transmitted through the air to your ear. A cell phone converts electrical energy into electromagnetic waves that carry information.

Visualize It!

7 Identify List the devices in the photograph that could be a load in an electric circuit.

_____

_____

_____

_____

_____

_____

Answers

5. *See students' pages for annotations.*

6. Students' answers will vary, but they should identify that some form of energy is converted to mechanical energy which, in turn, generates electrical energy.

7. computer, speakers, cell phone, electric bass guitar, clock, fan, lamp

Using Annotations

Underlining examples of each of the three parts of a circuit will reinforce this information for students. Extend the activity by having students work with a partner to review the examples that were underlined, and to classify each as an example of an energy source, a load, or an electrical conductor.

Building Reading Skills

Three-Panel Flip Chart After students have read the information about the components of a circuit, have them make a Three-Panel Flip Chart about conductors, loads, and energy sources. The insides of the chart should include statements describing the functions of each of the components of circuit.

🔵 *Online Resource: Three-Panel Flip Chart*

Formative Assessment

Ask: Why are power cords coated with a material that has different physical properties than the wire inside? The wires are coated with a material that is an insulator, so that people are protected from touching the wire and getting a shock.

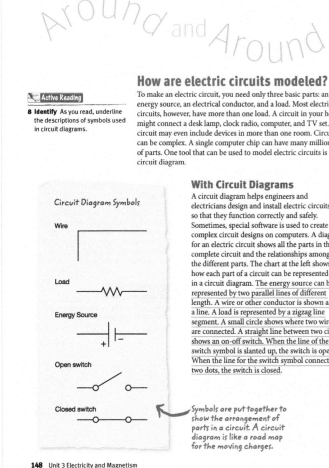

Around and Around

8 Identify As you read, underline the descriptions of symbols used in circuit diagrams.

How are electric circuits modeled?

To make an electric circuit, you need only three basic parts: an energy source, an electrical conductor, and a load. Most electric circuits, however, have more than one load. A circuit in your home might connect a desk lamp, clock radio, computer, and TV set. The circuit may even include devices in more than one room. Circuits can be complex. A single computer chip can have many millions of parts. One tool that can be used to model electric circuits is a circuit diagram.

With Circuit Diagrams

A circuit diagram helps engineers and electricians design and install electric circuits so that they function correctly and safely. Sometimes, special software is used to create complex circuit designs on computers. A diagram for an electric circuit shows all the parts in the complete circuit and the relationships among the different parts. The chart at the left shows how each part of a circuit can be represented in a circuit diagram. The energy source can be represented by two parallel lines of different length. A wire or other conductor is shown as a line. A load is represented by a zigzag line segment. A small circle shows where two wires are connected. A straight line between two circles shows an on-off switch. When the line of the switch symbol is slanted up, the switch is open. When the line for the switch symbol connects two dots, the switch is closed.

Circuit Diagram Symbols

Wire

Load

Energy Source

Open switch

Closed switch

Symbols are put together to show the arrangement of parts in a circuit. A circuit diagram is like a road map for the moving charges.

148 Unit 3 Electricity and Magnetism

How does current stop and start?

Electric charges move continuously in the closed loop of an electric circuit. What do you do if you want the charges to stop flowing? You open the switch! A switch is a device that turns electrical devices on and off. A switch is usually made of a piece of conducting material that can move. When the switch is open, the circuit is open. That means it does not form a closed loop, so charges cannot flow. When you turn a light switch on, the switch closes the circuit. Charges flow through the light bulb. If you turn a light switch off, the switch opens the circuit, and the charges stop flowing.

9 Explain Why does an open light switch turn off the light?

Visualize It!

10 Identify Label the parts in this circuit diagram. Then draw a switch to match the circuit shown in the photograph.

A switch opens and closes a circuit to turn a light bulb off and on.

Lesson 3 Electric Circuits 149

Answers

8. *See students' pages for annotations.*

9. Sample answer: The open switch breaks the circuit so charges can't flow.

10. A. battery or energy source; B. light bulb or load Students should draw a straight line between the two circles to show a closed switch.

Learning Alert

When Charges Flow Some students may have difficulty understanding that charges can flow only through a circuit that is "closed," or complete. To help students remember this, arrange blocks in a circle. Designate one of the blocks as the switch. Pivot this block away from the circle to show students that if the switch is open, the circle is incomplete. When the switch is closed, the circle (that is, the circuit) is complete again.

Interpreting Visuals

Point out that the circuit diagrams shown on this page are a type of model. Encourage students to practice interpreting the symbols used in circuit diagrams by verbally describing the components of a circuit depicted by each symbol used in the diagram.

Formative Assessment

Use the light switch in your classroom to turn the lights off and then on. **Ask:** Use the information you have learned about electric circuits to explain what you have just observed. Sample answer: When the classroom light switch was turned off, the circuit containing the lights is open, and no charges flow. When the light switch is switched on, the circuit is closed. Electric current exists in the circuit, and the lights turn on.

All Together?

How do series circuits and parallel circuits differ?

Most electric circuits have more than one load. Simple electric circuits that contain one energy source and more than one load are classified as either a series circuit or a parallel circuit.

In Series Circuits, Charges Follow a Single Path

The three light bulbs shown below are connected in a series circuit. In a **series circuit**, all parts are connected in a row that forms one path for the electric charges to follow. The current is the same for all of the loads in a series circuit. All three light bulbs glow with the same brightness. However, adding a fourth bulb would lower the current in the circuit and cause all the bulbs to become dimmer. If one bulb burns out, the circuit is open and electric charges cannot flow through the circuit. So all of the bulbs go out.

Active Reading

11 Identify As you read this page and the next, underline what happens if you add a bulb to a series circuit and to a parallel circuit.

In Parallel Circuits, Charges Follow Multiple Paths

Think about what would happen if all of the lights in your home were connected in series. If you needed to turn on a light in your room, all other lights in the house would have to be turned on, too! Instead of being wired in series, circuits in buildings are wired in parallel. In a **parallel circuit**, electric charges have more than one path that they can follow. Loads in a parallel circuit are connected side by side. In the parallel circuit shown below, any bulb can burn out without opening the circuit.

Unlike the loads in a series circuit, the loads in a parallel circuit can have different currents. However, each load in a parallel circuit experiences the same voltage. For example, if three bulbs were hooked up to a 12-volt battery, each would have the full voltage of the battery. Each light bulb would glow at the same brightness no matter how many more bulbs were added to the circuit.

13 Compare In the table below, list the features of series and parallel circuits.

Series circuits	Parallel circuits

Visualize It!

12 Apply In these two circuit illustrations, draw an X over the bulbs that would not glow if the bulb closest to the battery burned out.

Series circuit with battery and switch

The bulbs are connected to one another in a single loop.

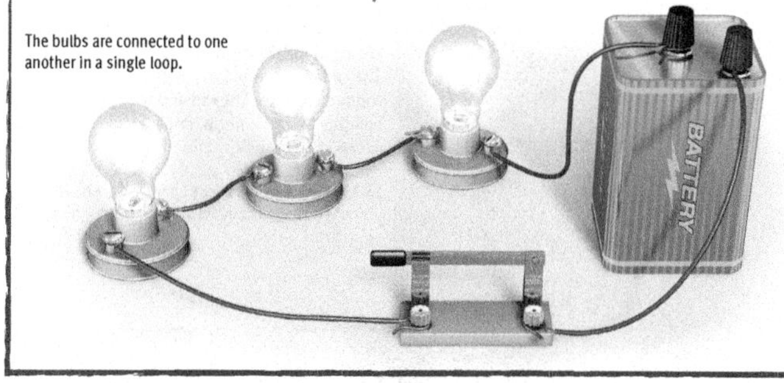

Parallel circuit with battery and switch

The bulbs are connected side by side.

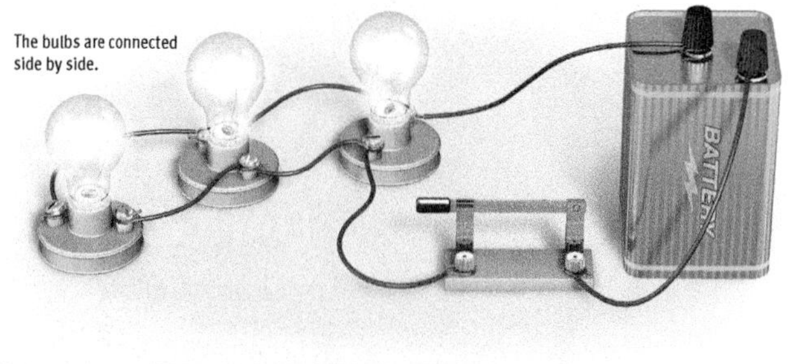

Answers

11. *See students' pages for annotations.*

12. In the first diagram, students should mark every bulb in the circuit with an X. In the second diagram, students should mark only the bulb closest to the battery.

13. Series: single path for charges; same current for all loads; break opens the whole circuit; Parallel: multiple paths for charges; current can vary among paths; break in one path does not affect others

Interpreting Visuals

Point out the illustrations of circuits shown on this page. Based on the illustrations, have students identify ways that series and parallel circuits are similar and ways that they are different. Record their responses on the board in two bulleted lists under the headings "Similarities" and "Differences." Then, have students read the information on these pages, and add to the lists on the board. Point out that some information is easier to obtain by looking at the illustrations, while other information is easier to obtain by reading.

Formative Assessment

Ask: Why are most of the circuits found in homes parallel circuits? Most circuits found in homes are parallel circuits so that if one device (such as a light bulb) goes out, electric charges can still flow through the other parts of the circuit.

Learning Alert

Conservation of Charge Students may think that charges are "used up" as they pass through a circuit. Reinforce that charge must be conserved. Charges that enter a device, such as a light bulb, must also leave the device.

Safety First!

How can I use electricity safely?

You use many electrical devices every day. It is important to remember that electrical energy can be hazardous if it is not used correctly. Electric circuits in buildings have built-in safeguards to keep people safe. You can stay safe if you are careful to avoid electrical dangers and pay attention to warning signs and labels.

By Avoiding Exposure to Current

Active Reading

14 Identify As you read, underline the reason that electric currents can be harmful to people.

Pure water is a poor conductor of electric current. But water usually has substances such as salt dissolved in it. These substances make water a better conductor. This is especially true of fluids inside your body. The water in your body is a good conductor of electric current. This is why you should avoid exposure to current. Even small currents can cause severe burns, shock, and even death. A current can prevent you from breathing and stop your heart.

Following basic safety precautions will protect you from exposure to electric current. Never use electrical devices around water. Do not use any appliance if its power cord is worn or damaged. Always pay attention to warning signs near places with high-voltage transmission lines. You do not actually have to touch some high-voltage wires to receive a deadly shock. Even coming near high-voltage wires can do serious harm to your body.

A damaged cord exposes the metal wires that conduct electric charges.

Stay away from places where there is high-voltage electrical equipment.

DANGER
High Voltage
Trespassers may
be electrocuted

152

By Using Electrical Safety Devices

Damage to wires can cause a "short circuit," in which charges do not pass through all the loads. When this happens, current increases and wires can get hot enough to start a fire.

Fuses, circuit breakers, and ground fault circuit interrupters (GFCIs) are safety devices that act like switches. When the current is too high in a fuse, a metal strip that is part of the circuit heats up and melts. Circuit breakers are switches that open when the current reaches a certain level. A GFCI is a type of circuit breaker. GFCIs are often built into outlets that are used near water, such as in a kitchen or bathroom.

Active Reading **15 Identify** Name three safety devices that you might find in electric circuits at home.

_____

_____

Fuses

When the current is too high in the fuse, the metal strip melts and opens the circuit.

Ground fault circuit interrupter (GFCI)

The lightning rod attached to the top of this building helps to protect it from a lightning strike.

By Taking Precautions during a Lightning Storm

When lightning strikes, electric charges can travel between a cloud and the ground. Lightning often strikes objects that are taller than their surroundings, such as skyscrapers, trees, barns, or even a person in an open field. During a thunderstorm, be sure to stay away from trees and other tall objects. The best place to seek shelter during a thunderstorm is indoors.

Many buildings have lightning rods. These are metal rods at the highest part of the building. The rod is connected to the ground by a thick conducting wire. The rod and wire protect the building by *grounding* it, or providing a path that allows charges to flow into the ground.

16 Infer What would happen if there were no electrical path from the top of the building to the ground?

_____

_____

153

Answers

14. *See students' pages for annotations.*

15. fuse, circuit breaker, and ground fault circuit interrupter

16. Sample answer: Electric current could flow through the building and the objects and people inside it.

Learning Alert

High Voltage Wires On these pages, students will read about the dangers of high-voltage transmission lines. Explain that electricity is transmitted over long distances at higher voltages than are used in homes. Step-up transformers increase the voltage for transmission, and step-down transformers decrease the voltage before it is delivered to homes and businesses. Using a high voltage for long-distance transmission decreases the amount of electricity lost due to resistance.

Formative Assessment

Ask: What are some basic safety rules to protect you from exposure to current? Sample answer: Do not use electrical devices when your hands are wet, make sure the insulation on power cords is not worn, and pay attention to warning signs near high-voltage transmission lines.

Probing Question   GUIDED inquiry

Analyzing The human heart beats in response to electric impulses generated within the body. Use this information to explain why exposure to external current can be dangerous. Sample answer: The external current can interfere with the internal electric impulses that regulate the human heartbeat, causing the heart to beat irregularly or to stop beating.

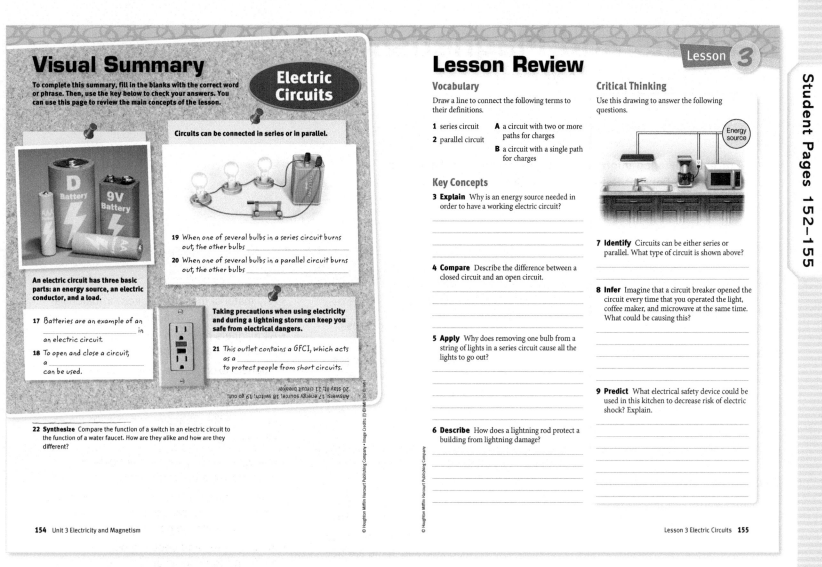

Visual Summary

Electric Circuits

To complete this summary, fill in the blanks with the correct word or phrase. Then, use the key below to check your answers. You can use this page to review the main concepts of the lesson.

An electric circuit has three basic parts: an energy source, an electric conductor, and a load.

17 Batteries are an example of an _____ in an electric circuit.

18 To open and close a circuit, a _____ can be used.

Circuits can be connected in series or in parallel.

19 When one of several bulbs in a series circuit burns out, the other bulbs _____

20 When one of several bulbs in a parallel circuit burns out, the other bulbs _____

Taking precautions when using electricity and during a lightning storm can keep you safe from electrical dangers.

21 This outlet contains a GFCI, which acts as a _____ to protect people from short circuits.

Answers: 17 energy source; 18 switch; 19 go out; 20 stay lit; 21 circuit breaker

22 Synthesize Compare the function of a switch in an electric circuit to the function of a water faucet. How are they alike and how are they different?

Lesson Review

Lesson 3

Vocabulary

Draw a line to connect the following terms to their definitions.

1 series circuit   **A** a circuit with two or more paths for charges

2 parallel circuit   **B** a circuit with a single path for charges

Key Concepts

3 Explain Why is an energy source needed in order to have a working electric circuit?

4 Compare Describe the difference between a closed circuit and an open circuit.

5 Apply Why does removing one bulb from a string of lights in a series circuit cause all the lights to go out?

6 Describe How does a lightning rod protect a building from lightning damage?

Critical Thinking

Use this drawing to answer the following questions.

Energy source

7 Identify Circuits can be either series or parallel. What type of circuit is shown above?

8 Infer Imagine that a circuit breaker opened the circuit every time that you operated the light, coffee maker, and microwave at the same time. What could be causing this?

9 Predict What electrical safety device could be used in this kitchen to decrease risk of electric shock? Explain.

Visual Summary Answers

17. energy source

18. switch

19. go out

20. stay lit

21. circuit breaker

22. Sample answer: They are alike because both stop and start a flow. The faucet starts a flow of water, and the switch starts a flow of electric charges. They are different because a valve closes to block the flow and a switch opens to break the circuit.

Lesson Review Answers

1. B

2. A

3. The energy source is the source of electrical energy that allows charges to flow through the circuit.

4. Sample answer: Electric charges flow through a closed circuit but cannot flow through an open circuit.

5. The lights are connected in a row, and removing one bulb opens the circuit.

6. Lighting strikes the rod and is conducted along a metal pathway into the ground.

7. a parallel circuit

8. Sample answer: The current in the circuit is too high.

9. Sample answer: Replacing wall outlets in a kitchen with outlets that contain GFCIs would break the circuit if water, which conducts electric current, and a person came in contact with the outlet.

Magnets and Magnetism

Essential Question What is magnetism?

Professional Development

For more detailed information about the topics in this lesson, refer to the Content Refresher in the Unit Opener pages.

Opening Your Lesson

Begin the lesson by assessing students' prerequisite and prior knowledge.

Prerequisite Knowledge

- Atoms are composed of small particles that have a charge. Protons have a positive charge, and electrons have a negative charge.
- Electric current is the flow of electrons.

Accessing Prior Knowledge

Have students discuss magnets and magnetism. Invite students to make a tri-fold FoldNote KWL chart about what they know about magnets and magnetism.

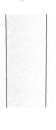

Optional Online resource: KWL support

Customize Your Opening

- ☐ **Accessing Prior Knowledge,** above
- ☐ **Print Path** Engage Your Brain, SE p. 157
- ☐ **Print Path** Active Reading, SE p. 157
- ☐ **Digital Path** Lesson Opener

Key Topics/Learning Goals	Supporting Concepts
Properties of Magnets 1 Describe the properties of magnets. 2 Explain what magnetic poles and magnetic fields are. 3 Describe how magnets attract and repel.	• Any material that attracts iron or materials containing iron is a magnet. • All magnets have two poles, called magnetic poles, that have opposing magnetic qualities. • Magnets exert forces on each other and are surrounded by a magnetic field. • Magnets contain spinning electrical charges that generate attractive or repulsive forces. Like poles repel, and opposite poles attract.
Properties of Magnetic Fields 1 Explain what causes magnetic fields and magnetism. 2 Tell why some materials are magnetic and some are not. 3 Tell how domains can cause materials to be magnetic.	• Electrons moving around the nucleus of an atom induce a magnetic field. • In most materials, the magnetic fields of the individual atoms cancel each other out, so these materials are not magnetic. • In iron, nickel, and cobalt, groups of atoms are found together in areas called domains in which the north and south poles of atoms line up and induce a strong magnetic field.
Types of Magnets 1 Distinguish between different types of magnets based on their magnetic properties.	• Ferromagnets are made of iron, nickel, cobalt, or mixtures thereof and have strong magnetic properties. • Electromagnets are produced by electric current. • Some materials can be magnetized by rubbing one pole of an existing magnet in one direction along the new material.
Earth's Magnetic Field 1 Tell how Earth acts as a magnet. 2. Tell how Earth's geographic and magnetic poles differ.	• As Earth rotates, its outer core flows, and its atoms' electrons induce a magnetic field. • Earth's magnetic poles mark the points on the planet's surface where its magnetic forces are the strongest.

Options for Instruction

Two parallel paths provide coverage of the Essential Questions, with a strong **Inquiry** strand woven into each. Follow the **Print Path,** the **Digital Path,** or your customized combination of print, digital, and inquiry.

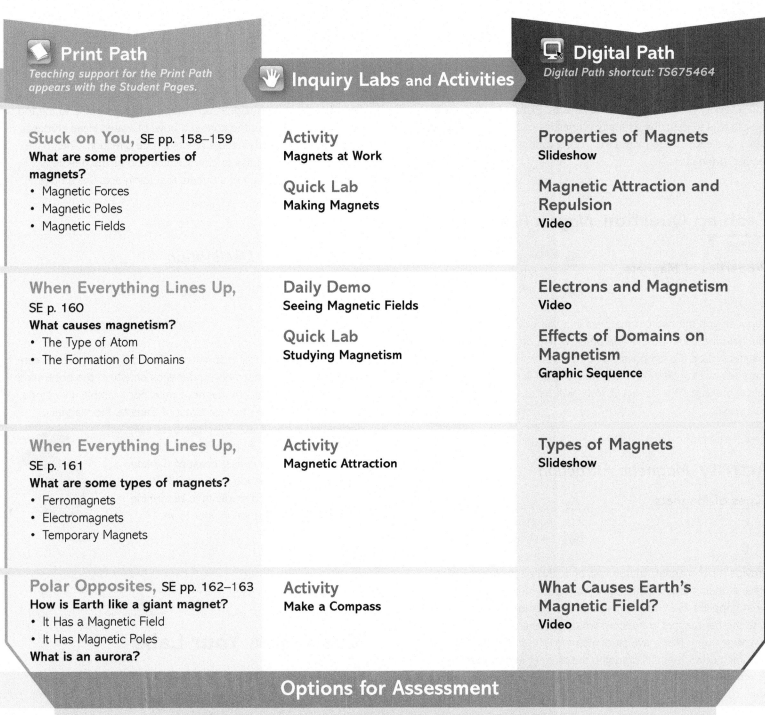

Print Path
Teaching support for the Print Path appears with the Student Pages.

Inquiry Labs and Activities

Digital Path
Digital Path shortcut: TS675464

Stuck on You, SE pp. 158–159
What are some properties of magnets?
- Magnetic Forces
- Magnetic Poles
- Magnetic Fields

Activity
Magnets at Work

Quick Lab
Making Magnets

Properties of Magnets
Slideshow

Magnetic Attraction and Repulsion
Video

When Everything Lines Up,
SE p. 160
What causes magnetism?
- The Type of Atom
- The Formation of Domains

Daily Demo
Seeing Magnetic Fields

Quick Lab
Studying Magnetism

Electrons and Magnetism
Video

Effects of Domains on Magnetism
Graphic Sequence

When Everything Lines Up,
SE p. 161
What are some types of magnets?
- Ferromagnets
- Electromagnets
- Temporary Magnets

Activity
Magnetic Attraction

Types of Magnets
Slideshow

Polar Opposites, SE pp. 162–163
How is Earth like a giant magnet?
- It Has a Magnetic Field
- It Has Magnetic Poles
What is an aurora?

Activity
Make a Compass

What Causes Earth's Magnetic Field?
Video

Options for Assessment

See the Evaluate page for options, including Formative Assessment, Summative Assessment, and Unit Review.

Engage and Explore

Activities and Discussion

Activity *Magnets at Work*

Engage

Properties of Magnets

👥 small groups
🕐 10 min
🔍 **GUIDED** inquiry

Give each student group two bar magnets, some small metal objects, and a variety of small nonmetallic objects. Explain to students that their task is to describe as many properties of the magnets as they can. Have each group record their observations and report their results to the class.

Probing Question *Magnet Power*

Engage

Properties of Magnets

👥 small groups or whole class
🕐 10 min
🔍 **GUIDED** inquiry

Suppose you put two bar magnets in a line with the north pole of one touching the south pole of the other. Where do you think this double magnet will be the strongest? The two bar magnets put together will act the same as a single magnet. The strongest force will be at each pole.

Activity *Magnetic Attraction*

Types of Magnets

👥 pairs or small groups
🕐 15 min
🔍 **DIRECTED** inquiry

Provide a bar magnet, an iron nail, and several steel paper clips. Have students touch the paper clips with the iron nail and record what happens. No paper clips stick. Have students touch the clips with the bar magnet and record what happens. All paper clips stick to the magnet. Next have students drag one end of the bar magnet 50 times down the nail, dragging the magnet in only one direction. Touch the nail to the clips. What happens? One or more paper clips stick to the nail.

Activity *Make a Compass*

Earth's Magnetic Fields

👥 pairs
🕐 10–20 min
🔍 **GUIDED** inquiry

Have students drag a needle—in only one direction—across one end of a strong bar magnet 50 times. Tape the needle to the top of a flat cork and put the cork in a bowl of water. Have students watch the cork as the needle points in one direction. Then have students use a compass to check which end of the needle is pointing north. Explain to students that Earth acts like a huge magnet.

Discussion *Declination*

Earth's Magnetic Fields

👥 whole class
🕐 10–20 min
🔍 **GUIDED** inquiry

Explain to students that magnetic declination, the angle between true north and magnetic north, depends on where the observer is with respect to the north magnetic pole. For example, in Victoria, British Columbia, on the west coast of Canada, the magnetic declination is about 20° E—a compass will point 20° east of true north. In St. John's, Newfoundland, on the east coast of Canada, the magnetic declination is about 23° W. Encourage interested students to determine the magnetic declination in your town.

©Comstock/Getty Images

Customize Your Labs

📄 *See the Lab Manual for lab datasheets.*

🖱 *Go Online for editable lab datasheets.*

Levels of **Inquiry**

DIRECTED inquiry
introduces inquiry skills
within a structured
framework.

GUIDED inquiry
develops inquiry skills
within a supportive
environment.

INDEPENDENT inquiry
deepens inquiry skills
with student-driven
questions or procedures.

Labs and Demos

◐ ◻ Daily Demo *Seeing Magnetic Fields*

Engage

**Properties of
Magnetic Fields**

👥 small groups
🕐 10 min
🔬 GUIDED inquiry

PURPOSE **To show magnetic field patterns**

MATERIALS

- sheet of paper
- iron filings
- bar magnet
- transparency
- horseshoe magnet

Have students gather around. Place a sheet of paper on the table
or desk, and place the bar magnet on top of it. Cover the magnet
with a transparency. Sprinkle the area near the magnet with iron
filings. Have students make observations. Discuss with students
what they notice. The filings will arrange to show the magnetic
lines of force. Clear the transparency and
put down a horseshoe magnet. Sprinkle iron
filings again and have students observe the
lines of force. Again, discuss with students
what they notice. Tell students that the force
that caused the patterns of filings to form is
magnetism.

©Marmaduke St. John/Alamy

Quick Lab *Making Magnets*

Engage

Properties of Magnets

👥 pairs
🕐 20 min
🔬 DIRECTED inquiry

PURPOSE **To observe the effect of bar magnets on non-magnetized
objects**

MATERIALS

- bar magnet
- sewing needles (6)
- plastic bowl
- foam squares (6)
- water

See the Lab Manual or go Online for planning information.

Quick Lab *Studying Magnetism*

Engage

**Properties of
Magnetic Fields**

👥 small groups
🕐 20 min
🔬 DIRECTED inquiry

PURPOSE **To investigate the effect of distance and barrier type on
the attraction of a magnet and a metal object**

MATERIALS

- aluminum foil
- wooden board
- cardboard
- wool cloth
- bar magnet
- paper
- paper clip
- metric ruler
- tape
- thread (80 cm length)

See the Lab Manual or go Online for planning information.

Activities and Discussion

- ☐ **Activity** Magnets at Work
- ☐ **Activity** Magnetic Attraction
- ☐ **Probing Question** Magnet Power
- ☐ **Activity** Make a Compass
- ☐ **Discussion** Declination

Labs and Demos

- ☐ **Daily Demo** Seeing Magnetic Fields
- ☐ **Quick Lab** Making Magnets
- ☐ **Quick Lab** Studying Magnetism

Your Resources

Explain Science Concepts

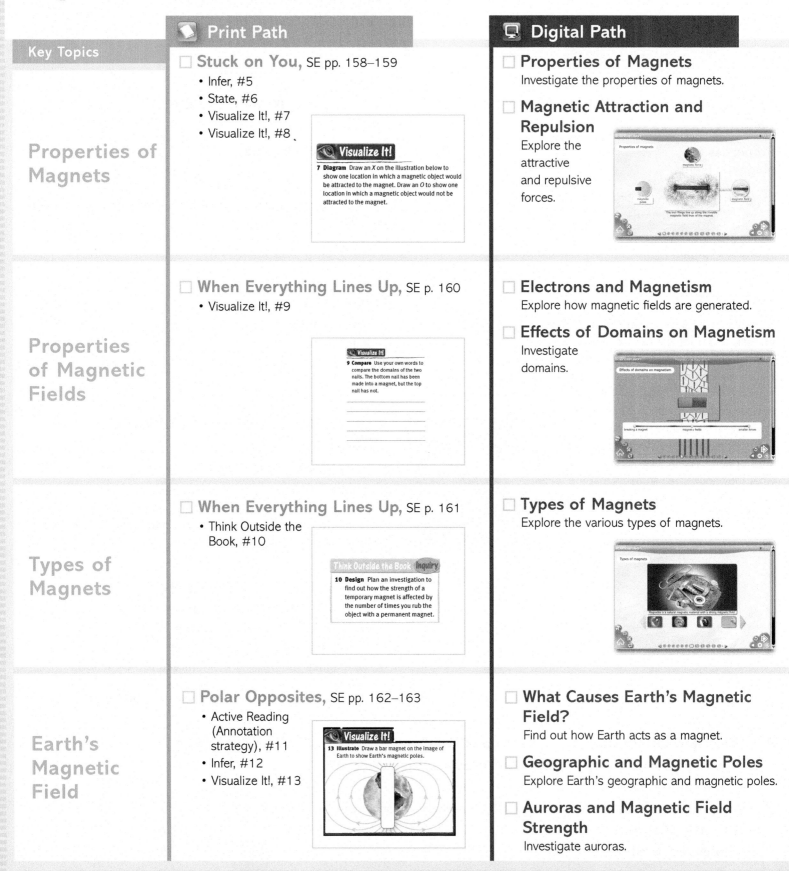

Key Topics	Print Path	Digital Path
Properties of Magnets	☐ **Stuck on You,** SE pp. 158–159 • Infer, #5 • State, #6 • Visualize It!, #7 • Visualize It!, #8 **Visualize It!** **7 Diagram** Draw an *X* on the illustration below to show one location in which a magnetic object would be attracted to the magnet. Draw an *O* to show one location in which a magnetic object would not be attracted to the magnet.	☐ **Properties of Magnets** Investigate the properties of magnets. ☐ **Magnetic Attraction and Repulsion** Explore the attractive and repulsive forces.
Properties of Magnetic Fields	☐ **When Everything Lines Up,** SE p. 160 • Visualize It!, #9 **Visualize It!** **9 Compare** Use your own words to compare the domains of the two nails. The bottom nail has been made into a magnet, but the top nail has not.	☐ **Electrons and Magnetism** Explore how magnetic fields are generated. ☐ **Effects of Domains on Magnetism** Investigate domains.
Types of Magnets	☐ **When Everything Lines Up,** SE p. 161 • Think Outside the Book, #10 **Think Outside the Book** Inquiry **10 Design** Plan an investigation to find out how the strength of a temporary magnet is affected by the number of times you rub the object with a permanent magnet.	☐ **Types of Magnets** Explore the various types of magnets.
Earth's Magnetic Field	☐ **Polar Opposites,** SE pp. 162–163 • Active Reading (Annotation strategy), #11 • Infer, #12 • Visualize It!, #13 **Visualize It!** **13 Illustrate** Draw a bar magnet on the image of Earth to show Earth's magnetic poles.	☐ **What Causes Earth's Magnetic Field?** Find out how Earth acts as a magnet. ☐ **Geographic and Magnetic Poles** Explore Earth's geographic and magnetic poles. ☐ **Auroras and Magnetic Field Strength** Investigate auroras.

Basic *Magnetic Maze*

Properties of Magnets

    small groups or individuals

    varied

Magnetic Force Arrange the desks to make a maze in your room. Label two adjacent walls of the room "North" and the opposite adjacent walls "South." Have students maneuver through the maze by holding a bar magnet in the proper position to pull and push them through the maze according to the labels on the walls.

Advanced *Electron Spin*

Properties of Magnetic Fields

    individuals

    15 min

Quick Research Electrons have a property called *spin* that produces a small magnetic field. Encourage interested students to research spin and find out whether magnetic fields or magnetism would be possible if all motion, including the motion of electrons, could be stopped. (Remind students that stopping all motion at the subatomic level is not theoretically possible.) Their research may include topics such as absolute zero, electrons, domains, and the spin property.

ELL *Diagramming Magnets*

Types of Magnets

    individuals

    15 min

Guide students to draw three different types of magnets: a ferromagnet, an electromagnet, and a temporary magnet. Have students use oral language to describe each type of magnet to a classmate.

ELL *Learning Poles*

Earth's Magnetic Fields

    Individuals or pairs

    15 min

Use a Compass Give each student a compass and a magnet. Help the students see the magnetic needle of the compass pointing north. You might have to point out to students how to orient the compass so that the letter N on the face of the compass is under the pointer. Next have students observe the effect of the north and south poles of a magnet on the compass needle.

magnet	**magnetic force**
magnetic pole	**magnetic field**

Previewing Vocabulary

    whole class   10 min

Word Families Have students create a table for the terms that contain the word *magnetic*. They should complete their tables by writing definitions for these terms in their own words. Students should include the following in their tables: magnetic force, magnetic pole and magnetic field.

Reinforcing Vocabulary

    individuals   ongoing

Magnet Word To help students remember the vocabulary terms in the lesson and any other words that give them difficulty, have them write each word in a magnet. Around the magnet on the lines, have students write words and phrases that are associated with each term.

Customize Your Core Lesson

Core Instruction

☐ **Print Path** choices

☐ **Digital Path** choices

Vocabulary

☐ **Previewing Vocabulary** Word Families

☐ **Reinforcing** Magnet Word

Differentiated Instruction

☐ **Basic** Magnetic Maze

☐ **Advanced** Electron Spin

☐ **ELL** Diagramming Magnets

☐ **ELL** Learning Poles

Your Resources

Extend Science Concepts

Reinforce and Review

Activity *Inside/Outside Circles*

Synthesizing Key Topics   👥 whole class   🕐 20 min

Inside/Outside Circles Help students review the material by following these steps:

1 After students have read the lesson, give each an index card with a question from the text. Students write their answers on the back of the index cards. Check the answers or provide a key to make sure they are correct. Have students adjust incorrect answers.

2 Students pair up and form two circles. One partner is in an inside circle; the other is in an outside circle. The students in the inside circle face out, and the students in the outside circle face in.

3 Each student in the inside circle asks his or her partner the question on the index card. The partner answers. If the answer is incorrect, the student in the inside circle teaches the other student the correct answer. Repeat this step with the outside-circle students asking the questions.

4 Have each student on the outside circle rotate one person to the right. He or she faces a new partner and gets a new question. Students rotate after each pair of questions. (You can vary the rotation by moving more than one person, moving to the left, and so on, but try to make sure that partners are always new.)

Graphic Organizer

Synthesizing Key Topics   👥 individuals   🕐 10 min

Cluster Diagram After students have studied the lesson, ask them to create a cluster diagram with the following terms: *properties of magnets, magnetism, types of magnets,* and *Earth as a magnet.*

🌐 *Optional Online resource: Cluster Diagram*

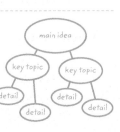

Going Further

Social Studies Connection

Synthesizing Key Topics   👥 individuals or pairs   🕐 20 min

Demonstrate Records from the first century BCE show that the Chinese knew that the mineral lodestone (magnetite) would align to the north. But not until about 1,200 years later were floating compasses used for navigation. Have students research early compasses. Demonstrate to the class how a compass works by building a 3D magnetic field viewer by dropping fine bits of steel wool into a bottle of mineral oil and exposing it to a magnet.

Biology Connection

Synthesizing Key Topics   👥 individuals   🕐 15 min

Research Scientists think that birds and other animals, such as sea turtles, may use Earth's magnetic field to help them navigate. Have students research which animals might find their way using Earth's magnetic field and investigate the evidence scientists have found that supports the idea. Students should prepare a one-page summary of their findings.

Customize Your Closing

☁️ *See the Assessment Guide for quizzes and tests.*

🌐 *Go Online to edit and create quizzes and tests.*

Reinforce and Review

☐ **Activity** Inside/Outside Circles

☐ **Graphic Organizer** Cluster Diagram

☐ **Print Path** Visual Summary, SE p. 164

☐ **Print Path** Lesson Review, SE p. 165

☐ **Digital Path** Lesson Closer

Evaluate Student Mastery

Formative Assessment

See the teacher support below the Student Pages for additional Formative Assessment questions.

Ask the following questions to assess student mastery of the material. **What is a magnet?** A magnet is any material that attracts iron or things made of iron. **What causes magnetism?** The arrangement of domains in an object determines whether the object is magnetic. **How does Earth act as a magnet?** Like a magnet, Earth has a magnetic field. Earth also has a north magnetic pole and a south magnetic pole. Earth's magnetic poles can attract another magnet, such as a compass needle.

Reteach

Formative assessment may show that students need reinforcement for certain topics. The resources below are recommended for reteaching. If students were introduced to a topic through the Print path, you can also use the Digital Path to reteach, or vice versa.

🎧 *Can be assigned to individual students*

Properties of Magnets
Quick Lab Making Magnets
Activity Magnets at Work 🎧

Properties of Magnetic Fields
Daily Demo Seeing Magnetic Fields
Quick Lab Studying Magnetism

Types of Magnets
ELL Diagramming Magnets 🎧

Earth's Magnetic Fields
ELL Learning Poles 🎧

Summative Assessment

Alternative Assessment
Magnetic Madness

🎧 *Online resources: student worksheet, optional rubrics*

Magnets and Magnetism

Take Your Pick: *Magnetic Madness*

1. Work on your own or with a partner.
2. Choose items below for a total of 10 points. Check your choices.
3. Have your teacher approve your plan.
4. Submit or present your results.

2 Points

_____ **Magnetic Properties** Name three properties of all magnets. Name two things a magnetic force can do.

_____ **Earth's Magnetic Field** Explain what scientists think causes Earth's magnetic field.

5 Points

_____ **Floating Objects** Explain how you could use magnets to make a small object appear to float in air.

_____ **Illustrating Domains** Draw a bar of non-magnetized iron metal. Show what the domains look like. Draw a bar of magnetized iron metal. Show what these domains look like. Use your own words to compare how these bars are alike and how they are different.

_____ **Making Magnets** Write instructions to tell someone how to make a temporary magnet. Have someone follow your instructions.

_____ **Other Planets** Data gathered have revealed that most planets have magnetic fields. For example, Saturn's magnetic field is 1,000 times stronger than Earth's. Find information about the magnetic field of one other planet and present your findings to the class.

8 Points

_____ **Magnetic Technology** Research a device that uses magnets such as a computer disk, maglev train, magnetic traffic lights, or the magnetic strip on a credit card. Prepare a poster to show what the device does and how it works.

_____ **Earth as a Magnet** Explain how Earth is similar to a giant bar magnet and how it is different. Use words and diagrams in your explanation. Remember to explain the difference between the Earth's geographic poles and its magnetic poles.

Going Further
☐ Social Studies Connection
☐ Biology Connection

Formative Assessment
☐ Strategies Throughout TE
☐ Lesson Review SE

Summative Assessment
☐ Alternative Assessment *Magnetic Madness*
☐ Lesson Quiz
☐ Unit Tests A and B
☐ Unit Review SE End-of-Unit

Your Resources

_____

_____

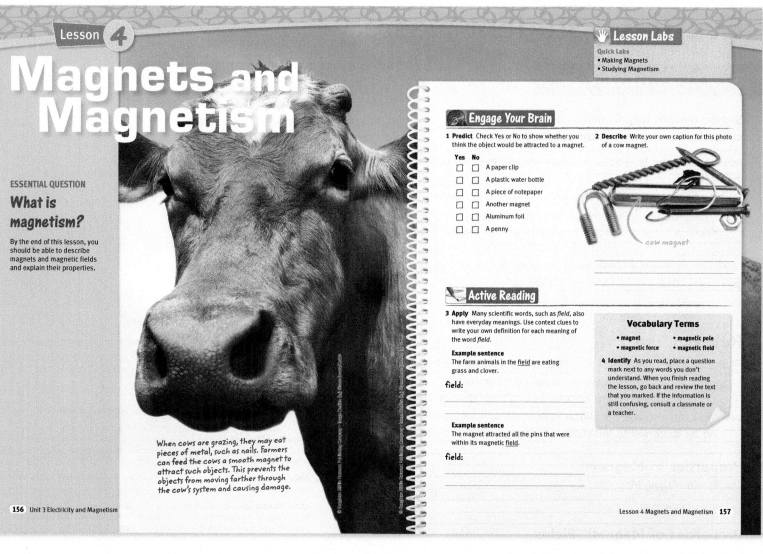

Answers

Answers for 1–3 should represent students' current thoughts, even if incorrect.

1. Yes; No; No; Yes; No; No

2. Sample answer: This magnet sits inside a cow's stomach and attracts and holds metal objects near it. The magnet protects the cow's system.

3. A field is an open area of ground.

   A magnetic field is the area surrounding a magnet.

4. *See students' pages for annotations.*

Opening Your Lesson

Discuss student responses to items 1 and 2 to assess students' prerequisite knowledge and to estimate what they already know about magnets and magnetism.

Prerequisites Students should already know that all matter is made up of atoms and that electrons move around atoms and have a negative charge. Students should also know that electric current is the flow of electric charges.

Learning Alert

Everyday Magnets Students are probably familiar with refrigerator magnets, but they may not realize just how many commonly used devices rely on magnets. A speaker in a sound system uses a permanent magnet and an electromagnet to produce sound. Many types of data storage systems are based on magnetic materials. Magnetic strips add convenience and security to credit and debit cards. Some traffic intersections rely on the interaction between metal vehicle bodies and electromagnetic fields to sense when vehicles are approaching.

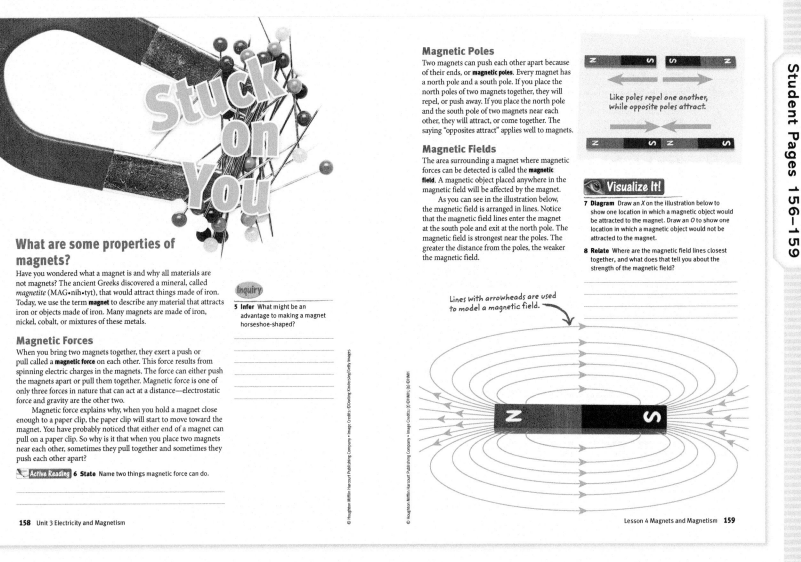

Student Pages 156–159

What are some properties of magnets?

Have you wondered what a magnet is and why all materials are not magnets? The ancient Greeks discovered a mineral, called *magnetite* (MAG•nih•tyt), that would attract things made of iron. Today, we use the term **magnet** to describe any material that attracts iron or objects made of iron. Many magnets are made of iron, nickel, cobalt, or mixtures of these metals.

Magnetic Forces

When you bring two magnets together, they exert a push or pull called a **magnetic force** on each other. This force results from spinning electric charges in the magnets. The force can either push the magnets apart or pull them together. Magnetic force is one of only three forces in nature that can act at a distance—electrostatic force and gravity are the other two.

Magnetic force explains why, when you hold a magnet close enough to a paper clip, the paper clip will start to move toward the magnet. You have probably noticed that either end of a magnet can pull on a paper clip. So why is it that when you place two magnets near each other, sometimes they pull together and sometimes they push each other apart?

Active Reading 6 **State** Name two things magnetic force can do.

Inquiry

5 **Infer** What might be an advantage to making a magnet horseshoe-shaped?

158 Unit 3 Electricity and Magnetism

Magnetic Poles

Two magnets can push each other apart because of their ends, or **magnetic poles**. Every magnet has a north pole and a south pole. If you place the north poles of two magnets together, they will repel, or push away. If you place the north pole and the south pole of two magnets near each other, they will attract, or come together. The saying "opposites attract" applies well to magnets.

Magnetic Fields

The area surrounding a magnet where magnetic forces can be detected is called the **magnetic field**. A magnetic object placed anywhere in the magnetic field will be affected by the magnet.

As you can see in the illustration below, the magnetic field is arranged in lines. Notice that the magnetic field lines enter the magnet at the south pole and exit at the north pole. The magnetic field is strongest near the poles. The greater the distance from the poles, the weaker the magnetic field.

Like poles repel one another, while opposite poles attract.

Visualize It!

7 **Diagram** Draw an *X* on the illustration below to show one location in which a magnetic object would be attracted to the magnet. Draw an *O* to show one location in which a magnetic object would not be attracted to the magnet.

8 **Relate** Where are the magnetic field lines closest together, and what does that tell you about the strength of the magnetic field?

Lines with arrowheads are used to model a magnetic field.

Lesson 4 Magnets and Magnetism 159

Answers

5. Sample answer: The pull of the magnet is concentrated to one side so it can easily be used to pick things up.

6. push or pull

7. The student should place the X somewhere on the magnetic lines of force. The student should place the O outside the magnetic lines of force.

8. Sample answer: The lines are closest together near the poles, showing that the force is strongest there.

Building Reading Skills: Main Idea

An important reading strategy is being able to identify the main idea and the supporting details of a passage. Direct students' attention to the question at the top of the page. Have them read it aloud. **Ask:** What will this page be about? properties of magnets Then have students read the page and write down the main ideas and supporting details in a Layered Book FoldNote. **Ask:** What is one property of a magnet? Bringing two magnets together exerts a force on each magnet. **Ask:** What are some other properties of magnets? Sample answers: Every magnet has a north pole and a south pole; magnets have magnetic fields, or regions where the magnetic force can be detected.

🌐 *Online Resource: Layered Book FoldNote*

Probing Question DIRECTED Inquiry

Analyzing Is it possible to make a magnet with only one pole by cutting it? No. If you cut a magnet, you get two new magnets, each with two poles. If you place small magnets together you get one large magnet with two poles. You may want to tell students that scientists have predicted the existence of magnetic monopoles, or isolated N and/or S magnetic poles. Although a magnetic monopole has not yet been found, it does not mean they don't exist. Some scientists have devoted years to this very search!

When Everything Lines Up

What causes magnetism?

Some materials are magnetic. Some are not. For example, you know that a magnet can pick up some metal objects such as paper clips and iron nails. But it cannot pick up paper, plastic, or even pennies or aluminum foil. What causes the difference? Whether a material is magnetic or not depends on the material's atoms.

The Type of Atom

All matter is made of atoms. Electrons are negatively charged particles of atoms. As an electron moves in an atom, it makes, or induces, a magnetic field. The electron will then have a north and a south magnetic pole. In most atoms, such as copper and aluminum, the magnetic fields of the individual electrons cancel each other out. These materials are not magnetic.

But the magnetic fields of the electrons in iron, nickel, and cobalt atoms do not completely cancel each other out. As a result, atoms of these materials have small magnetic fields. These materials are magnetic.

If you were to cut a magnet into two pieces, each piece would be a magnet with a north and a south pole. And if you were to break those two magnets into pieces, each would still have a north and a south pole. It does not matter how many pieces you make. Even the smallest magnet has two poles.

The Formation of Domains

In materials such as iron, nickel, and cobalt, groups of atoms form tiny areas called *domains*. The north and south poles of the atoms in a domain line up and make a strong magnetic field.

Domains are like tiny magnets within an object. The domains in an object determine whether the object is magnetic. When a magnetic material is placed in a magnetic field, most of the domains point toward the same direction, forming a magnetic field around the entire object. In other materials, there are no domains to line up because the atoms have no magnetic fields. These materials cannot become magnetized.

Domains before magnetization

Domains after magnetization

Visualize It!

9 Compare Use your own words to compare the domains of the two nails. The bottom nail has been made into a magnet, but the top nail has not.

160 Unit 3 Electricity and Magnetism

What are some types of magnets?

There are different types of magnets. Some materials are naturally magnetic, such as the mineral magnetite. Some materials can be turned into either permanent or temporary magnets.

Ferromagnets

A material that can be turned into a magnet is called *ferromagnetic* (fehr•oh•mag•NET•ik). Natural materials such as iron, nickel, cobalt, or mixtures of these materials have strong magnetic properties. They are considered ferromagnets.

A ferromagnetic material can be turned into a permanent magnet when placed in a strong magnetic field. Permanent magnets are difficult to make, but they keep their magnetic properties longer. Magnets can be made into various shapes such as bar magnets, disc magnets, and horseshoe magnets.

Electromagnets

Strong magnets are used to pick up metals in scrap yards, as shown in the photo below. To get a magnet powerful enough to do this, an *electromagnet* is used. An electromagnet is an iron core wrapped with electrical wire. When an electric current is in the wire, a magnetic field forms. When the current is turned off, the magnetic field stops. The strength of an electromagnet depends on the strength of the electric current.

Temporary Magnets

Some materials, such as soft iron, can be made into magnets temporarily when placed in a strong magnetic field. The material's domains line up, and the material is magnetized. You can make a temporary magnet by rubbing one pole of a strong magnet in one direction on a magnetic material, for example, a pair of scissors. The domains line up in the scissors, and it becomes a temporary magnet. Over time, the domains will lose their alignment. Banging or dropping a temporary magnet can also make it lose its magnetism.

This electromagnet uses electricity to produce a magnetic field.

Think Outside the Book Inquiry

10 Design Plan an investigation to find out how the strength of a temporary magnet is affected by the number of times you rub the object with a permanent magnet.

Lesson 4 Magnets and Magnetism 161

Answers

9. The domains in the unmagnetized nail are pointed in different directions. The domains in the magnetized nail are mostly pointing in the same direction.

10. Sample answer: Rub the magnet once, and find how many paper clips it can pick up. Rub it twice, and find how many paper clips it can pick up. Record your results. Continue for 3, 4, and 5 rubs.

Formative Assessment

Ask: Why are some iron objects magnetic while others are not? Iron objects are magnetic if most of their domains are aligned. If the domains are randomly arranged, the objects aren't magnetic. **Ask:** How are temporary magnets different from permanent magnets? Temporary magnets are easy to magnetize but quickly lose their magnetization. Permanent magnets are difficult to magnetize but retain their magnetic properties for a long time.

Interpreting Visuals

Observing What do the domains of the nonmagnetic nail look like? The domains in the nonmagnetic nail point in all different directions. What do the domains of the magnetic nail look like? The domains are all aligned in the same direction.

Probing Question DIRECTED Inquiry

Comparing How is the pole of a magnet similar to an electric charge? Magnetic poles and electric charges can both attract and repel one another. *Analyzing* What might be some advantages of electromagnets over permanent magnets? Electromagnets can be turned on and off. The strength of the electromagnet can be controlled because it depends on the strength of the electric current.

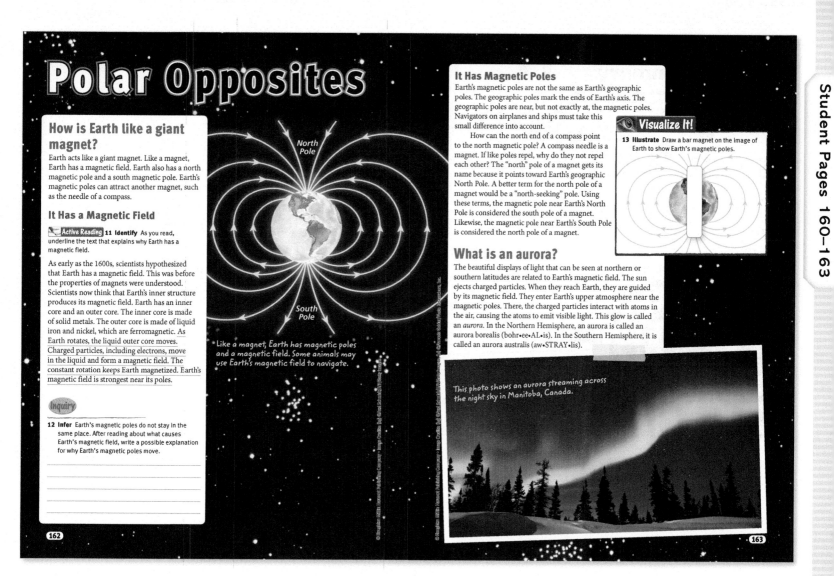

Polar Opposites

How is Earth like a giant magnet?

Earth acts like a giant magnet. Like a magnet, Earth has a magnetic field. Earth also has a north magnetic pole and a south magnetic pole. Earth's magnetic poles can attract another magnet, such as the needle of a compass.

It Has a Magnetic Field

Active Reading **11 Identify** As you read, underline the text that explains why Earth has a magnetic field.

As early as the 1600s, scientists hypothesized that Earth has a magnetic field. This was before the properties of magnets were understood. Scientists now think that Earth's inner structure produces its magnetic field. Earth has an inner core and an outer core. The inner core is made of solid metals. The outer core is made of liquid iron and nickel, which are ferromagnetic. As Earth rotates, the liquid outer core moves. Charged particles, including electrons, move in the liquid and form a magnetic field. The constant rotation keeps Earth magnetized. Earth's magnetic field is strongest near its poles.

Inquiry

12 Infer Earth's magnetic poles do not stay in the same place. After reading about what causes Earth's magnetic field, write a possible explanation for why Earth's magnetic poles move.

North Pole

South Pole

Like a magnet, Earth has magnetic poles and a magnetic field. Some animals may use Earth's magnetic field to navigate.

It Has Magnetic Poles

Earth's magnetic poles are not the same as Earth's geographic poles. The geographic poles mark the ends of Earth's axis. The geographic poles are near, but not exactly at, the magnetic poles. Navigators on airplanes and ships must take this small difference into account.

How can the north end of a compass point to the north magnetic pole? A compass needle is a magnet. If like poles repel, why do they not repel each other? The "north" pole of a magnet gets its name because it points toward Earth's geographic North Pole. A better term for the north pole of a magnet would be a "north-seeking" pole. Using these terms, the magnetic pole near Earth's North Pole is considered the south pole of a magnet. Likewise, the magnetic pole near Earth's South Pole is considered the north pole of a magnet.

What is an aurora?

The beautiful displays of light that can be seen at northern or southern latitudes are related to Earth's magnetic field. The sun ejects charged particles. When they reach Earth, they are guided by its magnetic field. They enter Earth's upper atmosphere near the magnetic poles. There, the charged particles interact with atoms in the air, causing the atoms to emit visible light. This glow is called an *aurora*. In the Northern Hemisphere, an aurora is called an aurora borealis (bohr•ee•AL•is). In the Southern Hemisphere, it is called an aurora australis (aw•STRAY•lis).

Visualize It!

13 Illustrate Draw a bar magnet on the image of Earth to show Earth's magnetic poles.

This photo shows an aurora streaming across the night sky in Manitoba, Canada.

162

163

Answers

11. *See students' pages for annotations.*

12. Sample answer: The moving outer core of Earth would change the position of the magnetic pole over time.

13. Students should draw a bar magnet with its south pole at the top and its north pole at the bottom.

Probing Questions

Forming a Hypothesis Why are auroras more commonly seen in places such as Alaska and southern Australia than in places such as Florida and Mexico? Auroras are most commonly seen near Earth's magnetic poles. Because Alaska and southern Australia are close to Earth's magnetic poles, people living in those places are more likely to see auroras than are people living in Florida and Mexico, which are far away from the Earth's magnetic poles.

Learning Alert ⚠ MISCONCEPTION ⚠

Students often get confused when told that the north pole of a magnet points to Earth's magnetic north pole. Some sources explain that one or the other of them is actually a south pole. Historically, because of the lack of knowledge about the causes of magnetism when it was first recognized, the poles of a magnet were labeled "north" and "south." However, once an understanding was reached regarding the attraction of opposite forces, the poles of magnets became more properly labeled as "north-seeking" and "south-seeking" poles.

Visual Summary

To complete this summary, fill in each blank with the correct word or phrase. Then, use the key below to check your answers. You can use this page to review the main concepts of the lesson.

Magnets and Magnetism

A magnet is any material that attracts iron or any substance that contains iron.

14 Magnetic materials exert _____ and have magnetic _____ and _____

15 If the _____ of a material are lined up, the object will be magnetic.

There are different types of magnets.

16 A material such as iron is _____

17 A(n) _____ is a magnet produced by electricity.

18 An object can become a(n) _____ magnet by rubbing the object with the end of a magnet.

Earth acts like a magnet because it has properties similar to those of magnets.

19 Earth has a _____ and north and south _____

Answers: 14 forces, poles, fields; 15 domains; 16 ferromagnetic; 17 electromagnet; 18 temporary; 19 magnetic field, magnetic poles

20 Synthesis Explain how a compass can be used to find north.

Lesson Review

Vocabulary

Draw a line to connect the following terms to their definitions.

1 magnet
2 magnetic force
3 magnetic pole
4 magnetic field

A a magnet's push or pull
B the end of a magnet where the force is the strongest
C the lines of force surrounding a magnet
D a metal object that attracts iron or nickel

Key Concepts

5 List What are three properties of a magnet?

6 Explain What causes some materials to have magnetic fields?

7 Identify List three types of magnets.

8 Describe How is Earth like a magnet?

9 Describe How do auroras form?

Critical Thinking

Use this drawing to answer the following question.

10 Illustrate The metal on the left has been magnetized, and the metal on the right has not. Draw the arrows in the domains of both.

11 Contrast What is the difference between the geographic North Pole and the magnetic north pole?

12 Explain If opposite poles repel each other, why does the north end of a compass point to the North Pole?

13 Apply Food manufacturers want to prevent small bits of metal from entering their product. How might magnets be used?

© Houghton Mifflin Harcourt Publishing Company • Image Credits: ©HMH

© Houghton Mifflin Harcourt Publishing Company

Visual Summary Answers

14. forces, poles, fields

15. domains

16. ferromagnetic

17. electromagnet

18. temporary

19. magnetic field, magnetic poles

20. Sample answer: Earth has a magnetic field. A compass has a floating magnetized needle. The north-seeking pole of the compass needle will be attracted to Earth's south magnetic pole. Since Earth's south magnetic pole and the geographic North Pole are near each other, the needle points close to north.

Lesson Review Answers

1. a metal object that attracts iron or nickel; 2: a magnet's push or pull; 3: the end of a magnet where the force is the strongest; 4: the lines of force surrounding a magnet

5. exerts magnetic force, has magnetic poles, has a magnetic field

6. For some materials, all the domains are lined up, producing a magnetic field around the entire object.

7. permanent magnets, electromagnets, temporary magnets

8. It has a magnetic field and magnetic poles.

9. Charged particles from the sun are forced near Earth's magnetic poles and interact with Earth's atmosphere.

10. The arrows on the left should mostly point in the same direction. The arrows on the right should point in random directions.

11. The geographic North Pole and the magnetic north pole are on opposite sides of the planet.

12. The north end of the compass points to the south magnetic pole of Earth, which is near Earth's North Pole.

13. Sample answer: pass the food under a large magnet before packaging to remove any bits of metal in the product

S.T.E.M. Engineering & Technology

Building an Electric Circuit

Purpose To build, test, and modify an electric circuit

Learning Goals
- Design a technological solution to a problem.
- Test and modify a prototype to achieve the desired result.

Academic Vocabulary
electric circuit, parallel circuit, series circuit, circuit diagram

Prerequisite Knowledge
- Understanding of electric charges and electric currents
- Basic understanding of electric circuits

Materials
- batteries
- battery holders
- masking tape or duct tape
- 3 1.5-volt lamp bulbs
- 3 small lamp bulb holders
- 3 switches
- wires

Teacher Note The batteries used in this activity should be D-cell flashlight batteries.

Content Refresher

Electric Circuits Electric circuits may be complex, but they always have an energy source (such as a battery), a load (the bulb or another object that will do work), and wires to carry electric charges through the circuit.

The rate of flow of charges in a circuit is called the **current**. Current is measured in amperes, abbreviated amps. The force pushing the electrons along a path is called the **voltage**. Voltage is measured in volts. The power outlets in the walls of your school deliver 120 volts.

21st Century SKILLS — Theme: Civic Literacy

Activities focusing on 21st Century Skills are included for this feature and can be found on the following pages.

These activities focus on the following skills:
- **Communication and Collaboration**
- **Media Literacy**
- **Social and Cross-Cultural Skills**

You can learn more about the 21st Century Skills in the front matter of this Teacher's Edition.

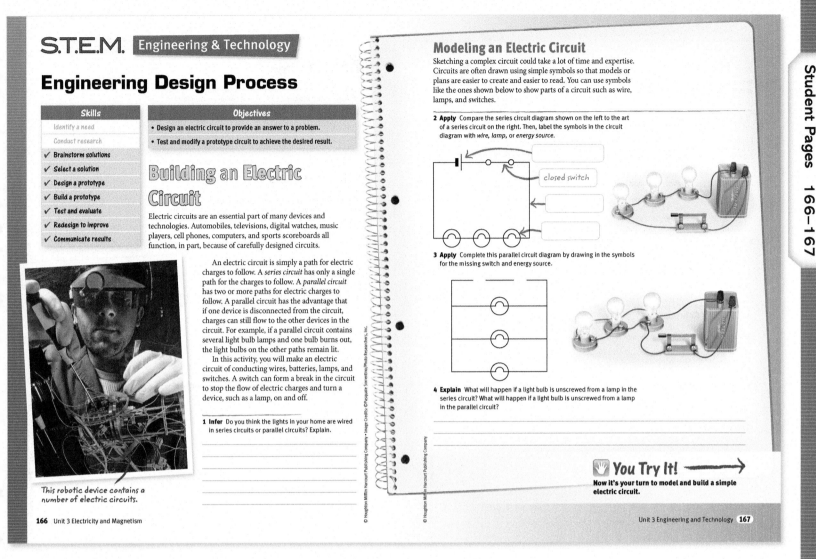

Answers

1. Sample answer: I think my home is wired in parallel circuits because when one light burns out or is turned off, the others do not go off.

2. From top to bottom: energy source; wire; lamp

3. Students should draw symbols corresponding to a switch and energy source. Symbols should match those provided in the series circuit diagram shown in question 2.

4. If a light bulb is unscrewed from the series circuit, all of the lights will go out. If a light bulb is unscrewed from the parallel circuit, that light will go out but the other two lights will remain lit.

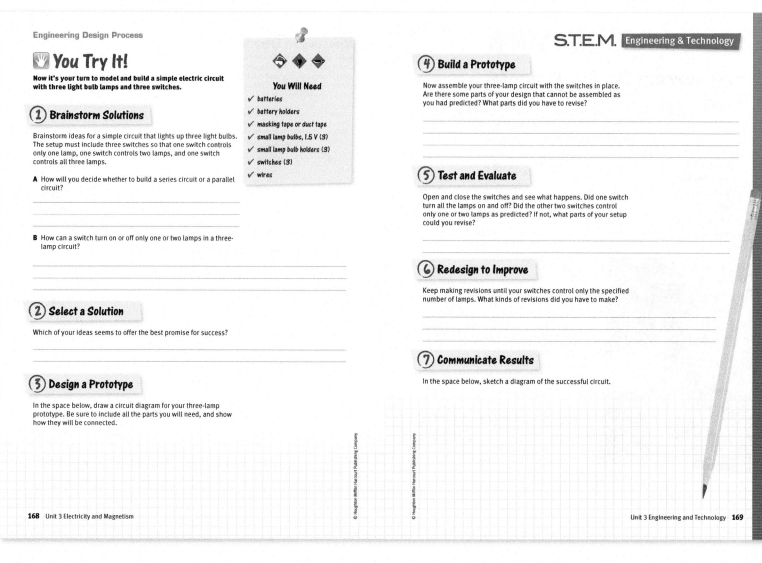

✋ You Try It!

Now it's your turn to model and build a simple electric circuit with three light bulb lamps and three switches.

1 Brainstorm Solutions

Brainstorm ideas for a simple circuit that lights up three light bulbs. The setup must include three switches so that one switch controls only one lamp, one switch controls two lamps, and one switch controls all three lamps.

A How will you decide whether to build a series circuit or a parallel circuit?

_____

_____

B How can a switch turn on or off only one or two lamps in a three-lamp circuit?

_____

_____

_____

2 Select a Solution

Which of your ideas seems to offer the best promise for success?

_____

3 Design a Prototype

In the space below, draw a circuit diagram for your three-lamp prototype. Be sure to include all the parts you will need, and show how they will be connected.

You Will Need

✓ batteries
✓ battery holders
✓ masking tape or duct tape
✓ small lamp bulbs, 1.5 V (3)
✓ small lamp bulb holders (3)
✓ switches (3)
✓ wires

S.T.E.M. Engineering & Technology

4 Build a Prototype

Now assemble your three-lamp circuit with the switches in place. Are there some parts of your design that cannot be assembled as you had predicted? What parts did you have to revise?

_____

_____

_____

5 Test and Evaluate

Open and close the switches and see what happens. Did one switch turn all the lamps on and off? Did the other two switches control only one or two lamps as predicted? If not, what parts of your setup could you revise?

_____

_____

_____

6 Redesign to Improve

Keep making revisions until your switches control only the specified number of lamps. What kinds of revisions did you have to make?

_____

_____

_____

7 Communicate Results

In the space below, sketch a diagram of the successful circuit.

Answers

1. A. I need to be able to have some lamps on while others are turned off, so I will need to build a parallel circuit.

   B. The switch has to be wired in parallel with the lamp or lamps that it should turn on or off.

2. A parallel circuit will allow some lights to be on while others can be turned off. The switches must be wired in parallel with the lamp or lamps they control.

3. Students' sketches should include all the necessary parts and the connections between them. Students' prototype diagrams may not yet be accurate.

4. Sample answer: The shape is not exactly the same, but the parts all are in the same order.

5. Sample answer: Switch 1 works one lamp and switch 3 works all three lamps. I have to revise where switch 2 is placed.

6. Sample answer: I had to make only one revision. I moved switch 2 so it breaks the circuit for two lamps.

7. Sample answer: Students' sketches should show a complete circuit in which one switch controls one lamp, one switch controls two lamps, and one switch controls three lamps.

21st Century SKILLS

Learning and Innovation Skills

👥 pairs   🕐 20 min

Communication and Collaboration Have pairs of students work together to develop methods (perhaps employing timers, motion detectors, occupancy sensors, and other types of switches) to help city buildings conserve electricity. Encourage students to listen attentively to their partner's ideas, to be respectful of diverse opinions and willing to compromise, and to share responsibility for the final design. Invite students to explain their ideas to the class.

Information, Media, and Technology Skills

👥 small groups   🕐 ongoing

Media Literacy Invite small groups of students to put together a computer slideshow, a video, or another type of multimedia presentation that explains to students in other parts of the world how to make an electric circuit. Students should prepare the presentation so that viewers who speak languages other than English can understand the information.

Life and Career Skills

👥 small groups   🕐 20 min

Social and Cross-Cultural Skills Invite students to work together to design a plan for a battery-powered electric circuit to be used in a school that does not have access to electricity. Explain that the students in the school sometimes need light on cloudy days or when they stay late to work on a project. Encourage group members from other parts of the world to share their thoughts in order to develop new ideas and increase innovation and quality of work, and encourage all students to respond open-mindedly to different ideas from group members. Have students share their ideas with the class.

Differentiated Instruction

Basic *Improving a Circuit*

👥 pairs   🕐 15 min

Challenge pairs of students to take their circuit one step further by using four bulbs and four switches. Ask student pairs to brainstorm ways in which the switches and bulbs could be arranged to complete the circuit. Have pairs explain their circuits and ideas to the class.

Advanced *Wiring the Ultimate Room*

👥 individuals or pairs   🕐 30 min

Invite interested students to design the ultimate circuit for a room. The circuit should have several bulbs, several switches (including three-way switches), and perhaps other components (such as motors, fans, heaters, or music players) that are powered by electrical energy. Have students explain how their electric circuit works and what a person can control using the switches in their room.

ELL *Circuit Diagrams*

👥 individuals or pairs   🕐 10 min

Have students make circuit diagrams showing how series and parallel circuits work. Students should label their diagrams in two languages so that students who speak another language will understand. Students can also write a paragraph explaining how the circuits work.

Customize Your Feature

- [ ] **21st Century Skills** Learning and Innovation Skills
- [ ] **21st Century Skills** Information, Media, and Technology Skills
- [ ] **21st Century Skills** Life and Career Skills
- [ ] **Basic** Improving a Circuit
- [ ] **Advanced** Wiring the Ultimate Room
- [ ] **ELL** Circuit Diagrams

Electromagnetism

Essential Question What is electromagnetism?

🍎 **Professional Development**

For more detailed information about the topics in this lesson, refer to the Content Refresher in the Unit Opener pages.

Opening Your Lesson

Begin the lesson by assessing students' prerequisite and prior knowledge.

Prerequisite Knowledge

- Basic knowledge of magnets and magnetism
- Basic knowledge of electric current and electric circuits

Accessing Prior Knowledge

Ask: What are some characteristics of magnets? Sample answers: They have north and south poles; opposite poles attract; like poles repel; they attract objects that contain iron, nickel, and cobalt.

Ask: What is needed to complete a simple electric circuit? A wire must make a closed loop between a battery's positive and negative ends.

Customize Your Opening

- ☐ **Accessing Prior Knowledge,** above
- ☐ **Print Path** Engage Your Brain, SE p. 171, #1–2
- ☐ **Print Path** Active Reading, SE p. 171, #3–4
- ☐ **Digital Path** Lesson Opener

Key Topics/Learning Goals	Supporting Concepts
Electromagnetism 1 Describe electromagnetism.	• Electromagnetism is the interaction between electricity and magnetism.
Electromagnets 1 Describe a solenoid and how it works. 2 Describe what an electromagnet is and how one is constructed.	• A solenoid is a coil of wire with an electric current in it. • When a solenoid is wrapped around an iron core, an electromagnet is formed. An electromagnet is a coil that has a soft iron core and that acts as a magnet when an electric current is in the coil.
Uses of Electromagnets 1 Describe some ways in which electromagnets are used in everyday life.	• Powerful electromagnets can be used to lift heavy objects made of iron. • A galvanometer is an instrument that detects, measures, and determines the direction of a small electric current. • An electric motor converts electrical energy into mechanical energy.
Induction 1 Explain how a magnetic field can make an electric current through induction. 2 Explain how induction is used in generators. 3 Describe transformers.	• An electric current is made when a magnet moves in a coil of wire or when a wire moves between the poles of a magnet. • A generator uses induction to change mechanical energy into electrical energy. • A transformer is a device that increases (step-up) or decreases (step-down) the voltage of alternating current.

Options for Instruction

Two parallel paths provide coverage of the Essential Questions, with a strong Inquiry strand woven into each.
Follow the Print Path, the Digital Path, or your customized combination of print, digital, and inquiry.

Print Path
Teaching support for the Print Path appears with the Student Pages.

Inquiry Labs and Activities

Digital Path
Digital Path shortcut: TS675474

Magnetic Attraction, SE p. 172
What is electromagnetism?
• The Interaction Between Magnets and Electricity
• Magnetism Produced by Electricity

Daily Demo
Magnetic Fields

Activity
Electromagnetic Relationships

☐ **Electromagnetism**
Interactive Graphics

Magnetic Attraction, SE p. 173
How can you make a magnet using a current?
• With a Solenoid
• With an Electromagnet

Quick Lab
Building an Electromagnet

Activity
Electromagnetic Carousel

☐ **What Is an Electromagnet?**
Video

Magnetic Attraction, SE p. 174
What are some uses for electromagnets?

Let's Motor!, SE pp. 176–177
How do motors work?
• Motors Use Electromagnets

S.T.E.M. Lab
Building a Speaker

☐ **Electric Motor**
Graphic Sequence

☐ **Electromagnets Around You**
Slideshow

A New Generation,
SE pp.178–181
What are some uses for induction?
• To Change Voltage
• To Generate Electricity

Quick Lab
Making an Electric Generator

Activity
Generating Diagrams

☐ **Magnets Can Produce Electricity**
Slideshow

☐ **Motors vs. Generators**
Slideshow

☐ **Two Kinds of Transformers**
Interactive Graphics

Options for Assessment

See the Evaluate page for options, including Formative Assessment, Summative Assessment, and Unit Review.

Engage and Explore

Activities and Discussion

Activity *Electromagnetic Relationships*

Electromagnetism

- 👥 individuals, then pairs
- 🕐 15 min
- 🔍 **GUIDED** inquiry

Magnet Word Have students create a Magnet Word graphic organizer for the word *electromagnetism*. Ask students which two words they think of when they see the term. electricity and magnetism Have students label the left side of the magnet with *electro-* and the right side with *-magnetism*. On the *electro-* side, they should draw pictures and write words associated with electricity. On the *-magnetism* side, they should write words and draw pictures related to magnets. After completing the graphic organizer, encourage students to share their work with a partner.

🌐 *Optional Online resources: Magnet Word support*

Discussion *Conversion Misconceptions*

Introducing Key Topics

- 👥 whole class
- 🕐 10 min
- 🔍 **DIRECTED** inquiry

Mnemonic Devices Students may confuse the terms *motor* and *generator*. To help clarify the difference, show students that Electrical Energy to Mechanical Energy = Motor (or "E-E-M-E-M," which resembles the sound a motor makes). Next, show students that Mechanical Energy to Electrical Energy = Generator (or "M-E-E-E-Generator"). Create a poster for each of these, and display them for the lesson.

Activity *Generating Diagrams*

Induction

- 👥 pairs
- 🕐 20 min
- 🔍 **GUIDED** inquiry

Discuss with students how generators use magnets to produce electricity. List some of the different types of power generators, such as wind turbines, hydroelectric plants, and nuclear and fossil fuel burning plants. Remind students that all of these methods of generating electricity rely on converting movement to electricity. Have each pair choose a type of power generator and then discuss and draw a diagram illustrating how the method produces electricity.

Take It Home *Electromagnetic Devices*

Uses of Electromagnets

- 👥 adult-student pairs
- 🕐 15 min
- 🔍 **GUIDED** inquiry

Students work with an adult to identify objects at home that use electromagnets to produce movement. Tell students that they should briefly explain to the adult what an electromagnet is and how it relates to motors.

🌐 *Optional Online resource: student worksheet*

Customize Your Labs

🔷 *See the Lab Manual for lab datasheets.*

🌐 *Go Online for editable lab datasheets.*

Levels of **Inquiry**   **DIRECTED** inquiry   **GUIDED** inquiry   **INDEPENDENT** inquiry
introduces inquiry skills   develops inquiry skills   deepens inquiry skills
within a structured   within a supportive   with student-driven
framework.   environment.   questions or procedures.

Labs and Demos

⊘ ▣ S.T.E.M. Lab *Building a Speaker*

Electromagnets, Uses of Electromagnets

   👥 small groups
   🕐 45 min
   inquiry **GUIDED** and **INDEPENDENT** inquiry

Students will set up a speaker and investigate which variables will affect the volume of sound outputted by the speaker.

PURPOSE **To describe the relationship between electricity and magnetism and how this relationship affects our world**

MATERIALS

- cable, 1/8 inch input
- cup, paper
- magnets, different strengths (3)
- paper clip
- pencil
- radio (or mp3 player)

- ruler, metric
- tape, masking
- wire, 2 m long enameled (magnet), ends stripped
- wire, insulated with alligator clips (2)

⊘ ▣ Quick Lab *Building an Electromagnet*

Electromagnets

   👥 pairs
   🕐 15 min
   inquiry **DIRECTED** inquiry

Students will build an electromagnet and observe how it works.

PURPOSE **To observe that an electromagnet displays magnetic properties when an electric current is in the wire**

MATERIALS

- batteries, D-cell (2)
- nail, iron
- tape, electrical
- wire, insulated
- paper clip

Daily Demo *Magnetic Fields*

Engage ▶

Introducing Key Topics

   👥 whole class
   🕐 10–15 min
   inquiry **GUIDED** inquiry

Use this short demo after you have discussed electromagnetism.

PURPOSE **To demonstrate a magnetic field**

MATERIALS

- compass
- 6 V battery
- insulated copper wire

1 Connect one end of the wire to the positive battery terminal. Wrap the wire around the compass. Connect the other end of the wire to the negative battery terminal to start the flow of electric charges. The electric current in the wire will cause the magnetic compass needle to move.

2 **Analyzing Ask:** What types of forces could cause the compass needle to move? The electric current creates a magnetic field that causes the compass needle to move.

3 Now reverse the direction of the current in the coil around the compass. **Ask:** What did you observe?

⊘ ▣ Quick Lab *Making an Electric Generator*

PURPOSE **To construct a generator that uses electromagnetic induction**

See the Lab Manual or go Online for planning information.

Activities and Discussion

- ☐ **Activity** Electromagnetic Relationships
- ☐ **Activity** Generating Diagrams
- ☐ **Take It Home** Electromagnetic Devices

Labs and Demos

- ☐ **S.T.E.M. Lab** Building a Speaker
- ☐ **Quick Lab** Building an Electromagnet
- ☐ **Daily Demo** Magnetic Fields
- ☐ **Quick Lab** Making an Electric Generator

Your Resources

Explain Science Concepts

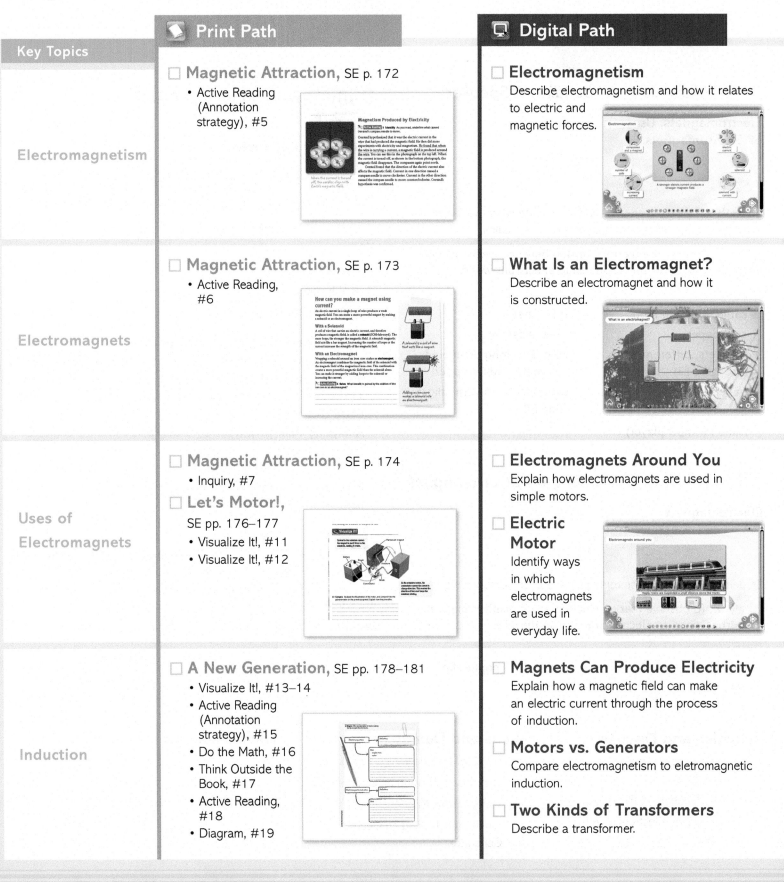

Key Topics	Print Path	Digital Path
Electromagnetism	☐ **Magnetic Attraction**, SE p. 172 • Active Reading (Annotation strategy), #5	☐ **Electromagnetism** Describe electromagnetism and how it relates to electric and magnetic forces.
Electromagnets	☐ **Magnetic Attraction**, SE p. 173 • Active Reading, #6	☐ **What Is an Electromagnet?** Describe an electromagnet and how it is constructed.
Uses of Electromagnets	☐ **Magnetic Attraction**, SE p. 174 • Inquiry, #7 ☐ **Let's Motor!**, SE pp. 176–177 • Visualize It!, #11 • Visualize It!, #12	☐ **Electromagnets Around You** Explain how electromagnets are used in simple motors. ☐ **Electric Motor** Identify ways in which electromagnets are used in everyday life.
Induction	☐ **A New Generation**, SE pp. 178–181 • Visualize It!, #13–14 • Active Reading (Annotation strategy), #15 • Do the Math, #16 • Think Outside the Book, #17 • Active Reading, #18 • Diagram, #19	☐ **Magnets Can Produce Electricity** Explain how a magnetic field can make an electric current through the process of induction. ☐ **Motors vs. Generators** Compare electromagnetism to eletromagnetic induction. ☐ **Two Kinds of Transformers** Describe a transformer.

Basic *Electromagnetic Diagram*

Electromagnets

👥 individuals

🕐 15–20 min

To reinforce how to build an electromagnet, have students draw a diagram that includes all the major parts of an electromagnet. Remind students to label all the parts and use directional arrows. Encourage students to include a brief description of how an electromagnet works.

Variation Students can also label the parts on a predrawn image of an electromagnet.

Advanced *Alternating or Direct?*

Uses of Electromagnets

👥 individual, then large groups

🕐 varied

Debate Have students research the "War of the Currents" to see how Thomas Edison and George Westinghouse each fought to have his system of generating electrical energy adopted. Then have a class debate, and choose students to advocate for either the AC or the DC electric system. At the end of the debate, conduct a secret ballot among the class to see which side presented its case most convincingly.

🌐 *Optional Online rubric: Class Discussion*

ELL *Faraday Another Way*

Induction

👥 whole class

🕐 10–15 min

Faraday's Experiment Students may benefit from an oral review of Faraday's experiment using simpler language. Create a transparency of the visual of the experiment from the text. After students have read the passage about the experiment, ask them to follow along on the transparency as you narrate Faraday's experiment for them again. Write key terms on the board, and check comprehension frequently by asking questions.

electromagnetism   solenoid   electromagnet
electric motor   transformer   electric generator
electromagnetic induction

Previewing Vocabulary

👥 individuals

🕐 ongoing

Key-Term Fold To help students remember the vocabulary words in the lesson, help them make a Key-Term Fold FoldNote. Students can write the terms on the outside beforehand. Then as they read the lesson, they can add definitions, examples, or illustrations on the inside.

🌐 *Online resource: Key-Term Fold support*

Reinforcing Vocabulary

👥 individuals

🕐 25 min

Frame Game Many of the terms in this lesson are particularly challenging and will probably be unfamiliar to students. Have students create frame game organizers for each term. Students can add pictures, definitions, or examples in the frame.

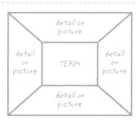

🌐 *Optional Online resource: Frame Game support*

Customize Your Core Lesson

Core Instruction

☐ **Print Path** choices
☐ **Digital Path** choices

Vocabulary

☐ **Previewing Vocabulary** Key-Term Fold
☐ **Reinforcing Vocabulary** Frame Game

Your Resources

Differentiated Instruction

☐ **Basic** Electromagnetic Diagram
☐ **Advanced** Alternating or Direct?
☐ **ELL** Faraday Another Way

Extend Science Concepts

Reinforce and Review

Activity *Electromagnetic Carousel*

Synthesizing Key Topics
👥 small groups
🕐 15–20 min

Carousel Review

1 Arrange chart paper in different parts of the room. (This strategy can be done on notebook paper if that is all that is available.) On each sheet of paper, write a question to preview or review content. Use the key topics, learning goals, and supporting concepts as guides.

2 Divide the class into small groups and assign each group a chart. Give each group a different-colored marker.

3 Groups review their question, discuss their answer, and write a response.

4 After five to ten minutes, each group rotates to the next station. Groups put a check by each answer they agree with, comment on answers they don't agree with, and add their own answers. Continue until all groups have reviewed all charts.

Graphic Organizer

Synthesizing Key Topics
👥 individuals
🕐 20–30 min

Mind Map Instruct students to create a Mind Map to connect key ideas from the lesson. Students should write the term *electromagnetism* in the center of the map. Then, as they review each section of the lesson, students should write details that relate to electromagnetism in the branches of the map.

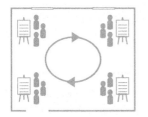

🌐 *Optional Online resource: Mind Map support*

Going Further

Life Science Connection

Synthesizing Key Topics
👥 individuals or pairs
🕐 varied

Living Motors Green gyms are exercise programs in which participants enhance the outdoor environment while targeting their own fitness. Activities include gardening and conservation-type work. Encourage students to research green gyms. Then have students design and create a brochure advertising their own green gym.

Earth Science Connection

Induction
👥 pairs or individuals
🕐 10–15 min

Geothermal Energy Another energy source for generators in some electric power plants is geothermal energy. Geothermal energy comes from hot magma deep within Earth. In some areas, magma rises near Earth's surface. Groundwater may be heated by magma to form hot springs, geysers, and steam vents. Geothermal power plants capture steam produced by magma and use it to generate electrical energy. Help students create a two-column chart listing the pros and cons of using renewable energy sources, such as solar, wind, tidal, and geothermal, to produce electricity. Then encourage students to share their ideas with the class.

🌐 *Optional Online resource: Two-Column Chart support*

Customize Your Closing

📄 *See the Assessment Guide for quizzes and tests.*

🌐 *Go Online to edit and create quizzes and tests.*

Reinforce and Review

☐ **Activity** Electromagnetic Carousel

☐ **Graphic Organizer** Mind Map

☐ **Print Path** Visual Summary, SE p. 182

☐ **Print Path** Lesson Review, SE p. 183

☐ **Digital Path** Lesson Closer

Evaluate Student Mastery

Formative Assessment

See the teacher support below the Student Pages for additional Formative Assessment questions.

Ask students to briefly summarize the discoveries of Hans Christian Oersted and Michael Faraday. Sample answer: Oersted discovered that electric current running through a wire produces a changing magnetic field. Faraday's discovery proved the opposite—that a changing magnetic field could produce an electric current.

Reteach

Formative assessment may show that students need reinforcement for certain topics. The resources below are recommended for reteaching. If students were introduced to a topic through the Print Path, you can also use the Digital Path to reteach and vice versa.
🎧 *Can be assigned to individual students*

Electromagnetism
Activity Electromagnetic Relationships 🎧
Graphic Organizer Mind Map 🎧

Electromagnets
Quick Lab Building an Electromagnet
Basic Electromagnetic Diagram 🎧

Electromagnetic Induction
Activity Generating Diagrams 🎧
Quick Lab Making an Electric Generator

Uses of Electromagnets
Take It Home Electromagnetic Devices
S.T.E.M. Lab Building a Speaker

Summative Assessment

Alternative Assessment
Electromagnetic Activities

🌐 *Online resources: student worksheet, optional rubric*

Electromagnetism

Climb the Pyramid: *Electromagnetic Activities*
Climb the pyramid to show what you have learned about electromagnetism.

1. Work on your own, with a partner, or with a small group.
2. Choose one item from each layer of the pyramid. Check your choices.
3. Have your teacher approve your plan.
4. Submit or present your results.

___ **Model**
Use craft supplies to create a model of one of the devices you learned about in this lesson, such as an electromagnet, a motor, a generator, or a transformer. Include a key that explains what each part of the model represents, as well as a paragraph explaining how your device works.

___ **Crossword Puzzle**
Write a crossword puzzle for the important terms in this lesson. Include the vocabulary words, as well as ten additional terms from the text.

___ **Game**
Play "What Am I" with one or more people. On index cards, write all of the vocabulary words from the lesson plus ten additional words from the lesson. Place the cards face down in a pile. One player draws a card and looks at it. The other players ask "yes" and "no" questions to determine which term the first player is.

___ **Play**
Write and act out a two-part play that reenacts the discoveries of Hans Christian Oersted and Michael Faraday. The play should focus on what each scientist discovered about electromagnetism.

___ **Newspaper Article**
Imagine you are a newspaper reporter working in the past. Write an article about one of the discoveries about electromagnetism that are featured in this lesson. Include illustrations or diagrams if it improves your article.

___ **Letter**
Design a new device that uses electromagnetism or plan improvements to an existing device by using electromagnets. Write a letter to André-Marie Ampère that describes your device. Make sure your letter includes a detailed illustration of your design.

Going Further
☐ Life Science Connection
☐ Earth Science Connection
☐ Print Path Why It Matters, SE p. 175

Formative Assessment
☐ Strategies Throughout TE
☐ Lesson Review SE

Summative Assessment
☐ Alternative Assessment Electromagnetic Activities
☐ Lesson Quiz
☐ Unit Tests A and B
☐ Unit Review SE End-of-Unit

Your Resources

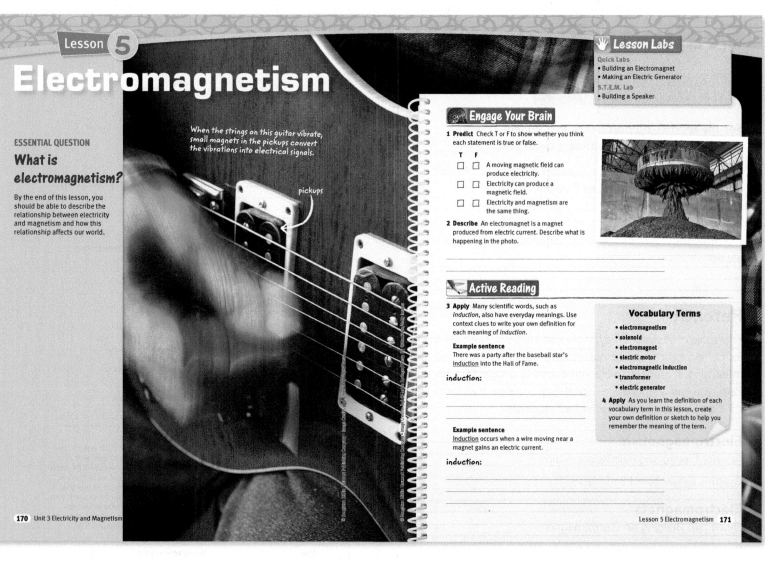

Answers

Answers for 1–3 should represent students' current thoughts, even if incorrect.

1. T; T; F

2. The electromagnet is more powerful than a bar magnet and runs on electricity.

3. bringing someone into an organization; production of electric current from magnetism

4. Students should define or sketch each vocabulary term in the lesson.

Opening Your Lesson

Discuss student responses to items 1 and 2 to assess students' prerequisite knowledge and to estimate what they already know about electromagnetism.

Prerequisites Students should already know the basic principles of how magnets work. Students should also know how electric current and electric circuits work.

Accessing Prior Knowledge DRTA Before beginning the lesson, you may wish to have students conduct a Textbook DRTA. Begin by explaining to students that DRTA stands for **D**irected **R**eading/**T**hinking **A**ctivity. To complete the activity, students need to 1) preview the selection, 2) write what they know, what they think they know, and what they think they'll learn about electromagnetism, 3) read the selection, and 4) write what they learned. At the end of the lesson, discuss whether students' expectations were reasonable and whether they learned additional information that they did not anticipate.

🌐 *Optional Online resource: Textbook DRTA support*

MAGNETIC ATTRACTION

What is electromagnetism?

Electromagnetism is a relationship between electricity and magnetism. **Electromagnetism** results when electric currents and magnetic fields interact with each other.

The Interaction Between Magnets and Electricity

In 1820, physicist Hans Christian Oersted of Denmark made an interesting discovery by accident. He discovered that there is a connection between electricity and magnetism. No one at the time knew that electricity and magnetism were related. One day while preparing for a lecture, he brought a compass close to a wire carrying an electric current. Oersted was surprised to see the compass needle move. A compass needle is a magnet. It usually points north because of Earth's magnetic field. However, the compass moved because it was affected by a magnetic field other than Earth's.

The compasses show that an electric current produces a circular magnetic field around the wire.

Magnetism Produced by Electricity

Active Reading 5 **Identify** As you read, underline what caused Oersted's compass needle to move.

Oersted hypothesized that it was the electric current in the wire that had produced the magnetic field. He then did more experiments with electricity and magnetism. He found that when the wire is carrying a current, a magnetic field is produced around the wire. You can see this in the photograph on the top left. When the current is turned off, as shown in the bottom photograph, the magnetic field disappears. The compasses again point north.

Oersted found that the direction of the electric current also affects the magnetic field. Current in one direction caused a compass needle to move clockwise. Current in the other direction caused the compass needle to move counterclockwise. Oersted's hypothesis was confirmed.

When the current is turned off, the needles align with Earth's magnetic field.

How can you make a magnet using current?

An electric current in a single loop of wire produces a weak magnetic field. You can make a more powerful magnet by making a solenoid or an electromagnet.

With a Solenoid

A coil of wire that carries an electric current, and therefore produces a magnetic field, is called a **solenoid** (SOH•luh•noyd). The more loops, the stronger the magnetic field. A solenoid's magnetic field acts like a bar magnet. Increasing the number of loops or the current increases the strength of the magnetic field.

With an Electromagnet

Wrapping a solenoid around an iron core makes an **electromagnet**. An electromagnet combines the magnetic field of the solenoid with the magnetic field of the magnetized iron core. This combination creates a more powerful magnetic field than the solenoid alone. You can make it stronger by adding loops to the solenoid or increasing the current.

Active Reading 6 **Solve** What benefit is gained by the addition of the iron core in an electromagnet?

_____

_____

A solenoid is a coil of wire that acts like a magnet.

Adding an iron core makes a solenoid into an electromagnet.

Electromagnets lift this maglev train off the tracks and move it forward.

Answers

5. *See students' pages for annotations.*

6. It makes a weak magnet stronger.

Building Reading Skills

Text Structure: Cause and Effect Now that students have been introduced to the idea of electromagnetism, ask them to predict how someone might make a magnet that can be switched on and off. Suggest that they apply the cause-and-effect relationship of electromagnetism after analyzing the text. Sample answer: Because electromagnets rely on electricity to make them magnetic, the presence of an electric current controls whether the magnet is on or off. Disconnecting the electricity would turn the electromagnet off.

🌐 *Optional Online resource: Text Structure: Cause and Effect support*

Formative Assessment

Ask: What did Oersted discover in 1820? Oersted discovered that electric current produces a magnetic field and that the direction of the magnetic field is dependent on the direction of the current. **Ask:** How does an electromagnet work? An iron core has current-carrying wire wrapped around it. The current causes the iron core to become magnetic. The entire coil-wrapped mechanism becomes an electromagnet.

What are some uses for electromagnets?

Electromagnets are used in many devices that you may use every day. A solenoid around an iron piston makes a doorbell ring. Huge electromagnets are used in industry to move metal. Small electromagnets drive electric motors in objects from hair dryers to speakers. Physicists use electromagnets in "atom smashers" to study the tiny particles and high energies that make up an atom.

To Lift Metal Objects

Electromagnets are useful for lifting and moving large metal objects containing iron. When current runs through the solenoid coils, it creates a magnetic field that attracts the metal objects. Turning off the current turns off the magnetic field so that the metal can be easily dropped in a new place. Powerful electromagnets can raise a maglev train above its track. Just as poles of a bar magnet repel each other, electromagnets in the train and track repel each other when the electric current is turned on.

To Measure Current

A *galvanometer* (gal•vuh•NAHM•ih•ter) is a device that measures the strength and direction of an electric current in a wire. A galvanometer contains an electromagnet between the poles of a permanent magnet, such as a horseshoe magnet. When current is applied to the electromagnet, the two magnetic fields interact and cause the electromagnet to turn. The indicator, attached to the electromagnet, moves to one side of the zero on the scale, indicating the strength and direction of the current. The parts of a simple galvanometer are shown below.

Inquiry

7 Infer What is one advantage of using an electromagnet to move loads of metal?

_____

_____

Industrial electromagnets can lift tons of metal.

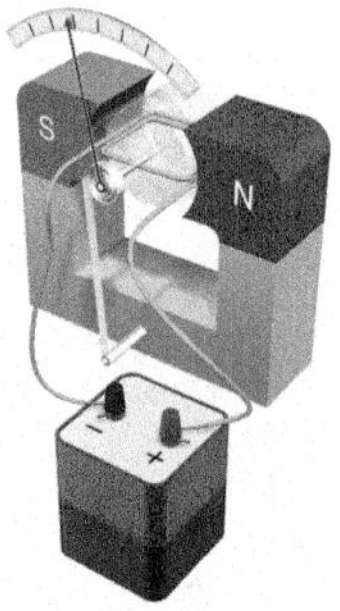

The indicator on a galvanometer shows current direction and strength.

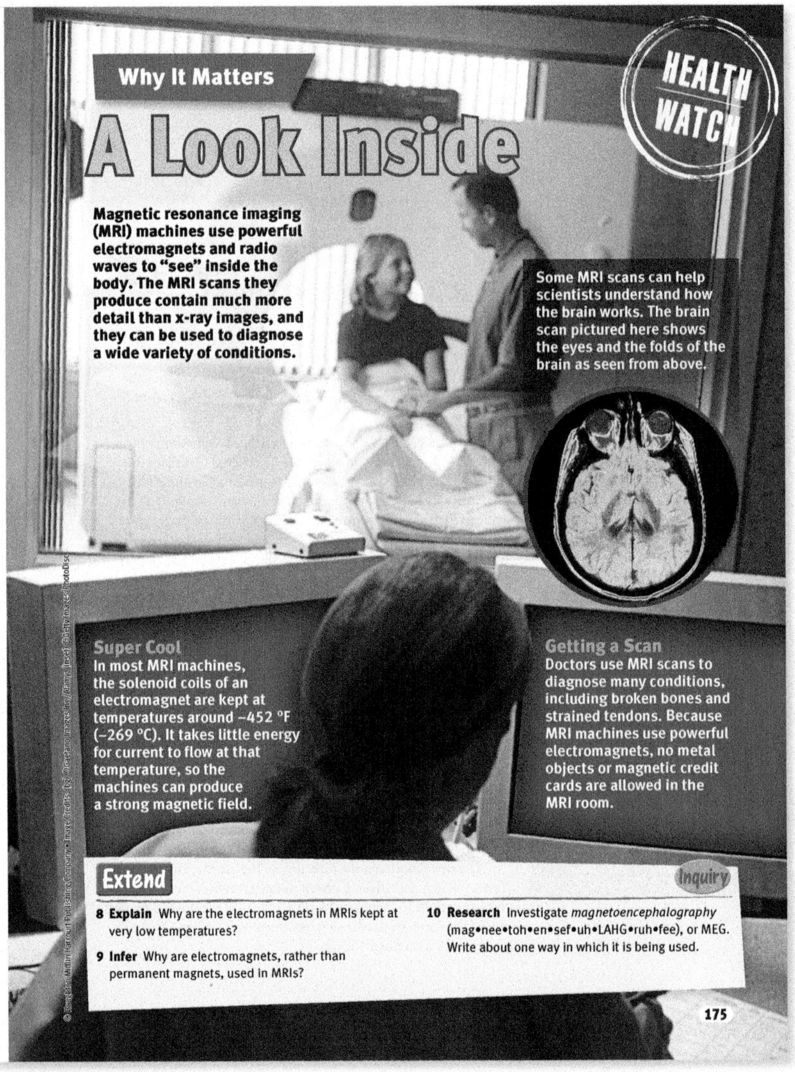

Why It Matters

HEALTH WATCH

A Look Inside

Magnetic resonance imaging (MRI) machines use powerful electromagnets and radio waves to "see" inside the body. The MRI scans they produce contain much more detail than x-ray images, and they can be used to diagnose a wide variety of conditions.

Some MRI scans can help scientists understand how the brain works. The brain scan pictured here shows the eyes and the folds of the brain as seen from above.

Super Cool
In most MRI machines, the solenoid coils of an electromagnet are kept at temperatures around −452 °F (−269 °C). It takes little energy for current to flow at that temperature, so the machines can produce a strong magnetic field.

Getting a Scan
Doctors use MRI scans to diagnose many conditions, including broken bones and strained tendons. Because MRI machines use powerful electromagnets, no metal objects or magnetic credit cards are allowed in the MRI room.

Extend

Inquiry

8 Explain Why are the electromagnets in MRIs kept at very low temperatures?

9 Infer Why are electromagnets, rather than permanent magnets, used in MRIs?

10 Research Investigate *magnetoencephalography* (mag•nee•toh•en•sef•uh•LAHG•ruh•fee), or MEG. Write about one way in which it is being used.

Answers

7. Sample answer: When current is switched off, the magnetic force disappears, and the metal can be released.

8. Electric charges flow more easily in a superconductor, so it can produce a stronger magnetic field.

9. Electromagnets are used because they can be turned on and off and because they can be made more powerful than permanent magnets.

10. Research results will vary.

Building Reading Skills

Visualize Text Once students have read how electromagnets are used, ask them to visualize the examples. Have volunteers explain what they think each device does and how electromagnets are used in them. You may encourage other students to draw a picture showing how they think each example works and how each uses electromagnets. **Ask:** How does visualizing help you understand what you're learning about? Sample answers: It helps me stop and think. It helps me to figure things out.

Why It Matters

Explain to students that the tube of an MRI machine contains electromagnets much like the simple solenoids they've learned about. **Ask:** How are an MRI and a simple solenoid similar? Sample answers: They both form a tubular shape. They both rely on electric current. Explain that the hydrogen atoms in the human body act like compasses in the presence of a strong magnetic field. When the magnetic field is removed, the hydrogen atoms return to their original positions and emit a radio signal while doing so. These radio waves are what an MRI detects and what allows the machine to see inside us.

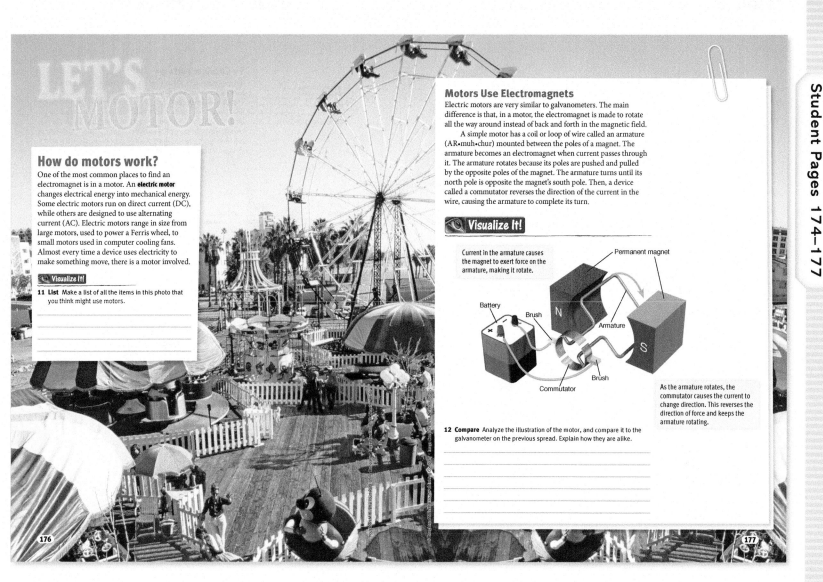

LET'S MOTOR!

How do motors work?

One of the most common places to find an electromagnet is in a motor. An **electric motor** changes electrical energy into mechanical energy. Some electric motors run on direct current (DC), while others are designed to use alternating current (AC). Electric motors range in size from large motors, used to power a Ferris wheel, to small motors used in computer cooling fans. Almost every time a device uses electricity to make something move, there is a motor involved.

Visualize It!

11 List Make a list of all the items in this photo that you think might use motors.

176

Motors Use Electromagnets

Electric motors are very similar to galvanometers. The main difference is that, in a motor, the electromagnet is made to rotate all the way around instead of back and forth in the magnetic field.

A simple motor has a coil or loop of wire called an armature (AR·muh·chur) mounted between the poles of a magnet. The armature becomes an electromagnet when current passes through it. The armature rotates because its poles are pushed and pulled by the opposite poles of the magnet. The armature turns until its north pole is opposite the magnet's south pole. Then, a device called a commutator reverses the direction of the current in the wire, causing the armature to complete its turn.

Visualize It!

Current in the armature causes the magnet to exert force on the armature, making it rotate.

Permanent magnet

Battery

Brush

N

Armature

S

Commutator

Brush

As the armature rotates, the commutator causes the current to change direction. This reverses the direction of force and keeps the armature rotating.

12 Compare Analyze the illustration of the motor, and compare it to the galvanometer on the previous spread. Explain how they are alike.

177

Answers

11. Sample answer: carousel, Ferris wheel, bumblebee ride, car ride

12. Both contain an electromagnet that rotates between the poles of another magnet.

Learning Alert

AC versus DC Students may not have seen the acronyms *AC* and *DC* before in a scientific context. Explain to students that *DC* stands for *Direct Current,* and *AC* stands for *Alternating Current.* Direct current is an electric charge that flows in one direction only. Direct current is produced by batteries and by DC generators, such as a cell phone charger. Alternating current is a flow of electric charge that reverses direction at regular intervals. The current that enters homes and schools is an alternating current.

Interpreting Visuals

Have students closely study the diagram of the motor after reading the text. Ask students to use the diagram to describe how electric energy from the battery is used to make the armature move. Electric current from the battery moves through the wires and then to the armature. This causes the armature to become an electromagnet. Since magnets surround the armature, its poles are repelled by the like poles in the magnet. The commutator keeps changing the poles of the electromagnet so that it continually moves.

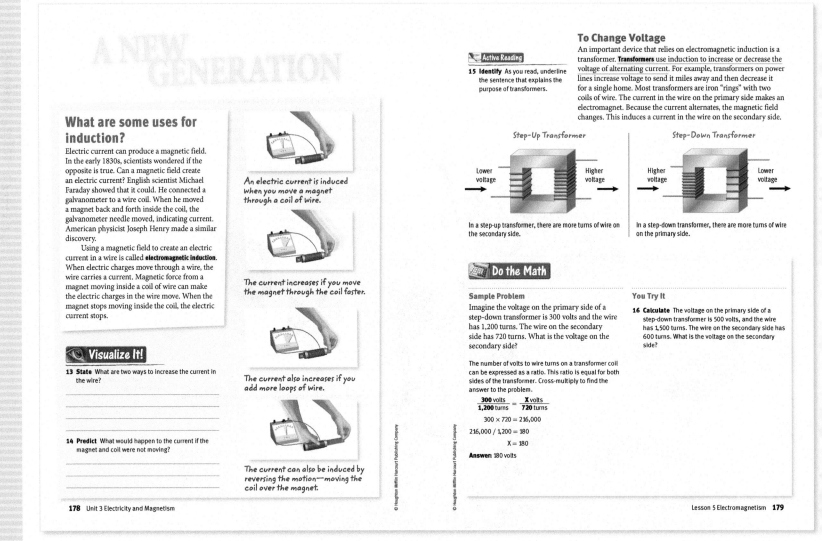

A NEW GENERATION

What are some uses for induction?

Electric current can produce a magnetic field. In the early 1830s, scientists wondered if the opposite is true. Can a magnetic field create an electric current? English scientist Michael Faraday showed that it could. He connected a galvanometer to a wire coil. When he moved a magnet back and forth inside the coil, the galvanometer needle moved, indicating current. American physicist Joseph Henry made a similar discovery.

Using a magnetic field to create an electric current in a wire is called **electromagnetic induction**. When electric charges move through a wire, the wire carries a current. Magnetic force from a magnet moving inside a coil of wire can make the electric charges in the wire move. When the magnet stops moving inside the coil, the electric current stops.

An electric current is induced when you move a magnet through a coil of wire.

The current increases if you move the magnet through the coil faster.

The current also increases if you add more loops of wire.

The current can also be induced by reversing the motion—moving the coil over the magnet.

Visualize It!

13 State What are two ways to increase the current in the wire?

_____

14 Predict What would happen to the current if the magnet and coil were not moving?

_____

178 Unit 3 Electricity and Magnetism

To Change Voltage

An important device that relies on electromagnetic induction is a transformer. **Transformers** use induction to increase or decrease the voltage of alternating current. For example, transformers on power lines increase voltage to send it miles away and then decrease it for a single home. Most transformers are iron "rings" with two coils of wire. The current in the wire on the primary side makes an electromagnet. Because the current alternates, the magnetic field changes. This induces a current in the wire on the secondary side.

Active Reading

15 Identify As you read, underline the sentence that explains the purpose of transformers.

Step-Up Transformer

Lower voltage → Higher voltage

In a step-up transformer, there are more turns of wire on the secondary side.

Step-Down Transformer

Higher voltage → Lower voltage

In a step-down transformer, there are more turns of wire on the primary side.

Do the Math

Sample Problem

Imagine the voltage on the primary side of a step-down transformer is 300 volts and the wire has 1,200 turns. The wire on the secondary side has 720 turns. What is the voltage on the secondary side?

The number of volts to wire turns on a transformer coil can be expressed as a ratio. This ratio is equal for both sides of the transformer. Cross-multiply to find the answer to the problem.

$$\frac{300 \text{ volts}}{1,200 \text{ turns}} = \frac{X \text{ volts}}{720 \text{ turns}}$$

$$300 \times 720 = 216,000$$

$$216,000 / 1,200 = 180$$

$$X = 180$$

Answer: 180 volts

You Try It

16 Calculate The voltage on the primary side of a step-down transformer is 500 volts, and the wire has 1,500 turns. The wire on the secondary side has 600 turns. What is the voltage on the secondary side?

Lesson 5 Electromagnetism 179

Answers

13. Move the magnet or the coil faster; increase the number of loops in the coil.

14. It would drop to zero.

15. *See students' pages for annotations.*

16. 200 volts

Formative Assessment

Ask: Why is induction considered to be the opposite of the process that produces an electromagnet? To make an electromagnet, you use electric current to produce a magnetic field. The process of induction uses a changing magnetic field to produce an electric current. **Ask:** What is the difference between a step-up transformer and a step-down transformer? The difference is the number of coils on the primary and secondary sides. A step-up transformer has more coils on the secondary side and therefore has a greater voltage output than input.

Do the Math

Step-Up/Step-Down Have students discuss how they know the transformers in the Do the Math examples are step-down transformers and not step-up transformers. In both examples, the wire wraps around the primary coil more times than the secondary coil. In the sample, the voltage on the primary coil is 300, and the voltage on the secondary coil is less—180 volts. Ask students how they can use this information to help them evaluate the accuracy of the answer they get in their You Try It calculation. The voltage on the secondary coil should be lower than the voltage on the primary coil (500 volts).

To Generate Electricity

Did you know that most of the electricity you use every day comes from electromagnetic induction? **Electric generators** use induction to change mechanical energy into electrical energy. You can think of electric generators as being the "opposite" of electric motors.

In all different types of power plants, mechanical energy is used to rotate turbines. The turbines turn magnets inside coils of wire, generating electricity. Many power plants use rising steam to turn the turbines. The steam is produced from burning fossil fuels or using nuclear reactions to heat water. Other sources of mechanical energy to turn turbines are blowing wind, falling water, and ocean tides and waves.

Generators induce electric current when a magnet moves in a coil of wire or when a wire moves between the poles of a magnet. In a simple generator, a wire loop at the end of a rod moves through the magnetic field of a magnet. In the first half of the turn, one side of the loop moves downward. In the second half of the turn, the part of the loop that was moving down now moves upward, and the current reverses, creating alternating current.

Think Outside the Book

17 Research Find out what type of mechanical energy is used to generate electricity for your community. Share this information with somebody at home.

Active Reading 18 Summarize How does the function of a generator relate to the function of a motor?

Generating Electricity

A generator induces electric current in wire that is moving in a magnetic field. A crank would be used to turn the wire in this generator.

The wire is rotated between the poles of a magnet, generating current.

The current in the rotating wire is transferred to metal rings.

The current can then be sent to other devices such as a light bulb.

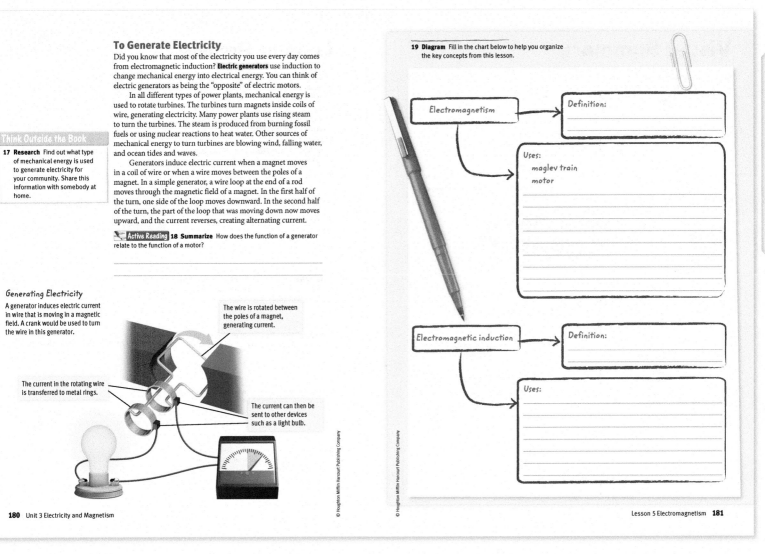

19 Diagram Fill in the chart below to help you organize the key concepts from this lesson.

Electromagnetism → Definition:

Uses:
maglev train
motor

Electromagnetic induction → Definition:

Uses:

Answers

17. Research results will vary.

18. They are opposites.

19. Electromagnetism: Definition: the interaction between electricity and magnetism; Uses: maglev train, motor, doorbell, industrial electromagnet, atom smasher, MRI machine, galvanometer; Electromagnetic induction: Definition: using a magnetic field to create an electric current; Uses: transformer, generator

Learning Alert ⚠️ MISCONCEPTION ⚠️

Motor and Generator Some students may think that both motors and generators produce electricity because they are made of the same parts. Point out that a generator changes mechanical energy into electrical energy (as happens at a power plant), and a motor changes electrical energy into mechanical energy (as in a fan). Have students explain the difference between a motor and a generator in their own words. Sample answer: A generator uses movement to produce electrical energy, while a motor uses electrical energy to produce movement.

Probing Questions DIRECTED Inquiry

Analyzing What role does kinetic energy play in the production of electricity? Kinetic energy turns the turbine in a generator.

Applying What other sources of mechanical energy might you be able to use to produce electricity? Sample answers: a treadmill, a bicycle, a hamster wheel, a hand crank What would be some of the pros and cons of using these sources of mechanical energy? Sample answers: Pros: It would be inexpensive and easy to use. Cons: Some of them require physical activity, so the person (or hamster) would get tired after doing it for a long time. It probably would not produce very much electricity.

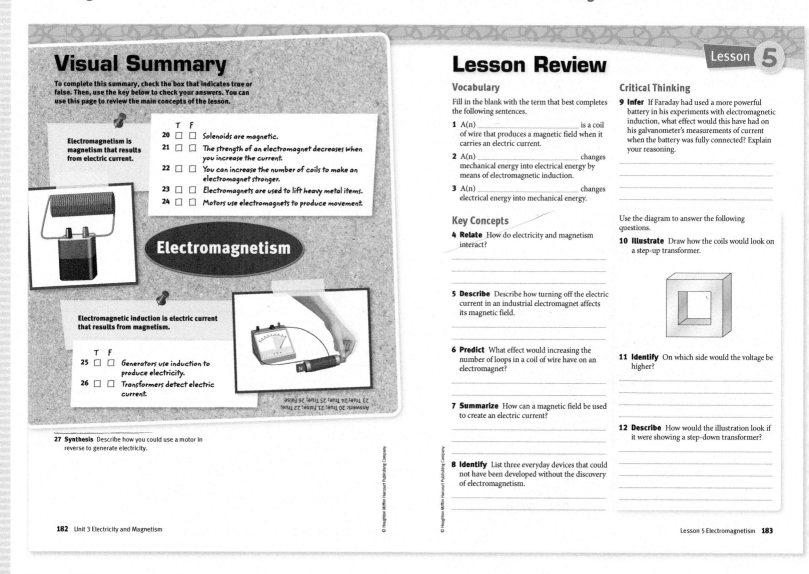

Visual Summary

To complete this summary, check the box that indicates true or false. Then, use the key below to check your answers. You can use this page to review the main concepts of the lesson.

Electromagnetism is magnetism that results from electric current.

	T	F	
20	☐	☐	Solenoids are magnetic.
21	☐	☐	The strength of an electromagnet decreases when you increase the current.
22	☐	☐	You can increase the number of coils to make an electromagnet stronger.
23	☐	☐	Electromagnets are used to lift heavy metal items.
24	☐	☐	Motors use electromagnets to produce movement.

Electromagnetism

Electromagnetic induction is electric current that results from magnetism.

	T	F	
25	☐	☐	Generators use induction to produce electricity.
26	☐	☐	Transformers detect electric current.

Answers: 20 True; 21 False; 22 True; 23 True; 24 True; 25 True; 26 False

27 Synthesis Describe how you could use a motor in reverse to generate electricity.

182 Unit 3 Electricity and Magnetism

© Houghton Mifflin Harcourt Publishing Company

Lesson Review

Lesson ⑤

Vocabulary

Fill in the blank with the term that best completes the following sentences.

1 A(n) _____ is a coil of wire that produces a magnetic field when it carries an electric current.

2 A(n) _____ changes mechanical energy into electrical energy by means of electromagnetic induction.

3 A(n) _____ changes electrical energy into mechanical energy.

Key Concepts

4 Relate How do electricity and magnetism interact?

5 Describe Describe how turning off the electric current in an industrial electromagnet affects its magnetic field.

6 Predict What effect would increasing the number of loops in a coil of wire have on an electromagnet?

7 Summarize How can a magnetic field be used to create an electric current?

8 Identify List three everyday devices that could not have been developed without the discovery of electromagnetism.

Critical Thinking

9 Infer If Faraday had used a more powerful battery in his experiments with electromagnetic induction, what effect would this have had on his galvanometer's measurements of current when the battery was fully connected? Explain your reasoning.

Use the diagram to answer the following questions.

10 Illustrate Draw how the coils would look on a step-up transformer.

11 Identify On which side would the voltage be higher?

12 Describe How would the illustration look if it were showing a step-down transformer?

Lesson 5 Electromagnetism **183**

© Houghton Mifflin Harcourt Publishing Company

Visual Summary Answers

20. T
21. F
22. T
23. T
24. T
25. T
26. F
27. Sample answer: You could manually turn the armature of a motor. Electricity would be produced in the wire because moving a wire inside a magnet produces electric current.

Lesson Review Answers

1. solenoid
2. generator
3. electric motor
4. Electric currents produce magnetic fields, and magnetic fields produce electricity.
5. The magnetic field disappears.
6. It would make the magnet stronger.
7. The magnet can move in a coil of wire, or the wire can move between the poles of a magnet.
8. Answers might include any motorized toy or appliance such as dishwasher, hair dryer, and washing machine.

9. A stronger battery would have had no effect when the wire was parallel with the magnetic field lines. The meter would still only register current when the battery was connected or disconnected.
10. The drawing should show more turns in the secondary side.
11. The voltage would be higher on the secondary side.
12. There would be more turns on the primary side.

Electronic Technology

Essential Question What are electronics, and how have they changed?

Professional Development

For more detailed information about the topics in this lesson, refer to the Content Refresher in the Unit Opener pages.

Opening Your Lesson

Begin the lesson by assessing students' prerequisite and prior knowledge.

Prerequisite Knowledge

- The structure of an atom and how electrons work
- Basic knowledge of electric charges and current
- Properties of electromagnetic waves

Accessing Prior Knowledge

Use a diagram of an atom to review the structure of an atom. Label the atom and include the electrons. **Ask:** What is an atom made up of? protons, neutrons, and electrons **Ask:** What are two types of charged particles? protons and electrons **Ask:** What makes up electric current? Electric charges moving in a wire make up electric current.

Customize Your Opening

- ☐ **Accessing Prior Knowledge,** above
- ☐ Print Path Engage Your Brain, SE p. 185
- ☐ Print Path Active Reading, SE p. 185
- ☐ **Digital Path** Lesson Opener

Key Topics/Learning Goals

Electronic Devices

1 Explain what makes something an electronic versus an electrical device.
2 Describe an integrated circuit.

Coded Information

1 Identify how signals transmit information.
2 Explain analog and digital signals, and give an example of each.

Computer Technology

1 Describe a computer's basic structure and functions.
2 Describe the development of computers.

Supporting Concepts

- An electrical device is one that produces, transports, or is powered by electrical energy.
- An electronic device manipulates the flow of electrons for its operation and requires an outside power source.
- An integrated circuit is an entire circuit that has many components on a single tiny sheet of specially treated silicon.

- A signal is anything that can be used to send information using another signal, called a carrier.
- There are two kinds of signals or codes: digital and analog.
- An analog signal is a signal whose properties can change continuously in a given range.
- A digital signal is one that is represented as a sequence of separate values called binary numbers.

- A modern computer is an electronic device that performs tasks by following instructions given to it.
- In 1945, the U.S. Army completed final assembly of a computer called ENIAC.
- The introduction of the integrated circuit enabled computer size to be greatly reduced.
- Today, a single integrated circuit in a pocket calculator can do everything that ENIAC could do and more.

Options for Instruction

Two parallel paths provide coverage of the Essential Questions, with a strong Inquiry strand woven into each.
Follow the Print Path, the Digital Path, or your customized combination of print, digital, and inquiry.

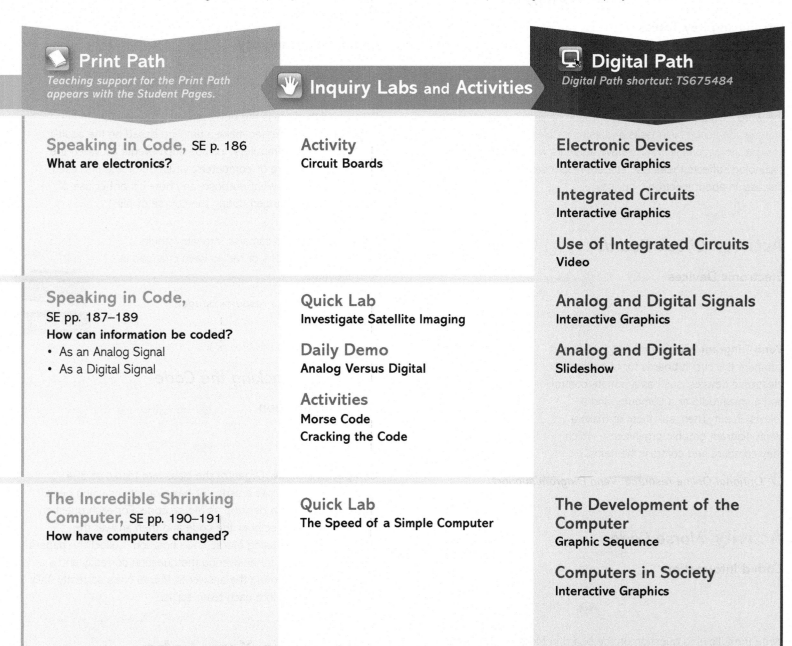

Print Path
Teaching support for the Print Path appears with the Student Pages.

Inquiry Labs and Activities

Digital Path
Digital Path shortcut: TS675484

Speaking in Code, SE p. 186
What are electronics?

Activity
Circuit Boards

Electronic Devices
Interactive Graphics

Integrated Circuits
Interactive Graphics

Use of Integrated Circuits
Video

Speaking in Code,
SE pp. 187–189
How can information be coded?
• As an Analog Signal
• As a Digital Signal

Quick Lab
Investigate Satellite Imaging

Daily Demo
Analog Versus Digital

Activities
Morse Code
Cracking the Code

Analog and Digital Signals
Interactive Graphics

Analog and Digital
Slideshow

The Incredible Shrinking Computer, SE pp. 190–191
How have computers changed?

Quick Lab
The Speed of a Simple Computer

The Development of the Computer
Graphic Sequence

Computers in Society
Interactive Graphics

Options for Assessment

See the Evaluate page for options, including Formative Assessment, Summative Assessment, and Unit Review.

Engage and Explore

Activities and Discussion

Discussion *What Is Technology?*

Introducing Key Topics

👥 whole class
🕐 10 min
Inquiry DIRECTED inquiry

Write the word technology on the board. Ask students to define the word. Sample answer: the application of knowledge, tools, and materials to accomplish tasks and solve problems; objects that are used to accomplish tasks Have students write three ways that technology affects them. Use student responses to launch a class discussion about electronic devices.

Activity *Circuit Boards*

Electronic Devices

👥 small groups
🕐 15 min
Inquiry GUIDED inquiry

Venn Diagram Allow students to study and compare the circuit boards for two different electronic devices, such as a remote control and a small radio or a computer and a television set. Then, ask them to make a Venn diagram graphic organizer in which they compare and contrast the items.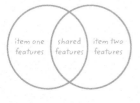

🌀 *Optional Online resource: Venn Diagram support*

Activity *Morse Code*

Coded Information

👥 individuals, whole class
🕐 15 min
Inquiry DIRECTED inquiry

Write the following question on the board in Morse code: "What is your first name?" Have the students use the Morse code table in their books to decipher the question and write an answer in Morse code. Explain to students that the telegraph machine was one of the first electronic devices used for communication. Invite students to suggest additional questions in Morse code that the class can answer.

Take It Home *An Oral History of Computers*

Computer Technology

👥 student-adult pairs
🕐 20 min
Inquiry GUIDED inquiry

With an adult, discuss the development of computers in his or her lifetime. Together, make a timeline based on the adult's experience with computers. Include such events as: when the adult became aware of computers, when he or she first used computers and for what purpose, and how his or her use of computers has changed during the course of his or her lifetime.

Variation Students can also interview adults about how televisions or radios have changed in their lifetime.

🌀 *Optional Online resource: student worksheet*

Activity *Cracking the Code*

Coded Information

👥 small groups
🕐 15 min
Inquiry GUIDED inquiry

Competitive Game Organize the class into teams of 3–4 students. Ask the class a series of basic questions using pencil taps and drags on a desktop as Morse code. For each question, groups must first decipher the code and then answer the question on paper using Morse code notation. Collect the papers and give one point for answering the question correctly and a second point for writing the answer in Morse code correctly. Tally up the total points that each team earns.

Customize Your Labs

📄 *See the Lab Manual for lab datasheets.*

🌀 *Go Online for editable lab datasheets.*

Levels of **Inquiry**

| **DIRECTED** inquiry | **GUIDED** inquiry | **INDEPENDENT** inquiry |
| introduces inquiry skills within a structured framework. | develops inquiry skills within a supportive environment. | deepens inquiry skills with student-driven questions or procedures. |

Labs and Demos

Daily Demo *Analog Versus Digital*

Engage

Coded Information

- 👥 whole class
- 🕐 10 min
- (Inquiry) **GUIDED** inquiry

Use this short demo after you have read the difference between analog and digital signals.

PURPOSE **To compare an analog and a digital recording**

MATERIALS

- cassette tape of a song (or any analog recording)
- CD of same song (or any digital recording)
- cassette/CD player

1 Tell students that they are going to listen to the same recording on a cassette tape and then on a CD. Explain that you will not be telling them which recording is the cassette and which is the CD.

2 Direct students to listen carefully to see if they notice a difference between the two recordings. **Ask:** Do you notice any difference? Explain. Sample answer: Yes, the digital recording is clearer than the analog recording.

3 Use student responses to launch a discussion on coded information. Most students will comment on the superior sound quality of the CD.

Variation You can also use a vinyl record and a record player as an example of an analog recording.

⊘ 🗏 Quick Lab *Investigate Satellite Imaging*

Coded Information

- 👥 pairs
- 🕐 15 min
- (Inquiry) **GUIDED** inquiry

Students will use binary code to send or receive a color image.

PURPOSE **To identify how signals transmit information and describe how binary code works**

MATERIALS

- graphing paper
- plain paper
- colored pens or pencils

⊘ 🗏 Quick Lab *The Speed of a Simple Computer*

Computer Technology

- 👥 individuals
- 🕐 15 min
- (Inquiry) **DIRECTED** inquiry

Students will investigate how solving mathematical problems with a calculator compares to solving problems without a calculator.

PURPOSE **To compare human calculation speed and accuracy to those done by computer**

MATERIALS

- calculator
- analog clock with a second hand (or stop watch)

Activities and Discussion

- ☐ **Discussion** What Is Technology?
- ☐ **Activity** Circuit Boards
- ☐ **Activity** Morse Code
- ☐ **Take It Home** An Oral History...
- ☐ **Activity** Cracking the Code

Labs and Demos

- ☐ **Daily Demo** Analog Versus Digital
- ☐ **Quick Lab** Investigate Satellite Imaging
- ☐ **Quick Lab** The Speed of a Simple Computer

Your Resources

Explain Science Concepts

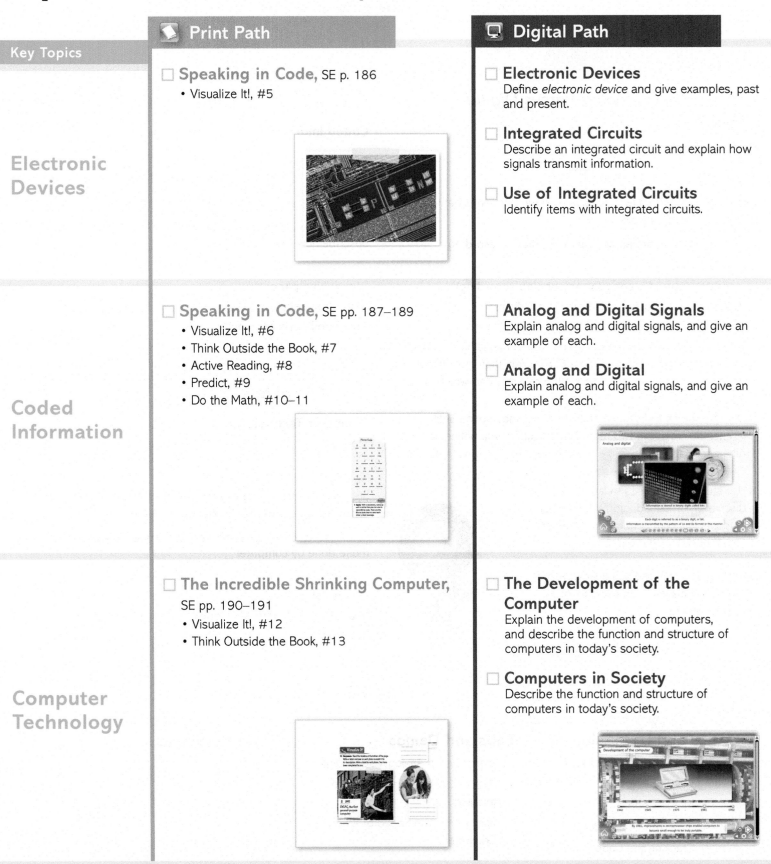

Key Topics	📖 Print Path	🖥 Digital Path
Electronic Devices	☐ **Speaking in Code,** SE p. 186 • Visualize It!, #5	☐ **Electronic Devices** Define *electronic device* and give examples, past and present. ☐ **Integrated Circuits** Describe an integrated circuit and explain how signals transmit information. ☐ **Use of Integrated Circuits** Identify items with integrated circuits.
Coded Information	☐ **Speaking in Code,** SE pp. 187–189 • Visualize It!, #6 • Think Outside the Book, #7 • Active Reading, #8 • Predict, #9 • Do the Math, #10–11	☐ **Analog and Digital Signals** Explain analog and digital signals, and give an example of each. ☐ **Analog and Digital** Explain analog and digital signals, and give an example of each.
Computer Technology	☐ **The Incredible Shrinking Computer,** SE pp. 190–191 • Visualize It!, #12 • Think Outside the Book, #13	☐ **The Development of the Computer** Explain the development of computers, and describe the function and structure of computers in today's society. ☐ **Computers in Society** Describe the function and structure of computers in today's society.

Basic *The Flow of Information*

Computer Technology | 👥 individuals | 🕐 10 min

Process Chart Help students create a process chart graphic organizer using the information in the text that describes the primary things that computers do. input information, store and process information, output information Students can also draw the parts of the computer responsible for each thing next to the corresponding box.

step 1
↓
step 2
↓
step 3

Advanced *ENIAC*

Computer Technology | 👥 individuals or pairs | 🕐 varied

Explain to students that ENIAC was developed for use by the U.S. Army during World War II. Ask students to find out what ENIAC was to be used for in the war and what plans were made for ENIAC after the war. Have interested students create a computer presentation to share their information. ENIAC was originally developed by the military as a faster method for calculating the settings needed to correctly fire various types of weapons under various conditions. Although development took only 2.5 years, the war had ended by the time ENIAC was finished. ENIAC was used during the Cold War to perform calculations for the design of a hydrogen bomb. The military also recommended ENIAC for use in areas of research that demand complex calculations, such as aerodynamics and weather prediction.

🌐 *Optional Online rubric: Multimedia Presentation*

ELL *Computer Image*

Computer Technology | 👥 individuals or pairs | 🕐 varied

Poster Remind students that all computers perform the same four basic functions: input information, process information, store information, and output the information. Tell students to create a poster that shows the components of the computer that perform these functions. For example, a keyboard is an input device.

Variation Students could also design a futuristic computer and show how their computers will do each of the four functions.

🌐 *Optional Online rubric: Posters and Displays*

electronic device | integrated circuit | analog signal
digital signal | computer

Previewing Vocabulary

👥 whole class | 🕐 5 min

Distinguishing Terms Tell students to use the following information to help them distinguish between analog and digital signals.

• An analog signal is a signal whose properties change without a break or jump between values, similar to the way that a dimmer switch allows you to continuously change the brightness of the light.

• A digital signal is a signal that does not change continuously, similar to the way a regular light switch can either be on or off.

Reinforcing Vocabulary

👥 individuals or pairs | 🕐 10 min

Concentrating on Vocabulary Have students write each vocabulary term in this section on a separate index card. Then, have students write the definition or an example of each term on a second set of index cards. Have students play a game of "concentration," turning over one card from each set each time, matching each vocabulary term to its definition. When students find a "match," have them pronounce the word and read the definition or the example aloud.

Customize Your Core Lesson

Core Instruction

☐ **Print Path** choices

☐ **Digital Path** choices

Vocabulary

☐ **Previewing Vocabulary** Distinguishing Terms

☐ **Reinforcing Vocabulary** Concentrating on Vocabulary

Differentiated Instruction

☐ **Basic** The Flow of Information

☐ **Advanced** ENIAC

☐ **ELL** Computer Image

Your Resources

Extend Science Concepts

Activity *Electronic Technology Review*

Synthesizing Key Topics   👥 whole class
                               🕐 20 min

Inside/Outside Circles Help students review the material by following these steps:

1 After students have read the lesson, give each an index card with a question from the text. Questions can include: "What type of device manipulates the flow of electrons for its operation and requires an outside power source?" "How is an analog signal different from a digital signal?" "What are the four functions of a computer?" Students write their answers on the back of the index cards. Check the answers or provide a key to make sure they are correct. Have students adjust incorrect answers.

2 Students pair up and form two circles. One partner is in an inside circle; the other is an outside circle. The students in the inside circle face out, and the students in the outside circle face in.

3 Each student in the inside circle asks his or her partner the question on the index card. The partner answers. If the answer is incorrect, the student in the inside circle teaches the other student the correct answer. Repeat this step, with the outside-circle students asking the questions.

4 Have each student on the outside circle rotate one person to the right. He or she faces a new partner and gets a new question. (You can vary the rotation by moving more than one person, moving to the left, and so on, but try to make sure that partners are always new.)

Graphic Organizer

Synthesizing Key Topics   👥 individuals or pairs
                               🕐 15–20 min

Mind Map After students have studied the lesson, ask them to create a mind map and include the following terms: *electronic devices, electrical devices, uses energy, analog signals, digital signals, computer,* and *integrated circuits.* Encourage students to include examples of electronic devices that rely on analog signals and those that use digital signals.

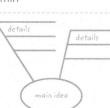

🔘 *Optional Online resource: Mind Map support*

Health Connection

Synthesizing Key Topics   👥 whole class
                               🕐 10 min

Discussion Explain to students that people who spend long hours working at a computer or playing video games may face health hazards. Discuss with students some of the health problems associated with prolonged computer use, such as eyestrain, headache, backache, and repetitive motion syndrome. Ask students if they know of anyone who has computer-related illnesses and what solutions those people found. Discuss ways to prevent some of these hazards.

Earth Science Connection

Synthesizing Key Topics   👥 individuals
                               🕐 15 min

Draw a Diagram Tell students that a seismograph is a device used by scientists to record waves made by earthquakes. This device makes wavy lines on paper that record ground movement. Ask interested students to research and then draw an example of a seismogram that shows changes in the wave. Ask them to explain why this is an example of an analog signal.

Customize Your Closing

🔲 *See the Assessment Guide for quizzes and tests.*

🔘 *Go Online to edit and create quizzes and tests.*

Reinforce and Review

☐ **Activity** Electronic Technology Review

☐ **Graphic Organizer** Mind Map

☐ **Print Path** Visual Summary, SE p. 192

☐ **Print Path** Lesson Review, SE p. 193

☐ **Digital Path** Lesson Closer

Evaluate Student Mastery

Formative Assessment

See the teacher support below the Student Pages for additional Formative Assessment questions.

Discuss with students the criteria that make a piece of equipment an electronic device. Ask the following questions to assess student mastery of the material. **Ask:** What are some examples of electronic devices? Sample answer: television remotes, computers, calculators **Ask:** How can information be coded in electronic devices? as analog and digital signals **Ask:** Describe how these signals work. An analog signal is a signal whose properties can change continuously in a given range, and a digital signal is one that is represented as a sequence of separate values called binary numbers. **Ask:** How have computers changed? Sample answers: Computers have gotten smaller and their processing speeds faster.

Reteach

Formative assessment may show that students need reinforcement for certain topics. The resources below are recommended for reteaching. If students were introduced to a topic through the Print Path, you can also use the Digital Path to reteach, or vice versa.
🎧 *Can be assigned to individual students*

Electronic Devices
Activity Circuit Boards
Graphic Organizer Mind Map 🎧

Coded Information
Activity Cracking the Code

Computer Technology
ELL Computer Image 🎧

Summative Assessment

Alternative Assessment
Bit by Bit

🎧 *Online resources: student worksheet; optional rubrics*

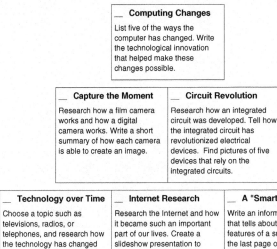

Electronic Technology

Climb the Pyramid: *Bit by Bit*

1. Work on your own, with a partner, or with a small group.
2. Choose one item from each layer of the pyramid. Check your choices.
3. Have your teacher approve your plan.
4. Submit or present your results.

__ Computing Changes
List five of the ways the computer has changed. Write the technological innovation that helped make these changes possible.

__ Capture the Moment
Research how a film camera works and how a digital camera works. Write a short summary of how each camera is able to create an image.

__ Circuit Revolution
Research how an integrated circuit was developed. Tell how the integrated circuit has revolutionized electrical devices. Find pictures of five devices that rely on the integrated circuits.

__ Technology over Time
Choose a topic such as televisions, radios, or telephones, and research how the technology has changed over time. Then create a timeline tracing the history of this technology using both descriptions and images.

__ Internet Research
Research the Internet and how it became such an important part of our lives. Create a slideshow presentation to share your findings.

__ A "Smart" Phone?
Write an informational brochure that tells about some of the features of a smartphone. On the last page of the brochure show how a smartphone is similar to a computer, and how it is different.

Going Further
- ☐ Health Connection
- ☐ Earth Science Connection

Formative Assessment
- ☐ Strategies Throughout TE
- ☐ Lesson Review SE

Summative Assessment
- ☐ Alternative Assessment Bit by Bit
- ☐ Lesson Quiz
- ☐ Unit Tests A and B
- ☐ Unit Review SE End-of-Unit

Your Resources

_____

_____

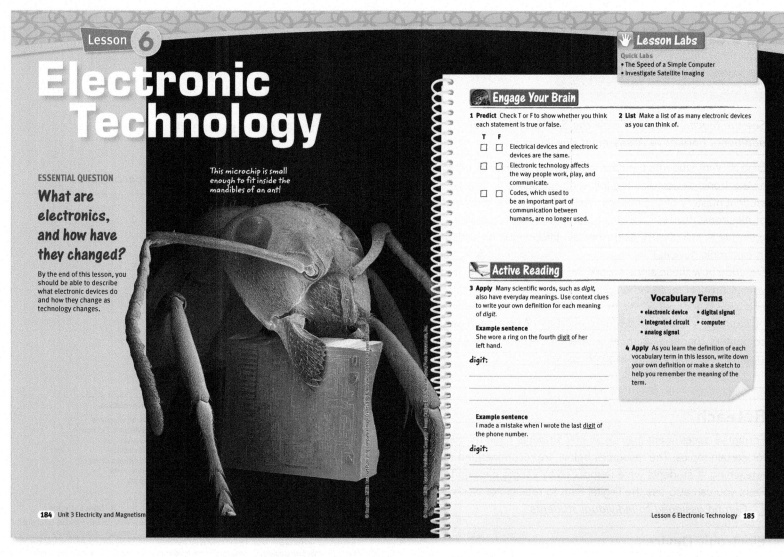

Answers

Answers for 1–3 should represent students' current thoughts, even if incorrect.

1. F; T; F

2. Sample answer: phone, computer, camera

3. finger; a number from 0 to 9

4. Students should define or sketch each vocabulary term in the lesson.

Opening Your Lesson

Discuss student responses to items 1 and 2 to assess their prerequisite knowledge and to estimate what they already know about electronic technology.

Prerequisites Students should already know the structure of an atom and how electrons work. Students should have a general knowledge about electric charges and current.

Learning Alert

Artificial Intelligence Some students may think that computers are more intelligent than people. Remind students that although computers are capable of functioning at extremely high speeds, they can currently perform only functions that have been programmed into them by people. Poll the students to see how many have heard of the computer rule GIGO (garbage in—garbage out) then discuss the meaning of the rule. Allow interested students to research artificial intelligence and report their findings to the class.

Speaking in Code

What are electronics?

Electronic devices like computers are not the same as electrical devices like toasters. Both use electrical energy. But electronic devices can perform more sophisticated tasks than electrical devices can. **Electronic devices** are able to control the flow of electrons using *integrated circuits*. An **integrated circuit** is a single, tiny chip of specially treated silicon containing many circuit parts. Integrated circuits carry out instructions, or programs, by controlling current.

A TV remote control is an example of an electronic device. Imagine that you push a button on the remote control to change the channel. A signal goes to integrated circuits inside the remote control. The circuits process the information and send an infrared signal to the TV. The signal tells the TV to change channels.

Integrated circuits, or microchips, are tiny silicon-based chips that can process information.

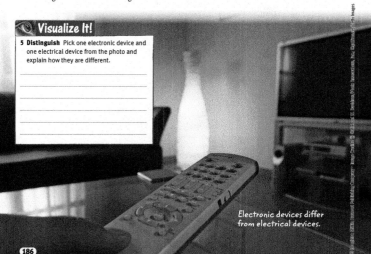

Visualize It!

5 Distinguish Pick one electronic device and one electrical device from the photo and explain how they are different.

_____

_____

_____

_____

Electronic devices differ from electrical devices.

186

How can information be coded?

A signal is a pattern that contains coded information. For example, when you speak, information is coded in the pattern of sounds you make. Your voice is the carrier of the signal, and a listener interprets it. Morse code is a signal that uses dashes and dots to represent letters of the alphabet. People used to send telegraph messages in Morse code using wires as the carrier. Electronics also use coded signals. The two kinds of signals they use are *analog signals* and *digital signals*.

As an Analog Signal

Signals that change continuously in a given range are called **analog signals**. For example, a dimmer switch sends an analog electrical signal to a light fixture. You slide a dimmer switch up or down in one continuous motion. As you move the switch up or down, the amount of electric current supplied to the lighting goes up or down. If you move the switch just a little bit, the lighting changes just a little bit. A record also produces an analog signal. A record needle moves up and down continuously as it moves over a record's grooves. The up-and-down movements are turned into sound waves by the record player. As the record groove changes, the sound changes.

Visualize It!

6 Identify What are the carriers of the analog signals in the examples shown below?

_____

_____

A dimmer switch is an example of a device that sends an analog signal.

Some people think the analog signals used by records and record players produce a richer sound than digital media.

Lesson 6 Electronic Technology **187**

Morse Code

A •— B —••• C —•—• D —••
E • F ••—• G ——• H ••••
I •• J •——— K —•— L •—••
M —— N —• O ——— P •——•
Q ——•— R •—• S ••• T —
U ••— V •••— W •—— X —••—
Y —•—— Z ——••

Think Outside the Book *Inquiry*

7 Apply With a classmate, come up with a carrier that you can use to send Morse code. Then use the Morse code chart to send each other a short message.

Answers

5. Sample answer: The TV is an electronic device and the lamp is an electrical device. The TV can process information and the lamp cannot.

6. dimmer switch: electric current; record: grooves

7. Students may use a visual signal, such as blinking, or an audible signal, such as tapping their desks, to send their messages.

Learning Alert

Looking for Light Students may think that the red LED on a TV remote control is what sends signals to the television. Most remote controls have two LEDs—one clear and one red. When a button on the remote control is pushed, the clear LED sends signals to the television. At the same time, the red LED flashes to indicate that the remote control is working.

Probing Question GUIDED *Inquiry*

Analyzing Ask students to think of several methods of sending messages. Sample answers: letter, e-mail, telephone, and texting Then, ask students to compare the equipment needed and the cost, speed, and reliability of each method. How has technology changed the transmission of information? Sample answer: It has sped up the transmission of information.

Formative Assessment

Ask: How are electronic devices different from electrical devices? Electronic devices have the ability to process information using integrated circuits. **Ask:** What are some examples of electronic devices? Sample answer: television, computer, smart phone

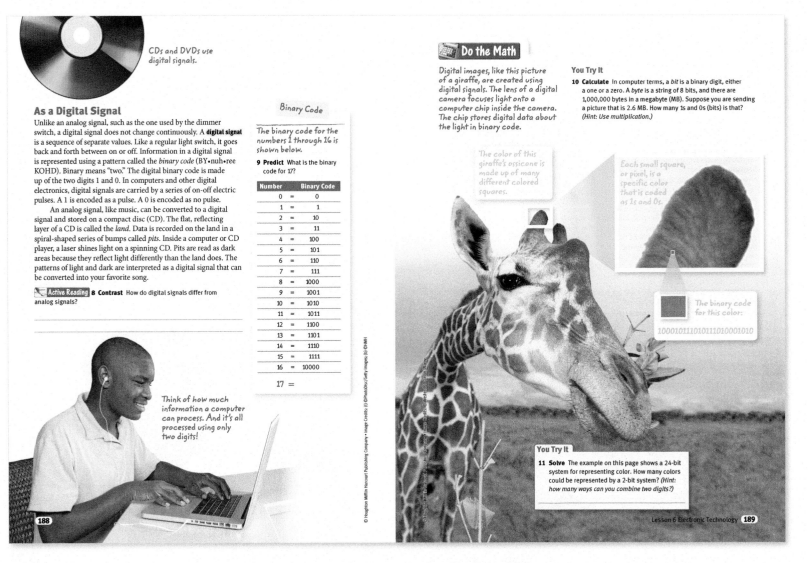

CDs and DVDs use digital signals.

As a Digital Signal

Unlike an analog signal, such as the one used by the dimmer switch, a digital signal does not change continuously. A **digital signal** is a sequence of separate values. Like a regular light switch, it goes back and forth between on or off. Information in a digital signal is represented using a pattern called the *binary code* (BY•nuh•ree KOHD). Binary means "two." The digital binary code is made up of the two digits 1 and 0. In computers and other digital electronics, digital signals are carried by a series of on-off electric pulses. A 1 is encoded as a pulse. A 0 is encoded as no pulse.

An analog signal, like music, can be converted to a digital signal and stored on a compact disc (CD). The flat, reflecting layer of a CD is called the *land*. Data is recorded on the land in a spiral-shaped series of bumps called *pits*. Inside a computer or CD player, a laser shines light on a spinning CD. Pits are read as dark areas because they reflect light differently than the land does. The patterns of light and dark are interpreted as a digital signal that can be converted into your favorite song.

Active Reading **8 Contrast** How do digital signals differ from analog signals?

Think of how much information a computer can process. And it's all processed using only two digits!

Binary Code

The binary code for the numbers 1 through 16 is shown below.

9 Predict What is the binary code for 17?

Number		Binary Code
0	=	0
1	=	1
2	=	10
3	=	11
4	=	100
5	=	101
6	=	110
7	=	111
8	=	1000
9	=	1001
10	=	1010
11	=	1011
12	=	1100
13	=	1101
14	=	1110
15	=	1111
16	=	10000
17	=	

Do the Math

Digital images, like this picture of a giraffe, are created using digital signals. The lens of a digital camera focuses light onto a computer chip inside the camera. The chip stores digital data about the light in binary code.

You Try It

10 Calculate In computer terms, a *bit* is a binary digit, either a one or a zero. A *byte* is a string of 8 bits, and there are 1,000,000 bytes in a megabyte (MB). Suppose you are sending a picture that is 2.6 MB. How many 1s and 0s (bits) is that? *(Hint: Use multiplication.)*

The color of this giraffe's ossicone is made up of many different colored squares.

Each small square, or pixel, is a specific color that is coded as 1s and 0s.

The binary code for this color:
100010111010111010001010

You Try It

11 Solve The example on this page shows a 24-bit system for representing color. How many colors could be represented by a 2-bit system? *(Hint: how many ways can you combine two digits?)*

188

Lesson 6 Electronic Technology 189

Answers

8. Digital signals are a pattern of 0s and 1s; analog signals change continuously.

9. 10001

10. 2.6 megabytes × 1,000,000 = 2,600,000 bytes; 2,600,000 bytes × 8 = 20,800,000 bits

11. four colors

Probing Questions GUIDED Inquiry

Making Inferences Does a mercury thermometer provide information in an analog or digital way? Explain your reasoning. A mercury thermometer provides information in an analog way. The mercury rises or falls in a continuous manner as the temperature changes. What advantage does a digital signal have over an analog signal? Sample answer: Digital code allows more information to be stored in a smaller amount of space. For example, an 8 GB MP3 player can store thousands of minutes of music, while the average 700 MB CD can store approximately 500 minutes of music (depending on bit rate).

Do the Math

Students may need help setting up the unit conversion. Explain to students that they will need to perform two steps to go from megabytes to bits. First they will have to convert megabytes to bytes, and then they will have to convert bytes to bits. To convert megabytes to bytes, they will multiply the number of megabytes by 1,000,000. Students should find that there are 2,600,000 bytes in 2.6 MB. To convert bytes to bits, they will need to multiply the number of bytes by 8. Students should find that there are 20,800,000 bits, or ones and zeros, in 2.6 MB. Challenge students to solve this problem using pencil and paper. Then they can check their answers with a calculator.

The Incredible Shrinking Computer

How have computers changed?

A **computer** is any electronic device that performs tasks by following instructions given to it. Computers receive information, called *input*, through keyboards, touchscreens, or other devices. The input can be processed through a central processor or stored in memory. Computers output information through monitors, printers, or other devices.

Computers have changed greatly over time, as shown below. Today's computers include *smartphones*, cell phones that have functions such as Internet access, cameras, and built-in applications.

Visualize It!

12 Sequence Read the timeline at the bottom of the page. Write a letter and year on each photo to match it to its description. Write a label for each photo. Two have been completed for you.

B 1945
ENIAC, the first general-purpose computer

C 1958
The first integrated circuit

Think Outside the Book Inquiry

13 Create Design a new electronic device for tomorrow's classrooms. Create a poster describing the advantages of your technology.

| 1800 | 1945 | | 1965 | 1985 | 2005 |

A In 1801, French weaver Joseph Marie Jacquard invented wooden punch cards to program which pattern a loom would weave. The presence of a hole meant the loom needle could go through, and the absence of a hole meant it could not, similar to the 1s and 0s of modern software.

B In 1945, engineers completed one of the first general-purpose computers, the Electronic Numerical Integrator and Computer (ENIAC), for the U.S. Army. Punch cards delivered information to be processed by almost 18,000 vacuum tubes inside the 33-ton machine.

C In 1958, developers introduced the integrated circuit, which allowed the development of much smaller computers.

D In 1965, the first commercially successful tabletop computer came on the market. It could sit on a table, but it was too expensive for home computing. It cost what the average person might earn in 15 years!

E In the mid-1970s, personal computers like those used today first appeared. They had monitors, keyboards, and hard drives. These computers could store, process, and output information for people in their homes or businesses.

F In the early 2000s, the first touchscreen smartphones came on the market. Smartphones combined the features of a telephone with a computer. People could make phone calls, send e-mail or messages, and surf the Internet from almost anywhere.

190 Unit 3 Electricity and Magnetism

Lesson 6 Electronic Technology 191

Answers

12. Left to right (left page): D 1965, First successful tabletop computer; F early 2000s, Smartphone; (right page): A 1801, Jacquard loom; E mid-1970s, Early personal computer

13. Students' designs will vary.

Interpreting Visuals

Point out the timeline shown on these pages. Based on the timeline, have students identify some of the ways that the first computers were different from the computers of today. Sample answer: The first computers were much larger and had slower processing speeds.

Learning Alert

Bigger Isn't Better Students may mistakenly assume that a physically large computer must have greater capabilities than a smaller computer does. Remind students that the early digital computers of the late 1950s had RAM (random access memory) capacities of 8,000 to 64,000 words—a vast improvement over the 1,000-word RAM capacity of the much larger UNIVAC computer.

Formative Assessment

Ask: What is a computer's basic function? A computer performs tasks by following instructions given to it. **Ask:** How did the integrated circuit change the structure of the computer? It allowed for the development of much smaller computers. It also led to the development of the microchip.

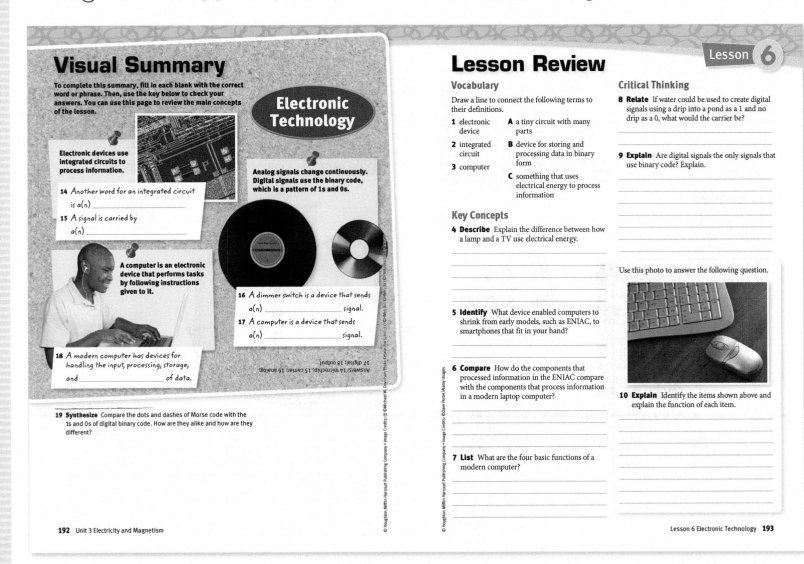

Visual Summary Answers

14. microchip
15. carrier
16. analog
17. digital
18. output
19. Sample answer: Both send information with binary signals. Morse Code uses two kinds of symbols, dots and dashes, and can be sent by different carriers. Digital code uses 1s and 0s and is carried by electric current that is either on or off.

Lesson Review Answers

1. C
2. A
3. B
4. Sample answer: A lamp converts electrical energy to mechanical energy to do work; a TV uses electrical energy to process information.
5. integrated circuits or microprocessor chip
6. Sample answer: ENIAC processed information with vacuum tubes, but modern laptops process information with tiny integrated circuits.
7. receive input (or information); process input (or information); store input (or information); output information

8. water waves
9. Sample answer: No, any signal that has only two states uses the binary code. For example, Morse code is a binary code because it has only two options.
10. Sample answer: The items are a keyboard and a mouse. They are both input devices, because they use signals to enter information into the computer.

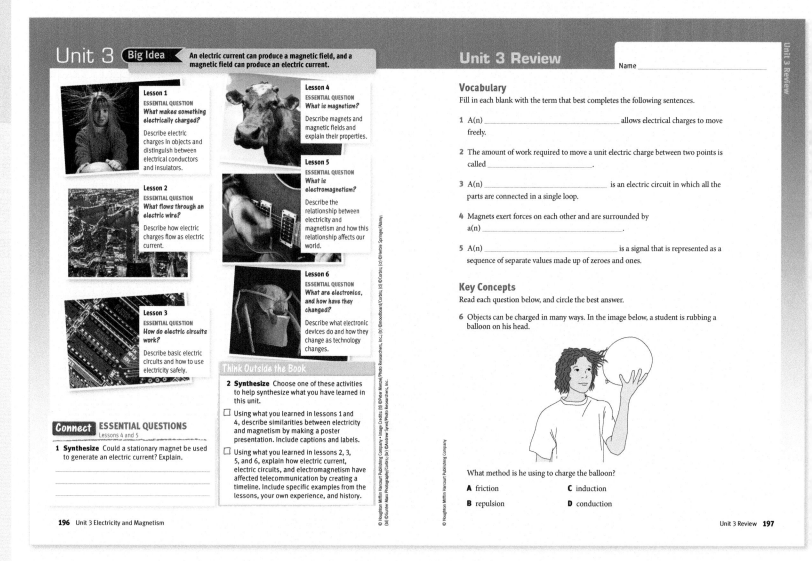

Unit Summary Answers

1. A stationary magnet can generate an electric current if the wire coil is in motion.

2. Option 1: Student presentations may include one or more of the following:

   • Electric charge can be positive (+) or negative (−). A magnet's poles have opposing magnetic qualities.

   • Like charges repel one another, and unlike charges attract one another. Electric charges within magnets create attractive and repulsive forces.

   • An uncharged object can become charged by coming into contact with a charged object. Some materials can be magnetized by rubbing one pole of an existing magnet in one direction along the new material.

   Option 2: Answers will vary depending on examples chosen by students.

Unit Review Response to Intervention

A Quick Grading Chart follows the Answers. See the Assessment Guide for more detail about correct and incorrect answer choices. Refer back to the Lesson Planning pages for activities and assignments that can be used as remediation for students who answer questions incorrectly.

Answers

1. electrical conductor An electrical conductor allows charges to flow freely, while an electrical insulator does not allow electric charges to flow freely. (Lesson 1)

2. voltage The higher the voltage of an electric current, the greater the amount of energy the charges release as they move. (Lesson 2)

3. series circuit If one part of a series circuit breaks, there is no current throughout the circuit. (Lesson 3)

Unit 3 Review continued

Name _____

7 Which of the following is an electrical insulator?

A copper   **C** aluminum

B rubber   **D** iron

8 Which of the following wires has the lowest resistance?

A a short, thick copper wire at 25 °C

B a long, thick copper wire at 35 °C

C a long, thin copper wire at 35 °C

D a short, thin iron wire at 25 °C

9 There are many devices in the home that use electricity. Below is a diagram of four common electrical devices.

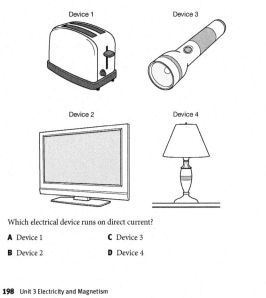

Device 1   Device 3

Device 2   Device 4

Which electrical device runs on direct current?

A Device 1   **C** Device 3

B Device 2   **D** Device 4

198   Unit 3 Electricity and Magnetism

10 The diagram below shows two examples of electrical circuits.

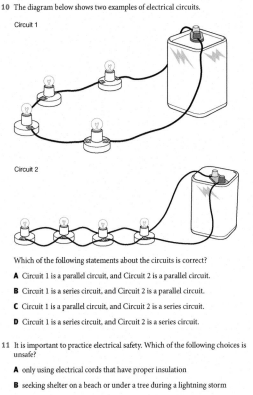

Circuit 1

Circuit 2

Which of the following statements about the circuits is correct?

A Circuit 1 is a parallel circuit, and Circuit 2 is a parallel circuit.

B Circuit 1 is a series circuit, and Circuit 2 is a parallel circuit.

C Circuit 1 is a parallel circuit, and Circuit 2 is a series circuit.

D Circuit 1 is a series circuit, and Circuit 2 is a series circuit.

11 It is important to practice electrical safety. Which of the following choices is unsafe?

A only using electrical cords that have proper insulation

B seeking shelter on a beach or under a tree during a lightning storm

C keeping electrical appliances away from sinks and bathtubs

D using ground fault circuit interrupters (GFCIs) in the home

Unit 3 Review   **199**

Answers *(continued)*

4. magnetic field Magnetic forces can be detected in a magnetic field. (Lesson 4)

5. digital signal Digital signals are made up of digits (0s and 1s), which are made up of a series of electric pulses. (Lesson 6)

6. Answer A is correct because when using friction by rubbing, electrons are transferred from one object to another. (Lesson 1)

7. Answer B is correct because rubber is an electrical insulator. (Lesson 1)

8. Answer A is correct because wires made of copper are good electric conductors, thick wires have less resistance than thin wires, and lower temperatures are less resistant than higher temperatures. (Lesson 2)

9. Answer C is correct because a battery-powered device like a flashlight runs on direct current (DC). (Lesson 2)

10. Answer B is correct because circuit 1 is a series circuit, and circuit 2 is a parallel circuit. (Lesson 3)

11. Answer B is correct because during a lightning storm you should not seek shelter on a beach or under a tree. You should seek shelter inside. (Lesson 3)

12. Answer D is correct because the load converts the energy to heat and light. (Lesson 3)

13. Answer C is correct because a hand-held compass does not contain an electromagnet. (Lesson 5)

14. Answer D is correct because gaining or losing electrons will affect an object's charge. (Lesson 1)

15. Answer B is correct because the microprocessor chip replaced the large vacuum tubes so that computers, which at one time were as large as a room, could be made much smaller. (Lesson 6)

16. Answer B is correct because binary code is a digital signal composed of 1s and 0s. (Lesson 6)

Unit 3 Review continued

Name_____

12 Here is a diagram of a simple electric circuit. There are four elements to the circuit. They are labeled Circuit Element 1, Circuit Element 2, Circuit Element 3, and Circuit Element 4.

Circuit Element 1

Circuit Element 2

Circuit Element 4

Circuit Element 3

What part of an electric circuit changes the electrical energy into another form of energy?

A Circuit Element 1   **C** Circuit Element 3

B Circuit Element 2   **D** Circuit Element 4

13 Which of the following does not use an electromagnet?

A electric motor   **C** hand-held compass

B galvanometer   **D** doorbell

14 An object can become electrically charged if it gains or loses which particles?

A volts   **C** atoms

B neutrons   **D** electrons

15 Over time, computer size has been greatly reduced because of the introduction of which component?

A memory device   **C** monitor

B microprocessor chip   **D** mouse

16 Binary code is an example of which of the following?

A an analog system   **C** an electronic device

B a digital signal   **D** an integrated circuit

17 Below is an image of a magnet showing the magnetic field.

C   **N**   A   **S**

B   D

Where is the magnetic force the strongest?

A Position A   **C** Position C

B Position B   **D** Position D

Critical Thinking

Answer the following questions in the space provided.

18 Describe three properties of magnets.

_____

_____

_____

_____

_____

19 List two ways in which the strength of an electromagnet can be increased.

_____

_____

_____

_____

Answers *(continued)*

17. Answer C is correct because the magnetic fields are strongest at the magnetic poles. (Lesson 4)

18. Key Elements:

   • Magnets attract objects made of iron and other magnets.

   • Magnets have two poles called magnetic poles (north and south) that have opposing magnetic qualities. Like poles repel, and opposite poles attract.

   • Magnets are surrounded by a magnetic field. (Lesson 4)

19. Key Elements:

   • Increase the number of loops of wire in the coil around the magnet.

   • Increase the electric current running through the wire. (Lesson 5)

20. Key Elements:

   • Earth's geographic poles mark the ends of the imaginary axis about which the planet rotates. Earth's magnetic poles are near the geographic poles and mark the points on the planet's surface where its magnetic forces are the strongest.

   • The north-seeking end of a compass points to the north magnetic pole. Navigators must take the angle of difference between the geographic and magnetic poles into account when plotting a course. (Lesson 4)

21. Key Elements:

   • Electromagnetic induction is the process of creating a current in a circuit by changing a magnetic field. Passing a magnet through a coil of wire can generate an electric current.

   • A solenoid is a coil of wire with an electric current running through it. When a solenoid is wrapped around an iron core, an electromagnet is formed.

Unit 3 Review continued

20 The image below shows Earth and its magnetic field.

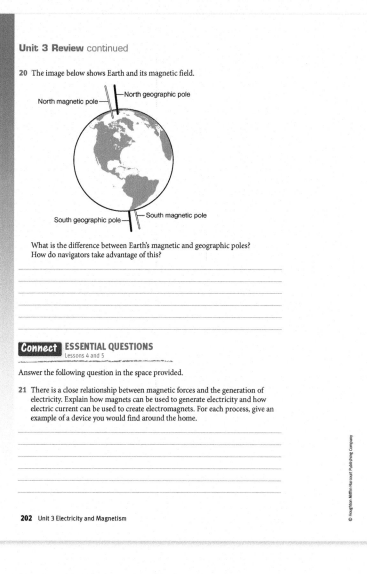

What is the difference between Earth's magnetic and geographic poles? How do navigators take advantage of this?

_____

_____

_____

_____

_____

_____

Connect ESSENTIAL QUESTIONS
Lessons 4 and 5

Answer the following question in the space provided.

21 There is a close relationship between magnetic forces and the generation of electricity. Explain how magnets can be used to generate electricity and how electric current can be used to create electromagnets. For each process, give an example of a device you would find around the home.

_____

_____

_____

_____

_____

_____

202 Unit 3 Electricity and Magnetism

Answers (continued)

- An electric generator uses electromagnetic induction to change mechanical energy into electrical energy.
- A doorbell uses two solenoids. (Lessons 4, 5)

Quick Grading Chart

Use the chart below for quick test grading. The lesson correlations can help you target reteaching for missed items.

Item	Answer	Cognitive Complexity	Lesson
1.	—	Low	1
2.	—	Low	2
3.	—	Low	3
4.	—	Low	4
5.	—	Low	6
6.	A	Moderate	1
7.	B	Moderate	1
8.	A	Moderate	2
9.	C	Moderate	2
10.	B	Moderate	3
11.	B	Moderate	3
12.	D	Moderate	3
13.	C	Moderate	5
14.	D	Moderate	1
15.	B	Moderate	6
16.	B	Moderate	6
17.	C	Moderate	4
18.	—	Moderate	4
19.	—	Moderate	5
20.	—	Moderate	4
21.	—	Moderate	4, 5

Cognitive Complexity refers to the demand on thinking associated with an item, and may vary with the answer choices, the number of steps required to arrive at an answer, and other factors, but not the ability level of the student.

Teacher Notes

Resources

Handbook

References

Mineral Properties

Here are five steps to take in mineral identification:

1 Determine the color of the mineral. Is it light-colored, dark-colored, or a specific color?

2 Determine the luster of the mineral. Is it metallic or non-metallic?

3 Determine the color of any powder left by its streak.

4 Determine the hardness of your mineral. Is it soft, hard, or very hard? Using a glass plate, see if the mineral scratches it.

5 Determine whether your sample has cleavage or any special properties.

TERMS TO KNOW	DEFINITION
adamantine	a non-metallic luster like that of a diamond
cleavage	how a mineral breaks when subject to stress on a particular plane
luster	the state or quality of shining by reflecting light
streak	the color of a mineral when it is powdered
submetallic	between metallic and nonmetallic in luster
vitreous	glass-like type of luster

Silicate Minerals

Mineral	Color	Luster	Streak	Hardness	Cleavage and Special Properties
Beryl	deep green, pink, white, bluish green, or yellow	vitreous	white	7.5–8	1 cleavage direction; some varieties fluoresce in ultraviolet light
Chlorite	green	vitreous to pearly	pale green	2–2.5	1 cleavage direction
Garnet	green, red, brown, black	vitreous	white	6.5–7.5	no cleavage
Hornblende	dark green, brown, or black	vitreous	none	5–6	2 cleavage directions
Muscovite	colorless, silvery white, or brown	vitreous or pearly	white	2–2.5	1 cleavage direction
Olivine	olive green, yellow	vitreous	white or none	6.5–7	no cleavage
Orthoclase	colorless, white, pink, or other colors	vitreous	white or none	6	2 cleavage directions
Plagioclase	colorless, white, yellow, pink, green	vitreous	white	6	2 cleavage directions
Quartz	colorless or white; any color when not pure	vitreous or waxy	white or none	7	no cleavage

Nonsilicate Minerals

Mineral	Color	Luster	Streak	Hardness	Cleavage and Special Properties
Native Elements					
Copper	copper-red	metallic	copper-red	2.5–3	no cleavage
Diamond	pale yellow or colorless	adamantine	none	10	4 cleavage directions
Graphite	black to gray	submetallic	black	1–2	1 cleavage direction
Carbonates					
Aragonite	colorless, white, or pale yellow	vitreous	white	3.5–4	2 cleavage directions; reacts with hydrochloric acid
Calcite	colorless or white to tan	vitreous	white	3	3 cleavage directions; reacts with weak acid; double refraction
Halides					
Fluorite	light green, yellow, purple, bluish green, or other colors	vitreous	none	4	4 cleavage directions; some varieties fluoresce
Halite	white	vitreous	white	2.0–2.5	3 cleavage directions
Oxides					
Hematite	reddish brown to black	metallic to earthy	dark red to red-brown	5.6–6.5	no cleavage; magnetic when heated
Magnetite	iron-black	metallic	black	5.5–6.5	no cleavage; magnetic
Sulfates					
Anhydrite	colorless, bluish, or violet	vitreous to pearly	white	3–3.5	3 cleavage directions
Gypsum	white, pink, gray, or colorless	vitreous, pearly, or silky	white	2.0	3 cleavage directions
Sulfides					
Galena	lead-gray	metallic	lead-gray to black	2.5–2.8	3 cleavage directions
Pyrite	brassy yellow	metallic	greenish, brownish, or black	6–6.5	no cleavage

References

Geologic Time Scale

Geologists developed the geologic time scale to represent the 4.6 billion years of Earth's history that have passed since Earth formed. This scale divides Earth's history into blocks of time. The boundaries between these time intervals (shown in millions of years ago or mya in the table below), represent major changes in Earth's history. Some boundaries are defined by mass extinctions, major changes in Earth's surface, and/or major changes in Earth's climate.

The four major divisions that encompass the history of life on Earth are Precambrian time, the Paleozoic era, the Mesozoic era, and the Cenozoic era. The largest divisions are eons. **Precambrian time** is made up of the first three eons, over 4 billion years of Earth's history.

The **Paleozoic era** lasted from 542 mya to 251 mya. All major plant groups, except flowering plants, appeared during this era. By the end of the era, reptiles, winged insects, and fishes had also appeared. The largest known mass extinction occurred at the end of this era.

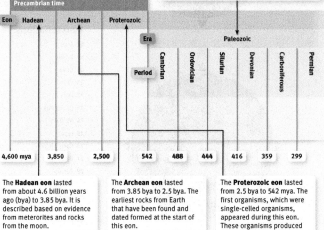

The **Hadean eon** lasted from about 4.6 billion years ago (bya) to 3.85 bya. It is described based on evidence from meteorites and rocks from the moon.

The **Archean eon** lasted from 3.85 bya to 2.5 bya. The earliest rocks from Earth that have been found and dated formed at the start of this eon.

The **Proterozoic eon** lasted from 2.5 bya to 542 mya. The first organisms, which were single-celled organisms, appeared during this eon. These organisms produced so much oxygen that they changed Earth's oceans and Earth's atmosphere.

Divisions of Time

The divisions of time shown here represent major changes in Earth's surface and when life developed and changed significantly on Earth. As new evidence is found, the boundaries of these divisions may shift. The Phanerozoic eon is divided into three eras. The beginning of each of these eras represents a change in the types of organisms that dominated Earth. And, each era is commonly characterized by the types of organisms that dominated the era. These eras are divided into periods, and periods are divided into epochs.

The **Mesozoic era** lasted from 251 mya to 65.5 mya. During this era, many kinds of dinosaurs dominated land, and giant lizards swam in the ocean. The first birds, mammals, and flowering plants also appeared during this time. About two-thirds of all land species went extinct at the end of this era.

The **Phanerozoic eon** began 542 mya. We live in this eon.

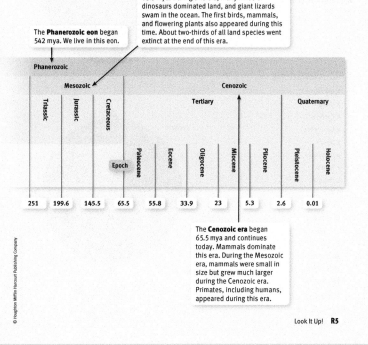

The **Cenozoic era** began 65.5 mya and continues today. Mammals dominate this era. During the Mesozoic era, mammals were small in size but grew much larger during the Cenozoic era. Primates, including humans, appeared during this era.

Star Charts for the Northern Hemisphere

A star chart is a map of the stars in the night sky. It shows the names and positions of constellations and major stars. Star charts can be used to identify constellations and even to orient yourself using Polaris, the North Star.

Because Earth moves through space, different constellations are visible at different times of the year. The star charts on these pages show the constellations visible during each season in the Northern Hemisphere.

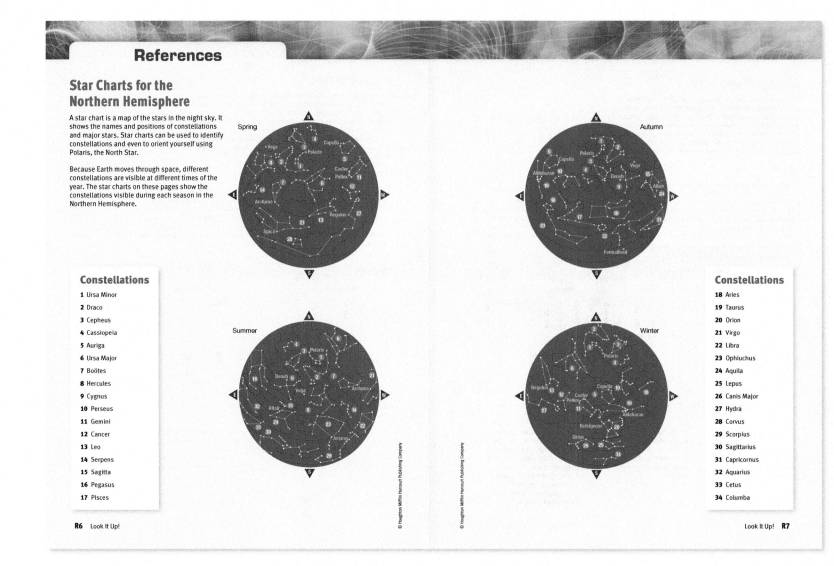

Constellations

1 Ursa Minor
2 Draco
3 Cepheus
4 Cassiopeia
5 Auriga
6 Ursa Major
7 Boötes
8 Hercules
9 Cygnus
10 Perseus
11 Gemini
12 Cancer
13 Leo
14 Serpens
15 Sagitta
16 Pegasus
17 Pisces

Constellations

18 Aries
19 Taurus
20 Orion
21 Virgo
22 Libra
23 Ophiuchus
24 Aquila
25 Lepus
26 Canis Major
27 Hydra
28 Corvus
29 Scorpius
30 Sagittarius
31 Capricornus
32 Aquarius
33 Cetus
34 Columba

References

World Map

LEGEND

Boundary

— Tectonic plate boundary

Elevation and Depth

Elevation (meters)

8,850
5,000
2,500
1,000
500
0

Depth (meters)

-500
-1,000
-2,500
-5,000
-10,900

© Houghton Mifflin Harcourt Publishing Company

© Houghton Mifflin Harcourt Publishing Company

R8   Look It Up!

Look It Up!   R9

References

Classification of Living Things

Domains and Kingdoms

All organisms belong to one of three domains: Domain Archaea, Domain Bacteria, or Domain Eukarya. Some of the groups within these domains are shown below. (Remember that genus names are italicized.)

Domain Archaea

The organisms in this domain are single-celled prokaryotes, many of which live in extreme environments.

Archaea		
Group	Example	Characteristics
Methanogens	*Methanococcus*	produce methane gas; can't live in oxygen
Thermophiles	*Sulpholobus*	require sulphur; can't live in oxygen
Halophiles	*Halococcus*	live in very salty environments; most can live in oxygen

Domain Bacteria

Organisms in this domain are single-celled prokaryotes and are found in almost every environment on Earth.

Bacteria		
Group	Example	Characteristics
Bacilli	*Escherichia*	rod shaped; some bacilli fix nitrogen; some cause disease
Cocci	*Streptococcus*	spherical shaped; some cause disease; can form spores
Spirilla	*Treponema*	spiral shaped; cause diseases such as syphilis and Lyme disease

Domain Eukarya

Organisms in this domain are single-celled or multicellular eukaryotes.

Kingdom Protista Many protists resemble fungi, plants, or animals, but are smaller and simpler in structure. Most are single celled.

Protists		
Group	Example	Characteristics
Sarcodines	*Amoeba*	radiolarians; single-celled consumers
Ciliates	*Paramecium*	single-celled consumers
Flagellates	*Trypanosoma*	single-celled parasites
Sporozoans	*Plasmodium*	single-celled parasites
Euglenas	*Euglena*	single celled; photosynthesize
Diatoms	*Pinnularia*	most are single celled; photosynthesize
Dinoflagellates	*Gymnodinium*	single celled; some photosynthesize
Algae	*Volvox*	single celled or multicellular; photosynthesize
Slime molds	*Physarum*	single celled or multicellular; consumers or decomposers
Water molds	powdery mildew	single celled or multicellular; parasites or decomposers

Kingdom Fungi Most fungi are multicellular. Their cells have thick cell walls. Fungi absorb food from their environment.

Fungi		
Group	Examples	Characteristics
Threadlike fungi	bread mold	spherical; decomposers
Sac fungi	yeast; morels	saclike; parasites and decomposers
Club fungi	mushrooms; rusts; smuts	club shaped; parasites and decomposers
Lichens	British soldier	a partnership between a fungus and an alga

Kingdom Plantae Plants are multicellular and have cell walls made of cellulose. Plants make their own food through photosynthesis. Plants are classified into divisions instead of phyla.

Plants		
Group	Examples	Characteristics
Bryophytes	mosses; liverworts	no vascular tissue; reproduce by spores
Club mosses	*Lycopodium*; ground pine	grow in wooded areas; reproduce by spores
Horsetails	rushes	grow in wetland areas; reproduce by spores
Ferns	spleenworts; sensitive fern	large leaves called fronds; reproduce by spores
Conifers	pines; spruces; firs	needlelike leaves; reproduce by seeds made in cones
Cycads	*Zamia*	slow growing; reproduce by seeds made in large cones
Gnetophytes	*Welwitschia*	only three living families; reproduce by seeds
Ginkgoes	*Ginkgo*	only one living species; reproduce by seeds
Angiosperms	all flowering plants	reproduce by seeds made in flowers; fruit

Kingdom Animalia Animals are multicellular. Their cells do not have cell walls. Most animals have specialized tissues and complex organ systems. Animals get food by eating other organisms.

Animals		
Group	Examples	Characteristics
Sponges	glass sponges	no symmetry or specialized tissues; aquatic
Cnidarians	jellyfish; coral	radial symmetry; aquatic
Flatworms	planaria; tapeworms; flukes	bilateral symmetry; organ systems
Roundworms	*Trichina*; hookworms	bilateral symmetry; organ systems
Annelids	earthworms; leeches	bilateral symmetry; organ systems
Mollusks	snails; octopuses	bilateral symmetry; organ systems
Echinoderms	sea stars; sand dollars	radial symmetry; organ systems
Arthropods	insects; spiders; lobsters	bilateral symmetry; organ systems
Chordates	fish; amphibians; reptiles; birds; mammals	bilateral symmetry; complex organ systems

References

Periodic Table of the Elements

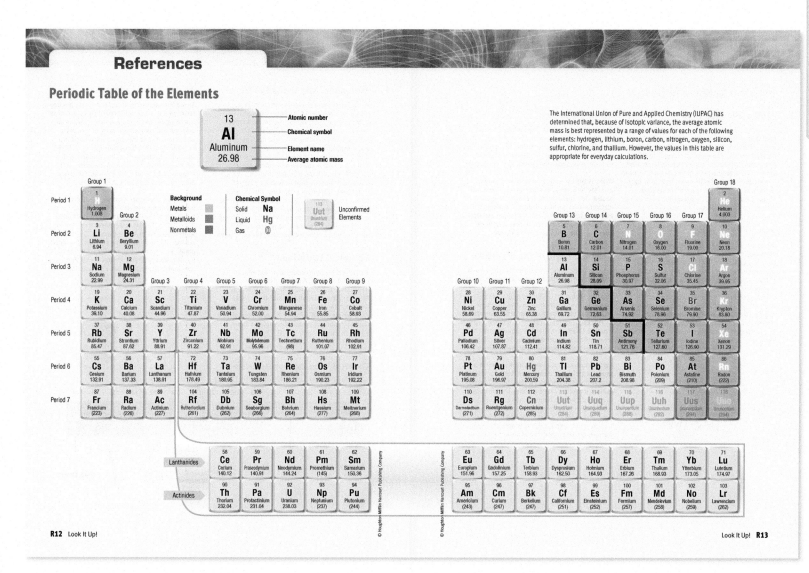

The International Union of Pure and Applied Chemistry (IUPAC) has determined that, because of isotopic variance, the average atomic mass is best represented by a range of values for each of the following elements: hydrogen, lithium, boron, carbon, nitrogen, oxygen, silicon, sulfur, chlorine, and thallium. However, the values in this table are appropriate for everyday calculations.

Physical Science Refresher

Atoms and Elements

Every object in the universe is made of matter. **Matter** is anything that takes up space and has mass. All matter is made of atoms. An **atom** is the smallest particle into which an element can be divided and still be the same element. An **element**, in turn, is a substance that cannot be broken down into simpler substances by chemical means. Each element consists of only one kind of atom. An element may be made of many atoms, but they are all the same kind of atom.

Atomic Structure

Atoms are made of smaller particles called **electrons**, **protons**, and **neutrons**. Electrons have a negative electric charge, protons have a positive charge, and neutrons have no electric charge. Together, protons and neutrons form the **nucleus**, or small dense center, of an atom. Because protons are positively charged and neutrons are neutral, the nucleus has a positive charge. Electrons move within an area around the nucleus called the **electron cloud**. Electrons move so quickly that scientists cannot determine their exact speeds and positions at the same time.

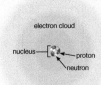

electron cloud

nucleus — proton

neutron

Atomic Number

To help distinguish one element from another, scientists use the atomic numbers of atoms. The **atomic number** is the number of protons in the nucleus of an atom. The atoms of a certain element always have the same number of protons.

When atoms have an equal number of protons and electrons, they are uncharged, or electrically neutral. The atomic number equals the number of electrons in an uncharged atom. The number of neutrons, however, can vary for a given element. Atoms of the same element that have different numbers of neutrons are called **isotopes**.

Periodic Table of the Elements

In the periodic table, each element in the table is in a separate box. And the elements are arranged from left to right in order of increasing atomic number. That is, an uncharged atom of each element has one more electron and one more proton than an uncharged atom of the element to its left. Each horizontal row of the table is called a **period**. Changes in chemical properties of elements across a period correspond to changes in the electron arrangements of their atoms.

Each vertical column of the table is known as a **group**. A group lists elements with similar physical and chemical properties. For this reason, a group is also sometimes called a family. The elements in a group have similar properties because their atoms have the same number of electrons in their outer energy level. For example, the elements helium, neon, argon, krypton, xenon, and radon all have similar properties and are known as the noble gases.

Molecules and Compounds

When two or more elements join chemically, they form a **compound**. A compound is a new substance with properties different from those of the elements that compose it. For example, water, H_2O, is a compound formed when hydrogen (H) and oxygen (O) combine. The smallest complete unit of a compound that has the properties of that compound is called a **molecule**. A chemical formula indicates the elements in a compound. It also indicates the relative number of atoms of each element in the compound. The chemical formula for water is H_2O. So, each water molecule consists of two atoms of hydrogen and one atom of oxygen. The subscript number after the symbol for an element shows how many atoms of that element are in a single molecule of the compound.

Chemical Equations

A chemical reaction occurs when a chemical change takes place. A chemical equation describes a chemical reaction using chemical formulas. The equation indicates the substances that react and the substances that are produced. For example, when carbon and oxygen combine, they can form carbon dioxide, shown in the equation below: $C + O_2 \longrightarrow CO_2$

Acids, Bases, and pH

An **ion** is an atom or group of chemically bonded atoms that has an electric charge because it has lost or gained one or more electrons. When an acid, such as hydrochloric acid, HCl, is mixed with water, it separates into ions. An **acid** is a compound that produces hydrogen ions, H^+, in water. The hydrogen ions then combine with a water molecule to form a hydronium ion, H_3O^+. A **base**, on the other hand, is a substance that produces hydroxide ions, OH^-, in water.

To determine whether a solution is acidic or basic, scientists use pH. The **pH** of a solution is a measure of the hydronium ion concentration in a solution. The pH scale ranges from 0 to 14. Acids have a pH that is less than 7. The lower the number, the more acidic the solution. The middle point, pH = 7, is neutral, neither acidic nor basic. Bases have a pH that is greater than 7. The higher the number is, the more basic the solution.

The pH of Some Common Materials

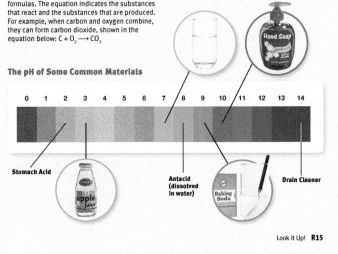

0 1 2 3 4 5 6 7 8 9 10 11 12 13 14

Stomach Acid

Antacid (dissolved in water)

Baking Soda

Drain Cleaner

Hand Soap

References

Physical Laws and Useful Equations

Law of Conservation of Mass

Mass cannot be created or destroyed during ordinary chemical or physical changes.

The total mass in a closed system is always the same no matter how many physical changes or chemical reactions occur.

Law of Conservation of Energy

Energy can be neither created nor destroyed.

The total amount of energy in a closed system is always the same. Energy can be changed from one form to another, but all of the different forms of energy in a system always add up to the same total amount of energy, no matter how many energy conversions occur.

Law of Universal Gravitation

All objects in the universe attract each other by a force called gravity. The size of the force depends on the masses of the objects and the distance between the objects.

The first part of the law explains why lifting a bowling ball is much harder than lifting a marble. Because the bowling ball has a much larger mass than the marble does, the amount of gravity between Earth and the bowling ball is greater than the amount of gravity between Earth and the marble.

The second part of the law explains why a satellite can remain in orbit around Earth. The satellite is placed at a carefully calculated distance from Earth. This distance is great enough to keep Earth's gravity from pulling the satellite down, yet small enough to keep the satellite from escaping Earth's gravity and wandering off into space.

Newton's Laws of Motion

Newton's first law of motion states that an object at rest remains at rest, and an object in motion remains in motion at constant speed and in a straight line unless acted on by an unbalanced force.

The first part of the law explains why a football will remain on a tee until it is kicked off or until a gust of wind blows it off. The second part of the law explains why a bike rider will continue moving forward after the bike comes to an abrupt stop. Gravity and the friction of the sidewalk will eventually stop the rider.

Newton's second law of motion states that the acceleration of an object depends on the mass of the object and the amount of force applied.

The first part of the law explains why the acceleration of a 4 kg bowling ball will be greater than the acceleration of a 6 kg bowling ball if the same force is applied to both balls. The second part of the law explains why the acceleration of a bowling ball will be greater if a larger force is applied to the bowling ball. The relationship of acceleration (a) to mass (m) and force (F) can be expressed mathematically by the following equation:

$$acceleration = \frac{force}{mass}, \ or \ a = \frac{F}{m}$$

This equation is often rearranged to read $force = mass \times acceleration$, or $F = m \times a$

Newton's third law of motion states that whenever one object exerts a force on a second object, the second object exerts an equal and opposite force on the first.

This law explains that a runner is able to move forward because the ground exerts an equal and opposite force on the runner's foot after each step.

© Houghton Mifflin Harcourt Publishing Company

Average speed

$$average \ speed = \frac{total \ distance}{total \ time}$$

Example:
A bicycle messenger traveled a distance of 136 km in 8 h. What was the messenger's average speed?

$$\frac{136 \ km}{8 \ h} = 17 \ km/h$$

The messenger's average speed was **17 km/h.**

Average acceleration

$$average \ acceleration = \frac{final \ velocity - starting \ velocity}{time \ it \ takes \ to \ change \ velocity}$$

Example:
Calculate the average acceleration of an Olympic 100 m dash sprinter who reached a velocity of 20 m/s south at the finish line. The race was in a straight line and lasted 10 s.

$$\frac{20 \ m/s - 0 \ m/s}{10 \ s} = 2 \ m/s/s$$

The sprinter's average acceleration was **2 m/s/s south.**

Pressure

Pressure is the force exerted over a given area. The SI unit for pressure is the pascal. Its symbol is Pa.

$$pressure = \frac{force}{area}$$

Net force
Forces in the Same Direction

When forces are in the same direction, add the forces together to determine the net force.

Example:
Calculate the net force on a stalled car that is being pushed by two people. One person is pushing with a force of 13 N northwest, and the other person is pushing with a force of 8 N in the same direction.

$$13 \ N + 8 \ N = 21 \ N$$

The net force is **21 N northwest.**

Forces in Opposite Directions

When forces are in opposite directions, subtract the smaller force from the larger force to determine the net force. The net force will be in the direction of the larger force.

Example:
Calculate the net force on a rope that is being pulled on each end. One person is pulling on one end of the rope with a force of 12 N south. Another person is pulling on the opposite end of the rope with a force of 7 N north.

$$12 \ N - 7 \ N = 5 \ N$$

The net force is **5 N south.**

Example:
Calculate the pressure of the air in a soccer ball if the air exerts a force of 10 N over an area of 0.5 m².

$$pressure = \frac{10N}{0.5 \ m^2} = \frac{20N}{m^2} = 20 \ Pa$$

The pressure of the air inside the soccer ball is **20 Pa.**

© Houghton Mifflin Harcourt Publishing Company

A How-To Manual for Active Reading

This book belongs to you, and you are invited to write in it. In fact, the book won't be complete until you do. Sometimes you'll answer a question or follow directions to mark up the text. Other times you'll write down your own thoughts. And when you're done reading and writing in the book, the book will be ready to help you review what you learned and prepare for tests.

Active Reading Annotations

Before you read, you'll often come upon an Active Reading prompt that asks you to underline certain words or number the steps in a process. Here's an example.

Active Reading

12 Identify In this paragraph, number the sequence of sentences that describe replication.

Marking the text this way is called **annotating**, and your marks are called **annotations**. Annotating the text can help you identify important concepts while you read.

There are other ways that you can annotate the text. You can draw an asterisk (*) by vocabulary terms, mark unfamiliar or confusing terms and information with a question mark (?), and mark main ideas with a double underline. And you can even invent your own marks to annotate the text!

Other Annotating Opportunities

Keep your pencil, pen, or highlighter nearby as you read, so you can make a note or highlight an important point at any time. Here are a few ideas to get you started.

- Notice the headings in red and blue. The blue headings are questions that point to the main idea of what you're reading. The red headings are answers to the questions in the blue ones. Together these headings outline the content of the lesson. After reading a lesson, you could write your own answers to the questions.

- Notice the bold-faced words that are highlighted in yellow. They are highlighted so that you can easily find them again on the page where they are defined. As you read or as you review, challenge yourself to write your own sentence using the bold-faced term.

- Make a note in the margin at any time. You might
  - Ask a "What if" question
  - Comment on what you read
  - Make a connection to something you read elsewhere
  - Make a logical conclusion from the text

Use your own language and abbreviations. Invent a code, such as using circles and boxes around words to remind you of their importance or relation to each other. Your annotations will help you remember your questions for class discussions, and when you go back to the lesson later, you may be able to fill in what you didn't understand the first time you read it. Like a scientist in the field or in a lab, you will be recording your questions and observations for analysis later.

Active Reading Questions

After you read, you'll often come upon Active Reading questions that ask you to think about what you've just read. You'll write your answer underneath the question. Here's an example.

Active Reading

8 Describe Where are phosphate groups found in a DNA molecule?

This type of question helps you sum up what you've just read and pull out the most important ideas from the passage. In this case the question asks you to **describe** the structure of a DNA molecule that you have just read about. Other times you may be asked to do such things as **apply** a concept, **compare** two concepts, **summarize** a process, or **identify a cause-and-effect** relationship. You'll be strengthening those critical thinking skills that you'll use often in learning about science.

Reading and Study Skills

Using Graphic Organizers to Take Notes

Graphic organizers help you remember information as you read it for the first time and as you study it later. There are dozens of graphic organizers to choose from, so the first trick is to choose the one that's best suited to your purpose. Following are some graphic organizers to use for different purposes.

To remember lots of information	To relate a central idea to subordinate details	To describe a process	To make a comparison
• Arrange data in a Content Frame • Use Combination Notes to describe a concept in words and pictures	• Show relationships with a Mind Map or a Main Idea Web • Sum up relationships among many things with a Concept Map	• Use a Process Diagram to explain a procedure • Show a chain of events and results in a Cause-and-Effect Chart	• Compare two or more closely related things in a Venn Diagram

Content Frame

1 Make a four-column chart.

2 Fill the first column with categories (e.g., snail, ant, earthworm) and the first row with descriptive information (e.g., group, characteristic, appearance).

3 Fill the chart with details that belong in each row and column.

4 When you finish, you'll have a study aid that helps you compare one category to another.

Combination Notes

1 Make a two-column chart.

2 Write descriptive words and definitions in the first column.

3 Draw a simple sketch that helps you remember the meaning of the term in the second column.

Mind Map

1 Draw an oval, and inside it write a topic to analyze.

2 Draw two or more arms extending from the oval. Each arm represents a main idea about the topic.

3 Draw lines from the arms on which to write details about each of the main ideas.

Main Idea Web

1 Make a box and write a concept you want to remember inside it.

2 Draw boxes around the central box, and label each one with a category of information about the concept (e.g., definition, formula, descriptive details).

3 Fill in the boxes with relevant details as you read.

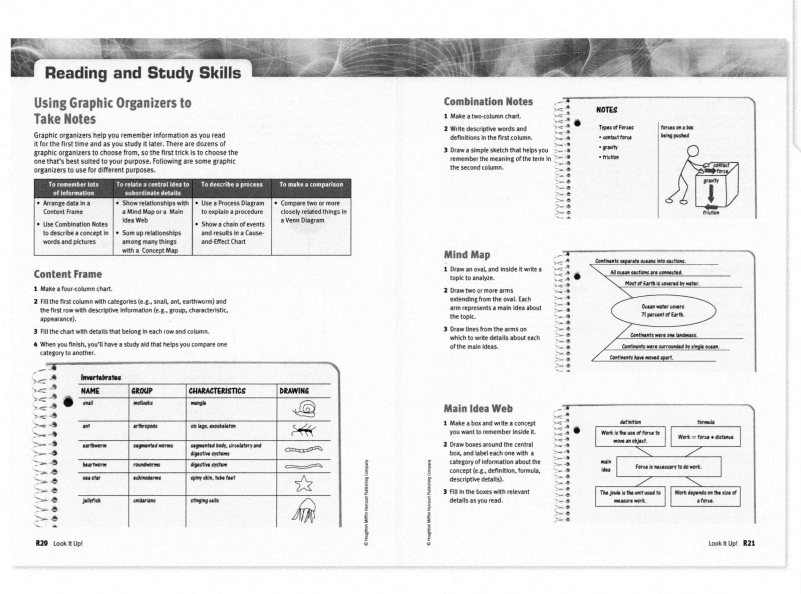

Reading and Study Skills

Concept Map

1 Draw a large oval, and inside it write a major concept.

2 Draw an arrow from the concept to a smaller oval, in which you write a related concept.

3 On the arrow, write a verb that connects the two concepts.

4 Continue in this way, adding ovals and arrows in a branching structure, until you have explained as much as you can about the main concept.

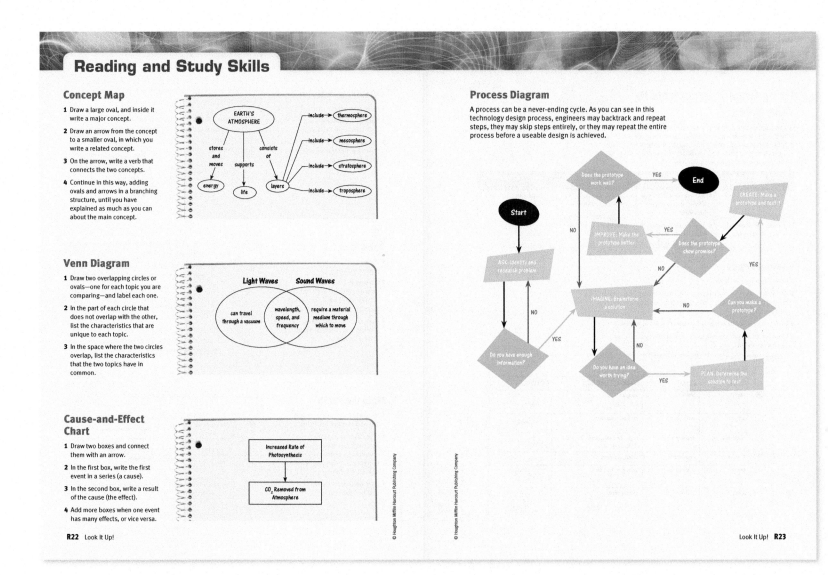

Venn Diagram

1 Draw two overlapping circles or ovals—one for each topic you are comparing—and label each one.

2 In the part of each circle that does not overlap with the other, list the characteristics that are unique to each topic.

3 In the space where the two circles overlap, list the characteristics that the two topics have in common.

Cause-and-Effect Chart

1 Draw two boxes and connect them with an arrow.

2 In the first box, write the first event in a series (a cause).

3 In the second box, write a result of the cause (the effect).

4 Add more boxes when one event has many effects, or vice versa.

Process Diagram

A process can be a never-ending cycle. As you can see in this technology design process, engineers may backtrack and repeat steps, they may skip steps entirely, or they may repeat the entire process before a useable design is achieved.

Reading and Study Skills

Using Vocabulary Strategies

Important science terms are highlighted where they are first defined in this book. One way to remember these terms is to take notes and make sketches when you come to them. Use the strategies on this page and the next for this purpose. You will also find a formal definition of each science term in the Glossary at the end of the book.

Description Wheel

1 Draw a small circle.

2 Write a vocabulary term inside the circle.

3 Draw several arms extending from the circle.

4 On the arms, write words and phrases that describe the term.

5 If you choose, add sketches that help you visualize the descriptive details or the concept as a whole.

Four Square

1 Draw a small oval and write a vocabulary term inside it.

2 Draw a large rectangle around the oval, and divide the rectangle into four smaller squares.

3 Label the smaller squares with categories of information about the term, such as: definition, characteristics, examples, non-examples, appearance, and root words.

4 Fill the squares with descriptive words and drawings that will help you remember the overall meaning of the term and its essential details.

Definition	Characteristics
any living thing	needs food, water, air; needs energy; grows, develops, reproduces
ORGANISM	
Examples	Non-Examples
dogs, cats, birds, insects, flowers, trees	rocks, water, dirt

Frame Game

1 Draw a small rectangle, and write a vocabulary term inside it.

2 Draw a larger rectangle around the smaller one. Connect the corners of the larger rectangle to the corners of the smaller one, creating four spaces that frame the word.

3 In each of the four parts of the frame, draw or write details that help define the term. Consider including a definition, essential characteristics, an equation, examples, and a sentence using the term.

Magnet Word

1 Draw horseshoe magnet, and write a vocabulary term inside it.

2 Add lines that extend from the sides of the magnet.

3 Brainstorm words and phrases that come to mind when you think about the term.

4 On the lines, write the words and phrases that describe something essential about the term.

Word Triangle

1 Draw a triangle, and add lines to divide it into three parts.

2 Write a term and its definition in the bottom section of the triangle.

3 In the middle section, write a sentence in which the term is used correctly.

4 In the top section, draw a small picture to illustrate the term.

© Houghton Mifflin Harcourt Publishing Company

Science Skills

Safety in the Lab

Before you begin work in the laboratory, read these safety rules twice. Before starting a lab activity, read all directions and make sure that you understand them. Do not begin until your teacher has told you to start. If you or another student are injured in any way, tell your teacher immediately.

Dress Code

Eye Protection

Hand Protection

Clothing Protection

- Wear safety goggles at all times in the lab as directed.
- If chemicals get into your eyes, flush your eyes immediately.
- Do not wear contact lenses in the lab.
- Do not look directly at the sun or any intense light source or laser.
- Do not cut an object while holding the object in your hand.
- Wear appropriate protective gloves as directed.
- Wear an apron or lab coat at all times in the lab as directed.
- Tie back long hair, secure loose clothing, and remove loose jewelry.
- Do not wear open-toed shoes, sandals, or canvas shoes in the lab.

Glassware and Sharp Object Safety

Glassware Safety

Sharp Objects Safety

- Do not use chipped or cracked glassware.
- Use heat-resistant glassware for heating or storing hot materials.
- Notify your teacher immediately if a piece of glass breaks.
- Use extreme care when handling all sharp and pointed instruments.
- Cut objects on a suitable surface, always in a direction away from your body.

Chemical Safety

Chemical Safety

- If a chemical gets on your skin, on your clothing, or in your eyes, rinse it immediately (shower, faucet or eyewash fountain) and alert your teacher.
- Do not clean up spilled chemicals unless your teacher directs you to do so.
- Do not inhale any gas or vapor unless directed to do so by your teacher.
- Handle materials that emit vapors or gases in a well-ventilated area.

Electrical Safety

Electrical Safety

- Do not use equipment with frayed electrical cords or loose plugs.
- Do not use electrical equipment near water or when clothing or hands are wet.
- Hold the plug housing when you plug in or unplug equipment.

Heating and Fire Safety

Heating Safety

- Be aware of any source of flames, sparks, or heat (such as flames, heating coils, or hot plates) before working with any flammable substances.
- Know the location of lab fire extinguishers and fire-safety blankets.
- Know your school's fire-evacuation routes.
- If your clothing catches on fire, walk to the lab shower to put out the fire.
- Never leave a hot plate unattended while it is turned on or while it is cooling.
- Use tongs or appropriate insulated holders when handling heated objects.
- Allow all equipment to cool before storing it.

Wafting

Plant and Animal Safety

Plant Safety

Animal Safety

- Do not eat any part of a plant.
- Do not pick any wild plants unless your teacher instructs you to do so.
- Handle animals only as your teacher directs.
- Treat animals carefully and respectfully.
- Wash your hands thoroughly after handling any plant or animal.

Cleanup

Proper Waste Disposal

Hygienic Care

- Clean all work surfaces and protective equipment as directed by your teacher.
- Dispose of hazardous materials or sharp objects only as directed by your teacher.
- Keep your hands away from your face while you are working on any activity.
- Wash your hands thoroughly before you leave the lab or after any activity.

Science Skills

Designing, Conducting, and Reporting an Experiment

An experiment is an organized procedure to study something under specific conditions. Use the following steps of the scientific method when designing or conducting a controlled experiment.

1 Identify a Research Problem

Every day, you make observations by using your senses to gather information. Careful observations lead to good questions, and good questions can lead you to an experiment. Imagine, for example, that you pass a pond every day on your way to school, and you notice green scum beginning to form on top of it. You wonder what it is and why it seems to be growing. You do a little research to find out what is already known. A good place to start a research project is at the library. A library catalog lists all of the resources available to you at that library and often those found elsewhere. Begin your search by using:

• keywords or main topics.

• similar words, or synonyms, of your keyword.

The types of resources that will be helpful to you will depend on the kind of information you are interested in. And, some resources are more reliable for a given topic than others. Some different kinds of useful resources are:

• magazines and journals (or periodicals)—articles on a topic.

• encyclopedias—a good overview of a topic.

• books on specific subjects—details about a topic.

• newspapers—useful for current events.

The Internet can also be a great place to find information. Some of your library's reference materials may even be online. When using the Internet, however, it is especially important to make sure you are using appropriate and reliable sources. Websites of universities and government agencies are usually more accurate and reliable than websites created by individuals or businesses. Decide which sources are relevant and reliable for your topic. If in doubt, check with your teacher.

Take notes as you read through the information in these resources. You will probably come up with many questions and ideas for which you can do more research as needed. Once you feel you have enough information, think about the questions you have on the topic. Then, write down the problem that you want to investigate. Your notes might look like these.

Research Questions	Research Problem	Library and Internet Resources
• How do algae grow? • How do people measure algae? • What kind of fertilizer would affect the growth of algae? • Can fertilizer and algae be used safely in a lab? How?	How does fertilizer affect the algae in a pond?	Pond fertilization: initiating an algal bloom – from University of California Davis website. Blue-Green algae in Wisconsin waters—from the Department of Natural Resources of Wisconsin website.

As you gather information from reliable sources, record details about each source, including author name(s), title, date of publication, and/or web address. Make sure to also note the specific information that you use from each source. Staying organized in this way will be important when you write your report and create a bibliography or works cited list. Recording this information and staying organized will help you credit the appropriate author(s) for the information that you have gathered.

Representing someone else's ideas or work as your own, (without giving the original author credit), is known as plagiarism. Plagiarism can be intentional or unintentional. The best way to make sure that you do not commit plagiarism is to always do your own work and to always give credit to others when you use their words or ideas.

Current scientific research is built on scientific research and discoveries that have happened in the past. This means that scientists are constantly learning from each other and combining ideas to learn more about the natural world through investigation. But, a good scientist always credits the ideas and research that they have gathered from other people to those people. There are more details about crediting sources and creating a bibliography under step 9.

2 Make a Prediction

A prediction is a statement of what you expect will happen in your experiment. Before making a prediction, you need to decide in a general way what you will do in your procedure. You may state your prediction in an if-then format.

Prediction

If the amount of fertilizer in the pond water is increased, then the amount of algae will also increase.

© Houghton Mifflin Harcourt Publishing Company

Science Skills

3 Form a Hypothesis

Many experiments are designed to test a hypothesis. A hypothesis is a tentative explanation for an expected result. You have predicted that additional fertilizer will cause additional algae growth in pond water; your hypothesis should state the connection between fertilizer and algal growth.

Hypothesis
- The addition of fertilizer to pond water will affect the amount of algae in the pond.

4 Identify Variables to Test the Hypothesis

The next step is to design an experiment to test the hypothesis. The experimental results may or may not support the hypothesis. Either way, the information that results from the experiment may be useful for future investigations.

Experimental Group and Control Group

An experiment to determine how two factors are related has a control group and an experimental group. The two groups are the same, except that the investigator changes a single factor in the experimental group and does not change it in the control group.

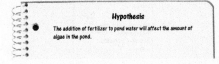

Experimental Group: two containers of pond water with one drop of fertilizer solution added to each

Control Group: two containers of the same pond water sampled at the same time but with no fertilizer solution added

Variables and Constants

In a controlled experiment, a variable is any factor that can change. Constants are all of the variables that are kept the same in both the experimental group and the control group.

The independent variable is the factor that is manipulated or changed in order to test the effect of the change on another variable. The dependent variable is the factor the investigator measures to gather data about the effect.

Independent Variable	Dependent Variable	Constants
Amount of fertilizer in pond water	Growth of algae in the pond water	• Where and when the pond water is obtained • The type of container used • Light and temperature conditions where the water is stored

R30 Look It Up!

© Houghton Mifflin Harcourt Publishing Company

5 Write a Procedure

Write each step of your procedure. Start each step with a verb, or action word, and keep the steps short. Your procedure should be clear enough for someone else to use as instructions for repeating your experiment.

Procedure
1. Use the masking tape and the marker to label the containers with your initials, the date, and the identifiers "Jar 1 with Fertilizer," "Jar 2 with Fertilizer," "Jar 1 without Fertilizer," and "Jar 2 without Fertilizer."
2. Put on your gloves. Use the large container to obtain a sample of pond water.
3. Divide the water sample equally among the four smaller containers.
4. Use the eyedropper to add one drop of fertilizer solution to the two containers labeled, "Jar 1 with Fertilizer," and "Jar 2 with Fertilizer".
5. Cover the containers with clear plastic wrap. Use the scissors to punch ten holes in each of the covers.
6. Place all four containers on a window ledge. Make sure that they all receive the same amount of light.
7. Observe the containers every day for one week.
8. Use the ruler to measure the diameter of the largest clump of algae in each container, and record your measurements daily.

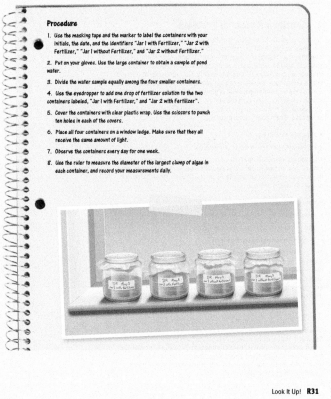

© Houghton Mifflin Harcourt Publishing Company

Look It Up! R31

Science Skills

6 Experiment and Collect Data

Once you have all of your materials and your procedure has been approved, you can begin to experiment and collect data. Record both quantitative data (measurements) and qualitative data (observations), as shown below.

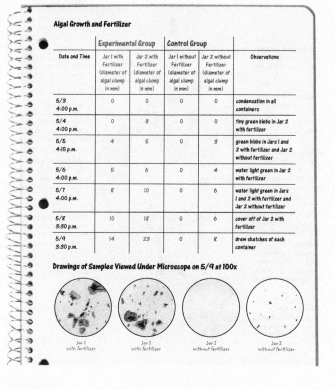

Algal Growth and Fertilizer

Date and Time	Experimental Group		Control Group		Observations
	Jar 1 with Fertilizer (diameter of algal clump in mm)	Jar 2 with Fertilizer (diameter of algal clump in mm)	Jar 1 without Fertilizer (diameter of algal clump in mm)	Jar 2 without Fertilizer (diameter of algal clump in mm)	
5/3 4:00 p.m.	0	0	0	0	condensation in all containers
5/4 4:00 p.m.	0	3	0	0	tiny green blobs in Jar 2 with fertilizer
5/5 4:15 p.m.	4	5	0	3	green blobs in Jars 1 and 2 with fertilizer and Jar 2 without fertilizer
5/6 4:00 p.m.	5	6	0	4	water light green in Jar 2 with fertilizer
5/7 4:00 p.m.	8	10	0	6	water light green in Jars 1 and 2 with fertilizer and Jar 2 without fertilizer
5/8 3:30 p.m.	10	18	0	6	cover off of Jar 2 with fertilizer
5/9 3:30 p.m.	14	23	0	8	drew sketches of each container

Drawings of Samples Viewed Under Microscope on 5/9 at 100x

Jar 1 with Fertilizer   Jar 2 with Fertilizer   Jar 1 without Fertilizer   Jar 2 without Fertilizer

© Houghton Mifflin Harcourt Publishing Company

7 Analyze Data

After you complete your experiment, you must analyze all of the data you have gathered. Tables, statistics, and graphs are often used in this step to organize and analyze both the qualitative and quantitative data. Sometimes, your qualitative data are best used to help explain the relationships you see in your quantitative data.

Computer graphing software is useful for creating a graph from data that you have collected. Most graphing software can make line graphs, pie charts, or bar graphs from data that has been organized in a spreadsheet. Graphs are useful for understanding relationships in the data and for communicating the results of your experiment.

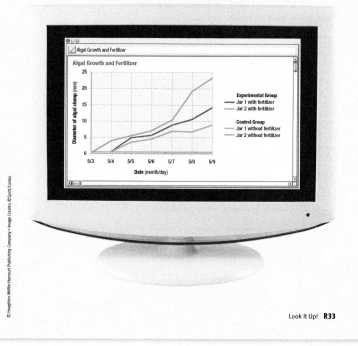

© Houghton Mifflin Harcourt Publishing Company • Image Credits: ©Spirit/Corbis

Science Skills

8 Make Conclusions

To draw conclusions from your experiment, first, write your results. Then, compare your results with your hypothesis. Do your results support your hypothesis? What have you learned?

Conclusion

More algae grew in the pond water to which fertilizer had been added than in the pond water to which fertilizer had not been added. My hypothesis was supported. I conclude that it is possible that the growth of algae in ponds can be influenced by the input of fertilizer.

9 Create a Bibliography or Works Cited List

To complete your report, you must also show all of the newspapers, magazines, journals, books, and online sources that you used at every stage of your investigation. Whenever you find useful information about your topic, you should write down the source of that information. Writing down as much information as you can about the subject can help you or someone else find the source again. You should at least record the author's name, the title, the date and where the source was published, and the pages in which the information was found. Then, organize your sources into a list, which you can title Bibliography or Works Cited.

Usually, at least three sources are included in these lists. Sources are listed alphabetically, by the authors' last names. The exact format of a bibliography can vary, depending on the style preferences of your teacher, school, or publisher. Also, books are cited differently than journals or websites. Below is an example of how different kinds of sources may be formatted in a bibliography.

BOOK: Hauschultz, Sara. Freshwater Algae. Brainard, Minnesota: Northwoods Publishing, 2011.

ENCYCLOPEDIA: Lasure, Sedona. "Algae is not all just pond scum." Encyclopedia of Algae. 2009.

JOURNAL: Johnson, Keagan. "Algae as we know it." Sci Journal, vol 64. (September 2010): 201-211.

WEBSITE: Dout, Bill. "Keeping algae scum out of birdbaths." Help Keep Earth Clean. News. January 26, 2011. <www.SaveEarth.org>.

Using a Microscope

Scientists use microscopes to see very small objects that cannot easily be seen with the eye alone. A microscope magnifies the image of an object so that small details may be observed. A microscope that you may use can magnify an object 400 times—the object will appear 400 times larger than its actual size.

Body The body separates the lens in the eyepiece from the objective lenses below.

Nosepiece The nosepiece holds the objective lenses above the stage and rotates so that all lenses may be used.

High-Power Objective Lens This is the largest lens on the nosepiece. It magnifies an image approximately 40 times.

Stage The stage supports the object being viewed.

Diaphragm The diaphragm is used to adjust the amount of light passing through the slide and into an objective lens.

Mirror or Light Source Some microscopes use light that is reflected through the stage by a mirror. Other microscopes have their own light sources.

Eyepiece Objects are viewed through the eyepiece. The eyepiece contains a lens that commonly magnifies an image ten times.

Coarse Adjustment This knob is used to focus the image of an object when it is viewed through the low-power lens.

Fine Adjustment This knob is used to focus the image of an object when it is viewed through the high-power lens.

Low-Power Objective Lens This is the smallest lens on the nosepiece. It magnifies images about 10 times.

Arm The arm supports the body above the stage. Always carry a microscope by the arm and base.

Stage Clip The stage clip holds a slide in place on the stage.

Base The base supports the microscope.

Science Skills

Measuring Accurately

Precision and Accuracy

When you do a scientific investigation, it is important that your methods, observations, and data be both precise and accurate.

Low precision: The darts did not land in a consistent place on the dartboard.

Precision, but not accuracy: The darts landed in a consistent place, but did not hit the bull's eye.

Prescision and accuracy: The darts landed consistently on the bull's eye.

Precision

In science, *precision* is the exactness and consistency of measurements. For example, measurements made with a ruler that has both centimeter and millimeter markings would be more precise than measurements made with a ruler that has only centimeter markings. Another indicator of precision is the care taken to make sure that methods and observations are as exact and consistent as possible. Every time a particular experiment is done, the same procedure should be used. Precision is necessary because experiments are repeated several times and if the procedure changes, the results might change.

Example

Suppose you are measuring temperatures over a two-week period. Your precision will be greater if you measure each temperature at the same place, at the same time of day, and with the same thermometer than if you change any of these factors from one day to the next.

Accuracy

In science, it is possible to be precise but not accurate. *Accuracy* depends on the difference between a measurement and an actual value. The smaller the difference, the more accurate the measurement.

Example

Suppose you look at a stream and estimate that it is about 1 meter wide at a particular place. You decide to check your estimate by measuring the stream with a meter stick, and you determine that the stream is 1.32 meters wide. However, because it is difficult to measure the width of a stream with a meter stick, it turns out that your measurement was not very accurate. The stream is actually 1.14 meters wide. Therefore, even though your estimate of about 1 meter was less precise than your measurement, your estimate was actually more accurate.

Graduated Cylinders

How to Measure the Volume of a Liquid with a Graduated Cylinder

- Be sure that the graduated cylinder is on a flat surface so that your measurement will be accurate.

- When reading the scale on a graduated cylinder, be sure to have your eyes at the level of the surface of the liquid.

- The surface of the liquid will be curved in the graduated cylinder. Read the volume of the liquid at the bottom of the curve, or meniscus (muh-NIHS-kuhs).

- You can use a graduated cylinder to find the volume of a solid object by measuring the increase in a liquid's level after you add the object to the cylinder.

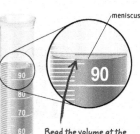

meniscus

Read the volume at the bottom of the meniscus. The volume is 96 mL.

Metric Rulers

How to Measure the Length of a Leaf with a Metric Ruler

1 Lay a ruler flat on top of the leaf so that the 1-centimeter mark lines up with one end. Make sure the ruler and the leaf do not move between the time you line them up and the time you take the measurement.

2 Look straight down on the ruler so that you can see exactly how the marks line up with the other end of the leaf.

3 Estimate the length by which the leaf extends beyond a marking. For example, the leaf below extends about halfway between the 4.2-centimeter and 4.3-centimeter marks, so the apparent measurement is about 4.25 centimeters.

4 Remember to subtract 1 centimeter from your apparent measurement, since you started at the 1-centimeter mark on the ruler and not at the end. The leaf is about 3.25 centimeters long (4.25 cm − 1 cm = 3.25 cm).

Triple Beam Balance

This balance has a pan and three beams with sliding masses, called riders. At one end of the beams is a pointer that indicates whether the mass on the pan is equal to the masses shown on the beams.

How to Measure the Mass of an Object

1 Make sure the balance is zeroed before measuring the mass of an object. The balance is zeroed if the pointer is at zero when nothing is on the pan and the riders are at their zero points. Use the adjustment knob at the base of the balance to zero it.

2 Place the object to be measured on the pan.

3 Move the riders one notch at a time away from the pan. Begin with the largest rider. If moving the largest rider one notch brings the pointer below zero, begin measuring the mass of the object with the next smaller rider.

4 Change the positions of the riders until they balance the mass on the pan and the pointer is at zero. Then add the readings from the three beams to determine the mass of the object.

300 g	position of largest rider
90 g	position of middle rider
+ 3 g	position of smallest rider
393 g	mass of beaker and water

pan

largest rider (300 g)

middle rider (90 g)

beams

smallest rider (3 g)

Using the Metric System and SI Units

Scientists use International System (SI) units for measurements of distance, volume, mass, and temperature. The International System is based on powers of ten and the metric system of measurement.

Basic SI Units		
Quantity	Name	Symbol
length	meter	m
volume	liter	L
mass	gram	g
temperature	kelvin	K

SI Prefixes		
Prefix	Symbol	Power of 10
kilo-	k	1000
hecto-	h	100
deca-	da	10
deci-	d	0.1 or $\frac{1}{10}$
centi-	c	0.01 or $\frac{1}{100}$
milli-	m	0.001 or $\frac{1}{1000}$

Changing Metric Units

You can change from one unit to another in the metric system by multiplying or dividing by a power of 10.

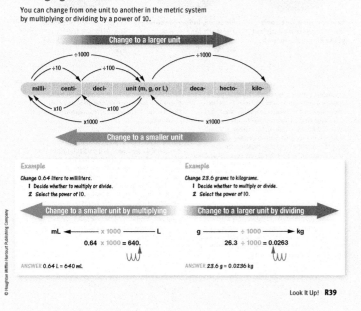

Change to a larger unit

÷1000 ÷1000
÷10 ÷100

milli- centi- deci- unit (m, g, or L) deca- hecto- kilo-

x10 x100
x1000 x1000

Change to a smaller unit

Example

Change 0.64 liters to milliliters.
1 Decide whether to multiply or divide.
2 Select the power of 10.

Change to a smaller unit by multiplying

mL ◄——— x 1000 ——— L

0.64 x 1000 = 640.

ANSWER 0.64 L = 640 mL

Example

Change 23.6 grams to kilograms.
1 Decide whether to multiply or divide.
2 Select the power of 10.

Change to a larger unit by dividing

g ——— ÷ 1000 ——► kg

26.3 ÷ 1000 = 0.0263

ANSWER 23.6 g = 0.0236 kg

Science Skills

Converting Between SI and U.S. Customary Units

Use the chart below when you need to convert between SI units and U.S. customary units.

SI Unit	From SI to U.S. Customary			From U.S. Customary to SI		
Length	When you know	multiply by	to find	When you know	multiply by	to find
kilometer (km) = 1000 m	kilometers	0.62	miles	miles	1.61	kilometers
meter (m) = 100 cm	meters	3.28	feet	feet	0.3048	meters
centimeter (cm) = 10 mm	centimeters	0.39	inches	inches	2.54	centimeters
millimeter (mm) = 0.1 cm	millimeters	0.04	inches	inches	25.4	millimeters
Area	When you know	multiply by	to find	When you know	multiply by	to find
square kilometer (km²)	square kilometers	0.39	square miles	square miles	2.59	square kilometers
square meter (m²)	square meters	1.2	square yards	square yards	0.84	square meters
square centimeter (cm²)	square centimeters	0.155	square inches	square inches	6.45	square centimeters
Volume	When you know	multiply by	to find	When you know	multiply by	to find
liter (L) = 1000 mL	liters	1.06	quarts	quarts	0.95	liters
	liters	0.26	gallons	gallons	3.79	liters
	liters	4.23	cups	cups	0.24	liters
	liters	2.12	pints	pints	0.47	liters
milliliter (mL) = 0.001 L	milliliters	0.20	teaspoons	teaspoons	4.93	milliliters
	milliliters	0.07	tablespoons	tablespoons	14.79	milliliters
	milliliters	0.03	fluid ounces	fluid ounces	29.57	milliliters
Mass	When you know	multiply by	to find	When you know	multiply by	to find
kilogram (kg) = 1000 g	kilograms	2.2	pounds	pounds	0.45	kilograms
gram (g) = 1000 mg	grams	0.035	ounces	ounces	28.35	grams

Temperature Conversions

Even though the kelvin is the SI base unit of temperature, the degree Celsius will be the unit you use most often in your science studies. The formulas below show the relationships between temperatures in degrees Fahrenheit (°F), degrees Celsius (°C), and kelvins (K).

$$°C = \frac{5}{9} (°F - 32) \qquad °F = \frac{9}{5} °C + 32 \qquad K = °C + 273$$

Examples of Temperature Conversions		
Condition	**Degrees Celsius**	**Degrees Fahrenheit**
Freezing point of water	0	32
Cool day	10	50
Mild day	20	68
Warm day	30	86
Normal body temperature	37	98.6
Very hot day	40	104
Boiling point of water	100	212

Math Refresher

Performing Calculations

Science requires an understanding of many math concepts. The following pages will help you review some important math skills.

Mean

The mean is the sum of all values in a data set divided by the total number of values in the data set. The mean is also called the *average*.

Example

Find the mean of the following set of numbers: 5, 4, 7, and 8.

Step 1   Find the sum.

   5 + 4 + 7 + 8 = 24

Step 2   Divide the sum by the number of numbers in your set. Because there are four numbers in this example, divide the sum by 4.

   24 ÷ 4 = 6

Answer   The average, or mean, is 6.

Median

The median of a data set is the middle value when the values are written in numerical order. If a data set has an even number of values, the median is the mean of the two middle values.

Example

To find the median of a set of measurements, arrange the values in order from least to greatest. The median is the middle value.

   13 mm   14 mm   16 mm   21 mm   23 mm

Answer   The median is 16 mm.

Mode

The mode of a data set is the value that occurs most often.

Example

To find the mode of a set of measurements, arrange the values in order from least to greatest and determine the value that occurs most often.

   13 mm, 14 mm, 14 mm, 16 mm,
   21 mm, 23 mm, 25 mm

Answer   The mode is 14 mm.

A data set can have more than one mode or no mode. For example, the following data set has modes of 2 mm and 4 mm:

   2 mm   2 mm   3 mm   4 mm   4 mm

The data set below has no mode, because no value occurs more often than any other.

   2 mm   3 mm   4 mm   5 mm

Math Refresher

Ratios

A **ratio** is a comparison between numbers, and it is usually written as a fraction.

Example

Find the ratio of thermometers to students if you have 36 thermometers and 48 students in your class.

Step 1   Write the ratio.

$$\frac{36 \text{ thermometers}}{48 \text{ students}}$$

Step 2   Simplify the fraction to its simplest form.

$$\frac{36}{48} = \frac{36 \div 12}{48 \div 12} = \frac{3}{4}$$

The ratio of thermometers to students is 3 to 4 or 3:4.

Proportions

A **proportion** is an equation that states that two ratios are equal.

$$\frac{3}{1} = \frac{12}{4}$$

To solve a proportion, you can use cross-multiplication. If you know three of the quantities in a proportion, you can use cross-multiplication to find the fourth.

Example

Imagine that you are making a scale model of the solar system for your science project. The diameter of Jupiter is 11.2 times the diameter of the Earth. If you are using a plastic-foam ball that has a diameter of 2 cm to represent the Earth, what must the diameter of the ball representing Jupiter be?

$$\frac{11.2}{1} = \frac{x}{2 \text{ cm}}$$

Step 1   Cross-multiply.

$$\frac{11.2}{1} = \frac{x}{2}$$

$$11.2 \times 2 = x \times 1$$

Step 2   Multiply.

$$22.4 = x \times 1$$

$$x = 22.4 \text{ cm}$$

You will need to use a ball that has a diameter of 22.4 cm to represent Jupiter.

Rates

A **rate** is a ratio of two values expressed in different units. A unit rate is a rate with a denominator of 1 unit.

Example

A plant grew 6 centimeters in 2 days. The plant's rate of growth was $\frac{6 \text{ cm}}{2 \text{ days}}$.

To describe the plant's growth in centimeters per day, write a unit rate.

Divide numerator and denominator by 2:

$$\frac{6 \text{ cm}}{2 \text{ days}} = \frac{6 \text{ cm} \div 2}{2 \text{ days} \div 2}$$

Simplify: $= \frac{3 \text{ cm}}{1 \text{ day}}$

Answer   The plant's rate of growth is 3 centimeters per day.

Percent

A **percent** is a ratio of a given number to 100. For example, 85% = 85/100. You can use percent to find part of a whole.

Example

What is 85% of 40?

Step 1   Rewrite the percent as a decimal by moving the decimal point two places to the left.

$$0.85$$

Step 2   Multiply the decimal by the number that you are calculating the percentage of.

$$0.85 \times 40 = 34$$

85% of 40 is 34.

Decimals

To **add** or **subtract decimals**, line up the digits vertically so that the decimal points line up. Then, add or subtract the columns from right to left. Carry or borrow numbers as necessary.

Example

Add the following numbers: 3.1415 and 2.96.

Step 1   Line up the digits vertically so that the decimal points line up.

$$\begin{array}{r} 3.1415 \\ + \ 2.96 \\ \hline \end{array}$$

Step 2   Add the columns from right to left, and carry when necessary.

$$\begin{array}{r} 3.1415 \\ + \ 2.96 \\ \hline 6.1015 \end{array}$$

The sum is 6.1015.

Fractions

A **fraction** is a ratio of two nonzero whole numbers.

Example

Your class has 24 plants. Your teacher instructs you to put 5 plants in a shady spot. What fraction of the plants in your class will you put in a shady spot?

Step 1   In the denominator, write the total number of parts in the whole.

$$\frac{?}{24}$$

Step 2   In the numerator, write the number of parts of the whole that are being considered.

$$\frac{5}{24}$$

So, $\frac{5}{24}$ of the plants will be in the shade.

Math Refresher

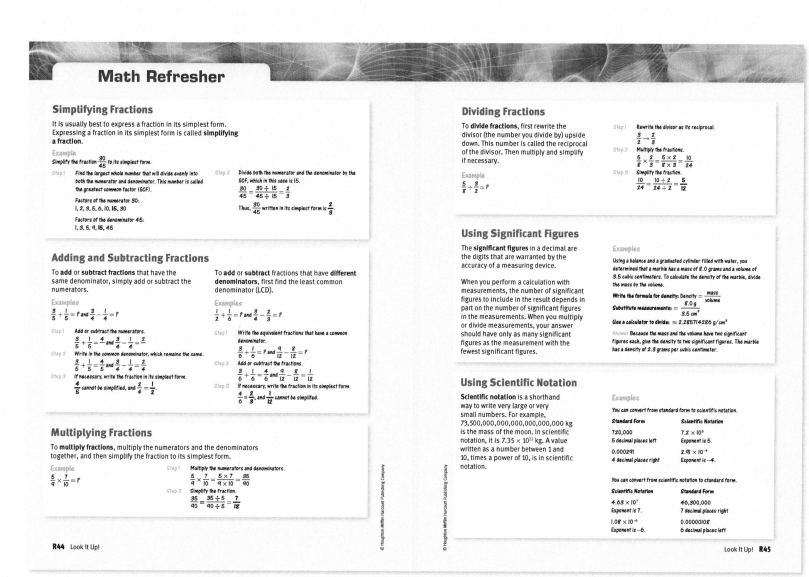

Simplifying Fractions

It is usually best to express a fraction in its simplest form. Expressing a fraction in its simplest form is called **simplifying a fraction**.

Example

Simplify the fraction $\frac{30}{45}$ to its simplest form.

Step 1 Find the largest whole number that will divide evenly into both the numerator and denominator. This number is called the greatest common factor (GCF).

Factors of the numerator 30:
1, 2, 3, 5, 6, 10, 15, 30

Factors of the denominator 45:
1, 3, 5, 9, 15, 45

Step 2 Divide both the numerator and the denominator by the GCF, which in this case is 15.
$$\frac{30}{45} = \frac{30 \div 15}{45 \div 15} = \frac{2}{3}$$

Thus, $\frac{30}{45}$ written in its simplest form is $\frac{2}{3}$.

Adding and Subtracting Fractions

To **add** or **subtract fractions** that have the same denominator, simply add or subtract the numerators.

Examples

$\frac{3}{5} + \frac{1}{5} = ?$ and $\frac{3}{4} - \frac{1}{4} = ?$

Step 1 Add or subtract the numerators.
$\frac{3}{5} + \frac{1}{5} = \frac{4}{5}$ and $\frac{3}{4} - \frac{1}{4} = \frac{2}{4}$

Step 2 Write in the common denominator, which remains the same.
$\frac{3}{5} + \frac{1}{5} = \frac{4}{5}$ and $\frac{3}{4} - \frac{1}{4} = \frac{2}{4}$

Step 3 If necessary, write the fraction in its simplest form.
$\frac{4}{5}$ cannot be simplified, and $\frac{2}{4} = \frac{1}{2}$.

To **add** or **subtract** fractions that have **different denominators**, first find the least common denominator (LCD).

Examples

$\frac{1}{2} + \frac{1}{6} = ?$ and $\frac{3}{4} - \frac{2}{6} = ?$

Step 1 Write the equivalent fractions that have a common denominator.
$\frac{3}{6} + \frac{1}{6} = ?$ and $\frac{9}{12} - \frac{8}{12} = ?$

Step 2 Add or subtract the fractions.
$\frac{3}{6} + \frac{1}{6} = \frac{4}{6}$ and $\frac{9}{12} - \frac{8}{12} = \frac{1}{12}$

Step 3 If necessary, write the fraction in its simplest form.
$\frac{4}{6} = \frac{2}{3}$, and $\frac{1}{12}$ cannot be simplified.

Multiplying Fractions

To **multiply fractions**, multiply the numerators and the denominators together, and then simplify the fraction to its simplest form.

Example

$\frac{5}{9} \times \frac{7}{10} = ?$

Step 1 Multiply the numerators and denominators.
$\frac{5}{9} \times \frac{7}{10} = \frac{5 \times 7}{9 \times 10} = \frac{35}{90}$

Step 2 Simplify the fraction.
$\frac{35}{90} = \frac{35 \div 5}{90 \div 5} = \frac{7}{18}$

Dividing Fractions

To **divide fractions**, first rewrite the divisor (the number you divide by) upside down. This number is called the reciprocal of the divisor. Then multiply and simplify if necessary.

Example

$\frac{5}{8} \div \frac{3}{2} = ?$

Step 1 Rewrite the divisor as its reciprocal.
$\frac{3}{2} \rightarrow \frac{2}{3}$

Step 2 Multiply the fractions.
$\frac{5}{8} \times \frac{2}{3} = \frac{5 \times 2}{8 \times 3} = \frac{10}{24}$

Step 3 Simplify the fraction.
$\frac{10}{24} = \frac{10 \div 2}{24 \div 2} = \frac{5}{12}$

Using Significant Figures

The **significant figures** in a decimal are the digits that are warranted by the accuracy of a measuring device.

When you perform a calculation with measurements, the number of significant figures to include in the result depends in part on the number of significant figures in the measurements. When you multiply or divide measurements, your answer should have only as many significant figures as the measurement with the fewest significant figures.

Examples

Using a balance and a graduated cylinder filled with water, you determined that a marble has a mass of 8.0 grams and a volume of 3.5 cubic centimeters. To calculate the density of the marble, divide the mass by the volume.

Write the formula for density: Density $= \frac{mass}{volume}$

Substitute measurements: $= \frac{8.0\,g}{3.5\,cm^3}$

Use a calculator to divide: $\approx 2.285714286\,g/cm^3$

Answer Because the mass and the volume have two significant figures each, give the density to two significant figures. The marble has a density of 2.3 grams per cubic centimeter.

Using Scientific Notation

Scientific notation is a shorthand way to write very large or very small numbers. For example, 73,500,000,000,000,000,000,000 kg is the mass of the moon. In scientific notation, it is 7.35×10^{22} kg. A value written as a number between 1 and 10, times a power of 10, is in scientific notation.

Examples

You can convert from standard form to scientific notation.

Standard Form	Scientific Notation
720,000	7.2×10^5
5 decimal places left	Exponent is 5.
0.000291	2.91×10^{-4}
4 decimal places right	Exponent is -4.

You can convert from scientific notation to standard form.

Scientific Notation	Standard Form
4.63×10^7	46,300,000
Exponent is 7.	7 decimal places right
1.08×10^{-6}	0.00000108
Exponent is -6.	6 decimal places left

Math Refresher

Making and Interpreting Graphs

Circle Graph

A circle graph, or pie chart, shows how each group of data relates to all of the data. Each part of the circle represents a category of the data. The entire circle represents all of the data. For example, a biologist studying a hardwood forest in Wisconsin found that there were five different types of trees. The data table at right summarizes the biologist's findings.

Wisconsin Hardwood Trees	
Type of tree	Number found
Oak	600
Maple	750
Beech	300
Birch	1,200
Hickory	150
Total	3,000

How to Make a Circle Graph

1 To make a circle graph of these data, first find the percentage of each type of tree. Divide the number of trees of each type by the total number of trees, and multiply by 100%.

$$\frac{600 \text{ oak}}{3,000 \text{ trees}} \times 100\% = 20\%$$

$$\frac{750 \text{ maple}}{3,000 \text{ trees}} \times 100\% = 25\%$$

$$\frac{300 \text{ beech}}{3,000 \text{ trees}} \times 100\% = 10\%$$

$$\frac{1,200 \text{ birch}}{3,000 \text{ trees}} \times 100\% = 40\%$$

$$\frac{150 \text{ hickory}}{3,000 \text{ trees}} \times 100\% = 5\%$$

2 Now, determine the size of the wedges that make up the graph. Multiply each percentage by 360°. Remember that a circle contains 360°.

$$20\% \times 360° = 72° \qquad 25\% \times 360° = 90°$$

$$10\% \times 360° = 36° \qquad 40\% \times 360° = 144°$$

$$5\% \times 360° = 18°$$

3 Check that the sum of the percentages is 100 and the sum of the degrees is 360.

$$20\% + 25\% + 10\% + 40\% + 5\% = 100\%$$

$$72° + 90° + 36° + 144° + 18° = 360°$$

4 Use a compass to draw a circle and mark the center of the circle.

5 Then, use a protractor to draw angles of 72°, 90°, 36°, 144°, and 18° in the circle.

6 Finally, label each part of the graph, and choose an appropriate title.

A Community of Wisconsin Hardwood Trees

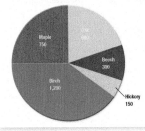

Line Graphs

Line graphs are most often used to demonstrate continuous change. For example, Mr. Smith's students analyzed the population records for their hometown, Appleton, between 1910 and 2010. Examine the data at right.

Because the year and the population change, they are the variables. The population is determined by, or dependent on, the year. Therefore, the population is called the **dependent variable,** and the year is called the **independent variable.** Each year and its population make a **data pair**. To prepare a line graph, you must first organize data pairs into a table like the one at right.

Population of Appleton, 1910–2010	
Year	Population
1910	1,800
1930	2,500
1950	3,200
1970	3,900
1990	4,600
2010	5,300

How to Make a Line Graph

1 Place the independent variable along the horizontal (x) axis. Place the dependent variable along the vertical (y) axis.

2 Label the x-axis "Year" and the y-axis "Population." Look at your greatest and least values for the population. For the y-axis, determine a scale that will provide enough space to show these values. You must use the same scale for the entire length of the axis. Next, find an appropriate scale for the x-axis.

3 Choose reasonable starting points for each axis.

4 Plot the data pairs as accurately as possible.

5 Choose a title that accurately represents the data.

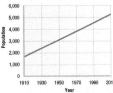

Population of Appleton, 1910–2010

How to Determine Slope

Slope is the ratio of the change in the y-value to the change in the x-value, or "rise over run."

1 Choose two points on the line graph. For example, the population of Appleton in 2010 was 5,300 people. Therefore, you can define point A as (2010, 5,300). In 1910, the population was 1,800 people. You can define point B as (1910, 1,800).

2 Find the change in the y-value. (y at point A) − (y at point B) = 5,300 people − 1,800 people = 3,500 people

3 Find the change in the x-value. (x at point A) − (x at point B) = 2010 − 1910 = 100 years

4 Calculate the slope of the graph by dividing the change in y by the change in x.

$$slope = \frac{change \ in \ y}{change \ in \ x}$$

$$slope = \frac{3,500 \text{ people}}{100 \text{ years}}$$

$$slope = 35 \text{ people per year}$$

In this example, the population in Appleton increased by a fixed amount each year. The graph of these data is a straight line. Therefore, the relationship is **linear**. When the graph of a set of data is not a straight line, the relationship is **nonlinear**.

Math Refresher

Bar Graphs

Bar graphs can be used to demonstrate change that is not continuous. These graphs can be used to indicate trends when the data cover a long period of time. A meteorologist gathered the precipitation data shown here for Summerville for April 1–15 and used a bar graph to represent the data.

Precipitation in Summerville, April 1–15			
Date	Precipitation (cm)	Date	Precipitation (cm)
April 1	0.5	April 9	0.25
April 2	1.25	April 10	0.0
April 3	0.0	April 11	1.0
April 4	0.0	April 12	0.0
April 5	0.0	April 13	0.25
April 6	0.0	April 14	0.0
April 7	0.0	April 15	6.50
April 8	1.75		

How to Make a Bar Graph

1 Use an appropriate scale and a reasonable starting point for each axis.

2 Label the axes, and plot the data.

3 Choose a title that accurately represents the data.

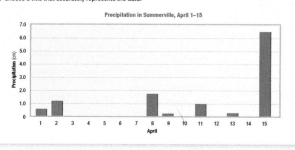
Precipitation in Summerville, April 1–15

Glossary

Pronunciation Key							
Sound	Symbol	Example	Respelling	Sound	Symbol	Example	Respelling
ă	a	pat	PAT	ŏ	ah	bottle	BAHT'l
ā	ay	pay	PAY	ō	oh	toe	TOH
âr	air	care	KAIR	ô	aw	caught	KAWT
ä	ah	father	FAH•ther	ôr	ohr	roar	ROHR
är	ar	argue	AR•gyoo	oi	oy	noisy	NOYZ•ee
ch	ch	chase	CHAYS	ŏŏ	u	book	BUK
ĕ	e	pet	PET	ōō	oo	boot	BOOT
ĕ (at end of a syllable)	eh	settee lessee	seh•TEE leh•SEE	ou	ow	pound	POWND
ĕr	ehr	merry	MEHR•ee	s	s	center	SEN•ter
ē	ee	beach	BEECH	sh	sh	cache	CASH
g	g	gas	GAS	ŭ	uh	flood	FLUHD
ĭ	i	pit	PIT	ûr	er	bird	BERD
ĭ (at end of a syllable)	ih	guitar	gih•TAR	z	z	xylophone	ZY•luh•fohn
ī	y eye (only for a complete syllable)	pie island	PY EYE•luhnd	z	z	bags	BAGZ
				zh	zh	decision	dih•SIZH•uhn
îr	ir	hear	HIR	ə	uh	around broken focus	uh•ROWND BROH•kuhn FOH•kuhs
j	j	germ	JERM	ər	er	winner	WIN•er
k	k	kick	KIK	th	th	thin they	THIN THAY
ng	ng	thing	THING	w	w	one	WUHN
ngk	ngk	bank	BANGK	wh	hw	whether	HWETH•er

Glossary

A

acceleration (ak·sel·uh·RAY·shuhn) the rate at which velocity changes over time; an object accelerates if its speed, direction, or both change (22)
aceleración la tasa a la que la velocidad cambia con el tiempo; un objeto acelera si su rapidez cambia, si su dirección cambia, o si tanto su rapidez como su dirección cambian

analog signal (AN·uh·lawg SIG·nuhl) a signal whose properties can change continuously in a given range (187)
señal análoga una señal cuyas propiedades cambian continuamente en un rango determinado

Archimedes' principle (ar·kuh·MEE·deez PRIN·suh·puhl) the principle that states that the buoyant force on an object in a fluid is an upward force equal to the weight of the volume of fluid that the object displaces (62)
principio de Arquímedes el principio que establece que la fuerza flotante de un objeto que está en un fluido es una fuerza ascendente cuya magnitud es igual al peso del volumen del fluido que el objeto desplaza

atmospheric pressure (at·muh·SFIR·ik PRESH·er) the pressure caused by the weight of the atmosphere (58)
presión atmosférica la presión producida por el peso de la atmósfera

B

buoyant force (BOY·uhnt FOHRS) the upward force that keeps an object immersed in or floating on a liquid (62)
fuerza boyante la fuerza ascendente que hace que un objeto se mantenga sumergido en un líquido o flotando en él

C

centripetal acceleration (sen·TRIP·ih·tl ak·sel·uh·RAY·shuhn) the acceleration directed toward the center of a circular path (25)
aceleración centrípeta la aceleración que se dirige hacia el centro de un camino circular

computer (kuhm·PYOO·ter) an electronic device that can accept data and instructions, follow the instructions, and output the results (190)
computadora un aparato electrónico que acepta información e instrucciones, sigue instrucciones, y produce una salida para los resultados

D

digital signal (DIJ·ih·tl SIG·nuhl) a signal that can be represented as a sequence of discrete values (188)
señal digital una señal que se puede representar como una secuencia de valores discretos

E

electric charge (ee·LEK·trik CHARJ) a fundamental property that leads to the electromagnetic interactions among particles that make up matter (128)
carga eléctrica una propiedad fundamental que determina las interacciones electromagnéticas entre las partículas que forman la materia

electric circuit (ee·LEK·trik SER·kit) a set of electrical components connected such that they provide one or more complete paths for the movement of charges (146)
circuito eléctrico un conjunto de componentes eléctricos conectados de modo que proporcionen una o más rutas completas para el movimiento de las cargas

electric current (ee·LEK·trik KER·uhnt) the rate at which electric charges pass a given point (138)
corriente eléctrica la tasa a la que las cargas eléctricas pasan por un punto dado

electric generator (ee·LEK·trik JEN·uh·ray·ter) a device that converts mechanical energy into electrical energy (180)
generador eléctrico un aparato que transforma la energía mecánica en energía eléctrica

electric motor (ee·LEK·trik MO·ter) a device that converts electrical energy into mechanical energy (176)
motor eléctrico un aparato que transforma la energía eléctrica en energía mecánica

electrical conductor (ee·LEK·trik·kuhl kuhn·DUHK·ter) a material in which charges can move freely (132)
conductor eléctrico un material en el que las cargas se mueven libremente

electrical insulator (ee·LEK·trih·kuhl IN·suh·lay·ter) a material in which charges cannot move freely (132)
aislante eléctrico un material en el que las cargas no pueden moverse libremente

electromagnet (ee·lek·troh·MAG·nit) a coil that has a soft iron core and that acts as a magnet when an electric current is in the coil (173)
electroimán una bobina que tiene un centro de hierro suave y que funciona como un imán cuando hay una corriente eléctrica en la bobina

electromagnetic induction (ee·lek·troh·mag·NET·ik in·DUHK·shuhn) the process of creating a current in a circuit by changing a magnetic field (178)
inducción electromagnética el proceso de crear una corriente en un circuito por medio de un cambio en el campo magnético

electromagnetism (ee·lek·troh·MAG·nih·tiz·uhm) the interaction between electricity and magnetism (172)
electromagnetismo la interacción entre la electricidad y el magnetismo

electronic device (ee·lek·TRAHN·ik dih·VYS) a device that produces or is powered by a flow of electrons and contains an integrated circuit (186)
dispositivo electrónico dispositivo con un circuito integrado, que produce o cuyo funcionamiento depende de un flujo de electrones

energy (EN·er·jee) the ability to cause change (82)
energía la capacidad de producir un cambio

F

fluid (FLOO·id) a nonsolid state of matter in which the atoms or molecules are free to move past each other, as in a gas or liquid (56)
fluido un estado no sólido de la materia en el que los átomos o moléculas tienen libertad de movimiento, como en el caso de un gas o un líquido

force (FOHRS) a push or a pull exerted on an object in order to change the motion of the object; force has size and direction (30)
fuerza una acción de empuje o atracción que se ejerce sobre un objeto con el fin de cambiar su movimiento; la fuerza tiene magnitud y dirección

free fall (FREE FAWL) the motion of a body when only the force of gravity is acting on the body (48)
caída libre el movimiento de un cuerpo cuando la única fuerza que actúa sobre él es la fuerza de gravedad

fulcrum (FUL·kruhm) the point on which a lever pivots (108)
fulcro el punto sobre el que pivota una palanca

G-H

gravity (GRAV·ih·tee) a force of attraction between objects that is due to their masses (44)
gravedad una fuerza de atracción entre dos objetos debido a sus masas

I-J

inclined plane (in·KLYND PLAYN) a simple machine that is a straight, slanted surface, which facilitates the raising of loads; a ramp (112)
plano inclinado una máquina simple que es una superficie recta e inclinada, que facilita el levantamiento de cargas; una rampa

inertia (ih·NER·shuh) the tendency of an object to resist a change in motion unless an outside force acts on the object (34)
inercia la tendencia de un objeto a resistir un cambio en el movimiento a menos que actúe una fuerza externa sobre el objeto

Integrated circuit

integrated circuit (in·tih·GRAY·tid SER·kit) a circuit whose components are formed on a single semiconductor (186)
circuito integrado un circuito cuyos componentes están formados en un solo semiconductor

K

kinetic energy (kih·NET·ik EN·er·jee) the energy of an object that is due to the object's motion (90)
energía cinética la energía de un objeto debido al movimiento del objeto

L

lever (LEV·er) a simple machine that consists of a bar that pivots at a fixed point called a fulcrum (108)
palanca una máquina simple formada por una barra que gira en un punto fijo llamado fulcro

M

machine (muh·SHEEN) a device that helps do work by changing the magnitude and/or direction of an applied force (104)
máquina un dispositivo que ayuda a realizar trabajos cambiando la magnitud y/o la dirección de una fuerza aplicada

magnet (MAG·nit) any material that attracts iron or materials containing iron (158)
imán cualquier material que atrae hierro o materiales que contienen hierro

magnetic field (MAG·net·ik FEELD) a region where a magnetic force can be detected (159)
campo magnético una región donde puede detectarse una fuerza magnética

magnetic force (MAG·net·ik FOHRS) the force of attraction or repulsion generated by moving or spinning electric charges (158)
fuerza magnética la fuerza de atracción o repulsión generadas por cargas eléctricas en movimiento o que giran

magnetic pole (MAG·net·ik POHL) one of two points, such as the ends of a magnet, that have opposing magnetic qualities (159)
polo magnético uno de dos puntos, tales como los extremos de un imán, que tienen cualidades magnéticas opuestas

mechanical advantage (mih·KAN·ih·kuhl ad·VAN·tij) a number that tells how many times a machine multiplies input force (106)
ventaja mecánica un número que indica cuántas veces una máquina multiplica su fuerza de entrada

mechanical efficiency (mih·KAN·ih·kuhl ih·FISH·uhn·see) a quantity, usually expressed as a percentage, that measures the ratio of work output to work input in a machine (107)
eficiencia mecánica una cantidad, generalmente expresada como un porcentaje, que mide la relación entre el trabajo de entrada y el trabajo de salida en una máquina

mechanical energy (mih·KAN·ih·kuhl EN·er·jee) the sum of an object's kinetic energy and potential energy due to gravity or elastic deformation; does not include chemical energy or nuclear energy (94)
energía mecánica la suma de las energías cinética y potencial de un objeto debido a la gravedad o a la deformación elástica; no incluye la energía química ni nuclear

motion (MOH·shuhn) an object's change in position relative to a reference point (8)
movimiento el cambio en la posición de un objeto respecto a un punto de referencia

net force (NET FOHRS) the combination of all of the forces acting on an object (32)
fuerza neta la combinación de todas las fuerzas que actúan sobre un objeto

O

orbit (OHR·bit) the path that a body follows as it travels around another body in space (48)
órbita la trayectoria que sigue un cuerpo al desplazarse alrededor de otro cuerpo en el espacio

P–Q

parallel circuit (PAIR·uh·lel SER·kit) a circuit in which the parts are joined in branches such that the voltage across each part is the same (151)
circuito paralelo un circuito en el que las partes están unidas en ramas de manera tal que el voltaje entre cada parte es la misma

pascal (pa·SKAL) the SI unit of pressure (symbol, Pa) (57)
pascal la unidad de presión del sistema internacional de unidades (símbolo: Pa)

position (puh·ZISH·uhn) the location of an object (6)
posición la ubicación de un objeto

potential energy (puh·TEN·shuhl EN·er·jee) the energy that an object has because of the position, condition, or chemical composition of the object (92)
energía potencial la energía que tiene un objeto debido a su posición, condición, o composición química

power (POW·er) the rate at which work is done or energy is transformed (84)
potencia la tasa a la que se realiza un trabajo o a la que se transforma la energía

pressure (PRESH·er) the amount of force exerted per unit area of a surface (56)
presión la cantidad de fuerza ejercida en una superficie por unidad de área

pulley (PUL·ee) a simple machine that consists of a wheel over which a rope, chain, or wire passes (111)
polea una máquina simple formada por una rueda sobre la cual pasa una cuerda, cadena, o cable

R

reference point (REF·er·uhns POYNT) a location to which another location is compared (6)
punto de referencia una ubicación con la que se compara otra ubicación

resistance (rih·ZIS·tuhns) in physical science, the opposition presented to the current by a material or device (140)
resistencia en ciencias físicas, la oposición que un material o aparato presenta a la corriente

S

semiconductor (sem·ee·kuhn·DUHK·ter) an element or compound that conducts electric current better than an insulator does but not as well as a conductor does (133)
semiconductor un elemento o compuesto que conduce la corriente eléctrica mejor que un aislante, pero no tan bien como un conductor

series circuit (SIR·eez SER·kit) a circuit in which the parts are joined one after another such that the current in each part is the same (150)
circuito en serie un circuito en el que las partes están unidas una después de la otra de manera tal que la corriente en cada parte es la misma

solenoid (SOH·luh·noyd) a coil of wire with an electric current in it (173)
solenoide una bobina de alambre que tiene una corriente eléctrica

speed (SPEED) the distance traveled divided by the time interval during which the motion occurred (9)
rapidez la distancia que un objeto se desplaza dividida entre el intervalo de tiempo durante el cual ocurrió el movimiento

static electricity (STAT·ik ee·lek·TRIS·ih·tee) electric charge at rest; generally produced by friction or induction (131)
electricidad estática carga eléctrica en reposo; por lo general se produce por fricción o inducción

T–U

transformer (trans·FOHR·mer) a device that increases or decreases the voltage of alternating current (179)
transformador un aparato que aumenta o disminuye el voltaje de la corriente alterna

V

vector (VEK·ter) a quantity that has both size and direction (15)
vector una cantidad que tiene tanto magnitud como dirección

velocity (vuh·LAHS·ih·tee) the speed of an object in a particular direction (15)
velocidad la rapidez de un objeto en una dirección dada

voltage (VOHL·tij) the amount of work to move a unit electric charge between two points; expressed in volts (140)
voltaje la cantidad de trabajo necesario para transportar una unidad de carga eléctrica entre dos puntos; se expresa en voltios

W–Z

wheel and axle (WEEL AND AK·suhl) a simple machine consisting of two circular objects of different sizes; the wheel is the larger of the two circular objects, and the axle is attached to the center of the wheel (110)
rueda y eje una máquina simple formada por dos objetos circulares de diferentes tamaños; la rueda es el más grande de los dos objetos circulares, y el eje está sujeto al centro de la rueda

work (WERK) the transfer of energy to an object by using a force that causes the object to move in the direction of the force (80)
trabajo la transferencia de energía a un objeto mediante una fuerza que hace que el objeto se mueva en la dirección de la fuerza

COMMON CORE

State STANDARDS FOR ENGLISH LANGUAGE ARTS

Correlations

This table shows correlations to the *Reading Standards for Literacy in Science and Technical Subjects* for grades 6–8.

Go online at thinkcentral.com for correlations of all *ScienceFusion* Modules to Common Core State Standards for Mathematics and to the rest of the *Common Core State Standards for English Language Arts*.

Grade 6–8 Standard Code	Citations for Module K "Introduction to Science and Technology"

READING STANDARDS FOR LITERACY IN SCIENCE AND TECHNICAL SUBJECTS

Key Ideas and Details

RST.6–8.1 Cite specific textual evidence to support analysis of science and technical texts.

Student Edition pp. 25, 75, 113
Teacher Edition pp. 98, 117

RST.6–8.2 Determine the central ideas or conclusions of a text; provide an accurate summary of the text distinct from prior knowledge or opinions.

Student Edition pp. 25, 32, 60, 75, 113, 132, 137, 149, 157, 163, 171, 189
Teacher Edition pp. 17, 21, 22, 35, 51, 61, 62, 98, 106, 117, 128, 130, 161, 178, 179, 206, 213, 237, 240. Also use "Synthesizing Key Topics" items in the Extend Science Concepts sections of the Teacher Edition.

RST.6–8.3 Follow precisely a multistep procedure when carrying out experiments, taking measurements, or performing technical tasks.

Student Edition pp. 83, 90–91
Teacher Edition p. 94
Other Use the Lab Manual, Project-Based Assessments, Video-Based Projects, and the Virtual Labs.

Craft and Structure

RST.6–8.4 Determine the meaning of symbols, key terms, and other domain-specific words and phrases as they are used in a specific scientific or technical context relevant to *grades 6–8 texts and topics.*

Student Edition pp. 5, 17, 31, 43, 63, 64, 77, 93, 115, 131, 141, 153, 169, 181
Teacher Edition p. 111. Also use "Previewing Vocabulary" and "Reinforcing Vocabulary" items in the Explain Science Concepts sections of the Teacher Edition.

Grade 6–8 Standard Code (continued)	Citations for Module K "Introduction to Science and Technology"
RST.6–8.5 Analyze the structure an author uses to organize a text, including how the major sections contribute to the whole and to an understanding of the topic.	*Student Edition* p. 75 *Teacher Edition* pp. 51, 128, 213, 237, 240
RST.6–8.6 Analyze the author's purpose in providing an explanation, describing a procedure, or discussing an experiment in a text.	*Student Edition* pp. 25, 75 *Teacher Edition* pp. 14, 47, 98

Integration of Knowledge and Ideas

RST.6–8.7 Integrate quantitative or technical information expressed in words in a text with a version of that information expressed visually (e.g., in a flowchart, diagram, model, graph, or table).	*Student Edition* pp. 3, 35, 54, 66–67, 81, 122–123, 144, 147, 158, 159 *Teacher Edition* pp. 21, 40, 53, 54, 123, 194, 201, 206, 208, 224, 237, 240. Also use the "Graphic Organizer" items in the Teacher Edition. *Other* Use the lessons in the Digital Path.
RST.6–8.8 Distinguish among facts, reasoned judgment based on research findings, and speculation in a text.	*Student Edition* pp. 13, 25, 74–75, 113 *Teacher Edition* pp. 14, 17, 98
RST.6–8.9 Compare and contrast the information gained from experiments, simulations, video, or multimedia sources with that gained from reading a text on the same topic.	*Student Edition* pp. 113, 137, 163 *Teacher Edition* pp. 40, 79, 117 *Other* Use the Lab Manual, Project-Based Assessments, Video-Based Projects, and the lessons in the Digital Path.

Range of Reading and Level of Text Complexity

RST.6–8.10 By the end of grade 8, read and comprehend science/technical texts in the grades 6–8 text complexity band independently and proficiently.	*Student Edition* pp. 3, 22, 75, 90, 113, 132, 137, 149, 157, 163, 171, 189. Also use all lessons in the Student Edition. *Teacher Edition* pp. 47, 48, 61, 62, 117

Bibliography

This bibliography is a compilation of trade books that can supplement the materials covered in *ScienceFusion* Grades 6–8. Many of the books are recommendations of the National Science Teachers Association (NSTA) and the Children's Book Council (CBC) as outstanding science trade books for children. These books were selected because they meet the following rigorous criteria: they are of literary quality and contain substantial science content; the theories and facts are clearly distinguished; they are free of gender, ethnic, and socioeconomic bias; and they contain clear, accurate, up-to-date information. Several selections are award-winning titles, or their authors have received awards.

As with all materials you share with your class, we suggest you review the books first to ensure their appropriateness. While titles are current at time of publication, they may go out of print without notice.

Grades 6–8

Acids and Bases (Material Matters/Express Edition) by Carol Baldwin (Heinemann-Raintree, 2005) focuses on the properties of acids and bases with photographs and facts.

Acids and Bases by Eurona Earl Tilley (Chelsea House, 2008) provides a thorough, basic understanding of acid and base chemistry, including such topics as naming compounds, writing formulas, and physical and chemical properties.

Across the Wide Ocean: The Why, How, and Where of Navigation for Humans and Animals at Sea by Karen Romano Young (Greenwillow, 2007) focuses on navigational tools, maps, and charts that researchers and explorers use to learn more about oceanography. AWARD-WINNING AUTHOR

Adventures in Sound with Max Axiom, Super Scientist (Graphic Science Series) by Emily Sohn (Capstone, 2007) provides information about sound through a fun graphic novel.

Air: A Resource Our World Depends on (Managing Our Resources) by Ian Graham (Heinemann-Raintree, 2005) examines this valuable natural resource and answers questions such as "How much does Earth's air weigh?" and "Why do plants need wind?"

The Alkaline Earth Metals: Beryllium, Magnesium, Calcium, Strontium, Barium, Radium (Understanding the Elements of the Periodic Table) by Bridget Heos (Rosen Central, 2009) describes the characteristics of these metals, including their similar physical and molecular properties.

All About Light and Sound (Mission: Science) by Connie Jankowski (Compass Point, 2010) focuses on the importance of light and sound and how without them we could not survive.

Alternative Energy: Beyond Fossil Fuels by Dana Meachen Rau (Compass Point, 2010) discusses the ways that water, wind, and sun provide a promising solution to our energy crisis and encourages readers to help the planet by conserving energy. AWARD-WINNING AUTHOR

Amazing Biome Projects You Can Build Yourself (Build it Yourself Series) by Donna Latham (Nomad, 2009) provides an overview of eight terrestrial biomes, including characteristics about climate, soil, animals, and plants.

Archaea: Salt-Lovers, Methane-Makers, Thermophiles, and Other Archaeans (A Class of Their Own) by David M. Barker (Crabtree, 2010) provides interesting facts about different types of archaeans.

The Art of Construction: Projects and Principles for Beginning Engineers and Architects by Mario Salvadori (Chicago Review, 2000) explains how tents, houses, stadiums, and bridges are built, and how to build models of such structures using materials found around the house. AWARD-WINNING AUTHOR

Astronomy: Out of This World! by Simon Basher and Dan Green (Kingfisher, 2009) takes readers on a journey of the universe and provides information about the planets, stars, galaxies, telescopes, space missions, and discoveries.

At the Sea Floor Café: Odd Ocean Critter Poems by Leslie Bulion (Peachtree, 2011) provides poetry to educate students about how ocean creatures search for food, capture prey, protect their young, and trick their predators.

Battery Science: Make Widgets That Work and Gadgets That Go by Doug Stillinger (Klutz, 2003) offers an array of activities and gadgets to get students excited about electricity.

The Biggest Explosions in the Universe by Sara Howard (BookSurge, 2009) tells the story of stars in our universe through fun text and captivating photographs.

Biology: Life as We Know It! by Simon Basher and Dan Green (Kingfisher, 2008) offers information about all aspects of life from the animals and plants to the minuscule cells, proteins, and DNA that bring them to life.

Birds of a Feather by Jane Yolen (Boyds Mills Press, 2011) offers facts and information about birds through fun poetry and beautiful photographs. AWARD-WINNING AUTHOR

Blackout!: Electricity and Circuits (Fusion) by Anna Claybourne (Heinemann-Raintree, 2005) provides an array of facts about electricity and how we rely on it for so many things in everyday life. AWARD-WINNING AUTHOR

Cell Division and Genetics by Robert Snedden (Heinemann, 2007) explains various aspects of cells and the living world, including what happens when cells divide and how characteristics are passed on from one generation to another. AWARD-WINNING AUTHOR

Chemistry: Getting a Big Reaction by Dan Green and Simon Basher (Kingfisher, 2010) acts as a guide about the chemical "characters" that fizz, react, and combine to make up everything around us.

Cool Stuff Exploded by Chris Woodford (Dorling Kindersley, 2008) focuses on today's technological marvels and tomorrow's jaw-dropping devices. OUTSTANDING SCIENCE TRADE BOOK

Disaster Deferred: How New Science Is Changing Our View of Earthquake Hazards in the Midwest by Seth Stein (Columbia University, 2010) discusses technological innovations that make earthquake prediction possible.

The Diversity of Species (Timeline: Life on Earth) by Michael Bright (Heinemann, 2008) explains how and why things on Earth have genetic and physical differences and how they have had and continue to have an impact on Earth.

Drip! Drop!: How Water Gets to Your Tap by Barbara Seuling (Holiday House, 2000) introduces students to JoJo and her dog, Willy, who explain the water cycle and introduce fun experiments about filtration, evaporation, and condensation. AWARD-WINNING AUTHOR

Eat Fresh Food: Awesome Recipes for Teen Chefs by Rozanne Gold (Bloomsbury, 2009) includes more than 80 recipes and places a strong emphasis on fresh foods throughout the book.

Eco-Tracking: On the Trail of Habitat Change (Worlds of Wonder) by Daniel Shaw (University of New Mexico, 2010) recounts success stories of young people involved in citizen science efforts and encourages others to join in to preserve nature's ecosystems.

Electric Mischief: Battery-Powered Gadgets Kids Can Build by Alan Bartholomew (Kids Can Press, 2002) offers a variety of fun projects that include making battery connections and switches and building gadgets such as electric dice and a bumper car.

Electricity (Why It Works) by Anna Claybourne (QED Publishing, 2008) provides information about electricity in an easy-to-follow manner. AWARD-WINNING AUTHOR

Electricity and Magnetism (Usborne Understand Science) by Peter Adamczyk (Usborne, 2008) explains the basics about electricity and magnetism, including information about static electricity, electric circuits, and electromagnetism.

Energy Transfers (Energy Essentials) by Nigel Saunders and Steven Chapman (Raintree, 2005) explains the different types of energy, how they can change, and how different forms of energy help us in our everyday lives.

The Everything Machine by Matt Novak (Roaring Brook, 2009) tells the silly story of a machine that does everything for a group of people until they wake up one day and discover that the machine has stopped working. AWARD-WINNING AUTHOR

Experiments with Plants and Other Living Things by Trevor Cook (PowerKids, 2009) provides fun, hands-on experiments to teach students about flowers, plants, and biology.

Exploring the Oceans: Seafloor by John Woodward (Heinemann, 2004) takes readers on a virtual tour through the bottom part of the ocean, highlighting the plants and animals that thrive in this environment.

Extreme Structures: Mega Constructions of the 21st Century (Science Frontiers) by David Jefferis (Crabtree, 2006) takes a look at how some of the coolest buildings in the world were built and what other kinds of structures are being planned for the future. AWARD-WINNING AUTHOR

Fascinating Science Projects: Electricity and Magnetism by Bobbi Searle (Aladdin, 2002) teaches the concepts of electricity and magnetism through dozens of projects and experiments and color illustrations.

Fizz, Bubble and Flash!: Element Explorations and Atom Adventures for Hands-on Science Fun! by Anita Brandolini, Ph.D. (Williamson, 2003) introduces chemistry to students in a nonintimidating way and focuses on the elements and the periodic table. PARENTS' CHOICE

Floods: Hazards of Surface and Groundwater Systems (The Hazardous Earth) by Timothy M. Kusky (Facts on File, 2008) explores the processes that control the development and flow in river and stream systems and when these processes become dangerous.

Fossils (Geology Rocks!) by Rebecca Faulkner (Raintree, 2008) educates students about rock formation and the processes and characteristics of rocks and fossils.

Friends: True Stories of Extraordinary Animal Friendships by Catherine Thimmesh (Houghton Mifflin Harcourt, 2011) depicts true stories of unlikely animal friendships, including a wild polar bear and a sled dog as well as a camel and a Vietnamese pig. AWARD-WINNING AUTHOR

The Frog Scientist (Scientists in the Field) by Pamela S. Turner (Houghton Mifflin Harcourt, 2009) follows a scientist and his protégés as they research the effects of atrazine-contaminated water on vulnerable amphibians. BOOKLIST EDITORS' CHOICE

From Steam Engines to Nuclear Fusion: Discovering Energy (Chain Reactions) by Carol Ballard (Heinemann-Raintree, 2007) tells the fascinating story of energy, from the heat produced by a simple fire to the extraordinary power contained in an atom.

Fully Charged (Everyday Science) by Steve Parker (Heinemann-Raintree, 2005) explains how electricity is generated, harnessed, and used and also the difference between electricity, including static electricity, and electronics. AWARD-WINNING AUTHOR

Galileo for Kids: His Life and Ideas by Richard Panchyk (Chicago Review, 2005) includes experiments that demonstrate scientific principles developed by the astronomer Galileo.

Genes and DNA by Richard Walker (Kingfisher, 2003) offers an abundance of information about characteristics of genes, gene function, DNA technology, and genetic engineering, as well as other fascinating topics. NSTA TRADE BOOK; OUTSTANDING SCIENCE TRADE BOOK

Hands-on Science Series: Simple Machines by Steven Souza and Joseph Shortell (Walch, 2001) investigates the concepts of work, force, power, efficiency, and mechanical advantage.

How Animals Work by David Burnie (Dorling Kindersley, 2010) provides vivid photographs and intriguing text to describe various animals and their characteristics, diets, and families. AWARD-WINNING AUTHOR

How Does an Earthquake Become a Tsunami? (How Does it Happen?) by Linda Tagliaferro (Heinemann-Raintree, 2009) describes the changes in water, waves, and tides that occur between an earthquake and a tsunami. AWARD-WINNING AUTHOR

How the Future Began: Machines by Clive Gifford (Kingfisher, 1999) acts as a guide to historical and current developments in the field of machinery, including mass production, computers, robots, microengineering, and communications technology. AWARD-WINNING AUTHOR

How Scientists Work (Simply Science) by Natalie M. Rosinsky (Compass Point, 2003) discusses the scientific method, equipment, and procedures and also describes how scientists compile information and answer questions.

How to Clean a Hippopotamus: A Look at Unusual Animal Partnerships by Steve Jenkins and Robin Page (Houghton Mifflin Harcourt, 2010) explores animal symbiosis with fun illustrations and a close-up, step-by-step view of some of nature's most fascinating animal partnerships. ALA NOTABLE BOOK

Human Spaceflight (Frontiers in Space) by Joseph A. Angelo (Facts on File, 2007) examines the history of space exploration and the evolution of space technology from the dawn of the space age to the present time.

The Hydrosphere: Agent of Change by Gregory L. Vogt, Ed.D. (Twenty-First Century, 2006) discusses the impact this 20-mile-thick sphere has had on the surface of the planet and the processes that go on there, including the ability of Earth to sustain life. AWARD-WINNING AUTHOR

In Rivers, Lakes, and Ponds (Under the Microscope) by Sabrina Crewe (Chelsea Clubhouse, 2010) educates readers about the microscopic critters that live in these various bodies of water.

A Kid's Guide to Climate Change and Global Warming: How to Take Action! by Cathryn Berger Kaye, M.A. (Free Spirit, 2009) encourages students to learn about the climate changes happening around the world and to get involved to help save our planet.

Lasers (Lucent Library of Science and Technology) by Don Nardo (Lucent, 2003) discusses the scientific discovery and development of lasers—high-intensity light—and their use in our daily lives. AWARD-WINNING AUTHOR

Leonardo's Horse by Jean Fritz (Putnam, 2001) tells the story of Leonardo da Vinci—the curious and inquisitive artist, engineer, and astronomer—who created a detailed horse sculpture for the city of Milan. ALA NOTABLE BOOK; NOTABLE SOCIAL STUDIES TRADE BOOK; NOTABLE CHILDREN'S BOOK IN THE LANGUAGE ARTS

Light: From Sun to Bulbs by Christopher Cooper (Heinemann, 2003) invites students to investigate the dazzling world of physical science and light through fun experiments. AWARD-WINNING AUTHOR

Magnetism and Electromagnets (Sci-Hi: Physical Science) by Eve Hartman (Raintree, 2008) offers colorful illustrations, photographs, quizzes, charts, graphs, and text to teach students about magnetism.

Making Good Choices About Nonrenewable Resources (Green Matters) by Paula Johanson (Rosen Central, 2009) focuses on the different types of nonrenewable natural resources, alternative resources, conservation, and making positive consumer choices.

Making Waves: Sound (Everyday Science) by Steve Parker (Heinemann-Raintree, 2005) describes what sound is, how it is formed and used, and properties associated with sound, such as pitch, speed, and volume. AWARD-WINNING AUTHOR

The Manatee Scientists: Saving Vulnerable Species (Scientists in the Field Series) by Peter Lourie (Houghton Mifflin Harcourt, 2011) discusses three species of manatees and the importance of preserving these mammals. AWARD-WINNING AUTHOR

The Man Who Named the Clouds by Julie Hannah and Joan Holub (Albert Whitman, 2006) tells the story of 18th-century English meteorologist Luke Howard and also discusses the ten classifications of clouds.

Medicine in the News (Science News Flash) by Brian R. Shmaefsky, Ph.D. (Chelsea House, 2007) focuses on medical advancements that are in the news today and the innovative tools that are used for diagnosis and treatment.

Metals and Metalloids (Periodic Table of the Elements) by Monica Halka, Ph.D., and Brian Nordstrom, Ed.D. (Facts on File, 2010), offers information about the physics, chemistry, geology, and biology of metals and metalloids.

Meteorology: Ferguson's Careers in Focus by Ferguson (Ferguson, 2011) profiles 18 different careers pertaining to the science of the atmosphere and its phenomena.

The Microscope (Great Medical Discoveries) by Adam Woog (Lucent, 2003) recounts how the microscope has had an impact on the history of medicine.

Microscopes and Telescopes: Great Inventions by Rebecca Stefoff (Marshall Cavendish Benchmark, 2007) describes the origin, history, development, and societal impact of the telescope and microscope. OUTSTANDING SCIENCE TRADE BOOK

Mighty Animal Cells by Rebecca L. Johnson (Millbrook, 2007) takes readers on a journey to discover how people and animals grow from just one single cell. AWARD-WINNING AUTHOR

Moon (Eyewitness Books) by Jacqueline Mitton (Dorling Kindersley, 2009) offers information about our planet's mysterious nearest neighbor, from the moon's waterless seas and massive craters to its effect on Earth's ocean tides and its role in solar eclipses. AWARD-WINNING AUTHOR

MP3 Players (Let's Explore Technology Communications) by Jeanne Sturm (Rourke, 2010) discusses the technological advances in music in our society.

Nanotechnologist (Cool Science Careers) by Ann Heinrichs (Cherry Lake, 2009) provides information about nanotechnologists—scientists who work with materials on a subatomic or atomic level.

Ocean: An Illustrated Atlas by Sylvia A. Earle (National Geographic, 2008) provides an overview on the ocean as a whole, each of the major ocean basins, and the future of the oceans. AWARD-WINNING AUTHOR

Oceans (Insiders) by Beverly McMillan and John A. Musick (Simon & Schuster, 2007) takes readers on a 3-D journey of the aquatic universe—exploring the formation of waves and tsunamis as well as the plant and animal species that live beneath the ocean's surface.

Organic Chemistry and Biochemistry (Facts at Your Fingertips) by Graham Bateman (Brown Bear, 2011) provides diagrams, experiments, and testing aids to teach students the basics about organic chemistry and biochemistry.

An Overcrowded World?: Our Impact on the Planet (21st Century Debates) by Rob Bowden (Heinemann, 2002) investigates how and why the world's population is growing so fast, the effects of this growth on wildlife and habitats, and the pressure on resources, and suggests ways of controlling growth.

The Pebble in My Pocket: A History of Our Earth by Meredith Hooper (Viking, 1996) follows the course of a pebble, beginning 480 million years ago, through a fiery volcano and primordial forest and along the icy bottom of a glacier and how it looks today as the result of its journey. AWARD-WINNING AUTHOR

The Periodic Table: Elements with Style! by Simon Basher and Adrian Dingle (Kingfisher, 2007) offers information about the different elements that make up the periodic table and their features and characteristics.

Phenomena: Secrets of the Senses by Donna M. Jackson (Little, Brown, 2008) focuses on the senses and how to interpret them and discusses ways that technology is changing how we experience the world around us. AWARD-WINNING AUTHOR

Pioneers of Light and Sound (Mission: Science) by Connie Jankowski (Compass Point, 2010) focuses on various scientists and their accomplishments and achievements.

Planet Animal: Saving Earth's Disappearing Animals by B. Taylor (Barron's, 2009) focuses on the planet's most endangered animals, their relationships to the environment, and steps that are being taken to try to save these animals from extinction.

Plant and Animal Science Fair Projects (Biology Science Projects Using the Scientific Method) by Yael Calhoun (Enslow, 2010) provides an array of experiments about plants and animals and describes the importance of the scientific method, forming a hypothesis, and recording data for any given project.

Plant Secrets: Plant Life Processes by Anna Claybourne (Heinemann-Raintree, 2005) includes informative text, vivid photographs, and detailed charts about characteristics of various plants. AWARD-WINNING AUTHOR

Polar Regions: Human Impacts (Our Fragile Planet) by Dana Desonie (Chelsea House, 2008) focuses on pollutants and global warming in the Arctic and Antarctic and future dangers that will occur if our planet continues on its current path.

Potato Clocks and Solar Cars: Renewable and Non-renewable Energy by Elizabeth Raum (Raintree, 2007) explores various topics, including alternative energy sources, fossil fuels, and sustainable energy.

The Power of Pressure (How Things Work) by Andrew Dunn (Thomson Learning, 1993) explains how water pressure and air work and how they are used in machines.

Protists and Fungi (Discovery Channel School Science) by Katie King and Jacqueline A. Ball (Gareth Stevens, 2003) focuses on the appearance, behavior, and characteristics of various protists and fungi, using examples of algae, mold, and mushrooms.

Protozoans, Algae and Other Protists by Steve Parker (Compass Point, 2010) introduces readers to the parts, life cycles, and reproduction of various types of protists, from microscopic protozoans to seaweedlike algae, and some of the harmful effects protists have on humans. AWARD-WINNING AUTHOR

Sally Ride: The First American Woman in Space by Tom Riddolls (Crabtree, 2010) focuses on the growth and impact of Sally Ride Science—an educational program founded by the astronaut to encourage girls to pursue hobbies and careers in science.

Science and Technology in 20th Century American Life by Christopher Cumo (Greenwood, 2008) takes readers on a history of technology from agricultural implements through modern computers, telecommunications, and skateboards.

Sedimentary Rock (Geology Rocks!) by Rebecca Faulkner (Raintree, 2008) educates students about rock formation and the processes and characteristics of sedimentary rock.

Shaping the Earth by Dorothy Hinshaw Patent (Clarion/Houghton Mifflin, 2000) combines vivid photographs with informative text to explain the forces that have created the geological features on Earth's surface. AWARD-WINNING AUTHOR

Silent Spring by Rachel Carson (Houghton Mifflin, 2002) celebrates marine biologist and environmental activist Rachel Carson's contribution to Earth through an array of essays.

Skywalkers: Mohawk Ironworkers Build the City by David Weitzman (Flash Point, 2010) focuses on the ironworkers who constructed bridges and skyscrapers in New York and Canada. AWARD-WINNING AUTHOR

Sustaining Earth's Energy Resources (Environment at Risk) by Ann Heinrichs (Marshall Cavendish, 2010) offers information on Earth's sources of nonrenewable and renewable energy, how they are used, and their disadvantages and benefits.

Team Moon: How 400,000 People Landed Apollo 11 on the Moon by Catherine Thimmesh (Houghton Mifflin, 2006) tells the story of the first moon landing and celebrates the dedication, ingenuity, and perseverance of the people who made this event happen. ALA NOTABLE BOOK; ORBIS PICTUS HONOR; NOTABLE CHILDREN'S BOOK IN THE LANGUAGE ARTS; ALA BEST BOOK FOR YOUNG ADULTS; GOLDEN KITE HONOR

The Top of the World: Climbing Mount Everest by Steve Jenkins (Houghton Mifflin, 1999) describes the conditions and terrain of Mount Everest, attempts that have been made to scale this peak, and information about the equipment and techniques of mountain climbing. ALA NOTABLE BOOK; SLJ BEST BOOK; BOSTON GLOBE–HORN BOOK AWARD; ORBIS PICTUS HONOR

Transmission of Power by Fluid Pressure: Air and Water by William Donaldson (Nabu, 2010) describes the transmission of fluid pressure as it pertains to the elements of air and water in the world of motion, forces, and energy.

Tsunami: The True Story of an April Fools' Day Disaster by Gail Langer Karwoski (Darby Creek, 2006) offers a variety of viewpoints about the wave that struck Hawaii in 1946. NOTABLE SOCIAL STUDIES TRADE BOOK

Vapor, Rain, and Snow: The Science of Clouds and Precipitation (Weatherwise) by Paul Fleisher (Lerner, 2010) answers an array of questions about water, such as "How does a cloud form?" and "Why do ice cubes shrink in the freezer?" AWARD-WINNING AUTHOR

Water Supplies in Crisis (Planet in Crisis) by Russ Parker (Rosen Central, 2009) describes a world where safe drinking water is not readily available, polluted water brings disease, and lakes are disappearing.

Weird Meat-Eating Plants (Bizarre Science) by Nathan Aaseng (Enslow, 2011) provides information about a variety of carnivorous plants, reversing the food chain's usual order. AWARD-WINNING AUTHOR

What Are Igneous Rocks? (Let's Rock!) by Molly Aloian (Crabtree, 2010) explains how granite, basalt, lava, silica, and quartz are formed after hot molten rock cools.

What's Living Inside Your Body? by Andrew Solway (Heinemann, 2004) offers information about an array of viruses, germs, and parasites that thrive inside the human body.

Why Should I Bother to Keep Fit? (What's Happening?) by Kate Knighton and Susan Meredith (Usborne, 2009) motivates students to get fit and stay fit.

The World of Microbes: Bacteria, Viruses, and Other Microorganisms (Understanding Genetics) by Janey Levy (Rosen Classroom, 2010) describes the world of microbes, a history of microbiology, and the characteristics of both harmful and beneficial bacteria.

Written in Bone: Buried Lives of Jamestown and Colonial Maryland by Sally M. Walker (Carolrhoda, 2009) describes the way that scientists used forensic anthropology to investigate colonial-era graves near Jamestown, Virginia. ALA NOTABLE BOOK; OUTSTANDING SCIENCE TRADE BOOK; NOTABLE SOCIAL STUDIES TRADE BOOK

You Blink Twelve Times a Minute and Other Freaky Facts About the Human Body by Barbara Seuling (Picture Window, 2009) provides fun and unusual facts about various ailments, medical marvels, and body parts and their functions. AWARD-WINNING AUTHOR

Correlation to
ScienceSaurus

*ScienceSaurus, **A Student Handbook,*** is a "mini-encyclopedia" that students can use to find out more about unit topics. It contains numerous resources including concise content summaries, an almanac, many tables, charts, and graphs, history of science, and a glossary. ***ScienceSaurus*** is available from Houghton Mifflin Harcourt..

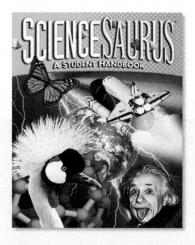

ScienceFusion Page References	Topics	*ScienceFusion* Grades 6-8
Scientific Investigation, pp. 1–19		
	Scientific Inquiry	Mod K, Unit 1, Lessons 1-3
		Mod K, Unit 2, Lessons 1, 3
	Designing Your Own Investigations	Mod K, Unit 1, Lessons 2, 4
Working in the Lab, pp. 20–72		
	Laboratory Safety	Mod K, Unit 2, Lesson 2
	Glassware and Microscopes	Mod K, Unit 2, Lesson 2
	Measurement	Mod K, Unit 2, Lesson 2
Life Science, pp. 73–164		
	Structure of Life	Mod A, Unit 1, Lessons 1-3
		Mod A, Unit 2, Lessons 1, 3
	Human Biology	Mod C, Unit 1, Lessons 1-6
		Mod C, Unit 2, Lesson 1
	Physiology and Behavior	Mod A, Unit 1, Lesson 5
		Mod B, Unit 2, Lessons 3-6
	Genes and Heredity	Mod A, Unit 2, Lessons 2-6
	Change and Diversity of Life	Mod B, Unit 1, Lessons 2-4

ScienceFusion Page References	Topics	*ScienceFusion* Grades 6-8
Life Science, pp. 73–164 (continued)		
	Ecosystems	Mod D, Unit 1, Lessons 1-4
		Mod D, Unit 2, Lessons 1-4
		Mod D, Unit 2, Lesson 5
	Classification	Mod B, Unit 1, Lesson 5
		Mod B, Unit 2, Lessons 3, 5
Earth Science, pp. 165–248		
	Geology	Mod E, Unit 4, Lesson 1
		Mod E, Unit 3, Lessons 1-3
		Mod E, Unit 4, Lessons 2-5
		Mod E, Unit 1, Lessons 2-4
		Mod E, Unit 2, Lessons 1-4
		Mod E, Unit 1, Lessons 3, 5
	Oceanography	Mod F, Unit 1, Lesson 1
		Mod F, Unit 2, Lessons 1, 3
	Meteorology	Mod F, Unit 3, Lesson 1
		Mod F, Unit 1, Lesson 2
		Mod F, Unit 4, Lesson 1, 2, 3, 6
	Astronomy	Mod G, Unit 3, Lessons 1-3
		Mod G, Unit 2, Lessons 2-6
		Mod G, Unit 1, Lessons 1-3
Physical Science, pp. 249–321		
	Matter	Mod H, Unit 1, Lessons 1-6
		Mod H, Unit 3, Lessons 1-4
		Mod H Unit 4, Lessons 1-3
		Mod H, Unit 5, Lessons 1-3

ScienceFusion Page References	Topics	ScienceFusion Grades 6-8
Physical Science, pp. 249–321 (continued)		
	Forces and Motion	Mod I, Unit 1, Lessons 1-5
		Mod I, Unit 2, Lessons 1-3
	Energy	Mod H, Unit 2, Lessons 1-4
		Mod I, Unit 3, Lessons 1-5
		Mod J, Unit 1, Lessons 1, 2
		Mod J, Unit 2, Lessons 1, 2
		Mod J, Unit 3, Lessons 1-4
Natural Resources and the Environment, pp. 322–353		
	Earth's Natural Resources	Mod D, Unit 3, Lessons 2-5
	Resource Conservation	Mod D, Unit 3, Lesson 5
	Solid Waste and Pollution	Mod D, Unit 4, Lessons 1-4 Mod F, Unit 4, Lesson 7
Science, Technology, and Society, pp. 354–373		
	Science and Technology	Mod A, Unit 2, Lesson 7
		Mod G, Unit 4, Lesson 2
		Mod I, Unit 3, Lesson 6
		Mod J, Unit 2, Lesson 3
		Mod J, Unit 3, Lesson 5
	Science and Society	Mod K, Unit 1, Lesson 4
		Mod K, Unit 3, Lesson 6

ScienceFusion Page References	Topics	*ScienceFusion* Grades 6-8
Almanac, pp. 374–438		
	Scientific Numbers	May be used with all units.
	Using Data Tables and Graphs	Mod K, Unit 2, Lesson 1
	Solving Math Problems in Science	May be used with all units.
	Classroom and Research Skills	May be used with all units.
	Test-Taking Skills	May be used with all units.
	References	May be used with all units.
Yellow Pages, pp. 439–524		
	History of Science Timeline	See People in Science features.
	Famous Scientists	See People in Science features.
	Greek and Latin Word Roots	Glossary
	Glossary of Scientific Terms	Glossary

Index

Key:

Teacher Edition page numbers follow the Student Edition page numbers and are printed in blue type.
Student Edition page numbers for highlighted definitions are printed in **boldface** type.
Student Edition page numbers for illustrations, maps, and charts are printed in *italics*.

Example:

Student Edition Pages	Teacher Edition Pages

atom, *352*, 352–355, 364–372, **367**; 355, 395, 397, 401, 443, 445